A RECORD OF
BRITISH
WARTIME
FOOTBALL

A RECORD OF
BRITISH
WARTIME
FOOTBALL

Brian McColl

Published by Brian McColl
2014

First Published 2014

ISBN 978-1-291-84089-6

www.scottish-football-historical-archive.com

CONTENTS

ix   **Introduction**

Part 1 – The Great War

3   1914-15
19   1915-16
37   1916-17
55   1917-18
69   1918-19

Part 2 – The Second World War

85   1939-40
107   1940-41
133   1941-42
157   1942-43
183   1943-44
213   1944-45
243   1945-46

Appendices

269   Non-Participating League Clubs
    Representative and Friendly Matches
272   1914-1919
275   1939-1946
284   International Matches
285   Military Competitions
287   Index of Competitions

To Anne Marie,
for being so forgiving of me for my endless scribblings

Introduction

In the 1970s, I came across a list of war-time winners in an old football yearbook. I've been intrigued ever since as to how those competitions were organized, who played whom and when, what were the final scores and how did the cups pan out. Hopefully these questions, and more besides, have been answered within these pages.

Throughout this book, I have used the club names that were in use at the time; for instance both Arsenal and Sheffield Wednesday were called The Arsenal and The Wednesday respectively during The Great War. Also to differentate it from Bradford City, Bradford has latterly had 'Park Avenue' added to its name. However this book has, like the club's contemporaries, referred to it as simply Bradford.

This book is the result of seven months of extensive research of contemporary newspapers, both national and local,

The Times
The Sunday Post
The Scotsman
Glasgow Herald
Burnley News
Bath Chronicle
Birmingham Gazette
Western Daily Press
Dundee Courier
Aberdeen Journal

As expected, there were a number of missing results that the above papers didn't report. These have been supplied thanks to the help and kindness of a number of fellow historians, most of whom are members of the excellent history section on the Non League Matters forum (www.nonleaguematters.co.uk); 'HibeeJibee', Keith 'Southend Statto', John Gibbes, Stephen Byrne, Craig Tyreman, John Treleven, Tom McGouran, John Duffy, Peter Holme (of the National Football Museum). Thanks are also extended to Davy Allan and Tom McGouran.

However there are two gentlemen I would like to single out for special praise.

Phil Newport, who aided greatly with information for the Great War period and the 1939-40 season

Norman Nicol, without whose help this book may never have finished. His help in digging out those elusive Scottish WWI results, proofreading the ongoing work, his unwavering eyes noting typos etc, his help with the troublesome 1940-41 season... I could go on!

Unfortunately there are a very small number of dates and/or results in the Southern League Second Division of 1914-15 and of some Irish games from the Second World War that were not found before the date of publication. Some of the local cup results are also missing. Research for these is ongoing and all new material will be posted on my website at scottish-football-historical-archive.com.

During the Great War, although the Football League officially abolished points for wins and draws, newspapers of the time continued to print tables and declare champions.

And although the various championships during the Second World War were unofficial, the Football League published final tables in their annual yearbooks. However as the League itself cannot account for the veracity of these tables, they were crossed-checked with the results I had and all inconsistencies and errors have been rectified. Therefore some of the tables included within this book may differ slightly from other published sources.

This is primarily a statistical work. As such any narrative has been kept to a minimum. However for those seeking to read more into the background of the game during World War 2, I thoroughly recommend the following books, **Soccer at War** by Jack Rollin, **Gas Masks for Goal Posts** by Anton Rippon, and for the immediate aftermath, **Football's War and Peace - The Tumulteous Season of 1946-47** by Thomas Taw. These excellent works are all available through the usual mediums. Lastly, John Ross Schleppi wrote a brilliant thesis on English war-time football in 1971. This can be downloaded for free from the internet by typing his name into your browser.

Brian McColl
May 2014

PART 1

THE GREAT WAR

1914-1918

AND THE VICTORY SEASON 1918-19

The Heart of Midlothian War Memorial in Edinburgh

1914-15

1914-15

The League season in Britain continued as normal despite the necessary restrictions. However, although the FA Cup continued, the Scottish FA Cup was abandoned after the preliminary Qualifying Cup had been completed.

WINNERS OF THE PRINCIPAL COMPETITIONS

FA Cup	Sheffield United
Football League –	
First Division	Everton
Second Division	Derby County
Southern League –	
First Division	Watford
Second Division	Stoke
Welsh FA Cup	Wrexham
Scottish League –	
First Division	Celtic
Second Division	Cowdenbeath
Irish FA Cup	Linfield
Irish League	Belfast Celtic
Gold Cup	Shelbourne

The Football League 1914-15

FIRST DIVISION

	Aston Villa	Blackburn R	Bolton W	Bradford	Bradford C	Burnley	Chelsea	Everton	Liverpool	Manchester C	Manchester U	Middlesbrough	Newcastle U	Notts Co	Oldham Ath	Sheffield U	Sunderland	The Wednesday	Tottenham H	WBA
Aston Villa	X	2 Apr 2-1	26 Dec 1-2	5 Dec 1-2	13 Feb 0-0	17 Oct 3-3	3 Oct 2-1	10 Oct 3-3	3 Feb 1-5	3 Apr 6-2	21 Aug 4-1	19 Dec 3-3	13 Mar 5-0	31 Oct 2-1	2 Sep 2-1	17 Apr 0-0	14 Nov 1-0	5 Sep 1-3	16 Jan 0-0	27 Feb 3-1
Blackburn Rovers	25 Dec 1-2	X	26 Sep 2-2	2 Jan 2-2	29 Mar 2-1	28 Nov 6-0	14 Nov 3-2	7 Nov 1-3	13 Mar 2-1	21 Sep 4-2	3 Oct 0-1	23 Jan 3-3	24 Apr 4-0	12 Dec 2-3	13 Feb 5-1	12 Feb 4-1	1 Sep 1-2	27 Oct 3-1	10 Apr 4-1	31 Oct 2-1
Bolton Wanderers	1 Jan 2-2	7 Sep 3-2	X	2 Apr 3-2	14 Nov 3-5	13 Mar 3-1	14 Apr 3-1	31 Oct 0-0	25 Dec 0-1	19 Sep 2-3	12 Sep 3-0	12 Dec 4-0	10 Apr 0-0	3 Oct 1-2	2 Jan 2-0	26 Aug 0-1	10 Mar 1-1	17 Oct 0-3	28 Nov 4-2	27 Feb 1-1
Bradford	10 Apr 2-2	5 Sep 1-2	7 Oct 1-2	X	28 Apr 3-0	31 Oct 2-2	17 Oct 3-0	14 Apr 3-1	12 Dec 1-0	24 Apr 3-1	5 Apr 5-0	27 Mar 2-0	14 Nov 1-0	16 Jan 3-1	25 Dec 1-1	28 Nov 2-0	19 Sep 2-1	17 Oct 1-1	13 Mar 5-1	3 Oct 1-4
Bradford City	10 Oct 3-0	21 Nov 3-0	20 Mar 4-2	24 Oct 3-2	X	2 Jan 0-0	9 Sep 2-2	26 Dec 0-1	10 Mar 3-2	6 Apr 0-0	7 Nov 4-2	26 Sep 1-1	23 Jan 1-1	3 Apr 3-1	24 Apr 1-0	6 Feb 1-1	5 Dec 3-1	17 Oct 1-0	12 Sep 2-2	19 Dec 5-0
Burnley	22 Feb 2-1	3 Apr 3-2	21 Nov 5-0	6 Mar 2-0	5 Sep 0-1	X	5 Apr 2-0	7 Sep 1-0	24 Oct 3-0	18 Jan 1-2	20 Mar 3-0	6 Feb 4-0	26 Sep 2-0	5 Dec 0-0	7 Nov 2-3	10 Oct 1-2	17 Apr 2-1	19 Dec 2-3	23 Jan 3-1	25 Dec 0-2
Chelsea	6 Feb 3-1	20 Mar 1-3	7 Nov 2-1	1 Apr 0-1	2 Apr 2-0	28 Dec 1-4	X	19 Dec 2-0	10 Oct 3-1	25 Dec 0-0	19 Apr 1-3	23 Jan 2-2	12 Sep 0-3	21 Nov 4-1	24 Oct 2-2	26 Sep 0-3	3 Apr 4-1	5 Dec 0-0	2 Jan 1-1	17 Apr 4-1
Everton	26 Sep 0-0	7 Nov 1-3	22 Mar 5-3	10 Oct 4-1	25 Dec 1-1	2 Apr 0-2	26 Aug 2-2	X	6 Feb 1-3	12 Dec 4-1	24 Oct 4-2	12 Sep 3-0	2 Jan 2-3	20 Mar 3-4	17 Mar 0-4	23 Jan 0-1	21 Nov 7-1	3 Apr 0-1	1 Jan 1-1	5 Dec 2-1
Liverpool	28 Nov 3-6	5 Apr 3-0	2 Sep 4-3	17 Apr 2-1	17 Oct 2-1	27 Feb 3-0	13 Feb 2-3	3 Oct 0-5	X	13 Mar 3-2	26 Dec 1-1	14 Nov 2-2	29 Mar 1-1	5 Sep 1-2	19 Dec 2-1	12 Apr 2-1	16 Jan 2-1	19 Sep 2-1	31 Oct 7-2	24 Mar 3-1
Manchester City	25 Nov 1-0	6 Feb 1-3	23 Jan 2-1	19 Dec 2-3	1 Sep 4-1	12 Sep 1-0	26 Dec 2-1	17 Apr 0-1	5 Dec 1-1	X	2 Jan 1-1	24 Oct 1-1	10 Oct 1-1	22 Feb 0-0	5 Apr 0-0	7 Nov 0-0	6 Mar 2-0	20 Mar 4-0	26 Sep 2-1	3 Apr 4-0
Manchester United	26 Aug 1-0	19 Sep 2-0	16 Jan 4-1	1 Jan 1-2	13 Mar 1-0	14 Nov 0-2	31 Oct 2-2	27 Feb 1-2	2 Apr 2-0	6 Sep 0-0	X	10 Apr 2-2	28 Nov 1-0	30 Jan 2-2	2 Sep 1-3	12 Dec 1-2	3 Oct 3-0	13 Feb 2-0	27 Mar 1-1	17 Oct 0-0
Middlesbrough	7 Nov 1-1	19 Dec 1-4	17 Apr 0-0	21 Nov 1-3	3 Feb 3-0	3 Oct 1-1	19 Sep 3-0	16 Jan 5-1	20 Mar 3-0	27 Feb 1-0	5 Dec 1-1	X	17 Oct 1-1	25 Dec 1-0	3 Apr 4-1	1 Mar 2-2	1 Jan 2-3	6 Apr 3-1	13 Feb 7-5	5 Sep 2-0
Newcastle United	28 Apr 3-0	17 Apr 2-1	5 Dec 1-2	3 Mar 1-1	19 Sep 1-0	14 Apr 1-2	17 Mar 2-0	5 Sep 0-1	7 Nov 0-0	13 Feb 2-1	3 Apr 2-0	3 Mar 1-2	X	19 Dec 1-1	21 Nov 1-2	24 Oct 4-3	25 Dec 2-5	9 Sep 0-0	3 Oct 4-0	2 Sep 1-2
Notts County	5 Apr 1-1	10 Oct 1-1	17 Mar 0-0	12 Sep 1-2	28 Nov 0-0	10 Apr 0-0	28 Apr 2-0	14 Nov 0-0	2 Jan 3-1	17 Oct 0-2	26 Dec 4-2	26 Sep 5-1	24 Apr 1-0	X	23 Jan 2-1	2 Apr 3-1	27 Feb 2-1	31 Oct 1-2	12 Dec 1-2	1 Mar 1-1
Oldham Athletic	12 Dec 3-3	16 Jan 3-2	5 Sep 6-2	26 Dec 6-2	31 Oct 1-0	20 Apr 1-2	27 Feb 0-0	17 Oct 1-1	24 Apr 0-2	1 Jan 0-0	6 Apr 1-0	28 Nov 5-1	27 Mar 1-0	19 Sep 2-0	X	10 Apr 3-0	1 Feb 4-5	3 Oct 5-2	14 Nov 4-1	9 Mar 1-1
Sheffield United	20 Mar 3-0	26 Dec 1-2	19 Apr 3-1	3 Apr 3-2	3 Oct 1-1	13 Feb 1-0	8 Mar 1-1	19 Apr 1-1	21 Nov 1-0	29 Sep 2-1	17 Apr 0-0	31 Dec 0-1	27 Feb 1-0	28 Dec 1-0	5 Dec 3-0	X	5 Apr 1-1	5 Sep 0-1	17 Oct 1-1	16 Jan 2-0
Sunderland	2 Jan 4-0	20 Feb 5-1	10 Oct 4-3	23 Apr 3-3	10 Feb 1-1	12 Dec 2-1	28 Nov 2-1	6 Apr 0-3	12 Sep 2-2	31 Oct 0-2	6 Feb 1-0	2 Apr 4-1	26 Dec 2-4	24 Oct 3-1	26 Dec 1-2	2 Sep 3-2	X	13 Mar 3-1	24 Apr 5-0	14 Nov 1-2
The Wednesday	12 Sep 5-2	24 Oct 1-1	1 Mar 7-0	26 Sep 6-0	12 Dec 3-3	24 Apr 0-0	10 Apr 3-2	28 Nov 1-4	23 Jan 2-1	14 Nov 2-1	10 Oct 1-0	1 Sep 3-1	1 Jan 2-1	6 Mar 0-0	6 Feb 2-2	2 Apr 1-1	7 Nov 1-2	X	25 Dec 3-2	27 Mar 3-2
Tottenham Hotspur	24 Oct 0-2	5 Dec 0-4	3 Apr 4-2	7 Nov 3-0	16 Jan 0-0	19 Sep 1-3	5 Sep 1-1	2 Sep 1-3	6 Mar 1-1	15 Mar 2-2	21 Nov 2-0	10 Oct 3-3	2 Apr 0-0	20 Feb 2-0	20 Apr 1-1	19 Mar 1-1	19 Dec 0-6	26 Dec 6-1	X	28 Sep 2-0
West Bromwich Albion	23 Jan 2-0	6 Mar 0-0	24 Oct 3-0	6 Feb 1-0	24 Apr 3-0	26 Dec 3-0	12 Dec 2-0	10 Apr 1-2	26 Sep 4-0	28 Nov 0-1	20 Feb 0-0	2 Jan 1-0	5 Apr 2-0	7 Nov 4-1	10 Oct 0-0	12 Sep 1-1	20 Mar 1-2	21 Nov 0-0	6 Apr 3-2	X

The Football League 1914-15

FIRST DIVISION

Final Table

		P	W	D	L	F	A	Pts
1	Everton	38	19	8	11	76	47	46
2	Oldham Athletic	38	17	11	10	70	56	45
3	Blackburn Rovers	38	18	7	13	83	61	43
4	Burnley	38	18	7	13	61	47	43
5	Manchester City	38	15	13	10	49	39	43
6	Sheffield United	38	15	13	10	49	41	43
7	The Wednesday	38	15	13	10	61	54	43
8	Sunderland	38	18	5	15	81	72	41
9	Bradford	38	17	7	14	69	65	41
10	West Bromwich Albion	38	15	10	13	49	43	40
11	Bradford City	38	13	14	11	55	49	40
12	Middlesbrough	38	13	12	13	62	74	38
13	Liverpool	38	14	9	15	65	75	37
14	Aston Villa	38	13	11	14	62	72	37
15	Newcastle United	38	11	10	17	46	48	32
16	Notts County	38	9	13	16	41	57	31
17	Bolton Wanderers	38	11	8	19	68	84	30
18	Manchester United	38	9	12	17	46	62	30
19	Chelsea	38	8	13	17	51	65	29
20	Tottenham Hotspur	38	8	12	18	57	90	28

SECOND DIVISION

Final Table

		P	W	D	L	F	A	Pts
1	Derby County	38	23	7	8	71	33	53
2	Preston North End	38	20	10	8	61	42	50
3	Barnsley	38	22	3	13	51	51	47
4	Wolverhampton Wanderers	38	19	7	12	77	52	45
5	The Arsenal	38	19	5	14	69	41	43
6	Birmingham	38	17	9	12	62	39	43
7	Hull City	38	19	5	14	65	54	43
8	Huddersfield Town	38	17	8	13	61	42	42
9	Clapton Orient	38	16	9	13	50	48	41
10	Blackpool	38	17	5	16	58	57	39
11	Bury	38	15	8	15	61	56	38
12	Fulham	38	15	7	16	53	47	37
13	Bristol City	38	15	7	16	62	56	37
14	Stockport County	38	15	7	16	54	60	37
15	Leeds City	38	14	4	20	65	64	32
16	Lincoln City	38	11	9	18	46	65	31
17	Grimsby Town	38	11	9	18	48	76	31
18	Nottingham Forest	38	10	9	19	43	77	29
19	Leicester Fosse	38	10	4	24	47	88	24
20	Glossop	38	6	6	26	31	87	18

The Football League 1914-15

SECOND DIVISION

	Barnsley	Birmingham	Blackpool	Bristol City	Bury	Clapton Orient	Derby Co	Fulham	Glossop	Grimsby T	Huddersfield T	Hull C	Leeds City	Leicester Fosse	Lincoln C	Nottingham F	Preston NE	Stockport Co	The Arsenal	Wolves
Barnsley	X	8 Mar 2-1	13 Mar 1-2	3 Oct 2-1	17 Feb 2-0	26 Dec 1-0	2 Apr 1-0	3 Apr 2-2	20 Mar 2-0	19 Sep 0-0	30 Jan 1-0	17 Apr 1-0	19 Dec 2-1	31 Oct 1-0	5 Sep 3-1	27 Feb 3-0	17 Oct 2-1	5 Dec 2-0	1 Jan 1-0	21 Nov 2-1
Birmingham	12 Sep 2-0	X	28 Nov 3-0	24 Apr 1-1	25 Dec 1-0	6 Mar 1-0	20 Mar 0-2	1 Mar 1-0	23 Jan 11-1	10 Apr 3-0	12 Dec 1-0	24 Mar 2-2	24 Oct 6-3	2 Jan 2-0	21 Nov 2-0	28 Dec 3-0	5 Apr 1-1	10 Oct 0-1	7 Nov 3-0	26 Sep 1-2
Blackpool	7 Nov 1-1	14 Apr 3-1	X	1 Jan 2-0	12 Sep 3-4	6 Feb 5-1	6 Mar 2-1	19 Dec 2-2	21 Nov 3-0	17 Apr 5-0	2 Apr 3-2	2 Jan 1-2	23 Oct 1-0	24 Mar 1-2	20 Oct 0-0	10 Oct 3-0	26 Sep 0-2	5 Apr 4-2	20 Feb 0-2	5 Dec 1-0
Bristol City	6 Feb 3-1	19 Dec 2-3	2 Sep 2-1	X	2 Jan 1-0	21 Nov 3-0	5 Dec 2-3	24 Oct 0-0	10 Oct 3-1	26 Dec 7-0	5 Apr 0-1	7 Nov 5-2	20 Feb 1-0	26 Mar 1-0	17 Apr 2-1	23 Jan 1-2	12 Sep 4-0	6 Mar 0-2	3 Apr 1-1	20 Feb 0-1
Bury	10 Oct 1-2	26 Dec 1-3	25 Jan 2-2	5 Sep 2-1	X	3 Apr 3-0	17 Apr 2-0	6 Mar 1-0	20 Feb 5-0	2 Apr 2-2	1 Jan 3-1	20 Mar 0-1	21 Nov 0-0	6 Feb 3-1	14 Dec 1-1	26 Sep 4-2	23 Jan 0-0	7 Nov 2-1	5 Dec 3-1	24 Oct 4-1
Clapton Orient	25 Dec 4-2	31 Oct 1-1	3 Oct 2-0	27 Mar 2-0	28 Nov 2-2	X	17 Oct 0-1	2 Jan 2-1	5 Apr 5-2	13 Mar 2-1	14 Nov 3-1	23 Jan 0-3	26 Sep 2-0	24 Apr 2-0	27 Mar 3-1	12 Feb 0-0	10 Apr 1-1	12 Sep 3-0	13 Feb 1-0	1 Sep 1-1
Derby County	2 Sep 7-0	14 Nov 1-0	31 Oct 5-0	10 Apr 1-0	12 Dec 2-1	20 Feb 0-3	X	23 Jan 1-1	2 Jan 1-1	27 Mar 1-1	28 Nov 1-0	6 Feb 4-1	10 Oct 1-2	5 Apr 1-0	13 Mar 3-0	26 Dec 1-0	24 Apr 2-0	26 Sep 1-0	24 Oct 4-0	12 Sep 3-1
Fulham	28 Nov 2-0	3 Oct 2-3	24 Apr 0-1	27 Feb 1-2	31 Oct 6-3	5 Sep 4-0	19 Sep 2-0	X	23 Apr 2-0	13 Feb 2-1	17 Oct 2-3	6 Apr 4-1	9 Sep 1-0	27 Mar 109	29 Mar 3-1	14 Nov 2-1	13 Mar 0-2	26 Dec 1-0	16 Jan 0-1	12 Dec 0-1
Glossop	14 Nov 0-1	19 Sep 3-3	27 Mar 1-3	13 Feb 2-1	17 Oct 3-1	2 Apr 3-1	5 Sep 1-1	5 Dec 1-0	X	30 Jan 0-0	3 Oct 2-2	16 Mar 0-5	25 Dec 0-3	13 Mar 2-3	16 Jan 1-2	31 Oct 1-0	27 Feb 0-1	17 Apr 1-1	8 Sep 0-4	3 Apr 0-2
Grimsby Town	23 Jan 2-3	5 Dec 1-0	12 Dec 2-0	25 Dec 2-3	5 Apr 1-0	7 Nov 2-1	21 Nov 1-2	10 Nov 1-1	10 Oct 1-0	X	24 Apr 0-0	24 Oct 1-1	6 Mar 2-5	12 Sep 1-0	3 Apr 5-1	2 Jan 4-0	1 Sep 2-2	20 Feb 6-1	20 Mar 1-0	6 Feb 1-4
Huddersfield Town	26 Sep 1-0	17 Apr 0-0	26 Dec 5-0	6 Apr 5-3	8 Sep 0-1	20 Mar 1-1	3 Apr 0-0	20 Feb 2-2	6 Feb 0-1	19 Dec 3-1	X	31 Oct 1-0	7 Nov 1-0	21 Dec 3-1	5 Sep 0-1	12 Sep 4-0	2 Jan 3-1	24 Oct 2-1	21 Nov 3-0	10 Oct 2-0
Hull City	12 Dec 2-1	17 Oct 0-0	5 Sep 1-3	13 Apr 1-1	14 Nov 3-1	19 Sep 0-1	3 Oct 1-0	5 Oct 2-0	24 Apr 2-0	29 Apr 4-1	15 Apr 0-4	X	16 Jan 2-6	10 Apr 2-1	11 Mar 6-1	28 Nov 3-1	27 Mar 0-1	3 Sep 1-0	2 Apr 1-0	25 Dec 5-1
Leeds City	24 Apr 0-2	27 Feb 2-0	19 Sep 2-0	14 Nov 1-1	27 Mar 2-1	3 Feb 0-1	13 Feb 3-5	2 Sep 0-1	26 Sep 3-0	31 Dec 5-0	13 Oct 1-0	12 Sep 2-3	X	12 Dec 7-2	17 Oct 3-1	10 Apr 4-0	28 Nov 0-0	2 Jan 1-3	3 Oct 2-2	6 Apr 2-3
Leicester Fosse	6 Mar 0-1	5 Sep 1-0	27 Feb 2-2	25 Mar 1-3	3 Oct 1-3	30 Jan 1-1	28 Dec 0-6	21 Nov 0-2	7 Nov 3-2	16 Jan 2-0	19 Sep 1-2	5 Dec 1-1	17 Apr 5-1	X	2 Sep 2-2	17 Oct 3-1	13 Feb 2-3	3 Apr 5-4	25 Dec 1-4	20 Mar 0-3
Lincoln City	2 Jan 3-0	27 Mar 0-1	14 Nov 0-1	12 Dec 3-1	24 Apr 2-3	24 Oct 1-0	7 Nov 0-0	26 Sep 3-1	12 Sep 2-1	28 Nov 2-1	10 Apr 1-1	10 Oct 0-3	20 Feb 0-1	2 Apr 2-3	X	5 Apr 2-1	25 Dec 3-1	6 Feb 2-2	6 Mar 1-0	23 Jan 2-2
Nottingham Forest	24 Oct 2-1	2 Sep 2-1	13 Feb 0-1	19 Sep 0-1	4 Feb 2-3	17 Apr 0-1	25 Dec 2-2	20 Mar 2-2	6 Mar 1-0	5 Sep 4-2	16 Jan 3-2	3 Apr 1-0	5 Dec 3-1	20 Feb 1-3	1 Oct 3-2	X	3 Oct 1-1	21 Nov 1-1	18 Nov 1-1	7 Nov 3-1
Preston North End	20 Feb 5-2	2 Apr 2-0	30 Jan 1-0	11 Feb 4-1	19 Sep 2-0	5 Dec 2-2	19 Dec 1-3	7 Nov 2-1	24 Oct 1-0	7 Sep 3-0	5 Sep 1-1	21 Nov 2-1	3 Apr 2-0	10 Oct 1-0	26 Dec 0-0	6 Feb 2-2	X	20 Mar 2-0	17 Apr 3-0	6 Mar 5-3
Stockport County	10 Apr 1-2	13 Feb 3-1	25 Dec 0-2	31 Oct 2-2	13 Mar 1-0	16 Jan 2-0	30 Jan 3-2	2 Apr 0-2	12 Dec 2-1	17 Oct 1-1	27 Feb 2-1	1 Jan 3-0	5 Sep 3-1	28 Nov 3-0	3 Oct 1-0	27 Mar 1-0	14 Nov 2-1	X	19 Sep 1-1	24 Apr 2-2
The Arsenal	5 Apr 1-0	13 Mar 1-0	17 Oct 2-0	28 Nov 3-0	10 Apr 3-1	10 Oct 2-1	27 Feb 1-2	19 Sep 3-0	1 Sep 3-0	14 Nov 6-0	27 Mar 0-3	26 Sep 2-1	6 Feb 2-0	26 Dec 6-0	31 Oct 1-1	24 Apr 7-0	12 Dec 1-2	23 Jan 3-1	X	2 Jan 5-1
Wolverhampton Wanderers	27 Mar 1-0	19 Apr 0-0	10 Apr 2-0	17 Oct 2-2	27 Feb 1-1	7 Sep 0-0	16 Jan 0-1	17 Apr 2-0	28 Nov 4-0	3 Oct 0-1	13 Feb 4-1	26 Dec 1-2	5 Apr 5-1	14 Nov 7-0	19 Sep 3-1	13 Mar 5-1	31 Oct 2-0	19 Dec 4-1	5 Sep 1-0	X

The Southern Football League 1914-15

FIRST DIVISION

	Brighton & HA	Bristol Rovers	Cardiff C	Croydon Common	Crystal Palace	Exeter C	Gillingham	Luton T	Millwall	Northampton T	Norwich C	Plymouth Arg	Portsmouth	QPR	Reading	Southampton	Southend U	Swindon T	Watford	West Ham U
Brighton & Hove Albion	X	20 Mar 0-0	23 Jan 2-1	21 Nov 4-1	1 May 1-0	26 Sep 2-1	5 Sep 2-1	17 Mar 0-1	7 Nov 2-2	17 Apr 1-0	2 Apr 2-2	9 Sep 2-2	10 Oct 1-0	6 Mar 1-0	3 Apr 2-0	5 Dec 4-0	24 Oct 1-0	20 Feb 1-3	24 Apr 1-2	25 Dec 0-0
Bristol Rovers	14 Nov 4-0	X	27 Mar 0-1	6 Apr 3-0	5 Sep 1-1	28 Nov 2-1	13 Mar 2-1	10 Apr 1-0	7 Nov 2-2	3 Oct 2-3	31 Oct 4-2	17 Oct 3-2	12 Dec 2-3	25 Dec 1-3	19 Dec 3-3	17 Sep 3-1	28 Dec 4-1	24 Apr 1-0	13 Feb 2-3	27 Feb 1-0
Cardiff City	19 Sep 0-1	21 Nov 7-0	X	3 Apr 1-0	30 Jan 5-0	6 Feb 1-0	16 Jan 3-1	10 Oct 3-0	20 Mar 4-1	19 Dec 5-0	5 Sep 1-0	26 Dec 2-0	20 Feb 3-2	7 Nov 2-0	5 Dec 3-2	17 Apr 1-1	6 Mar 3-0	24 Oct 3-0	1 Jan 2-3	5 Apr 2-1
Croydon Common	27 Mar 1-0	5 Sep 0-3	28 Nov 0-1	X	19 Sep 1-1	10 Apr 0-0	14 Nov 8-1	12 Dec 1-1	2 Jan 2-1	13 Feb 4-1	13 Mar 4-1	27 Feb 2-2	16 Jan 1-1	5 Apr 1-0	30 Jan 4-1	3 Oct 4-1	26 Dec 1-1	2 Sep 0-0	17 Oct 0-1	31 Oct 1-2
Crystal Palace	12 Sep 0-2	2 Jan 1-0	26 Sep 0-2	11 Mar 1-5	X	10 Oct 0-0	5 Apr 1-0	24 Oct 2-3	26 Dec 0-0	6 Mar 1-1	28 Dec 2-1	3 Apr 2-1	7 Nov 1-0	19 Dec 2-2	6 Feb 4-1	3 Mar 1-2	5 Dec 1-1	21 Nov 3-1	20 Mar 0-1	17 Apr 2-1
Exeter City	24 Feb 1-0	3 Apr 1-0	3 Oct 2-0	5 Dec 3-1	13 Feb 1-1	X	19 Sep 2-0	20 Feb 1-2	21 Nov 0-1	23 Sep 2-1	16 Jan 2-0	5 Apr 2-0	24 Oct 1-1	20 Mar 0-1	17 Apr 0-1	19 Dec 1-2	7 Nov 7-1	6 Mar 0-1	26 Dec 4-1	5 Sep 3-1
Gillingham	2 Jan 1-3	7 Nov 0-1	12 Sep 1-1	20 Mar 2-2	2 Apr 3-0	23 Jan 0-0	X	26 Sep 2-4	6 Mar 0-0	5 Dec 2-2	25 Dec 3-3	19 Dec 0-0	6 Feb 3-1	24 Oct 0-1	21 Nov 0-5	3 Apr 4-3	20 Feb 1-0	10 Oct 4-0	17 Apr 2-3	9 Sep 4-0
Luton Town	3 Oct 0-1	21 Oct 3-1	13 Feb 2-1	17 Apr 2-1	27 Feb 1-2	17 Oct 0-2	30 Jan 3-1	X	28 Nov 0-2	25 Dec 1-1	19 Sep 1-1	5 Sep 2-1	6 Mar 0-2	16 Sep 2-4	30 Sep 1-2	9 Sep 3-2		7 Mar 3-4	5 Nov 2-2	10 Mar 1-2
Millwall	13 Mar 3-0	5 Apr 2-0	14 Nov 2-1	5 Sep 1-0	25 Dec 0-0	27 Mar 2-1	31 Oct 3-0	3 Apr 3-3	X	26 Sep 2-1	6 Apr 0-1	1 Mar 1-1	10 Apr 1-1	1 Sep 3-1	16 Jan 0-1	19 Sep 1-2	24 Apr 1-4	12 Dec 1-2	3 Oct 0-3	17 Oct 2-1
Northampton Town	12 Dec 2-1	6 Feb 2-0	24 Apr 2-5	10 Oct 3-2	31 Oct 3-1	28 Dec 1-1	10 Apr 4-0	26 Dec 0-3	1 May 5-0	X	28 Nov 4-1	14 Nov 1-1	5 Apr 1-0	23 Jan 1-1	20 Feb 2-1	24 Oct 2-0	9 Sep 1-0	2 Jan 2-3	13 Mar 1-1	27 Mar 1-1
Norwich City	5 Apr 2-1	6 Mar 5-1	2 Jan 2-1	7 Nov 1-1	10 Sep 2-1	12 Sep 3-1	26 Dec 4-0	23 Jan 5-1	24 Oct 1-3	3 Apr 0-1	X	17 Apr 2-0	26 Sep 0-0	24 Oct 2-1	20 Mar 0-2	21 Nov 0-0	10 Oct 1-1	6 Dec 1-1	5 Dec 2-0	19 Dec 0-0
Plymouth Argyle	2 Sep 2-0	20 Feb 3-0	25 Dec 2-0	24 Oct 1-2	28 Nov 1-4	2 Apr 1-3	24 Apr 3-2	2 Jan 3-3	10 Oct 0-0	20 Mar 0-1	12 Dec 2-2	X	12 Sep 2-2	6 Feb 1-1	6 Mar 1-1	7 Nov 0-2	26 Sep 1-0	23 Jan 3-1	21 Nov 1-1	10 Apr 1-0
Portsmouth	13 Feb 2-0	17 Apr 3-0	17 Oct 0-1	30 Sep 1-0	13 Mar 1-0	27 Feb 0-2	3 Oct 1-0	31 Oct 3-1	5 Dec 1-1	2 Apr 1-0	1 May 0-0	30 Jan 3-1	X	3 Apr 1-1	9 Sep 1-0	25 Dec 0-1	21 Nov 1-0	20 Mar 1-1	5 Sep 2-3	19 Sep 3-1
Queen's Park Rangers	31 Oct 0-1	26 Dec 2-1	13 Mar 3-0	2 Apr 1-0	24 Apr 3-2	14 Nov 0-2	27 Feb 3-0	27 Mar 0-3	28 Dec 0-1	19 Sep 0-0	17 Oct 1-1	3 Oct 1-1	28 Nov 1-2	X	5 Sep 0-1	16 Jan 4-3	12 Dec 4-2	10 Apr 4-2	18 Mar 2-5	13 Feb 1-1
Reading	28 Nov 3-1	3 Mar 3-1	10 Apr 1-2	26 Sep 4-1	3 Oct 3-0	12 Dec 1-0	2 Mar 1-0	24 Apr 4-0	9 Sep 0-2	17 Oct 2-1	14 Nov 1-0	31 Oct 2-0	2 Sep 1-1	2 Jan 2-2	X	13 Feb 0-1	5 Apr 2-0	25 Dec 2-2	23 Jan 1-1	13 Mar 3-1
Southampton	10 Apr 4-2	26 Sep 3-1	12 Dec 1-1	6 Feb 4-0	17 Oct 2-3	24 Apr 5-0	28 Nov 2-1	5 Sep 3-3	23 Jan 3-2	21 Apr 4-2	27 Mar 2-2	13 Mar 2-1	26 Dec 4-3	9 Sep 3-0	10 Oct 2-4	X	2 Jan 2-0	5 Apr 4-1	31 Oct 3-1	14 Nov 3-1
Southend United	27 Feb 2-2	9 Sep 2-0	31 Oct 2-1	10 Feb 1-0	10 Apr 2-3	13 Mar 0-2	17 Oct 1-1	14 Nov 1-0	19 Dec 0-0	1-2	13 Feb 4-1	1 May 3-1	27 Mar 0-2	17 Apr 1-1	2 Apr 0-2	5 Sep 4-0	X	28 Nov 1-0	19 Sep 0-0	3 Oct 0-1
Swindon Town	17 Oct 2-1	16 Sep 4-1	27 Feb 0-0	28 Dec 7-1	27 Mar 5-2	31 Oct 4-0	13 Feb 5-1	13 Mar 2-2	17 Apr 1-2	5 Sep 2-2	3 Oct 4-0	19 Sep 3-2	14 Nov 1-3	5 Dec 1-2	26 Dec 1-1	2 Apr 2-0	3 Apr 1-0	X	6 Apr 5-0	30 Jan 1-1
Watford	16 Sep 0-0	10 Oct 2-0	2 Sep 2-1	20 Feb 3-0	14 Nov 1-0	25 Dec 1-1	12 Dec 4-0	2 Apr 2-4	27 Feb 4-0	7 Nov 0-0	10 Apr 2-1	27 Mar 2-0	2 Jan 2-1	26 Sep 2-2	24 Oct 0-1	6 Mar 5-2	3 Feb 2-1	9 Sep 3-0	X	28 Nov 0-1
West Ham United	26 Dec 2-1	24 Oct 4-1	2 Apr 2-1	6 Mar 1-0	12 Dec 1-2	2 Jan 4-1	1 Sep 2-1	9 Sep 3-0	20 Feb 1-1	21 Nov 1-0	24 Nov 1-1	5 Dec 2-0	23 Jan 4-3	10 Oct 2-2	7 Nov 3-2	20 Mar 3-0	6 Jan 3-1	26 Sep 1-1	3 Apr 2-0	X

The Southern Football League 1914-15

FIRST DIVISION

Final Table

		P	W	D	L	F	A	Pts
1	Watford	38	22	8	8	68	46	52
2	Reading	38	21	7	10	68	43	49
3	Cardiff City	38	22	4	12	72	38	48
4	West Ham United	38	18	9	11	58	47	45
5	Northampton Town	38	16	11	11	56	51	43
6	Southampton	38	19	5	14	78	74	43
7	Portsmouth	38	16	10	12	54	42	42
8	Millwall	38	16	10	12	50	51	42
9	Swindon Town	38	15	11	12	77	59	41
10	Brighton & Hove Albion	38	16	7	15	46	47	39
11	Exeter City	38	15	8	15	50	41	38
12	QPR	38	13	12	13	55	56	38
13	Norwich City	38	11	14	13	53	56	36
14	Luton Town	38	13	8	17	61	73	34
15	Crystal Palace	38	13	8	17	47	61	34
16	Bristol Rovers	38	14	3	21	53	75	31
17	Plymouth Argyle	38	8	14	16	51	61	30
18	Southend United	38	10	8	20	44	64	28
19	Croydon Common	38	9	9	20	47	63	27
20	Gillingham	38	6	8	24	43	83	20

SECOND DIVISION

	Barry T	Brentford	Coventry C	Ebbw Vale	Llanelly	Merthyr T	Mid Rhondda	Newport Co	Pontypridd	Stalybridge Celtic	Stoke	Swansea T	Ton Pentre
Barry Town	X	12 Jan 0-1	26 Sep 2-0	13 Mar 8-0	28 Nov 3-0	14 Nov 0-0	12 Dec 1-0	13 Feb 3-1	2 Apr 2-2	31 Oct 0-1	23 Jan 0-0	2 Jan 1-2	17 Oct 1-1
Brentford	16 Jan 0-0	X	5 Sep 3-2	6 Mar 4-1	13 Mar 2-3			14 Nov 1-0	10 Apr 6-0		25 Dec 2-2	12 Dec 2-0	30 Jan 3-3
Coventry City	9 Jan 3-0	2 Jan	X	14 Nov 6-0	27 Mar 1-0	7 Nov 1-2	6 Mar 3-0	28 Nov 10-1	10 Apr 5-0	24 Oct 3-0	12 Sep 1-3	5 Apr 0-0	13 Feb 7-2
Ebbw Vale	21 Nov 2-1		20 Mar	X			6 Feb 0-0	22 Sep 3-2	20 feb	26 Dec 0-3	19 Sep 0-1	24 Oct 1-2	
Llanelly	3 Apr 1-0	7 Nov 3-0	21 Nov 1-2		X	10 Apr 1-0		6 Feb 6-1	26 Dec 6-0		20 Mar 1-2		17 Apr 1-2
Merthyr Town	20 Mar 3-0		13 Mar 3-0			X	27 Feb 3-0	23 Jan 2-1	10 Oct 2-1	17 Apr 1-1	6 Mar 2-0	26 Dec 2-1	3 Apr 2-0
Mid Rhondda	17 Apr 2-0		5 Dec 2-1	3 Oct 4-1	30 Jan 0-1		X	17 Oct 0-0	7 Nov 1-1		3 Apr 4-2	20 Mar	28 Nov 2-2
Newport County	5 Apr 2-0	20 Mar 5-0	3 Apr 0-1	30 Jan 3-0	3 Oct 2-0	19 Sep 1-0	20 Feb 3-1	X	6 Mar 1-1	5 Sep 0-1	5 Dec 8-0	16 Jan 1-0	19 Dec 1-2
Pontypridd	25 Dec 2-4		19 Sep 2-3	17 Oct 5-2	24 Oct 0-2		13 Mar 3-0	31 Oct 1-1	X	3 Apr 0-1	21 Nov 0-1		16 Jan 0-2
Stalybridge Celtic	6 Mar 3-2	13 Feb 3-1	27 Feb 2-0	24 Apr 4-0	30 Jan 1-0		12 Sep 2-0	2 Jan 1-0		X	17 Oct 1-0		20 Mar
Stoke	22 Sep 2-0	26 Dec 3-0	16 Jan 5-1	5 Apr 10-0	14 Nov 3-1	31 Oct 4-0	28 Nov 8-0	9 Jan 3-1	12 Dec 5-0	13 Mar 1-1	X	17 Sep 1-0	3 Oct 4-1
Swansea Town	27 Mar 4-0	8 Apr 8-0	2 Apr 1-0	27 Feb 5-2	6 Mar 1-1		14 Nov 4-0	13 Mar 2-0	28 Nov 1-0	3 Oct 3-2	24 Apr 1-0	X	
Ton Pentre	20 Feb 3-0		10 Oct 2-1	13 Feb 3-7	12 Dec 3-1			24 Apr 6-0		14 Nov 1-0	6 Feb 0-1		X

Abertillery, Leyton and Mardy all resigned during the season

		P	W	D	L	F	A	Pts
1	Stoke	24	17	4	3	62	15	38
2	Stalybridge Celtic	24	17	3	4	47	22	37
3	Merthyr Town	24	15	5	4	46	20	35
4	Swansea Town	24	16	1	7	48	21	33
5	Coventry City	24	13	2	9	56	33	28
6	Ton Pentre	24	11	6	7	42	43	28
7	Brentford	24	8	7	9	35	45	23
8	Llanelly	24	10	1	13	39	32	21
9	Barry	24	6	5	13	30	35	17
10	Newport County	24	7	3	14	27	42	17
11	Ponytpridd	24	5	6	13	31	58	16
12	Mid Rhondda	24	3	6	15	17	49	12
13	Ebbw Vale	24	3	1	20	23	88	7

The FA Challenge Cup 1914-15

First round
Played on 9 Jan
Blackpool v Sheffield United 1–2
Darlington v Bradford City 0–1
Bristol City v Cardiff City 2–0
Burnley v Huddersfield Town 3–1
Liverpool v Stockport County 3–0
Rochdale v Gillingham 2–0
South Shields v Fulham 1–2
Southampton v Luton Town 3–0
Reading v Wolverhampton Wanderers 0–1
Nottingham Forest v Norwich City 1–4
Aston Villa v Exeter City 2–0
The Wednesday v Manchester United 1–0
Bolton Wanderers v Notts County 2–1
Grimsby Town v Northampton Town 0–3
Middlesbrough v Goole Town 9–3
Derby County v Leeds City 1–2
Everton v Barnsley 3–0
Tottenham Hotspur v Sunderland 2–1
Queen's Park Rangers v Glossop 2–1
Brighton & Hove Albion v Lincoln City 2–1
Millwall v Clapton Orient 2–1
Hull City v West Bromwich Albion 1–0
Croydon Common v Oldham Athletic 0–3
Bradford v Portsmouth 1–0
Swansea Town v Blackburn Rovers 1–0
The Arsenal v Merthyr Town 3–0
Played on 9 Jan, replay on 16 Jan
Birmingham v Crystal Palace 2–2, 3–0
(both matches were played at St Andrews, Birmingham)
Bury v Plymouth Argyle 1–1, 2–1
Preston North End v Manchester City 0–0, 0–3
West Ham United v Newcastle United 2–2, 2–3
Chelsea v Swindon Town 1–1, 5–2 *(aet, 90 mins 2-2)*
Played on 16 Jan, replay on 23 Jan
Bristol Rovers v Southend United 0–0, 0–3

Second round
Played on 30 Jan
Burnley v Southend United 6–0
Bury v Bradford 0–1
The Wednesday v Wolverhampton Wanderers 2–0
Everton v Bristol City 4–0
Sheffield United v Liverpool 1–0
Manchester City v Aston Villa 1–0
Queen's Park Rangers v Leeds City 1–0
Fulham v Southampton 2–3
Norwich City v Tottenham Hotspur 3–2
Bradford City v Middlesbrough 1–0
Hull City v Northampton Town 2–1
Oldham Athletic v Rochdale 3–0
Chelsea v The Arsenal 1–0
Played on 30 Jan, replay on 6 Feb
Brighton & Hove Albion v Birmingham 0–0, 0–3
Newcastle United v Swansea Town 1–1, 2–0
Played on 30 Jan, replay on 6 Feb, second replay on 13 Feb
Bolton Wanderers v Millwall 0–0, 2-2, 4-1 *(third match played at Bolton)*

Third round
Played on 20 Feb
Birmingham v Oldham Athletic 2–3
The Wednesday v Newcastle United 1–2
Bolton Wanderers v Burnley 2–1
Sheffield United v Bradford 1–0
Manchester City v Chelsea 0–1
Queen's Park Rangers v Everton 1–2
Played on 20 Feb, replay on 27 Feb
Southampton v Hull City 2–2, 0-4
Played on 20 Feb, replay on 27 Feb, second replay on 3 Mar
Bradford City v Norwich City 1–1, 0-0, 2-0

Fourth round
Played on 6 Mar
Bolton Wanderers v Hull City 4–2
Bradford City v Everton 0–2
Played on 6 Mar, replay on 13 Mar
Oldham Athletic v Sheffield United 0–0, 0-3
Chelsea v Newcastle United 1–1, 1-0

Semi-final
Played on 27 Mar
Sheffield United v Bolton Wanderers 2-1
(at Villa Park, Birmingham)
Chelsea v Everton 2-0
(at Ewood Park, Blackburn)

Final
24 Apr 1915 at Old Trafford, Manchester
Att 49,557
Sheffield United 3 *(Simmons, Fazackerly, Kitchen)*
Chelsea 0

Sheffield United: Gough, Cook, English, Sturgess, Brelsford, Utley, Simmons, Fazackerley, Kitchen, Masterman, Evans
Chelsea: Molyneux, Bettridge, Harrow, Taylor, Logan, Walker, Ford, Halse, Thomson, Croal, McNeil

Other English and Welsh Competitions 1914-15

LANCASHIRE CUP

First round
Played on 21 Sep
Accrington Stanley v Nelson 0-3
South Liverpool v Southport Central 5-0
Played on 23 Sep
Chorley v Eccles Borough 2-4
Fleetwood v Rochdale 2-3
Heywood United v Barrow wo-scr

Second round
Played on 5 Oct
Blackburn Rovers v Blackpool 4-2
Burnley v Manchester United 5-0
Everton v Bury 1-1
REPLAY on 13 Oct
Bury v Everton 1-4
Manchester City v Liverpool 3-6
Oldham Athletic v Heywood United 3-2
Preston North End v Bolton Wanderers 1-0
Rochdale v Nelson 3-2
Played on 7 Oct
South Liverpool v Eccles Borough 4-1

Third round
Played on 19 Oct
Liverpool v Burnley 1-5
Oldham Athletic v Preston North End 3-0
Played on 20 Oct
Rochdale v South Liverpool 2-0
Played on 21 Oct
Everton v Blackburn Rovers 1-3

Semi-final
Played on 9 Nov
Burnley v Blackburn Rovers 2-1 *(at Turf Moor, Burnley)*
Rochdale v Oldham Athletic 2-0 *(at Gigg Lane, Bury)*

Final
Played on 7 Dec at Hyde Road, Manchester
Burnley v Rochdale 4-1

BIRMINGHAM CHARITY CUP
Played on 23 Sep
Aston Villa v Birmingham 2-3

LINCOLNSHIRE CUP

Final
Played on 1 May at Blundell Park, Cleethorpes
Lincoln City v Grimsby Town 3-2

LONDON CHALLENGE CUP

First round
Woolwich v Ilford
Played on 21 Sep
Nunhead v Tottenham Hotspur 1-2
The Arsenal v Tufnell Park 6-0
Queen's Park Rangers v Chelsea 1-0
West Ham United v Croydon Common 5-1
Millwall v Clapton Orient 3-1
Fulham v Brentford 0-1
Dulwich Hamlet v Crystal Palace 0-1

Second round
Played on 19 Oct
Crystal Palace v Tottenham Hotspur 3-1
The Arsenal v Queen's Park Rangers 2-1
West Ham United v Brentford 1-0
Millwall v Ilford 3-2

Semi-final
Played on 9 Nov
Crystal Palace v The Arsenal 0-2 *(at White Hart Lane)*
Millwall v West Ham United 1-0 *(at Stamford Bridge)*

Final
Played on 7 Dec at The Den
Millwall v The Arsenal 2-1

LIVERPOOL SENIOR CUP

Semi-final
Played on 28 Oct
Liverpool v South Liverpool 5-0

Final
Played on 25 Nov at Goodison Park, Liverpool
Liverpool v Tranmere Rovers 1-1
REPLAY on 10 Apr at Anfield Road, Liverpool
Liverpool v Tranmere Rovers 1-0

SUNDERLAND HOSPITAL CUP
Played on 23 Sep
Newcastle United v Sunderland 0-1

WELSH FA CUP
Matches involving Football League or Southern League clubs only

Preliminary round
Barry v Ynysddu wo-scr
Played on DATE UNKNOWN
Troedyrhiw v Mid Rhondda 0-2
Cardiff Albions v Mardy 0-6
Ystradmynach v Merthyr Town 0-11
Ton Pentre v Ebbw Vale 6-0
Newport County v Abertillery 3-0

First round
Played on DATE UNKNOWN
Bargoed v Mid Rhondda 0-1
Merthyr Town v Mardy 7-0
Gilfach v Barry 0-1 (protested?)

Second round
Played on DATE UNKNOWN
Merthyr Town v Mid Rhondda 1-0
Gilfach v Ton Pentre 1-7

Third round
Pontypridd v Cardiff City wo-scr
Swansea Town v Milford Town wo-scr
Llandrindod Wells v Merthyr Town scr-wo
Played on DATE UNKNOWN
Llanelly v Ton Pentre 3-1

Fourth round
Played on DATE UNKNOWN
Swansea Town v Pontypridd 2-1
Merthy Town v Llanelly 0-9

Semi-final
Played on DATE UNKNOWN
Swansea Town v llanelly 1-0 *(at Vetch Field, Swansea)*
Llandudno v Wrexham 1-3 *(at Llandudno)*

Final
Played on 15 Apr at The Racecourse, Wrexham
Wrexham v Swansea Town 1-1
REPLAY on 25 Apr at Ninian Park, Cardiff
Wrexham v Swansea Town 1-0

The Scottish Football League 1914-15

FIRST DIVISION

	Aberdeen	Airdrieonians	Ayr U	Celtic	Clyde	Dumbarton	Dundee	Falkirk	Hamilton Acad	Hearts	Hibernian	Kilmarnock	Morton	Motherwell	Partick Th	Queen's Park	Raith Rovers	Rangers	St Mirren	Third Lanark
Aberdeen	X	20 Mar 3-0	5 Jan 1-1	5 Dec 0-1	5 Sep 2-0	21 Nov 0-0	1 Jan 2-1	23 Jan 1-2	17 Jan 1-2	3 Apr 1-0	20 Apr 0-0	19 Feb 0-0	6 Dec 3-0	19 Feb 2-0	6 Sep 3-1	28 Mar 0-0	7 Nov 1-3	22 Nov 0-2	3 Oct 0-0	17 Oct 1-2
Airdrieonians	10 Oct 3-0	X	17 Apr 1-2	19 Dec 0-1	20 Feb 2-1	6 Feb 4-1	24 Oct 3-4	5 Dec 3-2	12 Sep 3-2	13 Mar 2-2	9 Jan 1-3	26 Jan 0-2	1 Sep 0-0	7 Nov 4-1	27 Mar 0-0	22 Aug 2-1	10 Apr 3-3	21 Nov 1-2	23 Jan 2-1	15 Aug 1-0
Ayr United	12 Sep 1-0	29 Aug 0-0	X	10 Oct 1-0	24 Apr 3-1	19 Dec 2-1	10 Apr 0-0	6 Mar 1-2	27 Mar 2-0	31 Oct 0-2	4 Jan 2-1	20 Feb 2-0	14 Nov 2-1	13 Mar 1-1	15 Aug 4-0	6 Feb 2-1	5 Dec 3-0	17 Oct 2-0	26 Sep 0-2	2 Jan 1-0
Celtic	10 Apr 1-0	3 Apr 3-0	21 Nov 4-0	X	28 Sep 3-0	20 Feb 1-0	3 Oct 6-0	17 Oct 1-0	26 Dec 3-1	30 Jan 1-1	6 Mar 5-1	4 Jan 2-0	5 Sep 6-2	22 Aug 1-0	9 Jan 6-1	12 Dec 5-1	27 Mar 3-1	31 Oct 2-1	6 Feb 2-1	14 Nov 1-0
Clyde	16 Jan 3-0	19 Sep 0-0	20 Mar 3-1	2 Jan 0-2	X	24 Oct 2-1	13 Feb 1-1	1 Jan 4-2	27 Feb 2-2	7 Nov 1-2	15 Aug 1-0	23 Jan 1-0	5 Dec 2-3	3 Apr 0-0	19 Dec 1-3	17 Apr 2-1	29 Aug 1-0	13 Mar 1-2	28 Nov 1-2	5 Apr 1-2
Dumbarton	30 Jan 3-2	17 Oct 1-4	5 Sep 1-2	28 Nov 1-4	26 Dec 2-1	X	19 Sep 1-1	24 Apr 0-1	13 Feb 0-1	3 Oct 3-2	20 Mar 1-0	3 Apr 1-0	27 Feb 3-2	10 Apr 1-0	5 Dec 0-2	9 Jan 3-1	1 Jan 3-1	14 Nov 1-1	22 Aug 2-4	31 Oct 2-1
Dundee	15 Aug 1-3	27 Feb 2-0	12 Dec 2-3	26 Sep 1-3	12 Apr 3-0	5 Oct 0-0	X	9 Jan 1-0	29 Aug 1-0	17 Oct 1-2	26 Dec 2-4	31 Oct 0-1	23 Jan 1-1	14 Nov 1-0	6 Feb 1-2	3 Apr 2-0	17 Apr 2-0	12 Sep 1-1	20 Feb 2-1	5 Dec 0-0
Falkirk	24 Oct 1-1	30 Jan 2-1	7 Nov 1-1	16 Jan 0-1	21 Nov 3-1	15 Aug 1-3	10 Oct 0-1	X	26 Sep 2-0	2 Jan 1-1	27 Mar 0-0	10 Apr 3-2	19 Dec 2-0	28 Aug 5-1	29 Aug 2-1	13 Feb 1-0	27 Feb 3-1	5 Sep 1-3	3 Apr 2-0	13 Mar 1-1
Hamilton Academical	14 Nov 3-0	6 Mar 0-1	22 Aug 2-1	24 Oct 0-1	3 Oct 3-2	10 Oct 4-1	19 Dec 2-0	20 Mar 0-1	X	28 Nov 1-3	6 Feb 2-2	13 Mar 0-0	19 Sep 1-1	1 Jan 0-3	7 Nov 2-2	23 Jan 3-0	5 Sep 1-1	3 Apr 4-3	9 Jan 5-2	20 Feb 4-2
Hearts	26 Sep 2-0	12 Dec 3-1	21 Sep 1-0	15 Aug 2-0	27 Mar 2-0	6 Mar 4-1	16 Jan 3-2	14 Nov 2-0	4 Jan 3-0	X	5 Dec 3-1	6 Feb 3-1	9 Jan 1-0	10 Oct 2-0	20 Mar 3-1	24 Oct 2-2	26 Dec 4-0	20 Feb 3-4	12 Sep 5-0	29 Aug 2-0
Hibernian	31 Oct 1-2	5 Sep 1-0	3 Oct 0-4	19 Sep 1-1	21 Sep 3-1	7 Nov 2-2	21 Nov 2-0	22 Aug 1-1	17 Oct 0-2	27 Feb 2-2	X	2 Jan 3-1	13 Mar 1-1	23 Jan 1-2	28 Nov 4-1	10 Apr 4-0	13 Feb 2-1	30 Jan 1-2	19 Dec 3-2	3 Apr 4-2
Kilmarnock	28 Nov 5-2	26 Dec 2-1	19 Sep 1-2	7 Nov 1-3	22 Aug 0-3	16 Jan 4-0	20 Mar 3-2	3 Oct 1-0	30 Jan 1-0	5 Sep 0-2	24 Oct 5-1	X	24 Apr 2-2	6 Mar 2-2	13 Feb 2-0	27 Feb 2-0	9 Jan 3-1	12 Dec 0-1	1 Jan 2-1	27 Mar 2-1
Morton	29 Aug 1-1	28 Nov 4-1	26 Dec 3-0	13 Feb 0-2	12 Dec 2-0	12 Sep 3-2	7 Sep 2-0	4 Nov 2-0	2 Jan 1-0	10 Apr 4-0	26 Sep 0-0	15 Aug 3-1	X	20 Mar 2-0	24 Oct 2-2	10 Oct 1-0	21 Nov 0-1	16 Jan 3-3	6 Mar 4-2	30 Jan 4-2
Motherwell	26 Dec 1-1	2 Jan 4-2	16 Jan 1-1	24 Apr 1-1	31 Oct 0-2	26 Sep 2-3	30 Jan 1-1	12 Dec 4-1	5 Dec 2-4	13 Feb 0-1	29 Aug 3-0	12 Sep 3-2	17 Oct 1-1	X	17 Apr 1-0	21 Nov 1-0	15 Aug 1-2	27 Feb 2-4	27 Mar 0-2	3 Oct 3-2
Partick Thistle	12 Dec 3-0	31 Oct 4-0	30 Jan 2-0	27 Feb 0-2	14 Nov 0-0	13 Mar 1-2	22 Aug 4-1	20 Feb 2-0	10 Apr 1-4	21 Nov 0-2	16 Jan 3-1	17 Oct 0-0	3 Apr 1-5	5 Sep 4-1	X	26 Dec 5-0	5 Jan 2-1	2 Jan 3-1	24 Apr 0-1	1 Jan 1-1
Queen's Park	13 Mar 3-1	16 Jan 0-1	28 Nov 1-1	5 Apr 0-3	17 Oct 0-1	29 Aug 2-2	2 Jan 0-3	12 Dec 1-2	31 Oct 0-2	19 Dec 0-4	14 Nov 0-2	5 Dec 1-0	27 Mar 0-2	20 Feb 0-3	3 Oct 0-2	X	30 Jan 1-3	24 Apr 0-4	15 Aug 4-1	6 Mar 1-2
Raith Rovers	2 Jan 5-1	3 Oct 3-0	3 Apr 0-0	5 Oct 2-2	6 Mar 2-0	12 Dec 1-2	28 Nov 1-1	31 Oct 1-3	16 Jan 1-3	22 Jan 1-3	12 Aug 1-3	14 Sep 3-0	20 Feb 1-1	6 Feb 2-1	23 Jan 2-2	19 Sep 1-2	X	10 Oct 1-2	17 Oct 2-2	19 Dec 1-1
Rangers	27 Mar 1-1	4 Jan 0-5	13 Feb 1-3	1 Jan 2-1	9 Jan 1-2	23 Jan 1-0	6 Mar 2-0	6 Feb 3-0	15 Aug 1-0	19 Sep 1-2	28 Sep 4-2	29 Aug 2-1	3 Oct 0-2	19 Dec 5-0	5 Apr 0-1	7 Nov 4-1	24 Oct 1-2	X	5 Dec 5-0	28 Nov 3-0
St Mirren	13 Feb 0-2	14 Nov 0-0	27 Feb 1-3	29 Aug 3-3	30 Jan 3-1	2 Jan 1-1	5 Sep 0-1	26 Dec 2-0	12 Dec 1-0	17 Apr 1-0	10 Oct 4-2	21 Nov 2-3	31 Oct 2-4	24 Oct 1-1	19 Sep 2-0	20 Mar 3-0	13 Mar 3-2	10 Apr 0-2	X	16 Jan 2-0
Third Lanark	27 Feb 0-1	13 Feb 0-2	24 Oct 2-1	17 Apr 0-4	6 Feb 1-1	13 Apr 1-0	25 Dec 7-0	19 Sep 0-0	27 Apr 1-2	23 Jan 2-2	12 Dec 2-2	10 Oct 3-2	22 Aug 3-3	9 Jan 1-0	28 Sep 4-0	5 Sep 1-1	26 Sep 3-0	26 Dec 1-1	7 Nov 0-0	X

The Scottish Football League 1914-15

FIRST DIVISION

		P	W	D	L	F	A	Pts
1	Celtic	38	30	5	3	91	25	65
2	Heart of Midlothian	38	27	7	4	83	32	61
3	Rangers	38	23	4	11	74	47	50
4	Morton	38	18	12	8	74	48	48
5	Ayr United	38	20	8	10	55	40	48
6	Falkirk	38	16	7	15	48	48	39
7	Partick Thistle	38	15	8	15	56	58	38
8	Hamilton Academical	38	16	6	16	60	55	38
9	St. Mirren	38	14	8	16	56	65	36
10	Hibernian	38	12	11	15	59	66	35
11	Airdrieonians	38	14	7	17	54	60	35
12	Dumbarton	38	13	8	17	51	66	34
13	Kilmarnock	38	15	4	19	55	59	34
14	Dundee	38	12	9	17	43	61	33
15	Aberdeen	38	11	11	16	39	52	33
16	Third Lanark	38	10	12	16	51	57	32
17	Clyde	38	12	6	20	44	59	30
18	Motherwell	38	10	10	18	49	66	30
19	Raith Rovers	38	9	10	19	53	68	28
20	Queen's Park	38	4	5	29	27	90	13

SECOND DIVISION

		P	W	D	L	F	A	Pts
1	Cowdenbeath	26	16	5	5	49	17	37
2	Leith	26	15	7	4	54	31	37
3	St Bernard's	26	18	1	7	66	34	37
4	East Stirlingshire	26	13	5	8	53	44	31
5	Clydebank	26	13	4	9	67	37	30
6	Dunfermline Athletic	26	13	2	11	49	39	28
7	Johnstone	26	11	5	10	41	52	27
8	St. Johnstone	26	10	6	10	56	53	26
9	Albion Rovers	26	9	7	10	37	42	25
10	Lochgelly United	26	9	3	14	43	60	21
11	Dundee Hibernian	26	8	3	15	48	61	19
12	Abercorn	26	5	7	14	35	65	17
13	Arthurlie	26	6	4	16	36	66	16
14	Vale of Leven	26	4	5	17	33	66	13

SECOND DIVISION

	Abercorn	Albion R	Arthurlie	Clydebank	Cowdenbeath	Dundee H	Dunfermline Ath	East Stirlingshire	Johnstone	Leith	Lochgelly U	St Bernard's	St Johnstone	Vale of Leven
Abercorn	X	12 Sep 1-0	20 Feb 1-2	3 Oct 4-2	26 Sep 2-2	17 Oct 4-2	6 Feb 1-2	7 Nov 3-3	22 Aug 1-1	6 Mar 1-1	5 Dec 0-1	15 Aug 1-3	9 Jan 3-1	28 Nov 3-1
Albion Rovers	14 Nov 0-0	X	17 Oct 2-0	28 Nov 2-2	12 Dec 0-1	31 Oct 3-0	19 Sep 3-0	2 Jan 4-2	29 Aug 2-2	3 Oct 1-1	16 Jan 2-1	26 Dec 1-1	27 Feb 4-1	6 Mar 4-1
Arthurlie	29 Aug 1-1	6 Feb 0-3	X	26 Dec 0-3	13 Feb 0-2	9 Jan 2-1	5 Dec 2-0	26 Sep 0-1	12 Dec 1-3	23 Jan 0-2	3 Apr 5-3	24 Oct 1-2	10 Oct 2-2	27 Feb 5-1
Clydebank	31 Oct 6-1	26 Sep 1-1	16 Jan 6-0	X	1 Jan 1-0	14 Nov 2-3	21 Nov 3-0	15 Aug 3-1	10 Oct 5-1	5 Dec 9-2	6 Mar 4-3	6 Feb 1-4	19 Dec 2-2	22 Aug 3-1
Cowdenbeath	21 Nov 5-0	24 Oct 2-0	7 Nov 5-1	20 Feb 2-1	X	12 Sep 3-0	22 Aug 3-1	19 Dec 2-1	2 Jan 3-0	30 Jan 0-1	6 Feb 2-0	5 Sep 2-0	17 Oct 1-0	5 Dec 3-0
Dundee Hibernian	16 Jan 2-1	19 Dec 3-3	22 Aug 3-3	19 Sep 1-3	28 Nov 2-2	X	7 Nov 0-2	24 Oct 1-3	1 Jan 3-0	21 Nov 4-0	3 Oct 1-0	10 Oct 3-1	2 Jan 3-1	13 Feb 2-1
Dunfermline Athletic	10 Oct 3-0	9 Jan 4-0	2 Jan 3-2	12 Dec 1-0	23 Jan 0-1	15 Aug 3-1	X	29 Aug 2-2	28 Nov 3-1	31 Oct 2-3	1 Jan 1-3	26 Sep 2-1	24 Oct 3-2	14 Nov 7-2
East Stirlingshire	12 Dec 3-2	22 Aug 0-0	17 Apr 3-0	27 mar 3-1	9 Jan 0-0	6 Feb 4-3	6 Mar 2-0	X	26 Dec 4-1	17 Oct 3-0	23 Jan 3-2	12 Sep 3-0	20 Feb 2-1	31 Oct 3-2
Johnstone	30 Jan 4-1	7 Nov 2-2	3 Oct 2-1	23 Jan 1-0	31 Oct 2-1	5 Dec 2-1	17 Oct 1-0	16 Jan 3-1	X	9 Jan 0-0	20 Feb 3-1	20 Mar 2-1	15 Aug 3-4	6 Feb 2-0
Leith	24 Oct 3-3	20 Feb 3-2	15 aug 3-2	29 Aug 0-2	10 Oct 0-0	26 Sep 4-2	12 Sep 1-0	3 Apr 1-0	14 Nov 3-0	X	2 Jan 5-0	28 Nov 5-0	6 Feb 3-0	26 Dec 4-1
Lochgelly United	20 Mar 4-0	10 Dec 1-0	13 mar 2-2	30 Jan 1-3	15 Aug 0-4	26 Dec 2-1	27 Mar 1-4	27 Feb 6-1	17 Apr 6-0	12 Dec 0-0	X	29 Aug 1-3	26 Sep 1-1	9 Jan 1-0
St Bernard's	27 Feb 4-0	21 Nov 6-0	30 Jan 2-1	17 Oct 1-0	13 Mar 5-1	23 Jan 2-1	19 Dec 3-2	13 Feb 4-2	6 Mar 2-0	22 Aug 6-0	10 Apr X	27 Mar 3-1	19 Sep 2-1
St Johnstone	26 Dec 4-0	23 Jan 4-1	24 Apr 2-3	7 Nov 4-3	20 Mar 2-1	29 Aug 3-1	3 Oct 2-2	30 jan 3-2	13 Feb 2-2	1 Jan 2-2	22 Aug 5-1	14 Nov 3-1	X	13 Mar 2-0
Vale of Leven	23 Jan 5-1	15 Aug 0-1	19 Dec 4-1	2 Jan 0-0	29 Aug 2-2	12 Dec 1-1	16 Jna 0-3	10 Oct 1-1	24 Oct 2-1	7 Nov 1-1	24 Apr 1-2	20 Feb 1-7	12 Sep 4-2	X

SECOND DIVISION CHAMPIONSHIP PLAY-OFF

Played on 10 Apr at East End Park, Dunfermline
Cowdenbeath v Leith 2-1
Played on 17 Apr at Easter Road, Edinburgh
Leith v St Bernard's 2-1
Played on 24 Apr at Easter Road, Edinburgh
Cowdenbeath v St Bernard's 3-1

Cowdenbeath were declared Second Division champions

Other Scottish Competitions 1914-15

WAR FUND SHIELD

First round
Played on 20 Oct
  Third Lanark v Rangers 0-4
Played on 27 Oct
  Queen's Park v Morton 0-3
Played on 3 Nov
  Clyde v St Mirren 0-1 *(at Ibrox Park, Glasgow)*
Played on 10 Nov
  Partick Thistle v Celtic 1-1
REPLAY on 1 Dec
  Celtic v Partick Thistle 2-1

Semi-final
Played on 15 Dec
  Rangers v Celtic 2-1 *(at Firhill Park, Glasgow)*
Played on 12 Apr
  Morton v St Mirren 2-1
(This also doubled as a Renfrewshire Cup tie)

Final
28 Apr 1915 at Firhill Park, Glasgow
Att 18,000
Morton 2 *(McLaughlin, Seymour)*
Rangers 1 *(Bennett)*

Morton: Bradford, ferrier, Ormonde, Wright, Stark, McLean, Torrance, Gourlay, McLaughlin, Stevenson, Seymour
Rangers: Lock, Craig, Muir, Gordon, Purcell, Bowie, Duncan, Cunningham, Bennett, Cairns, Paterson

GLASGOW CUP
First round
Played on 12 Sep
  Clyde v Celtic 2-0
  Partick Thistle v Third Lanark 1-0

Semi-final
Played on 26 Sep
  Rangers v Partick Thistle 0-2
  Clyde v Queen's Park 0-0
REPLAY on 6 Oct
  Queen's Park v Clyde 0-2

Final
Played on 10 Oct at Ibrox Park, Glasgow
  Clyde v Partick Thistle 1-1
REPLAY on 13 Oct at Ibrox Park, Glasgow
  Clyde v Partick Thistle 1-0

GLASGOW CHARITY CUP
First round
Played on 1 May
  Queen's Park v Celtic 1-2
  Third Lanark v Clyde 1-0

Semi-final
Played on 4 May
  Third Lanark v Rangers 0-3
Played on 5 May
  Celtic v Partick Thistle 1-1 *(Celtic won 4-3 on corners)*

Final
Played on 8 May at Ibrox Park, Glasgow
  Celtic v Rangers 3-2

DUNBARTONSHIRE CUP

	Clydebank	Dumbarton	Dumbarton Harp	Renton	Vale of Leven
Clydebank	X	21 Apr 0-2	9 Jan 5-0	24 Oct 1-0	3 Apr 3-0
Dumbarton		X	5 Apr 0-1	17 Apr 0-2	1 May 4-3
Dumbarton Harp		19 Apr 0-2	X	20 Feb 3-1	
Renton	13 Mar 2-0	28 Apr 3-1	6 Mar 3-1	X	10 Apr 3-7
Vale of Leven	17 Apr 2-0	27 Mar 0-0	20 Mar 5-0	21 Apr 2-1	X

		P	W	D	L	F	A	Pts
1	Vale of Leven	7	4	1	2	19	11	9
2	Renton	8	4	0	4	15	15	8
3	Dumbarton	7	3	1	3	9	9	7
4	Clydebank	6	3	0	2	9	6	6
5	Dumbarton Harp	6	2	0	4	9	6	4

FORFARSHIRE CUP
First round
  Dundee Hibernian v Arbroath Amateurs wo-scr
Played on 21 Nov
  Arbroath v Brechin City 3-0
Played on 12 Dec
  Forfar Athletic v Montrose 3-0

Semi-final
Played on 27 Feb
  Forfar Athletic v Arbroath 1-2
Played on 6 Mar
  Dundee Hibernian v Dundee 3-1

Final
Played on 27 Mar at Dens Park, Dundee
  Dundee Hibernian v Arbroath 2-0

Other Scottish Competitions 1914-15

AYRSHIRE CUP

First round
Due to be played on 23 Jan
  Beith v Hurlford
  Galston v Annbank

Semi-final
DATES unknown
  Stevenston United beat Beith
  Kilmarnock 'A' v beat Girvan Athletic or Maybole

Second round
Played on 6 Feb
  Kilmarnock ' A' v Galston 2-1
Due to be played on 6 Feb
  Girvan Athletic v Maybole
  Beith v Ardrossan Academy FP
  Stevenston United v Lanemark

Final
Played on 17 Apr at Riverside Park, Galston
  Stevenston United v Kilmarnock 0-0
REPLAY on 24 Apr at Riverside Park, Galston
  Stevenston United v Kilmarnock 2-1

Semi-final
Played on 26 Aug
  Albion Rovers v Motherwell 0-4
Played on 2 Sep
  Airdrieonians v Hamilton Academical 3-0

LANARKSHIRE CUP

Final
Played on 7 Jan at Douglas Park, Hamilton
  Airdrieonians v Motherwell 3-1

First round
Played on 18 Aug
  Bridge of Weir Athletic v Arthurlie
Played on 29 Aug
  Moorpark Crusaders v Paisley Grammar School FP 4-1

RENFREWSHIRE CUP

Semi-final
Played on 27 Mar
  Johnstone v Arthurlie 2-0
Played on 12 Apr
  Morton v St Mirren 2-1

Second round
DATES unknown
  Morton v Abercorn 8-2
  St Mirren v Moorpark Crusaders 4-1

Final – 2 legs
First leg played on 16 Apr , second leg on 17 Apr
  Johnstone v Morton 3-0, 0-4

Semi-final
Played on 28 Nov
  Aberdeen v Buckie Thistle 2-2
REPLAY on 19 Dec
  Buckie Thistle v Aberdeen 0-3

ABERDEENSHIRE CUP

Final
Played on 13 Mar at Pittodrie Park, Aberdeen
  Aberdeen v Peterhead 7-2

Semi-final
Played on 17 Aug
  Heart of Midlothian v Falkirk 3-2
Played on 19 Aug
  Hibernian v Raith Rovers 3-0

DUNEDIN CUP

Final
Played on 26 Aug at Tynecastle Park, Edinburgh
  Heart of Midlothian v Hibernian 6-0

NOTE the final was played at the start of 1915-16 season

EAST OF SCOTLAND CITY CUP

Semi-final
Due to be played on 20 Mar
  Leith Amateurs v St Bernard's
  Peebles Rovers v Leith

COMPETITION ABANDONED

ROBERTSON CUP

2 legs, first leg played on 24 Apr, second leg on 1 May
  Dundee v Aberdeen 1-0, 1-1

WILSON CUP

Played on 1 Jan at Easter Road, Edinburgh
  Hibernian v Heart of Midlothian 1-2

Semi-final
Played on 25 Dec
  Heart of Midlothian v Leith 1-1
REPLAY on 19 Apr
  Heart of Midlothian v Leith 6-1
Played on 21 Apr
  St Bernard's v Hibernian 0-2

EAST OF SCOTLAND SHIELD

Final
Played on 24 Apr at Tynecastle Park, Edinburgh
  Heart of Midlothian v Hibernian 1-0

Semi-final
Played on 1 May
  Heart of Midlothian v St Bernard's 2-3
  Hibernian v Leith 4-1

ROSEBERY CHARITY CUP

Final
Played on 8 May at Tynecastle Park, Edinburgh
  St Bernard's v Hibernian 4-3 *(aet, 90 mins 3-3)*

Other Scottish Competitions 1914-15

FIFE CUP

First round
DATE unknown
St Andrews University v Cowdenbeath

Second round
Kirkcaldy United v Lochgelly wo –scr
Lumphinnans v Raith Rovers scr-wo
Played on 13 Feb
Lochgelly United v Dunfermline Athletic 3-0
Played on 27 Feb
Cowdenbeath v East Fife 3-0 *(abandoned due to a snowstorm)*
REPLAY on 6 Mar
Cowdenbeath v East Fife 0-0
SECOND REPLAY on 27 Mar
Cowdenbeath v East Fife 0-0
THIRD REPLAY on 14 Apr at Stark's Park, Kirkcaldy
East Fife v Cowdenbeath 1-0

Semi-final
Played on 20 Mar
Raith Rovers v Kirkcaldy United 5-0 *(Protest upheld)*
REPLAY on 10 Apr
Raith Rovers v Kirkcaldy United 2-0 *(aet, 90 mins 0-0)*
Played on 21 Apr
Lochgelly United v East Fife 0-1

Final
Played on 28 Apr at Stark's Park, Kirkcaldy
Raith Rovers v East Fife 4-0

WEMYSS CUP

Semi-final
First round
Kirkcaldy United v Lochgelly wo-scr

Second round
Lochgelly United v Lumphinnans wo-scr
DATES unknown
Kirkcaldy United v Raith Rovers
St Andrews University v Dunfermline Athletic
Played on 27 Feb
Cowdenbeath v East Fife 3-0 *(abandoned)*
REPLAY on 3 Apr
Cowdenbeath v East Fife 3-1

Semi-final
Played on 5 Apr
Raith Rovers v Lochgelly United 3-2
Played on 17 Apr
Cowdenbeath v Dunfermline Athletic 1-1
REPLAY on 28 Apr
Cowdenbeath v Dunfermline Athletic 1-0

Final
Played on 30 Apr
Cowdenbeath v Raith Rovers *(aet, Raith won 1-0 on corners)*

PENMAN CUP

First round
Played on 16 Jan
Leith v Stenhousemuir 5-0
Played on 23 Jan
Broxburn United v Armadale 0-0
REPLAY on 13 Mar
Broxburn United v Armadale 0-3

Second round
Lumphinnans v Alloa Athletic scr-wo
Lochgelly v Bathgate scr-wo
Clackmannan v Cowdenbeath
Played on 1 Jan
East Stirlingshire v Kirkcaldy United 2-0
Played on 2 Jan
King's Park v Raith Rovers 3-2
Played on 27 Feb
Dunfermline Athletic v Leith 1-0 (abandoned due to the weather)
REPLAY on 20 Mar
Leith v Dunfermline Athletic 2-1
DATES unknown
East Fife v Lochgelly United
Armadale v Bo'ness

Third round
Alloa Athletic v Armadale or Bo'ness
East Fife v Bathgate
DATES unknown
East Stirlingshire v Leith
King's Park v Clackmannan or Cowdenbeath

Semi-final
East Stirlingshire v East Fife or Bathgate
King's Park v Alloa Athletic or Broxburn United

COMPETITION ABANDONED

PAISLEY CHARITY CUP

Semi-final
Played on 1 May
Johnstone v Arthurlie 4-3
Played on 8 May
St Mirren v Abercorn 3-1

Final
Played on 15 May at St Mirren Park, Paisley
St Mirren v Johnstone 1-0

Other Scottish Competitions 1914-15

SCOTTISH FA QUALIFYING CUP
Results of games involving Scottish Football League clubs only

First round
Paisley Grammar School FP v Abercorn scr-wo
Played on 5 Sep
Clackmannan v East Stirlingshire 0-4
Dundee Hibernian v Forfar Athletic 0-4
Kirkcaldy United v Dunfermline Athletic 1-0
Leith v Bathgate 3-1
Lochgelly United v Lumphinnans 3-0
St Johnstone v Crieff Morrisonians 6-2
Vale of Leven v Albion Rovers 3-1
Played on 5 Sep, REPLAY on 12 Sep
Clydebank v Arthurlie 2-2, 1-2
Played on 5 Sep, REPLAY on 12 Sep, SECOND REPLAY on 19 Sep at Clydeholm, Clydebank
Royal Albert v Johnstone 0-0, 0-0, 1-5

Second round
St Bernard's v Duns wo-scr
Played on 19 Sep
Arbroath v Cowdenbeath 1-4
Armadale v Leith 2-0
Arthurlie v Abercorn 2-1
Blairgowrie v St Johnstone 0-7
Lochgelly United v Brechin City 7-1
Tulloch v East Stirlingshire 1-5
Played on 26 Sep
Vale of Leven v Johnstone 1-0

Third round
Played on 3 Oct
Cowdenbeath v East Stirlingshire 1-3
Peebles Rovers v St Bernard's 1-3

Fourth round
Played on 17 Oct
Dumfries v Vale of Leven 1-0
Played on 24 Oct, REPLAY on 31 Oct, SECOND REPLAY on 7 Nov at East End Park, Dunfermline
Alloa v Lochgelly United 0-0, 2-2, 0-1

Fifth round
Played on 31 Oct
Arthurlie v Dumfries 2-0
St Johnstone v Forres Mechanics 5-0
Played on 31 Oct, REPLAY on 7 Nov
Broxburn United v St Bernard's 0-0, 0-4
Played on 14 Nov, REPLAYS on 21 Nov and 28 Nov
East Stirlingshire v Lochgelly United 1-1, 1-1, 0-4

Sixth round
Played on 14 Nov, REPLAYS on 21 Nov and 28 Nov
Arthurlie v Galston 2-2, 2-2, 0-4
Played on 21 Nov, REPLAY on 28 Nov
Forfar Athletic v St Johnstone 1-1, 0-1
Played on 5 Dec
St Bernard's v East Stirlingshire 2-1

Semi-final
Played on 12 Dec
St Johnstone v St Bernard's 1-4

Final
Played on 2 Jan at Ibrox Park, Glasgow
St Bernard's v Dykehead 2-2
Played on 9 Jan at Firhill Park, Glasgow
St Bernard's v Dykehead 1-1
Played on 2 Jan at Ibrox Park, Glasgow
St Bernard's v Dykehead 3-0

STIRLINGSHIRE CUP
First round
Played on 23 Jan
Falkirk v Stenhousemuir 1-0
Alloa Athletic v Clackmannan 1-1 *(protest upheld)*
REPLAY on 13 Feb
Alloa Athletic v Clackmannan 2-1

Semi-final
Played on 13 Mar
Alloa Athletic v King's Park 1-1
REPLAY on 20 Mar
King's Park v Alloa Athletic 2-0
Played on 20 Mar
Falkirk v East Stirlingshire 1-1

Final
Played on 3 Apr at Forthbank, Stirling
King's Park v Falkirk 1-1
REPLAY on 10 Apr at Forthbank, Stirling
King's Park v Falkirk 1-0

STIRLINGSHIRE CONSOLATION CUP
Semi-final
Played on 3 Apr
Stenhousemuir v Alloa Athletic 2-0
Played on 10 Apr
East Stirlingshire v Clackmannan 4-2

Final
Played on 1 May at Brockville Park, Falkirk
East Stirlingshire v Stenhousemuir 2-1

FALKIRK INFIRMARY SHIELD
Semi-final
Played on 8 May
Falkirk v East Stirlingshire 0-0 *(Falkirk won 4-1 on corners)*

Final
Played on 15 May at Brockville Park, Falkirk
Falkirk v Stenhousemuir 3-1

WISHAW CHARITY CUP
Played on 10 Apr
Motherwell v Wishaw Thistle 0-0

BLENHEIM CUP
2 legs, first leg played on 18 Aug, second leg on 20 Sep 1915
Leith v St Bernard's 2-0, 1-2

LOFTUS CUP
Round Robin Competition
Known results
21 Sep Dunfermline Athletic v Cowdenbeath 2-3
4 Jan Dunfermline Athletic v East Stirlingshire 5-1
30 Jan Dunfermline Athletic v Dundee Hibernian 6-0
3 Apr Dunfermline Athletic v St Johnstone 4-1
5 Apr Cowdenbeath v Dunfermline Athletic 3-1
17 Apr St Johnstone v Dundee Hibernian 3-2

Ireland 1914-15

IRISH FOOTBALL LEAGUE

	Belfast Celtic	Bohemians	Cliftonville	Distillery	Glenavon	Glentoran	Linfield	Shelbourne
Belfast Celtic	X	1-1	5-0	1-0	3-0	1-0	2-1	1-0
Bohemians	0-3	X	1-2	2-3	2-4	0-3	2-5	0-3
Cliftonville	1-3	2-0	X	0-1	3-1	0-3	1-2	1-3
Distillery	0-1	3-0	4-0	X	4-2	1-2	0-0	0-1
Glenavon	2-2	6-0	1-1	0-3	X	0-0	5-1	0-0
Glentoran	2-0	3-0	2-0	4-3	5-0	X	1-1	1-0
Linfield	0-0	5-2	3-0	3-0	1-1	3-0	X	2-2
Shelbourne	0-1	2-0	0-2	0-1	3-2	1-1	2-0	X

		P	W	D	L	F	A	Pts
1	Belfast Celtic	14	10	3	1	24	7	23
2	Linfield	14	9	3	2	27	10	21
3	Glentoran	14	6	5	3	27	18	17
4	Distillery	14	7	1	6	23	16	15
5	Shelbourne	14	6	3	5	17	12	15
6	Glenavon	14	3	5	6	24	28	11
7	Cliftonville	14	4	1	9	13	29	9
8	Bohemians	14	0	1	13	10	45	1

Semi-final
Belfast Celtic v Shelbourne 0-0, 1-0
Linfield v Distillery 2-0

IRISH FA CUP
Final
Played on 25 Mar at Solitude, Belfast
Linfield v Belfast Celtic 1-0

GOLD CUP
Semi-final
Played on 20 Feb
Linfield v Glenavon 2-0
Shelbourne v Distillery 2-1

First round
Glenavon received a bye
Played on 16 Jan
Cliftonville v Shelbourne 2-4
Belfast Celtic v Linfield 1-1
REPLAY on 13 Feb
Linfield v Belfast Celtic 6-0
Played on 13 Feb
Glentoran v Distillery 1-2

Final
Played on 25 Mar at Solitude, Belfast
Shelbourne v Linfield 1-0

1915-16

Two sections, Lancashire and Midland, replaced the national First and Second Divsions that existed pre-war. To fill in the spare dates, subsidiary tournaments were played in the latter stages of the season. The London members of the Football League combined with Southern League sides to form the London Combination. A similar competition was formed for the western clubs.

In Scotland, the Scottish Football League continued with their championship although the Second Division was suspended. Its clubs also combined with other non-League sides to form the West of Scotland and Eastern Leagues.

The Irish League suspended its competition and was replaced by the Belfast & District League.

WINNERS OF THE PRINCIPAL COMPETITIONS

Football League –	
Lancashire Principal	Manchester City
Lancashire Subsidiary 'North'	Burnley
Lancashire Subsidiary 'South'	Manchester City
Midland Principal	Nottingham Forest
Midland Subsidiary 'Northern'	Leeds City
Midland Subsidiary 'Midland'	Grimsby Town
Midland Subsidiary 'Southern'	Nottingham Forest
London Combination –	
Principal	Chelsea
Supplementary	Chelsea
South Western Combination	Portsmouth
Scottish League	Celtic
West of Scotland League	Vale of Leven
Eastern League	Armadale
Irish FA Cup	Linfield
Belfast & District League	Linfield
Belfast City Cup	Glentoran
Gold Cup	Linfield

The Football League 1915-16

LANCASHIRE SECTION

Principal Competition

	Blackpool	Bolton W	Burnley	Bury	Everton	Liverpool	Manchester City	Manchester United	Oldham Ath	Preston NE	Rochdale	Southport C	Stockport Co	Stoke
Blackpool	X	25 Sep 2-1	15 Jan 2-1	12 Feb 3-1	18 Dec 1-4	6 Nov 5-2	1 Jan 2-0	20 Nov 5-1	11 Sep 4-1	23 Oct 5-1	26 Feb 4-0	4 Dec 0-0	29 Jan 4-1	9 Oct 1-1
Bolton Wanderers	25 Dec 0-2	X	12 Feb 3-0	11 Dec 1-2	16 Oct 3-4	4 Sep 1-1	29 Jan 4-2	18 Sep 3-5	8 Jan 1-6	20 Nov 1-0	22 Jan 3-0	2 Oct 0-7	24 Apr 4-2	6 Nov 2-1
Burnley	16 Oct 5-2	13 Nov 3-0	X	2 Oct 2-2	5 Feb 2-1	25 Dec 3-3	19 Feb 3-1	8 Jan 7-4	30 Oct 4-0	11 Dec 4-1	4 Sep 6-1	22 Jan 5-0	18 Sep 1-1	27 Nov 3-2
Bury	13 Nov 1-2	11 Sep 4-2	1 Jan 3-0	X	4 Dec 0-3	23 Oct 2-1	18 Dec 0-3	5 Feb 2-1	27 Nov 1-2	9 Oct 2-1	30 Oct 3-1	19 Feb 1-1	15 Jan 4-1	25 Dec 4-2
Everton	18 Sep 4-2	15 Jan 2-1	6 Nov 1-2	4 Sep 5-0	X	26 Feb 0-1	23 Oct 4-2	11 Dec 2-0	2 Oct 2-3	12 Feb 2-0	8 Jan 3-2	25 Dec 2-0	20 Nov 2-5	29 Jan 4-1
Liverpool	5 Feb 1-0	4 Dec 3-3	25 Sep 5-2	22 Jan 2-1	27 Nov 4-1	X	11 Sep 0-1	30 Oct 0-2	19 Feb 0-2	1 Jan 0-2	16 Oct 2-2	13 Nov 4-2	9 Oct 0-0	18 Dec 2-0
Manchester City	2 Oct 3-0	30 Oct 1-2	20 Nov 1-0	18 Sep 5-4	22 Jan 2-1	11 Dec 2-1	X	25 Dec 2-1	16 Oct 2-2	26 Feb 8-0	5 Feb 4-1	8 Jan 5-2	4 Sep 3-1	12 Feb 4-2
Manchester United	19 Feb 1-1	18 Dec 1-0	9 Oct 3-7	6 Nov 1-1	11 Sep 2-4	29 Jan 1-1	25 Sep 1-1	X	4 Dec 2-0	15 Jan 4-0	13 Nov 2-0	27 Nov 0-0	23 Oct 3-0	1 Jan 1-2
Oldham Athletic	11 Dec 2-0	9 Oct 6-2	29 Jan 3-1	24 Apr 4-2	XX	20 Nov 1-2	15 Jan 1-2	4 Sep 3-2	X	6 Nov 1-1	25 Dec 2-3	18 Sep 2-1	12 Feb 5-3	23 Oct 1-3
Preston North End	22 Jan 1-2	19 Feb 1-3	11 Sep 0-5	8 Jan 3-1	13 Nov 0-2	2 Oct 1-2	27 Nov 3-2	16 Oct 0-0	5 Feb 0-1	X	18 Sep 1-2	30 Oct 0-5	25 Dec 0-1	4 Dec 2-3
Rochdale	27 Nov 2-3	23 Oct 2-4	4 Dec 1-0	29 Jan 2-1	9 Oct 1-2	15 Jan 3-1	6 Nov 0-2	12 Feb 2-2	25 Sep 0-0	18 Dec 2-4	X	11 Sep 1-0	1 Jan 0-1	19 Feb 3-1
Southport Central	4 Sep 2-0	1 Jan 3-1	23 Oct 1-1	20 Nov 1-0	25 Sep 2-1	12 Feb 5-5	9 Oct 0-2	26 Feb 5-0	18 Dec 2-3	29 Jan 1-0	11 Dec 2-2	X	6 Nov 3-2	15 Jan 1-1
Stockport County	30 Oct 2-1	27 Nov 4-2	18 Dec 0-2	16 Oct 0-2	19 Feb 3-1	8 Jan 1-3	4 Dec 1-1	22 Jan 3-1	13 Nov 2-0	25 Nov 5-0	2 Oct 2-0	5 Feb 1-0	X	11 Sep 3-1
Stoke	8 Jan 3-1	5 Feb 1-1	26 Feb 2-2	25 Sep 3-2	30 Oct 3-2	18 Sep 2-2	13 Nov 1-0	2 Oct 0-0	22 Jan 2-1	4 Sep 3-1	20 Nov 1-1	16 Oct 2-0	11 Dec 0-2	X

Stoke v Oldham Athletic on 27 Dec was abandoned after 45 minutes with the score at 1-1 and replayed at a later date
XX=Oldham Athletic v Everton on 1 Jan was abandoned after 50 minutes with the score at 0-1. The match was not fulfilled.

		P	W	D	L	F	A	Pts
1	Manchester City	26	16	3	7	61	35	35
2	Burnley	26	14	5	7	71	43	33
3	Blackpool	26	14	3	9	54	41	31
4	Everton	25	15	0	10	59	42	30
5	Oldham Athletic	25	13	3	9	52	44	29
6	Liverpool	26	11	7	8	48	42	29
7	Stockport County	26	13	3	10	47	43	29
8	Stoke	26	10	7	9	43	46	27
9	Southport Central	26	9	6	11	41	41	24
10	Bury	26	10	3	13	46	52	23
11	Manchester United	26	7	8	11	41	51	22
12	Bolton Wanderers	26	9	3	14	48	65	21
13	Rochdale	26	7	5	14	34	56	19
14	Preston North End	26	4	2	20	23	67	10

The Football League 1915-16

LANCASHIRE SECTION

Subsidiary Tournament

Northern Division

	Blackpool	Bolton W	Burnley	Bury	Preston NE	Southport C
Blackpool	X	25 Mar 3-1	11 Mar 1-2	8 Apr 4-2	22 Apr 2-0	21 Apr 3-1
Bolton Wanderers	29 Apr 1-2	X	8 Apr 2-0	1 Apr 4-3	11 Mar 1-6	18 Mar 2-0
Burnley	15 Apr 2-1	4 Mar 3-1	X	18 Mar 1-2	21 Apr 4-0	25 Mar 6-1
Bury	4 Mar 1-2	21 Apr 4-2	22 Apr 1-5	X	25 Mar 2-4	15 Apr 1-2
Preston North End	18 Mar 1-3	15 Apr 1-1	1 Apr 1-2	29 Apr 2-0	X	4 Mar 4-1
Southport Central	1 Apr 2-3	22 Apr 0-1	29 Apr 2-4	11 Mar 0-1	8 Apr 3-3	X

		P	W	D	L	F	A	Pts
1	Burnley	10	8	0	2	29	12	16
2	Blackpool	10	8	0	2	24	13	16
3	Preston North End	10	4	2	4	22	19	10
4	Bolton Wanderers	10	4	1	5	16	22	9
5	Bury	10	3	0	7	17	26	6
6	Southport Central	10	1	1	8	12	28	3

Southern Division

	Everton	Liverpool	Manchester City	Manchester United	Oldham Ath	Stockport Co
Everton	X	1 Apr 1-0	18 Mar 1-1	8 Apr 3-1	29 Apr 0-2	11 Mar 2-0
Liverpool	21 Apr 5-2	X	15 Apr 0-2	22 Apr 7-1	4 Mar 4-1	25 Mar 2-1
Manchester City	22 Apr 5-4	11 Mar 1-1	X	29 Apr 2-1	1 Apr 4-4	8 Apr 3-2
Manchester United	4 Mar 0-2	18 Mar 0-0	25 Mar 0-2	X	15 Apr 3-0	21 Apr 3-2
Oldham Athletic	25 Mar 1-2	8 Apr 2-1	21 Apr 4-3	11 Mar 1-0	X	22 Apr 0-0
Stockport County	15 Apr 1-2	29 Apr 2-1	4 Mar 2-0	1 Apr 5-3	18 Mar 4-2	X

		P	W	D	L	F	A	Pts
1	Manchester City	10	5	3	2	23	19	13
2	Everton	10	6	1	3	19	16	13
3	Liverpool	10	4	2	4	21	13	10
4	Oldham Athletic	10	4	2	4	17	21	10
5	Stockport County	10	4	1	5	19	18	9
6	Manchester United	10	2	1	7	12	24	5

The Football League 1915-16

MIDLAND SECTION

Principal Competition

	Barnsley	Bradford	Bradford City	Derby Co	Grimsby T	Huddersfield T	Hull City	Leeds City	Leicester F	Lincoln C	Nottingham F	Notts County	Sheffield United	The Wednesday
Barnsley	X	9 Oct 5-2	27 Nov 3-2	25 Sep 1-1	11 Sep 3-2	4 Dec 2-1	23 Oct 4-1	15 Jan 2-1	13 Jan 3-2	6 Nov 4-2	29 Jan 1-1	18 Dec 1-0	19 Feb 0-0	25 Apr 4-0
Bradford	8 Jan 6-0	X	30 Oct 3-1	27 Nov 2-3	13 Nov 2-0	5 Feb 3-0	25 Dec 1-2	18 Sep 4-3	16 Oct 1-2	11 Sep 4-0	2 Oct 1-0	19 Feb 4-0	22 Jan 0-1	4 Dec 1-2
Bradford City	21 Apr 6-2	29 Jan 4-0	X	15 Jan 5-0	1 Jan 0-0	27 Dec 1-0	12 Feb 8-4	6 Nov 3-0	4 Sep 2-0	18 Dec 3-0	20 Nov 0-0	9 Oct 1-2	11 Dec 1-2	23 Oct 0-1
Derby County	25 Dec 0-1	21 Apr 6-1	16 Oct 5-2	X	30 Oct 3-2	22 Jan 1-4	11 Dec 3-1	4 Sep 1-3	2 Oct 1-1	13 Nov 2-4	18 Sep 3-4	5 Feb 2-0	8 Jan 2-1	20 Nov 1-5
Grimsby Town	11 Dec 4-1	12 Feb 1-1	2 Oct 3-1	29 Jan 2-1	X	8 Jan 0-1	26 Feb 2-3	20 Nov 0-0	18 Sep 0-0	15 Jan 1-0	4 Sep 1-1	23 Oct 2-2	25 Dec 2-1	6 Nov 2-1
Huddersfield Town	4 Sep 2-1	6 Nov 2-1	25 Dec 0-0	23 Oct 4-1	9 Oct 4-1	X	20 Nov 1-0	12 Feb 5-1	11 Dec 2-1	1 Jan 5-0	25 Apr 2-0	15 Jan 2-1	18 Sep 2-2	29 Jan 2-2
Hull City	22 Jan 1-0	25 Sep 2-0	13 Nov 1-1	11 Sep 4-2	27 Nov 4-1	19 Feb 2-1	X	1 Jan 0-3	30 Oct 2-2	9 Oct 1-1	16 Oct 1-3	4 Dec 3-0	5 Feb 2-0	18 Dec 1-3
Leeds City	16 Oct 7-1	18 Dec 1-1	5 Feb 0-1	4 Dec 4-1	19 Feb 3-1	13 Nov 0-0	2 Oct 3-1	X	22 Jan 1-0	25 Sep 2-1	8 Jan 1-0	27 Nov 0-4	27 Dec 2-3	11 Sep 2-1
Leicester Fosse	12 Feb 2-2	15 Jan 2-1	4 Dec 2-1	1 Jan 2-0	18 Dec 2-0	11 Sep 3-0	29 Jan 4-0	23 Oct 4-0	X	19 Feb 1-1	6 Nov 1-3	27 Dec 2-1	27 Nov 2-5	9 Oct 3-1
Lincoln City	5 Feb 4-1	11 Dec 2-1	18 Sep 2-6	12 Feb 4-0	16 Oct 1-0	2 Oct 3-0	8 Jan 4-1	25 Dec 2-0	20 Nov 1-0	X	22 Jan 1-4	30 Oct 3-0	4 Sep 7-3	21 Apr 6-2
Nottingham Forest	30 Oct 5-0	1 Jan 0-0	19 Feb 0-2	18 Dec 5-0	4 Dec 2-0	27 Nov 2-0	15 Jan 4-1	9 Oct 2-0	5 Feb 1-0	23 Oct 3-2	X	11 Sep 3-5	13 Nov 2-0	27 Dec 1-0
Notts County	18 Sep 1-0	20 Nov 3-0	8 Jan 1-0	6 Nov 5-0	22 Jan 1-2	16 Oct 1-1	4 Sep 2-0	21 Apr 1-1	25 Dec 1-2	29 Jan 2-1	11 Dec 0-0	X	2 Oct 3-0	12 Feb 1-1
Sheffield United	20 Nov 1-0	23 Oct 2-2	11 Sep 0-1	9 Oct 2-0	25 Sep 6-1	18 Dec 5-1	6 Nov 3-0	29 Jan 4-1	25 Apr 1-1	4 Dec 4-1	12 Feb 3-1	1 Jan 1-1	X	15 Jan 1-1
The Wednesday	2 Oct 1-4	4 Sep 2-4	22 Jan 1-0	19 Feb 5-0	5 Feb 2-1	30 Oct 2-1	18 Sep 2-4	11 Dec 0-0	8 Jan 3-1	27 Nov 4-1	25 Dec 0-1	13 Nov 4-1	16 Oct 0-0	X

Barnsley v Huddersfield Town on 1 Jan was abandoned after 45 minutes with the score at 1-0 and replayed at a later date
Bradford City v Grimsby Town on 1 Jan was abandoned after 65 minutes with the score at 0-0. This was counted as the final score

		P	W	D	L	F	A	Pts
1	Nottingham Forest	26	15	5	6	48	25	35
2	Sheffield United	26	12	7	7	51	36	31
3	Huddersfield Town	26	12	5	9	43	36	29
4	Bradford City	26	12	4	10	52	32	28
5	Leicester Fosse	26	11	6	9	42	34	28
6	Barnsley	26	12	4	10	46	55	28
7	The Wednesday	26	11	5	10	46	43	27
8	Notts County	26	10	6	10	39	36	26
9	Lincoln City	26	12	2	12	54	54	26
10	Leeds City	26	10	5	11	39	43	25
11	Hull City	26	10	3	13	42	58	23
12	Bradford	26	9	4	13	46	46	22
13	Grimsby Town	26	7	6	13	31	46	20
14	Derby County	26	7	2	17	39	74	16

The Football League 1915-16

MIDLAND SECTION

Subsidiary Tournament

Northern Division

	Barnsley	Bradford	Bradford City	Huddersfield T	Leeds City	Rochdale
Barnsley	X	8 Apr 3-0	22 Apr 2-0	11 Mar 1-5	1 Apr 4-6	25 Mar 0-1
Bradford	4 Mar 4-1	X	24 Apr 4-2	25 Mar 2-0	15 Apr 0-1	22 Apr 5-2
Bradford City	18 Mar 4-0	1 Apr 0-4	X	8 Apr 2-2	29 Apr 2-4	11 Mar 5-0
Huddersfield Town	15 Apr 4-1	29 Apr 1-3	4 Mar 1-2	X	18 Mar 1-1	1 Apr 2-1
Leeds City	24 Apr 1-0	11 Mar 3-2	25 Mar 0-1	22 Apr 1-2	X	8 Apr 3-1
Rochdale	29 Apr 2-1	18 Mar 4-3	15 Apr 3-0	21 Apr 1-1	4 Mar 0-1	X

		P	W	D	L	F	A	Pts
1	Leeds City	10	7	1	2	21	13	15
2	Bradford	10	6	0	4	27	17	12
3	Huddersfield T	10	4	3	3	19	15	11
4	Bradford City	10	4	1	5	18	20	9
5	Rochdale	10	4	1	5	15	21	9
6	Barnsley	10	2	0	8	13	27	4

Southern Division

	Chesterfield T	Derby Co	Leicester F	Nottingham F	Notts County	Stoke
Chesterfield Town	X	29 Apr 1-6	1 Apr 3-1	18 Mar 2-1	15 Apr 0-1	4 Mar 3-0
Derby County	25 Mar 2-1	X	11 Mar 2-5	8 Apr 4-1	22 Apr 2-3	1 Apr 4-2
Leicester Fosse	24 Apr 2-2	15 Apr 3-2	X	29 Apr 1-3	4 Mar 0-0	18 Mar 2-1
Nottingham Forest	21 Apr 8-1	4 Mar 3-0	25 Mar 4-0	X	24 Apr 4-2	15 Apr 3-1
Notts County	11 Mar 1-1	18 Mar 3-1	8 Apr 1-1	1 Apr 2-0	X	29 Apr 3-0
Stoke	8 Apr 7-1	24 Apr 6-1	22 Apr 1-0	11 Mar 0-1	25 Mar 3-0	X

		P	W	D	L	F	A	Pts
1	Nottingham F	10	7	0	3	28	12	14
2	Notts County	10	5	3	2	16	12	13
3	Leicester Fosse	10	3	3	4	15	19	9
4	Stoke	10	4	0	6	21	18	8
5	Derby County	10	4	0	6	23	28	8
6	Chesterfield T	10	3	2	5	15	29	8

Midland Division

	Grimsby T	Hull C	Lincoln C	Rotherham Co	Sheffield United	The Wednesday
Grimsby Town	X	22 Apr 5-0	24 Apr 3-0	8 Apr 7-1	25 Mar 0-1	11 Mar 0-0
Hull City	18 Mar 2-5	X	15 Apr 2-1	24 Apr 4-1	4 Mar 5-2	29 Apr 1-0
Lincoln City	1 Apr 1-2	11 Mar 7-0	X	25 Mar 1-1	22 Apr 1-1	8 Apr 3-0
Rotherham County	4 Mar 3-2	1 Apr 4-2	29 Apr 4-1	X	15 Apr 1-0	18 Mar 0-2
Sheffield United	29 Apr 0-0	8 Apr 2-0	18 Mar 7-0	11 Mar 2-3	X	1 Apr 1-1
The Wednesday	15 Apr 2-1	25 Mar 0-2	4 Mar 2-2	22 Apr 3-2	24 Apr 0-1	X

		P	W	D	L	F	A	Pts
1	Grimsby Town	10	5	2	3	25	10	12
2	Sheffield United	10	4	3	3	17	11	11
3	Rotherham Co	10	5	1	4	20	24	11
4	Hull City	10	5	0	5	18	27	10
5	The Wednesday	10	3	3	4	10	13	9
6	Lincoln City	10	2	3	5	17	22	7

The London Football Combination 1915-16

Principal Competition

	Brentford	Chelsea	Clapton Orient	Croydon Common	Crystal Palace	Fulham	Millwall	QPR	The Arsenal	Tottenham H	Watford	West Ham U
Brentford	X	25 Dec 1-2	18 Dec 1-1	30 Oct 2-1	18 Sep 1-0	2 Oct 2-2	8 Jan 1-1	4 Dec 4-0	22 Jan 2-2	20 Nov 1-1	16 Oct 1-2	4 Sep 2-1
Chelsea	27 Dec 4-1	X	4 Sep 3-1	16 Oct 3-1	18 Dec 6-1	22 Jan 1-1	2 Oct 2-2	8 Jan 5-1	30 Oct 3-1	4 Dec 8-1	18 Sep 1-0	20 Nov 5-2
Clapton Orient	9 Oct 1-3	13 Nov 1-6	X	25 Sep 0-0	15 Jan 2-3	27 Dec 1-3	27 Nov 2-0	6 Nov 0-2	11 Dec 0-2	23 Oct 0-0	11 Sep 2-0	1 Jan 1-2
Croydon Common	15 Jan 2-2	1 Jan 0-2	4 Dec 3-3	X	4 Sep 2-1	18 Sep 3-2	18 Dec 1-0	20 Nov 0-1	23 Oct 1-4	27 Dec 0-0	2 Oct 1-2	6 Nov 1-1
Crystal Palace	27 Nov 1-0	9 Oct 1-5	30 Oct 1-2	13 Nov 4-2	X	8 Jan 2-2	25 Dec 0-1	16 Oct 1-0	11 Sep 3-1	11 Dec 4-2	22 Jan 1-1	25 Sep 2-0
Fulham	11 Dec 4-3	6 Nov 0-3	25 Dec 4-0	27 Nov 2-0	23 Oct 5-0	X	11 Sep 1-2	15 Jan 0-1	25 Sep 4-3	1 Jan 0-2	13 Nov 4-3	9 Oct 1-0
Millwall	23 Oct 3-3	11 Dec 1-0	18 Sep 0-1	9 Oct 6-3	27 Dec 4-1	20 Nov 0-0	X	4 Sep 3-1	1 Jan 3-0	6 Nov 3-2	4 Dec 4-0	15 Jan 1-0
Queen's Park Rangers	25 Sep 1-2	23 Oct 1-0	22 Jan 0-0	11 Sep 2-1	1 Jan 5-1	30 Oct 2-1	13 Nov 1-5	X	27 Nov 1-1	9 Oct 0-4	27 Dec 3-1	11 Dec 1-1
The Arsenal	6 Nov 3-1	15 Jan 0-6	2 Oct 2-0	8 Jan 4-2	20 Nov 2-2	4 Dec 2-1	16 Oct 1-1	18 Sep 2-1	X	4 Sep 2-0	18 Dec 3-1	27 Dec 3-2
Tottenham Hotspur	11 Sep 1-1	25 Sep 1-3	8 Jan 1-1	25 Dec 3-0	2 Oct 2-4	16 Oct 3-1	22 Jan 2-2	18 Dec 2-1	13 Nov 3-3	X	30 Oct 3-0	27 Nov 3-0
Watford	1 Jan 3-1	27 Nov 0-3	20 Nov 3-1	11 Dec 3-0	6 Nov 7-1	4 Sep 2-4	25 Sep 0-3	25 Dec 5-1	9 Oct 1-0	15 Jan 0-3	X	23 Oct 2-3
West Ham United	13 Nov 4-1	11 Sep 0-0	16 Oct 5-2	22 Jan 3-0	4 Dec 3-1	18 Dec 2-3	30 Oct 2-1	2 Oct 2-1	25 Dec 8-2	18 Sep 1-1	8 Jan 5-1	X

Both Watford v Tottenham Hotspur games were played at White Hart Lane, Tottenham

		P	W	D	L	F	A	Pts
1	Chelsea	22	17	3	2	71	18	37
2	Millwall	22	12	6	4	46	24	30
3	The Arsenal	22	10	5	7	43	46	25
4	West Ham United	22	10	4	8	47	35	24
5	Fulham	22	10	4	8	45	37	24
6	Tottenham Hotspur	22	8	8	6	38	35	24
7	Brentford	22	6	8	8	36	40	20
8	Queen's Park Rangers	22	8	3	11	27	41	19
9	Crystal Palace	22	8	3	11	35	55	19
10	Watford	22	8	1	13	37	46	17
11	Clapton Orient	22	4	6	12	22	44	14
12	Croydon Common	22	3	5	14	24	50	11

Supplementary Competition

Final Table

		P	W	D	L	F	A	Pts
1	Chelsea	14	10	1	3	50	15	21
2	West Ham United	14	9	2	3	32	16	20
3	Tottenham Hotspur	14	8	3	3	32	22	19
4	Fulham	14	9	0	5	38	19	18
5	Millwall	14	8	2	4	30	22	18
6	Crystal Palace	14	8	2	4	41	29	18
7	Watford	14	5	3	6	22	20	13
8	Brentford	14	5	2	7	29	33	12
9	Croydon Common	14	4	3	7	28	27	11
10	Clapton Orient	14	3	4	7	17	27	10
11	The Arsenal	14	3	4	7	19	31	10
12	Luton Town	14	4	1	9	31	44	9
13	Queen's Park Rangers	14	2	5	7	14	37	9
14	Reading	14	3	2	9	23	64	8

The London Football Combination 1915-16

Supplementary Competition

	Brentford	Chelsea	Clapton Orient	Croydon Common	Crystal Palace	Fulham	Luton Town	Millwall	QPR	Reading	The Arsenal	Tottenham H	Watford	West Ham U
Brentford	X			11 Mar 3-1	6 May 6-3	21 Apr 2-1	29 Apr 0-3		25 Mar 4-0		12 Feb 2-1			8 Apr 1-3
Chelsea		X		22 Apr 3-1	12 Feb 0-1	8 Apr 6-3	11 Mar 11-1		29 Apr 3-0		21 Apr 9-0			25 Mar 4-0
Clapton Orient			X	29 Apr 1-1	11 Mar 1-5	12 Feb 0-3	25 Mar 4-0		8 Apr 1-1		26 Feb 1-1			21 Apr 3-1
Croydon Common	15 Apr 0-0	1 Apr 1-4	5 Feb 3-0	X				19 Feb 1-2		24 Apr 10-2		18 Mar 3-3	4 Mar 3-0	
Crystal Palace	1 Apr 6-3	18 Mar 4-2	15 Apr 2-1		X			5 Feb 1-5		4 Mar 10-1		22 Apr 4-0	19 Feb 1-0	
Fulham	24 Apr 1-0	4 Mar 0-1	18 Mar 4-0			X		1 Apr 4-2		5 Feb 6-0		19 Feb 3-1	15 Apr 2-0	
Luton Town	5 Feb 4-3	15 Apr 1-1	19 Feb 1-2				X	4 Mar 1-2		18 Mar 9-2		1 Apr 1-2	22 Apr 3-1	
Millwall				25 Mar 3-0	29 Apr 2-2	26 Feb 1-7	8 Apr 3-0	X	21 Apr 6-2		11 Mar 2-0			12 Feb 1-0
Queen's Park Rangers	19 Feb 1-1	5 Feb 0-3	4 Mar 1-1					24 Apr 2-0	X	1 Apr 2-6		15 Apr 1-3	18 Mar 2-2	
Reading				21 Apr 4-2	8 Apr 1-1	29 Apr 0-4	12 Feb 4-2		22 Apr 1-2	X	25 Mar 1-1			11 Mar 0-4
The Arsenal	18 Mar 5-2	24 Apr 1-3	1 Apr 2-1					15 Apr 0-0	19 Feb 4-1		X	4 Mar 0-3	5 Feb 1-1	
Tottenham Hotspur				12 Feb 2-0	21 Apr 3-1	25 Mar 4-0	26 Feb 7-4	11 Mar 0-0		8 Apr 3-2		X		29 Apr 1-1
Watford				8 Apr 0-2	25 Mar 4-0	11 Mar 2-0	21 Apr 2-1		12 Feb 6-0		29 Apr 2-1		X	6 May 0-2
West Ham United	4 Mar 4-2	19 Feb 2-0	22 Apr 2-1					18 Mar 2-1	15 Apr 7-0			5 Feb 2-0	1 Apr 2-2	X

Both Watford v West Ham United games were played at Upton Park, West Ham. The 6 May game was scheduled as Watford's home match.

The South Western Football Combination 1915-16

	Bristol City	Bristol Rovers	Cardiff C	Newport Co	Portsmouth	Southampton	Swindon T
Bristol City	X	24 Apr 0-2	8 Apr 2-0	1 Jan 2-0	29 Jan 0-1	15 Jan 4-0	12 Feb 1-0
Bristol Rovers	21 Apr 1-1	X	1 Apr 0-2	15 Apr 3-0	18 Mar 2-1	10 Feb 2-4	4 Mar 0-0
Cardiff City	22 Jan 1-0	29 Jan 1-2	X	18 Mar 3-1	15 Apr 1-2	4 Mar 2-0	15 Jan 1-0
Newport County	5 Feb 4-0	15 Jan 0-3	11 Mar 1-5	X	8 Jan 1-3	1 Apr 0-0	NOT PLAYED
Portsmouth	4 Mar 3-0	12 Feb 3-0	25 Mar 4-0	12 Feb 4-0	X	21 Apr 0-2	29 Apr 6-1
Southampton	8 Jan 2-1	29 Apr 6-0	12 Feb 6-3	22 Jan 8-1	24 Apr 3-0	X	25 Mar 5-3
Swindon Town	15 Apr 1-2	22 Apr 2-2	8 Jan 0-2	8 Apr 1-0	1 Apr 1-2	18 Mar 3-1	X

		P	W	D	L	F	A	Pts
1	Portsmouth	12	9	0	3	29	11	18
2	Southampton	12	8	1	3	37	19	17
3	Cardiff City	12	7	0	5	21	18	14
4	Bristol Rovers	12	5	3	4	17	20	13
5	Bristol City	12	5	1	6	13	15	11
6	Swindon Town	11	2	2	7	12	22	6
7	Newport County	11	1	1	9	8	32	3

The Scottish Football League 1915-16

	Aberdeen	Airdrieonians	Ayr U	Celtic	Clyde	Dumbarton	Dundee	Falkirk	Hamilton Acad	Hearts	Hibernian	Kilmarnock	Morton	Motherwell	Partick Th	Queen's Park	Raith Rovers	Rangers	St Mirren	Third Lanark
Aberdeen	X	11 Dec 2-1	25 Sep 1-1	5 Feb 0-4	9 Oct 1-1	28 Aug 2-2	20 Nov 2-0	26 Feb 2-0	30 Oct 1-3	11 Mar 1-1	23 Oct 1-1	8 Jan 2-0	8 Apr 0-1	1 Apr 5-0	22 Jan 1-1	27 Sep 5-1	13 Nov 2-1	30 Apr 0-0	25 Dec 2-1	11 Sep 1-1
Airdrieonians	18 Sep 1-1	X	13 Nov 3-1	28 Aug 0-5	4 Dec 4-1	29 Jan 2-1	11 Sep 1-2	8 Jan 2-3	15 Jan 1-1	26 Feb 0-0	18 Dec 1-0	16 Oct 0-0	20 Nov 0-0	12 Feb 4-0	22 Apr 0-2	30 Oct 3-0	11 Mar 2-1	2 Oct 0-1	15 Apr 0-0	1 Apr 1-0
Ayr United	12 Feb 2-1	8 Aug 2-0	X	11 Dec 0-4	4 Jan 2-0	3 Jan 2-0	3 Jan 3-1	11 Mar 1-2	30 Apr 4-1	11 Sep 1-0	8 Jan 3-1	28 Aug 2-3	25 Dec 2-0	6 Nov 1-1	16 Oct 0-4	27 Nov 4-1	22 Jan 1-1	2 Oct 1-1	26 Feb 1-1	25 Mar 6-0
Celtic	6 Nov 3-1	25 Dec 6-0	29 Jan 3-1	X	27 Sep 5-0	12 Feb 6-0	26 Feb 3-0	4 Sep 2-1	11 Mar 5-1	22 Apr 0-0	15 Jan 3-1	20 Nov 2-0	1 Apr 0-0	21 Aug 3-1	30 Apr 5-0	4 Dec 6-2	15 Apr 6-0	1 Jan 2-2	23 Oct 0-2	24 Apr 4-1
Clyde	4 Mar 3-2	5 Feb 1-2	18 Mar 1-3	3 Jan 1-3	X	15 Apr 3-1	16 Oct 2-0	27 Nov 3-2	11 Dec 1-2	18 Sep 1-4	19 Feb 2-1	8 Apr 1-1	8 Jan 2-3	22 Jan 1-2	8 Apr 1-2	13 Nov 0-1	28 Aug 1-0	18 Dec 3-0	30 Oct 4-1	2 Oct 2-2
Dumbarton	25 Apr 2-1	23 Oct 3-1	4 Sep 0-3	8 Jan 1-2	6 Nov 2-1	X	2 Oct 1-1	18 Sep 3-1	26 Feb 7-0	5 Feb 1-1	8 Apr 2-1	30 Apr 1-1	22 Jan 1-1	25 Dec 0-0	11 Oct 2-0	9 Oct 2-4	4 Oct 2-4	21 Aug 1-3	4 Mar 2-0	20 Nov 1-1
Dundee	1 Jan 1-1	3 Jan 4-0	21 Aug 2-0	18 Sep 0-2	29 Jan 1-0	18 Mar 0-1	X	4 Mar 3-3	27 Nov 3-1	6 Nov 1-0	12 Feb 2-1	8 Apr 2-0	22 Apr 0-1	4 Sep 1-3	19 Feb 3-0	25 Sep 3-0	8 Dec 2-0	15 Jan 1-0	9 Oct 1-0	23 Oct 1-0
Falkirk	18 Dec 0-3	25 Mar 3-2	4 Dec 1-0	8 Apr 0-2	1 Jan 1-2	19 Feb 1-2	30 Oct 2-0	X	25 Sep 2-1	2 Oct 1-1	11 Sep 1-1	28 Aug 0-0	3 Jan 0-0	31 Dec 0-1	11 Mar 1-0	12 Feb 3-2	16 Oct 0-0	20 Nov 2-0	29 Jan 2-1	15 Jan 1-1
Hamilton Acad	18 Mar 2-0	30 Apr 2-1	4 Mar 2-3	16 Oct 2-3	21 Aug 3-1	18 Dec 1-1	5 Feb 4-4	15 Apr 0-1	X	22 Jan 3-2	4 Dec 3-2	2 Oct 5-2	4 Sep 5-2	20 Nov 3-1	8 Jan 1-0	25 Dec 5-2	18 Sep 2-0	1 Apr 0-1	19 Feb 4-1	6 Nov 2-1
Hearts	4 Dec 1-2	25 Sep 1-1	9 Oct 0-5	13 Nov 2-0	1 Apr 3-1	27 Nov 3-1	30 Apr 1-0	18 Apr 1-0	28 Mar 0-2	X	17 Apr 1-3	11 Sep 0-1	23 Oct 2-0	18 Dec 4-0	4 Mar 1-0	8 Apr 5-3	29 Jan 2-1	12 Apr 1-2	15 Apr 3-1	19 Feb 2-0
Hibernian	15 Aug 0-0	22 Jan 3-0	22 Apr 3-1	2 Oct 0-4	4 Sep 0-1	30 Oct 1-1	25 Dec 0-2	5 Feb 2-1	26 Apr 1-3	20 Sep 1-2	X	26 Feb 1-0	18 Sep 0-2	6 Nov 1-2	16 Oct 0-4	21 Aug 3-0	8 Jan 1-0	11 Mar 2-3	20 Nov 2-1	11 Dec 0-1
Kilmarnock	21 Aug 5-0	19 Feb 4-0	23 Oct 0-1	4 Mar 0-3	15 Jan 0-1	25 Sep 5-1	13 Nov 2-0	1 Apr 1-3	29 Jan 3-0	15 Apr 3-1	9 Oct 0-0	X	18 Mar 1-1	18 Sep 1-0	30 Oct 1-1	27 Nov 4-0	3 Jan 2-0	4 Sep 0-3	1 Jan 1-1	18 Dec 1-1
Morton	16 Oct 3-0	1 Jan 8-2	15 Jan 0-1	11 Sep 0-1	25 Sep 3-0	13 Dec 3-1	28 Aug 3-1	9 Oct 6-0	12 Feb 8-1	XX	29 Jan 5-1	18 Dec 2-0	X	30 Apr 1-0	25 Dec 0-1	26 Feb 5-0	30 Oct 4-0	4 Dec 2-0	11 Mar 3-0	15 Apr 2-0
Motherwell	27 Nov 2-2	9 Oct 3-2	15 Apr 0-3	15 Apr 1-3	23 Oct 2-2	11 Sep 4-2	11 Dec 3-0	13 Nov 1-1	1 Oct 0-3	30 Oct 1-3	4 Mar 1-1	11 Mar 1-1	19 Feb 2-3	X	28 Aug 2-2	22 Apr 2-1	15 Jan 1-4	29 Jan 2-2	25 Sep 3-1	5 Feb 3-4
Partick Thistle	2 Oct 3-0	6 Nov 4-1	1 Apr 1-1	18 Dec 0-4	24 Apr 2-3	15 Jan 0-0	4 Dec 2-0	23 Oct 5-2	9 Oct 0-1	4 Sep 0-2	18 Sep 4-1	12 Mar 4-0	21 Feb 3-2	26 Aug 3-1	X	29 Jan 5-0	20 Nov 2-0	15 Apr 5-2	19 Apr 4-0	1 Jan 1-0
Queen's Park	15 Jan 0-1	18 Mar 3-0	1 Jan 2-2	19 Feb 0-1	11 Mar 2-2	1 Apr 0-2	15 Apr 2-0	11 Dec 2-1	23 Oct 2-1	20 Nov 0-3	3 Jan 4-2	5 Feb 1-2	18 Dec 4-4	2 Oct 1-4	18 Sep 1-1	X	30 Apr 4-1	6 Nov 0-6	28 Aug 2-1	4 Mar 0-0
Raith Rovers	22 Apr 3-1	21 Aug 1-1	19 Feb 0-4	27 Nov 0-2	25 Dec 2-0	1 Jan 1-0	1 Apr 0-2	22 Jan 3-1	4 Jan 2-0	11 Dec 1-2	25 Sep 1-1	6 Nov 1-1	4 Mar 2-1	18 Mar 1-0	5 Feb 2-0	8 Sep 0-3	X	23 Oct 1-3	11 Sep 0-1	9 Oct 0-1
Rangers	19 Feb 4-0	4 Mar 3-0	18 Sep 5-2	30 Oct 3-0	22 Apr 2-2	20 Apr 2-2	10 Apr 3-2	25 Dec 1-0	13 Nov 3-0	16 Oct 0-4	27 Nov 4-2	22 Jan 3-1	5 Feb 1-0	8 Jan 4-1	3 Jan 0-1	24 Apr 6-0	8 Apr 3-0	X	11 Dec 4-0	28 Aug 4-0
St Mirren	4 Sep 3-2	27 Nov 2-4	18 Dec 1-0	18 Mar 0-5	12 Feb 1-0	16 Oct 1-2	22 Jan 1-2	6 Nov 2-1	22 Apr 5-0	21 Aug 4-1	1 Apr 3-1	4 Dec 3-0	2 Oct 1-3	8 Apr 5-0	13 Nov 1-2	8 Jan 1-1	26 Feb 2-0	17 Apr 1-1	X	18 Sep 1-0
Third Lanark	29 Jan 6-2	4 Sep 0-1	30 Oct 1-1	22 Jan 0-4	26 Feb 1-1	11 Mar 4-0	8 Jan 2-1	21 Aug 0-0	8 Apr 0-1	25 Dec 1-3	13 Nov 3-0	22 Apr 1-2	27 Nov 1-3	4 Dec 1-3	27 Sep 0-0	16 Oct 0-0	12 Feb 2-0	18 Mar 0-1	30 Apr 3-0	X

To enable the fixtures to be completed on time, two clubs played two fixtures on 15 April, Celtic beat Raith Rovers in the afternoon and then Motherwell at Fir Park in the evening. Motherwell had also lost at home to Ayr United earlier that day.
However, because Heart of Midlothian couldn't raise a team, their match at Greenock against Morton was never played, the only occasion in which a First Division fixture was unfulfilled.

The Scottish Football League 1915-16

Final Table

		P	W	D	L	F	A	Pts
1	Celtic	38	32	3	3	116	32	67
2	Rangers	38	25	6	7	87	39	56
3	Morton	37	22	7	8	86	35	51
4	Ayr United	38	20	8	10	72	45	48
5	Heart of Midlothian	37	20	6	11	66	45	46
6	Partick Thistle	38	19	8	11	65	41	46
7	Hamilton Academical	38	19	3	16	68	76	41
8	Dundee	38	18	4	16	56	49	40
9	Dumbarton	38	13	11	14	54	64	37
10	Kilmarnock	38	12	11	15	46	49	35
11	Aberdeen	38	11	12	15	51	64	34
12	Falkirk	38	12	9	17	45	61	33
13	St. Mirren	38	13	4	21	50	67	30
14	Motherwell	38	11	8	19	55	82	30
15	Airdrieonians	38	11	8	19	44	74	30
16	Third Lanark	38	9	11	18	40	56	29
17	Clyde	38	11	7	20	49	71	29
18	Queen's Park	38	11	6	21	53	100	28
19	Hibernian	38	9	7	22	44	71	25
20	Raith Rovers	38	9	5	24	30	65	23

The West of Scotland Football League 1915-16

	Abercorn	Albion Rovers	Arthurlie	Clydebank	Dumbarton Harp	Dykehead	Johnstone	Renton	Royal Albert	Stevenston United	Vale of Leven	Wishaw Thistle
Abercorn	X	11 Mar 4-3	28 Aug 2-0	25 Sep 3-4	4 Mar 3-1	9 Oct 3-1	15 Apr 3-4	11 Dec 3-5	29 Apr 1-1	11 Sep 1-2	5 Feb 1-2	29 Jan 3-0
Albion Rovers	22 Jan 5-2	X	5 Feb 2-1	23 Oct 0-1	6 Nov 2-2	21 Aug 2-1	4 Sep 1-0	25 Mar 3-0	1-0	25 Sep 1-0	9 Oct 0-0	19 Feb 2-1
Arthurlie	2 Oct 1-2	18 Sep 2-2	X	1 Apr 1-2	26 Feb 6-0	12 Feb 4-0	29 Jan 4-3	30 Oct 4-1	6 Nov 2-1	27 Nov 5-0	4 Sep 3-7	23 Oct 1-1
Clydebank	4-1	25 Dec 3-2	4 Mar 2-0	X	4 Sep 3-1	NOT PLAYED	6 Nov 1-0	18 Sep 7-0	16 Oct 3-1	2 Oct 0-1	21 Aug 1-3	30 Oct 2-0
Dumbarton Harp	1 Apr 4-2	28 Aug 4-0	16 Oct 3-2	15 Jan 1-3	X	30 Oct 3-5	12 Feb 4-1	11 Sep 4-1	2-1	19 Feb 5-0	11 Dec 0-2	25 Sep 3-1
Dykehead	18 Sep 4-0	29 Jan 2-4	29 Apr 3-1	28 Aug 3-3	2 Oct 3-2	X	16 Oct 2-1	1 Apr 5-1	NOT PLAYED	15 Apr 3-0	22 Jan 1-3	11 Sep 0-2
Johnstone	30 Oct 3-0	18 Dec 3-1	25 Sep 3-2	11 Sep 0-1	9 Oct 4-3	4 Dec 3-2	X	1-0	28 Aug 1-2	13 Nov 1-1	23 Oct 1-1	5 Feb 3-0
Renton	22 Apr 4-3	16 Oct 2-1	8 Apr 3-1	9 Oct 0-1	25 Dec 2-1	25 Sep 1-3	26 Feb 5-3	X	4 Sep 0-7	28 Aug 2-3	6 Nov 0-1	4 Mar 3-0
Royal Albert	26 Feb 1-2	30 Oct 1-1	11 Sep 6-2	25 Mar	21 Aug 2-1	23 Oct 5-2	2 Oct 2-0	15 Apr 4-3	X	29 Jan 2-1	25 Sep 2-2	9 Oct 4-1
Stevenston United	6 Nov 1-1	20 Nov 1-0	9 Oct 3-2	5 Feb 1-3	23 Oct 3-1	4 Sep 2-2	21 Aug 3-1	4 Dec 2-0	18 Sep 4-2	X	26 Feb 2-5	NOT PLAYED
Vale of Leven	16 Oct 3-1	11 Sep 2-0	4 Dec 6-0	12 Feb 1-1	18 Sep 4-2	25 Mar 4-2	1 Apr 1-4	2 Oct 4-1	19 Feb 5-0	30 Oct 1-2	X	28 Aug 5-1
Wishaw Thistle	4 Sep 2-1	2 Oct 4-1	21 Aug 5-3	22 Jan 3-2	4 Dec 2-2	2-2	18 Sep 1-1	NOT PLAYED	20 Nov 4-4	16 Oct 3-0	2-4	X

Abercorn v Johnstone was played at Johnstone
Johnstone v Renton on 22 Jan was abandoned at 3-0 and played at a later date

		P	W	D	L	F	A	Pts
1	Vale of Leven	22	16	4	2	66	27	36
2	Clydebank	20	15	2	3	47	22	32
3	Stevenston United	21	10	3	8	32	41	23
4	Royal Albert	20	9	4	7	48	38	22
5	Albion Rovers	22	9	4	9	34	36	22
6	Johnstone	22	9	3	10	41	40	21
7	Dykehead	20	8	3	9	46	46	19
8	Wishaw Thistle	20	6	5	9	35	46	17
9	Dumbarton Harp	22	8	2	12	49	52	18
10	Abercorn	22	7	2	13	42	55	16
11	Renton	21	7	0	14	34	61	14
12	Arthurlie	22	6	2	14	47	57	14

The Eastern Football League 1915-16

	Armadale	Bathgate	Broxburn United	Cowdenbeath	Dundee Hibernian	Dunfermline Athletic	East Fife	East Stirlingshire	Kirkcaldy United	Leith	Lochgelly United	St Bernard's
Armadale	X	2 Oct 4-0	20 Nov 2-0	6 Nov 2-1	15 Jan 3-0	8 Jan 1-0	9 Oct 5-1	28 Aug 3-2	11 Sep 6-0	26 Feb 5-1	18 Mar 1-0	23 Oct 2-0
Bathgate	21 Aug 0-1	X	13 Nov 2-0	4 Sep 2-1	9 Oct 5-2	19 Feb 7-1	5 Feb 3-0	30 Oct 2-0	27 Nov 5-1	15 Apr 3-0	16 Oct 1-2	29 Jan 1-2
Broxburn United	15 Apr 5-1	28 Aug 1-0	X	8 Jan 1-0	23 Oct 2-1	5 Feb 2-0	27 Nov 1-1	29 Apr 1-1	6 Nov 2-1	21 Aug 1-2	25 Sep 2-0	11 Sep 0-2
Cowdenbeath	25 Sep 2-3	26 Feb 1-2	12 Feb 1-0	X	27 Nov 3-0	30 Oct 3-0	28 Aug 1-1	16 Oct 1-0	18 Mar 2-0	2 Oct 2-0	11 Sep 0-1	13 Nov 2-1
Dundee Hibernian	16 Oct 1-2	11 Sep 0-3	18 Mar 3-0	25 Dec 0-4	X	2 Oct 2-1	13 Nov 2-5	20 Nov 2-1	22 Jan 1-0	30 Oct 0-2	28 Aug 4-5	4 Dec 5-2
Dunfermline Athletic	NOT PLAYED	6 Nov 2-3	4 Mar 3-3	9 Oct 1-1	15 Apr 4-1	X	25 Dec 1-2	11 Sep 2-2	23 Oct 4-3	4 Sep 7-1	27 Nov 0-0	25 Sep 5-4
East Fife	30 Oct 0-0	22 Apr 10-1	16 Oct 1-1	11 Mar 1-2	4 Sep 3-4	20 Nov 4-1	X	25 Sep 6-1	21 Aug 5-0	12 Feb 2-2	2 Oct 3-1	1 Jan 0-2
East Stirlingshire	5 Feb 1-0	18 Mar 1-0	4 Sep 2-1	18 Sep 2-3	*21 Aug 2-1*	13 Nov 4-1	23 Oct 1-3	X	9 Oct 4-1	6 Nov 4-0	15 Apr 5-2	27 Nov 1-2
Kirkcaldy United	13 Nov 2-5	12 Feb 0-3	2 Oct 1-3	20 Nov 1-5	18 Sep 3-3	28 Aug 1-3	18 Dec 2-1	15 Jan 0-1	X	16 Oct 4-1	30 Oct 0-3	15 Apr 1-3
Leith	27 Nov 0-0	23 Oct 2-1	9 Oct 1-2	5 Feb 1-1	25 Sep 2-1	NOT PLAYED	11 Sep 4-2	29 Jan 2-0	4 Mar 6-1	X	13 Nov 0-0	28 Aug 1-4
Lochgelly United	25 Dec 0-3	20 Nov 0-0	11 Mar 1-0	23 Oct 0-1	22 Apr 0-3	21 Aug 4-1	6 Nov 2-2	12 Feb 0-1	4 Sep 2-0	NOT PLAYED	X	9 Oct 1-2
St Bernard's	4 Sep 1-3	18 Sep 1-1	30 Oct 2-1	21 Aug 1-0	6 Nov 5-0	16 Oct 5-1	19 Feb 2-1	2 Oct 3-0	25 Dec 5-0	11 Dec 3-0	5 Feb 7-0	X

Lochgelly United v Leith (0-2) and Dunfermline Athletic v Armadale (0-0) on 22 Jan were both abandoned and replayed at a later date
Dunfermline Athletic v Dundee Hibernian on 12 Feb was abandoned at 2-0 and replayed at a later date
The Dundee Hibernian v Broxburn United match on 18 Mar also counted as a League Cup tie

		P	W	D	L	F	A	Pts
1	Armadale	21	17	2	2	52	17	36
2	St Bernard's	22	16	1	5	59	26	33
3	Cowdenbeath	22	12	3	7	38	20	27
4	Bathgate	22	12	2	8	45	30	26
5	East Fife	22	8	6	8	52	39	22
6	Broxburn United	22	9	4	9	29	29	22
7	East Stirlingshire	22	10	2	10	36	36	22
8	Leith	20	7	4	9	28	43	18
9	Lochgelly United	21	7	4	10	24	36	18
10	Dundee Hibernian	22	7	1	14	36	57	15
11	Dunfermline Athletic	20	5	4	11	38	53	14
12	Kirkcaldy United	22	2	1	19	22	73	5

EASTERN LEAGUE CUP

First round
Played on 8 Jan
East Stirlingshire v Lochgelly United 2-4
Played on 22 Jan
St Bernard's v East Fife 3-3
REPLAY on 26 Feb
East Fife v St Bernard's 1-5
Played on 29 Jan
Kirkcaldy United v Armadale 0-3
Broxburn United v Dundee Hibernian 0-0
REPLAY on 18 Mar
Dundee Hibernian v Broxburn United 3-0 *(This game also counted as a League match)*

Second round
Played on 4 Mar
Armadale v Cowdenbeath 4-0
Lochgelly United v Bathgate 0-3
Played on 1 Apr
St Bernard's v Dunfermline Athletic 3-0
Played on 8 Apr
Dundee Hibernian v Leith 0-3

Semi-final
Played on 8 Apr
Armadale v Bathgate 2-1
Played on 8 Apr
St Bernard's v Leith 2-2
REPLAY on 22 Apr
St Bernard's v Leith 2-0

Final
Played on 26 Apr at Tynecastle Park, Edinburgh
Armadale v St Bernard's 2-1

Other Scottish Competitions 1915-16

GLASGOW CUP

First round
Played on 11 Sep
Queen's Park v Rangers 1-4
Clyde v Partick Thistle 1-1 *(Partick won on penalties)*

Semi-final
Played on 26 Sep
Rangers v Partick Thistle 7-2
Celtic v Third Lanark 2-0

Final
Played on 9 Oct at Hampden Park, Glasgow
Celtic v Rangers 2-1

GLASGOW CHARITY CUP

First round
Played on 2 May
Queen's Park v Third Lanark 2-1
Played on 3 May
Partick Thistle v Clyde 3-1

Semi-final
Played on 6 May
Queen's Park v Partick Thistle 0-4 *(at Ibrox Park, Glasgow)*
Celtic v Rangers 3-0

Final
Played on 13 May at Hampden Park, Glasgow
Celtic v Partick Thistle 2-0

FORFARSHIRE CUP

First round
Forfar Athletic v Dundee Hibernian scr-wo
Played on 29 Jan
Arbroath v Brechin City 3-0

By this time Forfar Athletic and Montrose had closed down. The 2/7th Argyll and Sutherland Highlanders were based in Montrose and took over Montrose's place in the Forfarshire Cup.

Semi-final
Montrose v Dundee
Played on 19 Feb
Arbroath v Dundee Hibernian 1-1
REPLAY on 26 Feb
Dundee Hibernian v Arbroath 0-0
SECOND REPLAY on 11 Mar at Dens Park, Dundee
Dundee Hibernian v Arbroath 1-0

Final
Played on 1 Apr at Dens Park, Dundee
Montrose v Dundee Hibernian 2-0

AYR CHARITY CUP

Played on 3 May at Somerset Park, Ayr
Ayr United v Queen's Park 3-1

WILSON CUP

Played on 1 Jan at Tynecastle Park, Edinburgh
Heart of Midlothian v Hibernian 0-2

DUNBARTONSHIRE CHARITY CUP

Semi-final
Vale of Leven v Dumbarton
DATE unknown
Clydebank v Renton
REPLAY played on 6 May
Renton v Clydebank 0-1

Final
Played on 27 May
Clydebank v Vale of Leven 2-0

DUNBARTONSHIRE CUP

	Clydebank	Dumbarton H	Renton	Vale of Leven
Clydebank	X		13 Nov 6-0	11 Mar 1-1
Dumbarton Harp	18 Dec 1-1	X	27 Nov 4-0	
Renton	19 Feb 2-2		X	29 Jan 0-4
Vale of Leven	27 Nov 1-0	13 Nov 2-1	1 Jan 6-1	X

		P	W	D	L	F	A	Pts
1	Vale of Leven	5	4	1	0	14	3	9
2	Clydebank	5	1	3	1	10	5	5
3	Dumbarton Harp	3	1	1	1	6	3	3
4	Renton	5	0	1	4	3	22	1

GARDENERS CUP

	Armadale	Bathgate	Broxburn U	Leith	St Bernard's
Armadale	X	11 Mar 3-0			
Bathgate	21 Apr 3-1	X	22 Jan 2-1	18 Dec 2-0	15 Jan 2-1
Broxburn United		26 Apr 2-0	X	25 Dec 2-0	18 Dec 2-4
Leith		8 Jan 2-1	15 Jan 1-4	X	
St Bernard's			8 Apr 2-0	17 Apr 2-2	X

COMPETITION INCOMPLETE

Other Scottish Competitions 1915-16

LANARKSHIRE CUP

First round

Played on 6 Nov
Wishaw Thistle v Dykehead 3-3
REPLAY on 13 Nov
Dykehead v Wishaw Thistle 3-3
SECOND REPLAY on 26 Dec at Fir Park, Motherwell
Dykehead v Wishaw Thistle 1-1 (both went through)

Semi-final 2 legs

First leg played on 11 Mar , second on 18 Mar
Royal Albert v Dykehead 1-0, 1-4
First leg played on 18 Mar, second on 15 Apr
Wishaw Thistle v Albion Rovers 4-0, 0-2

Final

Played on 22 Apr at Douglas Park, Hamilton
Wishaw Thistle v Dykehead 2-0

RENFREWSHIRE VICTORIA CUP

	Abercorn	Arthurlie	Johnstone	Moorpark Crusaders	Paisley Academical
Abercorn	X	19 Feb 0-1	15 Jan 2-1		25 Dec 1-1
Arthurlie	13 Nov 2-2	X	25 Dec 4-1	18 Dec 10-3	8 Jan 7-0
Johnstone	8 Jan 5-1	11 Dec 4-0	X		
Moorpark Crusaders		22 Jan 0-6		X	
Paisley Academical		15 Apr 2-4			X

Abercorn v Arthurlie on 1 Jan was abandoned at 1-1 and replayed at a later date

FIFE CUP

First round

Played on 4 Dec
Cowdenbeath v Kirkcaldy United 8-0
Played on 15 Jan
East Fife v Lochgelly United 2-1

Semi-final

Played on 18 Dec
Cowdenbeath v Dunfermline Athletic 7-0
Played on 3 Apr
East Fife v Raith Rovers 0-1

Final

Played on 22 Apr at North End Park, Cowdenbeath
Cowdenbeath v Raith Rovers 2-0

BLENHEIM CUP

2 legs, first leg played on 20 Nov , second on 11 Mar
St Bernard's v Leith Athletic 0-1, 3-0
The first match was stopped after 83 mins due to fog

ROBERTSON CUP

2 legs, first leg played on 6 May , second on 13 May
Dundee v Aberdeen 3-4, 1-0

WEST FIFE CHARITY CUP

2 legs, first leg played on 6 May , second on 13 May
Cowdenbeath v Dunfermline Athletic 3-1, 2-1

FALKIRK INFIRMARY SHIELD

Played on 22 Apr at Brockville Park, Falkirk
Falkirk v East Stirlingshire 3-0

Other Scottish Competitions 1915-16

ROSEBERY CHARITY CUP

Semi-final
Played on 6 May
Heart of Midlothian v Leith Athletic 3-0
Hibernian v St Bernard's 6-1

Final
Played on 13 May at Tynecastle Park, Edinburgh
Heart of Midlothian v Hibernian 4-0

COATBRIDGE EXPRESS CUP

Final
Played on 29 Apr at Fir Park, Motherwell
Wishaw Thistle v Royal Albert 1-0

LINITHGOWSHIRE CUP

Semi-final
Bathgatr v Bo'ness wo-scr
Played on 1 Apr
Broxburn United v Armadale 0-1

Final
Played on 29 Apr at Volunteers Park, Armadale
Armadale v Bathgate 1-0

PAISLEY CHARITY CUP

Semi-final
Played on 6 May
Arthurlie v Abercorn 2-3

Final
Played on 13 May at St Mirren Park, Paisley
Abercorn v St Mirren 1-0

First round
Lochgelly United v Raith Rovers wo-scr
Played on 18 Sep
Armadale v Leith Athletic 2-0
Broxburn United v Bo'ness 5-0
East Fife v Dunfermline Athletic 3-2

Second round
Played on 4 Dec
Bathgate v Armadale 2-1
East Fife v Lochgelly United 3-0
Played on 11 Dec
East Stirlingshire v Broxburn United 3-0
Played on 1 Jan
Cowdenbeath v Kirkcaldy United 6-1

WEMYSS CUP

First round
Played on 11 Dec
Cowdenbeath v East Fife 4-1
Played on 29 Jan
Dunfermline Athletic v Lochgelly United 3-1

Semi-final
Played on 11 Mar
Dunfermline Athletic v Kirkcaldy United 3-1
Played on 19 Apr
Cowdenbeath v Raith Rovers 3-1

Final
Played on 29 Apr at North End Park, Cowdenbeath
Cowdenbeath v Dunfermline Athletic 1-0

MENZIES TROPHY

2 legs – first leg played on 27 Jan, second on 10 Feb
Bathgate v Armadale 1-4, 1-4

PENMAN CUP

Semi-final
Played on 25 Dec
East Stirlingshire v Bathgate 0-1
Played on 29 Jan
East Fife v Cowdenbeath 2-2 *(abandoned after 85 mins)*
REPLAY on 8 Apr
East Fife v Cowdenbeath 1-2

Final
Played on 22 Apr
Cowdenbeath v Bathgate 5-1

Ireland 1915-16

BELFAST & DISTRICT FOOTBALL LEAGUE

	Belfast United	Cliftonville	Distillery	Glenavon	Glentoran	Linfield
Belfast United	X	6 Nov 0-0	30 Oct 0-2	16 Oct 3-1	20 Nov 2-2	13 Nov 1-0
Cliftonville	25 Sep 2-1	X	13 Nov 0-2	9 Oct 0-0	18 Sep 1-0	27 Nov 0-2
Distillery	18 Sep 1-1	2 Oct 1-1	X	25 Sep 7-0	16 Oct 1-0	20 Nov 0-1
Glenavon	27 Nov 0-4	20 Nov 2-3	6 Nov 0-1	X	13 Nov 1-2	30 Oct 0-6
Glentoran	9 Oct 2-1	30 Oct 4-0	27 Nov 4-2	2 Oct 5-2	X	25 Sep 0-0
Linfield	2 Oct 3-1	16 Oct 1-0	9 Oct 2-1	18 Sep 2-1	6 Nov 0-0	X

		P	W	D	L	F	A	Pts
1	Linfield	10	7	2	1	17	4	16
2	Glentoran	10	5	4	1	20	10	14
3	Distillery	10	5	2	3	18	9	12
4	Belfast United	10	3	3	4	14	13	9
5	Cliftonville	10	2	4	4	7	14	8
6	Glenavon	10	0	1	9	7	33	1

BELFAST CITY CUP

	Belfast United	Cliftonville	Distillery	Glenavon	Glentoran	Linfield
Belfast United	X	11 Mar 4-1	4 Dec 1-0	11 Dec 5-2	5 Feb 1-5	18 Dec 1-0
Cliftonville	28 Dec 1-2	X	11 Dec 5-3	5 Feb 0-2	18 Dec 0-4	1 Jan 2-0
Distillery	1 Jan 1-3	8 Jan 3-0	X	18 Dec 4-0	4 Mar 0-1	25 Dec 3-2
Glenavon	8 Jan 3-5	25 Dec 3-2	15 Jan 1-2	X	1 Jan 4-5	28 Dec 0-3
Glentoran	25 Dec 0-0	15 Jan 3-1	28 Dec 2-1	4 Dec 5-1	X	11 Dec 3-0
Linfield	15 Jan 3-1	4 Dec 2-1	5 Feb 4-3	11 Mar 2-0	8 Jan 1-0	X

		P	W	D	L	F	A	Pts
1	Glentoran	10	8	1	1	28	9	17
2	Belfast United	10	7	1	2	23	16	15
3	Linfield	10	6	0	4	17	14	12
4	Distillery	10	4	0	6	20	19	8
5	Cliftonville	10	2	0	8	13	26	4
6	Glenavon	10	2	0	8	16	33	4

IRISH FA CUP

Semi-final
Played on 4 Mar
Belfast United v Linfield 0-1
Played on 11 Mar
Glentoran v Bohemians 4-2

Final
Played on 25 Mar at Celtic Park, Belfast
Linfield v Glentoran 1-1
REPLAY on 1 Apr at Grosvenor Park, Belfast
Linfield v Glentoran 1-0

Ireland 1915-16

GOLD CUP

	Belfast United	Cliftonville	Distillery	Glenavon	Glentoran	Linfield
Belfast United	X		24 Apr 1-4	6 May 1-1		25 Apr 1-3
Cliftonville	22 Apr 0-0	X				24 Apr 0-7
Distillery		6 May 3-1	X	25 Apr 2-0		
Glenavon		8 Apr 1-3		X	24 Apr 1-3	
Glentoran	8 Apr 2-2	25 Apr 0-1	22 Apr 0-0		X	
Linfield			8 Apr 1-1	22 Apr 4-1	6 May 1-1	X

NOTE all matches were played at neutral venues

		P	W	D	L	F	A	Pts
1=	Linfield	5	3	2	0	16	4	8
1=	Distillery	5	3	2	0	10	3	8
3	Glentoran	5	1	3	1	5	5	5
4	Cliftonville	5	2	1	2	5	11	5
5	Belfast United	5	0	3	2	5	10	3
6	Glenavon	5	0	1	4	4	13	1

PLAY-OFF MATCH
Played on 17 May at The Oval, Belfast
Linfield v Distillery 2-0

1916-17

The two sections, Lancashire and Midland, which had replaced the national First and Second Divsions in 1915 continued.

In Scotland, the Scottish Football League continued in an official capacity despite the restrictions. The non-League Western and Eastern Leagues catered for the ex-Scottish League sides from the Second Division

The Belfast & District League was continued as a replacement for the Irish League.

WINNERS OF THE PRINCIPAL COMPETITIONS

Football League –	
Lancashire Principal	Liverpool
Lancashire Subsidiary	Rochdale
Midland Principal	Leeds City
Midland Subsidiary	Bradford
London Combination	West Ham United
Scottish League	Celtic
West of Scotland League	Clydebank
Eastern League	Cowdenbeath
Irish FA Cup	Glentoran
Belfast & District League	Glentoran
Belfast City Cup	Glentoran
Gold Cup	Glentoran

The Football League 1916-17

LANCASHIRE SECTION

Principal Competition

	Blackburn R	Blackpool	Bolton W	Burnley	Bury	Everton	Liverpool	Manchester City	Manchester United	Oldham Ath	Port Vale	Preston NE	Rochdale	Southport C	Stockport Co	Stoke
Blackburn Rovers	X	9 Sep 4-0	20 Jan 5-1	1 Jan 1-4	17 Mar 2-2	6 Jan 1-5	3 Mar 0-2	16 Sep 2-1	11 Nov 1-2	3 Feb 1-1	14 Oct 4-0	28 Oct 3-2	30 Sep 6-1	16 Dec 4-0	25 Nov 2-4	9 Dec 1-1
Blackpool	23 Dec 2-1	X	17 Feb 5-3	16 Sep 1-1	11 Nov 1-1	20 Jan 1-1	14 Oct 0-1	6 Jan 3-1	30 Sep 2-2	17 Mar 9-0	3 Mar 4-0	2 Sep 5-1	3 Feb 0-2	1 Jan 0-2	28 Oct 0-2	25 Nov 1-1
Bolton Wanderers	7 Oct 0-0	4 Nov 4-1	X	17 Mar 3-1	30 Dec 2-3	21 Oct 1-3	28 Apr 1-0	27 Jan 2-2	9 Dec 5-1	3 Mar 2-2	11 Nov 3-2	25 Nov 6-2	10 Feb 1-3	13 Jan 0-0	9 Sep 1-1	23 Sep 9-2
Burnley	4 Nov 2-0	30 Dec 7-0	2 Dec 2-2	X	27 Jan 3-4	18 Nov 2-2	13 Jan 0-1	24 Feb 7-1	23 Sep 3-2	2 Sep 1-0	24 Mar 3-1	23 Dec 4-3	10 Mar 7-0	10 Feb 7-0	7 Oct 4-3	21 Oct 4-1
Bury	2 Dec 1-0	24 Feb 2-0	16 Sep 2-0	14 Oct 1-2	X	2 Sep 0-3	28 Oct 3-4	24 Mar 0-0	3 Feb 1-1	30 Sep 1-1	6 Jan 1-3	20 Jan 1-2	23 Dec 1-2	10 Mar 2-1	17 Feb 1-4	18 Nov 0-3
Everton	23 Sep 2-5	7 Oct 3-1	3 Feb 1-0	3 Mar 5-0	16 Dec 5-0	X	17 Mar 2-2	13 Jan 0-2	25 Nov 3-2	17 Feb 2-0	28 Oct 3-1	11 Nov 3-1	14 Oct 3-0	30 Dec 1-1	9 Dec 0-1	9 Sep 1-1
Liverpool	18 Nov 3-1	27 Jan 2-2	2 Sep 3-1	30 Sep 0-0	10 Feb 4-0	2 Dec 2-1	X	10 Mar 3-0	20 Jan 3-3	16 Sep 2-0	23 Dec 5-1	6 Jan 3-1	24 Mar 4-0	24 Feb 4-2	21 Oct 3-1	4 Nov 3-1
Manchester City	30 Dec 8-0	23 Sep 4-0	14 Oct 1-0	11 Nov 2-1	9 Dec 1-1	30 Sep 4-1	25 Nov 1-1	X	3 Mar 1-0	28 Oct 2-1	3 Feb 2-0	17 Feb 5-1	20 Jan 2-1	9 Sep 0-0	17 Mar 1-3	25 Dec 1-0
Manchester United	24 Feb 1-0	13 Jan 3-2	24 Mar 6-3	6 Jan 3-1	21 Oct 3-1	10 Mar 0-2	7 Oct 0-0	18 Nov 2-1	X	23 Dec 3-2	2 Sep 2-2	16 Sep 2-1	2 Dec 1-1	4 Nov 1-0	27 Jan 0-1	10 Feb 4-2
Oldham Athletic	21 Oct 2-0	2 Dec 1-1	18 Nov 2-1	16 Dec 2-1	13 Jan 1-4	4 Nov 2-3	30 Dec 0-1	10 Feb 2-1	9 Sep 0-2	X	10 Mar 3-0	9 Dec 2-1	24 Feb 1-0	27 Jan 1-0	23 Sep 1-1	7 Oct 1-1
Port Vale	27 Jan 3-1	18 Nov 11-1	24 Feb 2-0	9 Dec 2-6	23 Sep 2-2	10 Feb 1-1	9 Sep 0-0	21 Oct 0-1	6 Apr 3-0	25 Nov 4-0	X	17 Mar 1-1	4 Nov 1-1	7 Oct 1-3	30 Dec 1-2	13 Jan 1-2
Preston North End	10 Feb 0-2	16 Dec 2-1	10 Mar 1-2	9 Sep 4-5	7 Oct 3-1	24 Feb 2-2	23 Sep 0-1	4 Nov 2-2	30 Dec 3-2	24 Mar 4-2	2 Dec 2-1	X	18 Nov 1-2	21 Oct 1-1	13 Jan 2-0	27 Jan 1-1
Rochdale	13 Jan 3-0	21 Oct 4-1	28 Oct 0-6	25 Nov 1-2	9 Sep 2-0	27 Jan 2-1	9 Dec 3-2	7 Oct 2-2	17 Mar 2-0	11 Nov 4-1	17 Feb 1-3	3 Mar 1-2	X	23 Sep 1-1	16 Dec 4-0	30 Dec 0-1
Southport Central	2 Sep 2-3	9 Dec 2-0	30 Sep 3-0	28 Oct 3-0	25 Nov 2-1	16 Sep 1-0	11 Nov 1-3	23 Dec 0-0	17 Feb 0-1	14 Oct 5-3	20 Jan 3-1	3 Feb 2-2	6 Jan 3-0	X	3 Mar 1-1	17 Mar 0-2
Stockport County	10 Mar 7-1	10 Feb 6-0	6 Apr 2-0	20 Jan 1-0	4 Nov 1-1	24 Mar 5-1	3 Feb 0-0	2 Dec 0-0	14 Oct 1-0	6 Jan 2-0	16 Sep 5-3	30 Sep 1-1	2 Sep 3-0	18 Nov 1-0	X	24 Feb 2-1
Stoke	24 Mar 4-1	10 Mar 6-0	6 Jan 7-0	3 Feb 6-0	3 Mar 5-2	23 Dec 0-2	17 Feb 1-0	2 Sep 1-0	28 Oct 3-0	20 Jan 4-0	30 Sep 0-0	14 Oct 2-0	16 Sep 1-1	2 Dec 2-1	11 Nov 2-0	X

On 6 Apr Bolton Wanderers fielded two teams, one of which played a Lancashire Section Subsidiary Tournament match

The Football League 1916-17

Principal Competition

Final Table

		P	W	D	L	F	A	Pts
1	Liverpool	30	19	8	3	62	26	46
2	Stockport County	30	18	7	5	61	31	43
3	Stoke	30	16	7	7	64	36	39
4	Manchester City	30	14	9	7	49	29	37
5	Everton	30	15	7	8	62	41	37
6	Burnley	30	15	4	11	73	56	34
7	Manchester United	30	13	6	11	48	54	32
8	Rochdale	30	12	5	13	47	54	29
9	Southport Central	30	10	8	12	40	43	28
10	Bolton Wanderers	30	9	6	15	59	65	24
11	Blackburn Rovers	30	10	4	16	52	66	24
12	Preston North End	30	8	7	15	47	65	23
13	Bury	30	7	8	15	40	63	22
14	Oldham Athletic	30	8	6	16	36	65	22
15	Port Vale	30	7	7	16	50	60	21
16	Blackpool	30	6	7	17	44	80	19

MIDLAND SECTION

Principal Competition

Final Table

		P	W	D	L	F	A	Pts
1	Leeds City	30	18	10	2	68	29	46
2	Barnsley	30	15	8	7	65	41	38
3	Birmingham	30	14	9	7	56	38	37
4	Huddersfield Town	30	15	6	9	41	31	36
5	Bradford	30	14	6	10	51	32	34
6	Nottingham Forest	30	14	5	11	57	39	33
7	Notts County	30	13	6	11	47	52	32
8	Bradford City	30	12	7	11	41	41	31
9	Rotherham County	30	12	6	12	53	52	30
10	Sheffield United	30	11	7	12	43	47	29
11	Hull City	30	10	7	13	36	57	27
12	Chesterfield Town	30	11	4	15	59	62	26
13	The Wednesday	30	9	6	15	36	48	24
14	Grimsby Town	30	8	6	16	38	71	22
15	Leicester Fosse	30	6	7	17	29	53	19
16	Lincoln City	30	5	6	19	38	65	16

The Football League 1916-17

MIDLAND SECTION

Principal Competition

	Barnsley	Birmingham	Bradford	Bradford City	Chesterfield T	Grimsby T	Huddersfield T	Hull City	Leeds City	Leicester F	Lincoln C	Nottingham F	Notts County	Rotherham Co	Sheffield Utd	The Wednesday
Barnsley	X	27 Jan 2-1	14 Oct 3-0	2 Dec 3-0	17 Feb 6-2	2 Sep 2-2	30 Dec 1-1	28 Oct 8-2	18 Nov 4-1	26 Dec 5-0	30 Sep 6-1	10 Feb 0-1	16 Dec 4-0	16 Sep 1-1	3 Mar 2-0	13 Jan 2-0
Birmingham	21 Oct 2-0	X	30 Dec 1-2	17 Feb 1-1	6 Jan 2-2	3 Mar 3-0	2 Sep 2-1	7 Oct 4-2	3 Feb 1-1	18 Nov 2-1	28 Apr 0-0	20 Jan 1-0	2 Dec 4-0	26 Dec 1-3	4 Nov 5-0	16 Sep 4-1
Bradford	20 Jan 2-1	23 Sep 2-3	X	4 Nov 3-0	28 Apr 3-1	18 Nov 9-0	25 Dec 1-2	6 Jan 4-0	21 Oct 1-3	17 Feb 0-1	2 Sep 1-0	7 Oct 1-0	3 Mar 1-1	2 Dec 3-1	3 Feb 1-1	16 Dec 3-1
Bradford City	10 Mar 1-1	11 Nov 1-1	10 Feb 1-0	X	9 Sep 1-2	30 Dec 3-0	14 Oct 4-1	24 Feb 3-1	26 Dec 0-3	16 Sep 1-1	27 Jan 2-0	25 Nov 3-2	30 Sep 1-2	13 Jan 3-1	9 Dec 3-2	28 Oct 1-1
Chesterfield Town	11 Nov 1-1	30 Sep 0-3	16 Sep 3-1	16 Dec 3-0	X	13 Jan 4-5	24 Feb 5-3	14 Oct 5-0	25 Nov 3-4	30 Dec 2-0	10 Mar 3-3	28 Oct 0-3	27 Jan 3-1	10 Feb 1-2	25 Dec 3-0	2 Sep 1-1
Grimsby Town	9 Dec 2-2	25 Nov 3-0	24 Feb 0-2	23 Sep 1-3	7 Oct 1-3	X	28 Oct 2-1	10 Mar 2-3	9 Sep 1-6	6 Jan 1-3	10 Feb 1-0	26 Dec 1-1	14 Oct 3-3	27 Jan 1-0	23 Dec 2-0	11 Nov 1-0
Huddersfield Town	23 Sep 0-0	9 Dec 2-1	26 Dec 0-0	20 Jan 0-0	18 Nov 2-1	3 Feb 1-0	X	9 Sep 2-1	6 Jan 1-1	21 Oct 4-1	25 Nov 3-1	23 Dec 1-2	4 Nov 1-0	17 Feb 3-0	7 Oct 2-1	10 Mar 3-0
Hull City	3 Feb 0-1	13 Jan 0-1	30 Sep 1-1	18 Nov 1-0	20 Jan 3-1	2 Dec 2-0	16 Dec 0-1	X	4 Nov 1-1	3 Mar 2-1	16 Sep 2-1	21 Oct 3-1	25 Dec 2-0	2 Sep 0-0	17 Feb 1-1	30 Dec 1-0
Leeds City	24 Feb 3-0	28 Oct 1-1	27 Jan 0-0	25 Dec 1-0	3 Mar 1-0	16 Sep 1-0	30 Dec 1-0	10 Feb 1-1	X	2 Sep 2-2	13 Jan 3-1	11 Nov 3-1	16 Sep 5-1	30 Dec 2-0	2 Dec 2-0	14 Oct 1-0
Leicester Fosse	25 Dec 1-2	24 Feb 1-1	11 Nov 0-2	10 Apr 0-2	23 Sep 2-0	30 Sep 0-0	27 Jan 2-0	25 Nov 0-2	9 Dec 1-4	X	28 Oct 1-1	10 Mar 1-1	13 Jan 0-1	14 Oct 3-1	9 Sep 2-2	10 Feb 3-0
Lincoln City	6 Jan 0-1	9 Sep 3-2	9 Dec 1-1	21 Oct 1-2	2 Dec 1-3	4 Nov 1-1	3 Mar 0-1	23 Dec 1-1	7 Oct 2-5	3 Feb 3-1	X	23 Sep 1-2	17 Feb 1-2	18 Nov 2-0	20 Jan 0-2	26 Dec 4-0
Nottingham Forest	4 Nov 3-0	14 Oct 0-4	13 Jan 0-1	3 Mar 0-1	3 Feb 3-0	25 Dec 5-1	16 Sep 0-1	27 Jan 3-0	17 Feb 3-3	2 Dec 2-0	30 Dec 2-0	X	2 Sep 4-3	16 Dec 2-3	18 Nov 0-0	30 Sep 5-1
Notts County	9 Sep 1-1	10 Mar 1-1	25 Nov 2-1	6 Jan 1-0	21 Oct 1-4	20 Jan 2-3	10 Feb 2-1	26 Dec 7-1	23 Dec 1-0	7 Oct 5-1	11 Nov 0-4	9 Dec 2-2	X	28 Oct 2-2	23 Sep 2-0	24 Feb 1-0
Rotherham County	23 Dec 9-3	25 Dec 8-2	10 Mar 2-1	7 Oct 3-3	4 Nov 2-1	21 Oct 3-0	11 Nov 1-3	9 Dec 1-1	23 Sep 0-5	20 Jan 1-0	24 Feb 5-3	9 Sep 2-1	3 Feb 0-3	X	6 Jan 2-0	25 Nov 0-0
Sheffield United	25 Nov 1-3	10 Feb 0-0	28 Oct 2-1	2 Sep 4-1	26 Dec 4-1	16 Sep 5-3	13 Jan 1-0	11 Nov 4-1	10 Mar 2-2	16 Dec 1-0	14 Oct 5-1	24 Feb 1-4	30 Dec 0-1	30 Sep 1-0	X	27 Jan 1-0
The Wednesday	7 Oct 3-0	23 Dec 0-2	9 Sep 1-3	3 Feb 1-0	9 Dec 3-1	17 Feb 3-1	2 Dec 0-0	23 Sep 2-1	20 Jan 2-2	4 Nov 3-0	28 Apr 7-1	6 Jan 1-4	18 Nov 2-0	3 Mar 1-0	21 Oct 2-2	X

Three matches were abandoned but the results at the time stood and were not replayed:
Bradford v The Wednesday on 16 Dec after 65 minutes,
Lincoln City v Hull City on 23 Dec after 81 minutes
The Wednesday v Bradford City on 3 Feb after 85 minutes

On 28 Apr Lincoln City fielded two teams, one of which played a Midland Section Subsidiary Tournament match

The Football League 1916-17

LANCASHIRE SECTION

Subsidiary Tournament

GROUP A	Bolton W	Bury	Oldham Ath	Rochdale
Bolton Wanderers	X	21 Apr 6-0	1 Jan 0-3	31 Mar 0-1
Bury	7 Apr 2-3	X	14 Apr 0-1	6 Apr 0-2
Oldham Athletic	6 Apr 1-2	31 Mar 1-2	X	21 Apr 1-2
Rochdale	14 Apr 5-1	9 Apr 3-2	7 Apr 2-2	X

GROUP B	Everton	Liverpool	Southport C	Stockport Co
Everton	X	21 Apr 5-0	31 Mar 4-2	9 Apr 1-1
Liverpool	7 Apr 0-4	X	26 Dec 0-1	14 Apr 6-0
Southport Central	14 Apr 0-1	9 Apr 0-7	X	7 Apr 0-1
Stockport County	28 Apr 2-1	31 Mar 0-0	21 Apr 2-2	X

On 6 Apr Bolton Wanderers fielded two teams, one of which played a Lancashire Section Principal Tournament match

GROUP C	Blackburn R	Blackpool	Burnley	Preston NE
Blackburn Rovers	X	21 Apr 2-3	31 Mar 4-0	25 Dec 2-1
Blackpool	7 Apr 4-1	X	6 Apr 2-3	14 Apr 0-0
Burnley	14 Apr 4-1	25 Dec 4-0	X	7 Apr 0-0
Preston North End	26 Dec 3-1	31 Mar 2-1	21 Apr 2-3	X

GROUP D	Manchester City	Manchester United	Port Vale	Stoke
Manchester City	X	21 Apr 0-1	31 Mar 1-0	6 Apr 1-0
Manchester United	7 Apr 5-1	X	9 Apr 5-1	14 Apr 1-0
Port Vale	14 Apr 0-0	28 Apr 5-2	X	7 Apr 3-2
Stoke	9 Apr 5-0	31 Mar 2-1	21 Apr 2-0	X

		P	W	D	L	F	A	Pts
1	Rochdale	6	5	1	0	15	6	11
2	Everton	6	4	1	1	16	5	9
3	Burnley	6	4	1	1	14	9	9
4	Manchester United	6	4	0	2	15	9	8
5	Stockport County	6	2	3	1	6	10	7
6	Stoke	6	3	0	3	11	6	6
7	Preston North End	6	2	2	2	8	7	6
8	Bolton Wanderers	6	3	0	3	12	12	6
9	Liverpool	6	2	1	3	13	10	5
10	Oldham Athletic	6	2	1	3	9	8	5
11	Blackpool	6	2	1	3	10	12	5
12	Port Vale	6	2	1	3	9	12	5
13	Manchester City	6	2	1	3	3	11	5
14	Blackburn Rovers	6	2	0	4	11	15	4
15	Southport Central	6	1	1	4	5	15	3
16	Bury	6	1	0	5	6	16	2

The Football League 1916-17

MIDLAND SECTION

Subsidiary Tournament

GROUP A	Bradford	Bradford City	Huddersfield T	Leeds City
Bradford	X	14 Apr 3-0	31 Mar 2-0	17 Mar 1-1
Bradford City	24 Mar 2-2	X	7 Apr 1-2	21 Apr 1-5
Huddersfield Town	21 Apr 2-0	17 Mar 0-0	X	9 Apr 0-1
Leeds City	7 Apr 0-2	31 Mar 1-1	24 Apr 0-2	X

GROUP B	Barnsley	Rotherham Co	Sheffield United	The Wednesday
Barnsley	X	14 Apr 0-0	17 Mar 0-1	21 Apr 1-1
Rotherham County	24 Mar 3-5	X	31 Mar 0-3	9 Apr 2-1
Sheffield United	7 Apr 2-0	21 Apr 2-1	X	24 Mar 3-4
The Wednesday	31 Mar 2-2	1 Jan 2-3	14 Apr 2-1	X

GROUP C	Birmingham	Leicester F	Nottingham F	Notts County
Birmingham	X	24 Mar 5-1	9 Apr 4-3	31 Mar 1-1
Leicester Fosse	14 Apr 4-2	X	21 Apr 2-1	7 Apr 2-1
Nottingham Forest	6 Apr 3-3	31 Mar 1-0	X	14 Apr 2-3
Notts County	21 Apr 0-2	9 Apr 2-3	24 Mar 2-2	X

GROUP D	Chesterfield T	Grimsby T	Hull C	Lincoln C
Chesterfield Town	X	21 Apr 3-2	17 Mar 4-1	9 Apr 2-0
Grimsby Town	31 Mar 2-3	X	6 Apr 2-1	17 Mar 1-1
Hull City	7 Apr 5-1	9 Apr 2-2	X	21 Apr 2-1
Lincoln City	6 Apr 6-1	7 Apr 1-3	31 Mar 2-2	X

On 28 Apr Lincoln City fielded two teams, one of which played a Midland Section Principal Tournament match

		P	W	D	L	F	A	Pts
1	Bradford	6	3	2	1	10	5	8
2	Sheffield United	6	4	0	2	12	7	8
3	Birmingham	6	3	2	1	17	12	8
4	Leicester Fosse	6	4	0	2	12	12	8
5	Chesterfield Town	6	4	0	2	14	16	8
6	Huddersfield Town	6	3	1	2	6	4	7
7	Leeds City	6	2	2	2	8	7	6
8	Grimsby Town	6	2	2	2	12	11	6
9	Hull City	6	2	2	2	13	12	6
10	The Wednesday	6	2	2	2	12	12	6
11	Barnsley	6	1	3	2	8	9	5
12	Rotherham County	6	2	1	3	9	13	5
13	Lincoln City	6	1	2	3	11	11	4
14	Nottingham Forest	6	1	2	3	12	14	4
15	Notts County	6	1	2	3	9	12	4
16	Bradford City	6	0	3	3	5	13	3

The London Football Combination 1916-17

	Brentford	Chelsea	Clapton Orient	Crystal Palace	Fulham	Luton T	Millwall	Portsmouth	QPR	Southampton	The Arsenal	Tottenham H	Watford	West Ham U	Reading
Brentford	X	16 Sep 0-3	28 Oct 3-0	25 Nov 3-1	27 Jan 1-1	30 Sep 1-3	14 Oct 0-3	30 Dec 7-0	11 Nov 1-4	9 Sep 1-1	26 Apr 0-0	25 Dec 1-5	13 Jan 4-1	10 Feb 1-1	
Chelsea	9 Dec 7-2	X	27 Jan 1-0	9 Sep 4-1	11 Nov 4-0	30 Dec 1-4	13 Jan 4-0		10 Feb 3-0	23 Sep 3-0	30 Sep 3-0	25 Nov 2-4	28 Oct 3-2	25 Dec 1-1	14 Oct 6-0
Clapton Orient	20 Jan 5-2	4 Nov 0-2	X	21 Oct 2-2	23 Sep 0-3	18 Nov 1-7	2 Sep 3-0	25 Dec 1-1	23 Dec 2-1	9 Dec 1-2	3 Feb 2-2	6 Jan 1-2	2 Dec 1-1	7 Oct 0-4	
Crystal Palace	2 Sep 4-0	2 Dec 1-1	13 Jan 3-0	X	28 Oct 1-0		30 Dec 1-1	30 Sep 5-3	27 Jan 4-0	25 Dec 2-2	16 Sep 1-0	10 Feb 0-1	14 Oct 0-1	11 Nov 1-8	30 Sep 5-3
Fulham	4 Nov 2-0	3 Feb 2-0	10 Apr 2-1	20 Jan 4-3	X	26 Dec 5-1	2 Dec 0-1		7 Oct 2-0	23 Dec 8-1	18 Nov 2-0	21 Oct 2-1	16 Sep 7-0	6 Jan 0-2	2 Sep 9-0
Luton Town	23 Dec 5-2	7 Oct 1-4	10 Feb 2-3	23 Sep 3-1	25 Dec 1-0	X	27 Jan 5-2	28 Oct 2-2	25 Nov 6-0	21 Oct 3-1	6 Jan 1-4	9 Dec 1-3	11 Nov 3-2	9 Sep 3-4	
Millwall	6 Jan 3-0	21 Oct 0-0	28 Sep 3-0	7 Oct 3-2	9 Sep 3-2	4 Nov 2-1	X	3 Feb 2-0	9 Dec 2-1	18 Nov 3-1	20 Jan 1-0	23 Dec 3-3	25 Dec 3-0	23 Sep 1-4	
Portsmouth		6 Jan 2-1	26 Dec 2-0	23 Dec 2-2	11 Nov 3-4	20 Jan 0-4	11 Nov 0-1	X		4 Nov 0-1	21 Oct 1-0		10 Feb 3-0	9 Dec 1-2	
Queen's Park Rangers	3 Feb 2-0	18 Nov 1-2	30 Sep 0-0	4 Nov 1-0	30 Dec 1-7	2 Sep 1-4	16 Sep 0-4	2 Dec 1-7	X	6 Jan 4-0	25 Dec 2-3	20 Jan 1-1	17 Feb 2-1	21 Oct 0-4	
Southampton	2 Dec 3-1	16 Sep 2-0	16 Sep 1-1	26 Dec 2-2	30 Sep 4-3	13 Jan 3-1	10 Jan 1-3	27 Jan 1-0	14 Oct 2-1	X	30 Dec 0-1	11 Nov 1-0	2 Sep 5-0	28 Oct 3-0	
The Arsenal	23 Sep 0-0	23 Dec 2-1	11 Nov 4-0	9 Dec 1-2	10 Feb 3-2	14 Oct 2-1	28 Oct 1-0	13 Jan 1-0	26 Dec 0-0	7 Oct 3-3	X	9 Sep 1-1	27 Jan 1-1	25 Nov 0-2	
Tottenham Hotspur	26 Dec 5-2	2 Sep 0-2	14 Oct 4-2	18 Nov 3-1	13 Jan 1-0	16 Sep 2-3	30 Sep 1-4	31 Mar 10-0	28 Oct 4-5	3 Feb 3-1	2 Dec 4-1	X	30 Dec 3-0	28 Sep 1-2	
Watford	21 Oct 4-2	20 Jan 0-3	9 Sep 2-2	6 Jan 2-2	9 Dec 2-8	3 Feb 0-0	26 Dec 1-6	18 Nov 1-0	23 Sep 2-0	25 Nov 0-0	4 Nov 2-4	7 Oct 0-2	X	23 Dec 1-3	
West Ham United	18 Nov 4-0	26 Dec 2-0	30 Dec 6-1	3 Feb 1-0	14 Oct 2-0	2 Dec 2-0	10 Apr 0-2		13 Jan 5-3	20 Jan 1-1	2 Sep 2-1	4 Nov 5-1	30 Sep 2-2	X	16 Sep 5-1
Reading	7 Oct 0-2								9 Sep 2-3			23 Sep 2-4			X

Portsmouth replaced Reading from 21 October 1916 and took over their remaining fixtures.

Tottenham Hotspur v Portsmouth on 16 Dec was abandoned after 40 minutes with the score at 1-0 and replayed at a later date

West Ham United v Millwall on 16 Dec was abandoned after 50 minutes with the score at 1-0 and replayed at a later date

The London Football Combination 1916-17

Supplementary Fixtures

	Brentford	Chelsea	Clapton Orient	Crystal Palace	Fulham	Luton T	Millwall	Portsmouth	QPR	Southampton	The Arsenal	Tottenham H	Watford	West Ham U
Brentford	X	3 Mar 3-0			24 Feb 1-4	17 Mar 1-2	31 Mar 1-3		19 Apr 0-0				21 Apr 2-1	9 Apr 1-2
Chelsea	14 Apr 3-2	X			10 Mar 3-1	26 Apr 4-0	24 Feb 0-2		9 Apr 3-1		31 Mar 2-0		17 Mar 2-2	
Clapton Orient			X	31 Mar 1-4			24 Mar 1-2	10 Mar 6-1		6 Apr 4-0	14 Apr 1-3	28 Apr 0-8		24 Feb 3-4
Crystal Palace			17 Feb 3-0	X			30 Dec 1-1	9 Apr 3-2	21 Apr 3-0	24 Mar 4-2	17 Mar 1-0	7 Apr 0-3		3 Mar 3-1
Fulham	7 Apr 0-2	21 Apr 0-4			X	17 Feb 4-2	6 Apr 1-1		3 Mar 0-0	17 Mar 3-1			24 Mar 7-2	
Luton Town	28 Apr 6-0	24 Mar 0-2			31 Mar 2-3	X	10 Mar 3-1		24 Feb 2-0			14 Apr 5-4	9 Apr 3-0	
Millwall	17 Feb 2-3	7 Apr 2-1	25 Nov 2-0		9 Apr 2-0	21 Apr 6-0	X		17 Mar 1-0				3 Mar 2-2	
Portsmouth		21 Apr 3-0		6 Apr 2-1				X		3 Mar 1-0		17 Feb 2-4	7 Apr 8-3	17 Mar 2-5
Queen's Park Rangers	24 Mar 2-2	6 Apr 2-2		10 Mar 3-2	14 Apr 2-0	7 Apr 2-2	28 Apr 0-0		X					
Southampton		9 Apr 2-1		28 Apr 1-2				14 Apr 2-1		X	24 Feb 0-2	10 Mar 2-4		31 Mar 1-2
The Arsenal		17 Feb 3-0	3 Mar 3-1	28 Apr 4-0				24 Mar 2-1		7 Apr 2-2	X	9 Apr 3-2		21 Apr 2-1
Tottenham Hotspur			17 Mar 5-2	24 Feb 4-1			3 Mar 3-2	10 Apr 2-1		21 Apr 4-0	6 Apr 0-0	X		27 Jan 0-0
Watford	10 Mar 5-2	28 Apr 3-6			19 Apr 4-2	6 Apr 4-7	14 Apr 5-3	24 Feb 9-0	31 Mar 1-2				X	
West Ham United	6 Apr 2-0	7 Apr 2-0	14 Apr 2-1					28 Apr 5-2		17 Feb 5-2	10 Mar 2-3	24 Mar 3-0		X

		P	W	D	L	F	A	Pts
1	West Ham United	40	30	5	5	110	45	65
2	Millwall	40	26	6	8	85	48	58
3	Chelsea	40	24	5	11	93	48	53
4	Tottenham Hotspur	40	24	5	11	112	64	53
5	The Arsenal	40	19	10	11	62	47	48
6	Fulham	40	21	3	16	102	63	45
7	Luton Town	39	20	3	16	101	82	43
8	Crystal Palace	38	14	7	17	68	72	35
9	Southampton	39	13	8	18	57	80	34
10	Queen's Park Rangers	39	10	9	20	48	86	29
11	Watford	39	8	9	22	69	115	25
12	Brentford	40	9	7	24	56	99	25
13	Portsmouth	40	9	4	27	58	117	22
14	Clapton Orient	40	6	7	27	49	104	19

The Scottish Football League 1916-17

	Aberdeen	Airdrieonians	Ayr U	Celtic	Clyde	Dumbarton	Dundee	Falkirk	Hamilton Acad	Hearts	Hibernian	Kilmarnock	Morton	Motherwell	Partick Th	Queen's Park	Raith Rovers	Rangers	St Mirren	Third Lanark
Aberdeen	X	7 Oct 1-2	6 Jan 1-0	24 Mar 0-0	20 Jan 0-1	10 Mar 2-4	1 Jan 5-1	16 Dec 0-1	4 Nov 0-1	18 Nov 2-0	21 Apr 2-1	21 Oct 1-1	23 Sep 1-1	2 Dec 0-1	19 Aug 2-0	16 Sep 2-4	17 Feb 3-1	3 Feb 3-1	2 Sep 1-1	23 Dec 0-1
Airdrieonians	24 Feb 3-1	X	14 Apr 1-0	17 Mar 1-2	3 Feb 3-0	16 Sep 2-1	23 Dec 2-3	28 Apr 1-0	25 Nov 2-2	2 Sep 3-2	31 Mar 3-1	17 Feb 3-2	1 Jan 2-1	26 Aug 3-1	3 Mar 3-1	6 Jan 3-0	11 Nov 2-0	9 Dec 2-0	14 Oct 7-0	28 Oct 1-0
Ayr United	30 Sep 1-0	21 Oct 1-1	X	2 Sep 0-1	17 Feb 1-1	4 Nov 3-1	3 Feb 1-2	2 Jan 2-2	30 Dec 1-1	16 Mar 2-0	25 Nov 2-1	16 Feb 0-2	3 Mar 0-3	13 Dec 1-2	2 Dec 0-0	7 Apr 1-1	21 Apr 2-1	7 Oct 1-3	17 Mar 2-1	19 Aug 0-1
Celtic	25 Nov 1-0	9 Sep 3-1	9 Dec 5-0	X	2 Jan 0-0	20 Jan 1-1	17 Feb 2-0	30 Dec 2-0	10 Mar 6-1	30 Sep 1-0	26 Aug 3-1	21 Apr 0-2	21 Oct 0-0	6 Jan 0-0	18 Nov 0-0	3 Mar 3-2	3 Feb 5-0	28 Oct 0-0	31 Mar 3-0	9 Apr 2-0
Clyde	14 Oct 2-0	2 Dec 1-1	11 Nov 1-4	28 Apr 0-5	X	23 Dec 2-2	24 Mar 2-0	1 Jan 1-1	19 Aug 1-1	17 Mar 0-1	10 Feb 1-2	2 Sep 1-1	16 Dec 1-0	7 Apr 0-1	27 Jan 2-1	4 Nov 1-1	16 Sep 2-0	13 Jan 0-1	14 Apr 2-1	24 Feb 1-1
Dumbarton	28 Oct 1-1	21 Apr 1-1	24 Feb 3-1	7 Apr 1-3	6 Jan 5-1	X	11 Nov 4-3	31 Mar 1-1	3 Mar 0-0	3 Feb 4-1	9 Sep 2-1	25 Nov 1-1	7 Oct 1-4	23 Sep 3-1	16 Dec 2-1	30 Dec 0-2	1 Jan 1-1	17 Feb 0-3	26 Aug 2-1	9 Dec 2-3
Dundee	9 Sep 1-1	23 Sep 2-2	20 Jan 2-1	4 Nov 1-2	26 Aug 0-1	17 Mar 4-1	X	7 Oct 1-2	21 Jan 3-1	27 Jan 2-3	2 Apr 3-1	30 Dec 0-2	24 Feb 3-1	14 Apr 0-2	10 Mar 5-1	31 Mar 2-1	9 Dec 6-2	28 Apr 2-1	18 Nov 0-2	2 Dec 0-1
Falkirk	7 Apr 4-2	4 Nov 0-0	10 Mar 1-2	14 Oct 1-1	9 Dec 3-3	30 Sep 2-3	6 Jan 2-0	X	20 Jan 4-0	24 Mar 2-1	21 Oct 0-1	19 Aug 0-1	17 Feb 3-1	18 Nov 0-1	16 Sep 0-1	27 Jan 1-2	24 Feb 1-1	17 Mar 0-2	23 Dec 0-2	2 Sep 1-1
Hamilton Acad	17 Mar 4-1	13 Jan 1-0	24 Mar 2-1	16 Dec 0-4	31 Mar 2-1	18 Nov 3-1	7 Apr 2-4	9 Sep 1-1	X	28 Oct 1-0	24 Feb 4-1	3 Feb 3-0	6 Jan 0-1	1 Jan 0-1	23 Sep 0-1	26 Aug 2-0	28 Apr 3-1	21 Apr 3-1	2 Dec 1-1	17 Feb 1-1
Hearts	10 Feb 2-0	10 Mar 1-4	23 Dec 1-2	13 Jan 0-1	21 Oct 0-3	2 Dec 1-0	16 Dec 1-0	23 Sep 1-6	2 Jan 3-1	X	18 Sep 2-1	7 Apr 0-0	31 Mar 4-1	24 Feb 1-3	4 Nov 1-0	25 Nov 2-0	7 Oct 2-1	26 Aug 1-3	3 Mar 1-2	9 Sep 2-1
Hibernian	9 Dec 3-3	19 Aug 1-1	14 Oct 1-4	14 Apr 0-1	28 Oct 1-1	27 Jan 3-1	16 Sep 1-2	3 Feb 1-2	2 Sep 4-3	16 Apr 0-2	X	20 Jan 2-1	30 Dec 2-4	17 Feb 2-3	24 Mar 1-0	17 Mar 5-1	18 Nov 3-3	11 Nov 0-0	6 Jan 2-1	30 Sep 1-1
Kilmarnock	27 Jan 7-0	18 Nov 1-3	9 Sep 1-2	24 Feb 2-2	3 Mar 2-0	24 Mar 0-0	28 Oct 3-0	14 Apr 4-1	9 Dec 4-0	14 Oct 3-0	23 Sep 1-3	X	26 Aug 3-2	10 Mar 3-0	6 Jan 0-1	10 Feb 4-2	23 Dec 3-0	31 Mar 4-1	1 Jan 1-4	11 Nov 2-1
Morton	28 Apr 2-0	27 Jan 2-1	18 Nov 2-0	10 Feb 0-1	30 Sep 3-1	14 Apr 3-1	14 Oct 1-0	11 Nov 2-0	23 Dec 3-0	19 Feb 3-2	2 Dec 1-1	2 Jan 2-1	X	28 Oct 2-1	2 Sep 3-2	20 Jan 4-2	17 Mar 7-0	10 Mar 1-0	16 Sep 0-3	13 Jan 3-0
Motherwell	11 Nov 1-2	2 Jan 1-0	27 Jan 2-1	16 Sep 0-4	25 Nov 3-3	10 Feb 3-0	2 Sep 4-2	3 Mar 1-0	7 Oct 2-2	9 Dec 2-0	4 Nov 1-1	30 Sep 0-1	21 Apr 0-2	X	30 Dec 2-3	21 Oct 4-1	19 Aug 2-2	23 Dec 2-1	20 Jan 2-1	24 Mar 0-2
Partick Thistle	31 Mar 4-0	30 Sep 0-0	26 Aug 3-0	23 Dec 0-2	9 Apr 1-0	21 Oct 6-0	25 Nov 3-0	13 Jan 1-0	14 Oct 5-0	17 Feb 0-0	10 Mar 0-3	7 Oct 1-1	3 Feb 0-0	17 Mar 1-1	X	21 Apr 0-2	28 Oct 2-0	2 Jan 0-1	9 Dec 0-1	1 Jan 1-0
Queen's Park	13 Jan 2-1	24 Mar 0-5	1 Jan 3-2	11 Nov 1-3	10 Mar 2-2	19 Aug 1-0	30 Sep 2-2	28 Oct 1-1	14 Apr 4-2	28 Apr 1-1	23 Dec 0-1	2 Dec 0-1	9 Dec 3-4	3 Feb 0-0	24 Feb 2-1	X	2 Sep 3-1	9 Apr 1-4	17 Feb 1-2	14 Oct 3-4
Raith Rovers	2 Jan 3-0	10 Feb 0-2	23 Sep 1-3	2 Dec 1-4	30 Dec 1-1	14 Oct 0-3	3 Mar 3-2	26 Aug 0-6	30 Sep 0-1	20 Jan 1-4	13 Jan 2-1	4 Nov 0-4	9 Sep 1-2	31 Mar 2-1	14 Apr 3-1	16 Dec 2-0	X	11 Nov 1-4	27 Jan 1-1	10 Mar 0-1
Rangers	3 Mar 1-0	30 Dec 3-0	10 Feb 1-0	1 Jan 0-0	18 Nov 1-0	2 Sep 6-0	19 Aug 3-0	2 Dec 3-1	27 Jan 2-0	6 Jan 1-0	16 Dec 5-1	16 Sep 3-0	4 Nov 0-1	14 Oct 2-1	20 Jan 3-0	21 Apr 1-0	24 Mar 4-3	X	30 Sep 1-0	7 Apr 0-2
St Mirren	30 Dec 1-0	16 Dec 1-0	28 Oct 0-0	19 Aug 1-5	21 Apr 0-1	28 Apr 0-0	10 Mar 2-0	25 Nov 5-0	10 Feb 2-2	11 Nov 0-1	7 Oct 1-1	13 Jan 2-1	24 Mar 0-0	9 Sep 1-2	7 Apr 3-0	23 Sep 0-0	21 Oct 1-1	24 Feb	X	3 Feb 2-0
Third Lanark	26 Aug 2-0	20 Jan 1-0	31 Mar 4-3	27 Jan 0-0	14 Apr 1-0	2 Jan 1-1	21 Apr 0-0	10 Feb 5-4	16 Sep 3-1	30 Dec 1-1	3 Mar 1-1	17 Mar 3-0	25 Nov 0-0	16 Dec 2-1	28 Apr 2-0	7 Oct 4-1	6 Jan 0-1	21 Oct 1-1	4 Nov 1-0	X

To enable the fixtures to be completed on time, several clubs played two fixtures on one day. On 14 April, Clyde beat St Mirren in the afternoon then lost to Third Lanark in the evening. Then on 21 April, Queen's Park and Rangers met in the evening after playing off their afternoon fixtures with Partick Thistle and Hamilton Academical respectively.

The Scottish Football League 1916-17

Final Table

		P	W	D	L	F	A	Pts
1	Celtic	38	27	10	1	79	17	64
2	Morton	38	24	6	8	72	39	54
3	Rangers	38	24	5	9	68	32	53
4	Airdrieonians	38	21	8	9	71	38	50
5	Third Lanark	38	19	11	8	53	37	49
6	Kilmarnock	38	18	7	13	69	46	43
7	St. Mirren	38	15	10	13	49	43	40
8	Motherwell	38	16	6	16	57	59	38
9	Dumbarton	38	12	11	15	56	73	35
10	Partick Thistle	38	14	7	17	44	43	35
11	Hamilton Academical	38	13	9	16	54	73	35
12	Clyde	38	10	14	14	41	53	34
13	Falkirk	38	12	10	16	58	57	34
14	Heart of Midlothian	38	14	4	20	44	59	32
15	Ayr United	38	12	7	19	47	59	31
16	Dundee	38	13	4	21	58	71	30
17	Hibernian	38	10	10	18	57	72	30
18	Queen's Park	38	11	7	20	56	81	29
19	Raith Rovers	38	8	7	23	42	91	23
20	Aberdeen	38	7	7	24	36	68	21

The West of Scotland Football League 1916-17

	Abercorn	Albion Rovers	Arthurlie	Clydebank	Dumbarton Harp	Johnstone	Renton	Stevenston United	Vale of Leven	Dykehead	Royal Albert	Wishaw Thistle
Abercorn	X	9 Dec 2-0	4 Nov 1-0	16 Sep 0-0	26 Aug 2-1	18 Nov 1-1	14 Apr 5-1	27 Jan 3-0	3 Mar 4-3			30 Sep 1-1
Albion Rovers	23 Sep 1-1	X	30 Sep 2-3	10 Feb 1-1	9 Sep 1-2	30 Dec 3-1	24 Feb 5-1	4 Nov 2-2	16 Dec 0-0		10 Mar 2-0	19 Aug 4-1
Arthurlie	21 Oct 3-2	11 Nov 1-1	X	24 Feb 1-2	23 Sep 2-3	26 Aug 3-1	7 Oct 1-1	16 Sep 0-1	9 Sep 0-3	9 Dec 2-1		
Clydebank	19 Aug 1-0	2 Sep 4-0	27 Jan 2-0	X	11 Nov 1-0	23 Sep 5-1	9 Dec 3-3	17 Feb 2-1	7 Apr 4-0		25 Nov 4-1	7 Oct 3-0
Dumbarton Harp	24 Mar 4-1	23 Dec 1-0		31 Mar 2-1	X	27 Jan 2-0	3 Mar 1-0	10 Mar 4-0	16 Sep 0-1	18 Nov 3-1	30 Sep 3-0	2 Sep 4-1
Johnstone	13 Jan 2-2	16 Sep 1-0	3 Feb 1-1	16 Dec 3-1		X	6 Jan 1-1		30 Sep 0-2	2 Sep 1-0	9 Sep 7-1	
Renton	25 Nov 0-5	26 Aug 0-1		30 Sep 1-3	17 Mar 0-4	11 Nov 4-1	X	18 Nov 1-1	2 Sep 1-0			18 Sep 0-1
Stevenston United	11 Nov 3-0	3 Mar 2-0	16 Dec 1-0	26 Aug 2-0	7 Oct 2-1	21 Oct 4-0	9 Sep 2-0	X	30 Dec 3-1	30 Sep 5-0	2 Sep 3-1	25 Nov 2-0
Vale of Leven	7 Oct 3-0	20 Jan 1-0	25 Nov 6-1	17 Mar 0-3	9 Dec 4-2	10 Feb 1-1	14 Oct off	19 Aug 1-2	X		23 Sep 2-2	
Dykehead	9 Sep 2-5	25 Nov 1-0				7 Oct 2-0	23 Sep 1-0		11 Nov 2-3	X	26 Aug 3-3	
Royal Albert		7 Oct 1-1		28 Oct 0-2					18 Nov 1-0	4 Nov 0-0	X	
Wishaw Thistle				9 Sep 0-3			28 Oct 1-1	23 Sep 1-2	26 Aug 3-2			X

Dykehead, Royal Albert and Wishaw Thistle all resigned on the weekend of 2 Feb 1917 due to the war-time circumstances
Renton v Dumbarton Harp on 17 Mar was played at Dumbarton, Renton also fielding a side against Vale of Leven in the Dunbartonshire Cup.
Albion Rovers v Clydebank on 18 Nov was abandoned at 0-0 and replayed later
Stevenston United v Abercorn 6-0 on 10 Feb, was also reported as a West of Scotland League match

		P	W	D	L	F	A	Pts
1	Clydebank	16	10	3	3	33	15	23
2	Stevenston United	15	10	2	3	26	15	22
3	Dumbarton Harp	14	9	0	5	27	15	18
4	Abercorn	16	7	4	5	29	23	18
5	Vale of Leven	15	7	2	6	26	21	16
6	Albion Rovers	16	3	5	8	17	23	11
7	Arthurlie	14	3	3	8	16	27	9
8	Johnstone	14	2	5	7	14	30	9
9	Renton	14	2	4	8	14	33	8

WESTERN CUP

	Abercorn	Arthurlie	Clydebank	Johnstone	Stevenston U	Vale of Leven
Abercorn	X		20 Jan 1-3	28 Apr 2-2	6 Jan 1-1	
Arthurlie	17 Feb 2-1	X	6 Jan 0-1	24 Mar 7-0	20 Jan 1-1	
Clydebank	3 Feb 4-2	2 Dec 1-0	X		24 Mar 4-1	
Johnstone	31 Mar 1-0			X	10 Mar 1-1	17 Feb 1-0
Stevenston United	10 Feb 6-0	7 Apr 0-2	1 Jan 2-0	14 Apr 1-0	X	3 Feb 2-1
Vale of Leven	28 Oct 2-4	13 Jan 2-0	2 Jan 5-0		31 Mar 0-3	X

Abercorn v Stevenston on 2 Dec was abandoned at 2-1 after 80 mins and replayed later
Abercorn v Clydebank was played at Clydebank

Stevenston United were declared winners

The Eastern Football League 1916-17

	Armadale	Bathgate	Broxburn United	Cowdenbeath	Dundee Hibernian	Dunfermline Athletic	East Fife	East Stirlingshire	Lochgelly United	St Bernard's
Armadale	X	19 Aug 0-1	2 Sep 1-0	2 Dec 1-1		30 Sep 3-1	24 Feb 1-1	21 Oct 7-0	16 Sep 4-0	6-2
Bathgate	23 Sep 2-3	X		26 Aug 2-2	7 Oct 2-3	14 Oct 4-0	9 Sep 0-1	9 Dec 1-1		4 Nov 0-5
Broxburn United	25 Nov 2-2	21 Oct 2-1	X	9 Sep 0-3	23 Sep 1-2	NOT PLAYED	NOT PLAYED	4 Nov 1-1	30 Sep 1-0	26 Aug 1-0
Cowdenbeath	4 Nov 5-2	30 Sep 3-1	19 Aug 8-1	X	30 Dec 4-1	2 Sep 2-1	11 Nov 1-1	16 Sep 3-3	21 Oct 5-1	10 Feb 2-0
Dundee Hibernian	NOT PLAYED	2 Sep 1-2	11 Nov 0-0	16 Dec 1-2	X	16 Sep 3-0	14 Oct 1-3	30 Sep 2-0	19 Aug 5-1	25 Nov 1-2
Dunfermline Athletic	26 Aug 3-0	NOT PLAYED	7 Oct 3-2	1 Jan 1-0	21 Oct 3-2	X	23 Sep 1-0	10 Mar 2-0	4 Nov 1-0	9 Sep 1-1
East Fife	7 Oct 1-1	NOT PLAYED	NOT PLAYED	3 Feb 1-1	4 Nov 5-0	19 Aug 2-0	X	2 Sep 4-0	3 Mar 4-0	21 Oct 1-0
East Stirlingshire	9 Aug	11 Nov 7-0	3 Feb 2-1	7 Oct 0-1	26 Aug 3-1	28 Oct 3-2	NOT PLAYED	X		23 Sep 2-1
Lochgelly United	11 Nov 0-1			23 Sep 1-0	9 Sep 2-4	3 Feb 3-1	2-2	NOT PLAYED	X	7 Oct 0-3
St Bernard's	9 Dec 3-0	16 Sep 3-2	28 Oct 1-0	14 Oct 1-2	2 Dec 1-1	11 Nov 2-1	30 Sep 1-0	19 Aug 5-1	2 Sep 6-2	X

Due to a dispute, both games between East Fife and Broxburn United were called off and all four points awarded to East Fife
Broxburn United v East Stirlingshire on 4 Nov was stopped at 1-1 after 70 mins due to bad light
Cowdenbeath v East Fife on 11 Nov was stopped early at 1-1 stopped early

		P	W	D	L	F	A	Pts
1	Cowdenbeath	18	11	5	2	45	19	27
2	East Fife	14	7	5	2	26	9	23
3	St Bernard's	18	10	2	6	37	23	22
4	Armadale	17	7	6	4	36	26	20
5	Dundee Hibernian	17	6	3	8	29	33	15
6	Dunfermline Athletic	16	7	1	8	21	27	15
7	East Stirlingshire	15	5	4	6	28	35	14
8	Broxburn United	14	5	2	7	15	25	12
9	Bathgate	16	3	2	11	21	38	8
10	Lochgelly United	15	4	0	11	16	39	8

EASTERN LEAGUE CUP

First round
Played on 18 Nov
  St Bernard's v Bathgate 2-1
Played on 2 Dec
  Dunfermline Athletic v Lochgelly United 4-2

Second round
Played on 25 Nov
  Cowdenbeath v East Fife 3-1
Played on 2 Jan
  Armadale v East Stirlingshire 5-1
Played on 20 Jan
  St Bernard's v Broxburn United 3-0
Played on 3 Mar
  Dunfermline Athletic v Dundee Hibernian 7-0

Semi-final
  Armadale v Cowdenbeath
Played on 7 Apr
  Dunfermline Athletic v St Bernard's 1-2

Final
  St Bernard's v Armadale

COMPETITION UNFINISHED

Other Scottish Competitions 1916-17

GLASGOW CUP

First round
Played on 9 Sep
Queen's Park v Clyde 0-2
Partick Thistle v Rangers 0-2

Semi-final
Played on 23 Sep
Third Lanark v Clyde 0-4
Celtic v Rangers 3-0

Final
Played on 7 Oct at Celtic Park, Glasgow
Celtic v Clyde 3-2

GLASGOW CHARITY CUP

First round
Played on 5 May
Queen's Park v Clyde 1-0
Partick Thistle v Third Lanark 3-1

Semi-final
Played on 12 May
Queen's Park v Partick Thistle 4-1 (at Cathkin Park, Glasgow)
Celtic v Rangers 2-0

Final
Played on 19 May at Hampden Park, Glasgow
Queen's Park v Celtic 0-1

DUNBARTONSHIRE CUP

	Clydebank	Dumbarton Harp	Renton	Vale of Leven
Clydebank	X	30 Dec 3-1	4 Nov 4-0	
Dumbarton Harp	13 Jan 1-1	X	10 Feb 3-0	4 Nov 2-4
Renton	10 Mar 1-3	21 Oct 1-2	X	17 Mar
Vale of Leven	14 Apr 0-5	24 Feb 2-4	27 Jan 0-1	X

On 17 March, Renton fielded two sides, one of which was against Dumbarton Harp in the West of Scotland League

		P	W	D	L	F	A	Pts
1	Clydebank	5	4	1	0	16	3	9
2	Dumbarton Harp	6	3	1	2	13	11	7
3	Vale of Leven	4	1	0	3	6	12	2
4	Renton	5	1	0	4	3	12	2

Final
Played on 28 Apr at Boghead Park, Dumbarton
Clydebank v Dumbarton Harp 1-1
REPLAY on 2 Jan 1918 at Boghead Park, Dumbarton
Dumbarton harp v Clydebank 3-0

DUNBARTONSHIRE CHARITY CUP

First round
Played on 5 May
Clydebank v Renton 3-0

Semi-final
Played on 5 May
Vale of Leven v Dumbarton Harp 0-2
Played on 12 May
Dumbarton v Clydebank 3-1

Final
Played on 19 May at Boghead Park, Dumbarton
Dumbarton v Dumbarton Harp 3-0

LANARKSHIRE CUP

First round
Played on 21 Oct
Albion Rovers v Dykehead 2-0
Played on 28 Oct
Dykehead v Albion Rovers 4-1

Semi-final
Wishaw Thistle

Final
Wishaw Thistle won the Cup

LANARKSHIRE CHARITY CUP

Semi-final
Played on 5 May
Airdrieonians v Lanarkshire Select XI 2-0
Played on 12 May
Hamilton Academical v Motherwell 10-0

Final
Played on 19 May at Fir Park, Motherwell
Airdrieonians v Hamilton Academical 3-1

RENFREWSHIRE CUP

First round
Played on 24 Feb
Johnstone v Abercorn 0-1

COMPETITION ABANDONED

RENFREWSHIRE VICTORIA CUP

Known results
3 Mar Johnstone v Arthurlie 1-2
10 Mar Arthurlie v Abercorn 2-0
21 Apr Arthurlie v Abercorn 3-0

Final
Played on 7 Apr
Morton v Johnstone 4-0

Other Scottish Competitions 1916-17

EAST OF SCOTLAND SHIELD
Final

NOTE due to fixture congestion, this game was played in 1917-18 season

Played on 17 Sep 1917
Hibernian v Heart of Midlothian 4-0

ROSEBERY CHARITY CUP

Semi-final
Played on 5 May
Heart of Midlothian v Hibernian 3-0
Armadale v St Bernard's 2-2 *(aet, 90 mins 2-2, Armadale won 3-2 on corners, at Easter Road, Edinburgh)*

Final
Played on 12 May at Tynecastle Park, Edinburgh
Heart of Midlothian v Armadale 5-3

WILSON CUP
Played on 1 Jan at Easter Road, Edinburgh
Hibernian v Heart of Midlothian 3-0

FIFE CUP
Semi-final
Played on 17 Feb
Lochgelly United v Cowdenbeath 0-2
Played on 14 Apr
East Fife v Dunfermline Athletic 2-0

Final
Played on 28 Apr at North End Park, Cowdenbeath
Cowdenbeath v East Fife 0-0 *(aet, Cowdenbeath won 2-1 on corners)*

First round
Kirkcaldy United v Cowdenbeath scr-wo
Played on 7 Apr
East Fife v Raith Rovers 1-0 *(aet, 90 mins 0-0)*

WEST FIFE CHARITY CUP
2 legs – first leg played on 5 May, second on 19 May
Cowdenbeath v Dunfermline Athletic 2-0, 0-1

GARDENERS CUP

Semi-final – 2 legs
First leg played on 18 Nov, second on 31 Mar
Broxburn United v Armadale 0-4, 1-1
First leg played on 3 Feb, second on 31 Mar
St Bernard's v Bathgate 1-1, 0-1

Final
Played on 28 Apr at Bathgate
Armadale v Bathgate 3-2 *(aet, 90 mins 2-2)*

PAISLEY CHARITY CUP
2 legs, first leg played on 5 May, second on 12 May
St Mirren v Abercorn 4-1, 1-1

FALKIRK INFIRMARY SHIELD
Played on 5 May at Brockville park, Falkirk
Falkirk v East Stirlingshire 6-4

PENMAN CUP
Second round
Played on 18 Nov
East Fife v Lochgelly United 2-0
Played on 17 Feb
Armadale v St Bernard's 1-1
REPLAY on 3 Mar
St Bernard's v Armadale 1-1
Played on 3 Mar
Cowdenbeath v Raith Rovers 6-0
Played on 17 Mar
Bathgate v Broxburn United 3-1

First round
Played on 18 Nov
Cowdenbeath v Dunfermline Athletic 4-0 *(abandoned)*
REPLAY on 13 Jan
Cowdenbeath v Dunfermline Athletic 2-2
SECOND REPLAY on 20 Jan
Dunfermline Athletic v Cowdenbeath 2-2
THIRD REPLAY on 27 Jan
Dunfermline Athletic v Cowdenbeath 0-2
Played on 10 Feb
Broxburn United v East Stirlingshire 7-0

NOTE due to fixture congestion, the Semi-finals and final were held over to 1917-18 season.

Semi-final
Played on 17 Nov 1917
Bathgate v East Fife 1-1
Played on 17 Nov 1917
Cowdenbeath v Armadale 1-1
REPLAY on 15 Dec 1917
Armadale v Cowdenbeath 2-1

Final
Played on 2 Feb 1918 at North End Park, Cowdenbeath
East Fife v Armadale 1-0

Other Scottish Competitions 1916-17

WEMYSS CUP

First round
Kirkcaldy United v Dunfermline Athletic scr-wo
Played on 9 Dec
  Lochgelly United v East Fife 0-2

Semi-final
Played on 17 Mar
  Cowdenbeath v Dunfermline Athletic 1-1
REPLAY on 24 Mar
  Dunfermline Athletic v Cowdenbeath 0-1
Played on 24 Mar
  Raith Rovers v East Fife 0-2

Final
Played on 31 Mar at North End Park, Cowdenbeath
  Cowdenbeath v East Fife 0-0
REPLAY on 21 Apr at Bayview Park, Methil
  Cowdenbeath v East Fife 2-1

INTER COUNTY FOOTBALL LEAGUE

	Albion Rovers	Dumbarton Harp	Queen's Park Str	Renton	Stevenston United
Albion Rovers	X	17 Feb 0-1	27 Jan 3-1	17 Mar 4-0	
Dumbarton Harp	14 Apr 4-0	X	21 Apr 5-0		
Queen's Park Strollers	6 Jan 0-1		X	31 Mar 2-1	
Renton	3 Feb 2-2	3 Mar 0-1		X	
Stevenston United	3 Mar 2-0				X

FIFE FOOTBALL LEAGUE

	Cowdenbeath	Dunfermline Athletic	East Fife	Lochgelly U	Raith Rovers 'A'
Cowdenbeath	X				
Dunfermline Athletic		X			
East Fife			X	10 Feb 4-0	
Lochgelly United				X	21 Apr 2-5
Raith Rovers 'A'	3 Apr W-L		17 Feb 0-5	24 Feb 0-1	X

LINITHGOWSHIRE CUP

Semi-final – 2 legs
First leg played on 24 Mar, second on 7 Apr
  Broxburn United v Bathgate 2-0, 0-1

Final
Played on 21 Apr at Bathgate
  Armadale v Broxburn United 2-1

Ireland 1916-17

BELFAST & DISTRICT FOOTBALL LEAGUE

	Belfast United	Cliftonville	Distillery	Glenavon	Glentoran	Linfield
Belfast United	X	11 Nov 0-1	16 Sep 1-1	18 Nov 1-1	4 Nov 1-3	`21 Oct 0-3
Cliftonville	30 Sep 3-0	X	21 Oct 0-1	23 Sep 3-2	28 Oct 0-2	18 Nov 1-1
Distillery	28 Oct 1-1	9 Sep 1-0	X	30Sep 5-3	18 Nov 3-3	23 Sep 1-1
Glenavon	7 Oct 1-0	4 Nov 0-0	11 Nov 1-5	X	21 Oct 2-3	28 Oct 0-5
Glentoran	23 Sep 2-1	16 Sep 1-1	7 Oct 4-3	9 Sep 4-3	X	11 Nov 4-0
Linfield	9 Sep 3-2	7 Oct 2-0	4 Nov 0-2	16 Sep 2-0	30 Sep 2-2	X

		P	W	D	L	F	A	Pts
1	Glentoran	10	7	3	0	28	16	17
2	Distillery	10	5	4	1	23	14	14
3	Linfield	10	5	3	2	19	12	13
4	Cliftonville	10	3	3	4	9	10	9
5	Glenavon	10	1	2	7	13	28	4
6	Belfast United	10	0	3	7	7	19	3

BELFAST CITY CUP

	Belfast United	Cliftonville	Distillery	Glenavon	Glentoran	Linfield
Belfast United	X	2 Dec 3-2	6 Jan 0-1	30 Dec 2-0		20 Jan 0-3
Cliftonville		X	9 Dec 1-0	27 Jan 2-0	20 Jan 0-1	16 Dec 2-0
Distillery	16 Dec 2-0	30 Dec 1-0	X	23 Dec 4-0		
Glenavon			20 Jan 1-0	X	6 Jan 1-3	
Glentoran	27 Jan 3-2	23 Dec 3-1	2 Dec 1-0	16 Dec 7-0	X	30 Dec 2-0
Linfield	23 Dec 1-0	6 Jan 5-0	27 Jan 4-2		2 Dec 6-0	X

		P	W	D	L	F	A	Pts
1	Glentoran	8	7	0	1	20	10	14
3	Linfield	7	5	0	2	19	6	10
2	Distillery	8	4	0	4	10	7	8
4	Cliftonville	8	3	0	5	8	13	6
6	Belfast United	7	2	0	5	7	12	4
5	Glenavon	6	1	0	5	2	18	2

IRISH FA CUP

Semi-final
Played on 10 Mar
  Belfast Celtic v Bohemians 4-0
  Distillery v Glentoran 1-1
REPLAY on 17 Mar
  Glentoran v Distillery 3-1

Final
Played on 31 Mar
  Glentoran v Belfast Celtic 2-0

Ireland 1916-17

GOLD CUP

	Belfast United	Cliftonville	Distillery	Glenavon	Glentoran	Linfield
Belfast United	X			DRAW		
Cliftonville	W-L	X	NO GAME			
Distillery	W-L		X	W-L		21 Apr 0-3
Glenavon		L-W		X		
Glentoran	14 Apr 4-0	10 Apr 1-0	7 Apr 0-0	21 Apr 3-0	X	
Linfield	7 Apr 3-1	14 Apr 0-1		10 Apr 5-0	9 Apr 1-0	X

		P	W	D	L	F	A	Pts
1	Glentoran	5	4	1	0	8	0	9
3	Linfield	5	3	0	2	12	2	6
2	Cliftonville	4	3	0	1	6	2	6
4	Distillery	4	2	1	1	5	4	5
5	Belfast United	5	0	1	4	2	11	1
6	Glenavon	5	0	1	4	1	14	1

1917-18

The two sections, Lancashire and Midland, which had replaced the national First and Second Divsions in 1915 continued as in the previous season.

In Scotland, the Scottish Football League continued in an official capacity despite the restrictions. Again the non-League West of Scotland and Eastern Leagues catered for the ex-Scottish League sides from the Second Division

The Belfast & District League continued as a replacement for the Irish League.

WINNERS OF THE PRINCIPAL COMPETITIONS

Football League –	
Championship Cup	Leeds City
Lancashire Principal	Stoke
Lancashire Subsidiary	Liverpool
Midland Principal	Leeds City
Midland Subsidiary	Grimsby Town
London Combination	Chelsea
Scottish League	Rangers
West of Scotland League	Albion Rovers
Eastern League	Dundee
Irish FA Cup	Belfast Celtic
Belfast & District League	Linfield
Belfast City Cup	
Gold Cup	Linfield

The Football League 1917-18

LANCASHIRE SECTION

Principal Competition

	Blackburn R	Blackpool	Bolton W	Burnley	Bury	Everton	Liverpool	Manchester City	Manchester United	Oldham Ath	Port Vale	Preston NE	Rochdale	Southport C	Stockport Co	Stoke
Blackburn Rovers	X	2 Mar 2-2	12 Jan 1-3	29 Sep 3-1	3 Nov 1-4	16 Feb 0-6	1 Dec 1-6	29 Dec 0-4	1 Sep 0-5	13 Oct 0-2	16 Mar 1-5	9 Feb 0-1	26 Jan 1-3	15 Dec 0-1	15 Sep 1-6	17 Nov 1-8
Blackpool	9 Mar 4-1	X	2 Feb 0-5	29 Mar 1-0	15 Sep 1-0	5 Jan 1-0	3 Nov 0-6	16 Mar 1-0	15 Dec 2-3	1 Sep 3-2	19 Jan 0-1	23 Feb 1-0	22 Dec 1-3	17 Nov 1-1	29 Sep 3-1	13 Oct 0-5
Bolton Wanderers	5 Jan 5-2	9 Feb 1-1	X	3 Nov 8-0	29 Sep 4-1	16 Mar 2-3	15 Sep 0-3	16 Feb 1-0	17 Nov 4-2	15 Dec 3-5	22 Dec 0-2	26 Jan 4-0	2 Mar 1-1	13 Oct 1-1	1 Dec 1-3	1 Sep 2-5
Burnley	6 Oct 6-1	25 Dec 1-1	27 Oct 2-1	X	5 Jan 5-1	22 Sep 0-5	23 Feb 1-3	8 Dec 0-4	22 Dec 0-5	2 Feb 0-3	20 Oct 2-2	10 Nov 1-2	8 Sep 2-2	19 Jan 1-0	9 Mar 0-2	23 Mar 0-2
Bury	27 Oct 5-1	22 Sep 2-1	6 Oct 1-1	12 Jan 2-1	X	24 Nov 2-5	23 Mar 0-1	20 Oct 2-5	23 Feb 1-2	19 Jan 4-0	8 Dec 0-2	8 Sep 1-2	10 Nov 2-1	9 Mar 2-0	2 Feb 0-3	29 Dec 1-1
Everton	23 Feb 2-1	12 Jan 7-2	23 Mar 2-3	15 Sep 9-0	1 Dec 7-1	X	29 Sep 2-2	26 Jan 0-0	13 Oct 3-0	17 Nov 4-2	9 Mar 7-0	29 Dec 6-0	9 Feb 2-2	1 Sep 6-1	3 Nov 2-3	15 Dec 3-2
Liverpool	24 Nov 7-0	27 Oct 4-1	22 Sep 6-0	16 Feb 7-1	16 Mar 1-1	6 Oct 6-0	X	10 Nov 2-0	19 Jan 5-1	22 Dec 3-0	8 Sep 4-0	20 Oct 2-2	8 Dec 5-1	2 Feb 6-1	5 Jan 2-1	2 Mar 1-1
Manchester City	22 Dec 1-0	23 Mar 2-2	23 Feb 0-1	15 Dec 4-1	13 Oct 3-1	19 Jan 0-2	17 Nov 1-1	X	29 Sep 3-1	15 Sep 2-2	2 Feb 5-1	9 Mar 1-2	5 Jan 1-1	1 Dec 5-0	1 Sep 2-1	3 Nov 1-0
Manchester United	8 Sep 6-1	8 Dec 1-0	10 Nov 1-3	29 Dec 1-0	16 Feb 0-0	20 Oct 0-0	26 Jan 0-2	6 Oct 1-1	X	2 Mar 2-1	27 Oct 3-3	24 Nov 2-1	22 Sep 1-1	12 Jan 0-0	16 Mar 2-0	9 Feb 2-1
Oldham Athletic	20 Oct 2-0	8 Sep 1-1	8 Dec 6-3	9 Feb 6-2	26 Jan 1-0	10 Nov 1-3	29 Dec 3-3	22 Sep 0-0	9 Mar 2-0	X	24 Nov 1-1	6 Oct 1-3	27 Oct 2-1	23 Mar 3-1	23 Feb 1-0	12 Jan 2-2
Port Vale	23 Mar 0-2	26 Jan 4-0	29 Dec 1-2	13 Oct 5-2	15 Dec 2-2	2 Mar 0-1	1 Sep 2-3	9 Feb 0-2	3 Nov 2-2	1 Dec 2-0	X	12 Jan 3-0	16 Feb 1-1	15 Sep 1-1	17 Nov 0-4	29 Sep 0-2
Preston North End	2 Feb 2-0	16 Feb 2-1	19 Jan 2-0	17 Nov 0-0	1 Sep 1-0	22 Dec 0-1	13 Oct 0-6	2 Mar 0-2	1 Dec 0-0	29 Sep 5-1	5 Jan 1-0	X	16 Mar 3-4	3 Nov 4-2	15 Dec 0-1	15 Sep 2-3
Rochdale	19 Jan 6-0	29 Dec 6-3	9 Mar 5-2	1 Sep 9-0	17 Nov 7-5	2 Feb 2-2	15 Dec 1-0	12 Jan 1-4	15 Sep 3-0	3 Nov 1-0	23 Feb 2-0	23 Mar 4-3	X	29 Sep 6-0	13 Oct 0-1	1 Dec 0-0
Southport Central	8 Dec 2-1	10 Nov 0-2	20 Oct 6-2	26 Jan 2-0	2 Mar 1-3	8 Sep 0-2	9 Feb 1-3	24 Nov 0-0	5 Jan 3-0	16 Mar 1-0	22 Sep 2-4	27 Oct 1-0	6 Oct 2-2	X	22 Dec 3-2	16 Feb 0-2
Stockport County	22 Sep 6-0	6 Oct 3-1	24 Nov 2-3	2 Mar 0-0	9 Feb 3-2	27 Oct 0-0	12 Jan 1-0	8 Sep 0-1	23 Mar 2-1	16 Feb 2-0	10 Nov 2-2	8 Dec 1-0	20 Oct 2-0	29 Dec 6-0	X	26 Jan 0-3
Stoke	10 Nov 16-0	20 Oct 3-1	8 Sep 6-2	16 Mar 9-0	22 Dec 1-0	8 Dec 3-0	9 Mar 3-1	27 Oct 4-3	2 Feb 5-1	5 Jan 7-0	6 Oct 4-1	22 Sep 4-0	27 Apr 1-2	23 Feb 4-0	19 Jan 2-1	X

		P	W	D	L	F	A	Pts
1	Stoke	30	22	4	4	109	27	48
2	Liverpool	30	21	6	3	101	26	48
3	Everton	30	19	6	5	92	36	44
4	Manchester City	30	15	8	7	57	28	38
5	Stockport County	30	17	3	10	59	32	37
6	Rochdale	30	14	9	7	78	51	37
7	Bolton Wanderers	30	13	4	13	68	70	30
8	Manchester United	30	11	8	11	45	49	30
9	Oldham Athletic	30	11	6	13	50	59	28
10	Preston North End	30	12	3	15	38	53	27
11	Port Vale	30	9	8	13	47	58	26
12	Blackpool	30	10	5	15	46	70	25
13	Southport Central	30	8	6	16	33	69	22
14	Bury	30	8	5	17	46	64	21
15	Burnley	30	5	4	21	32	104	14
16	Blackburn Rovers	30	2	1	27	22	127	5

The Football League 1917-18

MIDLAND SECTION

Principal Competition

	Barnsley	Birmingham	Bradford	Bradford City	Grimsby T	Huddersfield T	Hull City	Leeds City	Leicester F	Lincoln C	Nottingham F	Notts County	Rotherham Co	Sheffield United	The Wednesday
Barnsley	X	6 Oct 3-3	12 Jan 1-0	24 Nov 1-2	22 Sep 4-0	27 Oct 2-1	2 Feb 1-3	8 Dec 3-4	16 Feb 1-0	8 Sep 1-0	2 Mar 1-0	13 Oct 0-0	26 Dec 1-2	22 Dec 3-6	10 Nov 3-2
Birmingham	29 Sep 3-1	X	20 Oct 2-0	22 Dec 2-1	8 Dec 0-1	26 Jan 2-1	1 Sep 2-1	17 Nov 3-1	25 Dec 0-0	2 Mar 5-0	1 Dec 1-1	12 Jan 7-2	16 Feb 2-0	3 Nov 4-1	2 Feb 4-1
Bradford	5 Jan 8-0	13 Oct 1-0	X	26 Dec 0-1	6 Oct 4-1	10 Nov 1-2	9 Mar 1-3	23 Feb 0-2	22 Dec 1-0	22 Sep 1-0	2 Apr 3-0	27 Oct 1-0	8 Sep 5-2	8 Dec 2-0	24 Nov 2-1
Bradford City	1 Dec 5-1	29 Dec 0-3	25 Dec 1-2	X	2 Mar 0-1	16 Feb 0-2	3 Nov 2-4	15 Sep 3-2	20 Oct 4-1	2 Feb 3-0	29 Sep 0-3	26 Jan 0-0	12 Jan 0-2	1 Sep 0-2	15 Dec 3-1
Grimsby Town	15 Sep 1-3	15 Dec 2-2	29 Sep 1-2	9 Mar 0-0	X	12 Jan 1-0	13 Apr 0-0	3 Nov 0-4	1 Dec 1-1	16 Feb 4-1	17 Nov 1-1	29 Dec 2-0	2 Feb 2-2	20 Oct 0-0	26 Jan 0-0
Huddersfield Town	3 Nov 5-0	19 Jan 4-2	17 Nov 1-0	23 Feb 2-2	5 Jan 2-0	X	29 Sep 4-2	26 Dec 1-3	15 Sep 1-2	1 Apr 4-0	1 Sep 2-1	2 Apr 2-1	8 Dec 1-1	1 Dec 3-1	2 Mar 4-0
Hull City	9 Feb 4-2	8 Sep 1-2	2 Mar 1-1	27 Oct 5-1	26 Dec 7-1	6 Oct 3-1	X	5 Jan 0-2	8 Dec 3-1	24 Nov 2-0	22 Dec 3-2	22 Sep 1-2	10 Nov 3-1	19 Jan 2-4	13 Oct 3-3
Leeds City	15 Dec 2-1	10 Nov 1-0	16 Feb 2-1	22 Sep 4-0	27 Oct 2-2	23 Mar 1-0	12 Jan 1-2	X	26 Jan 4-0	13 Oct 3-0	2 Feb 2-0	24 Nov 2-0	6 Oct 6-0	9 Mar 2-0	8 Sep 5-0
Leicester Fosse	23 Feb 5-1	26 Dec 3-0	29 Dec 2-0	13 Oct 2-0	24 Nov 6-1	22 Sep 4-1	15 Dec 3-1	19 Jan 2-4	X	10 Nov 4-0	5 Jan 2-0	8 Sep 1-0	27 Oct 2-0	9 Feb 1-2	6 Oct 1-2
Lincoln City	1 Sep 2-1	9 Mar 3-3	15 Sep 0-0	9 Feb 2-1	23 Feb 1-0	29 Dec 2-1	1 Dec 1-3	20 Oct 0-4	17 Nov 1-1	X	3 Nov 3-1	15 Dec 1-2	26 Jan 1-1	29 Sep 0-1	12 Jan 3-0
Nottingham Forest	9 Mar 1-0	24 Nov 2-1	26 Jan 0-0	6 Oct 2-0	10 Nov 5-0	8 Sep 3-0	29 Dec 5-1	9 Feb 0-1	12 Jan 2-0	27 Oct 0-1	X	26 Dec 0-0	13 Oct 1-3	23 Feb 0-1	22 Sep 3-1
Notts County	20 Oct 4-2	5 Jan 3-3	3 Nov 0-1	19 Jan 2-2	22 Dec 8-0	2 Feb 3-2	15 Sep 2-2	1 Dec 2-4	1 Sep 2-1	8 Dec 1-1	25 Dec 0-1	X	2 Mar 2-2	17 Nov 0-6	16 Feb 3-0
Rotherham County	25 Dec 4-1	23 Feb 1-0	1 Sep 2-2	5 Jan 2-3	9 Feb 1-1	15 Dec 3-1	17 Nov 1-2	29 Sep 0-3	3 Nov 4-2	19 Jan 2-0	20 Oct 1-3	9 Mar 2-2	X	15 Sep 0-1	29 Dec 0-0
Sheffield United	29 Dec 3-0	27 Oct 3-1	15 Dec 1-0	8 Sep 4-0	13 Oct 5-0	24 Nov 1-0	26 Jan 0-1	2 Mar 2-1	2 Feb 6-2	6 Oct 6-0	16 Feb 0-1	10 Nov 6-1	22 Sep 2-0	X	25 Dec 1-0
The Wednesday	17 Nov 4-2	9 Feb 0-2	1 Dec 3-1	8 Dec 3-0	27 Apr 1-1	9 Mar 3-1	20 Oct 4-3	1 Sep 0-1	29 Sep 1-3	5 Jan 7-2	15 Sep 0-3	23 Feb 2-1	22 Dec 3-3	26 Dec 3-1	X

Bradford v Nottingham Forest on 19 Jan was abandoned at half-time with the score 2-0 and replayed at a later date
Bradford City v Lincoln City on 2 Feb was abandoned just before the finish but the result was allowed to stand
Huddersfield Town v Notts County on 9 Feb was abandoned with the score 0-0 and replayed at a later date

		P	W	D	L	F	A	Pts
1	Leeds City	28	23	1	4	75	23	47
2	Sheffield United	28	20	1	7	66	27	41
3	Birmingham	28	14	6	8	59	38	34
4	Hull City	28	15	4	9	67	50	34
5	Nottingham Forest	28	13	4	11	41	28	30
6	Bradford	28	13	4	11	40	29	30
7	Leicester Fosse	28	13	3	12	52	43	29
8	Huddersfield Town	28	12	2	14	49	46	26
9	Rotherham County	28	8	9	11	42	52	25
10	Notts County	28	7	9	12	43	54	23
11	The Wednesday	28	9	5	14	45	59	23
12	Grimsby Town	28	5	11	12	24	62	21
13	Bradford City	28	8	4	16	34	55	20
14	Lincoln City	28	7	5	16	25	62	19
15	Barnsley	28	8	2	18	40	74	18

The Football League 1917-18

LANCASHIRE SECTION

Subsidiary Tournament

GROUP A	Everton	Liverpool	Southport C	Stockport Co
Everton	X	29 Mar 3-2	13 Apr 6-1	30 Mar 4-0
Liverpool	1 Jan 4-1	X	6 Apr 2-0	20 Apr 4-2
Southport Central	20 Apr 0-4	30 Mar 0-8	X	1 Jan 0-1
Stockport County	6 Apr 0-1	13 Apr 1-4	29 Mar 2-0	X

GROUP B	Manchester City	Manchester Utd	Port Vale	Stoke
Manchester City	X	29 Mar 3-0	6 Apr 1-0	20 Apr 2-0
Manchester United	1 Apr 2-0	X	13 Apr 2-0	30 Mar 2-1
Port Vale	30 Mar 1-4	20 Apr 3-0	X	29 Mar 0-2
Stoke	13 Apr 1-1	6 Apr 0-0	1 Apr 6-0	X

GROUP C	Blackburn R	Blackpool	Burnley	Preston NE
Blackburn Rovers	X	6 Apr 1-4	20 Apr 2-1	25 Dec 0-2
Blackpool	30 Mar 2-0	X	1 Dec 5-1	13 Apr 2-3
Burnley	13 Apr 3-0	24 Nov 3-1	X	6 Apr 1-1
Preston North End	26 Dec 1-0	20 Apr 1-4	30 Mar 2-1	X

GROUP D	Bolton W	Bury	Oldham Ath	Rochdale
Bolton Wanderers	X	1 Jan 4-0	30 Mar 2-0	13 Apr 2-1
Bury	25 Dec 2-2	X	20 Apr 1-1	6 Apr 1-4
Oldham Athletic	6 Apr 2-1	13 Apr 2-3	X	1 Apr 1-0
Rochdale	20 Apr 4-0	30 Mar 2-1	29 Mar 2-3	X

		P	W	D	L	F	A	Pts
1	Liverpool	6	5	0	1	24	7	10
2	Everton	6	5	0	1	19	7	10
3	Manchester City	6	4	1	1	11	4	9
4	Preston North End	6	4	1	1	10	8	9
5	Blackpool	6	4	0	2	18	9	8
6	Bolton Wanderers	6	3	1	2	11	9	7
7	Oldham Athletic	6	3	1	2	9	9	7
8	Manchester United	6	3	1	2	6	7	7
9	Stoke	6	2	2	2	10	5	6
10	Rochdale	6	3	0	3	13	8	6
11	Burnley	6	2	1	3	10	11	5
12	Bury	6	1	2	3	8	15	4
13	Stockport County	6	2	0	4	6	13	4
14	Port Vale	6	1	0	5	4	15	2
15	Blackburn Rovers	6	1	0	5	3	13	2
16	Southport Central	6	0	0	6	1	23	0

The Football League 1917-18

MIDLAND SECTION

Subsidiary Tournament

GROUP A	Gainsborough T	Grimsby T	Hull C	Lincoln C
Gainsborough Trinity	X	23 Mar 0-3	23 Feb 0-1	26 Dec 0-4
Grimsby Town	16 Mar 4-0	X	29 Mar 2-0	6 Apr 2-0
Hull City	16 Feb 4-2	1 Apr 2-2	X	16 Mar 4-2
Lincoln City	29 Mar 3-1	30 Mar 1-0	23 Mar 1-1	X

GROUP B	Birmingham	Leicester F	Nottingham F	Notts Co
Birmingham	X	20 Apr 1-0	16 Mar 0-0	6 Apr 3-2
Leicester Fosse	13 Apr 1-1	X	30 Mar 1-0	23 Mar 3-1
Nottingham Forest	23 Mar 1-0	6 Apr 2-0	X	1 Apr 0-3
Notts County	30 Mar 5-1	16 Mar 5-1	29 Mar 3-1	X

Grimsby Town v Hull City on 25 Dec was abandoned after 11 minutes
with the score 0-1 and replayed at a later date

GROUP C	Barnsley	Rotherham Co	Sheffield United	The Wednesday
Barnsley	X	16 Mar 3-0	6 Apr 1-1	1 Jan 4-1
Rotherham County	23 Mar 2-1	X	1 Apr 0-1	30 Mar 0-0
Sheffield United	30 Mar 2-3	1 Jan 4-1	X	16 Mar 0-5
The Wednesday	1 Apr 6-2	6 Apr 1-1	23 Mar 2-1	X

GROUP D	Bradford	Bradford City	Huddersfield T	Leeds City
Bradford	X	23 Mar 3-1	13 Apr 1-2	6 Apr 1-2
Bradford City	16 Mar 1-1	X	30 Mar 5-3	20 Apr 0-0
Huddersfield Town	20 Apr 3-1	6 Apr 1-1	X	16 Mar 4-2
Leeds City	30 Mar 3-1	13 Apr 0-0	23 Mar 1-0	X

		P	W	D	L	F	A	Pts
1	Grimsby Town	6	4	1	1	13	3	9
2	Notts County	6	4	0	2	19	9	8
3	The Wednesday	6	3	2	1	15	8	8
4	Hull City	6	3	2	1	12	9	8
5	Leeds City	6	3	2	1	8	6	8
6	Lincoln City	6	3	1	2	11	8	7
7	Huddersfield Town	6	3	1	2	13	11	7
8	Barnsley	6	3	1	2	14	12	7
9	Bradford City	6	1	4	1	8	8	6
10	Birmingham	6	2	2	2	6	9	6
11	Sheffield United	6	2	1	3	9	12	5
12	Leicester Fosse	6	2	1	3	6	10	5
13	Nottingham Forest	6	2	1	3	4	7	5
14	Rotherham County	6	1	2	3	4	10	4
15	Bradford	6	1	1	4	8	12	3
16	Gainsborough Trinity	6	0	0	6	3	19	0

LEAGUE CHAMPIONSHIP CUP
Played between the winners of the Lancashire Section and Midland Section Principal Competitions

First leg, 4 May 1918 at Elland Road, Leeds
Att 10,000
Leeds City 2 (Hibbert, Peart)
Stoke 0

Second leg, 11 May 1918 at Victoria Ground, Stoke
Att 10,000
Stoke 1 (Parker (pen))
Leeds City 0

Leeds City: T Hampson, Millership, W Hampson, Howison, Sherwin, Lamph, Goodwin, Cawley, Peart, Price, Hibbert
Stoke: Peers, Milne, Twemlow, Smith, Parker, Jones, Harrison, Whittingham, Howell, Herbert, Bridgett

Stoke: as first leg except Maddock for Milne, Tempest for Bridgett
Leeds City: as first leg

The London Football Combination 1917-18

	Brentford	Chelsea	Clapton Orient	Crystal Palace	Fulham	Millwall	QPR	The Arsenal	Tottenham H	West Ham U
Brentford	X	17 Nov 1-0; 9 Mar 0-1	1 Sep 1-0; 22 Dec 5-0	24 Nov 3-0; 16 Mar 0-2	20 Oct 1-3; 29 Mar 2-3	3 Nov 0-4; 23 Feb 3-0	25 Dec 1-1; 9 Feb 6-1	6 Oct 2-2; 26 Jan 3-2	15 Sep 5-2; 5 Jan 2-3	8 Dec 3-2; 30 Mar 3-7
Chelsea	22 Sep 3-1; 12 Jan 4-1	X	26 Dec 0-2; 9 Feb 3-0	10 Nov 0-1; 2 Mar 2-0	8 Dec 2-2; 30 Mar 7-0	1 Sep 3-4; 22 Dec 6-2	20 Oct 1-2; 29 Mar 1-0	24 Nov 4-3; 16 Mar 4-2	3 Nov 0-0; 23 Feb 3-0	6 Oct 4-3; 26 Jan 2-2
Clapton Orient	27 Oct 1-3; 16 Feb 1-1	25 Dec 1-4; 6 Apr 1-6	X	6 Oct 2-3; 26 Jan 0-0	22 Sep 1-5; 12 Jan 1-1	13 Oct 2-3; 2 Feb 0-1	24 Nov 1-2; 16 Mar 0-1	8 Sep 0-5; 29 Dec 1-2	15 Sep 2-4; 29 Mar 2-3	10 Nov 1-4; 2 Mar 1-3
Crystal Palace	29 Sep 4-0; 19 Jan 3-4	15 Sep 0-3; 5 Jan 0-0	1 Dec 3-1; 23 Mar 3-1	X	3 Nov 2-1; 23 Feb 5-2	15 Dec 1-5; 1 Apr 0-2	17 Nov 4-1; 9 Mar 1-4	13 Oct 2-0; 2 Feb 2-3	1 Sep 2-4; 22 Dec 2-3	26 Dec 4-0; 9 Feb 1-1
Fulham	15 Dec 2-0; 1 Apr 4-5	13 Oct 1-1; 2 Feb 0-2	17 Nov 3-0; 9 Mar 3-2	8 Sep 7-1; 29 Dec 1-1	X	29 Sep 3-1; 19 Jan 4-2	15 Sep 2-1; 5 Jan 1-0	25 Dec 1-1; 6 Apr 2-1	1 Dec 4-3; 23 Mar 0-3	27 Oct 1-1; 16 Feb 3-1
Millwall	8 Sep 1-3; 29 Dec 7-1	27 Oct 0-0; 16 Feb 0-4	8 Dec 2-1; 30 Mar 1-1	20 Oct 2-1; 29 Mar 1-3	24 Nov 2-1; 16 Mar 0-2	X	6 Oct 4-2; 26 Jan 0-1	10 Nov 2-2; 2 Mar 0-3	25 Dec 0-6; 6 Apr 0-1	22 Sep 2-3; 12 Jan 0-1
Queen's Park Rangers	26 Dec 0-4; 6 Apr 2-6	15 Dec 0-1; 1 Apr 1-2	29 Sep 2-0; 19 Jan 6-1	22 Sep 4-1; 12 Jan 2-1	10 Nov 2-3; 2 Mar 0-1	1 Dec 1-0; 23 Mar 4-1	X	27 Oct 2-0; 16 Feb 0-3	13 Oct 2-3; 2 Feb 2-7	8 Sep 0-3; 29 Dec 1-1
The Arsenal	1 Dec 4-1; 23 Mar 1-3	29 Sep 0-1; 19 Jan 4-1	3 Nov 3-1; 23 Feb 7-1	8 Dec 1-1; 30 Mar 3-0	26 Dec 1-1; 9 Feb 0-3	15 Sep 4-0; 5 Jan 1-0	1 Sep 2-0; 22 Dec 3-0	X	17 Nov 0-1; 9 Mar 4-1	20 Oct 2-2; 1 Apr 1-3
Tottenham Hotspur	10 Nov 6-1; 2 Mar 3-0	8 Sep 0-4; 29 Dec 2-0	20 Oct 2-1; 1 Apr 5-2	27 Oct 1-0; 16 Feb 8-0	6 Oct 1-0; 26 Jan 0-1	26 Dec 0-1; 9 Feb 4-2	8 Dec 0-1; 30 Mar 1-2	22 Sep 1-2; 12 Jan 4-1	X	24 Nov 2-0; 16 Mar 0-5
West Ham United	13 Oct 8-3; 2 Feb 7-2	1 Dec 1-1; 23 Mar 2-2	15 Sep 1-2; 5 Jan 3-0	25 Dec 2-1; 6 Apr 11-0	1 Sep 6-1; 22 Dec 0-3	17 Nov 0-0; 9 Mar 2-0	3 Nov 4-0; 23 Feb 4-0	15 Dec 3-2; 29 Mar 4-1	29 Sep 1-0; 19 Jan 2-2	X

		P	W	D	L	F	A	Pts
1	Chelsea	36	21	8	7	82	39	50
2	West Ham United	36	20	9	7	103	51	49
3	Fulham	36	20	7	9	75	60	47
4	Tottenham Hotspur	36	22	2	12	86	56	46
5	The Arsenal	36	16	5	15	76	57	37
6	Brentford	36	16	3	17	81	94	35
7	Crystal Palace	36	13	4	19	54	83	30
8	Queen's Park Rangers	36	14	2	20	48	73	30
9	Millwall	36	12	4	20	52	74	28
10	Clapton Orient	36	2	4	30	34	104	8

The Scottish Football League 1917-18

	Airdrieonians	Ayr U	Celtic	Clyde	Clydebank	Dumbarton	Falkirk	Hamilton Acad	Hearts	Hibernian	Kilmarnock	Morton	Motherwell	Partick Th	Queen's Park	Rangers	St Mirren	Third Lanark
Airdrieonians	X	22 Dec 4-1	3 Nov 2-0	8 Dec 3-0	12 Jan 1-2	16 Mar 0-0	15 Sep 3-1	13 Oct 2-1	9 Mar 0-1	16 Feb 3-0	10 Nov 0-1	20 Oct 1-1	29 Sep 3-1	2 Feb 0-1	18 Aug 2-4	23 Mar 1-2	1 Sep 1-0	24 Nov 0-3
Ayr United	8 Sep 1-2	X	29 Dec 1-2	22 Sep 1-3	9 Mar 1-2	10 Nov 0-1	13 Oct 4-0	25 Aug 2-0	23 Mar 1-1	27 Oct 2-2	24 Nov 0-3	8 Dec 0-1	2 Mar 1-3	15 Dec 0-0	16 Feb 0-2	26 Jan 0-2	12 Jan 2-1	2 Feb 2-2
Celtic	26 Jan 3-3	Aug 18 4-0	X	1 Sep 3-2	8 Dec 3-0	22 Dec 3-0	12 Jan 0-0	10 Nov 1-0	9 Feb 3-0	24 Nov 2-0	13 Oct 2-3	23 Feb 2-0	13 Apr 1-1	15 Sep 2-1	27 Oct 3-0	1 Jan 0-0	16 Mar 1-0	23 Mar 1-3
Clyde	25 Aug 3-1	30 Mar 4-0	2 Jan 1-4	X	29 Dec 0-3	3 Nov 0-4	2 Mar 1-0	9 Mar 1-3	1 Dec 3-0	20 Oct 2-5	15 Dec 1-2	5 Jan 0-2	2 Feb 0-2	24 Sep 0-0	29 Sep 1-1	16 Feb 0-3	17 Nov 1-2	20 Apr 2-0
Clydebank	6 Oct 3-3	29 Sep 3-1	2 Mar 1-2	18 Aug 0-4	X	31 Dec 1-2	1 Sep 1-1	9 Feb 2-1	3 Nov 3-1	16 Mar 2-0	23 Mar 1-0	13 Apr 1-2	15 Sep 1-2	20 Oct 1-2	1 Dec 3-1	5 Jan 1-1	15 Dec 4-1	17 Nov 2-2
Dumbarton	15 Dec 2-0	23 Feb 1-0	17 Nov 0-2	26 Jan 3-1	13 Oct 2-3	X	18 Aug 4-1	23 Mar 1-2	29 Dec 1-1	8 Dec 1-0	27 Oct 1-4	1 Sep 0-3	24 Nov 4-3	6 Apr 1-1	15 Sep 2-1	29 Sep 2-4	2 Mar 5-2	9 Feb 0-1
Falkirk	1 Dec 4-3	17 Nov 3-0	25 Aug 1-3	1 Jan 0-4	2 Feb 0-4	20 Aug 1-1	X	23 Feb 2-1	22 Sep 4-0	22 Dec 2-2	8 Sep 1-0	3 Nov 0-3	5 Jan 1-1	16 Feb 1-1	6 Apr 1-1	9 Mar 2-0	20 Oct 1-0	6 Oct 1-1
Hamilton Acad	29 Dec 1-1	5 Jan 0-3	16 Feb 1-2	15 Sep 2-0	24 Nov 3-3	20 Oct 2-0	29 Sep 1-1	X	17 Nov 3-0	18 Aug 1-0	6 Apr 4-1	22 Dec 2-1	1 Sep 3-3	13 Apr 2-2	2 Mar 1-2	8 Dec 1-2	2 Feb 2-1	3 Nov 4-0
Hearts	27 Oct 1-0	20 Oct 2-0	29 Sep 0-1	16 Mar 3-0	16 Feb 1-0	13 Apr 1-2	24 Nov 0-2	26 Jan 3-2	X	1 Sep 1-0	8 Dec 3-0	15 Sep 1-0	22 Dec 0-1	30 Mar 1-1	5 Jan 2-1	10 Nov 0-3	18 Aug 2-1	23 Feb 3-1
Hibernian	22 Sep 3-1	20 Apr 1-1	6 Apr 0-2	12 Jan 2-0	8 Sep 0-1	6 Oct 0-3	23 Mar 2-1	15 Dec 1-1	2 Feb 1-3	X	25 Aug 0-3	17 Nov 2-2	3 Nov 2-2	29 Dec 4-2	13 Oct 4-2	9 Feb 0-1	1 Dec 3-1	9 Mar 4-1
Kilmarnock	13 Apr 3-0	1 Sep 2-0	30 Mar 1-3	23 Feb 4-0	22 Sep 4-2	2 Feb 0-0	9 Feb 3-0	1 Dec 2-3	6 Oct 4-3	5 Jan 3-1	X	29 Sep 4-0	17 Nov 4-0	3 Nov 0-0	16 Mar 3-1	18 Aug 0-1	15 Sep 5-1	20 Oct 3-1
Morton	1 Jan 0-3	6 Apr 1-0	1 Dec 1-1	27 Oct 2-0	25 Aug 2-1	16 Feb 2-2	29 Dec 1-0	22 Dec 3-0	15 Sep 1-1	26 Dec 1-1	12 Jan 2-2	X	9 Mar 2-0	2 Feb 1-3	10 Nov 2-1	13 Oct 1-1	9 Feb 3-1	8 Sep 2-0
Motherwell	9 Feb 2-0	1 Dec 5-1	15 Dec 3-4	10 Nov 1-3	26 Jan 4-1	25 Aug 0-0	27 Oct 2-1	1 Jan 3-0	8 Sep 4-0	30 Mar 2-1	22 Sep 1-1	6 Oct 1-3	X	16 Mar 4-1	12 Jan 6-3	23 Feb 0-0	13 Oct 2-1	29 Dec 3-1
Partick Thistle	5 Jan 2-1	9 Feb 1-3	9 Mar 0-3	24 Nov 0-0	23 Feb 2-0	8 Sep 0-0	10 Nov 1-0	27 Oct 5-0	13 Oct 4-1	29 Sep 2-2	26 Jan 3-3	18 Aug 1-0	8 Dec 1-0	X	22 Dec 5-1	1 Sep 2-0	23 Mar 2-0	1 Jan 3-5
Queen's Park	30 Mar 3-0	1 Jan 0-0	2 Feb 0-2	9 Feb 4-2	22 Sep 3-1	9 Mar 2-0	8 Dec 5-0	6 Oct 2-1	25 Aug 4-0	23 Feb 2-0	29 Dec 3-0	23 Mar 3-0	20 Oct 2-2	17 Nov 2-0	X	24 Nov 2-3	3 Nov 1-1	15 Dec 3-3
Rangers	17 Nov 4-0	3 Nov 0-0	20 Oct 1-2	13 Apr 2-1	30 Mar 1-0	1 Dec 2-1	15 Dec 4-1	16 Mar 4-2	12 Jan 2-0	15 Sep 3-0	2 Mar 3-0	2 Feb 4-2	6 Apr 2-1	2 Jan 1-0	24 Sep 3-0	X	29 Dec 2-0	25 Aug 4-2
St Mirren	23 Feb 2-0	6 Oct 1-1	5 Jan 0-0	22 Dec 0-1	10 Nov 3-1	22 Sep 2-1	30 Mar 1-0	8 Sep 5-1	20 Apr 3-2	13 Apr 1-1	1 Jan 2-0	24 Nov 0-1	16 Feb 1-1	25 Aug 0-0	26 Jan 3-1	27 Oct 0-0	X	8 Dec 3-1
Third Lanark	2 Mar 2-2	15 Sep 1-1	24 Sep 0-2	13 Oct 3-0	27 Oct 0-1	5 Jan 4-1	26 Jan 4-0	12 Jan 2-1	6 Apr 2-3	10 Nov 1-0	16 Feb 1-1	16 Mar 1-2	18 Aug 2-4	1 Dec 0-1	1 Sep 5-0	22 Dec 0-1	29 Sep 1-2	X

		P	W	D	L	F	A	Pts
1	Rangers	34	25	6	3	66	24	56
2	Celtic	34	24	7	3	66	26	55
3	Kilmarnock	34	19	5	10	69	41	43
4	Morton	34	17	9	8	53	42	43
5	Motherwell	34	16	9	9	70	51	41
6	Partick Thistle	34	14	12	8	51	37	40
7	Dumbarton	34	13	8	13	48	49	34
8	Queen's Park	34	14	6	14	64	63	34
9	Clydebank	34	14	5	15	55	56	33
10	Heart of Midlothian	34	14	4	16	41	58	32
11	St. Mirren	34	11	7	16	42	50	29
12	Hamilton Academical	34	11	6	17	52	63	28
13	Third Lanark	34	10	7	17	56	62	27
14	Falkirk	34	9	9	16	38	58	27
15	Airdrieonians	34	10	6	18	46	58	26
16	Hibernian	34	8	9	17	42	57	25
17	Clyde	34	9	2	23	37	72	20
18	Ayr United	34	5	9	20	32	61	19

The West of Scotland Football League 1917-18

	Abercorn	Albion Rovers	Arthurlie	Dumbarton Harp	Johnstone	Renton	Stevenston United	Val of Leven
Abercorn	X	29 Sep 0-0	3 Nov 0-1	13 Oct 2-0	20 Oct 4-1	1 Sep 0-1	18 Aug 1-3	15 Sep 1-1
Albion Rovers	25 Aug 4-0	X	6 Oct 3-1	27 Oct 2-0	22 Sep 2-1	8 Sep 3-2	17 Nov 8-1	1 Dec 8-0
Arthurlie	8 Sep 1-2	1 Sep 0-2	X	24 Nov 7-1	13 Oct 3-1	29 Sep 2-1	27 Oct 3-1	17 Nov 3-0
Dumbarton Harp	22 Sep 3-1	3 Nov 3-2	25 Aug 5-3	X	8 Sep 4-0	10 Nov 1-1	6 Oct 3-0	20 Oct 4-1
Johnstone	27 Oct 1-1	18 Aug 2-2	15 Sep 1-1	29 Sep 1-1	X	17 Nov 1-3	2 Nov 2-0	1 Sep 3-2
Renton	24 Nov 2-0	20 Oct 3-2	1 Dec 2-0	15 Sep 2-1	6 Oct 5-1	X	22 Sep 1-3	25 Aug 1-0
Stevenston United	10 Nov 1-1	15 Sep 3-0	20 Oct 2-3	1 Sep 1-0	25 Aug 6-1	13 Oct 0-1	X	29 Sep 2-0
Vale of Leven	6 Oct 2-2	13 Oct 0-1	22 Sep 2-3	18 Aug 2-0	10 Nov 0-2	27 Oct 4-0	8 Sep 2-0	X

		P	W	D	L	F	A	Pts
1	Albion Rovers	14	9	2	3	39	16	20
2	Renton	14	9	1	4	25	19	19
3	Arthurlie	14	8	1	5	32	23	17
4	Dumbarton Harp	14	6	2	6	26	25	14
5	Stevenston United	14	6	1	7	23	26	13
6	Abercorn	14	3	5	6	15	21	11
7	Johnstone	14	3	4	7	18	34	10
8	Vale of Leven	14	3	2	9	16	30	8

WESTERN CUP

	Abercorn	Albion Rovers	Arthurlie	Dumbarton Harp	Johnstone	Renton	Stevenston United	Vale of Leven
Abercorn	X	16 Mar 3-1	23 Mar 1-3	17 Nov 2-0	2 Feb 3-3		1 Dec 1-2	15 Dec 2-1
Albion Rovers	2 Jan 1-0	X	2 Mar 3-1	26 Jan 3-4	15 Dec 1-0	6 Apr 0-0	5-2	29 Dec 8-0
Arthurlie	8 Dec 2-0	10 Nov 2-0	X	23 Feb 1-2	16 Mar 3-2	29 Dec 1-1	26 Jan 4-0	13 Apr 6-1
Dumbarton Harp	22 Dec 3-0	2 Feb 0-2		X	1 Dec 4-2	16 Mar 0-0	13 Apr 7-1	9 Mar 7-1
Johnstone		8 Dec 0-0	9 Mar 1-0	29 Dec 0-2	X	13 Apr 0-1	22 Dec 2-0	26 Jan 2-??
Renton	26 Jan 2-1	22 Dec 1-0	2 Feb 1-0	15 Dec 2-2	23 Feb 4-1	X	9 Mar 1-0	2 Jan 3-1
Stevenston United	1 Dec 1-0	23 Feb 2-5	15 Dec 1-2	23 Mar 1-??	24 Nov 2-1	9 Feb 1-2	X	
Vale of Leven	23 Feb 1-2	24 Nov 1-1	22 Dec 0-3	9 Feb 2-7	6 Apr ??-??	2 Mar 0-2		X

Renton v Albion Rovers on 22 Dec abandoned, result stood
Renton v Arthurlie on 16 Feb (score 2-1) was also reported as a Western League Cup match
Albion Rovers v Stevenston United on 16 Feb was abandoned after 63 mins at 3-0 and replayed at a later date

		P	W	D	L	F	A	Pts
1	Renton	13	9	4	0	20	7	22
2	Dumbarton Harp	12	8	2	2	38	16	18
3	Arthurlie	13	8	1	4	28	13	17
4	Albion Rovers	14	7	3	4	30	16	17
5	Abercorn	12	4	1	7	15	20	9
6	Johnstone	11	2	2	7	12	20	6
7	Stevenston United	11	3	0	8	12	30	6
8	Vale of Leven	10	0	1	9	8	41	1

Final
Played off between the clubs finishing in the top two places
Played on 20 Apr at Dumbarton
  Dumbarton Harp v Renton 2-0

NOTE this table does not include four of the results noted above.

The Eastern Football League 1917-18

	Armadale	Cowdenbeath	Dundee	Dundee Hibernian	Dunfermline Athletic	East Fife	Raith Rovers
Armadale	X	22 Sep 0-1 / 23 Mar 2-0	13 Oct 9-0 / 2 Jan 1-1	6 Oct 2-0 / 16 Feb 0-0	10 Nov 2-2 / 9 Mar 4-1	15 Sep 6-0 / NOT PLAYED	1 Sep 2-1 / NOT PLAYED
Cowdenbeath	25 Aug 1-1 / 9 Feb 3-0	X	29 Sep 5-0 / 8 Dec 0-3	3 Nov 5-0 / 30 Mar 3-0	20 Oct 4-0 / 23 Feb 2-0	10 Nov 0-1 / 16 Mar 4-0	15 Sep 2-0 / 26 Jan 0-0
Dundee	1 Dec 2-0 / 1 Jan 4-0	1 Sep 3-4 / 6 Apr 2-0	X	18 Aug 5-1 / 26 Jan 1-2	22 Sep 2-1 / 16 Mar 8-1	20 Oct 5-1 / 16 Feb 4-1	3 Nov 4-0 / 15 Dec 2-5
Dundee Hibernian	8 Sep 3-1 / 2 Jan 2-0	27 Oct 0-0 / 22 Dec 1-6	15 Sep 0-2 / 23 Feb 1-2	X	8 Dec 4-1 / 2 Feb 1-1	25 Aug 1-2 / 29 Dec 5-1	13 Oct 1-1 / 9 Mar 1-1
Dunfermline Athletic	29 Sep 6-3 / 2 Mar 1-3	18 Aug 3-2 / 5 Jan 0-1	27 Oct 1-2 / 23 Mar 0-2	1 Sep 3-1 / 9 Feb 0-3	X	24 Nov 4-0 / 15 Dec 4-2	17 Nov 2-4 / 30 Mar 1-2
East Fife	3 Nov 0-0 / NOT PLAYED	1 Dec 0-2 / 2 Mar 0-1	17 Nov 5-2 / 9 Mar 1-1	22 Sep 0-1 / 1 Jan 3-0	8 Sep 3-2 / 26 Jan 1-1	X	18 Aug 0-1 / 9 Feb 0-0
Raith Rovers	27 Oct 5-0 / NOT PLAYED	24 Nov 0-3 / 16 Feb 2-0	8 Sep 0-0 / 2 Feb 1-2	20 Oct 5-2 / 16 Mar 3-0	25 Aug 4-0 / 22 Dec 1-2	29 Sep 2-0 / 16 Mar 2-0	X

On 23 Mar, Armadale v Cowdenbeath was abandoned at 2-0 after Birrell of Cowdenbeath was attacked as he left the field after 73 mins. Armadale's ground was closed by the SFA from 8 April to 1 May 1918.

		P	W	D	L	F	A	Pts
1=	Cowdenbeath	24	15	3	6	49	18	33
1=	Dundee	24	15	3	6	59	40	33
3	Raith Rovers	22	11	5	6	40	24	27
4	Armadale	20	7	5	8	36	33	19
5	Dundee Hibernian	24	7	5	12	30	48	19
6	Dunfermline Athletic	24	6	3	15	37	61	15
7	East Fife	22	5	4	13	21	48	14

CHAMPIONSHIP DECIDER
Played at the start of 1918-19 season
2 legs – first leg played on 16 Aug 1918, second on 20 Aug 1918
Dundee v Cowdenbeath 2-1, 1-0

EASTERN LEAGUE CUP

First round
Dundee Hibernian beat Dunfermline Athletic
Armadale v Raith Rovers
East Fife beat Cowdenbeath
Dundee bye

Semi-final
Dundee Hibernian beat Armadale or Raith Rovers
Played on 13 Apr
Dundee v East Fife 1-1

Final
Played on 27 Apr at Dens Park, Dundee
Dundee v Dundee Hibernian 2-2

COMPETITION ABANDONED

Other Scottish Competitions 1917-18

WAR FUND SHIELD

Semi-final
Played on 27 Apr
  Celtic v Clydebank 2-0
  Rangers v Morton 1-3

Final
4 May 1918 at Hampden Park, Glasgow
Att 20,000
Celtic 1 *(Gallagher)*
Morton 0

Celtic: Shaw, McNair, Dodds, Jackson, McStay, Brown, Kelly, Gallagher, McLean, McMenemy, Browning
Morton: Bradford, Morrison, Ormonde, Lawrence, Wright, McLean, Grant, Robertsopn, McNab, Stevenson, Seymour

Qualifying round
Played on 9 Mar
  St Mirren v Kilmarnock 2-3 *(aet)*
Played on 30 Mar
  Morton v Third Lanark 3-1
Played on 6 Apr
  Clydebank v Airdrieonians 2-1

First round
Played on 20 Apr
  Celtic v Queen's Park 2-1
  Rangers v Partick Thistle 3-0
  Morton v Kilmarnock 7-1
  Motherwell v Clydebank 1-2

EAST OF SCOTLAND SHIELD
Final – 2 legs
First leg played on 17 Sep, second on 15 Apr
  Hibernian v Heart of Midlothian 4-0, 1-1

WILSON CUP
Played on 1 Jan at Tynecastle Park, Edinburgh
  Heart of Midlothian v Hibernian 1-3

DUNEDIN CUP
Semi-final
Played on 2 Jan
  Heart of Midlothian v Falkirk 1-3
  Hibernian v Raith Rovers 1-0

Final
Played on 27 Apr at Tynecastle Park, Edinburgh
  Hibernian v Falkirk 3-5

FIFE CUP
Final
Played on 6 Apr at North End Park, Cowdenbeath
  Dunfermline Athletic v Raith Rovers 1-1
REPLAY on 20 Apr at Stark's Park, Kirkcaldy
  Dunfermline Athletic v Raith Rovers 1-0

Semi-final
Played on 6 Oct
  Raith Rovers v Cowdenbeath 1-0
  Dunfermline Athletic v East Fife 1-1
REPLAY on 13 Oct
  East Fife v Dunfermline Athletic 1-2

RENFREWSHIRE VICTORIA CUP
Played on 2 Mar
  Johnstone v Abercorn 1-0
Played on 31 Dec
  Abercorn v Arthurlie 1-4

Final
Played on 30 Mar
  Arthurlie v Johnstone 2-1 *(protest upheld)*
REPLAY on 6 Apr
  Johnstone v Arthurlie 1-2 *(protest upheld)*
SECOND REPLAY at Cappielow Park, Greenock
  Arthurlie v Johnstone 3-2

RENFREWSHIRE CUP
First round
Played on 9 Feb
  Abercorn v Paisley Academical 6-0
  Arthurlie v Johnstone 1-2

Semi-final
  Morton beat Johnstone
Played on 6 Apr
  St Mirren v Abercorn 3-0

Final – 2 legs
First leg played on 6 May, second on 14 May
  St Mirren v Morton 3-1, 0-4

AYR CHARITY CUP
Played on 13 Apr at Hampden Park, Glasgow
  Queen's Park v Ayr United 1-2

FRASER CHARITY CUP
Played on 11 May at Clydeholm Park, Clydebank
  Clydebank v St Mirren 2-1

DUNBARTONSHIRE CHARITY CUP
Final
Played on 25 May at Boghead Park, Dumbarton
  Dumbarton v Renton 2-1 *aet*

Semi-final
Played on 11 May
  Vale of Leven v Renton 2-1
Played on 18 May
  Clydebank v Dumbarton 2-3 *aet*

Other Scottish Competitions 1917-18

GLASGOW CUP

First round
Played on 8 Sep
  Clyde v Rangers 0-0 *(Rangers won 14-2 on corners)*
  Queen's Park v Celtic 1-2

Semi-final
Played on 22 Sep
  Celtic v Rangers 0-3
  Partick Thistle v Third Lanark 1-0 *(at Ibrox Park, Glasgow)*

Final
Played on 6 Oct at Ibrox Park, Glasgow
  Rangers v Partick Thistle 4-1

GLASGOW CHARITY CUP

First round
Played on 11 May
  Queen's Park v Clyde 1-3
  Partick Thistle v Rangers 2-0 *(at Celtic Park, Glasgow)*

Semi-final
Played on 18 May
  Clyde v Partick Thistle 0-4
  Third Lanark v Celtic 1-2 *(at Hampden Park, Glasgow)*

Final
Played on 25 May at Hampden Park, Glasgow
  Celtic v Partick Thistle 2-0

LANARKSHIRE CUP

First round
Played on 2 Jan
  Albion Rovers v Motherwell 4-0 *(protest upheld)*
REPLAY on 23 Mar
  Albion Rovers v Motherwell 2-1
Played on 30 Mar
  Hamilton Academical v Dykehead 6-1

Semi-final
Played on 20 Apr
  Albion Rovers v Hamilton Academical 3-0
  Royal Albert v Airdrieonians 1-2

Final
Played on 27 Apr at Broomfield Park, Airdrie
  Airdrieonians v Albion Rovers 2-0

LANARKSHIRE CHARITY CUP

Played on 11 May
  Hamilton Academical v Motherwell 1-4

ROSEBERY CHARITY CUP

Final
Played on 18 May at Tynecastle Park, Edinburgh
  Heart of Midlothian v Hibernian 0-2

PENMAN CUP

First round
Dunfermline Athletic v Dundee
Played on 8 Dec
  Raith Rovers v Armadale 0-0
REPLAY on 23 Feb
  Armadale v Raith Rovers 2-0
Played on 6 Apr
  East Fife v Dundee Hibernian
REPLAY
  Dundee Hibernian v East Fife

Semi-final
Dundee Hibernian v Cowdenbeath
Played on 30 Mar
  Dundee v Armadale 3-0

Final
Played on 20 Apr at Dens Park, Dundee
  Dundee v Dundee Hibernian 2-0

WEST FIFE CHARITY CUP

2 legs – first leg played on 11 May, second on 25 May
Cowdenbeath v Dunfermline Athletic 3-0, 2-0

WEMYSS CUP

Semi-final
Played on 13 Apr
  Raith Rovers v Dunfermline Athletic 2-1

Final
Played on 27 Apr at Bayview park, Methil
  East Fife v Raith Rovers 2-0

PAISLEY CHARITY CUP

Played on 4 May at St Mirren Park, Paisley
St Mirren v Abercorn 3-0

Ireland 1917-18

BELFAST & DISTRICT FOOTBALL LEAGUE

	Belfast United	Cliftonville	Distillery	Glenavon	Glentoran	Linfield
Belfast United	X	22 Sep 1-1	17 Nov 1-0	29 Sep 4-1	27 Oct 1-3	20 Oct 0-1
Cliftonville	3 Nov 1-1	X	15 Sep 0-0	17 Nov 3-0	20 Oct 0-4	10 Nov 1-3
Distillery	6 Oct 3-2	27 Oct 3-2	X	8 Sep 5-0	10 Nov 0-2	3 Nov 2-2
Glenavon	10 Nov 1-0	6 Oct 1-0	20 Oct 0-1	X	3 Nov 1-4	27 Oct 2-0
Glentoran	15 Sep 2-1	8 Sep 0-0	29 Sep 2-0	22 Sep 1-0	X	6 Oct 0-0
Linfield	8 Sep 4-0	29 Sep 3-1	22 Sep 3-0	15 Sep 7-0	17 Nov 2-0	X

		P	W	D	L	F	A	Pts
1	Linfield	10	8	2	0	30	5	18
2	Glentoran	10	7	2	1	18	5	16
3	Distillery	10	4	2	4	14	14	10
4=	Cliftonville	10	1	4	5	9	16	6
4=	Belfast United	10	2	2	6	11	17	6
6	Glenavon	10	2	0	8	5	30	4

BELFAST CITY CUP

	Belfast United	Cliftonville	Distillery	Glenavon	Glentoran	Linfield
Belfast United	X		22 Dec 2-1	15 Dec 2-1		29 Dec 0-1
Cliftonville	24 Nov 2-1	X		22 Dec 2-0	19 Dec 0-2	
Distillery		1 Dec 3-0	X	22 Dec 1-0		
Glenavon			8 Dec 2-2	X		
Glentoran	1 Dec 5-1	8 Dec 4-0	15 Dec 1-1	24 Nov 4-1	X	
Linfield	8 Dec 6-1	15 Dec 3-0	24 Nov 1-1	1 Dec 2-1	22 Dec 1-0	X

IRISH FA CUP

First round
Played on 2 Feb
  Shelbourne v Bohemians 3-1
  Belfast United v Cliftonville 2-0

Second round
Played on 2 Feb
  Linfield v Glenavon 8-3
  Distillery v Linfield Swifts 3-0
  Belfast Celtic v Glentoran 0-0
REPLAY on 19 Feb
  Belfast Celtic v Glentoran 1-0
Played on 16 Feb
  Belfast United v Shelbourne 3-0

Semi-final
Played on 9 Mar
  Linfield v Distillery 3-0
  Belfast Celtic v Belfast United 2-1

Final
Played on 30 Mar at The Oval, Belfast
  Belfast Celtic v Linfield 0-0
REPLAY on 13 Apr at Solitude, Belfast
  Belfast Celtic v Linfield 0-0
SECOND REPLAY on 24 Apr at Grosvenor Park, Belfast
  Belfast Celtic v Linfield 2-0

Ireland 1917-18

GOLD CUP

	Belfast United	Cliftonville	Distillery	Glenavon	Glentoran	Linfield
Belfast United	X	W-L			23 Feb 2-2	1 Apr 1-2
Cliftonville		X			1 Apr 0-1	
Distillery	W-L	1-1	X	W-L		
Glenavon	DRAW	DRAW		X		
Glentoran			2 Apr 3-1	12 Apr 3-1	X	11 May 0-0
Linfield		2 Apr 3-0	23 Mar 2-0	23 Feb 7-0		X

		P	W	D	L	F	A	Pts
1	Linfield	5	4	1	0	14	1	9
2	Glentoran	5	3	2	0	9	4	8
3	Distillery	5	2	1	2	7	9	5
4	Belfast United	5	1	2	2	6	7	4
5	Cliftonville	5	0	2	3	1	6	2
6	Glenavon	5	0	2	3	2	11	2

1918-19

The two sections, Lancashire and Midland, which had replaced the national First and Second Divsions in 1915 continued. However, due to the war ending a number of other competitions commenced, the Northern and Midland Victory Leagues

In Scotland, the Scottish Football League and West of Scotland League both continued. However due to the dearth of clubs north of the River Forth, the Eastern League went into abeyance before recommencing in 1919.

The Belfast & District League continued as a replacement for the Irish League.

WINNERS OF THE PRINCIPAL COMPETITIONS

Football League –	
Championship Cup	Nottingham Forest
Lancashire Principal	Everton
Lancashire Subsidiary & Cup	Liverpool
Midland Principal	Nottingham Forest
Midland Subsidiary 'A'	Sheffield United
Midland Subsidiary 'B'	Birmingham
Midland Subsidiary 'C'	Bradford
Midland Subsidiary 'D'	Hull City
London Combination	Brentford
Midland Victory League	West Bromwich Albion
Northern Victory League	Middlesbrough
Scottish Victory Cup	St Mirren
Scottish League	Celtic
West of Scotland League	Dumbarton Harp
Irish FA Cup	Linfield
Belfast & District League	Belfast Celtic
Belfast City Cup	Glentoran / Belfast Celtic *shared*
Gold Cup	Linfield

The Football League 1918-19

LANCASHIRE SECTION

Principal Competition

	Blackburn R	Blackpool	Bolton W	Burnley	Bury	Everton	Liverpool	Manchester City	Manchester Utd	Oldham Ath	Port Vale	Preston NE	Rochdale	Southport V	Stockport Co	Stoke
Blackburn Rovers	X	16 Nov 0-3	11 Jan 2-3	12 Oct 3-4	2 Nov 0-1	28 Dec 1-4	14 Dec 1-2	1 Mar 2-1	28 Sep 1-1	25 Jan 2-2	29 Mar 6-0	25 Dec 0-0	15 Mar 4-2	14 Sep 2-3	30 Nov 0-4	26 Oct 0-6
Blackpool	23 Nov 2-0	X	7 Sep 1-4	8 Feb 1-1	25 Jan 3-2	7 Dec 1-3	10 Mar 3-2	19 Oct 0-3	28 Dec 2-2	9 Nov 3-1	21 Sep 1-1	5 Oct 1-2	21 Dec 5-1	22 Mar 5-0	22 Feb 2-0	11 Jan 1-6
Bolton Wanderers	18 Jan 3-0	14 Sep 2-1	X	2 Nov 2-1	1 Jan 2-1	1 Mar 3-6	26 Oct 2-2	29 Mar 3-1	30 Nov 3-1	15 Mar 2-1	18 Apr 2-1	25 Jan 2-4	8 Feb 3-2	16 Nov 3-2	28 Sep 3-1	14 Dec 1-1
Burnley	5 Oct 0-1	15 Feb 3-0	9 Nov 0-4	X	18 Jan 2-1	7 Sep 0-6	7 Apr 5-3	7 Feb 2-1	22 Feb 4-2	21 Dec 2-2	23 Nov 4-1	19 Oct 2-5	21 Sep 2-4	1 Feb 4-0	10 Mar 4-2	22 Mar 1-2
Bury	9 Nov 3-4	1 Feb 1-0	25 Dec 1-0	11 Jan 0-0	X	23 Nov 0-3	22 Feb 1-1	21 Sep 0-1	22 Mar 0-2	19 Oct 2-0	7 Sep 1-1	21 Dec 0-0	7 Dec 2-1	10 Mar 0-2	15 Feb 1-1	28 Dec 0-2
Everton	4 Jan 9-0	30 Nov 6-0	22 Feb 4-1	14 Sep 6-1	16 Nov 5-1	X	12 Oct 4-2	1 Feb 3-0	26 Oct 6-2	18 Jan 3-1	15 Feb 3-1	10 Mar 3-2	22 Mar 3-1	28 Sep 4-0	14 Dec 2-1	2 Nov 5-1
Liverpool	21 Dec 1-0	15 Mar 3-1	19 Dec 6-1	28 Dec 7-0	1 Mar 6-0	5 Oct 2-4	X	23 Nov 2-0	25 Jan 1-1	7 Dec 5-1	9 Nov 4-0	21 Sep 8-0	7 Sep 4-0	11 Jan 3-0	29 Mar 3-0	8 Feb 1-1
Manchester City	22 Feb 5-1	26 Oct 4-0	22 Mar 1-2	30 Nov 2-1	28 Sep 7-0	25 Jan 1-0	16 Nov 0-2	X	12 Oct 0-0	8 Feb 3-0	10 Mar 6-1	28 Dec 2-0	11 Jan 1-1	14 Dec 0-1	2 Nov 1-0	14 Sep 0-2
Manchester United	21 Sep 1-0	30 Apr 5-1	7 Dec 1-0	1 Mar 4-0	29 Mar 5-1	19 Oct 1-1	1 Feb 0-1	5 Oct 0-2	X	7 Sep 1-4	21 Dec 5-1	23 Nov 1-2	9 Nov 0-1	15 Feb 1-3	18 Jan 0-2	15 Mar 3-1
Oldham Athletic	1 Feb 4-0	2 Nov 1-1	10 Mar 3-1	14 Dec 3-1	26 Oct 0-2	11 Jan 0-3	30 Nov 0-2	15 Feb 0-3	8 Sep 0-2	X	22 Feb 6-0	22 Mar 1-2	28 Dec 0-1	12 Oct 0-0	16 Nov 1-3	28 Sep 3-1
Port Vale	22 Mar 3-2	28 Dec 1-1	28 Sep 3-1	16 Nov 4-2	14 Sep 2-1	8 Feb 0-1	2 Nov 0-2	15 Mar 1-5	14 Dec 3-1	1 Mar 3-1	X	11 Jan 1-0	25 Jan 2-0	30 Nov 2-0	26 Oct 2-2	12 Oct 1-8
Preston North End	26 Dec 2-2	12 Oct 3-1	1 Feb 0-0	26 Oct 4-2	14 Dec 1-1	15 Mar 2-3	28 Sep 0-2	10 Apr 2-1	16 Nov 4-2	29 Mar 0-2	18 Jan 0-2	X	1 Mar 3-1	2 Nov 1-0	14 Sep 0-3	30 Nov 0-1
Rochdale	10 Mar 3-1	14 Dec 1-0	15 Feb 2-2	28 Sep 2-1	30 Nov 0-2	29 Mar 1-3	14 Sep 1-2	18 Jan 4-5	2 Nov 1-3	29 Apr 5-0	1 Feb 2-0	22 Feb 1-2	X	26 Oct 5-2	12 Oct 4-1	16 Nov 3-2
Southport Vulcan	7 Sep 3-0	29 Mar 0-2	23 Nov 0-0	25 Jan 2-1	15 Mar 2-1	21 Sep 0-3	18 Jan 2-1	21 Dec 2-0	8 Feb 2-1	5 Oct 2-0	7 Dec 4-0	9 Nov 1-0	19 Oct 3-3	X	1 Apr 7-2	1 Mar 3-5
Stockport County	7 Dec 1-0	1 Mar 1-2	21 Sep 2-2	15 Mar 0-3	8 Feb 2-0	21 Dec 0-0	22 Mar 2-1	9 Nov 1-1	11 Jan 2-1	23 Nov 6-2	19 Oct 3-0	7 Sep 0-0	5 Oct 2-2	28 Dec 4-1	X	25 Jan 0-6
Stoke	19 Oct 7-0	18 Jan 2-1	21 Dec 7-1	29 Mar 2-1	4 Jan 3-1	9 Nov 0-2	15 Feb 3-1	7 Sep 3-0	8 Mar 1-2	21 Sep 1-0	5 Oct 3-2	7 Dec 5-0	23 Nov 1-1	22 Feb 0-2	1 Feb 1-0	X

		P	W	D	L	F	A	Pts
1	Everton	30	27	2	1	108	26	56
2	Stoke	30	20	3	7	84	36	43
3	Liverpool	30	19	4	7	82	33	42
4	Bolton Wanderers	30	15	6	9	58	58	36
5	Manchester City	30	15	3	12	57	36	33
6	Southport Vulcan	30	15	3	12	49	53	33
7	Preston North End	30	12	6	12	41	51	30
8	Stockport County	30	11	7	12	48	52	29
9	Manchester United	30	11	5	14	51	50	27
10	Rochdale	30	11	5	14	56	61	27
11	Blackpool	30	10	5	15	45	60	25
12	Port Vale	30	10	4	16	39	77	24
13	Burnley	30	10	3	17	54	76	23
14	Bury	30	7	6	17	27	58	20
15	Oldham Athletic	30	7	4	19	39	62	18
16	Blackburn Rovers	30	5	4	21	35	83	14

The Football League 1918-19

MIDLAND SECTION

Principal Competition

	Barnsley	Birmingham	Bradford	Bradford City	Coventry C	Grimsby T	Huddersfield T	Hull City	Leeds City	Leicester F	Lincoln C	Nottingham F	Notts County	Rotherham Co	Sheffield United	The Wednesday
Barnsley	X	7 Dec 2-1	15 Mar 0-1	5 Oct 0-0	22 Feb 6-2	21 Sep 2-4	9 Nov 2-4	8 Feb 3-4	18 Jan 0-1	21 Dec 3-2	7 Sep 2-6	22 Apr 3-2	23 Nov 1-0	26 Dec 1-0	1 Feb 2-0	26 Oct 0-1
Birmingham	30 Nov 7-0	X	19 Oct 2-0	4 Jan 5-1	16 Nov 3-1	1 Mar 4-0	25 Jan 1-0	2 Nov 5-1	28 Sep 4-2	25 Dec 0-2	15 Mar 3-0	14 Sep 2-3	11 Jan 0-7	21 Dec 2-0	12 Oct 4-1	15 Feb 4-2
Bradford	8 Mar 3-1	26 Oct 1-1	X	25 Dec 2-1	8 Feb 0-0	7 Dec 5-0	21 Sep 2-2	18 Jan 0-1	22 Feb 1-3	21 Apr 2-1	23 Nov 6-1	1 Feb 2-0	5 Oct 0-0	9 Nov 2-1	21 Dec 3-0	7 Sep 4-3
Bradford City	12 Oct 8-1	28 Dec 2-3	26 Dec 2-3	X	28 Sep 0-1	11 Jan 1-3	1 Mar 2-3	14 Sep 4-0	16 Nov 3-1	19 Oct 2-0	15 Feb 1-2	2 Nov 1-0	25 Jan 3-6	15 Mar 2-0	30 Nov 0-0	14 Dec 1-2
Coventry City	1 Mar 2-1	23 Nov 1-3	15 Feb 2-1	21 Sep 1-2	X	7 Sep 7-4	26 Oct 7-1	1 Feb 3-0	22 Apr 1-3	15 Mar 1-0	26 Dec 2-0	21 Dec 2-5	9 Dec 5-1	7 Dec 3-2	18 Jan 2-4	5 Oct 2-0
Grimsby Town	28 Sep 0-0	22 Feb 1-4	30 Nov 4-0	18 Jan 3-2	14 Sep 1-1	X	14 Dec 1-1	25 Dec 1-1	2 Nov 0-2	12 Oct 4-1	1 Feb 1-2	19 Oct 0-2	8 Mar 0-0	8 Feb 1-0	16 Nov 2-2	28 Dec 0-2
Huddersfield Town	2 Nov 2-1	1 Feb 1-0	28 Sep 0-0	22 Feb 1-1	19 Oct 4-1	21 Dec 1-0	X	12 Oct 1-0	26 Dec 0-1	16 Nov 2-0	21 Apr 0-0	30 Nov 0-0	8 Feb 1-1	18 Jan 5-1	14 Sep 1-0	15 Mar 2-1
Hull City	15 Feb 1-3	9 Nov 0-3	11 Jan 0-2	7 Sep 2-0	25 Jan 2-0	26 Dec 2-0	5 Oct 3-0	X	21 Dec 2-1	1 Mar 5-2	7 Dec 5-1	15 Mar 5-0	26 Oct 1-1	23 Nov 4-0	18 Apr 1-1	21 Sep 0-0
Leeds City	11 Jan 4-0	21 Sep 3-1	1 Mar 2-5	23 Nov 2-1	28 Dec 0-1	9 Nov 3-1	25 Dec 1-1	14 Dec 0-0	X	25 Jan 4-2	26 Oct 2-0	15 Feb 0-4	7 Sep 4-1	5 Oct 2-1	8 Mar 2-1	7 Dec 1-1
Leicester Fosse	14 Dec 2-1	26 Dec 0-4	28 Dec 1-2	26 Oct 3-2	8 Mar 2-2	5 Oct 5-3	23 Nov 3-1	22 Feb 3-2	1 Feb 0-0	X	21 Sep 2-0	18 Jan 0-1	7 Dec 3-0	7 Sep 4-1	8 Feb 2-1	9 Nov 7-3
Lincoln City	14 Sep 4-2	8 Mar 1-0	16 Nov 1-1	8 Feb 0-1	25 Dec 3-2	25 Jan 0-1	28 Dec 1-4	30 Nov 0-2	19 Oct 1-0	28 Sep 4-0	X	12 Oct 1-3	14 Dec 0-1	22 Feb 2-0	2 Nov 2-1	11 Jan 1-4
Nottingham Forest	28 Dec 2-0	7 Sep 1-0	25 Jan 3-0	9 Nov 6-1	14 Dec 0-1	26 Oct 6-1	7 Dec 1-0	8 Mar 2-1	8 Feb 0-2	11 Jan 1-1	5 Oct 1-1	X	25 Dec 2-0	21 Sep 3-1	22 Feb 3-1	23 Nov 3-1
Notts County	16 Nov 4-4	18 Jan 2-0	12 Oct 4-1	1 Feb 2-0	2 Nov 4-0	15 Mar 3-1	15 Feb 6-2	19 Oct 1-0	14 Sep 5-2	30 Nov 1-0	21 Dec 2-1	26 Dec 1-1	X	4 Jan 2-0	28 Sep 5-2	1 Mar 0-0
Rotherham County	25 Dec 2-4	14 Dec 0-2	2 Nov 1-1	8 Mar 2-2	30 Nov 1-1	15 Feb 2-0	11 Jan 2-1	16 Nov 2-2	12 Oct 0-3	14 Sep 0-3	1 Mar 0-0	28 Sep 1-1	28 Dec 0-1	X	19 Oct 2-4	25 Jan 1-1
Sheffield United	25 Jan 8-0	5 Oct 1-3	14 Dec 2-0	7 Dec 1-2	11 Jan 3-1	23 Nov 3-1	7 Sep 5-1	28 Dec 0-0	15 Mar 1-0	15 Feb 1-0	9 Nov 6-1	1 Mar 1-1	21 Sep 2-2	26 Oct 1-0	X	26 Dec 3-0
The Wednesday	19 Oct 2-0	8 Feb 0-1	14 Sep 2-3	21 Dec 1-0	12 Oct 3-0	22 Apr 5-2	8 Mar 1-3	28 Sep 3-1	30 Nov 0-2	2 Nov 0-2	18 Jan 4-2	16 Nov 1-2	22 Feb 2-2	1 Feb 0-0	25 Dec 4-0	X

Huddersfield Town v Nottingham Forest on 30 Nov was abandoned after 81 mins, but the result stood
Hull City v Sheffield United on 4 Jan was abandoned because of snow with the score at 6-1 and was replayed at a later date.

		P	W	D	L	F	A	Pts
1	Nottingham Forest	30	18	6	6	59	31	42
2	Birmingham	30	20	1	9	72	36	41
3	Notts County	30	16	9	5	65	38	41
4	Leeds City	30	17	4	9	53	38	38
5	Bradford	30	15	7	8	53	41	37
6	Huddersfield Town	30	13	8	9	45	45	34
7	Hull City	30	12	7	11	48	42	31
8	Sheffield United	30	12	6	12	56	47	30
9	Coventry City	30	13	4	13	55	59	30
10	Leicester Fosse	30	13	3	14	53	53	29
11	The Wednesday	30	11	6	13	49	49	28
12	Lincoln City	30	10	4	16	38	59	24
13	Bradford City	30	9	4	17	48	56	22
14	Barnsley	30	9	3	18	45	79	21
15	Grimsby Town	30	7	6	17	40	69	20
16	Rotherham County	30	2	8	20	23	60	12

The Football League 1918-19

LANCASHIRE SECTION

Subsidiary Competition
(Including the Lancashire Cup)

GROUP A	Blackburn R	Blackpool	Burnley	Preston NE
Blackburn Rovers	X	5 Apr 1-1	19 Apr 2-4	8 Feb 0-1
Blackpool	12 Apr 6-1	X	18 Apr 0-0	19 Apr 3-0
Burnley	26 Apr 5-1	25 Dec 5-1	X	12 Apr 1-3
Preston North End	15 Feb 1-1	26 Apr 0-2	5 Apr 1-0	X

		P	W	D	L	F	A	Pts
1	Blackpool	6	3	2	1	13	7	8
2	Burnley	6	3	1	2	15	8	7
3	Preston North End	6	3	1	2	6	7	7
4	Blackburn Rovers	6	0	2	4	6	18	2

GROUP B	Bolton W	Bury	Oldham Ath	Rochdale
Bolton Wanderers	X	12 Oct 3-1	12 Apr 3-1	26 Apr 2-1
Bury	5 Oct 1-5	X	19 Apr 0-1	5 Apr 0-3
Oldham Athletic	5 Apr 4-1	26 Apr 4-0	X	21 Apr 5-0
Rochdale	19 Apr 1-2	12 Apr 0-2	18 Apr 0-2	X

		P	W	D	L	F	A	Pts
1	Oldham Athletic	6	5	0	1	17	4	10
2	Bolton Wanderers	6	5	0	1	16	9	10
3	Rochdale	6	1	0	5	5	13	2
4	Bury	6	1	0	5	4	16	2

GROUP C	Manchester City	Manchester Utd	Port Vale	Stoke
Manchester City	X	18 Apr 3-0	26 Apr 4-1	5 Apr 1-0
Manchester United	21 Apr 2-4	X	12 Apr 2-1	19 Apr 0-1
Port Vale	19 Apr 0-1	5 Apr 1-3	X	28 Apr 4-1
Stoke	12 Apr 1-1	26 Apr 4-2	21 Apr 2-2	X

		P	W	D	L	F	A	Pts
1	Manchester City	6	5	1	0	14	4	11
2	Stoke	6	2	2	2	9	10	6
3	Manchester United	6	2	0	4	9	14	4
4	Port Vale	6	1	1	4	9	13	3

GROUP D	Everton	Liverpool	Southport C	Stockport Co
Everton	X	1 Jan 1-2	23 Apr 1-2	12 Apr 0-1
Liverpool	18 Apr 1-1	X	5 Apr 4-2	19 Apr 3-1
Southport Vulcan	19 Apr 4-1	12 Apr 0-2	X	18 Apr 0-1
Stockport County	5 Apr 0-1	26 Apr 1-1	21 Apr 3-1	X

		P	W	D	L	F	A	Pts
1	Liverpool	6	4	2	0	13	6	10
2	Stockport County	6	3	1	2	7	6	7
3	Southport Vulcan	6	2	0	4	9	12	4
4	Everton	6	1	1	4	5	10	3

LANCASHIRE CUP
Played between the four group winners of the Lancashire Section Subsidiary Competition

Semi-final
Played on 24 May
Blackpool v Liverpool 0-1
Manchester City v Oldham Athletic 1-1
REPLAY on 27 May
Oldham Athletic v Manchester City 1-0

Final
Played on 31 May at Old Trafford, Manchester
Att 21,605
Liverpool 3 *(Wadsworth, Lewis, Miller)*
Oldham Athletic 0

Liverpool: W.Scott, Longworth, Jenkinson, Bamber, W.Wadsworth, Mackinlay, H.Wadsworth, Chambers, J.Miller, Lewis, Pearson
Oldham Athletic: Matthews, Grundy, Stewart, Bradbury, Wilson, Wolstenholme, Goodwin, Walters, Pilkington, Gee, Wall

The Football League 1918-19

MIDLAND SECTION

Subsidiary Competition

GROUP A	Barnsley	Rotherham Co	Sheffield United	The Wednesday
Barnsley	X	29 Mar 4-3	1 Jan 2-2	19 Apr 1-2
Rotherham County	22 Mar 5-2	X	26 Apr 0-4	21 Apr 1-1
Sheffield United	21 Apr 2-1	19 Apr 3-0	X	29 Mar 1-0
The Wednesday	26 Apr 4-3	1 Jan 4-2	22 Mar 0-2	X

GROUP B	Birmingham	Leicester F	Nottingham F	Notts Co
Birmingham	X	19 Apr 3-0	29 Mar 1-0	5 Apr 0-3
Leicester Fosse	26 Apr 2-4	X	12 Apr 1-0	22 Mar 5-1
Nottingham Forest	22 Mar 1-3	5 Apr 0-2	X	18 Apr 3-2
Notts County	12 Apr 1-2	29 Mar 5-0	21 Apr 1-3	X

		P	W	D	L	F	A	Pts
1	Sheffield United	6	5	1	0	14	3	11
2	The Wednesday	6	3	1	2	11	10	7
3	Barnsley	6	1	1	4	13	18	3
4	Rotherham County	6	1	1	4	11	18	3

		P	W	D	L	F	A	Pts
1	Birmingham	6	5	0	1	13	7	10
2	Leicester Fosse	6	3	0	3	10	13	6
3	Notts County	6	2	0	4	13	13	4
4	Nottingham Forest	6	2	0	4	7	10	4

GROUP C	Bradford	Bradford City	Huddersfield T	Leeds City
Bradford	X	22 Apr 2-1	26 Apr 1-1	5 Apr 5-0
Bradford City	29 Mar 1-4	X	12 Apr 0-0	19 Apr 2-1
Huddersfield Town	19 Apr 0-0	5 Apr 5-0	X	29 Mar 1-0
Leeds City	12 Apr 3-1	26 Apr 3-0	22 Mar 3-0	X

GROUP D	Coventry C	Grimsby T	Hull C	Lincoln C
Coventry City	X	29 Mar 2-1	5 Apr 1-3	19 Apr 1-0
Grimsby Town	22 Mar 1-1	X	19 Apr 1-2	5 Apr 2-1
Hull City	12 Apr 0-1	26 Apr 3-1	X	29 Mar 1-2
Lincoln City	18 Apr 1-1	12 Apr 1-2	22 Mar 1-2	X

		P	W	D	L	F	A	Pts
1	Bradford	6	3	2	1	13	6	8
2	Huddersfield Town	6	2	3	1	7	4	7
3	Leeds City	6	3	0	3	10	9	6
4	Bradford City	6	1	1	4	4	15	3

		P	W	D	L	F	A	Pts
1	Hull City	6	4	0	2	11	7	8
2	Coventry City	6	3	2	1	7	6	8
3	Grimsby Town	6	2	1	3	8	10	5
4	Lincoln City	6	1	1	4	6	9	3

LEAGUE CHAMPIONSHIP CUP
Played between the winners of the Lancashire Section and Midland Section Principal Competitions

First leg, 10 May 1919 at City Ground, Nottingham
Att 25,000
Nottingham Forest 0
Everton 0

Second leg, 17 May 1919 at Goodison Park, Liverpool
Att
Everton 0
Nottingham Forest 1 *(Burton)*

Nottingham Forest: Hardy, Bulling, Jones, H Jones, Lowe, Wightman, Armstrong, Birch, Shea, Tinsley, Burton, Martin
Everton: Mitchell, J Smith, Robinson, Fleetwood, Wareing, Grenyer, Miller, Jeffries, Gault, Clennell, Harrison

Everton: as first leg except Quinn for Harrison
Nottingham Forest: as first leg

The London Football Combination 1918-19

	Brentford	Chelsea	Clapton Orient	Crystal Palace	Fulham	Millwall	QPR	The Arsenal	Tottenham H	West Ham U
Brentford	X	21 Sep 0-0 11 Jan 1-1	21 Dec 7-0 18 Apr 2-0	5 Oct 2-3 25 Jan 6-1	25 Dec 2-1 12 Apr 5-0	19 Oct 4-2 8 Feb 2-1	7 Dec 5-1 29 Mar 2-0	23 Nov 4-1 15 Mar 1-1	9 Nov 7-1 1 Mar 4-1	7 Sep 2-0 28 Dec 3-1
Chelsea	16 Nov 2-2 8 Mar 1-4	X	12 Oct 6-0 1 Feb 3-3	25 Dec 0-2 12 Apr 3-0	14 Sep 4-2 4 Jan 3-0	2 Nov 0-1 22 Feb 3-2	21 Dec 2-0 21 Apr 3-0	19 Oct 4-1 8 Feb 1-2	30 Nov 3-1 22 Mar 1-2	28 Sep 3-1 18 Jan 0-0
Clapton Orient	26 Oct 1-2 21 Apr 4-2	7 Dec 0-5 29 Mar 0-0	X	7 Sep 1-1 28 Dec 0-4	19 Oct 1-4 8 Feb 0-4	5 Oct 0-1 25 Jan 1-3	21 Sep 1-5 11 Jan 1-5	25 Dec 3-2 12 Apr 2-2	23 Nov 0-3 15 Mar 1-2	9 Nov 1-5 1 Mar 0-0
Crystal Palace	30 Nov 0-4 22 Mar 2-3	26 Dec 0-0 15 Feb 1-0	2 Nov 6-1 22 Feb 4-1	X	28 Sep 1-0 18 Jan 1-4	16 Nov 2-2 8 Mar 1-4	14 Sep 4-2 4 Jan 0-2	26 Oct 2-1 18 Apr 0-3	14 Dec 6-3 5 Apr 2-2	12 Oct 0-0 1 Feb 3-0
Fulham	26 Dec 1-4 15 Feb 3-2	9 Nov 1-2 1 Mar 6-2	14 Dec 5-1 5 Apr 2-0	23 Nov 5-1 15 Mar 1-1	X	7 Dec 0-1 29 Mar 2-0	5 Oct 3-3 25 Jan 1-0	21 Sep 1-2 11 Jan 3-1	7 Sep 2-2 28 Dec 3-1	26 Oct 2-2 18 Apr 1-1
Millwall	14 Dec 3-1 5 Apr 3-0	7 Sep 1-6 28 Dec 1-1	30 Nov 1-1 22 Mar 1-1	21 Sep 0-2 11 Jan 2-1	12 Oct 0-1 1 Feb 1-1	X	23 Nov 4-1 15 Mar 1-1	9 Nov 3-3 1 Mar 0-3	26 Oct 0-2 21 Apr 2-4	25 Dec 0-2 15 Feb 2-2
Queen's Park Rangers	12 Oct 2-1 1 Feb 0-0	26 Oct 2-2 18 Apr 3-2	16 Nov 3-1 8 Mar 5-2	9 Nov 3-2 1 Mar 3-2	30 Nov 0-3 22 Mar 0-1	28 Sep 1-0 18 Jan 3-0	X	7 Sep 3-3 28 Dec 0-2	25 Dec 1-1 15 Feb 7-1	14 Dec 1-0 5 Apr 1-3
The Arsenal	28 Sep 1-1 18 Jan 3-3	14 Dec 3-0 5 Apr 2-1	26 Dec 9-2 15 Feb 4-0	21 Dec 3-3 21 Apr 3-2	16 Nov 1-3 8 Mar 5-0	14 Sep 4-0 4 Jan 4-1	2 Nov 1-0 22 Feb 1-3	X	12 Oct 3-0 1 Feb 2-3	30 Nov 0-2 22 Mar 3-2
Tottenham Hotspur	14 Sep 1-1 4 Jan 1-1	5 Oct 2-1 25 Jan 1-1	28 Sep 2-0 18 Jan 2-4	19 Oct 2-0 8 Feb 4-2	2 Nov 1-0 22 Feb 0-2	21 Dec 0-3 18 Apr 2-2	26 Dec 0-0 12 Apr 2-3	7 Dec 1-0 29 Mar 0-1	X	16 Nov 1-4 8 Mar 0-1
West Ham United	2 Nov 1-3 22 Feb 2-1	23 Nov 3-1 15 Mar 3-3	14 Sep 3-1 4 Jan 7-0	7 Dec 2-0 29 Mar 1-3	21 Dec 2-1 21 Apr 2-1	26 Dec 2-0 12 Apr 3-2	19 Oct 4-1 8 Feb 0-4	5 Oct 1-4 25 Jan 1-2	21 Sep 0-1 11 Jan 2-0	X

		P	W	D	L	F	A	Pts
1	Brentford	36	20	9	7	94	46	49
2	The Arsenal	36	20	5	11	85	56	45
3	West Ham United	36	17	7	12	65	51	41
4	Fulham	36	17	6	13	70	55	40
5	Queen's Park Rangers	36	16	7	13	69	60	39
6	Chelsea	36	13	11	12	70	53	37
7	Crystal Palace	36	14	6	16	66	73	34
8	Tottenham Hotspur	36	13	8	15	52	72	34
9	Millwall	36	10	9	17	50	67	29
10	Clapton Orient	36	3	6	27	35	123	12

Other English Competitions 1918-19

MIDLAND VICTORY FOOTBALL LEAGUE

	Aston Villa	Derby Co	WBA	Wolverhampton W
Aston Villa	X	22 Mar 3-1	26 Apr 0-3	12 Apr 2-5
Derby County	29 Mar 3-2	X	12 Apr 1-0	19 Apr 4-0
West Bromwich Albion	19 Apr 5-1	5 Apr 3-1	X	29 Mar 0-1
Wolverhampton Wanderers	5 Apr 1-1	15 Mar 1-1	21 Apr 1-1	X

		P	W	D	L	F	A	Pts
1	West Bromwich Albion	6	3	1	2	12	5	7
2	Derby County	6	3	1	2	11	9	7
3	Wolverhampton Wanderers	6	2	3	1	9	9	7
4	Aston Villa	6	1	1	4	9	18	3

NORTHERN VICTORY FOOTBALL LEAGUE

	Darlington F	Durham C	Hartlepools U	Middlesbrough	Newcastle U	Scotswood	South Shields	Sunderland
Darlington Forge	X	18 Jan 0-0	25 Jan 1-7	22 Feb 0-2	26 Apr 0-4	12 Apr 1-0	28 Apr 4-2	8 Feb 0-1
Durham City	15 Feb 2-0	X	29 Mar 0-5	22 Mar 0-1	1 Feb 0-2	1 Mar 0-2	5 Apr 2-2	11 Jan 1-0
Hartlepools United	22 Mar 1-4	22 Feb 6-1	X	1 Feb 1-2	21 Apr 6-1	8 Feb 0-2	18 Jan 2-0	12 Apr 0-2
Middlesbrough	19 Apr 0-0	25 Jan 5-0	1 Mar 8-2	X	8 Feb 3-0	11 Jan 1-0	15 Feb 2-1	15 Mar 1-2
Newcastle United	1 Mar 0-2	12 Apr 2-0	11 Jan 0-0	29 Mar 0-1	X	15 Mar 2-2	19 Apr 1-1	25 Jan 4-3
Scotswood	1 Feb 5-0	26 Apr 2-2	5 Apr 4-1	8 Mar 1-2	18 Jan 2-3	X	22 Mar 4-2	22 Feb 2-2
South Shields	11 Jan 3-1	8 Feb 1-0	15 Mar 2-1	12 Apr 1-1	22 Feb 2-2	25 Jan 2-2	X	21 Apr 3-1
Sunderland	5 Apr 0-2	22 Apr 2-0	15 Feb 6-2	18 Jan 2-0	22 Mar 2-1	30 Apr 6-1	1 Feb 3-3	X

		P	W	D	L	F	A	Pts
1	Middlesbrough	14	10	1	3	29	12	21
2	Sunderland	14	8	2	4	32	20	18
3	South Shields	14	5	5	4	26	25	15
4	Scotswood	14	5	4	5	29	24	14
5	Newcastle United	14	5	4	5	21	23	14
6	Darlington Forge	14	5	2	7	15	27	12
7	Hartlepools United	14	5	1	8	34	33	11
8	Durham City	14	2	3	9	8	30	7

LONDON VICTORY CUP

First round
Played on 30 Dec
  Brentford v Clapton Orient 3-2
Played on 1 Jan
  Millwall v The Arsenal 0-1

Second round
Played on 17 Feb
  Crystal Palace v Brentford 1-0
Played on 20 Mar
  Chelsea v Queen's Park Rangers 2-0
Played on 24 Mar
  Tottenham Hotspur v West Ham United 3-1
Played on 31 Mar
  The Arsenal v Fulham 1-4

Semi-final
Played on 19 Apr
  Crystal Palace v Chelsea 0-4
  Tottenham Hotspur v Fulham 0-2

Final
28 Apr 1919 at Highbury Stadium, London
Att
Chelsea 3 *(Rutherford 2, Wilding)*
Fulham 0

Chelsea: Molyneux, Bettridge, harrow, Davidson, Dickie, N Middleboe, Ford, Whitehouse, Wilding, Rutherford, Vizard
Fulham: Smith, Blackman, Charlton, Russell, Torrance, McNeal, Harris, Carr, Elliott, McIntyre, Penn

WEST RIDING CUP

Semi-final
Played on 3 May
Leeds City v Bradford 2-1
Bradford City v Huddersfield Town 2-2 *(Huddersfield won on corners)*

Final at Valley Parade, Bradford
Played on 17 May
Leeds City v Huddersfield Town 0-0
Replayed on 25 May
Leeds City v Huddersfield Town 2-0

BASS CHARITY CUP

Final
Played on 17 May at Highfield Road, Coventry
Coventry City v Notts County 3-2

LIVERPOOL SENIOR CUP

Final
Played on 21 Apr at Anfield Road, Liverpool
Liverpool v Everton 1-5

DURHAM SENIOR CUP

Semi-final
Played on 19 Apr
Sunderland v Felling Colliery 8-1
Darlington Forge v Crook Town

Final
Played on 3 May at Darlington
Sunderland v Crook Town 8-0

The Scottish Football League 1918-19

	Airdrieonians	Ayr U	Celtic	Clyde	Clydebank	Dumbarton	Falkirk	Hamilton Acad	Hearts	Hibernian	Kilmarnock	Morton	Motherwell	Partick Th	Queen's Park	Rangers	St Mirren	Third Lanark
Airdrieonians	X	21 Dec 0-1	8 Feb 1-2	5 Oct 1-2	26 Apr 2-1	19 Oct 1-1	7 Dec 1-1	14 Sep 0-2	31 Aug 1-0	10 May 3-3	18 Jan 2-1	1 Jan 2-1	2 Nov 1-1	17 Aug 1-1	5 Apr 1-2	16 Nov 0-0	23 Nov 3-1	11 Jan 1-6
Ayr United	9 Nov 1-4	X	10 May 0-2	15 Feb 4-1	1 Feb 2-0	28 Dec 5-0	22 Feb 2-0	23 Nov 4-1	4 Jan 1-2	2 Nov 5-0	14 Dec 3-1	21 Sep 1-5	5 Oct 1-2	31 Aug 0-1	19 Oct 2-0	22 Mar 1-1	25 Jan 2-0	17 Aug 0-2
Celtic	21 Apr 3-0	7 Sep 1-0	X	2 Jan 2-0	11 Jan 3-1	14 Dec 2-0	19 Apr 4-0	15 Feb 4-1	9 Nov 1-1	28 Dec 2-0	1 Feb 2-1	24 Aug 1-1	25 Jan 0-0	22 Feb 2-1	22 Mar 2-0	19 Oct 0-3	2 Nov 1-0	30 Sep 3-1
Clyde	8 Mar 3-5	14 Sep 3-1	31 Aug 0-3	X	29 Mar 0-2	17 Aug 4-1	1 Jan 2-4	18 Jan 0-1	26 Oct 4-2	12 Oct 2-1	23 Nov 1-1	12 Apr 0-2	8 Feb 1-2	4 Jan 1-1	21 Dec 0-1	10 May 0-4	7 Dec 1-1	28 Sep 1-1
Clydebank	12 Oct 2-2	30 Nov 1-3	12 Apr 0-2	2 Nov 3-1	X	14 Sep 3-1	19 Oct 3-2	28 Sep 3-3	8 Feb 1-3	5 Apr 2-1	31 Aug 3-1	4 Jan 2-3	15 Feb 1-3	8 Mar 3-2	28 Dec 0-5	14 Dec 1-1	17 Aug 1-1	5 Oct 1-1
Dumbarton	15 Feb 0-0	7 Dec 0-0	26 Oct 0-5	22 Feb 1-0	31 Dec 1-1	X	2 Nov 1-2	9 Nov 1-2	21 Sep 1-2	23 Nov 4-0	8 Mar 0-1	18 Jan 0-1	24 Aug 2-0	21 Dec 1-1	5 Oct 0-0	1 Feb 0-2	11 Jan 0-0	5 Apr 4-3
Falkirk	7 Sep 1-0	26 Oct 4-4	28 Sep 1-2	24 Aug 1-3	18 Jan 0-0	4 Jan 5-1	X	12 Oct 3-1	21 Dec 0-0	1 Feb 1-1	9 Nov 0-1	30 Nov 1-2	22 Mar 2-3	5 Apr 2-2	8 Mar 2-3	12 Apr 0-4	7 Feb 1-2	14 Sep 4-5
Hamilton Acad	25 Jan 3-1	8 Feb 2-2	21 Dec 1-2	24 Apr 4-2	22 Mar 1-3	29 Mar 0-3	11 Jan 1-2	X	5 Oct 1-4	24 Aug 1-0	5 Apr 2-0	2 Nov 1-1	1 Jan 1-3	21 Sep 1-2	12 Apr 0-3	7 Sep 0-3	26 Oct 3-2	16 Nov 1-0
Hearts	28 Dec 0-0	12 Oct 2-3	28 Apr 2-3	22 Mar 3-0	7 Dec 2-1	3 May 2-0	16 Nov 5-0	1 Feb 4-1	X	11 Jan 3-1	2 Nov 1-4	5 Apr 1-1	7 Sep 0-0	28 Sep 1-0	15 Feb 2-2	24 Aug 1-4	14 Sep 0-0	23 Nov 2-0
Hibernian	26 Oct 2-1	8 Mar 0-1	17 Aug 0-3	30 Nov 3-1	21 Sep 1-2	8 Feb 1-0	14 Dec 2-1	22 Feb 1-2	19 Oct 1-3	X	4 Jan 1-4	5 Oct 0-3	21 Dec 0-3	18 Jan 0-2	26 Apr 1-0	25 Jan 1-2	9 Nov 1-2	31 Aug 1-5
Kilmarnock	21 Sep 3-1	16 Nov 2-3	12 Oct 1-1	25 Jan 5-3	15 Mar 2-3	28 Sep 0-0	28 Dec 0-0	7 Dec 5-0	22 Feb 2-2	7 Sep 7-1	X	22 Mar 0-1	30 Nov 0-2	26 Oct 0-3	24 Aug 1-0	11 Jan 1-0	1 Jan 1-3	8 Feb 0-1
Morton	28 Feb 3-2	29 Mar 1-1	8 Mar 0-0	28 Dec 3-0	26 Oct 2-2	31 Aug 3-1	25 Jan 4-0	14 Dec 3-3	17 Aug 2-0	15 Feb 9-2	14 Sep 2-2	X	11 Jan 6-2	7 Dec 3-0	9 Nov 3-3	23 Nov 1-0	2 Jan 3-1	12 Oct 1-1
Motherwell	1 Feb 1-3	18 Jan 4-0	7 Dec 3-2	14 Dec 3-2	9 Nov 1-1	26 Apr 3-0	23 Nov 2-1	31 Aug 1-1	8 Mar 1-2	14 Sep 0-0	17 Aug 1-2	19 Oct 2-0	X	12 Oct 1-1	4 Jan 3-1	28 Dec 1-2	28 Sep 1-2	22 Feb 1-1
Partick Thistle	22 Mar 0-1	11 Jan 1-3	23 Nov 0-1	30 Sep 1-1	24 Aug 3-1	25 Jan 1-3	5 Oct 4-2	19 Oct 6-3	14 Dec 3-1	21 Apr 2-0	15 Feb 4-0	1 Feb 2-1	12 Apr 2-0	X	2 Nov 2-1	2 Jan 1-0	28 Dec 5-1	1 Jan 1-2
Queen's Park	14 Dec 1-0	1 Jan 2-2	14 Sep 0-3	11 Jan 3-1	23 Nov 3-4	19 Apr 1-0	31 Aug 2-0	17 Aug 3-2	25 Jan 4-0	28 Sep 3-0	29 Mar 1-2	22 Feb 4-2	21 Apr 1-3	8 Feb 4-3	X	30 Sep 0-2	12 Oct 4-1	26 Oct 3-4
Rangers	4 Jan 2-1	28 Sep 6-2	1 Jan 1-1	9 Nov 3-0	22 Feb 3-0	12 Oct 3-0	17 Aug 1-0	8 Mar 3-0	1 Mar 3-2	7 Dec 5-1	21 Dec 8-0	8 Feb 1-0	26 Oct 0-0	14 Sep 2-0	18 Jan 4-0	X	31 Aug 2-0	21 Apr 4-0
St Mirren	22 Feb 1-2	24 Aug 1-1	18 Jan 0-4	19 Oct 1-1	21 Dec 2-1	22 Mar 2-0	21 Sep 3-1	4 Jan 2-0	10 May 3-3	3 May 3-1	5 Oct 1-5	7 Sep 2-2	5 Apr 1-0	19 Apr 1-1	1 Feb 1-1	15 Feb 2-2	X	14 Dec 0-0
Third Lanark	24 Aug 1-1	1 Mar 1-1	4 Jan 2-3	1 Feb 1-4	2 Jan 2-0	12 Apr 2-4	15 Feb 2-2	28 Dec 1-3	18 Jan 3-1	22 Mar 4-2	19 Oct 3-4	21 Dec 0-1	21 Sep 1-1	9 Nov 1-2	7 Dec 1-3	2 Nov 1-2	8 Mar 1-0	X

		P	W	D	L	F	A	Pts
1	Celtic	34	26	6	2	71	22	58
2	Rangers	34	26	5	3	86	16	57
3	Morton	34	18	11	5	76	40	47
4	Partick Thistle	34	17	7	10	62	43	41
5	Motherwell	34	14	10	10	51	40	38
6	Ayr United	34	15	8	11	62	53	38
7	Heart of Midlothian	34	14	9	11	59	52	37
8	Kilmarnock	34	14	7	13	61	59	35
9	Queen's Park	34	15	5	14	59	57	35
10	St. Mirren	34	10	12	12	43	55	32
11	Clydebank	34	12	8	14	54	65	32
12	Third Lanark	34	11	9	14	60	62	31
13	Airdrieonians	34	9	11	14	45	54	29
14	Hamilton Acad	34	11	5	18	49	75	27
15	Dumbarton	34	7	8	19	31	58	22
16	Clyde	34	7	6	21	45	75	20
17	Falkirk	34	6	8	20	46	73	20
18	Hibernian	34	5	3	26	30	91	13

The West of Scotland Football League 1918-19

	Abercorn	Albion Rovers	Arthurlie	Dumbarton Harp	Johnstone	Renton	Stevenston United	Vale of Leven
Abercorn	X	23 Nov 1-1	19 Oct 2-2	26 Oct 1-3	31 Aug 1-3	7 Dec 0-2	28 Sep 0-2	14 Sep 0-4
Albion Rovers	14 Dec 8-1	X	28 Sep 3-1	21 Sep 1-2	7 Sep 1-0	24 Aug 1-2	12 Oct 4-0	26 Oct 3-2
Arthurlie	5 Oct 0-1	31 Aug 2-4	X	9 Nov 2-3	23 Nov 0-0	21 Sep 1-2	7 Dec 4-1	7 Sep 2-2
Dumbarton Harp	30 Nov 3-1	17 Aug 1-0	12 Oct 4-0	X	14 Dec 2-1	19 Oct 0-0	14 Sep 3-0	28 Sep 1-1
Johnstone	12 Oct 2-1	2 Nov 0-1	14 Sep 4-0	24 Aug 2-4	X	26 Oct 2-1	17 Aug 2-2	5 Oct 1-0
Renton	9 Nov 3-1	14 Sep 0-1	14 Dec 1-0	31 Aug 0-1	28 Sep 2-2	X	30 Nov 1-0	12 Oct 4-0
Stevenston United	24 Aug 0-0	19 Oct 0-6	2 Nov 3-3	5 Oct 1-1	21 Sep 5-1	7 Sep 7-2	X	23 Nov 1-2
Vale of Leven	21 Sep 6-0	7 Dec 0-1	30 Nov 1-0	2 Nov 0-0	19 Oct 2-2	17 Aug 4-4	31 Aug 1-0	X

Abercorn v Arthurlie on 19 October was played at Cappielow Park, Greenock
Abercorn v Vale of Leven on 14 September played at Alexandria

		P	W	D	L	F	A	Pts
1	Dumbarton Harp	14	10	4	0	28	10	24
2	Albion Rovers	14	10	1	3	35	12	21
3	Renton	14	7	3	4	24	20	17
4	Vale of Leven	14	5	5	4	25	19	15
5	Johnstone	14	5	4	5	22	22	14
6	Stevenston United	14	3	4	7	22	30	10
7	Arthurlie	14	1	4	9	17	31	6
8	Abercorn	14	1	3	10	10	39	5

WESTERN CUP

	Abercorn	Albion Rovers	Arthurlie	Dumbarton Harp	Johnstone	Renton	Stevenston United	Vale of Leven
Abercorn	X		15 Mar 2-1	22 Feb 2-?	25 Jan 0-2		8 Feb 1-2	11 Jan 0-0
Albion Rovers	19 Apr 3-0	X	4 Jan 2-0	1 Feb 3-3	30 Nov 5-0	15 Feb 3-0	22 Feb 1-0	28 Dec 2-1
Arthurlie	18 Jan 1-0	21 Dec 0-0	X	11 Jan 0-2	22 Feb 1-2	1 Feb 1-4	8 Mar 0-2	15 Feb 1-4
Dumbarton Harp	12 Apr 7-6	8 Feb 3-0	29 Mar 3-0	X	22 Mar 5-1	26 Apr 1-0	12 Apr 7-0	19 Apr 1-1
Johnstone	12 Apr 0-6	18 Jan 0-1	28 Dec 4-1	7 Dec 1-2	X	11 Jan 1-2	12 Apr 0-0	1 Feb 1-0
Renton		29 Mar 2-1	12 Apr 1-2	29 Apr 1-1	8 Feb 2-0	X	15 Mar 3-1	22 Mar 0-0
Stevenston United	1 Feb 1-1	26 Apr 1-4	29 Mar 3-0	15 Feb 3-3		15 Mar ??-3	X	18 Jan 2-3
Vale of Leven	29 Mar 1-2	5 Apr 2-1	8 Feb 2-1	21 Dec 2-1	4 Jan 1-0	22 Feb 2-1	10 May 1-0	X

Dumbarton Harp v Renton on 23 Nov was reported as a Western Cup tie. Harp won 4-1, but apparently the match was protested and replayed on 26 Apr
Arthurlie v Albion Rovers on 21 Dec was abandoned at 1-1
Johnstone v Abercorn on 15 Feb was abandoned at 0-0 and replayed at a later date
Abercorn v Dumbarton Harp was played at Cappielow Park, Greenock

Dumbarton Harp were declared winners

Other Scottish Competitions 1918-19

VICTORY CUP

First round
Played on 1 Mar
Airdrieonians v Abercorn 5-1
Celtic v Vale of Leven 2-0
Clyde v Johnstone 2-0
Falkirk v Dumbarton Harp 3-0
Morton v Clydebank 2-1
Motherwell v Stevenston United 2-0
Partick Thistle v Renton 4-3
Queen's Park v Arthurlie 2-1
Played on 1 Mar, replays on 5 Mar
Kilmarnock v Albion Rovers 1-0 *aet*
St Mirren v Dumbarton 1-0 *aet*

Second round
Played on 15 Mar
Albion Rovers v Celtic 1-3
Hamilton Academical v Rangers 1-5
Hibernian v Ayr United 1-0
Motherwell v Morton 2-1 *aet*
Partick Thistle v Falkirk 2-0
Queen's Park v Airdrieonians 0-4
St Mirren v Clyde 3-2
Third Lanark v Heart of Midlothian 1-2

Third round
Played on 29 Mar
Airdrieonians v Rangers 1-0
Hibernian v Motherwell 2-0
Partick Thistle v Heart of Midlothian 0-2
St Mirren v Celtic 1-0

Semi-final
Played on 19 Apr
Heart of Midlothian v Airdrieonians 7-1
Hibernian v St Mirren 1-3

Final
26 Apr 1919 at Celtic Park, Glasgow
Att 45,000
St Mirren 3 *(Sunderland 2, Hodges)*
Heart of Midlothian 0
After extra time

St Mirren: O'hagan, Marshall, Fulton, Pirrie, McKenna, Anderson, Hodges, T Page, Clark, Sunderland, Thomson
Hearts: Black, Birrell, J Wilson, Preston, Mercer, Sharp, Sinclair, Miller, A Wilson, McCulloch, W Wilson

EAST OF SCOTLAND SHIELD
Final
Played on 7 May at Tynecastle Park, Edinburgh
Heart of Midlothian v Hibernian 1-0

ROSEBERY CHARITY CUP
Final
Played on 17 May at Tynecastle Park, Edinburgh
Heart of Midlothian v Hibernian 2-1

WILSON CUP
Played on 1 Jan at Easter Road, Edinburgh
REPLAY on 7 May at Tynecastle Park, Edinburgh
Hibernian v Heart of Midlothian 2-2, 0-1

NOTE The East of Scotland Shield also doubled as the replay for the Wilson Cup

DUNBARTONSHIRE CUP
Semi-final
Played on 1 Jan
Vale of Leven v Dumbarton Harp 1-2 *(abandoned after 85 mins)*
REPLAY on 6 May
Vale of Leven v Dumbarton Harp 1-1
Played on 3 May
Renton v Clydebank 1-1

Final
Played on 10 May at Clydeholm Park, Clydebank
Clydebank v Dumbarton Harp 2-1

FRASER CHARITY CUP
Played on 31 May at Clydeholm Park, Clydebank
Clydebank v Dumbarton 1-0

GLASGOW CUP
First round
Played on 7 Sep
Clyde v Partick Thistle 3-0
Queen's Park v Third Lanark 1-0

Semi-final
Played on 2 Sep
Celtic v Clyde 3-1
Played on 21 Sep
Rangers v Queen's Park 3-0

Final
Played on 5 Oct at Hampden Park, Glasgow
Rangers v Celtic 2-0

GLASGOW CHARITY CUP
First round
Played on 17 May
Third Lanark v Rangers 0-3 *(at Hampden Park, Glasgow)*
Partick Thistle v Clyde 2-2 *(Clyde won on corners)*

Semi-final
Played on 24 May
Queen's Park v Celtic 3-1
Rangers v Clyde 2-0

Final
Played on 31 May at Hampden Park, Glasgow
Queen's Park v Rangers 1-2

Other Scottish Competitions 1918-19

RENFREWSHIRE VICTORIA CUP
Played on 5 Apr
Morton v Johnstone 2-2

Final
Played on 3 May
Morton v Abercorn 2-0

LANARKSHIRE CUP
First round
Played on 9 Nov
Albion Rovers v Wishaw Thistle 11-0

Semi-final
Played on 2 Jan
Airdrieonians v Albion Rovers 0-0
REPLAY on 12 Apr
Airdrieonians v Albion Rovers 3-2
Played on 1 May
Hamilton Academical v Motherwell 3-1

Final
DATE unknown
Airdrieonians v Hamilton Academical

RENFREWSHIRE CUP
Final
Played on 3 May at Cappielow Park, Greenock
Morton v Abercorn 2-0

LANARKSHIRE CHARITY CUP
Played on 24 May
Airdrieonians v Albion Rovers 0-3

DUNBARTONSHIRE CHARITY CUP
Semi-final
Played on 17 May
Dumbarton Harp v Renton 5-1
Dumbarton v Vale of Leven 1-0 *(aet, at Clydeholm Park, Clydebank)*

Final
Played on DATE unknown
Dumbarton v Dumbarton Harp

AYR CHARITY CUP
Played on 17 May at Somerset Park, Ayr
Ayr United v Queen's Park 4-2

Ireland 1918-19

BELFAST & DISTRICT FOOTBALL LEAGUE

	Belfast Celtic	Belfast United	Cliftonville	Distillery	Glentoran	Linfield
Belfast Celtic	X	14 Sep 2-1	7 Sep 2-0	28 Sep 1-0	21 Sep 2-1	16 Nov 0-1
Belfast United	26 Oct 2-2	X	5 Oct 2-2	19 Oct 2-4	28 Sep 2-1	2 Nov 1-2
Cliftonville	19 Oct 0-3	16 Nov 0-1	X	2 Nov 1-1	14 Sep 1-0	9 Nov 2-3
Distillery	9 Nov 0-1	7 Sep 2-0	21 Sep 1-1	X	5 Oct 0-0	26 Oct 0-2
Glentoran	2 Nov 0-2	9 Nov 1-0	26 Oct 2-0	16 Nov 3-2	X	7 Sep 1-0
Linfield	5 Oct 2-0	21 Sep 3-1	28 Sep 1-0	14 Sep 1-1	19 Oct 0-2	X

		P	W	D	L	F	A	Pts
1=	Belfast Celtic	10	7	1	2	15	7	15
1=	Linfield	10	7	1	2	15	8	15
3	Glentoran	10	5	1	4	11	9	11
4	Distillery	10	2	4	4	11	12	8
5	Belfast United	10	2	2	6	12	19	6
6	Cliftonville	10	1	3	6	7	16	5

TEST MATCH
Played on 16 Apr at Grosvenor Park, Belfast
Belfast Celtic v Linfield 1-0
Belfast Celtic were declared champions

BELFAST CITY CUP

		P	W	D	L	F	A	Pts
1=	Glentoran	10	6	3	1	22	19	15
1=	Belfast Celtic	10	6	3	1	16	7	15
3	Linfield	10	5	1	4	14	10	11
4	Cliftonville	10	3	3	4	11	14	9
5	Distillery	10	1	5	4	17	18	7
6	Belfast United	10	1	1	8	8	29	3

After a Test Match was drawn, Glentoran and Belfast Celtic were declared joint winners

IRISH FA CUP

Semi-final
Played on 9 Mar
Glentoran v Belfast Celtic 2-0
Linfield v Shelbourne 2-0

Final
Played on 29 Mar at Celtic Park, Belfast
Linfield v Glentoran 1-1
REPLAY on 5 Apr at Grosvenor Park, Belfast
Linfield v Glentoran 0-0
SECOND REPLAY on 7 Apr at Solitude, Belfast
Linfield v Glentoran 2-1

GOLD CUP

		P	W	D	L	F	A	Pts
1	Linfield	5	3	2	0	11	3	8
2	Glentoran	5	2	1	2	6	3	5
	Belfast Celtic							
	Belfast United							
	Cliftonville							
	Distillery							

Known results

22 Feb Linfield v Glentoran 2-1
12 Apr Linfield v Distillery 3-1
21 Apr Cliftonville v Linfield 1-6
22 Apr Linfield v Belfast United 0-0
17 May Belfast Celtic v Linfield 0-0

12 Apr Belfast Celtic v Glentoran 0-0
21 Apr Glentoran v Belfast United 3-0
22 Apr Glentoran v Distillery 2-0
17 May Cliftonville v Glentoran 1-0

PART 2

THE SECOND WORLD WAR

1939-1945

AND THE VICTORY SEASON OF 1945-46

1939-40

After the declaration of war on 3 September all football in mainland Britain was suspended; the league season had lasted only a few weeks. However in England after a short break, regional divisions were formed covering the entire country. Each Football League group had between eight and twelve clubs apart from the League South which encompassed twenty clubs, subdivided into 'A' and 'B' sections; Luton Town were moved to the Midland grouping to achieve this. Although the fixtures were to last for the rest of the season, the South clubs managed to arrange a second series of competitions, 'C' which was composed of First and Second Division clubs and 'D' which was of Third Division content.

In Scotland, the Scottish Football League also re-arranged their competition into two regional competitions; West and North & East with a championship play-off between the two group winners.

Meanwhile, the Irish Football League managed to complete their season as usual.

WINNERS OF THE PRINCIPAL COMPETITIONS

Football League Cup	West Ham United
Football League –	
South 'A'	Arsenal
South 'B'	Queen's Park Rangers
South 'C'	Tottenham Hotspur
South 'D'	Crystal Palace
East Midland	Chesterfield
Midland	Wolverhampton Wanderers
Western	Stoke City
North Western	Bury
North Eastern	Huddersfield Town
South Western	Plymouth Argyle
Welsh FA Cup	Wellington Town
Scottish War Emergency Cup	Rangers
Scottish League –	
Championship	Rangers
West	Rangers
North & East	Falkirk
Irish FA Cup	Ballymena United
Irish League	Belfast Celtic
City Cup	Belfast Celtic
Gold Cup	Belfast Celtic

The Football League 1939-40

Results and standings at the time of the Declaration of War on 3 September 1939

FIRST DIVISION

Played on 26 Aug
Aston Villa v Middlesbrough 2-0
Chelsea v Bolton Wanderers 3-2
Everton v Brentford 1-1
Huddersfield Town v Blackpool 0-1
Manchester United v Grimsby Town 4-0
Portsmouth v Blackburn Rovers 2-1
Preston NE v Leeds United 0-0
Sheffield United v Liverpool 2-1
Stoke City v Charlton Athletic 4-0
Sunderland v Derby County 3-0
Wolverhampton Wanderers v Arsenal 2-2

Played on 28 Aug
Aston Villa v Everton 1-2
Blackpool v Brentford 2-1
Stoke City v Bolton Wanderers 1-2

Played on 29 Aug
Grimsby Town v Wolverhampton Wanderers 0-0

Played on 30 Aug
Arsenal v Blackburn Rovers 1-0
Chelsea v Manchester United 1-1
Derby County v Portsmouth 2-0
Leeds United v Charlton Athletic 0-1
Liverpool v Middlesbrough 4-1
Preston NE v Sheffield United 0-0
Sunderland v Huddersfield Town 1-2

Played on 2 Sep
Arsenal v Sunderland 5-2
Blackburn Rovers v Everton 2-2
Blackpool v Wolverhampton Wanderers 2-1
Bolton Wanderers v Portsmouth 2-1
Brentford v Huddersfield Town 1-0
Charlton Athletic v Manchester United 2-0
Derby County v Aston Villa 1-0
Grimsby Town v Preston NE 2-0
Leeds United v Sheffield United 0-1
Liverpool v Chelsea 1-0
Middlesbrough v Stoke City 2-2

SECOND DIVISION

Played on 26 Aug
Barnsley v Nottingham Forest 4-1
Burnley v Coventry City 1-1
Bury v Fulham 3-1
Chesterfield v Bradford 2-0
Leicester City v Manchester City 4-3
Luton Town v Sheffield Wednesday 3-0
Millwall v Newcastle United 3-0
Newport County v Southampton 3-1
Plymouth Argyle v West Ham United 1-3
Swansea Town v West Bromwich Albion 1-2
Tottenham Hotspur v Birmingham 1-1

Played on 28 Aug
Coventry City v West Bromwich Albion 3-3
Millwall v Plymouth Argyle 0-2
Sheffield Wednesday v Barnsley 3-1
West Ham United v Fulham 2-1

Played on 30 Aug
Birmingham v Leicester City 2-0
Bradford v Luton Town 0-3
Manchester City v Bury 1-1
Southampton v Swansea Town 1-3

Played on 31 Aug
Newport County v Tottenham Hotspur 1-1
Nottingham Forest v Newcastle United 2-0

Played on 2 Sep
Birmingham v Burnley 2-0
Bradford v Millwall 2-2
Coventry City v Barnsley 4-2
Fulham v Luton Town 1-1
Manchester City v Chesterfield 2-0
Newcastle United v Swansea Town 8-1
Nottingham Forest v Newport County 2-1
Sheffield Wednesday v Plymouth Argyle 0-1
Southampton v Bury 3-0
West Bromwich Albion v Tottenham Hotspur 3-4
West Ham United v Leicester City 0-2

FIRST DIVISION

		P	W	D	L	F	A	Pts
1	Blackpool	3	3	0	0	5	2	6
2	Sheffield United	3	2	1	0	3	1	5
3	Arsenal	3	2	1	0	8	4	5
4	Liverpool	3	2	0	1	6	3	4
5	Everton	3	1	2	0	5	4	4
6	Bolton Wanderers	3	2	0	1	6	5	4
7	Charlton Athletic	3	2	0	1	3	4	4
8	Derby County	3	2	0	1	3	3	4
9	Manchester United	3	1	1	1	5	3	3
10	Chelsea	3	1	1	1	4	4	3
11	Stoke City	3	1	1	1	7	4	3
12	Brentford	3	1	1	1	3	3	3
13	Grimsby Town	3	1	1	1	2	4	3
14	Sunderland	3	1	0	2	6	7	2
15	Aston Villa	3	1	0	2	3	3	2
16	Wolverhampton W	3	0	2	1	3	4	2
17	Huddersfield Town	3	1	0	2	2	3	2
18	Preston North End	3	0	2	1	0	2	2
19	Portsmouth	3	1	0	2	3	5	2
20	Leeds United	3	0	1	2	0	2	1
21	Blackburn Rovers	3	0	1	2	3	5	1
22	Middlesbrough	3	0	1	2	3	8	1

SECOND DIVISION

		P	W	D	L	F	A	Pts
1	Luton Town	3	2	1	0	7	1	5
2	Birmingham	3	2	1	0	5	1	5
3	Coventry City	3	1	2	0	8	6	4
4	Plymouth Argyle	3	2	0	1	4	3	4
5	West Ham United	3	2	0	1	5	4	4
6	Leicester City	3	2	0	1	6	5	4
7	Tottenham Hotspur	3	1	2	0	6	5	4
8	Nottingham Forest	3	2	0	1	5	5	4
9	Millwall	3	1	1	1	5	4	3
10	Newport County	3	1	1	1	5	4	3
11	Manchester City	3	1	1	1	6	5	3
12	West Bromwich Alb	3	1	1	1	8	8	3
13	Bury	3	1	1	1	4	5	3
14	Newcastle United	3	1	0	2	8	6	2
15	Chesterfield	2	1	0	1	2	2	2
16	Barnsley	3	1	0	2	7	8	2
17	Southampton	3	1	0	2	5	6	2
18	Sheffield Wed	3	1	0	2	3	5	2
19	Swansea Town	3	1	0	2	5	11	2
20	Fulham	3	0	1	2	3	6	1
21	Burnley	2	0	1	1	1	3	1
22	Bradford	3	0	1	2	2	7	1

The Football League 1939-40

THIRD DIVISION (NORTHERN SECTION)

Played on 26 Aug
Bradford City v Accrington Stanley 0-2
Darlington v Southport 1-0
Doncaster Rovers v Rochdale 2-0
Gateshead v Crewe Alexandra 0-3
Hartlepools United v Barrow 1-1
Hull City v Lincoln City 2-2
Oldham Athletic v Carlisle United 3-1
Stockport County v Halifax Town 0-3
Tranmere Rovers v Rotherham United 3-1
Wrexham v New Brighton 2-0
York City v Chester 2-2

Played on 28 Aug
Barrow v Accrington Stanley 1-2
Halifax Town v Oldham Athletic 2-0
Lincoln City v Darlington 0-2
Rotherham United v York City 2-1

Played on 29 Aug
Rochdale v Wrexham 1-0
Southport v Tranmere Rovers 3-3

Played on 30 Aug
Chester v Doncaster Rovers 1-0
Gateshead v Hartlepools United 3-0
New Brighton v Bradford City 2-1

Played on 2 Sep
Accrington Stanley v Oldham Athletic 2-0
Barrow v Bradford City 2-2
Carlisle United v Stockport County 2-0
Chester v Tranmere Rovers 2-0
Crewe Alexandra v Hartlepools United 0-0
Halifax Town v Wrexham 1-1
Lincoln City v Gateshead 4-3
New Brighton v Doncaster Rovers 4-2
Rochdale v York City 1-0
Rotherham United v Darlington 2-2
Southport v Hull City 1-1

THIRD DIVISION (SOUTHERN SECTION)

Played on 26 Aug
Aldershot v Bristol City 0-1
Brighton & Hove Albion v Port Vale 0-0
Bristol Rovers v Reading 2-2
Clapton Orient v Ipswich Town 2-2
Exeter City v Torquay United 2-2
Mansfield Town v Crystal Palace 4-5
Northampton Town v Swindon Town 1-0
Norwich City v Cardiff City 1-2
Notts County v Bournemouth & Boscombe Athletic 1-1
Queen's Park Rangers v Watford 2-2
Southend United v Walsall 3-2

Played on 28 Aug
Northampton Town v Exeter City 1-2

Played on 30 Aug
Bournemouth & BA v Queen's Park Rangers 2-2
Brighton & Hove Albion v Aldershot 2-1
Bristol City v Norwich City 1-2
Ipswich Town v Bristol Rovers 2-0
Reading v Crystal Palace 5-0
Swindon Town v Cardiff City 0-1
Torquay United v Walsall 0-0
Watford v Mansfield Town 1-2

Played on 31 Aug
Clapton Orient v Southend United 0-0

Played on 2 Sep
Bournemouth & BA v Northampton Town 10-0
Bristol City v Brighton & Hove Albion 3-3
Cardiff City v Notts County 2-4
Crystal Palace v Bristol Rovers 3-0
Ipswich Town v Norwich City 1-1
Port Vale v Exeter City 0-1
Reading v Southend United 1-0
Swindon Town v Aldershot 2-2
Torquay United v Mansfield Town 2-2
Walsall v Queen's Park Rangers 1-0
Watford v Clapton Orient 1-1

THIRD DIVISION (NORTHERN SECTION)

		P	W	D	L	F	A	Pts
1	Accrington Stanley	3	3	0	0	6	1	6
2	Halifax Town	3	2	1	0	6	1	5
3	Chester	3	2	1	0	5	2	5
4	Darlington	3	2	1	0	5	2	5
5	New Brighton	3	2	0	1	6	5	4
6	Rochdale	3	2	0	1	2	2	4
7	Crewe Alexandra	2	1	1	0	3	0	3
8	Wrexham	3	1	1	1	3	2	3
9	Tranmere Rovers	3	1	1	1	6	6	3
10	Lincoln City	3	1	1	1	6	7	3
11	Rotherham United	3	1	1	1	5	6	3
12	Carlisle United	2	1	0	1	3	3	2
13	Hull City	2	0	2	0	3	3	2
14	Gateshead	3	1	0	2	6	7	2
15	Barrow	3	0	2	1	4	5	2
16	Doncaster Rovers	3	1	0	2	4	5	2
17	Southport	3	0	2	1	4	5	2
18	Oldham Athletic	3	1	0	2	3	5	2
19	Hartlepools United	3	0	2	1	1	4	2
20	York City	3	0	1	2	3	5	1
21	Bradford City	3	0	1	2	3	6	1
22	Stockport County	2	0	0	2	0	5	0

THIRD DIVISION (SOUTHERN SECTION)

		P	W	D	L	F	A	Pts
1	Reading	3	2	1	0	8	2	5
2	Exeter City	3	2	1	0	5	3	5
3	Notts County	2	2	0	0	6	3	4
4	Ipswich Town	3	1	2	0	5	3	4
5	Brighton & Hove Albion	3	1	2	0	5	4	4
6	Cardiff City	3	2	0	1	5	5	4
7	Crystal Palace	3	2	0	1	8	9	4
8	Bournemouth & BA	3	1	1	1	13	4	3
9	Bristol City	3	1	1	1	5	5	3
10	Mansfield Town	3	1	1	1	8	8	3
11	Norwich City	3	1	1	1	4	4	3
12	Clapton Orient	3	0	3	0	3	3	3
13	Southend United	3	1	1	1	3	3	3
14	Torquay United	3	0	3	0	4	4	3
15	Walsall	3	1	1	1	3	3	3
16	Queen's Park Rangers	3	0	2	1	4	5	2
17	Watford	3	0	2	1	4	5	2
18	Northampton Town	3	1	0	2	2	12	2
19	Aldershot	3	0	1	2	3	5	1
20	Swindon Town	3	0	1	2	2	4	1
21	Bristol Rovers	3	0	1	2	2	7	1
22	Port Vale	2	0	1	1	0	1	1

The Football League 1939-40

SOUTH (A)

	Arsenal	Charlton Athletic	Clapton Orient	Crystal Palace	Millwall	Norwich City	Southend United	Tottenham Hotspur	Watford	West Ham U
Arsenal	X	21 Oct 8-4	25 Dec 3-0	4 Nov 5-0	13 Jan 4-1	30 Dec 2-2	16 Dec 5-1	18 Nov 2-1	8 Feb 2-2	2 Dec 3-0
Charlton Athletic	1 Jan 2-6	X	4 Nov 8-1	30 Dec 5-4	2 Dec 2-4	18 Nov 1-1	28 Oct 8-1	13 Jan 1-5	16 Dec 5-1	8 Feb 2-5
Clapton Orient	28 Oct 1-6	26 Dec 2-7	X	18 Nov 5-3	27 Jan 1-2	13 Jan 1-1	11 Nov 5-1	2 Dec 2-1	15 Feb 1-2	16 Dec 1-6
Crystal Palace	26 Dec 0-3	11 Nov 3-4	6 Jan 1-1	X	16 Dec 4-1	2 Dec 1-0	25 Nov 4-2	28 Feb 1-1	28 Oct 3-3	17 Jan 0-3
Millwall	25 Nov 3-3	20 Jan 5-2	9 Dec 1-1	25 May 7-2	X	21 Oct 1-1	26 Dec 6-1	25 Dec 5-1	6 Jan 1-1	11 Nov 2-2
Norwich City	11 Nov 1-1	29 Feb 1-3	25 Nov 4-0	13 Apr 5-2	7 Mar 1-3	X	13 May 3-2	16 Dec 5-2	26 Dec 3-2	28 Oct 5-3
Southend United	3 Apr 0-5	25 Dec 0-2	30 Dec 7-0	13 Jan 3-1	4 Nov 1-2	9 Dec 2-4	X	21 Oct 1-2	2 Dec 1-2	18 Nov 3-2
Tottenham Hotspur	25 Jan 0-1	25 Nov 4-2	20 Jan 2-3	9 Dec 1-3	28 Oct 3-0	27 May 2-2	17 Jan 2-4	X	11 Nov 8-2	26 Dec 0-1
Watford	9 Dec 1-3	13 Mar 3-0	21 Oct 1-2	25 Dec 5-1	18 Nov 2-0	4 Nov 4-1	20 Jan 4-0	30 Dec 6-1	X	13 Jan 3-1
West Ham United	20 Jan 3-0	9 Dec 4-3	22 Feb 4-1	21 Oct 2-6	30 Dec 6-2	25 Dec 4-1	6 Jan 4-0	4 Nov 2-1	25 Nov 5-0	X

On 23 December 1939, Charlton Athletic v Arsenal (0-0), Clapton Orient v Watford (2-1) (both after 57 mins) and Tottenham Hotspur v Southend United (3-4) and Norwich City v Millwall (2-5) (after 61 mins), and on 6 January 1940 Norwich City v Charlton Athletic (1-0) (after 15 mins) were all abandoned, to be replayed at a later date.

SOUTH (B)

	Aldershot	Bournemouth & BA	Brentford	Brighton & HA	Chelsea	Fulham	Portsmouth	Queen's Park Rangers	Reading	Southampton
Aldershot	X	2 Dec 1-4	25 Nov 1-0	23 Dec 5-1	7 Mar 5-2	26 Dec 3-3	11 Nov 4-4	6 Jan 1-3	28 Oct 1-1	16 Dec 3-0
Bournemouth & Boscombe Ath	20 Jan 2-0	X	27 Jan 2-2	28 Oct 6-1	16 Dec 2-2	11 Nov 2-1	6 Jan 5-0	25 Nov 3-0	26 Dec 2-1	23 Dec 3-2
Brentford	13 Jan 4-3	9 Dec 5-2	X	18 Nov 4-1	21 Oct 2-2	14 Feb 2-5	25 Dec 4-0	30 Dec 0-7	2 Dec 3-0	4 Nov 3-1
Brighton & Hove Albion	21 Oct 4-0	25 Dec 1-3	6 Jan 3-2	X	4 Nov 5-1	20 Jan 1-1	9 Dec 1-2	4 May 3-1	25 Nov 1-2	30 Dec 9-4
Chelsea	9 Dec 2-2	22 Feb 4-3	25 Jan 3-2	26 Dec 3-2	X	6 Jan 1-1	25 Nov 1-0	20 Jan 0-0	11 Nov 3-0	28 Oct 6-2
Fulham	4 Nov 3-1	30 Dec 5-2	16 Dec 2-4	2 Dec 7-4	18 Nov 1-3	X	21 Oct 2-1	25 Dec 3-8	13 May 6-2	13 Jan 4-1
Portsmouth	30 Dec 4-2	18 Nov 3-5	28 Oct 3-1	27 Jan 5-1	13 Jan 1-2	23 Dec 3-1	X	4 Nov 2-1	16 Dec 1-2	2 Dec 4-1
Queen's Park Rangers	18 Nov 4-1	13 Jan 2-1	11 Nov 1-0	16 Dec 3-2	2 Dec 3-2	28 Oct 2-2	26 Dec 5-2	X	1 Jan 3-0	8 Feb 4-1
Reading	25 Dec 7-2	4 Nov 6-3	20 Jan 3-1	13 Jan 1-0	30 Dec 1-5	9 Dec 6-1	8 Jun 2-2	21 Oct 2-0	X	18 Nov 5-3
Southampton	14 Mar 2-3	21 Oct 1-2	26 Dec 2-3	11 Nov 3-2	25 Dec 5-3	25 Nov 5-2	20 Jan 2-0	9 Dec 1-2	6 Jan 5-6	X

On 23 December 1939 Chelsea v Brentford 3-4 was abandoned after 65 mins, and replayed later.

SOUTH (A)

		P	W	D	L	F	A	Pts
1	Arsenal	18	13	4	1	62	22	30
2	West Ham United	18	12	1	5	57	33	25
3	Millwall	18	8	5	5	46	38	21
4	Watford	18	9	3	6	44	38	21
5	Norwich City	18	7	6	5	41	36	20
6	Charlton Athletic	18	8	1	9	61	58	17
7	Crystal Palace	18	5	3	10	39	56	13
8	Clapton Orient	18	5	3	10	28	60	13
9	Tottenham Hotspur	18	5	2	11	37	43	12
10	Southend United	18	4	0	14	30	61	8

SOUTH (B)

		P	W	D	L	F	A	Pts
1	QPR	18	12	2	4	49	26	26
2	Bournemouth & BA	18	11	2	5	52	37	24
3	Chelsea	18	9	5	4	45	37	23
4	Reading	18	10	2	6	47	42	22
5	Brentford	18	8	2	8	42	41	18
6	Fulham	18	7	4	7	50	51	18
7	Portsmouth	18	7	2	9	37	42	16
8	Aldershot	18	5	4	9	38	50	14
9	Brighton & HA	18	5	1	12	42	53	11
10	Southampton	18	4	0	14	41	64	8

The Football League 1939-40

SOUTH (C)

	Arsenal	Brentford	Charlton Athletic	Chelsea	Fulham	Millwall	Portsmouth	Southampton	Tottenham Hotspur	West Ham United
Arsenal	X	10 Feb 3-1	25 Mar 1-1	23 Mar 3-0	22 May 2-1	24 Feb 4-1	13 Apr 3-2	1 Jun 5-0	24 Apr 2-4	16 Mar 2-3
Brentford	6 Apr 2-4	X	18 May 2-1	2 Mar 1-1	30 Mar 5-0	17 Apr 1-1	22 Mar 3-1	16 Mar 5-0	4 May 2-3	17 Feb 4-3
Charlton Athletic	22 Mar 1-2	24 Feb 3-2	X	10 Feb 3-3	18 Apr 7-5	9 Mar 1-1	1 Jun 4-2	30 Mar 4-1	13 Apr 2-4	5 Jun 0-0
Chelsea	17 Apr 2-2	11 May 0-2	6 Apr 1-4	X	22 Mar 1-4	24 Apr 2-1	9 Mar 4-1	17 Feb 5-1	24 Feb 0-2	30 Mar 3-10
Fulham	2 Mar 1-1	3 Jun 3-5	16 Mar 2-0	25 Mar 4-3	X	13 Apr 2-0	10 Feb 3-2	6 Jun 1-2	23 Mar 2-3	27 May 2-1
Millwall	13 May 0-2	23 Mar 4-1	4 May 4-2	16 Mar 2-3	17 Feb 2-0	X	8 Apr 3-4	6 Apr 5-2	25 Mar 1-1	2 Mar 4-0
Portsmouth	25 May 1-1	25 Mar 1-3	2 Mar 1-3	4 May 3-1	6 Apr 0-3	30 Mar 1-1	X	23 Mar 3-1	16 Mar 1-2	13 May 1-1
Southampton	9 Mar 3-2	10 Apr 4-1	8 Jun 1-3	13 Apr 3-0	24 Feb 0-4	10 Feb 2-2	24 Apr 1-0	X	18 May 3-3	22 Mar 1-6
Tottenham Hotspur	30 Mar 1-1	9 Mar 1-1	17 Feb 2-0	25 May 3-2	10 Apr 3-1	22 Mar 1-2	11 May 4-1	2 Mar 4-1	X	6 Apr 2-6
West Ham United	18 Apr 2-1	13 Apr 1-1	23 Mar 2-0	4 May 4-2	9 Mar 5-0	3 Jun 1-2	24 Feb 4-1	25 Mar 2-2	10 Feb 2-0	X

Chelsea v Brentford was played at Brentford on 11 May

SOUTH (D)

	Aldershot	Bournemouth & BA	Brighton & HA	Clapton Orient	Crystal Palace	Norwich City	Queen's Park Rangers	Reading	Southend United	Watford
Aldershot	X	9 Mar 3-2	27 Apr 4-1	24 Feb 4-1	1 Jun 3-2	30 Mar 4-1	10 Apr 0-1	22 Mar 2-2	18 May 1-0	6 Apr 2-3
Bournemouth & Boscombe Ath	8 Jun 2-1	X	23 Mar 5-0	16 Mar 4-0	30 Mar 2-3	NOT PLAYED	3 Apr 1-0	6 Apr 3-1	25 Mar 6-1	2 Mar 1-1
Brighton & Hove Albion	13 May 2-2	17 Apr 3-3	X	8 Jun 3-0	10 Feb 1-3	22 Mar 3-3	9 Mar 1-2	24 Feb 3-0	10 Apr 1-3	1 Jun 2-2
Clapton Orient	4 May 4-3	11 Apr 2-0	2 Mar 5-1	X	22 Mar 0-1	6 Apr 4-3	30 Mar 4-3	4 Apr 0-3	9 Mar 5-1	17 Feb 1-1
Crystal Palace	16 Mar 3-4	18 May 6-0	6 Apr 10-0	25 Mar 7-1	X	2 Mar 2-0	13 May 2-2	17 Feb 5-1	23 Mar 5-2	29 May 2-1
Norwich City	4 Apr 3-2	24 Feb 4-3	25 Mar 3-0	10 Feb 2-2	8 Jun 1-3	X	25 May 3-1	9 Mar 5-2	1 Jun 1-3	23 Mar 2-0
Queen's Park Rangers	23 Mar 3-1	1 Jun 5-0	20 Apr 5-4	18 May 4-0	24 Feb 2-5	16 Mar 0-0	X	23 May 2-1	10 Feb 3-1	25 Mar 2-0
Reading	25 Mar 1-0	10 Feb 1-4	18 May 3-1	23 Mar 0-2	8 Apr 2-4	29 May 2-1	2 Mar 4-1	X	24 Apr 1-1	16 Mar 5-2
Southend United	2 Mar 2-2	22 Mar 2-1	16 Mar 8-2	25 May 3-0	5 Jun 3-0	17 Feb 3-0	6 Apr 0-1	30 Mar 4-2	X	8 Jun 2-2
Watford	10 Feb 3-0	25 May 7-1	30 Mar 4-2	11 May 2-2	9 Mar 5-2	18 May 0-0	22 Mar 1-1	1 May 3-0	24 Feb 4-2	X

Bournemouth v Norwich, scheduled for 5 June, was never played.

SOUTH (C)		P	W	D	L	F	A	Pts
1	Tottenham H	18	11	4	3	43	30	26
2	West Ham U	18	10	4	4	53	28	24
3	Arsenal	18	9	5	4	41	26	23
4	Brentford	18	8	4	6	42	34	20
5	Millwall	18	7	5	6	35	30	19
6	Charlton Athletic	18	7	4	7	39	36	18
7	Fulham	18	8	1	9	38	42	17
8	Southampton	18	5	3	10	28	54	13
9	Chelsea	18	4	3	11	33	53	11
10	Portsmouth	18	3	3	12	26	45	9

SOUTH (D)		P	W	D	L	F	A	Pts
1	Crystal Palace	18	13	1	4	65	30	27
2	QPR	18	10	3	5	38	28	23
3	Watford	18	7	7	4	41	29	21
4	Southend United	18	8	3	7	41	37	19
5	Aldershot	18	7	3	8	38	36	17
6	Clapton Orient	18	7	3	8	33	45	17
7	Bournemouth & BA	17	7	2	8	38	40	16
8	Norwich City	17	6	4	7	32	34	16
9	Reading	18	6	2	10	31	43	14
10	Brighton & Hove Albion	18	2	4	12	30	65	8

The Football League 1939-40

EAST MIDLAND

	Barnsley	Chesterfield	Doncaster Rovers	Grimsby Town	Lincoln City	Mansfield Town	Nottingham Forest	Notts County	Rotherham United	Sheffield United	Sheffield Wednesday
Barnsley	X	30 Mar 3-1	6 Apr 1-1	23 Dec 4-1	24 Feb 1-7	4 Nov 2-1	22 Mar 3-0	25 Nov 2-1	11 Nov 2-2	1 Jun 3-1	16 Mar 2-0
Chesterfield	2 Dec 5-2	X	23 Mar 3-1	6 Apr 5-0	21 Oct 8-0	20 Jan 4-0	29 May 6-1	16 Mar 3-1	4 May 6-1	9 Mar 5-0	11 Nov 4-0
Doncaster Rovers	9 Dec 1-1	25 Nov 2-4	X	6 Jan 2-0	2 Mar 3-1	16 Mar 4-2	24 Feb 4-3	11 Nov 2-1	18 May 2-1	1 Jan 1-2	21 Oct 2-2
Grimsby Town	13 Apr 0-0	9 Dec 1-0	1 Jun 7-4	X	11 Nov 7-3	21 Oct 2-1	8 Jun 4-3	30 Mar 3-2	16 Mar 3-1	22 Mar 2-0	4 Nov 3-2
Lincoln City	28 Oct 1-3	25 Mar 1-4	20 Apr 3-2	9 Mar 4-1	X	2 Dec 3-2	23 Mar 1-0	4 May 3-4	6 Jan 0-1	18 Nov 1-2	22 Mar 4-2
Mansfield Town	25 May 3-2	18 May 3-1	18 Nov 2-1	4 May 4-1	30 Mar 4-5	X	9 Mar 3-0	13 Jan 6-4	9 Dec 1-1	28 Oct 4-2	25 Nov 5-3
Nottingham Forest	25 Mar 1-0	6 Jan 2-2	28 Oct 1-1	13 May 1-1	25 Nov 0-1	11 Nov 6-2	X	25 May 6-2	30 Mar 4-1	26 Mar 4-1	9 Dec 1-1
Notts County	23 Mar 0-6	18 Nov 1-4	9 Mar 4-0	2 Dec 1-2	1 Jun 3-0	22 Mar 2-2	2 Mar 4-3	X	21 Oct 2-0	6 Apr 3-0	18 May 1-4
Rotherham United	9 Mar 0-4	28 Oct 1-1	26 Mar 3-1	18 Nov 2-1	11 May 3-1	6 Apr 1-2	2 Dec 1-0	25 Mar 3-2	X	23 Mar 0-4	2 Mar 1-1
Sheffield United	6 Jan 2-1	13 Apr 1-2	25 May 3-0	18 May 3-0	16 Mar 1-0	8 Jun 2-2	21 Oct 3-0	9 Dec 7-1	25 Nov 5-0	X	30 Mar 4-3
Sheffield Wednesday	18 Nov 1-1	26 Dec 2-1	4 May 1-3	23 Mar 2-1	9 May 2-2	23 Dec 2-0	6 Apr 2-1	28 Oct 1-1	13 Jan 0-1	2 Dec 2-3	X

EAST MIDLAND

		P	W	D	L	F	A	Pts
1	Chesterfield	20	14	2	4	69	23	30
2	Sheffield United	20	12	1	7	46	34	25
3	Barnsley	20	10	5	5	43	29	25
4	Grimsby Town	20	10	2	8	40	44	22
5	Mansfield Town	20	9	3	8	49	48	21
6	Doncaster Rovers	20	7	4	9	37	45	18
7	Lincoln City	20	9	0	11	41	53	18
8	Rotherham United	20	7	4	9	24	42	18
9	Sheffield Wednesday	20	5	5	10	33	41	15
10	Nottingham Forest	20	5	4	11	37	43	14
11	Notts County	20	6	2	12	40	57	14

The Football League 1939-40

WESTERN

	Chester	Crewe Alexandra	Everton	Liverpool	Manchester City	Manchester United	New Brighton	Port Vale	Stockport County	Stoke City	Tranmere Rovers	Wrexham
Chester	X	6 Jan 1-0	18 Nov 3-2	18 May 4-0	6 Apr 0-3	28 Oct 0-4	2 Dec 1-1	2 Mar 0-3	23 Dec 8-1	23 Mar 3-3	25 Mar 2-2	9 Mar 4-1
Crewe Alexandra	1 Jun 3-1	X	23 Mar 2-1	22 Mar 3-6	23 Dec 1-2	9 Mar 1-4	6 Apr 0-4	10 Feb 1-3	20 Apr 3-1	2 Dec 4-2	28 Oct 5-1	18 Nov 7-0
Everton	16 Mar 5-0	25 Nov 6-2	X	30 Mar 1-3	11 Nov 3-1	6 Jan 3-2	24 Feb 3-0	9 Dec 3-1	3 Apr 7-0	21 Oct 4-4	17 Apr 5-3	22 May 1-2
Liverpool	20 Jan 1-1	1 Jan 7-3	2 Dec 2-2	X	25 May 3-2	18 Nov 1-0	23 Dec 6-2	28 Oct 1-1	11 May 4-3	6 Apr 1-2	29 May 8-3	23 Mar 0-0
Man City	9 Dec 4-1	13 May 6-2	9 Mar 2-2	6 Jan 3-7	X	10 Feb 1-0	23 Mar 2-3	18 May 7-0	2 Dec 6-6	18 Nov 1-1	13 Apr 5-1	28 Oct 6-1
Man United	24 Feb 5-1	11 Nov 5-1	1 Jun 0-3	16 Mar 1-0	21 Oct 0-4	X	6 May 6-0	25 Nov 8-1	6 Apr 6-1	20 Jan 4-3	30 Mar 6-1	23 Dec 5-1
New Brighton	30 Mar 4-2	9 Dec 6-1	28 Oct 0-1	1 Jun 0-0	25 Nov 1-3	18 May 6-0	X	6 Jan 2-2	18 Nov 4-2	9 Mar 3-1	22 Mar 5-2	10 Feb 4-1
Port Vale	4 May 3-1	21 Oct 6-1	6 Apr 2-1	24 Feb 3-8	11 May 2-5	23 Mar 1-3	13 May 3-0	X	9 Mar 6-2	6 May 1-2	18 Nov 6-2	2 Dec 1-0
Stockport County	25 May 1-3	2 Mar 4-1	29 May 1-2	21 Oct 0-3	30 Mar 1-1	9 Dec 4-7	16 Mar 4-1	11 Nov 2-1	X	24 Feb 1-5	25 Nov 5-0	6 Jan 0-1
Stoke City	25 Nov 2-0	30 Mar 1-1	10 Feb 1-0	9 Dec 3-1	16 Mar 2-1	25 May 3-2	11 Nov 4-1	25 Mar 5-1	28 Oct 4-2	X	6 Jan 1-0	2 Mar 3-1
Tranmere Rovers	21 Oct 1-2	24 Feb 7-2	23 Dec 2-9	11 Nov 1-3	4 May 1-6	2 Dec 2-4	20 Jan 2-4	16 Mar 1-5	23 Mar 2-2	13 May 5-1	X	6 Apr 2-2
Wrexham	11 Nov 2-2	16 Mar 5-0	20 Jan 0-0	25 Nov 2-1	24 Feb 3-2	13 May 3-2	21 Oct 6-4	30 Mar 1-0	4 May 4-2	4 Nov 5-0	9 Dec 5-0	X

		P	W	D	L	F	A	Pts
1	Stoke City	22	13	5	4	57	41	31
2	Liverpool	22	12	5	5	66	40	29
3	Everton	22	12	4	6	64	33	28
4	Manchester United	22	14	0	8	74	41	28
5	Manchester City	22	12	4	6	73	41	28
6	Wrexham	22	10	5	7	45	50	25
7	New Brighton	22	10	3	9	55	52	23
8	Port Vale	22	10	2	10	52	56	22
9	Chester	22	7	5	10	40	51	19
10	Crewe Alexandra	22	6	1	15	44	79	13
11	Stockport County	22	4	3	15	45	79	11
12	Tranmere Rovers	22	2	3	17	41	93	7

The Football League 1939-40

NORTH WESTERN

	Accrington Stanley	Barrow	Blackburn Rovers	Blackpool	Bolton Wanderers	Burnley	Bury	Carlisle United	Oldham Athletic	Preston North End	Rochdale	Southport
Accrington Stanley	X	2 Dec 2-2	18 Nov 2-2	25 Nov 2-3	6 Jan 1-1	29 May 1-2	23 Dec 3-5	27 Apr 1-6	28 Oct 1-2	24 May 1-5	9 Mar 4-1	6 Apr 1-1
Barrow	26 Dec 3-3	X	28 Oct 2-0	9 Mar 1-4	22 Mar 4-2	6 Jan 5-2	18 Nov 1-3	25 May 6-3	18 May 5-1	1 Jun 1-4	10 Feb 1-1	25 Nov 3-0
Blackburn Rovers	16 Mar 0-2	25 Mar 2-4	X	21 Oct 1-1	25 Nov 3-1	9 Dec 1-1	2 Mar 1-2	27 May 1-1	6 Jan 1-3	30 Mar 0-3	3 Jun 4-2	11 Nov 5-0
Blackpool	23 Mar 8-1	11 Nov 5-4	10 Feb 3-2	X	30 Mar 3-1	13 Apr 5-0	28 Oct 1-1	6 Jan 2-2	13 May 11-2	9 Dec 3-0	24 Apr 7-2	16 Mar 3-1
Bolton Wanderers	18 May 4-1	6 Apr 2-0	23 Mar 2-0	2 Dec 3-1	X	10 Apr 5-1	11 May 0-1	28 Oct 4-1	13 Jan 3-0	13 Apr 1-0	18 Nov 4-0	23 Dec 2-1
Burnley	1 Jun 7-0	21 May 2-0	6 Apr 0-0	23 Dec 1-1	21 Oct 1-1	X	9 Mar 1-2	18 Nov 8-0	23 Mar 4-3	24 Feb 1-0	2 Dec 3-1	20 Jan 7-3
Bury	4 May 7-0	16 Mar 5-2	13 Apr 2-1	24 Feb 1-2	20 Jan 4-1	11 Nov 5-0	X	25 Nov 4-2	9 Dec 2-0	21 Oct 1-2	6 Jan 3-1	30 Mar 4-0
Carlisle United	21 Oct 0-0	2 Dec 1-0	23 Dec 1-2	1 Jun 3-1	24 Feb 2-3	16 Mar 3-4	23 Mar 3-3	X	2 Dec 1-2	11 Nov 1-5	6 Apr 1-2	25 Mar 1-2
Oldham Athletic	4 Nov 3-1	17 Feb 8-2	28 May 2-5	8 Jun 4-2	11 Nov 2-2	25 Nov 3-1	6 Apr 3-2	30 Mar 8-1	X	16 Mar 3-2	23 Dec 0-3	21 Oct 4-3
Preston North End	20 Jan 3-1	23 Dec 3-2	2 Dec 2-0	6 Apr 1-1	4 May 1-3	28 Oct 2-1	10 Feb 3-2	9 Mar 3-2	18 Nov 6-1	X	23 Mar 5-0	18 May 5-0
Rochdale	11 Nov 5-1	21 Oct 1-3	20 Jan 1-5	28 May 3-3	16 Mar 2-2	30 Mar 1-1	18 May 2-3	9 Dec 3-1	25 May 3-1	25 Nov 1-1	X	24 Feb 1-2
Southport	9 Dec 3-2	23 Mar 3-3	9 Mar 4-1	18 Nov 0-3	13 May 1-8	25 May 1-1	2 Dec 1-2	22 Mar 4-0	10 Feb 0-0	6 Jan 1-2	28 Oct 3-2	X

On 27 January 1940 Barrow v Oldham 1-2 was abandoned after 50 mins and replayed at a later date.
Blackburn v Barrow (played at Barrow) and Accrington v Carlisle (played at Carlisle)

		P	W	D	L	F	A	Pts
1	Bury	22	16	2	4	64	30	34
2	Preston North End	22	15	2	5	58	27	32
3	Blackpool	22	13	6	3	73	36	32
4	Bolton Wanderers	22	13	4	5	55	30	30
5	Oldham Athletic	22	11	2	9	55	61	24
6	Burnley	22	9	6	7	49	43	24
7	Barrow	22	8	4	10	53	57	20
8	Blackburn Rovers	22	6	5	11	37	40	17
9	Rochdale	22	5	5	12	38	58	15
10	Southport	22	5	4	13	34	62	14
11	Carlisle United	22	4	4	14	38	68	12
12	Accrington Stanley	22	2	6	14	31	73	10

The Football League 1939-40

NORTH EASTERN

	Bradford	Bradford City	Darlington	Halifax Town	Hartlepools United	Huddersfield Town	Hull City	Leeds United	Middlesbrough	Newcastle United	York City
Bradford	X	11 May 2-1	NOT PLAYED	26 Dec 3-0	20 May 2-0	13 Apr 1-3	25 Nov 2-1	9 Dec 3-1	11 Nov 3-0	16 Mar 2-1	25 May 2-3
Bradford City	4 Nov 4-3	X	18 Nov 4-0	21 Oct 5-1	23 Mar 4-0	6 Apr 0-1	9 Mar 4-0	NOT PLAYED	18 May 1-4	26 Mar 3-1	2 Dec 2-1
Darlington	18 May 4-2	16 Mar 4-4	X	26 Mar 2-1	2 Dec 4-0	23 Dec 0-4	21 Oct 2-0	11 Nov 1-3	25 Mar 8-0	4 Nov 1-2	6 Apr 5-3
Halifax Town	25 Dec 2-3	2 Mar 2-2	28 Oct 2-4	X	9 Mar 3-1	23 Mar 2-3	18 May 0-1	25 May 3-2	6 Apr 1-1	23 Dec 3-4	18 Nov 1-4
Hartlepools United	22 Mar 0-4	25 Nov 4-1	30 Mar 3-1	11 Nov 3-2	X	1 Jun 2-2	24 Feb 3-2	16 Mar 2-1	25 May 1-2	21 Oct 1-2	25 Dec 1-2
Huddersfield Town	21 Oct 4-1	9 Dec 1-1	25 May 8-2	25 Nov 1-2	25 Mar 4-1	X	16 Mar 1-0	30 Mar 2-1	24 Feb 4-2	11 Nov 2-0	1 Jun 1-0
Hull City	23 Mar 4-1	25 May 3-0	8 Jun 4-4	6 Jan 2-0	28 Oct 2-3	18 Nov 1-5	X	4 Nov 0-3	2 Dec 3-0	6 Apr 3-1	25 Mar 4-1
Leeds United	6 Apr 5-2	28 Oct 3-0	9 Mar 3-2	NOT PLAYED	18 Nov 2-1	2 Dec 0-0	1 Jun 3-1	X	23 Dec 3-1	8 Jun 1-3	23 Mar 3-1
Middlesbrough	9 Mar 3-3	6 Jan 3-0	16 Dec 8-1	9 Dec 3-1	2 Mar 2-0	28 Oct 2-2	30 Mar 2-3	13 Apr 1-1	X	25 Nov 1-2	1 Jun 6-1
Newcastle United	18 Nov 2-3	8 Jun 4-4	22 Mar 3-0	29 May 6-1	10 Feb 3-0	9 Mar 3-5	9 Dec 3-0	6 Jan 3-0	23 Mar 3-5	X	28 Oct 9-2
York City	4 May 3-2	30 Mar 0-1	9 Dec 2-1	16 Mar 3-1	18 May 2-1	3 Jun 1-0	11 Nov 3-1	25 Nov 1-1	21 Oct 1-3	23 Mar 1-1	X

On 8 June 1940, Newcastle played two games simultaneously, at Bradford and at Leeds

		P	W	D	L	F	A	Pts
1	Huddersfield Town	20	15	4	1	54	22	34
2	Newcastle United	20	12	1	7	59	42	25
3	Bradford	19	10	2	7	47	38	22
4	Middlesbrough	20	9	4	7	49	42	22
5	Leeds United	18	9	3	6	36	27	21
6	Bradford City	19	8	4	7	41	37	20
7	Hull City	20	8	1	11	35	41	17
8	York City	20	8	1	11	36	51	17
9	Darlington	19	6	3	10	44	56	15
10	Hartlepool United	20	6	1	13	27	47	13
11	Halifax Town	19	3	2	14	28	53	8

The Football League 1939-40

SOUTH WESTERN

	Bristol City	Bristol Rovers	Cardiff City	Newport County	Plymouth Argyle	Swansea Town	Swindon Town	Torquay United
Bristol City	X	11 Nov 0-3 / 6 Apr 0-1	21 Oct 1-1 / 22 Mar 3-2	26 Dec 1-3 / 24 Feb 6-2	16 Dec 1-0 / 23 Mar 3-4	2 Dec 3-1 / 25 Mar 2-0	4 Nov 2-6 / 10 Feb 5-1	13 Jan 1-3 / 18 May 2-2
Bristol Rovers	30 Dec 4-2 / 9 Mar 4-4	X	6 Jan 7-0 / 1 Jun 3-3	28 Oct 2-3 / 22 Mar 3-5	25 Nov 1-2 / 2 Mar 1-1	9 Dec 1-3 / 16 Mar 6-2	25 Dec 3-4 / 20 Jan 5-2	23 Dec 2-2 / 30 Mar 3-2
Cardiff City	9 Dec 7-3 / 16 Mar 5-2	18 Nov 0-0 / 24 Feb 1-1	X	13 Jan 1-0 / 13 May 4-1	4 Nov 1-0 / 10 Feb 0-0	28 Oct 2-2 / 18 May 2-2	30 Dec 1-1 / 6 Apr 1-1	25 Nov 2-2 / 9 Mar 1-1
Newport County	25 Dec 1-1 / 4 May 4-1	16 Dec 0-1 / 25 Mar 0-2	25 Nov 3-1 / 25 May 4-1	X	7 Jun 6-3 / 8 Jun 5-2	23 Dec 2-2 / 30 Mar 1-5	21 Oct 0-2 / 18 May 5-2	11 Nov 1-0 / 1 Jun 11-0
Plymouth Argyle	28 Oct 6-0 / 3 Feb 10-3	13 Jan 2-0 / 13 May 4-1	23 Dec 6-2 / 30 Mar 4-1	25 Nov 2-0 / 9 Mar 3-0	X	11 Nov 3-0 / 17 Feb 3-1	18 Nov 2-1 / 24 Feb 4-2	21 Oct 4-0 / 26 Dec 1-1
Swansea Town	13 May 6-2 / 8 Jun 4-1	21 Oct 0-0 / 27 Jan 2-2	16 Dec 4-0 / 23 Mar 1-0	4 Nov 1-2 / 10 Feb 2-2	30 Dec 1-0 / 6 Apr 0-2	X	25 Nov 1-3 / 2 Mar 2-1	18 Nov 5-1 / 24 Feb 2-1
Swindon Town	23 Dec 7-2 / 30 Mar 1-3	2 Dec 3-3 / 26 Dec 1-1	11 Nov 2-2 / 20 Apr 2-2	9 Dec 2-1 / 16 Mar 3-3	6 Jan 2-0 / 11 May 2-2	13 Jan 4-1 / 25 May 4-0	X	28 Oct 2-0 / 4 May 1-3
Torquay United	25 Nov 3-3 / 2 Mar 3-0	4 Nov 2-1 / 10 Feb 5-1	20 Jan 5-0 / 11 May 2-4	30 Dec 6-2 / 6 Apr 4-3	9 Dec 5-2 / 27 Jan 1-0	6 Jan 3-2 / 5 Jun 7-2	16 Dec 5-1 / 23 Mar 4-3	X

		P	W	D	L	F	A	Pts
1	Plymouth Argyle	28	16	4	8	72	41	36
2	Torquay United	28	14	6	8	73	62	34
3	Bristol Rovers	28	9	10	9	62	55	28
4	Newport County	28	12	4	12	70	63	28
5	Swindon Town	28	10	8	10	66	63	28
6	Swansea Town	28	10	6	12	54	60	26
7	Cardiff City	28	6	13	9	45	63	25
8	Bristol City	28	7	5	16	57	92	19

The Football League 1939-40

MIDLAND

	Birmingham	Coventry City	Leicester City	Luton Town	Northampton Town	Walsall	WBA	Wolverhampton W
Birmingham	X	30 Dec 2-4 / 6 Apr 2-0	13 Jan 3-3 / 20 May 0-0	4 Nov 2-1 / 10 Feb 2-4	2 Dec 1-1 / 9 Mar 3-1	16 Dec 2-1 / 23 Mar 2-1	18 Nov 2-2 / 24 Feb 1-6	21 Oct 3-2 / 10 Apr 0-1
Coventry City	11 Nov 3-1 / 5 Jun 0-0	X	23 Dec 0-1 / 30 Mar 4-1	25 Mar 10-2 / 1 Jun 5-1	9 Dec 1-4 / 16 Mar 6-3	25 Nov 4-3 / 2 Mar 4-1	28 Oct 6-3 / 8 Jun 4-0	6 Jan 0-3 / 13 Apr 1-1
Leicester City	25 Nov 1-3 / 2 Mar 2-1	4 Nov 4-2 / 30 May 1-3	X	16 Dec 3-3 / 23 Mar 1-2	6 Jan 1-1 / 8 Jun 2-0	21 Oct 6-1 / 1 Jun 0-0	30 Dec 2-5 / 6 Apr 5-2	20 Jan 1-2 / 25 May 3-1
Luton Town	26 Mar 4-5 / 30 Mar 1-4	2 Dec 7-0 / 9 Mar 1-5	28 Oct 4-2 / 18 May 5-1	X	13 Jan 6-2 / 13 May 3-2	6 Jan 1-0 / 4 May 3-4	9 Dec 4-5 / 16 Mar 3-6	11 Nov 2-2 / 1 May 3-0
Northampton Town	20 Jan 3-0 / 1 May 1-3	21 Oct 1-1 / 26 Mar 2-0	18 Nov 2-2 / 24 Feb 4-2	25 Nov 2-1 / 2 Mar 1-1	X	30 Dec 6-1 / 6 Apr 2-2	4 Nov 1-1 / 5 Jun 1-2	16 Dec 1-2 / 23 Mar 2-0
Walsall	28 Oct 1-2 / 8 Jun 1-8	13 Jan 0-2 / 25 May 2-1	9 Dec 4-3 / 16 Mar 3-2	18 Nov 4-6 / 24 Feb 4-4	11 Nov 1-1 / 11 May 1-0	X	2 Dec 0-2 / 9 Mar 1-1	23 Dec 3-5 / 30 Mar 1-2
West Bromwich Albion	26 Dec 3-0 / 25 Mar 4-1	16 Dec 3-1 / 23 Mar 3-1	11 Nov 1-0 / 26 Mar 5-1	21 Oct 3-1 / 13 Apr 3-1	23 Dec 4-1 / 30 Mar 4-1	20 Jan 7-2 / 14 May 2-3	X	25 Nov 5-0 / 2 Mar 1-1
Wolverhampton Wanderers	9 Dec 6-2 / 16 Mar 3-1	18 Nov 4-0 / 24 Feb 1-0	2 Dec 5-0 / 9 Mar 5-1	30 Dec 4-1 / 6 Apr 6-1	28 Oct 7-2 / 1 Jun 1-0	4 Nov 4-1 / 18 May 1-5	13 Jan 2-0 / 13 May 5-4	X

Due to restrictions, Birmingham had to play all but one of their games away from their St Andrews ground, the exception being the game against Walsall on 23 March 1940 when they were allowed to play at home.

		P	W	D	L	F	A	Pts
1	Wolverhampton Wanderers	28	19	3	6	76	44	41
2	West Bromwich Albion	28	18	4	6	87	51	40
3	Coventry City	28	13	3	12	68	57	29
4	Birmingham	28	12	5	11	56	60	29
5	Luton Town	28	10	4	14	76	88	24
6	Northampton Town	28	7	8	13	48	59	22
7	Leicester City	28	7	6	15	51	71	20
8	Walsall	28	7	5	16	51	83	19

Football League (War) Cup 1939-40

Preliminary round
Played on 13 Apr
Brighton & Hove Albion v Clapton Orient 1-2
Mansfield Town v Notts County 3-5
Northampton Town v Watford 1-1
REPLAY on 17 Apr
Watford v Northampton Town 2-1
Southend United v Queen's Park Rangers 1-0
Bournemouth & Boscombe Athletic v Bristol City 5-1
Bristol Rovers v Aldershot 2-0
Cardiff City v Reading 1-1
REPLAY on 18 Apr
Reading v Cardiff City 1-0
Port Vale v Walsall 2-2
REPLAY on 15 Apr
Walsall v Port Vale 6-0
Swindon Town v Torquay United 1-1
REPLAY on 17 Apr
Torquay United v Swindon Town 5-0
Barrow v Carlisle United 1-0
New Brighton v Crewe Alexandra 2-1
Rochdale v Accrington Stanley 3-0
Southport v Oldham Athletic 1-1
REPLAY on 17 Apr
Oldham Athletic v Southport 0-1
Wrexham v Stockport County 3-0
Darlington v Gateshead 2-0
Doncaster Rovers v Rotherham United 0-0
REPLAY on 15 Apr
Rotherham United v Doncaster Rovers 1-0 *(aet 90 mins 0-0)*
Hartlepools United v Halifax Town 2-1
Hull City v Lincoln City 1-0
York City v Bradford City 6-4

First round – 2 legs
First leg played on 20 Apr, second leg on 27 Apr
South (A)
Arsenal v Notts County 4-0, 5-1
Crystal Palace v Tottenham Hotspur 4-1, 1-2
Fulham v Brentford 4-1, 2-1
Leicester City v Clapton Orient 5-2, 0-2
Nottingham Forest v Charlton Athletic 1-0, 3-1
Norwich City v Millwall 2-1, 1-1
Southend United v Watford 3-2, 3-1
West Ham United v Chelsea 3-2, 2-0
South (B)
Coventry City v Luton Town 3-0, 1-2
Newport County v Birmingham 2-2, 2-5
Plymouth Argyle v Bournemouth & Boscombe Athletic 0-1, 1-4
Southampton v Bristol Rovers 1-1, 1-3
Swansea Town v Walsall 2-0, 1-2
Torquay United v Reading 2-0, 0-3 aet
West Bromwich Albion v Portsmouth 3-1, 2-3
North (A)
Barrow v Liverpool 2-0, 2-1
Blackburn Rovers v Bolton Wanderers 5-1, 3-1
Blackpool v Southport 4-0, 4-2
Chester v Burnley 1-3, 0-3
Everton v Preston North End 3-1, 2-2
Manchester United v Manchester City 0-1, 2-0

New Brighton v Stoke City 1-4, 1-2
Rochdale v Bury 1-0, 1-1
Wrexham v Wolverhampton Wanderers 1-1, 0-3
North (B)
Barnsley v Hartlepools United 3-0, 1-1
Bradford v Newcastle United 2-0, 0-3
Chesterfield v Huddersfield Town 2-1, 0-2
Leeds United v Sheffield Wednesday 6-3, 2-3
Middlesbrough v Grimsby Town 4-1, 1-3
Sheffield United v Rotherham United 0-0, 3-0
Sunderland v Darlington 1-1, 3-2
York City v Hull City 1-1, 0-1

Second round – 2 legs
First leg played on 4 May, second leg on 11 May
Arsenal v Crystal Palace 3-1, 2-0
Leicester City v West Ham United 1-1, 0-3
Norwich City v Fulham 1-1, 0-1
Nottingham Forest v Southend United 3-1, 1-0
Birmingham v Reading 2-0, 2-0
Bournemouth & Boscombe Athletic v West Bromwich Albion 1-2, 1-3
Bristol Rovers v Swansea Town 6-0, 0-3
Wolverhampton Wanderers v Coventry City 0-2, 2-5
Barrow v Stoke City 0-2, 1-6
Blackburn Rovers v Manchester United 1-2, 3-1
Burnley v Blackpool 1-2, 1-3
Everton v Rochdale 5-1, 2-4
Barnsley v Sheffield United 3-0, 0-1
Huddersfield Town v Hull City 1-1, 1-0
Middlesbrough v Newcastle United 2-2, 1-2
Sunderland v Leeds United 0-0, 1-0

Third round
Played on 18 May
Arsenal v Birmingham 1-2
Barnsley v Blackpool 0-1
Coventry City v West Bromwich Albion 0-1 *(aet 90 mins 0-0)*
Everton v Stoke City 1-0
Fulham v Nottingham Forest 2-0
Huddersfield v West Ham United 3-3 (aet)
REPLAY on 22 May
West Ham United v Huddersfield 3-1
Newcastle United v Bristol Rovers 1-0

Fourth round
Played on 25 May
Blackburn Rovers v West Bromwich Albion 2-1
Blackpool v Newcastle United 0-2
Fulham v Everton 5-2
West Ham United v Birmingham 4-2

Semi-final
Played on 1 Jun
Blackburn Rovers v Newcastle United 1-0
Fulham v West Ham United 3-4

Final
Football League War Cup 1939-40
Played on 8 Jun 1940 at Wembley Stadium, London
Att 42,399
West Ham United 1 *(Small)*
Blackburn Rovers 0

West Ham United: Conway, Bicknell, C Walker, Fenton, R Walker, Cockcroft, Small, Macaulay, Foreman, Goulden, Foxall
Blackburn R: Barron, Hough, Crook, Whiteside, Pryde, Chivers, Rogers, Butt, Weddle, Clarke, Guest

Other English & Welsh Competitions 1939-40

LANCASHIRE CUP

First round
Played on 4 Nov
Barrow v Bury 3-4
Blackburn Rovers v Rochdale 2-1
Blackpool v Southport 4-1
Bolton Wanderers v Liverpool 1-3
Burnley v Everton 2-3
Accrington Stanley bye
New Brighton bye

Second round
Played on 16 Dec
Accrington Stanley v Oldham Athletic 7-1
Blackburn Rovers v Everton 0-6
Bury v Blackpool 5-3
Played on 13 Jan
New Brighton v Liverpool 4-1

Semi-final
Played on 25 Mar
Bury v Accrington Stanley 4-0
Played on 10 Apr
Everton v Liverpool 4-1

Final
Played on 8 Jun
Bury v Everton 2-4

LIVERPOOL SENIOR CUP

First round
Played on 16 Dec
New Brighton v Southport 2-3

Semi-final
Played on 2 Mar
Liverpool v Southport 5-1
Played on 13 Jan, replay on 2 Mar
Everton v Tranmere Rovers 4-4, 6-3 *aet*

Final
Played on 13 May
Everton v Liverpool 6-3

CHESHIRE BOWL

Final
Played on 11 May
Chester v Tranmere Rovers 5-1

STAFFORDSHIRE CUP

Final
Played on 23 Mar, replay on 25 Mar
Walsall v Stafford Rangers 2-2, 5-3

WELSH FA CUP
(Games involving Football League clubs only)

Fourth round
Played on 16 Dec
Wrexham v Wellington Town 1-2
Rhyl v New Brighton 1-4
Southport v South Liverpool 2-1
Newport County v Lovell's Athletic 1-1, 0-2
Cardiff City v Ebbw Vale 3-0
Swansea Town v Haverfordwest Athletic wo-disq

Fifth round
Played on 3 Feb
Barry Town v Newport County 2-3
Played on 2 Mar
New Brighton v Llandudno 4-1
Played on 20 Jan
Swansea Town v Gwynfi Welfare 7-2

Sixth round
Played on 2 Mar
Cardiff City v Newport County 1-1
Newport County v Cardiff City 5-0
Played on 9 Mar
Swansea Town v Aberystwyth Town 2-0
Played on 25 Mar
New Brighton v Southport 1-0
Chester v Wellington Town 1-3

Semi-final
Played on 4 May
Wellington Town v New Brighton 0-0
New Brighton v Wellington Town 2-4 *(at Shrewsbury)*
Swansea Town v Newport County 1-0

Final
Played on 1 Jun at Shrewsbury
Swansea Town v Wellington Town 0-4

The Scottish Football League 1939-40

Results and standings at the time of the Declaration of War on 3 September 1939

FIRST DIVISION

Played on 12 Aug
Aberdeen v Celtic 3-1
Albion Rovers v Ayr United 5-0
Alloa Athletic v St Johnstone 3-0
Clyde v Falkirk 4-6
Cowdenbeath v Third Lanark 2-1
Hamilton Academical v Arbroath 2-0
Heart of Midlothian v Partick Thistle 1-1
Kilmarnock v Motherwell 3-3
Queen of the South v Hibernian 2-1
Rangers v St Mirren 5-1

Played on 19 Aug
Arbroath v Alloa Athletic 5-2
Ayr United v Rangers 0-4
Celtic v Heart of Midlothian 2-0
Falkirk v Cowdenbeath 7-1
Hibernian v Clyde 3-2
Motherwell v Aberdeen 3-0
Partick Thistle v Albion Rovers 2-1
St Johnstone v Kilmarnock 0-3
St Mirren v Queen of the South 3-3
Third Lanark v Hamilton Academical 2-2

Played on 22 Aug
Partick Thistle v Heart of Midlothian 2-2
St Mirren v Rangers 0-0
Third Lanark v Cowdenbeath 4-2

Played on 23 Aug
Arbroath v Hamilton Academical 2-0
Ayr United v Albion Rovers 2-1
Celtic v Aberdeen 1-3
Falkirk v Clyde 4-2
Hibernian v Queen of the South 3-1
Motherwell v Kilmarnock 4-2
St Johnstone v Alloa Athletic 4-0

Played on 26 Aug
Aberdeen v Hibernian 3-1
Albion Rovers v St Mirren 0-0
Alloa Athletic v Motherwell 3-2
Clyde v St Johnstone 2-0
Cowdenbeath v Celtic 1-2
Hamilton Academical v Falkirk 2-1
Heart of Midlothian v Ayr United 6-2
Kilmarnock v Third Lanark 0-1
Rangers v Arbroath 3-1
Queen of the South v Partick Thistle 3-0

Played on 2 Sep
Arbroath v Kilmarnock 1-2
Ayr United v Hamilton Academical 6-1
Celtic v Clyde 1-0
Falkirk v Queen of the South 2-1
Hibernian v Albion Rovers 3-5
Motherwell v Heart of Midlothian 2-4
Partick Thistle v Alloa Athletic 2-0
St Johnstone v Aberdeen 3-0
St Mirren v Cowdenbeath 4-0
Third Lanark v Rangers 1-2

SECOND DIVISION

Played on 12 Aug
Brechin City v St Bernard's 0-0
Dundee v Raith Rovers 5-1
East Fife v Morton 3-0
East Stirlingshire v Montrose 4-1
Edinburgh City v Dundee United 2-3
Forfar Athletic v King's Park 3-5
Leith Athletic v Dumbarton 1-2
Queen's Park v Airdrieonians 2-0
Stenhousemuir v Dunfermline Athletic 0-0

Played on 19 Aug
Airdrieonians v Dundee 2-4
Dumbarton v East fife 3-3
Dundee United v Stenhousemuir 4-2
Dunfermline Athletic v Queen's Park 3-3
King's Park v Leith Athletic 3-1
Montrose v Edinburgh City 2-2
Morton v East Stirlingshire 3-0
Raith Rovers v Brechin City 2-0
St Bernard's v Forfar Athletic 6-2

Played on 26 Aug
Brechin City v King's Park 1-1
Dundee v Dumbarton 3-1
East Fife v St Bernard's 5-1
East Stirlingshire v Dundee United 1-1
Edinburgh City v Morton 3-0
Forfar Athletic v Airdrieonians 1-3
Leith Athletic v Dunfermline Athletic 0-2
Queen's Park v Raith Rovers 2-1
Stenhousemuir v Montrose 1-0

Played on 2 Sep
Airdrieonians v East Fife 2-1
Dumbarton v Edinburgh City 3-2
Dundee United v Leith Athletic 0-2
Dunfermline Athletic v Brechin City 5-2
King's Park v East Stirlingshire 2-2
Montrose v Forfar Athletic 4-1
Morton v Dundee 1-1
Raith Rovers v Stenhousemuir 1-3
St Bernard's v Queen's Park 0-0

FIRST DIVISION

		P	W	D	L	F	A	Pts
1	Rangers	5	4	1	0	14	3	9
2	Falkirk	5	4	0	1	20	10	8
3	Aberdeen	5	3	0	2	9	9	6
4	Celtic	5	3	0	2	7	8	6
5	Heart of Midlothian	5	2	2	1	14	9	6
6	Partick Thistle	5	2	2	1	7	7	6
7	Motherwell	5	2	1	2	14	12	5
8	Hamilton Academical	5	2	1	2	7	11	5
9	Third Lanark	5	2	1	2	9	8	5
10	Queen of the South	5	2	1	2	10	9	5
11	Albion Rovers	5	2	1	2	12	7	5
12	St Mirren	5	1	3	1	8	8	5
13	Kilmarnock	5	2	1	2	10	9	5
14	Hibernian	5	2	0	3	11	13	4
15	Alloa Athletic	5	2	0	3	8	13	4
16	Arbroath	5	2	0	3	9	9	4
17	St Johnstone	5	2	0	3	7	8	4
18	Ayr United	5	2	0	3	10	17	4
19	Clyde	5	1	0	4	10	14	2
20	Cowdenbeath	5	1	0	4	6	14	2

SECOND DIVISION

		P	W	D	L	F	A	Pts
1	Dundee	4	3	1	0	13	5	7
2	Dunfermline Athletic	4	2	2	0	10	5	6
3	King's Park	4	2	2	0	11	7	6
4	East Fife	4	2	1	1	12	6	5
5	Queen's Park	4	1	3	0	7	5	5
6	Stenhousemuir	4	2	1	1	6	5	5
7	Dundee United	4	2	1	1	8	7	5
8	Dumbarton	4	2	1	1	9	9	5
9	East Stirlingshire	4	1	2	1	7	7	4
10	St Bernard's	4	1	2	1	7	7	4
11	Airdrieonians	4	2	0	2	7	8	4
12	Edinburgh City	4	1	1	2	9	8	3
13	Montrose	4	1	1	2	7	8	3
14	Raith Rovers	4	1	1	2	8	12	3
15	Morton	4	1	1	2	4	7	3
16	Leith Athletic	4	1	0	3	4	7	2
17	Brechin City	4	0	2	2	3	8	2
18	Forfar Athletic	4	0	0	4	7	18	0

The Scottish Football League 1939-40

WEST DIVISION

	Airdrieonians	Albion R	Ayr U	Celtic	Clyde	Dumbarton	Hamilton A	Kilmarnock	Morton	Motherwell	Partick Th	QOS	Queen's Park	Rangers	St Mirren	Third Lanark
Airdrieonians	X	1 Jan 1-4	30 Mar 4-1	6 Jan 0-1	21 Oct 1-6	2 Dec 3-2	8 Apr 1-1	4 Nov 3-0	18 May 3-2	13 Jan 5-2	16 Dec 1-2	10 Feb 4-1	22 Apr 3-3	18 Nov 0-1	13 May 4-2	10 May 4-2
Albion Rovers	6 Apr 0-1	X	28 Oct 2-1	25 Nov 3-2	20 Apr 2-1	17 Apr 3-1	27 Apr 1-2	30 Dec 2-3	23 Dec 3-1	2 Jan 4-0	17 Feb 4-2	4 May 2-3	9 Dec 5-2	16 May 3-3	3 Apr 2-1	11 Nov 2-0
Ayr United	30 Dec 2-1	10 Apr 2-0	X	27 Apr 1-0	18 Nov 3-2	11 May 4-4	24 Apr 2-2	13 Apr 2-3	21 Oct 0-1	20 Apr 0-1	2 Dec 7-0	1 Jan 2-1	10 Feb 1-2	4 Nov 0-2	16 Dec 2-3	23 Mar 2-4
Celtic	20 Apr 4-2	23 Apr 3-1	13 Jan 1-3	X	9 Apr 4-1	23 Mar 4-0	21 Oct 3-4	18 Nov 1-1	10 Feb 0-3	30 Dec 2-2	9 Mar 1-1	4 Nov 0-3	13 Apr 4-4	6 Apr 1-2	2 Dec 2-1	16 Dec 1-2
Clyde	2 Apr 2-0	6 Jan 5-0	17 Feb 1-1	28 Oct 2-0	X	11 Nov 3-3	30 Mar 5-3	27 Apr 1-2	30 Apr 0-3	25 Nov 8-2	6 Apr 2-2	23 Dec 2-2	16 Mar 1-1	9 Dec 0-1	16 Apr 3-1	25 Mar 4-0
Dumbarton	4 May 0-1	4 Nov 4-1	9 Dec 2-1	23 Dec 1-5	10 Feb 1-2	X	18 Nov 1-2	10 Apr 2-2	1 Jan 3-2	16 Mar 0-1	30 Mar 0-0	13 Apr 1-3	21 Oct 1-3	24 Apr 2-3	6 Jan 3-2	27 Apr 3-1
Hamilton Academical	28 Oct 5-0	13 Jan 2-1	27 Mar 4-2	3 Apr 5-0	30 Dec 3-2	17 Feb 4-2	X	20 Apr 0-0	16 Mar 2-2	6 Apr 2-3	11 Nov 6-4	9 Dec 3-6	3 May 3-1	23 Dec 2-0	2 Jan 3-4	17 Apr 4-0
Kilmarnock	25 May 1-5	30 Mar 6-2	2 Jan 3-1	17 Feb 3-2	13 Jan 1-2	28 Oct 5-0	6 Jan 1-4	X	9 Dec 4-2	11 Nov 1-1	25 Nov 5-2	16 Mar 1-3	23 Dec 2-1	15 May 3-1	6 Apr 3-1	2 Apr 1-2
Morton	2 Jan 2-1	23 Mar 2-3	3 Apr 4-1	11 Nov 1-1	2 Dec 2-1	6 Apr 5-0	16 Dec 1-2	11 May 2-0	X	28 Oct 3-3	13 Apr 3-0	20 Apr 4-0	13 Jan 2-2	30 Dec 3-0	25 Nov 3-2	17 Feb 3-2
Motherwell	27 Apr 0-2	18 May 2-1	6 Jan 3-3	30 Mar 2-0	24 Apr 1-1	16 Dec 5-1	1 Jan 1-1	10 Feb 2-1	25 May 2-1	X	15 Mar 6-1	18 Nov 2-1	4 Nov 4-1	21 Oct 0-1	11 May 1-4	6 Dec 6-2
Partick Thistle	16 Mar 3-2	18 Nov 0-1	1 May 2-0	9 Dec 4-2	1 Jan 3-2	30 Dec 0-4	10 Feb 1-1	24 Apr 5-2	4 Nov 1-0	23 Dec 1-3	X	21 Oct 2-2	10 Apr 6-0	25 May 1-3	18 May 3-1	20 Apr 4-1
Queen of the South	11 Nov 4-2	2 Dec 4-2	6 Apr 3-0	17 Apr 1-3	18 May 2-2	2 Jan 3-1	11 May 3-2	16 Dec 4-2	6 Jan 3-0	27 Mar 4-1	23 Mar 4-1	X	9 Mar 4-2	13 Jan 1-2	28 Oct 1-1	25 Nov 6-3
Queen's Park	25 Nov 1-2	7 May 1-3	11 Nov 5-4	25 Mar 1-4	16 Dec 1-1	2 Apr 4-1	2 Dec 3-2	18 May 0-1	27 Apr 3-3	16 Apr 2-2	28 Oct 4-3	30 Dec 1-2	X	20 Apr 2-3	17 Feb 1-3	1 Jan 4-2
Rangers	17 Feb 3-1	16 Dec 2-1	17 Apr 3-1	1 Jan 1-1	8 May 3-1	25 Nov 2-1	18 May 2-2	2 Dec 4-1	30 Jan 1-0	20 Jan 1-2	25 Mar 2-2	27 Apr 5-1	6 Jan 4-0	X	11 Nov 4-0	28 Oct 6-0
St Mirren	23 Dec 3-2	21 Oct 2-1	16 Mar 2-0	4 May 2-1	4 Nov 1-1	20 Apr 1-2	13 Apr 2-1	1 Jan 3-3	23 Apr 0-3	9 Dec 1-3	27 Apr 3-1	9 Apr 1-1	18 Nov 3-0	10 Feb 4-6	X	30 Dec 5-3
Third Lanark	9 Dec 1-4	10 Feb 2-2	23 Dec 1-1	16 Mar 4-2	12 Apr 2-4	27 Mar 3-2	4 Nov 1-1	21 Oct 3-2	18 Nov 3-1	1 May 1-1	6 Jan 2-0	24 Apr 1-1	6 Apr 3-0	22 Apr 0-1	30 Mar 2-1	X

		P	W	D	L	F	A	Pts
1	Rangers	30	22	4	4	72	36	48
2	Queen of the South	30	17	6	7	77	55	40
3	Hamilton Academical	30	15	8	7	78	55	38
4	Motherwell	30	15	8	7	64	56	38
5	Morton	30	14	5	11	64	46	33
6	Albion Rovers	30	15	2	13	62	60	32
7	Clyde	30	11	9	10	68	51	31
8	Kilmarnock	30	13	5	12	63	63	31
9	Airdrieonians	30	14	2	14	63	61	30
10	Partick Thistle	30	10	6	14	57	74	26
11	St Mirren	30	11	4	15	59	66	26
12	Third Lanark	30	10	5	15	53	78	25
13	Celtic	30	9	6	15	55	61	24
14	Queen's Park	30	7	7	16	55	82	21
15	Ayr United	30	7	5	18	50	66	19
16	Dumbarton	30	7	4	19	48	78	18

The Scottish Football League 1939-40

NORTH & EAST DIVISION

	Aberdeen	Alloa	Arbroath	Cowdenbeath	Dundee	Dundee United	Dunfermline A	East Fife	Falkirk	Hearts	Hibernian	King's Park	Raith R	St Bernard's	St Johnstone	Stenhousemuir
Aberdeen	X	27 Jan 3-1	6 Apr 5-2	13 Jan 8-1	30 Apr 3-0	24 Apr 3-1	10 Feb 3-0	20 Apr 2-2	2 Jan 6-2	16 Mar 3-0	4 Nov 3-3	9 Mar 5-2	21 Oct 5-1	18 Nov 3-3	23 Dec 5-1	2 Dec 6-1
Alloa Athletic	28 Oct 0-3	X	27 Apr 1-1	25 Nov 2-1	9 Mar 2-2	30 Dec 2-1	16 Mar 2-3	17 Feb 3-1	6 Jan 0-2	11 Nov 2-3	M23 2-3	13 Apr 1-3	9 Dec 3-1	2 Dec 5-0	2 Apr 4-1	1 Jan 3-1
Arbroath	1 Jan 2-1	13 Jan 1-1	X	11 Nov 0-6	17 Feb 3-1	26 Apr 5-2	23 Mar 1-3	28 Oct 2-2	30 Mar 1-2	13 Apr 2-2	16 Dec 0-0	3 Apr 5-2	4 May 0-2	9 Dec 0-4	17 Apr 1-2	25 Nov 2-1
Cowdenbeath				X	6 Jan 1-1	4 Nov 4-2					23 Dec 2-3	2 Jan 0-4	2 Dec 5-2	18 Nov 5-3	21 Oct 4-0	
Dundee	30 Dec 3-1	4 Nov 1-1	18 Nov 9-3		X	6 Apr 2-1	8 Apr 2-2	13 Jan 2-0	18 May 4-2	9 Dec 4-6	21 Oct 2-1	16 Dec 5-0	10 Feb 2-3	2 Jan 2-2	4 May 7-2	17 Apr 7-1
Dundee United	25 Nov 3-5	30 Mar 5-0	6 Jan 4-2		1 Jan 2-1	X	2 Dec 5-2	25 May 3-2	27 Apr 1-3	17 Feb 3-2	11 May 1-3	28 Oct 1-0	23 Dec 1-1	16 Mar 1-0	11 Nov 2-2	3 Apr 10-2
Dunfermline Athletic	11 Nov 4-3	16 Dec 2-4	23 Dec 4-0	1 Jan 3-0	28 Oct 2-0	18 May 2-0	X	3 Apr 6-4	9 Dec 4-3	25 Nov 5-2	13 Jan 2-1	17 Apr 2-0	30 Mar 3-4	20 Apr 3-1	17 Feb 2-3	13 Apr 4-2
East Fife	6 Jan 1-4	18 Nov 2-3	10 Apr 6-2	30 Dec 2-4	27 Apr 3-0	2 Jan 3-6	21 Oct 1-8	X	4 Nov 2-5	4 May 1-2	13 Apr 4-3	23 Mar 6-1	6 Apr 3-2	10 Feb 2-1	9 Dec 4-4	16 Dec 9-3
Falkirk	13 Apr 0-1	20 Apr 2-1	30 Dec 3-0	28 Oct 9-0	25 Nov 6-1	13 Jan 4-2	6 May 0-0	17 Apr 3-0	X	3 Apr 7-1	2 Dec 3-3	11 Nov 5-2	16 Dec 5-0	23 Mar 8-1	1 Jan 4-0	17 Feb 4-1
Heart of Midlothian	16 Dec 3-2	10 Feb 7-2	2 Jan 7-2		11 May 2-3	18 Nov 9-2	25 May 2-0	2 Dec 6-3	21 Oct 2-3	X	6 Apr 4-0	20 Apr 7-2	10 Apr 4-3	4 Nov 2-2	13 Jan 3-0	30 Dec 8-2
Hibernian	18 May 2-0	23 Dec 3-0	16 Mar 2-4	3 Apr 6-0	9 Dec 6-2	27 Apr 2-3	25 Nov 2-5	4 May 5-6	1 Jan 5-6		X	17 Feb 2-1	6 Jan 4-1	30 Mar 3-1	28 Oct 3-3	11 Nov 1-2
King's Park	9 Dec 2-1	2 Jan 1-2	21 Oct 5-3		16 Mar 3-3	8 Apr 2-1	4 Nov 2-3	23 Dec 2-3	10 Feb 1-1	6 Jan 2-2	18 Nov 2-7	X	24 Apr 5-6	27 Mar 4-1	30 Mar 5-2	13 Jan 1-1
Raith Rovers	1 Apr 4-1	1 May 1-3	2 Dec 6-0		11 Nov 2-1	8 May 5-0	30 Dec 0-3	1 Jan 2-5	16 Mar 2-2	28 Oct 1-5	20 Apr 1-1	25 Nov 1-2	X	13 Jan 6-0	13 Apr 3-4	23 Mar 5-2
St Bernard's	17 Feb 3-1	4 May 2-0	9 Mar 2-0		13 Apr 0-0	16 Dec 4-2	14 May 1-3	11 Nov 2-1	23 Dec 1-2	15 Apr 0-2	30 Dec 1-6	6 Apr 3-4	27 Apr 1-0	X	25 Nov 1-1	28 Oct 6-2
St Johnstone	23 Mar 3-0	21 Oct 2-3	4 Nov 4-0	16 Dec 3-0	2 Dec 2-2	10 Feb 1-3	18 Nov 4-2	9 Mar 8-1	6 Apr 2-2	27 Apr 2-2	10 Apr 4-0	30 Dec 2-1	2 Dec 10-3	24 Apr 6-1	X	20 Apr 3-2
Stenhousemuir	4 May 0-0	6 Apr 2-3	24 Apr 2-0	9 Dec 2-5	23 Dec 0-3	21 Oct 0-1	2 Jan 3-0	16 Mar 0-2	18 Mar 3-8	30 Nov 1-0	27 Mar 2-1	27 Apr 2-3	4 Nov 5-0	10 Apr 4-0	6 Jan 3-3	X

Cowdenbeath resigned from the League on 6 Feb but their record was allowed to stand

		P	W	D	L	F	A	Pts
1	Falkirk	29	20	5	4	106	47	45
2	Dunfermline Athletic	29	19	2	8	80	55	40
3	Heart of Midlothian	29	18	4	7	104	66	40
4	Aberdeen	29	16	4	9	86	50	36
5	St Johnstone	29	13	8	8	84	69	34
6	Alloa Athletic	29	13	4	12	56	60	30
7	Dundee	29	11	8	10	70	62	30
8	Hibernian	29	12	5	12	82	65	29
9	Dundee United	29	12	2	15	68	77	26
10	East Fife	29	11	3	15	80	91	25
11	Raith Rovers	29	10	3	16	69	85	23
12	King's Park	29	9	4	16	62	88	22
13	St Bernard's	29	8	5	16	44	77	21
14	Arbroath	29	6	5	18	44	91	17
15	Stenhousemuir	29	7	3	19	52	98	17
16	Cowdenbeath	15	7	1	7	38	44	15

Other Scottish Competitions 1939-40

SCOTTISH LEAGUE CHAMPIONSHIP PLAY-OFF

Played on 1 Jun 1940 at Ibrox Park, Glasgow
Rangers 2 *(Venters, Little)*
Falkirk 1 *(Napier)*
Rangers: Dawson, Gray, Shaw, McKillop, Woodburn, Symon, Waddell, McPherson, Smith, Venters, Little
Falkirk: McKie, McPhee, Peat, A Miller, Shankly, Murray, keyes, W Miller, McCulloch, Napier, Dawson

WAR EMERGENCY CUP

First round – 2 legs
First leg played on 24 Feb, second on 2 Mar
Albion Rovers v Aberdeen 3-3, 1-0
Alloa Athletic v Rangers 1-4, 2-2
Celtic v Raith Rovers 4-2, 0-3
Clyde v East Fife 3-1, 0-1
Dumbarton v Arbroath 4-3, 2-0
Dundee v Third Lanark 1-1, 1-3
Falkirk v Hibernian 5-0, 0-4
Hamilton Academical v Stenhousemuir 7-1, 1-4
St Johnstone v Heart of Midlothian 2-1, 0-5
Kilmarnock v Ayr United 1-0, 2-2
King's Park v Motherwell 4-6, 2-3
Partick Thistle v Dundee United 2-4, 1-1
Queen's Park v Airdrieonians 3-2, 1-3
St Bernard's v Morton 1-5, 0-5
St Mirren v Queen of the South 6-0, 1-4

Second round
Played on 9 Mar, REPLAYS on 13 Mar
Clyde v Dunfermline Athletic 3-1
Dumbarton v Airdrieonians 0-2
Dundee United v Third Lanark 7-1
Falkirk v Rangers 0-0, 2-3
Hamilton Academical v St Mirren 0-2
Heart of Midlothian v Raith Rovers 2-1
Kilmarnock v Albion Rovers 2-1
Morton v Motherwell 1-1, 2-5

Third round
Played on 23 Mar
Dundee United v Kilmarnock 3-0
Motherwell v Clyde 3-0
Rangers v St Mirren 3-1
Airdrieonians v Heart of Midlothian 0-0
REPLAY on 27 Mar
Heart of Midlothian v Airdrieonians 2-2 *(aet, 90 mins 2-2, abandoned after 117 mins due to poor light)*
SECOND REPLAY on 1 Apr at Tynecastle Park, Edinburgh
Heart of Midlothian v Airdrieonians 3-4

Semi-final
Played on 13 Apr, REPLAY on 17 Apr
Rangers v Motherwell 4-1 *(at Hampden Park, Glasgow)*
Dundee United v Airdrieonians 0-0, 3-1 *(both games at Easter Road, Edinburgh)*

Final
4 May 1940 at Hampden Park, Glasgow
Att 71,000
Rangers 1 *(Smith)*
Dundee United 0

Rangers: Dawson, Gray, Shaw, Bolt, Woodburn, McKillop, Waddell, Thornton, Smith, Venters, Little
Dundee United: Thomson, Miller, Dunsmore, Baxter, Littlejohn, Robertson, Glen, Gardiner, Milne, Adamson, Frazer

FORFARSHIRE CUP

First round
Played on 30 Aug
Dundee v Dundee United 6-1
Montrose v Arbroath 0-1

Semi-final
Played on 30 Sep
Arbroath v Brechin City 3-1
Played on 7 Oct
Forfar Athletic v Dundee 2-5

Final
Played on 8 May at Dens Park, Dundee
Dundee v Arbroath 1-1
REPLAY at Gayfield Park, Arbroath
Arbroath v Dundee 2-0

DUMBARTONSHIRE CUP

Played on 30 Sep at Boghead Park, Dumbarton
Dumbarton v Vale of Leven 4-2

LANARKSHIRE CUP

Semi-final
Played on 14 Oct
Albion Rovers v Motherwell 1-4
Played on 22 May
Hamilton Academical v Airdrieonians 2-2

Final
Played on 31 May at Douglas Park, Hamilton
Hamilton Academical v Motherwell 0-1

GLASGOW CUP

First round
Played on 29 Sep
Partick Thistle v Rangers 1-4
Played on 30 Sep
Clyde v Third Lanark 0-1

Semi-final
Played on 30 Sep, replay on 7 Oct
Celtic v Queen's Park 2-2, 0-1
Played on 7 Oct, replay on 14 Oct
Rangers v Third Lanark 2-2, 2-1 *(both games at Ibrox Park, Glasgow)*

Final
Played on 25 Dec at Ibrox Park, Glasgow
Rangers v Queen's Park 3-1

GLASGOW CHARITY CUP

First round
Played on 18 May
Third Lanark v Celtic 2-3
Played on 21 May
Clyde v Partick Thistle 1-2

Semi-final
Played on 22 May
Rangers v Celtic 5-1
Played on 25 May
Queen's Park v Clyde 2-2 *(Clyde won 11-8 on corners)*

Final
Played on 29 May at Hampden Park, Glasgow
Rangers v Clyde 1-1 *(Rangers won 7-2 on corners)*

Other Scottish Competitions 1939-40

DEWAR SHIELD

Qualifying round
Played on 29 Apr 1939
St Johnstone v Blairgowrie 6-0
2 legs, first leg played in May 1938, second on 12 Aug 1938
Aberdeen v Buckie Thistle 5-2, 7-5

Semi-final
Played on 16 Aug
St Johnstone v Falkirk 0-3
Arbroath v Aberdeen 0-3

Final
Played on 30 Aug at Pittodrie Park, Aberdeen
Aberdeen v Falkirk 2-2
REPLAY on 30 Sep at Brockville Park, Falkirk
Falkirk v Aberdeen 1-2

EAST OF SCOTLAND SHIELD

Semi-final
Played on 29 Aug
St Bernard's v Hibernian 0-1
Played on 30 Aug
Heart of Midlothian v Leith Athletic 7-0

Final
Played on 15 May at Easter Road, Edinburgh
Hibernian v Heart of Midlothian 2-3

PAISLEY CHARITY CUP
Played on 1 Jun at St Mirren Park, Paisley
Clyde v St Mirren 3-0

WILSON CUP
Played on 16 Aug at Easter Road, Edinburgh
Hibernian v Heart of Midlothian 0-2

FALKIRK INFIRMARY SHIELD
Played on 25 May at Brockville Park, Falkirk
Falkirk v Stenhousemuir 3-6

RENFREWSHIRE CUP
Semi-final
Played on 25 Mar
Morton v Babcock & Wilcox 0-1 *(abandoned after 83 mins)*

FIFE CUP
First round
Played on 30 Aug
Raith Rovers v Burntisland Shipyard 6-0

Semi-final
Played on 14 Oct
Raith Rovers v Dunfermline Athletic 2-0

COMPETITION ABANDONED

AYRSHIRE CUP
1938-39 edition held over

Final
Played at Rugby Park, Kilmarnock, on 30 Aug, REPLAY at Somerset Park, Ayr, on 30 Sep
Kilmarnock v Ayr United 2-2, 1-3

First round – 2 legs
Dunfermline Athletic v Cowdenbeath
First leg played on 15 Aug, second on 7 Oct
St Bernard's v Leith Athletic 2-2, 1-4
First leg played on 30 Sep, second on 7 Oct
East Fife v Raith Rovers 3-0, 0-5
Played on 7 Oct
Alloa Athletic v King's Park 6-0

PENMAN CUP
Semi-final
Leith Athletic v Alloa Athletic or King's Park
Cowdenbeath or Dunfermline Athletic v Raith Rovers

COMPETITION ABANDONED

ROSEBERY CHARITY CUP

Semi-final
Played on 22 May
Heart of Midlothian v Leith Athletic 3-1
Played on 29 May
Hibernian v St Bernard's 2-2 *(Hibernian won 6-2 on corners)*

Final
Played on 1 June at Tynecastle Park, Edinburgh
Heart of Midlothian v Hibernian 2-5

STIRLINGSHIRE CUP

First round
Played on 16 Aug
King's Park v Alloa Athletic 3-1
Played on 26 Aug
Falkirk v Larbert Amateurs 5-0

Semi-final
Played on 30 Sep
King's Park v East Stirlingshire 4-3
Played on 7 Oct
Dumbarton v Falkirk 2-3

COMPETITION ABANDONED

Northern Ireland 1939-40

IRISH FOOTBALL LEAGUE

	Ards	Ballymena U	Bangor	Belfast Celtic	Cliftonville	Coleraine	Derry C	Distillery	Glenavon	Glentoran	Larne	Linfield	Newry T	Portadown
Ards	X	13 Jan 0-2	25 Mar 3-1	2 Dec 3-3	11 Nov 3-1	25 Dec 5-0	10 Feb 1-3	16 Mar 1-4	30 Mar 0-1	13 Apr 2-1	16 Dec 7-1	30 Dec 2-3	17 Feb 1-1	2 Mar 5-4
Ballymena United	6 Apr 5-0	X	2 Mar 6-0	27 Jan 1-5	26 Mar 4-3	2 Dec 6-1	6 Jan 4-1	17 Feb 4-0	16 Mar 2-2	26 Dec 2-3	18 Nov 5-1	16 Dec 2-1	25 Dec 8-2	3 Feb 2-1
Bangor	26 Dec 2-5	9 Dec 2-2	X	26 Mar 1-3	23 Dec 3-1	3 Feb 4-2	23 Mar 1-3	27 Jan 1-0	24 Feb 5-1	9 Mar 0-4	6 Apr 4-1	25 Nov 4-1	18 Nov 4-1	6 Jan 1-2
Belfast Celtic	24 Feb 3-0	13 Apr 3-3	30 Dec 6-0	X	10 Feb 6-2	25 Mar 6-1	25 Nov 3-0	25 Dec 4-0	13 Jan 4-2	11 Nov 4-2	16 Mar 0-0	30 Mar 5-0	2 Mar 12-0	16 Dec 0-0
Cliftonville	3 Feb 1-3	30 Dec 0-1	16 Mar 2-3	18 Nov 0-7	X	16 Dec 1-2	27 Jan 2-1	2 Mar 7-2	25 Mar 1-2	30 Mar 0-2	2 Dec 3-3	25 Dec 3-2	13 Jan 3-2	17 Feb 2-4
Coleraine	23 Mar 3-1	24 Feb 2-4	11 Nov 5-1	26 Dec 1-3	9 Mar 4-1	X	23 Dec 2-1	6 Apr 5-4	25 Nov 1-4	19 Dec 3-7	6 Jan 3-1	10 Feb 0-4	27 Jan 3-1	24 Feb 2-1
Derry City	18 Nov 6-2	30 Mar 5-2	25 Dec 5-2	17 Feb 0-0	13 Apr 6-1	16 Mar 0-0	X	16 Dec 2-1	30 Dec 9-0	13 Jan 3-2	2 Mar 6-0	25 Mar 1-2	3 Feb 4-1	2 Dec 3-5
Distillery	23 Dec 1-2	25 Nov 3-3	13 Apr 3-1	23 Mar 1-3	19 Dec 4-1	13 Jan 1-3	9 Mar 1-3	X	10 Feb 4-2	24 Feb 2-3	23 Mar 5-2	11 Nov 1-3	30 Mar 7-0	26 Dec 1-1
Glenavon	6 Jan 5-1	23 Dec 4-2	2 Dec 6-2	16 Apr 0-3	26 Dec 8-1	17 Feb 3-0	26 Mar 0-1	18 Nov 2-1	X	23 Mar 4-3	3 Feb 3-2	2 Mar 3-3	16 Dec 2-0	27 Jan 2-3
Glentoran	27 Jan 8-1	25 Mar 4-2	16 Dec 5-1	3 Feb 0-3	6 Jan 8-2	2 Mar 4-1	6 Apr 6-1	2 Dec 6-2	25 Dec 6-1	X	17 Feb 6-2	16 Mar 3-2	30 Dec 6-1	18 Nov 0-3
Larne	9 Mar 4-0	10 Feb 2-4	13 Jan 1-1	23 Dec 0-2	28 Oct 1-0	30 Mar 0-1	9 Dec 2-8	30 Dec 4-1	11 Nov 0-5	25 Nov 0-2	X	13 Apr 1-1	25 Mar 2-1	23 Mar 2-7
Linfield	26 Mar 4-0	9 Mar 2-1	17 Feb 1-1	6 Jan 0-2	23 Mar 5-1	18 Nov 3-1	26 Dec 3-1	3 Feb 3-1	9 Dec 5-5	24 Feb 1-2	27 Feb 5-5	X	2 Dec 3-0	6 Apr 0-5
Newry Town	25 Nov 2-0	23 Mar 1-3	10 Feb 3-0	9 Dec 0-1	6 Apr 3-1	13 Apr 1-1	11 Nov 2-0	6 Jan 1-1	9 Mar 3-2	26 Mar 1-9	26 Dec 1-1	24 Feb 3-4	X	23 Dec 1-1
Portadown	9 Dec 3-1	11 Nov 4-2	30 Mar 6-1	9 Mar 1-0	25 Nov 6-2	30 Dec 1-0	24 Feb 3-1	25 Mar 3-2	13 Apr 6-0	10 Feb 2-2	25 Dec 4-2	13 Jan 3-3	16 Mar 7-0	X

Glenavon v Portadown on 27 Jan was abandoned at 1-2 and replayed at a later date
NOTE dates shown in italics are the scheduled dates for these fixtures

		P	W	D	L	F	A	Pts
1	Belfast Celtic	26	20	5	1	91	18	45
2	Portadown	26	18	5	3	86	37	41
3	Glentoran	26	19	1	6	104	46	39
4	Ballymena United	26	15	4	7	82	52	34
5	Linfield	26	14	5	7	63	47	33
6	Derry City	26	14	2	10	73	46	30
7	Glenavon	26	13	3	10	69	68	29
8	Coleraine	26	11	2	13	47	68	24
9	Ards	26	9	2	15	49	72	20
10	Bangor	26	8	3	15	44	77	19
11	Distillery	26	6	3	17	53	70	15
12	Newry Town	26	5	5	16	32	86	15
13	Larne	26	4	5	17	36	83	13
14	Cliftonville	26	3	1	22	40	99	7

IRISH FA CUP

First round
Played on 20 Jan
  Ballymena United v Bangor 3-0
  Belfast Celtic v Cliftonville 3-0
  Coleraine v Dundela 1-1
  Glenavon v Glentoran 2-1
  Larne v Ards 3-0
  Linfield v Distillery 3-1
  Portadown v Derry City 2-2

Second round
Played on 24 Feb
  Ballymena United v Dundela 3-2
  Belfast Celtic v Derry City 3-0
  Belfast Celtic II v Glenavon 0-3
  Larne v Linfield 1-2

Semi-final
Played on 6 Apr
  Glenavon v Linfield 2-0
  Ballymena United v Belfast Celtic 2-0

Final
Played on 20 Apr at Windsor Park, Belfast
  Ballymena United v Glenavon 2-0

Northern Ireland 1939-40

CITY CUP

	Ards	Ballymena U	Bangor	Belfast Celtic	Cliftonville	Coleraine	Derry C	Distillery	Glenavon	Glentoran	Larne	Linfield	Newry T	Portadown
Ards	X							14 Oct 5-3					26 Aug 2-0	
Ballymena United		X		7 Oct 1-5	23 Sep 3-1			9 Sep 3-4		21 Oct 4-1				
Bangor	21 Oct 3-0	4 Nov 0-2	X						7 Oct 4-2		9 Sep 2-2			
Belfast Celtic	9 Sep 6-0			X								4 Nov 3-2	14 Oct 4-0	
Cliftonville					X		26 Aug 1-2	4 Nov 2-2				14 Oct 0-6		
Coleraine		26 Aug 3-1		21 Oct 2-3	7 Oct 2-0	X						9 Sep 1-3		
Derry City					14 Oct 1-1		X							4 Nov 0-0
Distillery								X	26 Aug 1-1		21 Oct 3-2			
Glenavon	23 Sep 2-1	14 Oct 4-4				4 Nov 6-1			X					
Glentoran			14 Oct 6-0	23 Sep 0-2	9 Sep 7-1		23 Sep 2-3			X			4 Nov 6-1	
Larne	4 Nov 1-4			26 Aug 2-2							X			14 Oct 1-0
Linfield			26 Aug 3-1				21 Oct 0-1				7 Oct 2-2	X		23 Sep 1-1
Newry Town							7 Oct 2-6		21 Oct 1-0		23 Sep 2-1		X	9 Sep 6-1
Portadown					21 Oct 4-0			7 Oct 3-1		26 Aug 1-1				X

Belfast Celtic were declared winners

Second round
Played on 28 Oct
  Belfast Celtic v Newry Town 1-1
  Linfield v Distillery 2-0
  Portadown v Coleraine 3-3

GOLD CUP
Final
  Belfast Celtic winners

1940-41

The Football League decided to continue with whatever clubs were willing to. Two large groupings, North Regional and South Regional were formed with over thirty clubs in each. The clubs were allowed to arrange their own fixtures, subject to approval from the League, with the only condition being that each First and Second Division club had to play at least from the Third Division. These were only arranged until Christmas when the situation would be reviewed. No points were awarded for wins and or draws, instead goal average would determine league positions. Travel restrictions meant most matches were local derbies and it wasn't uncommon to find some clubs meeting half a dozen times in a season.

League positions in late January were used to determine which clubs played in the first round of the League Cup, the lowest placed sides competing in a preliminary round. The results of these games were also included in the overall league tables.

After being excluded from the London Cup, several clubs formed a League South; these also doubled as South Regional games and counted towards both competitions. Likewise, a Western Regional League composed of Football League and non-League sides ran parallel to the Western Football League with matches between the League sides also counting towards the South Regional League.

Meanwhile Aston Villa competed in the non-League Birmingham & District League.

The Scottish Football League suspended itself for the duration of the war, but gave its permission for clubs to form their own competitions. Out of this came the Scottish Southern Football League which also organized a League Cup played on revolutionary lines as well as a Summer Cup. These competitions were run through until 1945 when the Scottish Football League re-formed. A league for northern clubs was put back a year because Dundee were unwilling to take part.

In Northern Ireland, the Irish Football League was replaced by the Northern Regional League after Belfast Celtic, Distillery, Glentoran and Linfield refused to take part.

WINNERS OF THE PRINCIPAL COMPETITIONS

Football League Cup	Preston North End
Football League –	
North Regional	Preston North End
South Regional	Crystal Palace
South	Brighton & Hove Albion
Western Regional League	Lovell's Athletic
Scottish Southern League	Rangers
Scottish Southern League Cup	Rangers
Irish FA Cup	Belfast Celtic
Northern Regional League	Belfast Celtic

The Football League 1940-41

NORTH REGIONAL LEAGUE

BARNSLEY

	31 Aug	Doncaster R	A	1-2
	7 Sep	Chesterfield	H	2-0
	14 Sep	Chesterfield	A	1-5
	21 Sep	Doncaster R	H	6-2
	28 Sep	Newcastle U	A	0-1
	5 Oct	Newcastle U	H	1-0
	12 Oct	Sheffield Wed	A	2-2
	19 Oct	Huddersfield T	A	2-1
	26 Oct	Sheffield Wed	H	5-0
	2 Nov	Leeds U	H	3-0
	9 Nov	Sheffield Utd	A	1-3
	16 Nov	Lincoln C	A	3-2
	23 Nov	Huddersfield T	H	4-1
	30 Nov	Sheffield Utd	H	1-4
	7 Dec	Leeds U	A	1-1
	14 Dec	Hull C	A	2-1
	21 Dec	Hull C	H	5-0
	25 Dec	Rotherham U	A	3-0
	25 Dec	Rotherham U	H	3-3
	28 Dec	Lincoln C	H	6-0
SC	11 Jan	Rotherham U	A	3-4
	18 Jan	Bradford City	A	5-1
	1 Feb	Everton	A	1-3
	1 Mar	Sheffield Wed	H	7-1
	5 Apr	Rotherham U	H	5-1
	12 Apr	Huddersfield T	H	4-3
	14 Apr	York C	H	1-1
	19 Apr	Middlesbrough	H	3-2
	26 Apr	Middlesbrough	A	2-3
	3 May	Chesterfield	H	3-2

BLACKBURN ROVERS

	31 Aug	Burnley	A	1-2
	7 Sep	Liverpool	H	0-3
	14 Sep	Liverpool	A	1-1
	21 Sep	Bury	H	3-2
	28 Sep	Wrexham	A	1-2
	5 Oct	Crewe Alex	A	4-1
	12 Oct	Rochdale	A	1-1
	19 Oct	Rochdale	H	2-0
	26 Oct	Manchester City	A	1-1
	2 Nov	Halifax T	A	1-1
	9 Nov	Burnley	H	1-1
	16 Nov	Manchester City	H	2-2
	23 Nov	Bury	A	1-3
	30 Nov	Crewe Alex	H	4-1
	7 Dec	Manchester Utd	H	5-5
	14 Dec	Oldham Ath	A	0-1
	21 Dec	Oldham Ath	H	3-2
	25 Dec	Preston NE	H	0-0
	28 Dec	Manchester Utd	A	0-9
La	4 Jan	Manchester Utd	H	0-2
La	11 Jan	Manchester Utd	A	0-0
	18 Jan	Bury	A	1-3
	25 Jan	Bury	H	3-1
	1 Feb	Burnley	A	1-2
	8 Feb	Halifax T	H	0-1
	15 Mar	Burnley	H	3-2
	29 Mar	Wrexham	H	3-2
	5 Apr	Wrexham	A	0-3
	12 Apr	Bury	H	4-0
	14 Apr	Halifax T	A	3-3
	26 Apr	Bolton W	A	0-2
	3 May	Preston NE	A	0-1

BLACKPOOL

La	4 Jan	Bury	H	3-2
La	11 Jan	Bury	A	2-1
La	18 Jan	Manchester City	A	4-2
La	25 Jan	Manchester City	H	2-1
	1 Mar	Chester	H	5-2
	8 Mar	Chester	A	3-4
	15 Mar	Liverpool	H	6-4
	22 Mar	Liverpool	A	6-2
	29 Mar	Manchester Utd	H	2-0
	5 Apr	Manchester Utd	A	3-2
	12 Apr	Liverpool	H	0-0
	14 Apr	Everton	A	2-2
	19 Apr	Oldham Ath	H	6-2
	26 Apr	Manchester City	A	0-2
	3 May	Manchester City	H	1-1
La	10 May	Burnley	A	0-1
	17 May	Preston NE	A	0-2
	24 May	Burnley	H	3-0
	31 May	Chester	H	4-2
	2 Jun	Preston NE	H	4-2

BOLTON W

La	4 Jan	Oldham Ath	H	2-1
La	11 Jan	Oldham Ath	A	2-3
La	18 Jan	Manchester Utd	H	3-2
La	25 Jan	Manchester Utd	A	1-4
	15 Mar	Bury	A	1-4
	22 Mar	Bury	H	5-1
	29 Mar	Southport	A	1-2
	12 Apr	Burnley	A	2-2
	14 Apr	Burnley	H	0-2
	19 Apr	Rochdale	A	3-1
	26 Apr	Blackburn R	H	2-0
	10 May	Chester	A	0-8
	17 May	Manchester City	H	1-1
	24 May	Manchester City	A	4-6
	31 May	Oldham Ath	H	3-1
	7 Jun	Oldham Ath	A	1-3

11 Jan, aet 5-3

BRADFORD

	31 Aug	Newcastle U	A	2-0
	7 Sep	Huddersfield T	A	1-1
	14 Sep	Halifax Town	H	0-0
	21 Sep	Hull City	A	1-2
	28 Sep	Bradford City	H	0-2
	5 Oct	Halifax Town	A	3-2
	12 Oct	Middlesbrough	H	0-2
	19 Oct	Middlesbrough	A	2-6
	26 Oct	Newcastle U	H	0-1
	2 Nov	Rochdale	A	1-1
	9 Nov	Oldham Ath	A	4-4
	16 Nov	Sheffield Utd	H	1-2
	23 Nov	Sheffield Utd	A	4-3
	30 Nov	Sheffield Wed	H	3-4
	7 Dec	Rochdale	H	2-4
	14 Dec	Bradford City	A	2-4
	21 Dec	Huddersfield T	H	3-2
	25 Dec	Leeds Utd	A	1-2
	28 Dec	York City	A	0-0
WR	11 Jan	York City	H	4-2
CC	18 Jan	Middlesbrough	A	3-5
	1 Feb	Grimsby T	A	3-0
	1 Mar	Lincoln C	H	4-0
	8 Mar	Bradford City	A	2-2
	15 Mar	Halifax T	A	2-2
	29 Mar	Bradford City	H	4-1
	5 Apr	Tranmere R	A	4-6
	14 Apr	Mansfield T	A	1-5
	19 Apr	Lincoln City	A	2-6
	26 Apr	Rotherham U	A	0-2
	3 May	Rotherham U	H	5-1

BRADFORD CITY

	31 Aug	Leeds U	A	2-2
	7 Sep	Hull C	H	4-5
	14 Sep	Doncaster R	A	1-2
	21 Sep	Halifax T	A	1-2
	28 Sep	Bradford	A	2-0
	5 Oct	Doncaster R	H	5-1
	12 Oct	Halifax T	A	1-5
	19 Oct	Leeds U	H	3-6
	26 Oct	Hull C	A	2-5
	2 Nov	York C	H	8-2
	9 Nov	Grimsby T	A	2-3
	16 Nov	Leeds U	A	0-6
	23 Nov	Middlesbrough	H	3-2
	30 Nov	Rotherham U	H	1-2
	7 Dec	York C	A	2-5
	14 Dec	Bradford	H	4-2
	25 Dec	Huddersfield T	H	0-5
	25 Dec	Huddersfield T	A	4-3
	28 Dec	Sheffield Wed	H	2-4
WR	11 Jan	Middlesbrough	A	2-8
	18 Jan	Barnsley	H	1-5
	1 Mar	Rotherham U	A	2-1
	8 Mar	Bradford	H	2-2
	15 Mar	Rochdale	A	1-2
	22 Mar	Stockport Co	H	9-3
	29 Mar	Bradford	A	1-4
	5 Apr	Grimsby T	H	2-4
	14 Apr	Stockport Co	A	2-5
	26 Apr	Rochdale	H	3-3

KEY: LC=League Cup; La=Lancashire Cup; MC=Midland Cup; SC=Sheffield Cup; CB=Cheshire Bowl
WR/CC West Riding Cup/Combined Counties Cup; Li=Liverpool Senior Cup

The Football League 1940-41

NORTH REGIONAL LEGUE

BURNLEY

	Date	Opponent	H/A	Score
	31 Aug	Blackburn R	H	2-1
	7 Sep	Rochdale	A	2-1
	14 Sep	Bury	A	0-0
	21 Sep	Crewe Alex	H	5-1
	28 Sep	Preston NE	A	2-6
	5 Oct	Stockport Co	H	2-2
	12 Oct	Manchester Utd	H	0-1
	19 Oct	Oldham Ath	A	1-6
	26 Oct	Oldham Ath	H	2-1
	2 Nov	Manchester Utd	A	1-4
	9 Nov	Blackburn R	A	1-1
	16 Nov	Chester	H	0-0
	23 Nov	Rochdale	H	0-1
	30 Nov	Bury	H	4-3
	7 Dec	Stockport Co	A	0-1
	14 Dec	Chester	A	4-3
	21 Dec	Southport	A	3-1
	25 Dec	Manchester City	H	2-2
	28 Dec	Preston NE	H	2-0
La	25 Jan	Everton	H	2-3
	1 Feb	Blackburn R	H	2-1
	1 Mar	Oldham Ath	A	0-2
	8 Mar	Oldham Ath	H	4-0
	15 Mar	Blackburn R	A	2-3
	22 Mar	Halifax T	A	2-2
	29 Mar	Sheffield Wed	A	2-0
	5 Apr	Sheffield Wed	H	2-0
	12 Apr	Bolton W	H	2-2
	14 Apr	Bolton W	A	2-0
	19 Apr	Halifax T	H	3-1
	26 Apr	Huddersfield T	A	3-0
La	3 May	Everton	A	1-0
La	10 May	Blackpool	H	1-0
La	17 May	Manchester Utd	H	0-1
	24 May	Blackpool	A	0-3

3 May, aet 2-0

BURY

	Date	Opponent	H/A	Score
	31 Aug	Oldham Ath	H	4-4
	7 Sep	Manchester Utd	A	0-0
	14 Sep	Burnley	H	0-0
	21 Sep	Blackburn R	A	2-3
	28 Sep	Rochdale	H	7-3
	5 Oct	Oldham Ath	A	4-3
	12 Oct	Liverpool	H	0-3
	19 Oct	Stockport Co	A	1-1
	26 Oct	Everton	A	1-3
	2 Nov	Everton	H	2-1
	9 Nov	Stockport Co	H	5-2
	16 Nov	Liverpool	A	0-3
	23 Nov	Blackburn R	H	3-1
	30 Nov	Burnley	A	3-4
	7 Dec	Preston NE	H	0-0
	14 Dec	Preston NE	A	2-2
	21 Dec	Manchester Utd	H	4-1
	25 Dec	Halifax T	H	5-5
	28 Dec	Rochdale	A	3-0
La	4 Jan	Blackpool	A	2-3
La	11 Jan	Blackpool	H	1-2
	18 Jan	Blackburn R	H	3-1
	25 Jan	Blackburn R	A	1-3
	1 Mar	Liverpool	H	2-5
	8 Mar	Manchester Utd	A	3-7
	15 Mar	Bolton W	H	4-1
	22 Mar	Bolton W	A	1-5
	29 Mar	Liverpool	H	1-5
	5 Apr	Liverpool	A	0-2
	12 Apr	Blackburn R	A	0-4
	14 Apr	Leeds U	A	2-2
	19 Apr	Huddersfield T	H	3-7
	26 Apr	Oldham Ath	A	0-2
	3 May	Oldham Ath	H	2-3
	10 May	Manchester Utd	H	5-1
	17 May	Huddersfield T	A	0-2
	31 May	Manchester City	H	2-3
	7 Jun	Manchester City	A	2-3

CHESTER

	Date	Opponent	H/A	Score
	31 Aug	Stockport Co	H	5-3
	7 Sep	Crewe Alex	A	3-0
	14 Sep	Stockport Co	A	0-4
	21 Sep	Everton	A	3-4
	28 Sep	Liverpool	H	0-2
	5 Oct	Liverpool	A	1-9
	12 Oct	Tranmere R	H	4-5
	19 Oct	Everton	H	1-0
	26 Oct	Crewe Alex	H	3-3
	2 Nov	Tranmere R	H	4-2
	9 Nov	Crewe Alex	H	6-0
	16 Nov	Burnley	A	0-0
	23 Nov	New Brighton	A	2-4
	30 Nov	Oldham Ath	A	0-0
	7 Dec	New Brighton	H	6-2
	14 Dec	Burnley	H	3-4
	25 Dec	Wrexham	A	1-2
	25 Dec	Wrexham	A	1-3
La	4 Jan	Southport	H	6-1
La	11 Jan	Southport	A	3-2
La	1 Feb	New Brighton	H	7-1
La	8 Feb	New Brighton	A	0-2
	1 Mar	Blackpool	A	2-5
	8 Mar	Blackpool	H	4-3
	22 Mar	Wrexham	A	2-5
	5 Apr	New Brighton	H	7-3
	12 Apr	Wrexham	H	1-1
	14 Apr	Preston NE	A	0-3
La	19 Apr	Manchester Utd	H	4-4
	26 Apr	Stoke C	A	2-1
	3 May	Stoke C	H	1-0
	10 May	Bolton W	H	8-0
CB	17 May	Tranmere R	A	1-1
	24 May	Liverpool	H	1-6
	31 May	Blackpool	A	2-4

19Apr, aet 4-6
17 May, aet 4-1

CHESTERFIELD

	Date	Opponent	H/A	Score
	7 Sep	Barnsley	A	0-2
	14 Sep	Barnsley	H	5-1
	21 Sep	Lincoln C	H	2-0
	28 Sep	Sheffield Wed	A	5-0
	5 Oct	Sheffield Utd	A	0-1
	12 Oct	Newcastle U	A	0-3
	19 Oct	Sheffield Utd	H	2-0
	26 Oct	Middlesbrough	A	3-0
	2 Nov	Newcastle U	H	5-1
	9 Nov	Lincoln C	A	0-2
	16 Nov	Huddersfield T	A	2-2
	23 Nov	Sheffield Wed	H	2-2
	30 Nov	Grimsby T	A	5-4
	7 Dec	Grimsby T	H	0-3
	14 Dec	Leeds U	H	3-0
	21 Dec	Rotherham U	A	3-0
	25 Dec	York C	H	2-0
	28 Dec	Leeds U	A	2-1
WR	4 Jan	Leeds U	H	2-4
WR	11 Jan	Leeds U	A	3-2
	1 Mar	Manchester Utd	H	1-1
	8 Mar	Stockport Co	A	0-1
	15 Mar	Doncaster R	H	5-0
	22 Mar	Doncaster R	A	1-0
	29 Mar	Everton	A	1-0
	5 Apr	Halifax T	A	0-0
	12 Apr	Sheffield Wed	A	1-3
	14 Apr	Notts County	H	3-0
	19 Apr	Everton	H	4-1
	26 Apr	Sheffield Wed	H	1-0
	3 May	Barnsley	A	2-3
	10 May	Sheffield Utd	H	1-1
	17 May	Stoke C	A	2-2
	24 May	Stoke C	H	5-1
	7 Jun	Mansfield T	A	4-1

CREWE ALEXANDRA

	Date	Opponent	H/A	Score
	7 Sep	Chesterfield	H	0-3
	14 Sep	Rochdale	H	1-1
	21 Sep	Burnley	A	1-5
	28 Sep	Tranmere R	H	2-3
	5 Oct	Blackburn R	H	1-4
	12 Oct	New Brighton	A	2-6
	19 Oct	New Brighton	H	2-3
	26 Oct	Chester	A	3-3
	2 Nov	Southport	H	3-3
	9 Nov	Chester	A	0-6
	16 Nov	Wrexham	A	1-3
	23 Nov	Southport	A	0-1
	30 Nov	Blackburn R	A	1-4
	7 Dec	Wrexham	H	3-2
	14 Dec	Wrexham	A	1-5
	21 Dec	Rochdale	A	0-1
	25 Dec	Tranmere R	A	2-1
	28 Dec	Wrexham	H	3-4
	11 Jan	Preston NE	H	1-4
CB	18 Jan	Stockport Co	A	1-2
	25 Jan	Rochdale	A	0-5
	8 Mar	Rochdale	H	2-5
	12 Apr	New Brighton	A	0-5
	19 Apr	New Brighton	H	2-5

DONCASTER ROVERS

	Date	Opponent	H/A	Score
	31 Aug	Barnsley	H	2-1
	7 Sep	Sheffield Utd	A	1-1
	14 Sep	Bradford City	H	2-1
	21 Sep	Barnsley	A	2-6
	28 Sep	Sheffield Utd	H	1-0
	5 Oct	Bradford City	A	1-5
	12 Oct	Hull C	H	4-2
	19 Oct	Grimsby T	A	2-3
	26 Oct	Huddersfield T	H	1-1
	2 Nov	Manchester City	H	0-4
	9 Nov	Sheffield Wed	H	4-4
	16 Nov	Hull C	A	4-5
	23 Nov	Grimsby T	H	6-0
	30 Nov	Huddersfield T	A	2-1
	7 Dec	Middlesbrough	A	2-2
	14 Dec	York C	A	4-1
	21 Dec	York C	H	9-2
	25 Dec	Lincoln C	H	0-0
	25 Dec	Lincoln C	A	1-3
	28 Dec	Middlesbrough	H	5-0
SC	11 Jan	Sheffield Wed	A	4-0
SC	18 Jan	Sheffield Utd	H	5-1
	8 Feb	Rotherham U	H	3-2
	8 Mar	Rotherham U	A	2-1
	15 Mar	Chesterfield	A	0-5
	22 Mar	Chesterfield	H	0-0
SC	29 Mar	Rotherham U	H	3-2
	5 Apr	Leeds U	H	1-4
	12 Apr	Halifax T	A	1-8
	26 Apr	Halifax T	H	2-2
	3 May	Mansfield T	H	2-1
	17 May	Mansfield T	A	1-6

KEY: LC=League Cup; La=Lancashire Cup; MC=Midland Cup; SC=Sheffield Cup; CB=Cheshire Bowl
WR/CC West Riding Cup/Combined Counties Cup; Li=Liverpool Senior Cup

The Football League 1940-41

NORTH REGIONAL LEAGUE

EVERTON

	Date	Opponent	H/A	Score
	31 Aug	Manchester City	A	0-0
	7 Sep	Manchester City	H	1-0
	14 Sep	Preston NE	A	2-2
	21 Sep	Chester	H	4-3
	28 Sep	Leeds U	H	5-1
	5 Oct	Southport	A	1-0
	12 Oct	Stockport Co	H	4-2
	19 Oct	Chester	A	0-1
	26 Oct	Bury	H	3-1
	2 Nov	Bury	A	1-2
	9 Nov	Manchester Utd	H	5-2
	16 Nov	Manchester Utd	A	0-0
	23 Nov	Tranmere R	A	9-0
	30 Nov	New Brighton	H	2-1
	7 Dec	Southport	H	2-1
	14 Dec	Tranmere R	A	8-2
	21 Dec	Preston NE	H	0-3
	25 Dec	Liverpool	A	1-3
La	4 Jan	Liverpool	A	2-1
La	11 Jan	Liverpool	H	4-1
La	25 Jan	Burnley	A	3-2
	1 Feb	Barnsley	H	3-1
	8 Feb	Liverpool	A	3-1
	29 Mar	Chesterfield	H	0-1
Li	5 Apr	Southport	A	5-3
	12 Apr	Manchester Utd	H	1-2
	14 Apr	Blackpool	H	2-2
	19 Apr	Chesterfield	A	1-4
	26 Apr	New Brighton	A	4-0
La	3 May	Burnley	H	0-1
	17 May	Oldham Ath	A	1-1
	24 May	Sheffield Utd	H	3-3
	31 May	Liverpool	A	2-2
	2 Jun	Liverpool	H	3-1

3 May, aet 0-2

GRIMSBY TOWN

	Date	Opponent	H/A	Score
	31 Aug	Lincoln C	A	2-2
	7 Sep	Lincoln C	H	2-1
	14 Sep	Rotherham U	A	0-1
	21 Sep	Sheffield Utd	A	1-6
	28 Sep	Middlesbrough	H	1-3
	12 Oct	Sheffield Utd	H	3-1
	19 Oct	Doncaster R	H	3-2
	26 Oct	Rotherham U	A	2-3
	9 Nov	Bradford City	H	3-2
	16 Nov	Newcastle U	A	1-3
	23 Nov	Doncaster R	A	0-6
	30 Nov	Chesterfield	H	4-5
	7 Dec	Chesterfield	A	3-0
	14 Dec	Middlesbrough	A	1-2
	25 Dec	Hull C	H	1-1
	28 Dec	Newcastle U	A	2-5
	4 Jan	Sheffield Utd	H	3-2
	11 Jan	Newcastle U	A	4-0
	18 Jan	Sheffield Wed	H	2-1
	1 Feb	Bradford	H	0-3
	22 Mar	Hull C	A	8-2
	29 Mar	Hull C	H	0-1
	5 Apr	Bradford City	A	4-2
	12 Apr	York C	A	2-3
	19 Apr	Rotherham U	H	5-3
	26 Apr	York C	H	2-0
	10 May	Mansfield T	A	1-3

HALIFAX TOWN

	Date	Opponent	H/A	Score
	31 Aug	Hull C	A	2-4
	7 Sep	Sheffield Wed	H	1-1
	14 Sep	Bradford	A	0-0
	21 Sep	Bradford City	A	2-1
	28 Sep	Huddersfield T	H	1-1
	5 Oct	Bradford	H	2-3
	12 Oct	Bradford City	H	5-1
	19 Oct	Sheffield Wed	A	0-4
	26 Oct	York C	H	2-1
	2 Nov	Blackburn R	H	1-1
	9 Nov	Hull C	H	3-0
	16 Nov	Oldham Ath	A	2-1
	23 Nov	Oldham Ath	A	0-1
	30 Nov	York C	A	2-2
	14 Dec	Huddersfield T	A	1-1
	21 Dec	Leeds U	H	2-2
	25 Dec	Bury	A	5-5
WR	4 Jan	Huddersfield T	H	1-2
WR	11 Jan	Huddersfield T	A	2-1
WR	18 Jan	Huddersfield T	H	1-4
	8 Feb	Blackburn R	A	1-0
	8 Mar	Huddersfield T	H	4-0
	15 Mar	Bradford	H	2-2
	22 Mar	Burnley	H	2-2
	5 Apr	Chesterfield	H	0-0
	12 Apr	Doncaster R	H	8-1
	14 Apr	Blackburn R	H	3-3
	19 Apr	Burnley	A	1-3
	26 Apr	Doncaster R	A	2-2
	3 May	Middlesbrough	H	4-2

HUDDERSFIELD TOWN

	Date	Opponent	H/A	Score
	31 Aug	Sheffield Wed	A	0-1
	7 Sep	Bradford	H	1-1
	14 Sep	Leeds U	A	2-5
	21 Sep	Sheffield Wed	H	5-0
	28 Sep	Halifax T	A	1-1
	5 Oct	Leeds U	H	1-1
	12 Oct	Manchester City	A	1-3
	19 Oct	Barnsley	H	1-2
	26 Oct	Doncaster R	A	1-1
	2 Nov	Sheffield Utd	H	3-0
	9 Nov	Rotherham U	A	0-1
	16 Nov	Chesterfield	H	2-2
	23 Nov	Barnsley	A	1-4
	30 Nov	Doncaster R	H	1-2
	7 Dec	Sheffield Utd	A	3-1
	14 Dec	Halifax T	H	1-1
	21 Dec	Bradford	A	2-3
	25 Dec	Bradford City	A	5-0
	25 Dec	Bradford City	H	3-4
	28 Dec	Manchester City	H	2-0
WR	4 Jan	Halifax T	A	2-1
WR	11 Jan	Halifax T	H	1-2
WR	18 Jan	Halifax T	A	4-1
	8 Mar	Halifax T	A	0-4
	22 Mar	Rochdale	H	11-0
	29 Mar	Oldham Ath	A	1-3
	5 Apr	Oldham Ath	H	1-0
	12 Apr	Barnsley	A	3-4
	14 Apr	Rotherham U	A	1-3
	19 Apr	Bury	A	7-3
	26 Apr	Burnley	H	0-3
CC	10 May	Leeds U	A	0-1
	17 May	Bury	H	2-0

HULL CITY

	Date	Opponent	H/A	Score
	31 Aug	Halifax T	H	4-2
	7 Sep	Bradford City	A	5-4
	14 Sep	York C	A	1-4
	21 Sep	Bradford	H	2-1
	28 Sep	York C	H	1-3
	5 Oct	Rotherham U	H	0-2
	12 Oct	Doncaster R	A	2-4
	19 Oct	Newcastle U	A	2-1
	26 Oct	Bradford City	H	5-2
	2 Nov	Lincoln c	A	1-1
	9 Nov	Halifax T	A	0-3
	16 Nov	Doncaster R	H	5-4
	23 Nov	Leeds U	A	2-3
	30 Nov	Lincoln C	H	1-2
	7 Dec	Newcastle U	A	1-3
	14 Dec	Barnsley	H	1-2
	21 Dec	Barnsley	A	0-5
	25 Dec	Grimsby T	A	1-1
	18 Jan	Leeds U	H	4-1
	25 Jan	York C	A	3-3
	22 Mar	Grimsby T	H	2-8
	29 Mar	Grimsby T	A	1-0
	5 Apr	Middlesbrough	H	0-8

LEEDS UNITED

	Date	Opponent	H/A	Score
	31 Aug	Bradford City	H	2-2
	7 Sep	Newcastle U	A	0-1
	14 Sep	Huddersfield T	H	5-2
	21 Sep	Manchester City	H	0-0
	28 Sep	Everton	A	1-5
	5 Oct	Huddersfield T	A	1-1
	12 Oct	Rotherham U	A	0-0
	19 Oct	Bradford City	A	6-3
	2 Nov	Barnsley	A	0-3
	9 Nov	Middlesbrough	H	2-1
	16 Nov	Bradford City	H	6-0
	23 Nov	Hull C	H	3-2
	30 Nov	Newcastle U	H	3-2
	7 Dec	Barnsley	H	1-1
	14 Dec	Chesterfield	A	0-3
	21 Dec	Halifax T	A	2-2
	25 Dec	Bradford	H	2-1
	28 Dec	Chesterfield	H	1-2
WR	4 Jan	Chesterfield	A	4-2
WR	11 Jan	Chesterfield	H	2-3
	18 Jan	Hull C	A	1-4
	22 Mar	Sheffield Wed	H	3-2
	29 Mar	Rochdale	A	3-2
	5 Apr	Doncaster R	A	4-1
	12 Apr	Manchester City	A	1-1
	14 Apr	Bury	H	2-2
	26 Apr	Sheffield Utd	H	2-0
	3 May	Newcastle U	A	2-3
CC	10 May	Huddersfield T	H	1-0
CC	17 May	Middlesbrough	A	2-3

KEY: LC=League Cup; La=Lancashire Cup; MC=Midland Cup; SC=Sheffield Cup; CB=Cheshire Bowl
WR/CC West Riding Cup/Combined Counties Cup; Li=Liverpool Senior Cup

The Football League 1940-41

NORTH REGIONAL LEAGUE

LINCOLN CITY

	Date	Opponent	H/A	Score
	31 Aug	Grimsby T	H	2-2
	7 Sep	Grimsby T	A	1-2
	14 Sep	Sheffield Utd	H	9-2
	21 Sep	Chesterfield	A	0-2
	28 Sep	Rotherham U	H	2-2
	5 Oct	York C	A	2-1
	12 Oct	York C	H	4-2
	26 Oct	Sheffield Utd	A	3-3
	2 Nov	Hull C	H	1-1
	9 Nov	Chesterfield	H	2-0
	16 Nov	Barnsley	H	2-3
	23 Nov	Rotherham U	A	3-0
	30 Nov	Hull C	A	2-1
	25 Dec	Doncaster R	A	0-0
	25 Dec	Doncaster R	H	3-1
	28 Dec	Barnsley	A	0-6
MC	11 Jan	Nottingham F	A	2-4
MC	18 Jan	Nottingham F	H	2-1
MC	1 Feb	Mansfield T	H	4-2
MC	8 Feb	Leicester C	A	1-4
	1 Mar	Bradford	A	0-4
	8 Mar	Sheffield Wed	H	4-1
	29 Mar	Mansfield T	H	3-1
	5 Apr	Mansfield T	A	1-1
MC	12 Apr	Leicester C	H	5-4
	14 Apr	Leicester C	A	1-1
	19 Apr	Bradford	H	6-2

LIVERPOOL

	Date	Opponent	H/A	Score
	31 Aug	Preston NE	H	3-3
	7 Sep	Blackburn R	A	3-0
	14 Sep	Blackburn R	H	1-1
	21 Sep	Preston NE	A	0-5
	28 Sep	Chester	A	2-0
	5 Oct	Chester	H	9-1
	12 Oct	Bury	H	3-0
	19 Oct	Manchester City	H	0-4
	26 Oct	Stockport Co	A	0-2
	2 Nov	Stockport Co	H	5-0
	9 Nov	Manchester City	A	1-5
	16 Nov	Bury	H	3-0
	23 Nov	Manchester Utd	H	2-2
	30 Nov	Manchester Utd	A	0-2
	7 Dec	Tranmere R	A	1-3
	14 Dec	New Brighton	H	6-4
	25 Dec	Everton	A	3-1
	28 Dec	Tranmere R	H	2-3
La	4 Jan	Everton	H	1-2
La	11 Jan	Everton	A	1-3
	18 Jan	Oldham Ath	A	3-0
	8 Feb	Everton	H	1-3
	1 Mar	Bury	A	5-2
	8 Mar	Wrexham	H	7-2
	15 Mar	Blackpool	A	4-6
	22 Mar	Blackpool	H	2-6
	29 Mar	Bury	A	5-1
	5 Apr	Bury	H	2-0
	12 Apr	Blackpool	A	0-0
	14 Apr	Southport	A	0-2
	26 Apr	Manchester Utd	H	2-1
	3 May	Manchester Utd	A	1-1
	17 May	Wrexham	A	3-4
	24 May	Chester	A	6-1
	31 May	Everton	H	2-2
	2 Jun	Everton	A	1-3
	7 Jun	Preston NE	A	1-6

MANCHESTER CITY

	Date	Opponent	H/A	Score
	31 Aug	Everton	H	0-0
	7 Sep	Everton	A	0-1
	14 Sep	New Brighton	H	5-2
	21 Sep	Leeds U	A	0-0
	28 Sep	Manchester Utd	H	4-1
	5 Oct	Manchester Utd	A	2-0
	12 Oct	Huddersfield T	H	3-1
	19 Oct	Liverpool	A	4-0
	26 Oct	Blackburn R	H	1-1
	2 Nov	Doncaster R	A	4-0
	9 Nov	Liverpool	H	5-1
	16 Nov	Blackburn R	A	2-2
	23 Nov	Preston NE	H	1-2
	30 Nov	Preston NE	A	4-4
	7 Dec	Oldham Ath	A	0-1
	14 Dec	Stockport Co	A	9-1
	21 Dec	Stockport Co	H	7-2
	25 Dec	Burnley	A	2-2
	28 Dec	Huddersfield T	A	0-2
La	4 Jan	Rochdale	H	9-1
La	11 Jan	Rochdale	A	6-1
La	18 Jan	Blackpool	H	2-4
La	25 Jan	Blackpool	A	1-2
	1 Feb	Oldham Ath	H	5-4
	8 Feb	Oldham Ath	A	5-2
	12 Apr	Leeds U	A	1-1
	14 Apr	Manchester Utd	H	1-7
	19 Apr	Wrexham	H	5-0
	26 Apr	Blackpool	H	2-0
	3 May	Blackpool	A	1-1
	10 May	Wrexham	A	0-0
	17 May	Bolton W	A	1-1
	24 May	Bolton W	H	6-4
	31 May	Bury	A	3-2
	7 Jun	Bury	H	3-2

MANCHESTER UNITED

	Date	Opponent	H/A	Score
	31 Aug	Rochdale	A	3-1
	7 Sep	Bury	H	0-0
	14 Sep	Oldham Ath	A	1-2
	21 Sep	Oldham Ath	H	2-3
	28 Sep	Manchester City	A	1-4
	5 Oct	Manchester City	H	0-2
	12 Oct	Burnley	A	1-0
	19 Oct	Preston NE	H	4-1
	26 Oct	Preston NE	A	1-3
	2 Nov	Burnley	H	4-1
	9 Nov	Everton	A	2-5
	16 Nov	Everton	H	0-0
	23 Nov	Liverpool	A	2-2
	30 Nov	Liverpool	H	2-0
	7 Dec	Blackburn R	A	5-5
	14 Dec	Rochdale	H	3-4
	21 Dec	Bury	A	1-4
	25 Dec	Stockport Co	A	3-1
	28 Dec	Blackburn R	H	9-0
La	4 Jan	Blackburn R	A	2-0
La	11 Jan	Blackburn R	H	0-0
La	18 Jan	Bolton W	A	2-3
La	25 Jan	Bolton W	H	4-1
	1 Mar	Chesterfield	A	1-1
	8 Mar	Bury	H	7-3
	22 Mar	Oldham Ath	A	1-0
	29 Mar	Blackpool	A	0-2
	5 Apr	Blackpool	H	2-3
	12 Apr	Everton	A	2-1
	14 Apr	Manchester City	A	7-1
La	19 Apr	Chester	A	4-4
	26 Apr	Liverpool	A	1-2
	3 May	Liverpool	H	1-1
	10 May	Bury	A	1-5
La	17 May	Burnley	A	1-0

19 Apr, aet, 90 mins 6-4

MIDDLESBROUGH

	Date	Opponent	H/A	Score
	31 Aug	York C	A	3-4
	7 Sep	York C	H	2-1
	14 Sep	Newcastle U	A	0-3
	21 Sep	Newcastle U	H	3-2
	28 Sep	Grimsby T	A	3-1
	5 Oct	Sheffield Wed	H	5-4
	12 Oct	Bradford	A	2-0
	19 Oct	Bradford	H	6-2
	26 Oct	Chesterfield	H	0-3
	2 Nov	Sheffield Wed	A	3-6
	9 Nov	Leeds U	A	1-2
	16 Nov	York C	H	6-4
	23 Nov	Bradford City	A	2-3
	7 Dec	Doncaster R	H	2-2
	14 Dec	Grimsby T	H	2-1
	25 Dec	Newcastle U	A	3-1
	28 Dec	Doncaster R	A	0-5
WR	11 Jan	Bradford City	H	8-2
CC	18 Jan	Bradford	H	5-3
	1 Feb	Newcastle U	A	2-6
	8 Feb	Newcastle U	H	4-3
	5 Apr	Hull C	A	8-0
	19 Apr	Barnsley	A	2-3
	26 Apr	Barnsley	H	3-2
	3 May	Halifax T	A	2-4
CC	17 May	Leeds U	H	3-2
	24 May	York C	A	4-2

NEW BRIGHTON

	Date	Opponent	H/A	Score
	31 Aug	Tranmere R	H	4-4
	7 Sep	Tranmere R	A	1-5
	14 Sep	Manchester City	A	2-5
	21 Sep	Wrexham	A	0-5
	28 Sep	Southport	H	5-3
	12 Oct	Crewe Alex	H	6-2
	19 Oct	Crewe Alex	A	3-2
	26 Oct	Wrexham	H	6-2
	2 Nov	Wrexham	A	2-4
	9 Nov	Southport	A	5-2
	16 Nov	Tranmere R	H	10-1
	23 Nov	Chester	H	4-2
	30 Nov	Everton	A	1-2
	7 Dec	Chester	A	2-6
	14 Dec	Liverpool	A	4-6
	25 Dec	Southport	A	4-2
La	4 Jan	Wrexham	A	5-3
La	11 Jan	Wrexham	H	6-1
	1 Feb	Chester	A	1-7
	8 Feb	Chester	H	2-0
	22 Mar	Southport	A	6-2
	29 Mar	Tranmere R	A	5-3
	5 Apr	Chester	A	3-7
	12 Apr	Crewe Alex	H	5-0
	19 Apr	Crewe Alex	A	5-2
	26 Apr	Everton	H	0-4

KEY: LC=League Cup; La=Lancashire Cup; MC=Midland Cup; SC=Sheffield Cup; CB=Cheshire Bowl
WR/CC West Riding Cup/Combined Counties Cup; Li=Liverpool Senior Cup

The Football League 1940-41

NORTH REGIONAL LEAGUE

NEWCASTLE UNITED

31 Aug	Bradford	H	0-2
7 Sep	Leeds U	H	1-0
14 Sep	Middlesbrough	H	3-0
21 Sep	Middlesbrough	A	2-3
28 Sep	Barnsley	H	1-0
5 Oct	Barnsley	A	0-1
12 Oct	Chesterfield	H	3-0
19 Oct	Hull C	A	1-2
26 Oct	Bradford	A	1-0
2 Nov	Chesterfield	A	1-5
9 Nov	York C	H	3-0
16 Nov	Grimsby T	H	3-1
23 Nov	York C	A	0-3
30 Nov	Leeds U	A	2-3
7 Dec	Hull C	H	3-1
25 Dec	Middlesbrough	H	1-3
28 Dec	Grimsby T	H	5-2
11 Jan	Grimsby T	A	0-4
25 Jan	Sheffield Wed	H	7-1
1 Feb	Middlesbrough	H	6-2
8 Feb	Middlesbrough	A	3-4
15 Mar	Sheffield Wed	A	0-2
10 May	Leeds U	H	3-2

OLDHAM ATHLETIC

	31 Aug	Bury	A	4-4
	7 Sep	Stockport Co	H	4-1
	14 Sep	Manchester Utd	A	2-1
	21 Sep	Manchester Utd	A	3-2
	28 Sep	Stockport County	A	5-1
	5 Oct	Bury	H	3-4
	12 Oct	Preston NE	A	0-3
	19 Oct	Burnley	H	6-1
	26 Oct	Burnley	A	1-2
	2 Nov	Preston North End	H	2-6
	9 Nov	Bradford	H	4-4
	16 Nov	Halifax T	H	1-2
	23 Nov	Halifax T	A	1-0
	30 Nov	Chester	H	0-0
	7 Dec	Manchester City	H	1-0
	14 Dec	Blackburn R	H	1-0
	21 Dec	Blackburn R	A	2-3
	25 Dec	Rochdale	A	3-2
La	4 Jan	Bolton W	A	1-2
La	11 Jan	Bolton W	H	3-2
	18 Jan	Liverpool	H	0-3
	1 Feb	Manchester City	A	4-5
	8 Feb	Manchester City	H	2-5
	1 Mar	Burnley	H	2-0
	8 Mar	Burnley	A	0-4
	22 Mar	Manchester Utd	H	0-1
	29 Mar	Huddersfield T	H	3-1
	5 Apr	Huddersfield T	A	0-1
	12 Apr	Preston NE	A	0-4
	14 Apr	Rochdale	A	4-0
	19 Apr	Blackpool	A	2-6
	26 Apr	Bury	H	2-0
	3 May	Bury	A	3-2
	10 May	Rochdale	H	5-0
	17 May	Everton	H	1-1
	31 May	Bolton W	A	1-3
	7 Jun	Bolton W	H	3-1

11 Jan, aet, 3-5

PRESTON NORTH END

31 Aug	Liverpool	A	3-3
7 Sep	Southport	H	1-0
14 Sep	Everton	H	2-2
21 Sep	Liverpool	H	5-0
28 Sep	Burnley	H	6-2
5 Oct	Rochdale	A	1-2
12 Oct	Oldham Ath	H	3-0
19 Oct	Manchester Utd	A	1-4
26 Oct	Manchester Utd	H	3-1
2 Nov	Oldham Ath	A	6-2
9 Nov	Rochdale	H	5-0
16 Nov	Southport	A	3-1
23 Nov	Manchester City	A	2-1
30 Nov	Manchester City	H	4-4
7 Dec	Bury	A	0-0
14 Dec	Bury	H	2-2
21 Dec	Everton	A	3-0
25 Dec	Blackburn R	A	0-0
28 Dec	Burnley	A	0-2
4 Jan	Stockport Co	A	2-2
11 Jan	Crewe Alex	A	4-1
1 Feb	Tranmere R	A	3-2
8 Feb	Sheffield Utd	H	4-1
12 Apr	Oldham Ath	H	4-0
14 Apr	Chester	H	3-0
3 May	Blackburn R	H	1-0
17 May	Blackpool	H	2-0
2 Jun	Blackpool	A	2-4
7 Jun	Liverpool	H	6-1

ROCHDALE

	31 Aug	Manchester Utd	H	1-3
	7 Sep	Burnley	H	1-2
	14 Sep	Crewe Alex	A	1-1
	21 Sep	Stockport Co	A	0-4
	28 Sep	Bury	A	3-7
	5 Oct	Preston NE	H	2-1
	12 Oct	Blackburn R	H	1-1
	19 Oct	Blackburn R	A	0-2
	26 Oct	Southport	A	3-2
	2 Nov	Bradford	H	1-1
	9 Nov	Preston NE	A	0-5
	16 Nov	Stockport Co	H	5-3
	23 Nov	Burnley	A	1-0
	30 Nov	Southport	H	10-0
	7 Dec	Bradford	A	4-2
	14 Dec	Manchester Utd	A	4-3
	21 Dec	Crewe Alex	H	1-0
	25 Dec	Oldham Ath	A	2-3
	28 Dec	Bury	H	0-3
La	4 Jan	Manchester City	A	1-9
La	11 Jan	Manchester City	H	1-6
	25 Jan	Crewe Alex	H	5-1
	8 Mar	Crewe Alex	A	5-2
	15 Mar	Bradford City	H	2-1
	22 Mar	Huddersfield T	A	0-11
	29 Mar	Leeds U	H	2-3
	5 Apr	Stockport Co	A	1-1
	12 Apr	Stockport Co	H	3-1
	14 Apr	Oldham Ath	A	0-4
	19 Apr	Bolton W	H	1-3
	26 Apr	Bradford City	A	3-3
	10 May	Oldham Ath	A	0-5

ROTHERHAM UNITED

	31 Aug	Sheffield Utd	H	3-3
	14 Sep	Grimsby T	H	1-0
	21 Sep	York C	H	3-0
	28 Sep	Lincoln C	A	2-2
	5 Oct	Hull C	A	2-0
	12 Oct	Leeds U	H	0-0
	19 Oct	York C	A	1-3
	26 Oct	Grimsby T	H	3-2
	9 Nov	Huddersfield T	H	1-0
	16 Nov	Sheffield Wed	A	1-1
	23 Nov	Lincoln C	H	0-3
	30 Nov	Bradford City	A	4-2
	7 Dec	Sheffield Wed	H	1-0
	21 Dec	Chesterfield	H	0-3
	25 Dec	Barnsley	H	0-3
	25 Dec	Barnsley	A	3-3
	28 Dec	Sheffield Utd	H	2-0
	4 Jan	Sheffield Wed	A	2-4
SC	11 Jan	Barnsley	H	4-3
	8 Feb	Doncaster R	A	2-3
	1 Mar	Bradford City	H	1-2
	8 Mar	Doncaster R	H	1-2
	29 Mar	Doncaster R	A	2-3
	5 Apr	Barnsley	A	1-5
	12 Apr	Mansfield T	A	1-0
	14 Apr	Huddersfield T	H	3-1
	19 Apr	Grimsby T	A	3-5
	26 Apr	Bradford	H	2-0
	3 May	Bradford	A	1-5

SHEFFIELD UNITED

	31 Aug	Rotherham U	A	3-3
	7 Sep	Doncaster R	H	1-1
	14 Sep	Lincoln C	A	2-9
	21 Sep	Grimsby T	H	6-1
	28 Sep	Doncaster R	A	0-1
	5 Oct	Chesterfield	H	1-0
	12 Oct	Grimsby T	A	1-3
	19 Oct	Chesterfield	A	0-2
	26 Oct	Lincoln C	H	3-3
	2 Nov	Huddersfield T	A	0-3
	9 Nov	Barnsley	H	3-1
	16 Nov	Bradford	A	2-1
	23 Nov	Bradford	H	3-4
	30 Nov	Barnsley	A	4-1
	7 Dec	Huddersfield T	H	1-3
	25 Dec	Sheffield Wed	H	0-0
	28 Dec	Rotherham U	A	0-2
	4 Jan	Grimsby T	A	2-3
	11 Jan	Stockport Co	A	5-1
SC	18 Jan	Doncaster R	A	1-5
	8 Feb	Preston NE	A	1-4
	14 Apr	Sheffield Wed	A	1-3
	26 Apr	Leeds U	A	0-2
	10 May	Chesterfield	A	1-1
	24 May	Everton	A	3-3

KEY: LC=League Cup; La=Lancashire Cup; MC=Midland Cup; SC=Sheffield Cup; CB=Cheshire Bowl
WR/CC West Riding Cup/Combined Counties Cup; Li=Liverpool Senior Cup

The Football League 1940-41

NORTH REGIONAL LEAGUE

SHEFFIELD WEDNESDAY

	Date	Opponent	H/A	Score
	31 Aug	Huddersfield T	H	1-0
	7 Sep	Halifax T	A	1-1
	21 Sep	Huddersfield T	A	0-5
	28 Sep	Chesterfield	H	0-5
	5 Oct	Middlesbrough	A	4-5
	12 Oct	Barnsley	H	2-2
	19 Oct	Halifax T	H	4-0
	26 Oct	Barnsley	A	0-5
	2 Nov	Middlesbrough	H	6-3
	9 Nov	Doncaster R	A	4-4
	16 Nov	Rotherham U	H	1-1
	23 Nov	Chesterfield	A	0-2
	30 Nov	Bradford	H	4-3
	7 Dec	Rotherham U	A	0-1
	25 Dec	Sheffield Utd	A	0-0
	28 Dec	Bradford City	A	4-2
	4 Jan	Rotherham U	H	4-2
SC	11 Jan	Doncaster R	A	0-4
	18 Jan	Grimsby T	A	1-2
	25 Jan	Newcastle U	A	1-7
	1 Mar	Barnsley	A	1-7
	8 Mar	Lincoln C	A	1-4
	15 Mar	Newcastle U	H	2-0
	22 Mar	Leeds U	A	2-3
	29 Mar	Burnley	H	0-2
	5 Apr	Burnley	A	0-2
	12 Apr	Chesterfield	H	3-1
	14 Apr	Sheffield Utd	H	3-1
	19 Apr	Nottingham F	H	1-1
	26 Apr	Chesterfield	A	0-1

SOUTHPORT

	Date	Opponent	H/A	Score
	31 Aug	Wrexham	A	1-3
	7 Sep	Preston NE	A	0-1
	14 Sep	Tranmere R	H	4-1
	21 Sep	Tranmere R	A	3-7
	28 Sep	New Brighton	A	3-5
	5 Oct	Everton	H	0-1
	12 Oct	Wrexham	H	6-2
	19 Oct	Tranmere R	A	0-2
	26 Oct	Rochdale	H	2-3
	2 Nov	Crewe Alex	A	3-3
	9 Nov	New Brighton	H	2-5
	16 Nov	Preston NE	H	1-3
	23 Nov	Crewe Alex	H	1-0
	30 Nov	Rochdale	A	0-10
	7 Dec	Everton	A	1-2
	21 Dec	Burnley	H	1-3
	25 Dec	New Brighton	H	2-4
	28 Dec	Stockport Co	H	8-0
La	4 Jan	Chester	A	1-6
La	11 Jan	Chester	H	2-3
	25 Jan	Stockport Co	A	1-4
	22 Mar	New Brighton	H	2-6
	29 Mar	Bolton W	H	2-1
Li	5 Apr	Everton	H	3-5
	12 Apr	Tranmere R	A	0-3
	14 Apr	Liverpool	H	2-0
	19 Apr	Tranmere R	H	8-1
	26 Apr	Tranmere R	A	2-2

STOCKPORT COUNTY

	Date	Opponent	H/A	Score
	31 Aug	Chester	A	3-5
	7 Sep	Oldham Ath	A	1-4
	14 Sep	Chester	H	4-0
	21 Sep	Rochdale	H	4-0
	28 Sep	Oldham Ath	H	1-5
	5 Oct	Burnley	A	2-2
	12 Oct	Everton	A	2-4
	19 Oct	Bury	H	1-1
	26 Oct	Liverpool	H	2-0
	2 Nov	Liverpool	A	0-5
	9 Nov	Bury	A	2-5
	16 Nov	Rochdale	A	3-5
	23 Nov	Wrexham	H	2-1
	30 Nov	Wrexham	A	2-2
	7 Dec	Burnley	H	1-0
	14 Dec	Manchester City	H	1-9
	21 Dec	Manchester City	A	2-7
	25 Dec	Manchester Utd	H	1-3
	28 Dec	Southport	A	0-8
	4 Jan	Preston NE	H	2-2
	11 Jan	Sheffield Utd	H	1-5
	18 Jan	Crewe Alex	H	2-1
	25 Jan	Southport	H	4-1
	8 Mar	Chesterfield	H	1-0
	22 Mar	Bradford City	A	3-9
	5 Apr	Rochdale	H	1-1
	12 Apr	Rochdale	A	1-3
	14 Apr	Bradford City	H	5-2
	26 Apr	Wrexham	A	0-3

TRANMERE ROVERS

	Date	Opponent	H/A	Score
	31 Aug	New Brighton	A	4-4
	7 Sep	New Brighton	H	5-1
	14 Sep	Southport	A	1-4
	21 Sep	Southport	H	7-3
	28 Sep	Crewe Alex	A	3-2
	5 Oct	Wrexham	A	3-3
	12 Oct	Chester	A	5-4
	19 Oct	Southport	H	2-0
	2 Nov	Chester	H	2-4
	9 Nov	Wrexham	H	2-3
	16 Nov	New Brighton	A	1-10
	23 Nov	Everton	H	0-9
	7 Dec	Liverpool	H	3-1
	14 Dec	Everton	H	2-8
	21 Dec	Wrexham	A	1-5
	25 Dec	Crewe Alex	H	1-2
	28 Dec	Liverpool	A	3-2
	1 Feb	Preston NE	H	2-3
	29 Mar	New Brighton	H	3-5
	5 Apr	Bradford City	H	6-4
	12 Apr	Southport	H	3-0
	19 Apr	Southport	A	1-8
	26 Apr	Southport	H	2-2
CB	17 May	Chester	H	1-1

17 May, aet, 1-4

WREXHAM

	Date	Opponent	H/A	Score
	31 Aug	Southport	H	3-1
	21 Sep	New Brighton	H	5-0
	28 Sep	Blackburn R	H	2-1
	5 Oct	Tranmere R	H	3-3
	12 Oct	Southport	A	2-6
	26 Oct	New Brighton	A	2-6
	2 Nov	New Brighton	H	4-2
	9 Nov	Tranmere R	A	3-2
	16 Nov	Crewe Alex	H	3-1
	23 Nov	Stockport Co	A	1-2
	30 Nov	Stockport Co	H	2-2
	7 Dec	Crewe Alex	A	2-3
	14 Dec	Crewe Alex	H	5-1
	21 Dec	Tranmere R	H	5-1
	25 Dec	Chester	H	2-1
	25 Dec	Chester	A	3-1
	28 Dec	Crewe Alex	A	4-3
La	4 Jan	New Brighton	H	3-5
La	11 Jan	New Brighton	A	1-6
	8 Mar	Liverpool	A	2-7
	22 Mar	Chester	H	5-2
	29 Mar	Blackburn R	A	2-3
	5 Apr	Blackburn R	H	3-0
	12 Apr	Chester	A	1-1
	19 Apr	Manchester City	A	0-5
	26 Apr	Stockport Co	H	3-0
	10 May	Manchester City	H	0-0
	17 May	Liverpool	H	4-3
	3 Jun	Stoke C	H	3-3

YORK CITY

	Date	Opponent	H/A	Score
	31 Aug	Middlesbrough	H	4-3
	7 Sep	Middlesbrough	A	1-2
	14 Sep	Hull C	H	4-1
	21 Sep	Rotherham U	A	0-3
	28 Sep	Hull C	A	3-1
	5 Oct	Lincoln C	H	1-2
	12 Oct	Lincoln C	A	2-4
	19 Oct	Rotherham U	H	3-1
	26 Oct	Halifax T	A	1-2
	2 Nov	Bradford City	A	2-8
	9 Nov	Newcastle U	A	0-3
	16 Nov	Middlesbrough	A	4-6
	23 Nov	Newcastle U	H	3-0
	30 Nov	Halifax T	H	2-2
	7 Dec	Bradford City	H	5-2
	14 Dec	Doncaster R	A	1-4
	21 Dec	Doncaster R	A	2-9
	25 Dec	Chesterfield	A	0-2
	28 Dec	Bradford	H	0-0
WR	11 Jan	Bradford	A	2-4
	25 Jan	Hull C	H	3-3
	12 Apr	Grimsby T	H	3-2
	14 Apr	Barnsley	A	1-1
	26 Apr	Grimsby T	A	0-2
	24 May	Middlesbrough	H	2-4

KEY: LC=League Cup; La=Lancashire Cup; MC=Midland Cup; SC=Sheffield Cup; CB=Cheshire Bowl
WR/CC West Riding Cup/Combined Counties Cup; Li=Liverpool Senior Cup

The Football League 1940-41

NORTH REGIONAL LEAGUE

Final Table

		P	W	D	L	F	A	G Ave
1	Preston North End	29	18	7	4	81	37	2.189
2	Chesterfield	35	20	6	9	77	40	1.925
3	Manchester City	35	18	10	7	104	55	1.891
4	Barnsley	30	18	4	8	86	49	1.755
5	Everton	34	19	7	8	85	50	1.700
6	Blackpool	20	13	3	4	56	34	1.647
7	Manchester United	35	14	8	13	80	65	1.231
8	Lincoln City	27	13	7	7	65	53	1.226
9	Halifax Town	30	10	13	7	62	51	1.216
10	Newcastle United	23	12	0	11	49	41	1.195
11	Huddersfield Town	33	11	6	16	69	58	1.190
12	Middlesbrough	27	16	1	10	84	71	1.183
13	New Brighton	26	15	1	10	97	82	1.183
14	Burnley	35	17	7	11	61	53	1.151
15	Leeds United	30	13	8	9	62	54	1.148
16	Liverpool	37	15	6	16	91	81	1.123
17	Wrexham	29	15	5	9	78	71	1.099
18	Chester	35	14	6	15	94	89	1.056
19	Doncaster Rovers	32	15	7	10	77	74	1.041
20	Oldham Athletic	37	17	4	16	79	77	1.026
21	Grimsby Town	27	12	2	13	60	63	0.952
22	Bradford	31	9	7	15	64	74	0.865
23	Rotherham United	29	12	5	12	48	57	0.842
24	Blackburn Rovers	32	9	10	13	49	60	0.817
25	Bury	38	10	8	20	80	100	0.800
26	Bolton Wanderers	16	6	2	8	31	41	0.756
27	Sheffield United	25	6	6	13	44	60	0.733
28	Bradford City	29	8	3	18	72	99	0.727
29	Tranmere Rovers	24	9	4	11	63	88	0.716
30	Southport	28	7	2	19	61	86	0.709
31	York City	25	7	4	14	49	71	0.690
32	Rochdale	32	12	5	15	64	93	0.688
33	Sheffield Wednesday	30	9	6	15	50	76	0.658
34	Hull City	23	8	3	12	44	67	0.657
35	Stockport County	29	9	5	15	54	93	0.581
36	Crewe Alexandra	24	2	3	19	32	84	0.381

Standings calculated on goal average

The Football League 1940-41

SOUTH REGIONAL LEAGUE

ALDERSHOT

31 Aug	Bournemouth	A	4-3
7 Sep	Southampton	H	4-1
14 Sep	Watford	A	1-3
21 Sep	Watford	H	2-1
28 Sep	Portsmouth	H	2-3
5 Oct	Southampton	A	3-2
12 Oct	Bristol City	H	5-1
19 Oct	Portsmouth	A	3-1
26 Oct	Bristol City	A	0-6
2 Nov	Brighton & HA	H	5-1
9 Nov	Chelsea	H	5-3
23 Nov	Bournemouth	H	5-2
30 Nov	Brighton & HA	A	1-1
7 Dec	Norwich C	H	5-4
14 Dec	Norwich C	A	1-10
25 Dec	Reading	A	5-4
28 Dec	Chelsea	A	0-6
29 Mar	Millwall	H	0-3
26 Apr	Tottenham H	H	2-3
3 May	Fulham	H	3-3
10 May	QPR	H	5-1
24 May	Crystal Palace	H	0-3
31 May	Portsmouth	H	9-2
7 Jun	Watford	H	3-1

ARSENAL

31 Aug	Southend U	A	7-1
7 Sep	Fulham	H	5-0
14 Sep	Fulham	A	1-0
21 Sep	Brentford	H	3-1
28 Sep	QPR	A	2-3
5 Oct	Southend U	H	7-0
12 Oct	Tottenham H	A	3-2
19 Oct	Northampton T	H	5-4
26 Oct	Brentford	A	3-3
2 Nov	Charlton Athletic	A	2-2
16 Nov	Tottenham H	H	1-1
23 Nov	Northampton T	A	8-1
30 Nov	Crystal Palace	H	2-2
7 Dec	Charlton Athletic	A	0-5
14 Dec	QPR	H	3-2
21 Dec	Crystal Palace	A	3-3
25 Dec	West Ham U	A	2-4
28 Dec	Luton T	A	8-1
14 Apr	Chelsea	A	1-3

12 Oct, abandoned after 47 mins due to an air raid warning, result stood.

BIRMINGHAM

31 Aug	Nottingham Forest	A	3-2
7 Sep	Nottingham Forest	H	2-1
14 Sep	Cardiff C	A	2-5
21 Sep	Cardiff C	H	3-2
28 Sep	WBA	A	2-1
5 Oct	WBA	H	1-3
12 Oct	Mansfield T	A	1-4
19 Oct	Mansfield T	H	4-1
26 Oct	Leicester C	A	1-2
2 Nov	Leicester C	H	1-2
9 Nov	Stoke C	A	0-5
16 Nov	Stoke C	H	6-2
30 Nov	Notts County	A	3-3
7 Dec	Northampton T	A	1-2
25 Dec	Walsall	A	3-6
1 Mar	Luton T	A	5-2

BOURNEMOUTH & BOSCOMBE ATHLETIC

	31 Aug	Aldershot	H	3-4
	7 Sep	Bristol City	H	5-2
	12 Oct	Reading	H	1-1
	19 Oct	Reading	A	1-5
	2 Nov	Crystal Palace	H	3-2
	9 Nov	Portsmouth	A	2-4
	16 Nov	Portsmouth	H	4-3
	23 Nov	Aldershot	A	2-5
	30 Nov	Southampton	H	1-1
	7 Dec	Crystal Palace	A	0-6
	14 Dec	Bristol City	A	0-3
	21 Dec	Cardiff C	H	2-5
	25 Dec	Bristol City	H	7-1
	28 Dec	Cardiff C	A	1-5
LS	11 Jan	Southampton	H	5-3
LS	18 Jan	Watford	H	2-5
LS	25 Jan	Portsmouth	A	2-10
LS	1 Feb	Brighton & HA	A	1-2
LS	8 Feb	Southend U	H	3-0
LS	1 Mar	Southampton	H	3-3
LS	15 Mar	Brighton & HA	H	1-3
LS	22 Mar	Portsmouth	H	3-0
LS	29 Mar	Watford	A	0-5
HC	5 Apr	Southampton	H	1-1
LS	12 Apr	Southampton	H	4-2
LS	26 Apr	Luton T	H	2-1
HC	3 May	Southampton	H	2-3
LS	10 May	Portsmouth	A	0-5

BRENTFORD

31 Aug	Clapton Orient	H	2-2
7 Sep	Chelsea	A	1-2
14 Sep	Charlton Ath	H	1-1
21 Sep	Arsenal	A	1-3
5 Oct	Clapton Orient	A	0-1
12 Oct	Charlton Ath	A	4-1
19 Oct	Fulham	H	8-3
26 Oct	Arsenal	H	3-3
2 Nov	Portsmouth	H	3-1
16 Nov	West Ham U	H	0-2
23 Nov	Fulham	A	0-3
7 Dec	Reading	H	2-3
14 Dec	Millwall	A	0-3
21 Dec	Portsmouth	A	3-2
25 Dec	QPR	H	2-1
28 Dec	Millwall	H	3-2
15 Mar	Crystal Palace	H	2-3
22 Mar	Crystal Palace	A	0-5
19 Apr	Millwall	H	5-2
3 May	West Ham U	A	2-3
10 May	Fulham	H	2-3
17 May	Reading	A	4-1
24 May	Reading	H	3-1

BRIGHTON & HOVE ALBION

	31 Aug	Southampton	A	1-3
	7 Sep	Crystal Palace	A	2-5
	21 Sep	Southampton	H	0-0
	5 Oct	Portsmouth	A	1-5
	12 Oct	Southampton	H	0-0
	2 Nov	Aldershot	A	1-5
	23 Nov	Watford	H	1-1
	30 Nov	Aldershot	H	1-1
	7 Dec	Watford	A	0-4
	14 Dec	Charlton Ath	H	1-1
	25 Dec	Norwich C	A	0-18
	28 Dec	Crystal Palace	H	1-5
LS	25 Jan	Southend U	A	0-2
LS	1 Feb	Bournemouth	H	2-1
LS	8 Feb	Watford	A	2-2
LS	1 Mar	Portsmouth	H	4-0
LS	8 Mar	Southampton	H	3-1
LS	15 Mar	Bournemouth	A	3-1
LS	22 Mar	Luton T	H	7-4
LS	29 Mar	Portsmouth	A	2-3
LS	5 Apr	Southend U	A	2-2
LS	12 Apr	Luton T	A	3-3
LS	14 Apr	Southampton	H	6-3
LS	19 Apr	Southampton	H	3-1
LS	3 May	Watford	H	4-2

KEY: LS=League South; WR=Western Regional League; HC=Hampshire Cup; MC=Midland Cup

The Football League 1940-41

SOUTH REGIONAL LEAGUE

BRISTOL CITY

	31 Aug	Swansea T	H	1-1
	7 Sep	Bournemouth	A	2-5
	14 Sep	Walsall	H	2-0
	21 Sep	Walsall	A	1-4
	28 Sep	Cardiff C	A	2-2
	5 Oct	Cardiff C	H	1-0
	12 Oct	Aldershot	A	1-5
	19 Oct	Swansea T	A	1-0
	26 Oct	Aldershot	H	6-0
	2 Nov	Swansea T	H	4-1
	9 Nov	Swansea T	A	1-2
	23 Nov	Cardiff C	H	4-1
	30 Nov	Cardiff C	A	1-5
	7 Dec	Southampton	H	6-2
	14 Dec	Bournemouth	H	3-0
	25 Dec	Bournemouth	A	1-7
	28 Dec	Southampton	H	5-0
	11 Jan	Cardiff C	A	2-5
	8 Feb	Cardiff C	A	4-7
WR	8 Mar	Swansea T	H	7-1

CARDIFF CITY

	31 Aug	Reading	A	0-2
	7 Sep	Reading	H	2-2
	14 Sep	Birmingham	H	5-2
	21 Sep	Birmingham	A	2-3
	28 Sep	Bristol City	H	2-2
	5 Oct	Cardiff C	A	0-1
	12 Oct	Coventry C	A	2-5
	19 Oct	Coventry C	H	2-2
	26 Oct	Swansea T	H	8-0
	9 Nov	Southampton	A	3-1
	16 Nov	Southampton	H	1-1
	23 Nov	Cardiff C	A	1-4
	30 Nov	Bristol City	H	5-1
	7 Dec	Stoke C	A	1-5
	14 Dec	Stoke C	H	4-0
	21 Dec	Bournemouth	A	5-2
	25 Dec	Swansea T	H	3-1
	28 Dec	Bournemouth	H	5-1
	11 Jan	Bristol City	H	5-2
	25 Jan	Swansea T	H	3-2
	8 Feb	Bristol City	H	7-4
	10 May	Chester	H	1-2
	17 May	WBA	H	4-4
	24 May	Portsmouth	H	4-1

CHARLTON ATHLETIC

	31 Aug	Millwall	A	0-2
	7 Sep	Millwall	H	2-4
	14 Sep	Brentford	A	1-1
	21 Sep	QPR	A	0-2
	28 Sep	Tottenham H	A	3-1
	5 Oct	Fulham	H	3-0
	12 Oct	Brentford	H	1-4
	19 Oct	Tottenham H	H	4-0
	26 Oct	QPR	H	6-2
	2 Nov	Arsenal	A	2-2
	9 Nov	Fulham	A	2-1
	16 Nov	Chelsea	H	2-2
	23 Nov	West Ham U	A	0-4
	30 Nov	West Ham U	H	1-2
	7 Dec	Arsenal	H	5-0
	14 Dec	Brighton & HA	A	1-1
	21 Dec	Chelsea	H	1-3
	25 Dec	Crystal Palace	A	2-0
	28 Dec	Portsmouth	A	1-3

CHELSEA

	31 Aug	Crystal Palace	A	3-6
	7 Sep	Brentford	H	2-1
	14 Sep	Tottenham H	A	2-3
	21 Sep	Tottenham H	H	4-1
	5 Oct	West Ham U	H	1-1
	12 Oct	QPR	A	3-2
	19 Oct	QPR	H	3-1
	26 Oct	Millwall	A	1-3
	2 Nov	Millwall	H	2-2
	9 Nov	Aldershot	A	3-5
	16 Nov	Charlton Athletic	A	2-2
	23 Nov	Portsmouth	A	2-4
	30 Nov	Portsmouth	A	0-5
	7 Dec	West Ham U	A	2-6
	14 Dec	Crystal Palace	H	1-2
	21 Dec	Charlton Athletic	A	3-1
	25 Dec	Fulham	H	5-2
	28 Dec	Aldershot	H	6-0
	14 Apr	Arsenal	H	3-1
	26 Apr	Reading	A	3-2
	10 May	Cardiff C	A	2-1
	17 May	Northampton T	A	1-4
	24 May	West Ham U	A	3-3

CLAPTON ORIENT

	31 Aug	Brentford	A	2-2
	7 Sep	QPR	A	3-3
	14 Sep	Southend U	H	1-2
	28 Sep	West Ham U	H	3-3
	5 Oct	Brentford	H	1-0
	12 Oct	Fulham	A	1-3
	19 Oct	Crystal Palace	A	2-6
	2 Nov	QPR	H	0-3
	9 Nov	Reading	A	0-6
	16 Nov	Crystal Palace	H	2-4
	7 Dec	Luton T	A	0-4
	14 Dec	West Ham U	A	1-5
	21 Dec	Tottenham H	A	0-9
	25 Dec	Southend U	A	3-9
	28 Dec	Tottenham H	A	0-7

14 Sep, abandoned after 65 mins, result stood

COVENTRY CITY

	31 Aug	Leicester C	H	1-1
	7 Sep	Leicester C	A	2-0
	14 Sep	Reading	H	7-3
	21 Sep	Reading	A	2-3
	28 Sep	Notts County	H	1-1
	5 Oct	Notts County	A	3-1
	12 Oct	Cardiff C	H	5-2
	19 Oct	Cardiff C	A	2-2
	2 Nov	Northampton T	H	1-2
	9 Nov	WBA	A	4-1

KEY: LS=League South; WR=Western Regional League; HC=Hampshire Cup; MC=Midland Cup

[117]

The Football League 1940-41

SOUTH REGIONAL LEAGUE

CRYSTAL PALACE

	Date	Opponent	H/A	Score
	31 Aug	Chelsea	H	6-3
	7 Sep	Brighton & HA	H	5-2
	14 Sep	Millwall	A	0-1
	21 Sep	Norwich C	H	7-1
	28 Sep	Millwall	H	2-1
	5 Oct	Norwich C	A	1-3
	12 Oct	Watford	A	2-1
	19 Oct	Clapton Orient	H	6-2
	26 Oct	Southampton	A	4-1
	2 Nov	Bournemouth	A	2-3
	16 Nov	Clapton Orient	A	4-2
	23 Nov	Southend U	H	1-2
	30 Nov	Arsenal	A	2-2
	7 Dec	Bournemouth	H	6-0
	14 Dec	Chelsea	A	2-1
	21 Dec	Arsenal	H	3-3
	25 Dec	Charlton Athletic	H	0-2
	28 Dec	Brighton & HA	A	5-1
	8 Mar	Millwall	H	5-3
	15 Mar	Brentford	A	3-2
	22 Mar	Brentford	H	5-0
	29 Mar	Fulham	H	1-1
	10 May	Tottenham H	A	1-1
	17 May	Southend U	H	7-0
	24 May	Aldershot	A	3-0
	2 Jun	Reading	H	1-3
	7 Jun	Millwall	A	2-3

FULHAM

	Date	Opponent	H/A	Score
	31 Aug	QPR	H	3-1
	7 Sep	Arsenal	A	0-5
	14 Sep	Arsenal	H	0-1
	21 Sep	Millwall	A	1-4
	28 Sep	Luton T	H	3-3
	5 Oct	Charlton Athletic	A	0-3
	12 Oct	Clapton Orient	H	3-1
	19 Oct	Brentford	A	3-8
	26 Oct	Reading	H	1-1
	2 Nov	Reading	A	1-2
	9 Nov	Charlton Athletic	H	1-2
	16 Nov	QPR	A	5-2
	23 Nov	Brentford	H	3-0
	7 Dec	Millwall	H	3-5
	14 Dec	Luton T	A	4-3
	21 Dec	West Ham U	H	1-2
	25 Dec	Chelsea	A	2-5
	28 Dec	West Ham U	A	1-1
	8 Mar	Norwich C	A	0-2
	29 Mar	Crystal Palace	A	1-1
MC	5 Apr	Portsmouth	A	3-3
MC	14 Apr	Millwall	A	0-0
MC	26 Apr	West Ham U	A	1-0
MC	3 May	Aldershot	A	3-3
MC	10 May	Brentford	A	3-2
	17 May	Millwall	H	4-1
	24 May	Southend U	H	8-2
	31 May	Millwall	A	0-6
	2 Jun	QPR	A	3-2
	7 Jun	Tottenham H	A	1-2

LEICESTER CITY

	Date	Opponent	H/A	Score
	31 Aug	Coventry C	A	1-1
	7 Sep	Coventry C	H	0-2
	14 Sep	Nottingham Forest	A	3-6
	21 Sep	Nottingham Forest	H	2-2
	28 Sep	Stoke C	H	1-0
	5 Oct	Stoke C	A	3-3
	12 Oct	Luton T	A	0-2
	19 Oct	Luton T	H	4-0
	26 Oct	Birmingham	H	2-1
	2 Nov	Birmingham	A	2-1
	9 Nov	Mansfield T	H	3-2
	16 Nov	Mansfield T	A	2-4
	23 Nov	Walsall	A	0-5
	30 Nov	Walsall	H	1-1
	7 Dec	Notts County	H	6-0
	14 Dec	WBA	H	4-3
	21 Dec	WBA	A	5-4
	25 Dec	Northampton T	A	2-5
	25 Dec	Northampton T	H	7-2
	28 Dec	Notts County	A	2-4
MC	4 Jan	Stoke C	H	6-2
MC	11 Jan	Stoke C	A	5-3
MC	1 Feb	Nottingham Forest	H	6-2
MC	8 Feb	Lincoln C	H	4-1
MC	12 Apr	Lincoln C	A	4-5
	14 Apr	Lincoln C	H	1-1
	3 May	Walsall	H	2-0
	10 May	Walsall	A	1-3
	17 May	Tottenham H	H	1-2
	24 May	Tottenham H	A	0-3
	31 May	Northampton T	H	3-2

LUTON TOWN

	Date	Opponent	H/A	Score
	31 Aug	Northampton T	H	7-1
	7 Sep	Norwich C	A	2-2
	21 Sep	West Ham U	A	0-3
	28 Sep	Fulham	A	3-3
	5 Oct	Northampton T	A	1-7
	12 Oct	Leicester C	H	2-0
	19 Oct	Leicester C	A	0-4
	26 Oct	Norwich C	H	3-2
	2 Nov	Tottenham H	H	1-1
	9 Nov	Millwall	A	0-2
	16 Nov	Reading	H	1-1
	23 Nov	Tottenham H	A	1-2
	30 Nov	Reading	A	2-3
	7 Dec	Clapton Orient	H	4-0
	14 Dec	Fulham	H	3-4
	21 Dec	Millwall	H	2-4
	25 Dec	Watford	A	2-2
	25 Dec	Watford	H	4-1
	28 Dec	Arsenal	H	1-8
MC	4 Jan	Walsall	H	6-2
MC	11 Jan	Walsall	A	2-3
MC	25 Jan	Northampton T	H	2-2
MC	1 Feb	Northampton T	A	2-5
	1 Mar	Birmingham	H	2-5
LS	8 Mar	Portsmouth	A	2-9
LS	15 Mar	Norwich C	A	4-0
LS	22 Mar	Brighton & HA	A	4-7
LS	29 Mar	Southampton	H	3-1
LS	5 Apr	Watford	A	6-2
LS	12 Apr	Brighton & HA	H	3-3
LS	14 Apr	Norwich C	A	1-4
LS	19 Apr	Southend U	A	2-4
LS	26 Apr	Bournemouth	A	1-2
LS	3 May	Portsmouth	H	2-1
LS	10 May	Watford	A	1-0

MANSFIELD TOWN

	Date	Opponent	H/A	Score
	31 Aug	Norwich C	H	4-0
	7 Sep	Northampton T	A	1-6
	14 Sep	Stoke C	H	2-3
	21 Sep	Stoke C	A	0-5
	28 Sep	Northampton T	H	3-1
	12 Oct	Birmingham	H	4-1
	19 Oct	Birmingham	A	1-4
	26 Oct	Walsall	H	6-6
	2 Nov	Walsall	A	3-1
	9 Nov	Leicester C	A	2-3
	16 Nov	Leicester C	H	4-2
	23 Nov	WBA	A	2-4
	30 Nov	WBA	H	3-3
	14 Dec	Nottingham Forest	H	2-1
	21 Dec	Nottingham Forest	A	4-1
	25 Dec	Stoke C	H	7-2
MC	4 Jan	Northampton T	H	3-1
MC	11 Jan	Northampton T	A	3-3
MC	1 Feb	Lincoln C	A	1-4
	29 Mar	Lincoln C	A	1-3
	5 Apr	Lincoln C	H	1-1
	12 Apr	Rotherham U	H	0-1
	14 Apr	Bradford	H	5-1
	19 Apr	Walsall	A	1-1
	26 Apr	Walsall	H	2-2
	3 May	Doncaster R	A	1-2
	10 May	Grimsby T	H	3-1
	17 May	Doncaster R	H	6-1
	7 Jun	Chesterfield	H	1-4

MILLWALL

	Date	Opponent	H/A	Score
	31 Aug	Charlton Athletic	H	2-0
	7 Sep	Charlton Athletic	A	4-2
	14 Sep	Crystal Palace	H	1-0
	21 Sep	Fulham	H	4-1
	28 Sep	Crystal Palace	A	1-2
	5 Oct	Watford	H	3-0
	12 Oct	West Ham U	A	2-3
	19 Oct	West Ham U	H	2-2
	26 Oct	Chelsea	H	3-1
	2 Nov	Chelsea	A	2-2
	9 Nov	Luton T	H	2-0
	16 Nov	Watford	A	1-1
	23 Nov	QPR	H	3-1
	30 Nov	QPR	A	1-2
	7 Dec	Fulham	A	5-3
	14 Dec	Brentford	H	3-0
	21 Dec	Luton T	A	4-2
	25 Dec	Tottenham H	A	3-3
	28 Dec	Brentford	A	2-3
	8 Mar	Crystal Palace	A	3-5
	15 Mar	Tottenham H	A	1-0
	29 Mar	Aldershot	H	3-0
	12 Apr	Reading	A	1-4
	14 Apr	Fulham	H	0-0
	19 Apr	Brentford	A	2-5
	26 Apr	Northampton T	H	1-4
	3 May	Northampton T	A	1-5
	17 May	Fulham	A	1-4
	31 May	Fulham	H	6-0
	2 Jun	West Ham U	A	3-0
	7 Jun	Crystal Palace	H	3-2

KEY: LS=League South; WR=Western Regional League; HC=Hampshire Cup; MC=Midland Cup

The Football League 1940-41

SOUTH REGIONAL LEAGUE

NORTHAMPTON TOWN

	31 Aug	Luton T	A	1-7
	7 Sep	Mansfield T	H	6-1
	14 Sep	WBA	A	1-4
	21 Sep	WBA	H	1-1
	28 Sep	Mansfield T	A	1-3
	5 Oct	Luton T	H	7-1
	12 Oct	Nottingham For	A	0-1
	19 Oct	Arsenal	A	4-5
	26 Oct	Watford	H	2-1
	2 Nov	Coventry C	A	2-1
	16 Nov	Nottingham For	H	7-0
	23 Nov	Arsenal	H	1-8
	7 Dec	Birmingham	H	2-1
	21 Dec	Notts County	H	2-1
	25 Dec	Leicester C	H	5-2
	25 Dec	Leicester C	A	2-7
MC	4 Jan	Mansfield t	A	1-3
MC	11 Jan	Mansfield T	H	3-3
MC	25 Jan	Luton T	A	2-2
MC	1 Feb	Luton T	H	5-2
MC	15 Mar	Walsall	H	1-3
MC	22 Mar	Walsall	A	0-2
	12 Apr	WBA	H	3-1
	14 Apr	Stoke C	H	7-0
	19 Apr	WBA	A	2-3
	26 Apr	Millwall	A	4-1
	3 May	Millwall	H	5-1
	10 May	Stoke C	A	1-2
	17 May	Chelsea	H	4-1
	31 May	Leicester C	A	2-3

NORWICH CITY

	31 Aug	Mansfield T	A	0-4
	7 Sep	Fulham	A	2-2
	21 Sep	Crystal Palace	A	1-7
	28 Sep	Southend U	A	0-3
	5 Oct	Crystal Palace	H	3-1
	19 Oct	Southend U	H	8-4
	26 Oct	Luton T	A	2-3
	16 Nov	Southend U	A	3-3
	7 Dec	Aldershot	A	4-5
	14 Dec	Aldershot	H	10-1
	21 Dec	Southend U	H	3-0
	25 Dec	Brighton & HA	H	18-0
	8 Mar	Fulham	H	2-0
LS	15 Mar	Luton T	A	0-4
LS	29 Mar	Southend U	A	2-3
LS	12 Apr	Watford	A	0-7
LS	14 Apr	Luton T	H	4-1
LS	19 Apr	Watford	H	5-4
LS	3 May	Southend U	H	5-3

NOTTS COUNTY

	31 Aug	Stoke C	A	1-4
	7 Sep	Stoke C	H	3-2
	28 Sep	Coventry C	A	1-1
	5 Oct	Coventry C	H	1-3
	12 Oct	Walsall	A	2-3
	19 Oct	Walsall	H	4-2
	26 Oct	WBA	A	1-3
	2 Nov	WBA	A	3-2
	9 Nov	Walsall	A	4-11
	16 Nov	Walsall	H	2-1
	30 Nov	Birmingham	H	3-3
	7 Dec	Leicester C	A	0-6
	21 Dec	Northampton T	A	1-2
	25 Dec	Nottingham Forest	A	4-2
	28 Dec	Leicester C	H	4-2
	11 Jan	WBA	A	1-8
	25 Jan	Stoke C	A	2-2
	1 Feb	Stoke C	H	2-1
	15 Mar	Nottingham Forest	H	0-4
	12 Apr	Nottingham Forest	A	3-1
	14 Apr	Chesterfield	A	0-3

NOTTINGHAM FOREST

	31 Aug	Birmingham	H	2-3
	7 Sep	Birmingham	A	1-2
	14 Sep	Leicester C	H	6-3
	21 Sep	Leicester C	A	2-2
	28 Sep	Walsall	H	2-0
	5 Oct	Walsall	A	3-4
	12 Oct	Northampton T	H	1-0
	26 Oct	Stoke C	H	3-3
	2 Nov	Stoke C	A	0-5
	16 Nov	Northampton T	A	0-7
	7 Dec	WBA	A	0-5
	14 Dec	Mansfield T	A	1-2
	21 Dec	Mansfield T	H	1-4
	25 Dec	Notts County	H	2-4
	28 Dec	WBA	A	3-5
MC	11 Jan	Lincoln C	H	4-2
MC	18 Jan	Lincoln C	A	1-2
MC	1 Feb	Leicester C	A	2-6
	15 Mar	Notts County	A	4-0
	29 Mar	Stoke C	A	0-4
	5 Apr	Stoke C	H	3-2
	12 Apr	Notts County	H	1-3
	19 Apr	Sheffield Wed	A	1-1
	24 May	Walsall	A	7-6
	2 Jun	Leicester C	A	0-2

PORTSMOUTH

	31 Aug	Watford	A	2-1
	28 Sep	Aldershot	A	3-2
	5 Oct	Brighton & HA	H	5-1
	12 Oct	Southend U	A	0-0
	19 Oct	Aldershot	H	1-3
	26 Oct	Tottenham H	A	2-1
	2 Nov	Brentford	A	1-3
	9 Nov	Bournemouth	H	4-2
	16 Nov	Bournemouth	A	3-4
	23 Nov	Chelsea	H	4-2
	30 Nov	Chelsea	H	5-0
	21 Dec	Brentford	H	2-3
	25 Dec	Southampton	H	1-2
	28 Dec	Charlton Athletic	H	3-1
LS	25 Jan	Bournemouth	H	10-2
LS	1 Feb	Watford	H	7-1
LS	8 Feb	Southampton	H	5-2
LS	1 Mar	Brighton & HA	A	0-4
LS	8 Mar	Luton T	H	9-2
LS	15 Mar	Southampton	H	6-0
LS	22 Mar	Bournemouth	A	0-3
LS	29 Mar	Brighton & HA	H	3-2
	5 Apr	Fulham	H	3-3
LS	12 Apr	Southend U	A	1-3
LS	14 Apr	Southend U	H	1-2
LS	26 Apr	Watford	A	0-6
LS	3 May	Luton T	A	1-2
LS	10 May	Bournemouth	H	5-0
	24 May	Cardiff C	A	1-4
	31 May	Aldershot	A	2-9
HC	2 Jun	Southampton	H	8-1

QUEEN'S PARK RANGERS

	31 Aug	Fulham	A	1-3
	7 Sep	Clapton Orient	H	3-3
	21 Sep	Charlton Athletic	H	2-0
	28 Sep	Arsenal	H	3-2
	5 Oct	Tottenham H	H	1-1
	12 Oct	Chelsea	H	2-3
	19 Oct	Chelsea	A	1-3
	26 Oct	Charlton Athletic	A	2-6
	2 Nov	Clapton Orient	A	3-0
	16 Nov	Fulham	H	2-5
	23 Nov	Millwall	A	1-3
	30 Nov	Millwall	H	2-1
	7 Dec	Tottenham H	A	3-2
	14 Dec	Arsenal	A	2-3
	21 Dec	Reading	H	4-1
	25 Dec	Brentford	A	1-2
	28 Dec	Reading	A	0-2
	10 May	Aldershot	A	1-5
	17 May	Watford	H	4-2
	24 May	Watford	A	3-3
	31 May	West Ham U	H	1-5
	2 Jun	Fulham	H	2-3
	7 Jun	West Ham U	A	3-2

KEY: LS=League South; WR=Western Regional League; HC=Hampshire Cup; MC=Midland Cup

The Football League 1940-41

SOUTH REGIONAL LEAGUE

READING

	Date	Opponent	H/A	Score
	31 Aug	Cardiff C	H	2-0
	7 Sep	Cardiff C	A	2-2
	14 Sep	Coventry C	A	3-7
	21 Sep	Coventry C	H	3-2
	28 Sep	Swansea T	A	1-4
	5 Oct	Swansea T	H	4-0
	12 Oct	Bournemouth	A	1-1
	19 Oct	Bournemouth	H	5-1
	26 Oct	Fulham	A	1-1
	2 Nov	Fulham	H	2-1
	9 Nov	Clapton Orient	H	6-0
	16 Nov	Luton T	A	1-1
	23 Nov	Southampton	A	3-2
	30 Nov	Luton T	H	3-2
	7 Dec	Brentford	A	3-2
	14 Dec	Southampton	H	8-0
	21 Dec	QPR	A	1-4
	25 Dec	Aldershot	H	4-5
	28 Dec	QPR	H	2-0
	12 Apr	Millwall	H	4-1
	26 Apr	Chelsea	H	2-3
	3 May	WBA	H	6-3
	10 May	West Ham U	H	1-1
	17 May	Brentford	H	1-4
	24 May	Brentford	A	1-3
	2 Jun	Crystal Palace	A	3-1

SOUTHAMPTON

	Date	Opponent	H/A	Score
	31 Aug	Brighton & HA	H	3-1
	7 Sep	Aldershot	A	1-4
	21 Sep	Brighton & HA	A	0-0
	28 Sep	Watford	H	2-5
	5 Oct	Aldershot	H	2-3
	12 Oct	Brighton & HA	A	0-0
	19 Oct	Watford	A	2-3
	26 Oct	Crystal Palace	H	1-4
	2 Nov	Watford	H	0-4
	9 Nov	Cardiff C	H	1-3
	16 Nov	Cardiff C	A	1-1
	23 Nov	Reading	H	2-3
	30 Nov	Bournemouth	A	1-1
	7 Dec	Bristol City	A	2-6
	14 Dec	Reading	A	0-8
	21 Dec	Watford	A	2-4
	25 Dec	Portsmouth	A	2-1
	28 Dec	Bristol City	A	0-5
LS	11 Jan	Bournemouth	A	3-5
LS	25 Jan	Watford	A	1-7
LS	1 Feb	Southend U	A	4-6
LS	8 Feb	Portsmouth	A	2-5
LS	1 Mar	Bournemouth	A	3-3
LS	8 Mar	Brighton & HA	A	1-3
LS	15 Mar	Portsmouth	A	0-6
LS	22 Mar	Watford	A	0-2
LS	29 Mar	Luton T	A	1-3
HC	5 Apr	Bournemouth	A	1-1
LS	12 Apr	Bournemouth	A	2-4
LS	14 Apr	Brighton & HA	A	3-6
LS	19 Apr	Brighton & HA	A	1-3
LS	26 Apr	Southend U	A	4-1
HC	3 May	Bournemouth	A	3-2
HC	2 Jun	Portsmouth	A	1-8

SOUTHEND UNITED

	Date	Opponent	H/A	Score
	31 Aug	Aldershot	H	1-7
	14 Sep	Clapton Orient	A	2-1
	28 Sep	Norwich C	H	3-0
	5 Oct	Arsenal	A	0-7
	12 Oct	Portsmouth	H	0-0
	19 Oct	Norwich C	A	4-8
	26 Oct	West Ham U	A	0-11
	2 Nov	West Ham U	H	3-1
	16 Nov	Norwich C	A	3-3
	23 Nov	Crystal Palace	A	2-1
	30 Nov	Tottenham H	H	3-2
	14 Dec	Watford	H	1-3
	21 Dec	Norwich C	A	0-3
	25 Dec	Clapton Orient	H	9-3
	28 Dec	Watford	A	1-1
LS	11 Jan	Watford	A	2-8
LS	25 Jan	Brighton & HA	H	2-0
LS	1 Feb	Southampton	H	6-4
LS	8 Feb	Bournemouth	A	0-3
LS	15 Mar	Watford	H	2-3
LS	29 Mar	Norwich C	H	3-2
LS	5 Apr	Brighton & HA	A	2-2
LS	12 Apr	Portsmouth	H	3-1
LS	14 Apr	Portsmouth	A	2-1
LS	19 Apr	Luton T	H	4-2
LS	26 Apr	Southampton	H	1-4
LS	3 May	Norwich C	A	3-5
	17 May	Crystal Palace	A	0-7
	24 May	Fulham	A	2-8

14 Sep, abandoned after 65 mins, result stood
28 Sep, abandoned after 35 mins, result stood

STOKE CITY

	Date	Opponent	H/A	Score
	31 Aug	Notts County	H	4-1
	7 Sep	Notts County	A	2-3
	14 Sep	Mansfield T	A	3-2
	21 Sep	Mansfield T	H	5-0
	28 Sep	Leicester C	A	0-1
	5 Oct	Leicester C	H	3-3
	12 Oct	WBA	A	1-0
	19 Oct	Walsall	H	1-3
	26 Oct	Nottingham Forest	A	3-3
	2 Nov	Nottingham Forest	H	5-0
	9 Nov	Birmingham	H	5-0
	16 Nov	Birmingham	A	2-6
	7 Dec	Cardiff C	H	5-1
	14 Dec	Cardiff C	A	0-4
	21 Dec	Walsall	H	2-2
	25 Dec	Mansfield T	A	2-7
	28 Dec	Walsall	A	1-5
MC	4 Jan	Leicester C	A	2-6
MC	11 Jan	Leicester C	H	3-5
	25 Jan	Notts County	H	2-2
	1 Feb	Notts County	A	1-2
	1 Mar	Walsall	H	1-1
	8 Mar	Walsall	A	3-7
	15 Mar	WBA	A	2-2
	22 Mar	Walsall	H	0-2
	29 Mar	Nottingham Forest	H	4-0
	5 Apr	Nottingham Forest	A	2-3
	14 Apr	Northampton T	A	0-7
	26 Apr	Chester	H	1-2
	3 May	Chester	A	0-1
	10 May	Northampton T	H	2-1
	17 May	Chesterfield	H	2-2
	24 May	Chesterfield	A	3-3
	2 June	Wrexham	A	3-3
	7 Jun	Leicester C	A	1-2

SWANSEA TOWN

	Date	Opponent	H/A	Score
	31 Aug	Bristol City	A	1-1
	28 Sep	Reading	H	4-1
	5 Oct	Reading	A	0-4
	19 Oct	Bristol City	H	0-1
	26 Oct	Cardiff C	A	0-8
	2 Nov	Bristol City	A	1-4
	9 Nov	Bristol City	H	2-1
	25 Dec	Cardiff C	H	1-3
	25 Jan	Cardiff C	A	2-3
WR	8 Mar	Bristol City	A	1-7

TOTTENHAM HOTSPUR

	Date	Opponent	H/A	Score
	31 Aug	West Ham U	H	2-3
	7 Sep	West Ham U	A	4-1
	14 Sep	Chelsea	H	3-2
	21 Sep	Chelsea	A	1-4
	28 Sep	Charlton Athletic	H	1-3
	5 Oct	QPR	A	1-1
	12 Oct	Arsenal	H	2-3
	19 Oct	Charlton Athletic	A	0-4
	26 Oct	Portsmouth	H	1-2
	2 Nov	Luton T	A	1-1
	16 Nov	Arsenal	A	1-1
	23 Nov	Luton T	H	2-1
	30 Nov	Southend U	A	2-3
	7 Dec	QPR	H	2-3
	21 Dec	Clapton Orient	H	9-0
	25 Dec	Millwall	H	3-3
	28 Dec	Clapton Orient	H	7-0
	15 Mar	Millwall	H	0-1
	26 Apr	Aldershot	A	3-2
	10 May	Crystal Palace	H	1-1
	17 May	Leicester C	A	2-1
	24 May	Leicester C	H	3-0
	7 Jun	Fulham	H	2-1

12 Oct, abandoned after 47 mins, result stood

KEY: LS=League South; WR=Western Regional League; HC=Hampshire Cup; MC=Midland Cup

The Football League 1940-41

SOUTH REGIONAL LEAGUE

WALSALL

	Date	Opponent	H/A	Score
	31 Aug	WBA	A	1-3
	7 Sep	WBA	H	0-2
	14 Sep	Bristol City	A	0-2
	21 Sep	Bristol City	H	4-1
	28 Sep	Nottingham F	A	0-2
	5 Oct	Nottingham F	H	4-3
	12 Oct	Notts County	H	3-2
	19 Oct	Notts County	A	2-4
	26 Oct	Mansfield T	A	6-6
	2 Nov	Mansfield T	H	1-3
	9 Nov	Notts County	H	11-4
	16 Nov	Notts County	A	1-2
	23 Nov	Leicester C	H	5-0
	30 Nov	Leicester C	A	1-1
	21 Dec	Stoke C	A	2-2
	25 Dec	Birmingham	H	6-3
	28 Dec	Stoke C	H	5-1
MC	4 Jan	Luton t	A	2-6
MC	11 Jan	Luton T	H	3-2
	8 Feb	Stoke C	H	4-3
	1 Mar	Stoke C	A	1-1
	8 Mar	Stoke C	H	7-3
	15 Mar	Northampton T	A	3-1
	22 Mar	Northampton T	H	2-0
	29 Mar	WBA	A	1-4
	5 Apr	Stoke C	H	3-3
	19 Apr	Mansfield T	H	1-1
	26 Apr	Mansfield T	A	2-2
	3 May	Leicester C	A	0-2
	10 May	Leicester C	H	3-1
	24 May	Nottingham F	H	6-7
	31 May	Stoke C	H	10-3

WATFORD

	Date	Opponent	H/A	Score
	31 Aug	Portsmouth	H	1-2
	14 Sep	Aldershot	H	3-1
	21 Sep	Aldershot	A	1-2
	28 Sep	Southampton	A	5-2
	5 Oct	Millwall	A	0-3
	12 Oct	Crystal Palace	H	1-2
	19 Oct	Southampton	H	3-2
	26 Oct	Northampton T	A	1-2
	2 Nov	Southampton	A	4-0
	16 Nov	Millwall	H	1-1
	23 Nov	Brighton & HA	A	1-1
	7 Dec	Brighton & HA	H	4-0
	14 Dec	Southend U	A	3-1
	21 Dec	Southampton	H	4-2
	25 Dec	Luton T	H	2-2
	25 Dec	Luton T	A	1-4
	28 Dec	Southend U	H	1-1
LS	11 Jan	Southend U	H	8-2
LS	18 Jan	Bournemouth	A	5-2
LS	25 Jan	Southampton	H	7-1
LS	1 Feb	Portsmouth	A	1-7
LS	8 Feb	Brighton & HA	H	2-2
LS	15 Mar	Southend U	A	3-2
LS	22 Mar	Southampton	H	2-0
LS	29 Mar	Bournemouth	H	5-0
LS	5 Apr	Luton T	H	2-6
LS	12 Apr	Norwich C	H	7-0
	14 Apr	WBA	A	0-2
LS	19 Apr	Norwich C	A	4-5
LS	26 Apr	Portsmouth	H	6-0
LS	3 May	Brighton & HA	A	2-4
LS	10 May	Luton T	H	0-1
	17 May	QPR	A	2-4
	24 May	QPR	H	3-3
	7 Jun	Aldershot	A	1-3

WEST BROMWICH ALBION

	Date	Opponent	H/A	Score
	31 Aug	Walsall	H	3-1
	7 Sep	Walsall	A	2-0
	14 Sep	Northampton T	H	4-1
	21 Sep	Northampton T	A	1-1
	28 Sep	Birmingham	H	1-2
	5 Oct	Birmingham	A	3-1
	12 Oct	Stoke C	H	0-1
	19 Oct	Stoke C	A	3-1
	26 Oct	Notts County	H	3-1
	2 Nov	Notts County	H	2-3
	9 Nov	Coventry C	H	1-4
	23 Nov	Mansfield T	H	4-2
	30 Nov	Mansfield T	A	3-3
	7 Dec	Nottingham F	H	5-0
	14 Dec	Leicester C	A	3-4
	21 Dec	Leicester C	H	4-5
	28 Dec	Nottingham F	H	5-3
MC	11 Jan	Notts County	H	8-1
MC	8 Feb	Walsall	A	3-4
	15 Mar	Stoke C	H	2-2
	22 Mar	Stoke C	A	2-0
	29 Mar	Walsall	H	4-1
	5 Apr	Walsall	A	3-3
	12 Apr	Northampton T	A	1-3
	19 Apr	Northampton T	H	3-2
	3 May	Reading	A	3-6
	17 May	Cardiff C	A	4-4
	31 May	Walsall	A	3-10

WEST HAM UNITED

Date	Opponent	H/A	Score
31 Aug	Tottenham H	A	3-2
7 Sep	Tottenham H	H	1-4
21 Sep	Luton T	H	3-0
28 Sep	Clapton Orient	A	3-3
5 Oct	Chelsea	A	1-1
12 Oct	Millwall	H	3-2
19 Oct	Millwall	A	2-2
26 Oct	Southend U	H	11-0
2 Nov	Southend U	A	1-3
16 Nov	Brentford	A	2-0
23 Nov	Charlton Athletic	H	4-0
30 Nov	Charlton Athletic	A	2-1
7 Dec	Chelsea	H	6-2
14 Dec	Clapton Orient	H	5-1
21 Dec	Fulham	A	2-1
25 Dec	Arsenal	H	4-2
28 Dec	Fulham	H	1-1
14 Apr	Watford	H	2-0
26 Apr	Fulham	H	0-1
3 May	Brentford	H	3-2
10 May	Reading	A	1-1
24 May	Chelsea	H	3-3
31 May	QPR	A	5-1
2 Jun	Millwall	H	0-3
7 Jun	QPR	H	2-3

KEY: LS=League South; WR=Western Regional League; HC=Hampshire Cup; MC=Midland Cup

The Football League 1940-41

Final Table

		P	W	D	L	F	A	G Ave
1	Crystal Palace	27	16	4	7	86	44	1.955
2	West Ham United	25	14	6	5	70	39	1.795
3	Coventry City	10	5	3	2	28	16	1.750
4	Arsenal	19	10	5	4	66	38	1.737
5	Cardiff City	24	12	5	7	75	50	1.500
6	Reading	26	14	5	7	73	51	1.431
7	Portsmouth	31	16	2	13	98	71	1.380
8	Watford	35	15	6	14	96	72	1.333
9	Norwich City	19	9	2	8	73	55	1.327
10	Tottenham Hotspur	23	9	5	9	53	41	1.293
11	Millwall	31	16	5	10	73	57	1.281
12	Walsall	32	14	7	11	100	80	1.250
13	West Bromwich Albion	28	13	5	10	83	69	1.203
14	Leicester City	33	17	5	11	87	73	1.192
15	Northampton Town	30	14	3	13	84	71	1.183
16	Bristol City	20	10	2	8	55	48	1.146
17	Mansfield Town	29	12	6	11	76	68	1.118
18	Charlton Athletic	19	7	4	8	37	34	1.088
19	Aldershot	24	14	2	8	73	68	1.074
20	Brentford	23	9	3	11	51	51	1.000
21	Chelsea	23	10	4	9	57	58	0.983
22	Birmingham City	16	7	1	8	38	43	0.884
23	Fulham	30	10	7	13	62	73	0.849
24	Stoke City	35	9	9	17	76	92	0.826
25	Luton Town	35	11	7	17	82	100	0.820
26	Queen's Park Rangers	23	8	3	12	47	60	0.783
27	Brighton & Hove Albion	25	8	8	9	50	73	0.685
28	Bournemouth & Boscombe Athletic	28	9	4	15	61	90	0.678
29	Nottingham Forest	25	7	3	15	50	77	0.649
30	Notts County	21	8	3	10	42	66	0.636
31	Southend United	29	12	4	13	64	101	0.634
32	Southampton	34	4	6	24	52	121	0.430
33	Swansea Town	10	2	1	7	12	33	0.364
34	Clapton Orient	15	1	3	11	19	66	0.288

Standings based on goal average

The Football League 1940-41

SOUTH

Results from this competition also counted towards the South Regional League after it was recognized by the Football League on 1 February 1941.

	Bournemouth & BA	Brighton & HA	Luton Town	Norwich City	Portsmouth	Southampton	Southend United	Watford
Bournemouth & Boscombe Athletic	X	15 Mar 1-3	26 Apr 2-1		22 Mar 3-0	11 Jan 5-3 1 Mar 3-3 12 Apr 4-2	8 Feb 3-0	18 Jan 2-5
Brighton & Hove Albion	1 Feb 2-1	X	22 Mar 7-4		1 Mar 4-0	8 Mar 3-1 14 Apr 6-3 19 Apr 3-1	5 Apr 2-2	3 May 4-2
Luton Town		12 Apr 3-3	X	15 Mar 4-0	3 May 2-1	29 Mar 3-1		
Norwich City			14 Apr 4-1	X			3 May 5-3	19 Apr 5-4
Portsmouth	25 Jan 10-2 10 May 5-0	29 Mar 3-2	8 Mar 9-2		X	8 Feb 5-2 15 Mar 6-0	14 Apr 1-2	1 Feb 7-1
Southampton						X		
Southend United		25 Jan 2-0	19 Apr 4-2	29 Mar 3-2	12 Apr 3-1	1 Feb 6-4 26 Apr 1-4	X	15 Mar 2-3
Watford	29 Mar 5-0	8 Feb 2-2	5 Apr 2-6 10 May 0-1	12 Apr 7-0	26 Apr 6-0	25 Jan 7-1 22 Mar 2-0	11 Jan 8-2	X

		P	W	D	L	F	A	Pts
1	Brighton & Hove Albion	13	8	3	2	41	25	19
2	Watford	14	8	1	5	54	32	17
3	Portsmouth	13	7	0	6	48	29	14
4	Southend United	12	6	1	5	30	35	13
5	Luton Town	11	5	1	5	29	33	11
6	Bournemouth & Boscombe Ath	12	5	1	6	26	39	11
7	Norwich City	6	3	0	3	16	22	6
8	Southampton	13	1	1	11	25	54	3

Brighton finished top, but Watford claimed the championship by counting only the results of the matches that were played between the original six clubs, ie all above excluding Luton Town and Norwich City. The dispute was settled by the challenge match.

CHALLENGE MATCH FOR CHAMPIONSHIP
Played on 31 May, att 2,500
Brighton & Hove Albion v Watford 4-1

Western Regional League 1940-41

	Aberaman Athletic	Bath City	Bristol City	Cardiff City	Cardiff Corinthians	Lovell's Athletic
Aberaman Athletic	X	29 Mar 1-5	15 Mar 1-2	14 Apr 2-2	12 Apr 5-3	26 Apr 0-1
Bath City	19 Apr 2-0	X	24 May 2-3	5 Apr 2-1	15 Mar 9-2	22 Mar 1-3
Bristol City	22 Mar 2-4	12 Apr 3-2	X	NOT PLAYED	26 Apr 7-1	5 Apr 2-2
Cardiff City	NOT PLAYED	26 Apr 5-2	NOT PLAYED	X	NOT PLAYED	12 Apr 3-2
Cardiff Corinthians	5 Apr 1-4	8 Mar 0-4	19 Apr 0-2	26 Mar ??	X	21 May 1-4
Lovell's Athletic	NOT PLAYED	3 May 1-2	29 Mar 7-2	19 Apr 2-1	14 Apr 5-2	X

This league was formed in February 1941 and sanctioned on 6 March 1941 and also included four non-League clubs. Swansea Town retired from the competition on 19 March but their match against Bristol City on 8 March which they lost 7-1 was included in the South Regional League table

All of the fixtures were not played, but Lovell's Athletic were declared champions.

		P	W	D	L	F	A	Pts
1	Lovell's Athletic	9	6	1	2	27	14	13
2	Bath City	10	6	0	4	31	19	12
3	Bristol City	8	5	1	4	23	19	11
4	Aberaman Athletic	8	3	1	4	17	18	7
5	Cardiff City	5	2	1	2	13	10	5
6	Cardiff Corinthians	8	0	0	8	9	40	0

WESTERN REGIONAL LEAGUE CUP

First round
Played on 10 May
Aberaman Athletic v Lovell's Athletic 0-8
Played on 17 May
Bath City v Bristol City 0-4

Semi-final
Played on 31 May
Lovell's Athletic v Cardiff Corinthians 12-2
Scheduled to be played on 28 May
Bristol City v Cardiff City (Bristol City scratched as they couldn't raise a team)

Final
Played on 4 Jun
Lovell's Athletic v Cardiff City 6-1

The Football League (War) Cup 1940-41

Preliminary round - 2 legs
First leg played on 1 Feb, second leg on 8 Feb
Bolton Wanderers v Bradford City 6-0, 3-1
Southport v Crewe Alexandra 4-1, 6-3
Stockport County v Blackpool 1-3, 2-9
York City v Sheffield Wednesday 7-0, 1-2

First round – 2 legs
First leg played on 15 Feb, second leg on 22 Feb
Brighton & Hove Albion v Arsenal 1-4, 1-3
Chelsea v Portsmouth 3-1, 4-1
Clapton Orient v Aldershot 3-2, 0-4
Crystal Palace v Queen's Park Rangers 0-1, 2-3
Leicester City v Birmingham 3-3, 3-2
Luton Town v Northampton Town 4-5, 0-5
Mansfield Town v Stoke City 6-1, 0-2
Norwich City v West Ham United 2-1, 1-4
Notts County v West Bromwich Albion 4-0, 0-5
Reading v Bristol City 3-2, 2-1
Southampton v Brentford 2-2, 2-5
Southend United v Millwall 3-1, 1-2
Tottenham Hotspur v Bournemouth & Boscombe Athletic 4-1, 6-1
Walsall v Nottingham Forest 3-2, 1-8
Watford v Fulham 4-1, 1-2
Blackpool v Manchester City 1-4, 1-0
Blackburn Rovers v Oldham Athletic 2-0, 5-1
Bolton Wanderers v Burnley 3-1, 2-2
Bury v Preston North End 4-4, 1-2
Chester v Tranmere Rovers 2-0, 2-9
Chesterfield v Barnsley 1-4, 2-5
Hull City v Lincoln City 4-1, 2-3
Liverpool v Southport 2-3, 2-2
Manchester United v Everton 2-2, 1-2
New Brighton v Wrexham 2-1, 8-5
Newcastle United v Rochdale 1-2, 3-1
Sheffield United v Rotherham United 2-3, 3-0
York City v Bradford 3-2, 4-3
First leg played on 15 Feb, second leg on 1 Mar
Cardiff City v Swansea Town 3-2, 6-2
Grimsby Town Doncaster Rovers 1-0, 0-0
Halifax Town v Leeds United 2-3, 2-2
Huddersfield Town v Middlesbrough 2-2, 2-4

Second round – 2 legs
First leg played on 1 Mar, second leg 8 Mar
Aldershot v Queen's Park Rangers 2-1, 2-4
Brentford v Chelsea 2-2, 1-3
Nottingham Forest v Leicester City 0-2, 1-1
Southend United v West Ham United 2-1, 1-3
Tottenham Hotspur v Northampton Town 4-0, 3-1
Watford v Arsenal 0-4, 0-5
West Bromwich Albion v Mansfield Town 2-3, 2-6
Bolton Wanderers v Preston North End 1-4, 0-2
Everton v Southport 5-0, 5-0
Hull City v Sheffield United 1-0, 1-3 aet
Manchester City v Blackburn Rovers 5-2, 4-2
Tranmere Rovers v New Brighton 0-3, 4-0
York City v Newcastle United 1-1, 1-4
First leg played on 8 Mar, second leg on 15 Mar
Barnsley v Grimsby Town 1-1, 2-2 aet
(Barnsley qualified due to their superior league position at the time)
Middlesbrough v Leeds United 2-0, 2-2
Reading v Cardiff City 0-1, 1-4

Third round – 2 legs
First leg played on 15 Mar, second leg 22 Mar
Leicester City v Mansfield Town 2-2, 2-1
Queen's Park Rangers v Chelsea 2-0, 4-2
Everton v Manchester City 1-1, 0-2
Preston North End v Tranmere Rovers 12-1, 8-1
First leg played on 15 Mar, second leg on 29 Mar
West Ham United v Arsenal 0-1, 1-2
First leg played on 22 Mar, second leg on 29 Mar
Tottenham Hotspur v Cardiff City 3-3, 2-3
Middlesbrough v Newcastle United 0-1, 0-3
Sheffield United v Barnsley 3-1, 1-1

Fourth round – 2 legs
First leg played on 29 Mar, second leg 5 Apr
Queen's Park Rangers v Leicester City 2-1, 1-6
Manchester City v Preston North End 1-2, 0-3
First leg played on 5 Apr, second leg on 12 Apr
Arsenal v Tottenham Hotspur 2-1, 1-1
Sheffield United v Newcastle United 2-0, 0-4

Semi-final – 2 legs
First leg played on 19 Apr, second leg 26 Apr
Arsenal v Leicester City 1-0, 2-1
Preston North End v Newcastle United 2-0, 0-0

Football League War Cup 1940-41
Played on 10 May 1941 at Wembley Stadium, London
Att 60,000
Preston North End 1 *(McLaren)*
Arsenal 1 *(D Compton)*

Preston NE: Fairbrother, Gallimore, Scott, Shankley, Smith, A Beattie, Finney, McLaren, Dougal, R Beattie, H O'Donnell*
Arsenal: Marks, Scott, Hapgood, Crayston, Joy, Collett, Kirchen, Jones, L Compton, Bastin, D Compston

REPLAY
31 May 1941 at Ewood Park, Blackburn
Att 45,000
Preston North End 2 *(R Beattie 2)*
Arsenal 1 *(og)*

Preston NE: as first game except Mansley replaced Scott,
Arsenal: as first game except Drake replaced L Compston

Other English & Welsh Competitions 1940-41

LIVERPOOL SENIOR CUP

Semi-final
Played on 5 Apr
  Southport v Everton 3-5
  Liverpool v Tranmere Rovers (not played)

COMPETITION INCOMPLETE

COMBINED COUNTIES CUP
*Incorporating the West Riding County Cup**

First round – 2 legs
First leg played on 4 Jan, second leg on 11 Jan
  * Chesterfield v Leeds United 2-4, 3-2
  * Halifax Town v Huddersfield Town 1-2, 2-1
REPLAY on 18 Jan
  * Halifax Town v Huddersfield Town 1-4
Played on 11 Jan
  * Bradford v York City 4-2
  Middlesbrough v Bradford City 8-2

Semi-final
Played on 18 Jan
  Middlesbrough v Bradford 5-3
West Riding Cup Final, played on 10 May
  * Leeds United v Huddersfield Town 1-0

Final
Played on 17 May
  Middlesbrough v Leeds United 3-2

SHEFFIELD COUNTY CUP

Preliminary round
Played on 11 Jan
  Doncaster Rovers v Sheffield Wednesday 4-0

Semi-final
Played on 11 Jan
  Rotherham United v Barnsley 4-3
Played on 18 Jan
  Doncaster Rovers v Sheffield United 5-1

Final
Played on 29 Mar
  Doncaster Rovers v Rotherham United 3-2

CHESHIRE COUNTY BOWL

Semi-final
Played on 18 Jan
  Stockport County v Crewe Alexandra 2-1
Played on 17 May
  Tranmere Rovers v Chester 1-4 (aet 90 mins 1-1)

Final
Played on 6 Sep 1941
  Stockport County v Chester 2-4
  (Final held over to 1941-42 season)

MIDLAND CUP

First round – 2 legs
First leg played on 4 Jan, second leg on 11 Jan
  Leicester City v Stoke City 6-2, 5-3
  Luton Town v Walsall 6-2, 2-3
(NOTE both clubs appear in Round 2)
  Mansfield Town v Northampton Town 3-1, 3-3
(NOTE both clubs appear in Round 2)
First leg played on 11 Jan, second leg on 18 Jan
  Nottingham Forest v Lincoln City 4-2, 1-2
(NOTE both clubs appear in Round 2)
  West Bromwich Albion v Notts County 8-1
(NOTE second leg not played)

Second round
Played on 25 Jan
  Luton Town v Northampton Town 2-2
REPLAY Played on 1 Feb
  Northampton Town v Luton Town 5-2
Played on 1 Feb
  Leicester City v Nottingham Forest 6-2
  Lincoln City v Mansfield Town 4-2
Played on 8 Feb
  Walsall v West Bromwich Albion 4-3

Semi-final – 2 legs
First leg played on 8 Feb, second leg on 12 Apr
  Leicester City v Lincoln City 4-1, 4-5
First leg played on 15 Mar, second leg on 22 Mar
  Northampton Town v Walsall 1-3, 0-2

Final
Played on 3 May
  Leicester City v Walsall 2-0

HAMPSHIRE CUP

Semi-final
Played on 5 Apr
  Bournemouth & Boscombe Athletic v Southampton 1-1
REPLAY Played on 3 May
  Bournemouth & Boscombe Athletic v Southampton 2-3
Played on 17 May
  Portsmouth v Aldershot 10-5 *(aet, 90 mins 5-5)*

Final
Played on 2 Jun
  Portsmouth v Southampton 8-1

SOUTH WALES & MONMOUTHSHIRE CUP

Final
Played on 2 Jun
  Cardiff City v Lovell's Athletic 2-0

Other English Competitions 1940-41

LONDON CUP

Section A	Aldershot	Brentford	Chelsea	Crystal Palace	Fulham	QPR
Aldershot	X	12 Apr 2-2	4 Jan 1-0	1 Feb 3-3	15 Mar 3-1	8 Feb 2-4
Brentford	5 Apr 4-2	X	29 Mar 2-2	4 Jan 2-2	8 Feb 7-4	14 Apr 4-2
Chelsea	11 Jan 5-1	25 Jan 0-1	X	5 Apr 1-3	19 Apr 4-3	3 May 2-3
Crystal Palace	14 Apr 1-0	11 Jan 2-2	8 Feb 3-3	X	25 Jan 5-2	12 Apr 1-2
Fulham	22 Mar 2-4	1 Feb 4-1	12 Apr 4-0	1 Mar 1-4	X	4 Jan 4-1
Queen's Park Rangers	25 Jan 2-3	27 Apr 0-0	1 Feb 5-2	19 Apr 2-1	11 Jan 5-7	X

Fulham v Aldershot was played at Aldershot

	P	W	D	L	F	A	Pts
Brentford	10	4	5	1	25	20	13
C Palace	10	4	4	2	25	18	12
QPR	10	5	1	4	26	26	11
Aldershot	10	4	2	4	21	24	10
Fulham	10	4	0	6	32	34	8
Chelsea	10	2	2	6	19	26	6

Section B	Arsenal	Clapton Orient	Millwall	Reading	Tottenham	West ham U
Arsenal	X	8 Feb 15-2	24 May 5-2	11 Jan 0-1	21 May 0-3	17 May 3-0
Clapton Orient	1 Feb 3-3	X	1 Mar 0-1	25 Jan 0-4	11 Jan 1-9	19 Apr 2-3
Millwall	22 Mar 1-6	5 Apr 4-0	X	1 Feb 0-2	11 Jan 1-3	4 Jan 1-2
Reading	4 Jan 2-0	29 Mar 9-0	8 Feb 2-2	X	19 Apr 2-2	5 Apr 4-1
Tottenham Hotspur	3 May 3-3	4 Jan 3-0	25 Jan 4-0	14 Apr 2-2	X	1 Feb 1-2
West Ham United	25 Jan 1-3	12 Apr 8-1	11 Jan 2-1	22 Mar 1-1	8 Feb 3-2	X

Arsenal v Millwall was played at Millwall

	P	W	D	L	F	A	Pts
Reading	10	6	4	0	29	8	16
Tottenham	10	5	3	2	32	14	13
West Ham	10	6	1	3	23	19	13
Arsenal	10	5	2	3	38	18	12
Millwall	10	2	1	7	13	26	5
Clapton O	10	0	1	9	9	59	1

Semi -final
Played on 31 May
Reading v Crystal Palace 4-1
Tottenham Hotspur v Brentford 0-2

Final
Played on 7 Jun 1941 at Stamford Bridge, London
Att 9,000
Reading 3 (Sherwood, Chitty, Edelston)
Brentford 2 (Perry 2)

Reading: Mapson*, McPhie*, Fullwood, Young, Ratcliffe*, Layton, Chitty, Edelston. McPhee, Bradley, Sherwood
Brentford: Poland*, Brown, Poyser, Mackenzie*, James, Holliday, Hopkins, Townsend, Perry*, Wilkins, Bamford

LANCASHIRE CUP

First round – 2 legs
First leg played on 4 Jan, second leg on 11 Jan
Blackburn Rovers v Manchester United 0-2, 0-0
Blackpool v Bury 3-2, 2-1
Bolton Wanderers v Oldham Athletic 2-1, 5-3 *(aet, 90 mins 2-3)*
Chester v Southport 6-1, 3-2
Liverpool v Everton 1-2, 1-4
Manchester City v Rochdale 9-1, 6-1
Wrexham v New Brighton 3-5, 1-6

Second round – 2 legs
First leg played on 18 Jan, second leg on 25 Jan
Bolton Wanderers v Manchester United 3-2, 1-4
Manchester City v Blackpool 2-4, 1-2
First leg played on 25 Jan, second leg on 3 May
Burnley v Everton 2-3, 2-0 *(aet, 90 mins 1-0)*
First leg played on 1 Feb, second leg on 8 Feb
Chester v New Brighton 7-1, 0-2

Semi-final
Played on 19 Apr
Chester v Manchester United 4-6 *(aet, 90 mins 4-4)*
Played on 10 May
Burnley v Blackpool 1-0

Final
Played on 17 May
Burnley v Manchester United 0-1

The Scottish Southern Football League 1940-41

	Airdrieonians	Albion Rovers	Celtic	Clyde	Dumbarton	Falkirk	Hamilton Ac	Heart of Midlothian	Hibernian	Morton	Motherwell	Partick Thistle	Queen's Park	Rangers	St Mirren	Third Lanark
Airdrieonians	X	7 Sep 3-2	5 Oct 1-0	10 Aug 1-4	24 Aug 6-1	8 Feb 5-2	21 Sep 6-5	14 Dec 3-1	16 Nov 4-2	4 Jan 0-0	15 Feb 5-3	1 Feb 1-1	30 Nov 5-2	28 Dec 0-2	19 Oct 3-0	19 Apr 3-4
Albion Rovers	26 Apr 2-4	X	31 Aug 1-3	12 Oct 0-1	3 Mar 1-2	14 Sep 5-5	9 Nov 1-4	12 Aug 0-3	21 Dec 4-3	19 Aug 3-3	28 Sep 3-1	7 Dec 1-1	26 Oct 2-1	25 Jan 2-7	23 Nov 0-2	17 Aug 6-1
Celtic	11 Jan 2-0	14 Dec 2-0	X	12 Aug 1-1	21 Sep 1-0	12 Oct 2-2	10 Aug 2-2	24 Aug 2-1	26 Oct 0-4	30 Nov 2-0	25 Jan 4-1	8 Feb 5-1	28 Dec 5-1	7 Sep 0-0	9 Nov 0-0	22 Feb 4-3
Clyde	23 Nov 4-3	8 Jan 4-2	4 Jan 1-1	X	5 Oct 2-2	7 Dec 8-2	1 Feb 2-1	19 Oct 10-3	31 Aug 2-1	2 Nov 2-1	14 Sep 3-2	22 Aug 5-3	16 Nov 5-1	15 Feb 0-3	17 Aug 1-3	28 Sep 3-3
Dumbarton	7 Dec 3-3	8 Feb 4-1	21 Dec 2-3	11 Jan 2-1	X	1 Jan 2-1	22 Feb 5-1	9 Nov 1-4	28 Sep 2-0	25 Jan 2-4	17 Aug 2-3	23 Nov 2-0	12 Oct 2-1	26 Oct 1-4	14 Sep 3-4	31 Aug 6-4
Falkirk	2 Nov 1-1	28 Dec 2-0	8 Jan 0-1	24 Aug 3-2	7 Sep 3-3	X	4 Jan 5-0	30 Nov 3-3	15 Feb 2-2	14 Dec 6-3	16 Nov 6-3	19 Oct 4-1	21 Sep 4-1	10 Aug 1-3	5 Oct 2-0	1 Feb 5-0
Hamilton Academical	21 Dec 3-2	15 Feb 0-2	23 Nov 1-0	26 Oct 0-2	16 Nov 3-0	28 Sep 1-2	X	2 Nov 6-2	14 Sep 2-3	12 Oct 4-3	26 Aug 3-4	17 Aug 3-1	25 Jan 3-4	12 Aug 1-4	31 Aug 2-2	7 Dec 1-1
Heart Of Midlothian	31 Aug 0-2	16 Nov 3-1	7 Dec 2-1	25 Jan 3-5	15 Feb 3-1	17 Aug 2-3	8 Feb 5-2	X	28 Aug 3-5	26 Oct 3-3	23 Nov 1-1	21 Dec 2-1	3 Mar 1-0	12 Oct 1-1	28 Sep 5-1	14 Sep 4-2
Hibernian	12 Aug 2-2	21 Sep 1-1	1 Feb 2-0	14 Dec 2-2	26 Aug 3-1	9 Nov 7-1	28 Dec 3-1	7 Sep 2-1	X	24 Aug 2-1	2 Nov 3-3	5 Oct 4-0	10 Aug 3-2	30 Nov 1-0	8 Jan 2-4	19 Oct 2-2
Morton	28 Sep 3-3	5 Oct 4-0	17 Aug 2-0	8 Feb 2-6	19 Oct 2-1	31 Aug 1-1	8 Jan 3-3	1 Feb 1-1	7 Dec 3-1	X	21 Dec 1-0	14 Sep 3-1	9 Nov 5-0	22 Feb 2-4	1 Jan 1-2	23 Nov 4-1
Motherwell	9 Nov 2-0	9 Mar 6-0	19 Oct 5-1	28 Dec 4-6	30 Nov 4-1	12 Aug 3-1	7 Sep 2-4	10 Aug 2-3	8 Feb 3-0	21 Sep 1-1	X	18 Jan 2-4	14 Dec 2-0	24 Aug 2-3	1 Feb 4-1	5 Oct 3-0
Partick Thistle	26 Oct 3-3	24 Aug 1-0	26 Aug 3-2	7 Sep 3-3	10 Aug 5-2	25 Jan 4-0	30 Nov 0-0	21 Sep 4-2	11 Jan 1-2	28 Dec 2-2	12 Oct 3-0	X	4 Jan 4-0	14 Dec 1-4	22 Nov 3-2	15 Feb 2-3
Queen's Park	17 Aug 2-3	1 Feb 6-1	14 Sep 0-1	22 Feb 3-4	8 Jan 2-3	21 Dec 1-3	19 Oct 1-2	5 Oct 3-1	23 Nov 2-5	15 Feb 2-1	31 Aug 1-3	28 Sep 1-1	X	2 Nov 0-5	7 Dec 2-0	12 Aug 2-2
Rangers	14 Sep 2-0	19 Oct 2-0	1 Jan 2-3	9 Nov 3-2	1 Feb 1-1	23 Nov 4-0	5 Oct 2-0	18 Jan 3-0	17 Aug 5-1	16 Nov 5-4	7 Dec 2-3	31 Aug 3-1	8 Feb 1-1	X	21 Sep 3-0	26 Aug 0-3
St Mirren	25 Jan 1-1	10 Aug 1-1	15 Feb 1-0	30 Nov 2-2	28 Dec 4-0	11 Jan 3-4	14 Dec 3-3	4 Jan 0-1	12 Oct 4-4	7 Sep 2-2	26 Oct 2-0	16 Nov 1-0	24 Aug 2-1	21 Dec 2-0	X	3 Mar 3-2
Third Lanark	12 Oct 3-2	30 Nov 0-3	16 Nov 1-0	21 Sep 1-6	14 Dec 4-1	26 Oct 0-4	24 Aug 3-4	28 Dec 2-0	25 Jan 3-2	10 Aug 2-2	11 Jan 1-1	9 Nov 0-0	7 Sep 0-3	4 Jan 0-1	8 Feb 5-3	X

		P	W	D	L	F	A	Pts
1	Rangers	30	21	4	5	79	33	46
2	Clyde	30	18	7	5	99	61	43
3	Hibernian	30	14	7	9	74	61	35
4	Airdrieonians	30	13	8	9	75	62	34
5	Celtic	30	14	6	10	48	40	34
6	Falkirk	30	13	7	10	78	73	33
7	St Mirren	30	12	8	10	55	57	32
8	Motherwell	30	13	4	13	73	65	30
9	Heart of Midlothian	30	12	5	13	64	71	29
10	Morton	30	9	11	10	67	62	29
11	Hamilton Academical	30	11	6	13	67	75	28
12	Partick Thistle	30	9	8	13	55	62	26
13	Third Lanark	30	9	7	14	56	80	25
14	Dumbarton	30	10	4	16	58	78	24
15	Albion Rovers	30	6	5	19	45	80	17
16	Queen's Park	30	6	3	21	46	79	15

The Scottish Southern Football League Cup 1940-41

Section 1	Airdrieonians	Celtic	Motherwell	Partick Th
Airdrieonians	X	1 Mar 1-2	15 Mar 3-2	29 Mar 0-3
Celtic	22 Mar 3-1	X	8 Mar 3-2	15 Mar 2-4
Motherwell	5 Apr 1-4	29 Mar 4-2	X	1 Mar 3-0
Partick Thistle	8 Mar 4-2	5 Apr 0-1	22 Mar 4-4	X

		P	W	D	L	F	A	Pts
1	Celtic	6	4	0	2	13	12	8
2	Partick Th	6	3	1	2	15	12	7
3	Motherwell	6	2	1	3	16	16	5
4	Airdrieonians	6	2	0	4	11	15	4

Section 2	Albion R	Hamilton A	Morton	St Mirren
Albion Rovers	X	5 Apr 0-3	8 Mar 5-2	22 Mar 1-2
Hamilton Academical	15 Mar 1-1	X	22 Mar 2-1	8 Mar 5-5
Morton	29 Mar 5-1	1 Mar 2-4	X	15 Mar 0-1
St Mirren	1 Mar 4-1	29 Mar 4-1	5 Apr 4-2	X

		P	W	D	L	F	A	Pts
1	St Mirren	6	5	1	0	20	10	11
2	Hamilton Academical	6	3	2	1	16	13	8
3	Albion Rovers	6	1	1	4	9	17	3
4	Morton	6	1	0	5	12	17	2

Section 3	Dumbarton	Falkirk	Rangers	Third Lanark
Dumbarton	X	5 Apr 3-0	8 Mar 1-8	22 Mar 2-0
Falkirk	15 Mar 1-0	X	22 Mar 2-0	8 Mar 2-2
Rangers	29 Mar 6-3	1 Mar 4-0	X	15 Mar 3-0
Third Lanark	1 Mar 4-2	29 Mar 1-2	5 Apr 1-2	X

		P	W	D	L	F	A	Pts
1	Rangers	6	5	0	1	23	7	10
2	Falkirk	6	3	1	2	7	10	7
3	Dumbarton	6	2	0	4	11	19	4
4	Third Lanark	6	1	1	4	8	13	3

Section 4	Clyde	Hearts	Hibernian	Queen's Park
Clyde	X	5 Apr 1-0	1 Mar 2-4	29 Mar 3-1
Heart of Midlothian	15 Mar 3-1	X	29 Mar 5-2	1 Mar 3-0
Hibernian	22 Mar 5-4	8 Mar 3-2	X	5 Apr 0-0
Queen's Park	8 Mar 1-1	22 Mar 0-1	15 Mar 2-1	X

		P	W	D	L	F	A	Pts
1	Heart of Midlothian	6	4	0	2	14	7	8
2	Hibernian	6	3	1	2	15	15	7
3	Clyde	6	2	1	3	12	14	5
4	Queen's Park	6	1	2	3	4	9	4

Semi-final
Played on 19 Apr
Heart of Midlothian v Celtic 2-0 (at Easter Road, Edinburgh)
Rangers v St Mirren 4-1 (at Hampden Park, Glasgow)

Final
10 May 1941 at Hampden Park, Glasgow
Att 75,000
Rangers 1 *(Marshall)*
Heart of Midlothian 1 *(Woodburn og)*

Rangers: Dawson, Gray, Shaw, Bolt, Woodburn, Symon, Gillick, Thornton, Smith, Marshall, Johnstone
Hearts: Waugh, McClure, Miller, Philp, Dykes, Brown, Dougan, Walker, Hamilton, Massie, Christie

REPLAY on 17 May 1941 at Hampden Park, Glasgow
Att 60,000
Rangers 4 *(Venters, Smith, Thornton, Johnstone)*
Heart of Midlothian 2 *(Hamilton 2)*

Rangers: as first game except Venters for Marshall
Hearts: as first game

Other Scottish Competitions 1940-41

SUMMER CUP

First round – 2 legs
First leg played on 7 June, second on 14 June
Airdrieonians v Hamilton Academical 2-3, 2-4
Celtic v Hibernian 3-5, 0-1
Falkirk v Rangers 2-3, 1-3
Heart of Midlothian v Queen's Park 8-1,1-3
Morton v Clyde 1-2, 1-3
Motherwell v Dumbarton 2-2, 0-3
Partick Thistle v St Mirren 1-3, 1-3
Third Lanark v Albion Rovers 5-2,4-1

Second round – 2 legs
First leg played on 21 June, second on 28 June
Hamilton Academical v Rangers 1-3, 5-5
St Mirren v Heart of Midlothian 2-3, 1-5
Third Lanark v Dumbarton 0-1,0-4
First leg played on 21 June, second on 28 June, REPLAY at Ibrox Park, Glasgow
Hibernian v Clyde 1-2, 4-3, 2-1

Semi-final
Played on 5 July
Heart of Midlothian v Rangers 2-4 *(at Hampden Park, Glasgow)*
Hibernian v Dumbarton 1-0 *(at Tynecastle Park, Edinburgh)*

Final
12 Jul 1941 at Hampden Park, Glasgow
Att 37,000
Hibernian 3 *(Finnigan 2 (1 pen), Baxter)*
Rangers 2 *(Gillick, McIntosh)*

Hibernian: Kerr, Shaw, Hall, Busby, Baxter, Kean, Nutley, Finnigan, Milne, Combe, Caskie
Rangers: Dawson, Gray, Shaw, Bolt, Woodburn, Symon, McIntosh, Thornton, Gillick, Venters, Johnstone

GLASGOW CUP

First round
Played on 21 Aug
Third Lanark v Rangers 2-5
Played on 28 Aug
Celtic v Queen's Park 3-2

Semi-final
Played on 4 Sep
Rangers v Partick Thistle 1-0
Played on 11 Sep
Celtic v Clyde 1-0

Final
Played on 28 Sep at Ibrox Park, Glasgow
Rangers v Celtic 0-1

GLAGOW CHARITY CUP

First round
Played on 20 May
Partick Thistle v Clyde 7-5
Played on 21 May
Queen's Park v Celtic 2-5

Semi-final
Played on 24 May
Rangers v Third Lanark 3-1
Celtic v Partick Thistle 1-2

Final
Played on 31 May at Hampden Park, Glasgow
Rangers v Partick Thistle 3-0

RENFREWSHIRE CUP

Final
Played in early Sep 1941
St Mirren beat Morton

Played in 1940-41 season

WILSON CUP
Played on 14 Aug at Tynecastle Park, Edinburgh
Heart of Midlothian v Hibernian 3-2

DEWAR SHIELD

Qualifying round
Played on 25 Mar 1940
St Johnstone v Black Watch 6-1

COMPETITION ABANDONED

NORTHERN REGIONAL FOOTBALL LEAGUE

	Belfast Celtic	Cliftonville	Derry City	Distillery	Glenavon	Glentoran	Linfield	Portadown
Belfast Celtic	X	30 Nov 9-1 / 1 Mar 3-1	7 Dec 1-2 / 8 Mar 8-2	21 Dec 4-0 / 22 Mar 3-1	25 Jan 13-0 / 19 Apr 5-2	28 Dec 1-2 / 12 Apr 8-2	8 Feb 5-2 / 10 May 2-4	6-0 / 15 Feb 3-1
Cliftonville	4 Jan 0-1 / 1-3	X	8 Feb 2-5 / 10 May 4-5	19 Apr 1-3 / 25 Jan 1-7	3-2 / 1-1	21 Dec 1-3 / 22 Mar 0-4	23 Nov 0-5 / 3-4	7 Dec 0-8 / 8 Mar 2-5
Derry City	11 Jan 0-4 / 0-1	2-1 / 29 Mar 2-1	X	1-2 / 15 Feb 1-4	21 Dec 5-3 / 22 Mar 2-3	30 Nov 0-4 / 1 Mar 2-2	25 Jan 0-4 / 19 Apr 2-2	28 Dec 2-2 / 12 Apr 2-5
Distillery	1 Feb 2-7 / 3 May 0-0	14 Dec 7-1 / 5-1	6-0 / 5-2	X	23 Nov 5-0 / 2-2	8 Feb 6-3 / 10 May 2-3	7 Dec 5-1 / 8 Mar 2-3	4 Jan 2-2 / 1-2
Glenavon	5 Apr 1-5 / 14 Dec 1-6	1-2 / 15 Feb 6-3	1 Feb 6-1 / 3 May 3-4	28 Dec 2-1 / 12 Apr 0-1	X	7 Dec 1-0 / 8 Mar 1-1	XXX / 1-1	29 Mar 0-4 / 1-4
Glentoran	23 Nov 1-1 / 3-3	1 Feb 6-2 / 3 May 6-3	4 Jan 5-0 / 4-0	5-0 / 6-1	11 Jan 8-0 / 1-2	X	1-2 / 3-1	14 Dec 4-2 / 7-4
Linfield	1-0 / 29 Mar 0-2	28 Dec 2-1 / 12 Apr 3-1	14 Dec 7-2 / 1-2	11 Jan 1-1 / 1-3	30 Nov 2-0 / 1 Mar 6-1	1-4 / 15 Feb 3-3	X	1 Feb 2-0 / 3 May 3-4
Portadown	XXX / 2-2	11 Jan 5-1 / 4-2	6-2 / 29 Mar 4-0	3-1 / 1 Mar 1-1	8 Feb 8-0 / 10 May 3-1	25 Jan 6-5 / 19 Apr 4-3	21 Dec 1-4 / 22 Mar 3-3	X

Glenavon v Linfield and Portadown v Belfast Celtic games were not played.

		P	W	D	L	F	A	Pts
1	Belfast Celtic	27	19	4	4	104	32	42
2	Portadown	27	17	4	6	92	58	38
3	Glentoran	28	16	5	7	99	57	37
4	Linfield	27	14	4	9	67	51	32
5	Distillery	28	13	5	10	77	57	31
6	Derry City	28	8	3	17	48	100	19
7	Glenavon	27	6	4	17	40	95	16

IRISH FA CUP

First round
Played on 18 Jan
 Larne v Bangor 3-4
 Derry City v Royal Ulster Regiment 5-5
REPLAY on 22 Feb
 Derry City v Royal Ulster Regiment 3-2
Played on 22 Feb
 Belfast Celtic v Coleraine 11-1
 Crusaders v Portadown 1-7
 Distillery v Glentoran 3-0
 Glenavon v Glentoran II 5-0
 Linfield v Ards 4-1

Second round
Played on 15 Mar
 Belfast Celtic v Bangor 3-2
 Cliftonville v Glenavon 3-3
 Derry City v Distillery 0-1
 Portadown v Linfield 0-3

Semi-final
 Belfast Celtic v Glenavon 5-2
 Linfield v Distillery 3-3, 5-2

Final
Played on 26 Apr at Windsor Park, Belfast
 Belfast Celtic v Linfield 1-0

1941-42

The Football League's North and South competitions were subdivided into smaller regional sections with each club playing nine others home and away for an eighteen-match schedule which concluded at Christmas. However the refusal of the capital's clubs to compete in the official League South saw them expelled by the Football League. They organized themselves as the London Football League which had the effect of reducing the South competition to just thirteen clubs.

The League Cup was also reorganized; qualifying sections of ten games each was followed by the knock-out phase with all games in this and the local cups counting towards the League Championship which ran through the second half of the season.

Again, Aston Villa competed in the non-League Birmingham & District League.

The Scottish Southern League was joined by the North Eastern Football League. Because of its size, it was played over Autumn and Spring competitions, with bonus points being awarded in the latter.

A Northern Irish Northern Regional League also operated. There was also an international competition involving clubs from the Republic of Ireland.

WINNERS OF THE PRINCIPAL COMPETITIONS

Football League Cup	Wolverhampton Wanderers
Football League –	
North	Blackpool
League Championship	Manchester United
South	Leicester City
London League	Arsenal
London Cup	Brentford
Scottish Southern League	Rangers
Scottish Southern League Cup	Rangers
Scottish North Eastern League –	
First Series	Rangers 'A'
Second Series	Aberdeen
North Eastern League Cup –	
First Series	Aberdeen
Second Series	Dundee United
Irish FA Cup	Linfield
Northern Regional League	Belfast Celtic
Substitute Gold Cup	Glentoran
Inter City Cup	Dundalk

The Football League 1941-42

NORTH

	Barnsley	Chesterfield	Doncaster Rovers	Grimsby Town	Lincoln City	Mansfield Town	Rotherham United	Sheffield United	Sheffield Wednesday
Barnsley	X	15 Nov 1-0	27 Sep 2-4	30 Aug 2-1	20 Sep 1-2	25 Oct 3-1	25 Dec 7-1	18 Oct 2-1	6 Dec 4-3
Chesterfield	8 Nov 1-1	X	30 Aug 3-1	20 Dec 1-1	30 Aug 1-2	18 Oct 1-2	6 Dec 2-1	27 Sep 0-1	29 Nov 0-1
Doncaster Rovers	4 Oct 1-1	13 Sep 3-1	X	8 Nov 1-3	29 Nov 1-3	6 Sep 4-1	1 Nov 5-1	20 Dec 3-1	11 Oct 2-2
Grimsby Town	6 Sep 1-1	25 Dec 2-3	15 Nov 2-0	X	25 Oct 1-3	13 Dec 4-5	4 Oct 6-2	22 Nov 7-1	13 Sep 1-1
Lincoln City	13 Sep 3-2	6 Sep 5-1	22 Nov 3-1	1 Nov 1-1	X	25 Dec 6-0	11 Oct 3-0	13 Dec 3-0	4 Oct 6-0
Mansfield Town	1 Nov 0-3	11 Oct 2-4	30 Aug 4-1	6 Dec 1-3	20 Dec 0-5	X	29 Nov 4-1	20 Sep 2-3	8 Nov 4-0
Rotherham United	20 Dec 3-3	13 Dec 3-1	25 Oct 2-1	27 Sep 2-3	18 Oct 2-3	22 Nov 4-0	X	15 Nov 1-1	6 Sep 4-1
Sheffield United	11 Oct 2-1	4 Oct 2-2	25 Dec 5-2	29 Nov 0-0	6 Dec 9-0	13 Sep 1-2	8 Nov 5-1	X	1 Nov 3-3
Sheffield Wednesday	13 Dec 3-0	22 Nov 1-1	18 Oct 5-2	20 Sep 0-2	27 Sep 1-1	15 Nov 2-0	30 Aug 1-0	25 Oct 1-3	X

	Bradford	Bradford City	Gateshead	Huddersfield Town	Leeds United	Middlesbrough	Newcastle United	Sunderland	York City
Bradford	X	29 Nov 3-1	30 Aug 2-2	25 Dec 1-3	11 Oct 6-0	1 Nov 1-0	8 Nov 0-0	20 Sep 2-2	25 Dec 2-2
Bradford City	22 Nov 2-1	X	25 Oct 1-2	27 Sep 3-1	13 Dec 5-0	20 Dec 5-1	6 Sep 1-1	15 Nov 4-2	18 Oct 0-2
Gateshead	30 Aug 2-2	1 Nov 1-1	X	8 Nov 3-2	13 Sep 3-2	4 Oct 4-1	11 Oct 1-1	20 Dec 2-0	29 Nov 1-0
Huddersfield Town	13 Dec 3-0	4 Oct 4-1	15 Nov 3-1	X	20 Dec 4-2	6 Sep 2-4	13 Sep 5-0	22 Nov 1-0	25 Oct 5-1
Leeds United	18 Oct 4-0	6 Dec 4-2	20 Sep 5-1	25 Dec 2-1	X	8 Nov 2-3	29 Nov 5-2	27 Sep 1-2	30 Aug 2-0
Middlesbrough	25 Oct 0-2	25 Dec 6-0	27 Sep 1-1	30 Aug 3-1	15 Nov 1-2	X	6 Dec 0-7	18 Oct 2-2	20 Sep 5-2
Newcastle United	15 Nov 3-1	30 Aug 1-1	18 Oct 3-1	20 Sep 3-1	22 Nov 4-2	13 Dec 7-4	X	25 Oct 1-1	27 Sep 5-3
Sunderland	13 Sep 1-2	8 Nov 5-1	25 Dec 1-3	29 Nov 5-0	4 Oct 6-1	11 Oct 4-4	1 Nov 3-2	X	6 Dec 4-2
York City	20 Dec 2-3	11 Oct 3-3	22 Nov 3-4	1 Nov 1-5	6 Sep 1-0	13 Sep 9-5	4 Oct 2-2	13 Dec 1-4	X

On 25 December 1941, Bradford played their game against Huddersfield Town, which was postponed from 6 December, in the morning. Both clubs then played their scheduled matches in the afternoon against their respective opponents

The Football League 1941-42

NORTH

	Blackburn Rovers	Blackpool	Bolton Wanderers	Burnley	Bury	Halifax Town	Oldham Athletic	Preston North End	Rochdale	Southport
Blackburn Rovers	X	25 Oct 2-1	4 Oct 3-3	22 Nov 3-2	13 Sep 2-0	11 Oct 2-0	15 Nov 2-1	20 Dec 2-1	13 Dec 8-2	6 Sep 2-0
Blackpool	1 Nov 4-1	X	18 Oct 2-1	13 Dec 9-0	4 Oct 4-2	8 Nov 9-1	22 Nov 5-1	6 Sep 2-0	25 Dec 0-1	13 Sep 10-1
Bolton Wanderers	27 Sep 2-2	11 Oct 2-6	X	15 Nov 3-1	6 Sep 2-1	13 Sep 1-1	25 Oct 3-5	13 Dec 2-6	22 Nov 3-3	25 Dec 4-0
Burnley	29 Nov 0-0	6 Dec 2-2	8 Nov 2-1	X	1 Nov 9-3	6 Sep 0-1	25 Dec 1-1	4 Oct 1-0	13 Sep 3-1	11 Oct 4-2
Bury	20 Sep 0-3	27 Sep 0-5	30 Aug 4-4	25 Oct 3-3	X	20 Dec 3-1	18 Oct 5-0	22 Nov 0-4	15 Nov 2-3	13 Dec 6-1
Halifax Town	18 Oct 0-0	15 Nov 1-2	20 Sep 2-0	30 Aug 2-3	25 Dec 2-1	X	13 Dec 3-0	25 Oct 0-1	27 Sep 4-2	29 Nov 2-1
Oldham Athletic	8 Nov 2-2	29 Nov 0-3	1 Nov 2-0	20 Dec 5-2	11 Oct 5-5	6 Dec 6-2	X	13 Sep 1-1	6 Sep 3-0	4 Oct 3-1
Preston North End	25 Dec 1-2	30 Aug 3-1	6 Dec 4-2	27 Sep 2-1	29 Nov 4-0	1 Nov 6-2	20 Sep 7-0	X	18 Oct 6-0	8 Nov 2-0
Rochdale	6 Dec 2-2	20 Dec 0-5	29 Nov 1-0	20 Sep 1-1	8 Nov 1-0	4 Oct 2-2	30 Aug 3-2	11 Oct 1-5	X	1 Nov 4-2
Southport	30 Aug 3-2	20 Sep 1-5	20 Dec 3-2	18 Oct 1-1	6 Dec 6-2	22 Nov 2-3	27 Sep 4-3	15 Nov 1-5	25 Oct 4-1	X

	Chester	Everton	Liverpool	Manchester City	Manchester United	New Brighton	Stockport County	Stoke City	Tranmere Rovers	Wrexham
Chester	X	20 Sep 2-0	8 Nov 3-4	6 Dec 1-3	11 Oct 0-7	25 Dec 6-1	30 Aug 3-1	4 Oct 3-4	1 Nov 6-1	29 Nov 2-2
Everton	13 Sep 1-1	X	1 Nov 5-3	29 Nov 9-0	4 Oct 1-3	6 Dec 4-0	25 Dec 6-0	6 Sep 3-1	11 Oct 3-2	8 Nov 3-1
Liverpool	15 Nov 4-2	25 Oct 3-2	X	20 Sep 4-2	22 Nov 1-1	27 Sep 7-2	18 Oct 6-1	20 Dec 1-1	13 Dec 7-2	30 Aug 5-2
Manchester City	13 Dec 7-2	22 Nov 3-4	13 Sep 3-4	X	20 Dec 2-1	25 Oct 2-2	15 Nov 2-1	11 Oct 4-3	6 Sep 1-1	4 Oct 2-0
Manchester United	18 Oct 8-1	27 Sep 2-3	29 Nov 2-2	25 Dec 2-2	X	30 Aug 13-1	20 Sep 7-1	1 Nov 3-0	8 Nov 6-1	6 Dec 10-3
New Brighton	20 Dec 4-3	13 Dec 1-5	4 Oct 5-5	1 Nov 3-2	6 Sep 3-3	X	22 Nov 6-3	8 Nov 3-5	13 Sep 2-1	11 Oct 2-2
Stockport County	6 Sep 2-4	20 Dec 1-1	11 Oct 1-2	8 Nov 4-6	13 Sep 1-5	29 Nov 7-1	X	6 Dec 1-6	4 Oct 5-2	1 Nov 3-3
Stoke City	27 Sep 2-5	30Aug 8-3	25 Dec 4-3	18 Oct 5-0	25 Oct 1-1	15 Nov 4-0	13 Dec 3-1	X	22 Nov 9-0	20 Sep 5-2
Tranmere Rovers	25 Oct 1-0	18 Oct 0-4	6 Dec 1-2	30 Aug 5-2	15 Nov 1-1	20 Sep 1-1	27 Sep 4-0	29 Nov 2-7	X	25 Dec 4-2
Wrexham	22 Nov 1-1	15 Nov 0-4	6 Sep 5-3	27 Sep 3-5	13 Dec 3-4	18 Oct 2-2	25 Oct 6-1	13 Sep 1-7	20 Dec 2-6	X

Inter area matches

Played on 30 Aug
Sunderland v Sheffield United 7-1
Played on 6 Sep
Sheffield United v Sunderland 0-1
Played on 13 Sep
Bradford City v Rotherham United 0-2
Played on 20 Sep
Rotherham United v Bradford City 3-1
Played on 27 Sep
Mansfield Town v Bradford 1-2
Played on 4 Oct
Bradford v Mansfield Town 3-0

Played on 11 Oct
Huddersfield Town v Grimsby Town 5-1
Played on 18 Oct
Grimsby Town v Huddersfield Town 2-2
Played on 25 Oct
Chesterfield v Leeds United 3-0
Played on 1 Nov
Leeds United v Chesterfield 2-2
Played on 8 Nov
Lincoln City v York City 3-3
Played on 15 Nov
York City v Lincoln City 4-2

Played on 22 Nov
Barnsley v Middlesbrough 3-1
Played on 29 Nov
Middlesbrough v Barnsley 3-2
Played on 6 Dec
Gateshead v Doncaster Rovers 6-2
Played on 13 Dec
Doncaster Rovers v Gateshead 5-1
Played on 20 Dec
Sheffield Wednesday v Newcastle United 4-2
Played on 25 Dec
Newcastle United v Sheffield Wednesday 2-4

The Football League 1941-42

NORTH

Final Table

		P	W	D	L	F	A	Pts
1	Blackpool	18	14	1	3	75	19	29
2	Lincoln City	18	13	3	2	54	28	29
3	Preston North End	18	13	1	4	58	18	27
4	Manchester United	18	10	6	2	79	27	26
5	Stoke City	18	12	2	4	75	36	26
6	Everton	18	12	2	4	61	31	26
7	Blackburn Rovers	18	10	6	2	40	24	26
8	Liverpool	18	11	4	3	66	44	26
9	Gateshead	18	9	5	4	39	35	23
10	Sunderland	18	9	4	5	50	30	22
11	Huddersfield Town	18	10	1	7	48	33	21
12	Bradford	18	8	5	5	33	28	21
13	Grimsby Town	18	7	6	5	41	31	20
14	Barnsley	18	8	4	6	39	31	20
15	Newcastle United	18	7	6	5	46	39	20
16	Sheffield Wednesday	18	7	5	6	33	37	19
17	Manchester City	18	8	3	7	48	54	19
18	Sheffield United	18	7	4	7	39	38	18
19	Burnley	18	6	6	6	36	40	18
20	Halifax Town	18	7	3	8	29	41	17
21	Oldham Athletic	18	6	4	8	40	49	16
22	Rochdale	18	6	4	8	28	52	16
23	Chesterfield	18	5	5	8	27	31	15
24	Chester	18	6	3	9	45	53	15
25	Middlesbrough	18	6	3	9	44	56	15
26	Leeds United	18	7	1	10	36	46	15
27	Doncaster Rovers	18	6	2	10	39	46	14
28	Bradford City	18	5	4	9	32	42	14
29	Rotherham United	18	6	2	10	33	47	14
30	New Brighton	18	4	6	8	39	75	14
31	Tranmere Rovers	18	5	3	10	35	60	13
32	York City	18	4	4	10	41	55	12
33	Mansfield Town	18	6	0	12	29	50	12
34	Bolton Wanderers	18	3	5	10	35	48	11
35	Southport	18	5	1	12	33	61	11
36	Bury	18	3	3	12	37	59	9
37	Wrexham	18	2	5	11	40	69	9
38	Stockport County	18	2	2	14	34	73	6

The Football League 1941-42

LEAGUE CHAMPIONSHIP

BARNSLEY

	Date	Opponent	H/A	Score
LC	27 Dec	Bradford	H	5-2
LC	3 Jan	Bradford	A	1-1
LC	10 Jan	Grimsby T	H	0-0
LC	17 Jan	Grimsby T	A	0-2
LC	14 Feb	Leeds U	A	2-3
LC	21 Feb	Stockport Co	H	6-1
LC	28 Feb	Stockport Co	A	6-3
LC	14 Mar	Halifax T	A	4-2
LC	21 Mar	Leeds U	H	3-2
LC	28 Mar	Halifax T	H	6-0
LC	4 Apr	Grimsby T	H	1-2
LC	6 Apr	Grimsby T	A	1-1
	9 May	Sheffield United	H	5-1
	16 May	Rotherham U	A	5-1
	25 May	Rotherham U	H	3-2

BLACKBURN ROVERS

	Date	Opponent	H/A	Score
LC	27 Dec	Manchester City	H	3-0
LC	3 Jan	Manchester City	A	2-1
LC	10 Jan	Everton	A	0-0
LC	17 Jan	Everton	H	0-0
LC	31 Jan	New Brighton	A	5-0
LC	14 Feb	Bradford City	H	2-0
LC	21 Feb	Leeds U	H	1-0
LC	28 Feb	Leeds U	A	1-0
LC	7 Mar	New Brighton	H	5-1
La	14 Mar	Burnley	H	6-2
LC	21 Mar	Bradford City	A	0-5
`La	28 Mar	Burnley	A	0-2
LC	4 Apr	Manchester Utd	H	1-2
LC	6 Apr	Manchester Utd	A	1-3
	11 Apr	Preston NE	H	3-3
	18 Apr	Preston NE	A	0-2
	25 Apr	Liverpool	A	0-0
	2 May	Tranmere R	A	5-0
	9 May	Manchester Utd	H	1-1
	16 May	Manchester Utd	A	1-0
	23 May	Liverpool	A	2-2
La	30 May	Blackpool	A	1-7

BLACKPOOL

	Date	Opponent	H/A	Score
LC	27 Dec	Stockport Co	H	5-2
LC	3 Jan	Stockport Co	A	1-2
LC	10 Jan	Wolverhampton	H	6-1
LC	17 Jan	Wolverhampton	A	0-1
LC	24 Jan	Huddersfield T	A	3-3
LC	31 Jan	Huddersfield T	H	4-2
LC	7 Feb	Liverpool	H	6-2
LC	14 Feb	Liverpool	A	3-1
LC	21 Feb	Tranmere R	A	2-2
LC	28 Feb	Tranmere R	H	15-3
	7 Mar	Burnley	H	13-0
	14 Mar	Everton	A	2-2
	21 Mar	Burnley	A	6-0
	28 Mar	Stoke C	H	4-0
	11 Apr	Bolton W	H	7-1
	18 Apr	Bolton W	A	1-2
	25 Apr	Rochdale	A	0-2
	2 May	Rochdale	H	5-1
	9 May	Oldham Ath	A	8-2
	16 May	Oldham Ath	A	2-2
	25 May	Liverpool	H	8-2
La	30 May	Blackburn R	H	7-1

BOLTON WANDERERS

	Date	Opponent	H/A	Score
LC	27 Dec	Manchester U	A	1-3
LC	3 Jan	Manchester U	H	2-2
LC	10 Jan	Chester	H	1-0
LC	17 Jan	Chester	A	1-3
LC	14 Feb	Stoke C	A	1-3
LC	28 Feb	York C	H	4-3
LC	14 Mar	Bradford City	H	4-0
LC	21 Mar	Stoke C	H	1-1
LC	28 Mar	York C	A	1-2
	4 Apr	Halifax T	A	2-2
	6 Apr	Sheffield Wed	H	3-3
La	11 Apr	Blackpool	A	1-7
La	18 Apr	Blackpool	H	2-1
	25 Apr	Bury	A	0-2
	2 May	Bury	H	2-1

BOURNEMOUTH & BOSCOMBE ATHLETIC

	Date	Opponent	H/A	Score
LC	10 Jan	Bristol City	A	0-5
LC	17 Jan	Bristol City	H	2-2
LC	31 Jan	Southampton	H	3-4
LC	7 Feb	Cardiff C	H	2-1
LC	14 Feb	Cardiff C	A	0-6
LC	21 Feb	Southampton	A	2-2
LC	28 Feb	Southampton	H	2-0
LC	7 Mar	Southampton	A	0-1

BRADFORD

	Date	Opponent	H/A	Score
LC	27 Dec	Barnsley	A	2-5
LC	3 Jan	Barnsley	H	1-1
LC	10 Jan	Middlesbrough	H	1-1
LC	17 Jan	Middlesbrough	A	2-1
LC	24 Jan	Oldham Ath	A	2-5
LC	31 Jan	Rotherham U	H	5-5
LC	14 Feb	Oldham Ath	H	3-1
LC	21 Feb	Sunderland	H	3-0
LC	28 Feb	Sunderland	A	2-4
LC	21 Mar	Rotherham U	A	1-3
	28 Mar	Bradford City	A	2-2
LC	4 Apr	Middlesbrough	A	2-3
LC	6 Apr	Middlesbrough	H	2-0
LC	11 Apr	Sheffield Utd	H	2-0
LC	18 Apr	Sheffield Utd	A	1-2
LC	25 Apr	Sunderland	H	0-1
LC	2 May	Sunderland	A	2-2
CC	9 May	Chesterfield	H	0-2
	16 May	Huddersfield T	A	2-2

BRADFORD CITY

	Date	Opponent	H/A	Score
LC	27 Dec	Burnley	H	5-1
LC	3 Jan	Burnley	A	1-3
LC	10 Jan	Sheffield Wed	A	1-0
LC	14 Feb	Blackburn R	A	0-2
LC	21 Feb	Gateshead	A	0-1
LC	28 Feb	Gateshead	H	2-0
LC	14 Mar	Bolton W	A	0-4
LC	21 Mar	Blackburn R	H	5-0
	28 Mar	Bradford	H	2-2
LC	4 Apr	Huddersfield T	H	4-1
LC	6 Apr	Huddersfield T	A	1-2
LC	11 Apr	Sunderland	A	2-1
LC	18 Apr	Sunderland	H	4-6
CC	9 May	York C	A	1-2

BRISTOL CITY

	Date	Opponent	H/A	Score
LC	27 Dec	Swansea T	H	1-1
LC	3 Jan	Swansea T	A	3-1
LC	10 Jan	Bournemouth	H	5-0
LC	17 Jan	Bournemouth	A	2-2
LC	24 Jan	Cardiff C	H	8-3
LC	31 Jan	Cardiff C	A	2-0
LC	7 Feb	Swansea T	A	1-2
LC	14 Feb	Swansea T	H	1-1
	7 Mar	Luton T	H	2-3
	14 Mar	Swansea T	H	10-0
LC	21 Mar	Southampton	H	5-1
LC	28 Mar	Southampton	A	1-5
LC	4 Apr	Northampton T	A	0-3
LC	6 Apr	Northampton T	H	3-1
	11 Apr	Luton T	H	7-0
	23 May	Leicester C	A	1-5
	30 May	Leicester C	H	3-1

BURNLEY

	Date	Opponent	H/A	Score
LC	27 Dec	Bradford City	A	1-5
LC	3 Jan	Bradford City	H	3-1
LC	10 Jan	Manchester City	H	1-2
LC	17 Jan	Manchester City	A	0-5
LC	24 Jan	Stockport Co	H	6-0
LC	31 Jan	Stockport Co	A	0-0
LC	7 Feb	Everton	A	2-3
LC	14 Feb	Everton	H	1-0
LC	21 Feb	Sheffield Wed	A	1-3
LC	28 Feb	Sheffield Wed	H	3-0
	7 Mar	Blackpool	A	0-13
La	14 Mar	Blackburn R	A	2-6
	21 Mar	Blackpool	A	0-6
La	28 Mar	Blackburn R	H	2-0
LC	4 Apr	Liverpool	H	0-3
LC	6 Apr	Liverpool	A	1-4
	11 Apr	Huddersfield T	H	3-0
	25 Apr	Preston NE	H	3-0
	2 May	Preston NE	A	0-2

KEY: LC=League Cup; La=Lancashire Cup; MC=Midland Cup;
CC=Combined Counties Cup; Li=Liverpool Senior Cup

The Football League 1941-42

LEAGUE CHAMPIONSHIP

BURY

LC	27 Dec	Liverpool	A	0-4
LC	3 Jan	Liverpool	H	2-3
LC	10 Jan	New Brighton	H	10-5
LC	17 Jan	New Brighton	A	6-0
LC	21 Feb	Chesterfield	A	4-3
LC	28 Feb	Chesterfield	H	1-2
LC	14 Mar	Wrexham	A	0-3
LC	21 Mar	Sheffield Wed	A	2-2
LC	28 Mar	Sheffield Wed	H	8-2
LC	4 Apr	Southport	H	4-4
LC	6 Apr	Southport	A	1-2
	11 Apr	Rochdale	H	4-3
	18 Apr	Rochdale	A	1-4
	25 Apr	Bolton W	H	2-0
	2 May	Bolton W	A	1-2

CARDIFF CITY

LC	27 Dec	Southampton	A	5-2
LC	3 Jan	Southampton	H	9-1
LC	10 Jan	Swansea T	A	1-1
LC	17 Jan	Swansea T	H	1-1
LC	24 Jan	Bristol City	A	3-8
LC	31 Jan	Bristol City	H	0-2
LC	7 Feb	Bournemouth	A	1-2
LC	14 Feb	Bournemouth	H	6-0
LC	21 Feb	Swansea T	A	5-1
LC	28 Feb	Swansea T	H	8-1
	14 Mar	Luton T	H	2-0
	21 Mar	Swansea T	H	4-1
LC	4 Apr	Southampton	H	3-1
LC	6 Apr	Southampton	A	1-1
LC	11 Apr	WBA	H	1-1
LC	18 Apr	WBA	A	2-3
	25 Apr	Northampton T	H	0-1
	2 May	Northampton T	A	1-6
	25 May	Swansea T	H	4-1
	30 May	Luton T	H	2-4

CHESTER

LC	27 Dec	Wolverhampton W	A	1-2
LC	3 Jan	Wolverhampton W	H	1-3
LC	10 Jan	Bolton W	A	0-1
LC	17 Jan	Bolton W	H	3-1
LC	31 Jan	Walsall	H	4-3
LC	7 Feb	Preston NE	A	0-6
LC	14 Feb	Preston NE	H	2-2
LC	21 Feb	New Brighton	A	1-2
LC	28 Feb	New Brighton	H	5-0
LC	14 Mar	Walsall	A	2-0
La	21 Mar	Liverpool	H	1-3
	28 Mar	Tranmere R	A	1-1
LC	4 Apr	Wolverhampton W	A	1-3
LC	6 Apr	Wolverhampton W	H	0-1
	11 Apr	Oldham Athletic	A	3-2
	25 Apr	Stoke C	H	2-4
	2 May	Stoke C	A	2-2
La	9 May	Liverpool	A	0-3
	16 May	Wrexham	H	1-2
	25 May	Wrexham	A	4-0

CHESTERFIELD

LC	27 Dec	Leicester C	H	3-3
LC	3 Jan	Leicester C	A	1-4
LC	10 Jan	Nottingham For	A	0-1
LC	17 Jan	Nottingham For	H	1-0
LC	31 Jan	Stoke C	A	1-2
LC	7 Feb	Huddersfield T	A	0-3
LC	21 Feb	Bury	H	3-4
LC	28 Feb	Bury	A	2-1
LC	14 Mar	Stoke C	H	2-1
LC	21 Mar	Huddersfield T	H	2-1
	4 Apr	Mansfield T	H	5-2
	6 Apr	Mansfield T	A	2-0
	11 Apr	York C	A	1-3
CC	25 Apr	Halifax T	H	4-1
CC	2 May	Leeds U	A	0-1
CC	9 May	Bradford	A	2-0
CC	16 May	Halifax T	A	2-2
	25 May	Sheffield United	H	1-2

16 May, aet 2-5

DONCASTER ROVERS

LC	27 Dec	Lincoln C	A	3-9
LC	3 Jan	Huddersfield T	A	1-3
LC	10 Jan	Halifax T	H	2-1
LC	21 Feb	Grimsby T	H	1-2
LC	28 Feb	Huddersfield T	H	1-4
LC	14 Mar	Leeds U	A	1-6
LC	21 Mar	Lincoln C	H	0-2
LC	28 Mar	Leeds U	H	1-0
	18 Apr	Rotherham U	A	0-3

EVERTON

LC	27 Dec	Sheffield Wed	A	3-0
LC	3 Jan	Sheffield Wed	H	2-0
LC	10 Jan	Blackburn R	H	0-0
LC	17 Jan	Blackburn R	A	0-0
LC	31 Jan	Wolverhampton	H	2-1
LC	7 Feb	Burnley	H	3-2
LC	14 Feb	Burnley	A	0-1
LC	21 Feb	Oldham Athletic	A	0-1
LC	28 Feb	Oldham Athletic	H	4-0
LC	7 Mar	Wolverhampton	A	1-11
	14 Mar	Blackpool	H	2-2
La	21 Mar	Southport	H	3-1
	28 Mar	Oldham Athletic	A	2-1
LC	4 Apr	Preston NE	H	2-2
LC	6 Apr	Preston NE	A	1-1
LC	11 Apr	Liverpool	A	2-0
LC	18 Apr	Liverpool	H	0-1
LC	25 Apr	WBA	A	1-3
La	28 Apr	Southport	A	1-2
LC	2 May	WBA	H	1-5
La	9 May	Manchester City	A	0-2
La	16 May	Manchester City	H	6-1
Li	30 May	Liverpool	A	1-4

6 Apr, aet 2-1

GATESHEAD

LC	27 Dec	Newcastle U	H	2-2
LC	3 Jan	Newcastle U	A	2-4
LC	10 Jan	York C	H	3-2
LC	17 Jan	York C	A	3-3
LC	31 Jan	Sunderland	H	1-2
LC	14 Feb	Middlesbrough	H	1-3
LC	21 Feb	Bradford City	H	1-0
LC	28 Feb	Bradford City	A	0-2
LC	14 Mar	Middlesbrough	A	1-7
LC	21 Mar	Sunderland	A	1-5
	4 Apr	Newcastle U	H	4-0
	6 Apr	Newcastle U	A	2-0
	9 May	Newcastle U	A	2-6

GRIMSBY TOWN

LC	27 Dec	York C	H	0-0
LC	3 Jan	York C	A	2-3
LC	10 Jan	Barnsley	A	0-0
LC	17 Jan	Barnsley	H	2-0
LC	24 Jan	Lincoln C	A	2-1
LC	21 Feb	Doncaster R	A	2-1
LC	28 Feb	Halifax T	A	2-2
	14 Mar	Huddersfield T	H	1-2
LC	21 Mar	Halifax T	H	1-3
LC	28 Mar	Lincoln C	H	4-2
LC	4 Apr	Barnsley	A	2-1
LC	6 Apr	Barnsley	H	1-1
LC	11 Apr	Nottingham Forest	H	3-1
LC	18 Apr	Nottingham Forest	A	5-1
LC	25 Apr	Norwich C	A	0-1
LC	2 May	Norwich C	H	2-0
LC	9 May	Sunderland	A	0-0
LC	16 May	Sunderland	H	2-3

HALIFAX TOWN

LC	27 Dec	Huddersfield T	H	2-2
LC	3 Jan	Rotherham U	A	1-0
LC	10 Jan	Doncaster R	A	1-2
LC	17 Jan	Rotherham U	H	0-2
LC	21 Feb	Huddersfield T	A	0-1
LC	28 Feb	Grimsby T	H	2-2
LC	14 Mar	Barnsley	A	2-4
LC	21 Mar	Grimsby T	A	3-1
LC	28 Mar	Barnsley	A	0-6
	4 Apr	Bolton W	H	2-2
CC	6 Apr	Leeds U	H	6-1
CC	11 Apr	Leeds U	A	1-3
	18 Apr	York C	H	1-1
CC	25 Apr	Chesterfield	A	1-4
CC	2 May	Huddersfield T	H	1-1
	9 May	Huddersfield T	A	1-1
CC	16 May	Chesterfield	H	2-2
CC	23 May	York C	A	0-2
	30 May	York C	H	4-3

16 May, aet 5-2

**KEY: LC=League Cup; La=Lancashire Cup; MC=Midland Cup;
CC=Combined Counties Cup; Li=Liverpool Senior Cup**

The Football League 1941-42

LEAGUE CHAMPIONSHIP

HUDDERSFIELD TOWN

LC	27 Dec	Halifax T	A	2-2
LC	3 Jan	Doncaster R	H	3-1
LC	10 Jan	Sheffield United	H	3-1
LC	17 Jan	Sheffield United	A	1-2
LC	24 Jan	Blackpool	H	3-3
LC	31 Jan	Blackpool	A	2-4
LC	7 Feb	Chesterfield	H	3-0
LC	21 Feb	Halifax T	H	1-0
LC	28 Feb	Doncaster R	A	4-1
	14 Mar	Grimsby T	A	2-1
LC	21 Mar	Chesterfield	A	1-2
	28 Mar	Rotherham U	A	3-1
LC	4 Apr	Bradford City	A	1-4
LC	6 Apr	Bradford City	H	2-1
	11 Apr	Burnley	A	0-3
CC	18 Apr	Leeds U	H	5-1
CC	25 Apr	York C	A	2-2
CC	2 May	Halifax T	A	1-1
CC	9 May	Halifax T	H	1-1
CC	16 May	Bradford	H	2-2

LEEDS UNITED

LC	27 Dec	Rotherham U	A	1-3
LC	3 Jan	Lincoln City	H	5-1
LC	10 Jan	Rochdale	A	0-2
LC	17 Jan	Rochdale	H	5-0
LC	14 Feb	Barnsley	H	3-2
LC	21 Feb	Blackburn R	A	0-1
LC	28 Feb	Blackburn R	H	0-1
LC	14 Mar	Doncaster R	H	6-1
LC	21 Mar	Barnsley	A	2-3
LC	28 Mar	Doncaster R	A	0-1
	4 Apr	Sheffield Wed	H	1-2
CC	6 Apr	Halifax T	A	1-6
CC	11 Apr	Halifax T	H	3-1
CC	18 Apr	Huddersfield T	A	1-5
	25 Apr	Middlesbrough	A	3-2
CC	2 May	Chesterfield	H	1-0
CC	9 May	Middlesbrough	H	1-2

LEICESTER CITY

LC	27 Dec	Chesterfield	A	3-3
LC	3 Jan	Chesterfield	H	4-1
LC	10 Jan	Luton T	H	3-0
LC	17 Jan	Luton T	A	2-2
LC	14 Feb	WBA	A	2-3
LC	21 Feb	Norwich C	H	1-1
LC	28 Feb	Norwich C	A	3-6
LC	14 Mar	Sheffield Wed	H	5-1
LC	21 Mar	WBA	A	4-2
	28 Mar	Northampton T	A	1-1
LC	4 Apr	Norwich C	H	2-0
LC	6 Apr	Norwich C	A	0-2
	11 Apr	Sheffield Wed	A	1-4
	18 Apr	Sheffield Wed	H	0-1
	16 May	Northampton T	A	1-3
	23 May	Bristol City	H	5-1
	25 May	Northampton T	H	1-4
	30 May	Bristol City	A	1-3

6 Apr, aet 0-3

LINCOLN CITY

LC	27 Dec	Doncaster R	H	9-3
LC	3 Jan	Leeds U	A	1-5
LC	10 Jan	Mansfield T	H	7-2
LC	24 Jan	Grimsby T	H	1-2
LC	14 Feb	Nottingham F	H	0-3
LC	21 Feb	Rotherham U	A	1-0
LC	28 Feb	Rotherham U	H	4-2
LC	21 Mar	Doncaster R	A	2-0
LC	28 Mar	Grimsby T	A	2-4
LC	4 Apr	Nottingham F	H	6-5
LC	6 Apr	Nottingham F	A	2-4
	11 Apr	Mansfield T	A	8-1
	18 Apr	Mansfield T	H	2-2

LIVERPOOL

LC	27 Dec	Bury	H	4-0
LC	3 Jan	Bury	A	3-2
LC	10 Jan	Preston NE	A	2-1
LC	17 Jan	Preston NE	H	2-1
LC	7 Feb	Blackpool	A	2-6
LC	14 Feb	Blackpool	H	1-3
LC	21 Feb	Sheffield United	H	5-2
LC	28 Feb	Sheffield United	A	1-5
LC	14 Mar	Rochdale	A	8-2
La	21 Mar	Chester	A	3-1
LC	28 Mar	Rochdale	H	5-2
LC	4 Apr	Burnley	A	3-0
LC	6 Apr	Burnley	H	4-1
LC	11 Apr	Everton	H	0-2
LC	18 Apr	Everton	A	1-0
	25 Apr	Blackburn R	H	0-0
La	9 May	Chester	H	3-0
	16 May	Preston NE	A	2-0
La	23 May	Blackburn R	H	2-2
	25 May	Blackpool	A	2-8
Li	30 May	Everton	H	4-1

LUTON TOWN

LC	27 Dec	Mansfield T	A	3-3
LC	3 Jan	Mansfield T	H	2-1
LC	10 Jan	Leicester C	A	0-3
LC	17 Jan	Leicester C	H	2-2
LC	24 Jan	Norwich C	A	0-2
LC	31 Jan	Norwich C	H	3-2
LC	7 Feb	Southampton	A	0-3
LC	14 Feb	Southampton	H	1-6
LC	21 Feb	Northampton T	A	0-3
LC	28 Feb	Northampton T	H	1-5
	7 Mar	Bristol C	A	3-2
	14 Mar	Cardiff C	A	0-2
	28 Mar	Nottingham Forest	A	1-3
	11 Apr	Bristol City	A	0-7
	9 May	Northampton T	A	0-8
	30 May	Cardiff C	A	4-2

MANCHESTER CITY

LC	27 Dec	Blackburn R	A	0-3
LC	3 Jan	Blackburn R	H	1-2
LC	10 Jan	Burnley	A	2-1
LC	17 Jan	Burnley	H	5-0
LC	14 Feb	Rochdale	H	5-0
LC	21 Feb	Wolverhampton W	A	3-1
LC	28 Feb	Wolverhampton W	H	4-1
LC	14 Mar	Preston NE	H	0-3
LC	21 Mar	Rochdale	A	1-3
LC	28 Mar	Preston NE	A	0-0
LC	4 Apr	Blackpool	H	wo
LC	6 Apr	Blackpool	A	wo
LC	11 Apr	Southport	A	4-1
LC	18 Apr	Southport	H	3-0
LC	25 Apr	Wolverhampton W	A	0-2
LC	2 May	Wolverhampton W	H	1-0
La	9 May	Everton	H	2-0
La	16 May	Everton	A	1-6
	23 May	Manchester United	H	1-3

MANCHESTER UNITED

LC	27 Dec	Bolton W	H	3-1
LC	3 Jan	Bolton W	A	2-2
LC	10 Jan	Oldham Ath	H	1-1
LC	17 Jan	Oldham Ath	A	3-1
LC	31 Jan	Southport	A	3-1
LC	14 Feb	Sheffield United	A	2-0
LC	21 Feb	Preston NE	H	0-2
LC	28 Feb	Preston NE	A	3-1
LC	21 Mar	Sheffield United	H	2-2
LC	28 Mar	Southport	H	4-2
LC	4 Apr	Blackburn R	A	2-1
LC	6 Apr	Blackburn R	H	3-1
LC	11 Apr	Wolverhampton	A	5-4
LC	18 Apr	Wolverhampton	A	0-1
La	25 Apr	Oldham Athletic	H	5-1
La	2 May	Oldham Athletic	A	2-1
La	9 May	Blackburn R	A	1-1
La	16 May	Blackburn R	H	0-1
	23 May	Manchester City	A	3-1

18 Apr, aet 0-2

MANSFIELD TOWN

LC	27 Dec	Luton T	H	3-3
LC	3 Jan	Luton T	A	1-2
LC	10 Jan	Lincoln C	A	2-7
LC	21 Feb	WBA	A	1-3
LC	14 Mar	Nottingham F	H	1-3
LC	21 Mar	Walsall	A	0-1
LC	28 Mar	Walsall	H	2-0
	4 Apr	Chesterfield	A	2-5
	6 Apr	Chesterfield	H	0-2
	11 Apr	Lincoln C	H	1-8
	18 Apr	Lincoln A	A	2-2

**KEY: LC=League Cup; La=Lancashire Cup; MC=Midland Cup;
CC=Combined Counties Cup; Li=Liverpool Senior Cup**

The Football League 1941-42

LEAGUE CHAMPIONSHIP

MIDDLESBROUGH

LC	27 Dec	Sunderland	A	0-6
LC	3 Jan	Sunderland	H	3-0
LC	10 Jan	Bradford	A	1-1
LC	17 Jan	Bradford	H	1-2
LC	31 Jan	York C	H	3-3
LC	14 Feb	Gateshead	A	3-1
LC	21 Feb	Newcastle U	H	4-1
LC	28 Feb	Newcastle U	A	1-1
LC	14 Mar	Gateshead	H	7-1
LC	21 Mar	York C	A	1-1
	28 Mar	Sunderland	A	2-1
LC	4 Apr	Bradford	H	3-2
LC	6 Apr	Bradford	A	0-2
	11 Apr	Newcastle U	H	2-3
	18 Apr	Newcastle U	A	1-3
	25 Apr	Leeds U	H	2-3
	9 May	Leeds U	A	2-1
	16 May	York C	A	1-4

NEW BRIGHTON

LC	27 Dec	Southport	A	1-2
LC	3 Jan	Southport	H	4-3
LC	10 Jan	Bury	A	5-10
LC	17 Jan	Bury	H	0-6
LC	31 Jan	Blackburn R	H	0-5
LC	7 Feb	Tranmere R	A	2-0
LC	14 Feb	Tranmere R	H	3-1
LC	21 Feb	Chester	H	2-1
LC	28 Feb	Chester	A	0-5
LC	7 Mar	Blackburn R	A	1-5
	4 Apr	Tranmere R	H	5-0

NEWCASTLE UNITED

LC	27 Dec	Gateshead	A	2-2
LC	3 Jan	Gateshead	H	4-2
LC	10 Jan	Sunderland	A	2-2
LC	17 Jan	Sunderland	H	2-1
LC	7 Feb	Rotherham U	A	1-2
LC	14 Feb	Rotherham U	H	1-3
LC	21 Feb	Middlesbrough	A	1-4
LC	28 Feb	Middlesbrough	H	1-1
LC	14 Mar	Sheffield United	A	0-0
	21 Mar	Preston NE	H	4-4
LC	28 Mar	Sheffield United	H	1-6
	4 Apr	Gateshead	A	0-4
	6 Apr	Gateshead	H	0-2
	11 Apr	Middlesbrough	A	3-2
	18 Apr	Middlesbrough	H	3-1
	9 May	Gateshead	H	6-2
	25 May	Sunderland	H	2-2

NORTHAMPTON TOWN

LC	27 Dec	Norwich C	H	3-2
LC	3 Jan	Norwich C	A	1-4
LC	10 Jan	Walsall	H	6-1
LC	17 Jan	Walsall	A	2-1
LC	21 Feb	Luton T	H	3-0
LC	28 Feb	Luton T	A	5-1
LC	7 Mar	WBA	H	4-3
LC	14 Mar	WBA	A	2-2
LC	21 Mar	Nottingham For	A	1-0
	28 Mar	Leicester C	H	1-1
LC	4 Apr	Bristol City	H	3-0
LC	6 Apr	Bristol City	A	1-3
LC	11 Apr	Norwich C	H	3-4
LC	18 Apr	Norwich C	A	1-3
	25 Apr	Cardiff C	A	1-0
	2 May	Cardiff C	H	6-1
	9 May	Luton T	H	8-0
	16 May	Leicester C	H	3-1
	23 May	Stoke C	H	10-0
	25 May	Leicester C	A	4-1
	30 May	Stoke	A	2-3

NORWICH CITY

LC	27 Dec	Northampton T	A	2-3
LC	3 Jan	Northampton T	H	4-1
LC	24 Jan	Luton T	H	2-0
LC	31 Jan	Luton T	A	2-3
LC	21 Feb	Leicester C	A	1-1
LC	28 Feb	Leicester C	H	6-3
LC	4 Apr	Leicester C	A	0-2
LC	6 Apr	Leicester C	H	2-0
LC	11 Apr	Northampton T	A	4-3
LC	18 Apr	Northampton T	H	3-1
LC	25 Apr	Grimsby T	H	1-0
LC	2 May	Grimsby T	A	0-2

6 Apr, aet 3-0

NOTTINGHAM FOREST

LC	27 Dec	Sheffield United	H	3-3
LC	3 Jan	Sheffield United	A	1-2
LC	10 Jan	Chesterfield	H	1-0
LC	17 Jan	Chesterfield	A	0-1
LC	14 Feb	Lincoln C	A	3-0
LC	21 Feb	Stoke C	H	1-0
LC	28 Feb	Stoke C	A	3-1
LC	14 Mar	Mansfield T	A	3-1
LC	21 Mar	Northampton T	H	0-1
	28 Mar	Luton T	H	3-1
LC	4 Apr	Lincoln C	A	5-6
LC	6 Apr	Lincoln C	H	4-2
LC	11 Apr	Grimsby T	A	1-3
LC	18 Apr	Grimsby T	H	1-5
	2 May	Sheffield Wed	H	2-1
	9 May	Sheffield Wed	A	1-3

OLDHAM ATHLETIC

LC	27 Dec	Rochdale	A	0-1
LC	3 Jan	Rochdale	H	3-2
LC	10 Jan	Manchester Utd	A	1-1
LC	17 Jan	Manchester Utd	H	1-3
LC	31 Jan	Tranmere R	H	6-0
LC	14 Feb	Bradford	A	1-3
LC	21 Feb	Everton	H	1-0
LC	28 Feb	Everton	A	0-4
LC	14 Mar	Bradford	H	5-2
LC	21 Mar	Tranmere R	A	0-1
	28 Mar	Everton	H	1-2
LC	4 Apr	Sunderland	H	1-1
LC	6 Apr	Sunderland	A	2-3
	11 Apr	Chester	H	2-3
	25 Apr	Manchester Utd	A	1-5
	2 May	Manchester Utd	H	1-2
	9 May	Blackpool	H	2-8
	16 May	Blackpool	A	2-2

PRESTON NORTH END

LC	27 Dec	Tranmere R	H	7-1
LC	3 Jan	Tranmere R	A	3-3
LC	10 Jan	Liverpool	H	1-2
LC	17 Jan	Liverpool	A	1-2
LC	7 Feb	Chester	H	6-0
LC	14 Feb	Chester	A	2-2
LC	21 Feb	Manchester Utd	A	2-0
LC	28 Feb	Manchester Utd	H	1-3
LC	14 Mar	Manchester City	A	3-0
	21 Mar	Newcastle U	A	4-4
LC	28 Mar	Manchester City	H	0-0
LC	4 Apr	Everton	H	2-2
LC	6 Apr	Everton	A	1-1
	11 Apr	Blackburn R	A	3-3
	18 Apr	Blackburn R	H	2-0
	25 Apr	Burnley	A	0-3
	2 May	Burnley	H	2-0
	9 May	Stoke C	H	1-2
	16 May	Liverpool	H	0-2

6 Apr 1-2 aet

ROCHDALE

LC	27 Dec	Oldham Ath	H	1-0
LC	3 Jan	Oldham Ath	A	2-3
LC	10 Jan	Leeds U	H	2-0
LC	17 Jan	Leeds U	A	0-5
LC	14 Feb	Manchester City	A	0-5
LC	21 Feb	Southport	A	1-2
LC	14 Mar	Liverpool	H	2-8
LC	21 Mar	Manchester City	H	3-1
LC	28 Mar	Liverpool	A	2-5
La	11 Apr	Bury	A	3-4
La	18 Apr	Bury	H	4-1
La	25 Apr	Blackpool	H	2-0
La	2 May	Blackpool	A	1-5

KEY: LC=League Cup; La=Lancashire Cup; MC=Midland Cup;
CC=Combined Counties Cup; Li=Liverpool Senior Cup

The Football League 1941-42

LEAGUE CHAMPIONSHIP

ROTHERHAM UNITED

LC	27 Dec	Leeds U	H	3-1
LC	3 Jan	Halifax T	H	0-1
LC	17 Jan	Halifax T	A	2-0
LC	31 Jan	Bradford	A	5-5
LC	7 Feb	Newcastle U	H	2-1
LC	14 Feb	Newcastle U	A	3-1
LC	21 Feb	Lincoln C	H	0-1
LC	28 Feb	Lincoln C	A	2-4
LC	21 Mar	Bradford	H	3-1
	28 Mar	Huddersfield T	H	1-3
LC	4 Apr	Sheffield United	H	2-5
LC	6 Apr	Sheffield United	A	3-3
	18 Apr	Doncaster R	H	3-0
SC	16 May	Barnsley	H	1-5
	25 May	Barnsley	A	2-3

SHEFFIELD UNITED

LC	27 Dec	Nottingham F	A	3-3
LC	3 Jan	Nottingham F	H	2-1
LC	10 Jan	Huddersfield T	A	1-3
LC	17 Jan	Huddersfield T	H	2-1
LC	14 Feb	Manchester Utd	H	0-2
LC	21 Feb	Liverpool	A	2-5
LC	28 Feb	Liverpool	H	5-1
LC	14 Mar	Newcastle U	H	0-0
LC	21 Mar	Manchester Utd	A	2-2
LC	28 Mar	Newcastle U	A	6-1
LC	4 Apr	Rotherham U	A	5-2
LC	6 Apr	Rotherham U	H	3-3
LC	11 Apr	Bradford	A	0-2
LC	18 Apr	Bradford	H	2-1
	25 Apr	Sheffield Wed	H	3-0
	9 May	Barnsley	A	1-5
	25 May	Chesterfield	A	2-1

SHEFFIELD WEDNESDAY

LC	27 Dec	Everton	H	0-3
LC	3 Jan	Everton	A	0-2
LC	10 Jan	Bradford City	A	0-1
LC	21 Feb	Burnley	H	3-1
LC	28 Feb	Burnley	A	0-3
LC	14 Mar	Leicester C	A	1-5
LC	21 Mar	Bury	H	2-2
LC	28 Mar	Bury	A	2-8
	4 Apr	Leeds U	A	2-1
	6 Apr	Bolton W	A	3-3
	11 Apr	Leicester C	H	4-1
	18 Apr	Leicester C	A	1-0
	25 Apr	Sheffield United	A	0-3
	2 May	Nottingham F	A	1-2
	9 May	Nottingham F	H	3-1

SOUTHAMPTON

LC	27 Dec	Cardiff C	H	2-5
LC	3 Jan	Cardiff C	A	1-9
LC	31 Jan	Bournemouth	A	4-3
LC	7 Feb	Luton T	H	3-0
LC	14 Feb	Luton T	A	6-1
LC	21 Feb	Bournemouth	H	2-2
LC	28 Feb	Bournemouth	A	0-2
LC	7 Mar	Bournemouth	H	1-0
LC	21 Mar	Bristol City	A	1-5
LC	28 Mar	Bristol City	H	5-1
LC	4 Apr	Cardiff C	A	1-3
LC	6 Apr	Cardiff C	H	1-1

SOUTHPORT

LC	27 Dec	New Brighton	H	2-1
LC	3 Jan	New Brighton	A	3-4
LC	10 Jan	Tranmere R	A	2-1
LC	17 Jan	Tranmere R	H	2-4
LC	31 Jan	Manchester United	H	1-3
LC	7 Feb	Stockport County	H	5-0
LC	14 Feb	Stockport County	A	1-1
LC	21 Feb	Rochdale	H	2-1
La	21 Mar	Everton	A	1-3
LC	28 Mar	Manchester United	A	2-4
LC	4 Apr	Bury	A	4-4
LC	6 Apr	Bury	H	2-1
LC	11 Apr	Manchester City	H	1-4
LC	18 Apr	Manchester City	A	0-3
LC	25 Apr	Tranmere R	A	0-3
La	28 Apr	Everton	H	2-1

STOCKPORT COUNTY

LC	27 Dec	Blackpool	A	2-5
LC	3 Jan	Blackpool	H	2-1
LC	10 Jan	Wrexham	A	1-6
LC	17 Jan	Wrexham	H	2-2
LC	24 Jan	Burnley	A	0-6
LC	31 Jan	Burnley	H	0-0
LC	7 Feb	Southport	A	0-5
LC	14 Feb	Southport	H	1-1
LC	21 Feb	Barnsley	A	1-6
LC	28 Feb	Barnsley	H	3-6

STOKE CITY

LC	27 Dec	Walsall	A	4-1
LC	3 Jan	Walsall	H	8-0
LC	10 Jan	WBA	A	0-4
LC	17 Jan	WBA	H	2-1
LC	31 Jan	Chesterfield	H	2-1
LC	14 Feb	Bolton W	H	3-1
LC	21 Feb	Nottingham F	A	0-1
LC	28 Feb	Nottingham F	H	1-3
LC	14 Mar	Chesterfield	A	1-2
LC	21 Mar	Bolton W	A	1-1
	28 Mar	Blackpool	A	0-4
LC	4 Apr	WBA	H	5-3
LC	6 Apr	WBA	A	1-6
	11 Apr	Walsall	A	0-1
	18 Apr	Walsall	H	2-3
	25 Apr	Chester	H	4-2
	2 May	Chester	A	2-2
	9 May	Preston NE	A	2-1
	16 May	Northampton T	A	0-10
	30 May	Northampton T	H	3-2

SUNDERLAND

LC	27 Dec	Middlesbrough	H	6-0
LC	3 Jan	Middlesbrough	A	0-3
LC	10 Jan	Newcastle U	H	2-2
LC	17 Jan	Newcastle U	A	1-2
LC	31 Jan	Gateshead	A	2-1
LC	14 Feb	York C	H	8-3
LC	21 Feb	Bradford	A	0-3
LC	28 Feb	Bradford	H	4-2
LC	14 Mar	York C	A	2-2
LC	21 Mar	Gateshead	H	5-1
	28 Mar	Middlesbrough	H	1-2
LC	4 Apr	Oldham Athletic	A	1-1
LC	6 Apr	Oldham Athletic	H	3-2
LC	11 Apr	Bradford City	H	1-2
LC	18 Apr	Bradford City	A	6-4
LC	25 Apr	Bradford	A	1-0
LC	2 May	Bradford	H	2-2
LC	9 May	Grimsby T	H	0-0
LC	16 May	Grimsby T	A	3-2
LC	23 May	Wolverhampton W	H	2-2
	25 May	Newcastle U	A	2-2
LC	30 May	Wolverhampton W	A	1-4

SWANSEA TOWN

LC	27 Dec	Bristol City	A	1-1
LC	3 Jan	Bristol City	H	1-3
LC	10 Jan	Cardiff C	H	1-1
LC	17 Jan	Cardiff C	A	1-1
LC	7 Feb	Bristol City	H	2-1
LC	14 Feb	Bristol City	A	1-1
LC	21 Feb	Cardiff C	H	1-5
LC	28 Feb	Cardiff C	A	1-8
	14 Mar	Bristol City	A	0-10
	21 Mar	Cardiff C	A	1-4
	25 May	Cardiff C	A	1-4

KEY: LC=League Cup; La=Lancashire Cup; MC=Midland Cup;
CC=Combined Counties Cup; Li=Liverpool Senior Cup

The Football League 1941-42

LEAGUE CHAMPIONSHIP

TRANMERE ROVERS

LC	27 Dec	Preston NE	A	1-7
LC	3 Jan	Preston NE	H	3-3
LC	10 Jan	Southport	H	1-2
LC	17 Jan	Southport	A	4-2
LC	31 Jan	Oldham Ath	A	0-6
LC	7 Feb	New Brighton	H	0-2
LC	14 Feb	New Brighton	A	1-3
LC	21 Feb	Blackpool	H	2-2
LC	28 Feb	Blackpool	A	3-15
LC	21 Mar	Oldham Ath	H	1-0
	28 Mar	Chester	H	1-1
	4 Apr	New Brighton	H	0-5
	6 Apr	Wrexham	H	4-2
	25 Apr	Southport	H	3-0
	2 May	Blackburn R	H	0-5

WALSALL

LC	27 Dec	Stoke C	H	1-4
LC	3 Jan	Stoke C	A	0-8
LC	10 Jan	Northampton T	A	1-6
LC	17 Jan	Northampton t	H	1-2
LC	31 Jan	Chester	A	3-4
LC	21 Feb	Wrexham	A	0-1
LC	28 Feb	Wrexham	H	2-0
LC	14 Mar	Chester	H	0-2
LC	21 Mar	Mansfield T	H	1-0
LC	28 Mar	Mansfield T	A	0-2
	11 Apr	Stoke C	H	1-0
	18 Apr	Stoke C	A	3-2
	23 May	WBA	A	1-3

WEST BROMWICH ALBION

LC	27 Dec	Wrexham	H	6-4
LC	3 Jan	Wrexham	A	5-5
LC	10 Jan	Stoke C	H	4-0
LC	17 Jan	Stoke C	A	1-2
LC	14 Feb	Leicester C	H	3-2
LC	21 Feb	Mansfield T	H	3-1
LC	7 Mar	Northampton T	A	3-4
LC	14 Mar	Northampton T	H	2-2
LC	21 Mar	Leicester C	A	2-4
LC	4 Apr	Stoke C	A	3-5
LC	6 Apr	Stoke C	H	6-1
LC	11 Apr	Cardiff C	A	1-1
LC	18 Apr	Cardiff C	H	3-2
LC	25 Apr	Everton	H	3-1
LC	2 May	Everton	A	5-1
LC	9 May	Wolverhampton W	H	0-4
LC	16 May	Wolverhampton W	A	0-3
	23 May	Walsall	H	3-1

WOLVERHAMPTON WANDERERS

LC	27 Dec	Chester	H	2-1
LC	3 Jan	Chester	A	3-1
LC	10 Jan	Blackpool	A	1-6
LC	17 Jan	Blackpool	H	1-0
LC	31 Jan	Everton	A	1-2
LC	7 Feb	Wrexham	A	3-0
LC	14 Feb	Wrexham	H	4-1
LC	21 Feb	Manchester City	H	1-3
LC	28 Feb	Manchester City	A	1-4
LC	7 Mar	Everton	H	11-1
LC	4 Apr	Chester	H	3-1
LC	6 Apr	Chester	A	1-0
LC	11 Apr	Manchester Utd	A	4-5
LC	18 Apr	Manchester Utd	H	1-0
LC	25 Apr	Manchester City	H	2-0
LC	2 May	Manchester City	A	0-1
LC	9 May	WBA	A	4-0
LC	16 May	WBA	H	3-0
LC	23 May	Sunderland	A	2-2
LC	30 May	Sunderland	H	4-1

18 Apr, aet 2-0

WREXHAM

LC	27 Dec	WBA	A	4-6
LC	3 Jan	WBA	H	5-5
LC	10 Jan	Stockport County	H	6-1
LC	17 Jan	Stockport County	A	2-2
LC	7 Feb	Wolverhampton	H	0-3
LC	14 Feb	Wolverhampton	A	1-4
LC	21 Feb	Walsall	H	1-0
LC	28 Feb	Walsall	A	0-2
LC	14 Mar	Bury	A	3-0
	6 Apr	Tranmere R	A	2-4
	16 May	Chester	A	2-1
	23 May	Chester	H	0-4

YORK CITY

LC	27 Dec	Grimsby T	A	0-0
LC	3 Jan	Grimsby T	H	3-2
LC	10 Jan	Gateshead	A	2-3
LC	17 Jan	Gateshead	H	3-3
LC	31 Jan	Middlesbrough	A	3-3
LC	14 Feb	Sunderland	A	3-8
LC	28 Feb	Bolton W	A	3-4
LC	14 Mar	Sunderland	H	2-2
LC	21 Mar	Middlesbrough	H	1-1
LC	28 Mar	Bolton W	H	2-1
	11 Apr	Chesterfield	H	3-1
	18 Apr	Halifax T	A	1-1
	25 Apr	Huddersfield T	H	2-2
	9 May	Bradford City	H	2-1
	16 May	Middlesbrough	H	4-1
	23 May	Halifax T	H	2-0
	30 May	Halifax T	A	3-4

KEY: LC=League Cup; La=Lancashire Cup; MC=Midland Cup;
CC=Combined Counties Cup; Li=Liverpool Senior Cup

The Football League 1941-42

LEAGUE CHAMPIONSHIP

Final Table

		P	W	D	L	F	A	Pts	Pts Ave
1	Manchester United	19	12	4	3	44	25	28	33.895
2	Blackpool	22	14	4	4	108	34	32	33.455
3	Northampton Town	21	14	2	5	70	31	30	32.857
4	Liverpool	21	14	2	5	57	39	30	32.857
5	Wolverhampton Wanderers	20	13	1	6	52	29	27	31.050
6	Huddersfield Town	20	9	6	5	42	33	24	27.600
7	Blackburn Rovers	22	10	6	6	40	31	26	27.182
8	West Bromwich Albion	18	9	3	6	53	43	21	26.833
9	Grimsby Town	18	8	5	5	31	22	21	26.833
10	Sunderland	22	9	7	6	53	42	25	26.136
11	Cardiff City	20	9	4	7	59	38	22	25.300
12	Preston North End	19	6	7	6	41	30	19	23.000
13	Chesterfield	18	8	2	8	32	31	18	23.000
14	Middlesbrough	18	7	4	7	37	36	18	23.000
15	Everton	23	9	5	9	37	41	23	23.000
16	Stoke City	20	9	2	9	41	49	20	20.444
17	Leicester City	18	6	4	8	39	38	16	19.368
18	Bradford	19	5	6	8	35	40	16	18.158
19	Halifax Town	19	4	7	8	30	40	15	18.158
20	Burnley	19	7	1	11	29	53	15	23.000
21	Chester	20	6	3	11	34	41	15	17.250
22	Oldham Athletic	18	4	3	11	30	43	11	14.056

Rankings based upon 23 games. Only those clubs playing 18 games or more qualified for the championship

	P	W	D	L	F	A	Pts
Barnsley	15	9	3	3	48	23	21
Bolton Wanderers	15	5	4	6	26	33	14
Bournemouth & Boscombe Athletic	8	2	2	4	11	21	6
Bradford City	14	6	1	7	28	25	13
Bristol City	17	9	3	5	55	29	21
Bury	15	6	2	7	46	39	14
Doncaster Rovers	9	2	0	7	10	30	4
Gateshead	13	4	2	7	23	36	10
Leeds United	17	7	0	10	33	33	14
Lincoln City	13	7	1	5	45	33	15
Luton Town	16	4	2	10	20	54	10
Manchester City	17	9	1	7	33	26	19
Mansfield Town	11	1	2	8	15	36	4
New Brighton	11	5	0	6	23	38	10
Newcastle United	17	5	6	6	33	40	16
Norwich City	12	7	1	4	27	19	15
Nottingham Forest	16	8	1	7	32	30	17
Rochdale	13	5	0	8	23	39	10
Rotherham United	15	6	2	7	32	34	14
Sheffield United	17	8	4	5	39	33	20
Sheffield Wednesday	15	5	2	8	22	36	12
Southampton	12	5	2	5	27	32	12
Southport	16	6	2	8	30	38	14
Stockport County	10	1	3	6	12	38	5
Swansea Town	11	1	4	6	11	39	6
Tranmere Rovers	15	4	3	8	24	55	11
Walsall	13	4	0	9	14	34	8
Wrexham	12	4	2	6	26	32	10
York City	17	6	7	4	39	37	19

The Football League 1941-42

SOUTH

	Bournemouth & BA	Bristol City	Cardiff City	Leicester City	Luton Town	Northampton Town	Norwich City	Nottingham Forest	Southampton	Swansea Town	Walsall	WBA	Wolverhampton W
Bournemouth & Boscombe Athletic	X	13 Sep 2-1	1 Nov 3-2		4 Oct 1-0				11 Oct 6-1 29 Nov 5-0				
Bristol City	20 Sep 2-1	X	13 Dec 2-6			15 Nov 5-1			20 Dec 4-2	27 Sep 6-3 11 Oct 8-1	29 Nov 4-2		30 Aug 4-2
Cardiff City	25 Oct 0-2	6 Dec 8-2	X		8 Nov 6-1				27 Sep 5-3	22 Nov 1-0 25 Dec 2-1		6 Sep 1-1	18 Oct 2-0
Leicester City				X	18 Oct 7-2	25 Oct 1-0	30 Aug 1-1 6 Dec 6-1	22 Nov 3-0 25 Dec 2-0			15 Nov 6-0	20 Sep 3-2	27 Sep 2-0
Luton Town	27 Sep 3-1		15 Nov 2-0	11 Oct 3-2	X	20 Dec 3-3	20 Sep 1-4	30 Aug 5-1	25 Oct 2-1		6 Dec 1-2	29 Nov 4-5	
Northampton Town		8 Nov 5-2		1 Nov 0-1	25 Dec 8-1	X	27 Sep 3-1	20 Sep 4-3			30 Aug 3-2	13 Dec 4-1	22 Nov 1-2
Norwich City			6 Sep 0-0	13 Sep 8-1	4 Oct 3-1		X						
Nottingham Forest			29 Nov 0-1 20 Dec 2-3	6 Sep 4-1	13 Sep 2-3		8 Nov 0-2	X			18 Oct 4-0		6 Dec 0-0
Southampton	18 Oct 4-3 22 Nov 5-2	25 Dec 5-2	4 Oct 1-3		1 Nov 5-0				X				
Swansea Town		4 Oct 1-2	29 Nov 4-1							X	13 Sep 4-7		
Walsall		22 Nov 5-0	8 Nov 2-1	13 Dec 5-3	6 Sep 2-2			11 Oct 8-2		20 Sep 4-2	X	27 Sep 2-1	1 Nov 4-1 20 Dec 1-2
West Bromwich Alb			30 Aug 6-3	13 Sep 4-1	22 Nov 10-1	6 Dec 7-0				18 Oct 8-2	4 Oct 4-0	X	15 Nov 5-3
Wolverhampton Wanderers		6 Sep 1-2	11 Oct 0-3	4 Oct 0-0		29 Nov 2-1		13 Dec 7-0		25 Oct 1-0 25 Dec 4-3		8 Nov 2-8	X

		P	W	D	L	F	A	Pts	Ave Pts
1	Leicester City	17	11	3	3	40	17	25	26.471
2	West Bromwich Albion	13	9	1	3	62	26	19	26.308
3	Cardiff City	15	9	1	5	43	28	19	22.800
4	Norwich City	8	4	2	2	20	13	10	22.500
5	Bournemouth & Boscombe Ath	10	6	0	4	26	18	12	21.600
6	Bristol City	15	9	0	6	46	45	18	21.600
7	Walsall	18	9	1	8	49	45	19	19.000
8	Northampton Town	16	7	2	7	39	38	16	18.000
9	Wolverhampton Wanderers	16	6	2	8	27	36	14	15.750
10	Southampton	10	4	0	6	27	32	8	14.400
11	Luton Town	18	5	1	12	34	73	11	11.000
12	Nottingham Forest	13	2	1	10	18	39	5	6.923
13	Swansea Town	9	1	0	8	18	39	2	4.000

Ave Pts= average points calculated over 18 games

London Football League 1941-42

	Aldershot	Arsenal	Brentford	Brighton & HA	Charlton Ath	Chelsea	Clapton Orient	Crystal Palace	Fulham	Millwall	Portsmouth	QPR	Reading	Tottenham H	Watford	West Ham U
Aldershot	X	7 Feb 1-0	7 Mar 6-3	22 Nov 5-1	27 Sep 1-0	27 Dec 2-3	18 Oct 1-1	6 Dec 1-2	13 Dec 4-3	25 Oct 5-2	25 Dec 3-2	8 Nov 4-1	21 Feb 0-0	6 Sep 3-2	11 Oct 8-1	10 Jan 1-5
Arsenal	1 Nov 3-2	X	13 Dec 1-3	14 Mar 4-2	17 Jan 3-2	4 Oct 3-0	15 Nov 5-2	6 Sep 7-2	25 Dec 2-0	14 Feb 10-0	3 Jan 6-1	22 Nov 4-1	29 Nov 3-1	20 Sep 4-0	31 Jan 11-0	18 Oct 4-1
Brentford	29 Nov 5-1	30 Aug 4-1	X	27 Dec 4-2	8 Nov 2-1	1 Nov 3-1	3 Jan 5-2	4 Oct 1-2	17 Jan 2-3	14 Mar 4-3	31 Jan 2-5	20 Dec 4-3	13 Sep 3-2	18 Oct 1-4	28 Feb 5-3	15 Nov 0-5
Brighton & Hove Albion	28 Feb 1-5	6 Dec 2-3	20 Sep 2-2	X	1 Nov 3-5	31 Jan 8-2	25 Dec 4-1	27 Sep 2-2	10 Jan 3-7	29 Nov 5-0	18 Oct 2-1	30 Aug 2-5	20 Dec 1-5	17 Jan 5-2	15 Nov 2-2	14 Feb 1-3
Charlton Athletic	3 Jan 1-5	11 Oct 1-3	14 Feb 3-2	7 Feb 8-2	X	30 Aug 2-1	6 Sep 4-0	21 Feb 3-1	22 Nov 3-3	4 Oct 1-2	14 Mar 2-5	24 Jan 3-1	25 Oct 2-3	29 Nov 2-1	20 Sep 5-1	13 Sep 1-1
Chelsea	20 Sep 4-0	10 Jan 1-5	7 Feb 1-1	25 Oct 1-3	13 Dec 2-4	X	6 Dec 1-3	8 Nov 1-0	21 Feb 1-5	3 Jan 3-3	7 Mar 3-4	17 Jan 3-1	18 Oct 0-5	22 Nov 1-1	25 Dec 2-2	6 Sep 4-8
Clapton Orient	24 Jan 0-5	21 Feb 1-3	27 Sep 1-3	13 Sep 3-3	20 Dec 1-1	14 Mar 0-3	X	17 Jan 4-0	25 Oct 2-1	2 May 3-3	22 Nov 0-4	29 Nov 0-0	30 Aug 3-8	14 Feb 2-3	10 Jan 2-0	27 Dec 3-1
Crystal Palace	14 Mar 1-2	9 May 3-3	10 Jan 2-0	3 Jan 10-1	15 Nov 4-0	14 Feb 3-2	11 Oct 2-0	X	18 Oct 3-1	30 Aug 2-0	1 Nov 3-1	13 Sep 2-1	27 Dec 1-1	31 Jan 2-2	29 Nov 6-1	28 Feb 1-1
Fulham	30 Aug 2-6	13 Sep 2-5	11 Oct 4-3	4 Oct 2-3	28 Feb 4-7	15 Nov 1-4	31 Jan 5-1	23 May 4-3	X	20 Dec 4-3	14 Feb 2-7	27 Dec 0-3	27 Sep 2-2	1 Nov 2-2	14 Mar 1-3	29 Nov 1-3
Millwall	31 Jan 3-1	8 Nov 2-2	6 Dec 4-2	7 Mar 2-0	10 Jan 0-1	27 Sep 6-3	1 Nov 2-2	13 Dec 1-0	6 Sep 2-4	X	20 Sep 1-3	21 Feb 1-2	28 Feb 1-1	25 Dec 1-2	18 Oct 4-2	17 Jan 1-3
Portsmouth	13 Sep 2A2	27 Sep 1-5	25 Oct 2-1	24 Jan 5-3	6 Dec 7-2	29 Nov 2-3	28 Feb 16-1	7 Feb 3-1	8 Nov 5-3	27 Dec 3-2	X	10 Jan 3-1	11 Oct 1-0	15 Nov 1-2	20 Dec 7-1	13 Dec 1-0
Queen's Park Rangers	14 Feb 0-2	28 Feb 0-1	6 Sep 3-4	13 Dec 3-0	18 Oct 0-0	11 Oct 2-1	7 Mar 2-1	25 Dec 1-3	20 Sep 2-5	15 Nov 4-1	4 Oct 0-2	X	14 Mar 4-0	3 Jan 1-0	1 Nov 1-5	31 Jan 2-1
Reading	15 Nov 3-3	7 Mar 1-4	25 Dec 4-3	6 Sep 4-5	31 Jan 1-4	2 May 3-2	13 Dec 2-0	20 Jan 6-2	3 Jan 4-1	22 Nov 2-1	17 Oct 5-2	6 Dec 2-2	X	4 Oct 1-1	14 Feb 5-1	1 Nov 3-2
Tottenham Hotspur	20 Dec 1-1	27 Dec 1-2	25 Apr 2-1	11 Oct 1-2	7 Mar 2-0	28 Feb 2-0	8 Nov 2-0	25 Oct 1-1	2 May 7-1	13 Sep 3-0	21 Feb 1-1	27 Sep 3-1	10 Jan 2-1	X	30 Aug 5-0	6 Dec 1-1
Watford	25 Apr 1-5	25 Oct 3-1	22 Nov 1-6	21 Feb 7-1	27 Dec 1-2	13 Sep 1-3	4 Oct 2-2	7 Mar 2-1	6 Dec 3-5	9 May 1-0	6 Sep 1-5	2 May 0-5	8 Nov 0-0	13 Dec 1-2	X	27 Sep 0-8
West Ham United	4 Oct 3-0	24 Jan 3-0	21 Feb 2-1	8 Nov 4-0	25 Dec 2-2	20 Dec 5-0	20 Sep 3-1	22 Nov 0-5	7 Mar 1-1	11 Oct 4-2	30 Aug 1-3	25 Oct 2-0	25 Apr 2-1	14 Mar 2-3	3 Jan 4-1	X

		P	W	D	L	F	A	Pts
1	Arsenal	30	23	2	5	108	43	48
2	Portsmouth	30	20	2	8	105	59	42
3	West Ham United	30	17	5	8	81	44	39
4	Aldershot	30	17	5	8	85	56	39
5	Tottenham Hotspur	30	15	8	7	61	41	38
6	Crystal Palace	30	14	6	10	70	53	34
7	Reading	30	13	8	9	76	58	34
8	Charlton Athletic	30	14	5	11	72	64	33
9	Brentford	30	14	2	14	80	76	30
10	Queen's Park Rangers	30	11	3	16	52	59	25
11	Fulham	30	10	4	16	79	99	24
12	Brighton & Hove Albion	30	9	4	17	71	108	22
13	Chelsea	30	8	4	18	56	88	20
14	Millwall	30	7	5	18	53	82	19
15	Clapton Orient	30	5	7	18	42	94	17
16	Watford	30	6	4	20	47	114	16

Other English Competitions 1941-42

Qualifying Round Final Table
See League Championship for match results

		P	W	D	L	F	A	Pts	Pts Ave
1	Northampton Town	9	7	1	1	27	14	15	16.667
2	Blackburn Rovers	10	7	2	1	19	7	16	16.000
3	Manchester United	10	6	3	1	23	13	15	15.000
4	Blackpool	10	6	2	2	45	19	14	14.000
5	Barnsley	10	6	2	2	33	16	14	14.000
6	Liverpool	10	7	0	3	33	24	14	14.000
7	Bristol City	10	5	3	2	29	16	13	13.000
8	Nottingham Forest	9	5	1	3	15	9	11	12.222
9	Leicester City	9	4	3	2	27	19	11	12.222
10	Rotherham United	9	5	1	3	20	15	11	12.222
11	Grimsby Town	9	4	3	2	15	12	11	12.222
12	Cardiff City	10	5	2	3	39	19	12	12.000
13	Sunderland	10	5	2	3	30	19	12	12.000
14	Wolverhampton Wanderers	10	6	0	4	28	19	12	12.000
15	Huddersfield Town	10	5	2	3	23	16	12	12.000
16	Middlesbrough	10	4	4	2	24	17	12	12.000
17	Everton	10	5	2	3	15	16	12	12.000
18	Norwich City	6	3	1	2	17	11	7	11.667
19	Lincoln City	9	5	0	4	27	21	10	11.111
20	West Bromwich Albion	9	4	2	3	29	24	10	11.111
21	Preston North End	10	4	3	3	26	13	11	11.000
22	Manchester City	10	5	1	4	21	14	11	11.000
23	Stoke City	10	5	1	4	22	15	11	11.000
24	Sheffield United	10	4	3	3	23	19	11	11.000
25	Southampton	10	5	1	4	25	28	11	11.000
26	Bury	9	4	1	4	33	24	9	10.000
27	Bradford City	8	4	0	4	14	11	8	10.000
28	Southport	9	4	1	4	20	19	9	10.000
29	Oldham Athletic	10	4	1	5	18	17	9	9.000
30	Chester	10	4	1	5	19	20	9	9.000
31	Burnley	10	4	1	5	18	19	9	9.000
32	Bradford	10	3	3	4	22	26	9	9.000

All above qualified for the First round

		P	W	D	L	F	A	Pts	Pts Ave
33	York City	10	2	5	3	22	27	9	9.000
34	Chesterfield	10	4	1	5	15	20	9	9.000
35	Wrexham	9	3	2	4	22	23	8	8.889
36	Bolton Wanderers	9	3	2	4	16	17	8	8.889
37	Leeds United	10	4	0	6	22	15	8	8.000
38	Newcastle United	10	2	4	4	15	23	8	8.000
39	New Brighton	10	4	0	6	18	38	8	8.000
40	Bournemouth & Boscombe Athletic	8	2	2	4	11	21	6	7.500
41	Swansea Town	8	1	4	3	9	21	6	7.500
42	Halifax Town	9	2	2	5	11	20	6	6.667
43	Rochdale	9	3	0	6	13	29	6	6.667
44	Gateshead	10	2	2	6	15	30	6	6.000
45	Luton Town	10	2	2	6	12	30	6	6.000
46	Tranmere Rovers	10	2	2	6	16	42	6	6.000
47	Doncaster Rovers	8	2	0	6	10	27	4	5.000
48	Stockport County	10	1	3	6	12	38	5	5.000
49	Mansfield Town	7	1	1	5	10	19	3	4.286
50	Walsall	10	2	0	8	9	29	4	4.000
51	Sheffield Wednesday	8	1	1	6	8	25	3	3.750

Pts Ave – Rankings based upon average points over 10 games

Other English Competitions 1941-42

FOOTBALL LEAGUE (WAR) CUP

First round – 2 legs
First leg played on 4 Apr , second leg on 6 Apr
Barnsley v Grimsby Town 1-2, 1-1
Blackburn Rovers v Manchester United 1-2, 1-3
Bradford City v Huddersfield Town 4-1, 1-2
Burnley v Liverpool 0-3, 1-4
Bury v Southport 4-4, 1-2
Cardiff City v Southampton 3-1, 1-1
Everton v Preston North End 2-2, 2-1
Leicester City v Norwich City 2-0, 0-3
Lincoln City v Nottingham Forest 6-5, 2-4
Middlesbrough v Bradford 3-2, 0-2
Northampton Town v Bristol City 3-0, 1-3
Oldham Athletic v Sunderland 1-1, 2-3
Rotherham United v Sheffield United 2-5, 3-3
Stoke City v West Bromwich Albion 5-3, 1-6
Wolverhampton Wanderers v Chester 3-1, 1-0

Second round – 2 legs
First leg played on 11 Apr, second leg on 18 Apr
Bradford v Sheffield United 2-0, 1-2
Cardiff City v West Bromwich Albion 1-1, 2-3
Grimsby Town v Nottingham Forest 3-1, 5-1
Liverpool v Everton 0-2, 1-0
Manchester United v Wolverhampton Wanderers 5-4, 0-2
Northampton Town v Norwich City 3-4, 1-3
Southport v Manchester City 1-4, 0-3
Sunderland v Bradford City 1-2, 6-4

Third round – 2 legs
First leg played on 25 Apr , second leg on 2 May
Bradford v Sunderland 0-1, 2-2
Norwich City v Grimsby Town 1-0, 0-2
West Bromwich Albion v Everton 3-1, 5-1
Wolverhampton Wanderers v Manchester City 2-0, 0-1

Semi-final – 2 legs
First leg played on 9 May , second leg on 16 May
Sunderland v Grimsby Town 0-0, 3-2
West Bromwich Albion v Wolverhampton W 0-4, 0-3

Final – 2 legs
First leg, 23 May 1942 at Roker Park, Sunderland
Att 35,000
Sunderland 2 *(Stubbins, Carter)*
Wolverhampton Wanderers 2 *(Westcott 2)*

Sunderland: Heywood, Gorman, Eves, Housam, Hewison, Hastings, Spuhler, Stubbins*, Whitelum, Carter, Robinson*
Wolverhampton W: Sidlow, Dowen*,Robinson, Thornhill, Galley, Dorsett, Broome*, McIntosh, Westcott, Stevenson, Mullen

Second leg, 30 May 1942 at Molineux Grounds, Wolverhampton
Att 43,038
Wolverhampton Wanderers 4 *(Rowley 2, Westcott, Broome)*
Sunderland 1 *(Carter)*

Wolverhampton: as first leg except Taylor for Thornhill, Rowley* for Stevenson
Sunderland: as first leg

COMBINED COUNTIES CUP

First round
Played on 2 May
Halifax Town v Huddersfield Town 1-1
REPLAY on 9 May
Huddersfield Town v Halifax Town 1-2
Played on 9 May
Bradford v Chesterfield 0-2
York City v Bradford City 2-1
Leeds United v Middlesbrough 1-2

Semi-final
Played on 16 May
Halifax Town v Chesterfield 5-2 aet (90 mins 2-2)
York City v Middlesbrough 4-1

Final
Played on 23 May
York City v Halifax Town 2-0

LANCASHIRE CUP

First round – 2 legs
First leg played on 11 Apr, second leg on 18 Apr
Bury v Rochdale 4-3, 1-4
Blackpool v Bolton Wanderers 7-1, 1-2
First leg played on 14 Mar, second leg on 28 Mar
Blackburn Rovers v Burnley 6-2, 0-2
First leg played on 21 Mar, second leg on 28 Apr
Everton v Southport 3-1, 1-2
First leg played on 25 Apr, second leg on 2 May
Manchester United v Oldham Athletic 5-1, 2-1

Second round – 2 legs
First leg played on 21 Mar , second leg on 9 May
Chester v Liverpool 1-3, 0-3
First leg played on 25 Apr , second leg on 2 May
Rochdale v Blackpool 2-0, 1-5
First leg played on 9 May , second leg on 16 May
Manchester City v Everton 2-0, 1-6
Blackburn Rovers v Manchester United 1-1, 1-0

Semi-final
Played on 23 May
Liverpool v Blackburn Rovers 2-3
Everton v Blackpool
(Everton were disqualified for not moving the venue to Blackpool, who couldn't travel because of logistical problems)

Final
Played on 30 May at Bloomfield Road, Blackpool
Blackpool v Blackburn Rovers 7-1

LIVERPOOL SENIOR CUP
Played on 30 May
Liverpool v Everton 4-1

Other English Competitions 1941-42

LONDON CUP

Group 1	Arsenal	Brighton & HA	Clapton Orient	West Ham U
Arsenal	X	18 Apr 5-1	21 Mar 4-1	6 Apr 1-4
Brighton & Hove Albion	11 Apr 0-3	X	6 Apr 5-2	21 Mar 1-2
Clapton Orient	4 Apr 1-2	28 Mar 3-2	X	18 Apr 0-1
West Ham United	28 Mar 0-4	4 Apr 6-2	11 Apr 5-3	X

	P	W	D	L	F	A	Pts
Arsenal	6	5	0	1	19	7	10
West Ham United	6	5	0	1	18	11	10
Clapton Orient	6	1	0	5	10	19	2
Brighton & Hove Albion	6	1	0	5	11	21	2

Group 2	Aldershot	Brentford	Millwall	QPR
Aldershot	X	18 Apr 1-3	4 Apr 2-4	28 Mar 0-2
Brentford	21 Mar 6-2	X	28 Mar 3-3	11 Apr 1-0
Millwall	11 Apr 4-1	6 Apr 2-2	X	21 Mar 2-2
Queen's Park Rangers	6 Apr 1-2	4 Apr 1-2	18 Apr 2-0	X

	P	W	D	L	F	A	Pts
Brentford	6	4	2	0	17	9	10
Millwall	6	2	3	1	15	12	7
Queen's Park Rangers	6	2	1	3	8	7	5
Aldershot	6	1	0	5	8	20	2

Group 3	Charlton Ath	Reading	Tottenham H	Watford
Charlton Athletic	X	28 Mar 1-1	18 Apr 0-0	4 Apr 0-1
Reading	6 Apr 3-5	X	21 Mar 1-2	18 Apr 3-0
Tottenham Hotspur	11 Apr 0-3	4 Apr 2-1	X	28 Mar 5-2
Watford	21 Mar 1-4	11 Apr 6-0	6 Apr 0-0	X

	P	W	D	L	F	A	Pts
Charlton Athletic	6	3	2	1	13	6	8
Tottenham Hotspur	6	3	2	1	9	7	8
Watford	6	2	1	3	10	12	5
Reading	6	1	1	4	9	16	3

Group 4	Chelsea	Crystal Palace	Fulham	Portsmouth
Chelsea	X	21 Mar 3-3	6 Apr 2-2	18 Apr 0-0
Crystal Palace	4 Apr 0-3	X	18 Apr 3-4	28 Mar 0-2
Fulham	28 Mar 1-0	11 Apr 4-1	X	4 Apr 2-1
Portsmouth	11 Apr 2-0	6 Apr 2-1	21 Mar 9-1	X

	P	W	D	L	F	A	Pts
Portsmouth	6	4	1	1	16	4	9
Fulham	6	4	1	1	14	16	9
Chelsea	6	1	3	2	8	8	5
Crystal Palace	6	0	1	5	8	18	1

Semi-final
Played on 25 Apr at Stamford Bridge
  Charlton Athletic v Portsmouth 0-1
Played on 2 May at Stamford Bridge
  Arsenal v Brentford 0-0
REPLAY on 16 May at White Hart Lane
  Arsenal v Brentford 1-2

Final
Played on 30 May 1942
at Wembley Stadium, London
Att 72,000
Brentford 2 *(L Smith 2)*
Portsmouth 0

Brentford: Jackson*, Brown, Poyser, Mackenzie*, James, Sneddon*, Hopkins, Wilkins, Perry, Hunt*, L Smith
Portsmouth: Walker, Rookes, Rochford, Guthrie, Flewin, Wharton, Bullock*, Griffiths, Black*, Barlow, Parker

CUP WINNERS MATCH
Played between the winners of the League War Cup and the London Cup

Played on 6 Jun 1942 at Stamford Bridge, London
Att 20,174
Brentford 1 *(Collett)*
Wolverhampton Wanderers 1 *(Mullen)*

Brentford: Jackson*, Brown, Poyser, Mackenzie*, James, Collett*, Hopkins, Wilkins, Perry, Hunt*, L Smith
Wolverhampton W: Sidlow, Dowen*, Taylor, Robinson, Ashton, Dorsett, Broome*, McIntosh, Westcott, Stevenson, Mullen

The Scottish Southern Football League 1941-42

	Airdrieonians	Albion Rovers	Celtic	Clyde	Dumbarton	Falkirk	Hamilton Ac	Heart of Midlothian	Hibernian	Morton	Motherwell	Partick Thistle	Queen's Park	Rangers	St Mirren	Third Lanark
Airdrieonians	X	1 Jan 3-4	14 Feb 2-2	20 Dec 2-1	22 Nov 3-2	18 Oct 1-2	6 Dec 1-0	16 Aug 1-2	9 May 1-2	13 Sep 3-1	25 Oct 0-2	11 Oct 4-3	27 Sep 4-2	30 Aug 1-6	10 Jan 1-2	15 Nov 3-4
Albion Rovers	6 Sep 2-3	X	29 Nov 4-4	21 Feb 4-3	2 May 0-0	13 Dec 3-1	25 Apr 4-4	1 Nov 1-2	23 Aug 3-8	8 Nov 1-5	3 Jan 1-5	9 Aug 2-2	17 Jan 4-1	4 Oct 0-1	20 Sep 3-0	27 Dec 1-3
Celtic	8 Nov 3-3	16 Aug 4-2	X	13 Sep 5-2	6 Dec 4-2	21 Feb 2-0	20 Dec 2-1	22 Nov 4-4	17 Jan 2-1	27 Dec 3-0	4 Oct 1-2	25 Oct 1-1	30 Aug 2-0	1 Jan 0-2	31 Jan 3-0	1 Nov 3-1
Clyde	20 Sep 2-2	15 Nov 4-2	3 Jan 2-1	X	14 Feb 5-4	9 Aug 8-0	11 Oct 6-2	28 Apr 2-0	29 Nov 2-3	2 May 2-0	13 Dec 2-3	6 Sep 4-2	7 Feb 2-1	6 Apr 2-8	27 Dec 5-2	23 Aug 5-4
Dumbarton	9 Aug 3-5	18 Oct 5-2	23 Aug 2-5	8 Nov 6-0	X	6 Sep 0-1	1 Nov 3-2	31 Jan 3-3	3 Jan 2-1	4 Oct 3-1	27 Dec 2-1	20 Sep 2-7	21 Feb 2-1	17 Jan 3-3	13 Dec 5-1	29 Nov 1-5
Falkirk	2 May 3-0	30 Aug 2-4	15 Nov 0-1	22 Nov 4-3	1 Jan 3-1	X	13 Sep 5-1	27 Sep 2-6	25 Oct 1-2	16 Aug 5-2	18 Apr 1-0	10 Jan 2-1	6 Dec 3-5	20 Sep 2-2	14 Feb 2-0	11 Oct 3-2
Hamilton Academical	23 Aug 3-2	25 Oct 1-6	20 Sep 3-3	17 Jan 3-0	9 May 4-1	3 Jan 2-2	X	2 May 2-1	13 Dec 2-2	21 Feb 1-2	6 Sep 4-2	27 Dec 3-6	4 Oct 0-2	8 Nov 2-3	29 Nov 3-4	9 Aug 3-4
Heart Of Midlothian	29 Nov 2-1	18 Apr 2-2	9 Aug 3-0	4 Oct 4-1	25 Oct 7-4	27 Dec 7-0	18 Oct 6-2	X	6 Sep 2-4	17 Jan 1-2	20 Sep 2-1	23 Aug 4-1	8 Nov 3-2	21 Feb 0-1	15 Jan 8-2	13 Dec 1-5
Hibernian	1 Nov 4-1	6 Dec 5-2	11 Oct 1-3	16 Aug 1-4	13 Sep 4-0	31 Jan 2-0	30 Aug 4-0	1 Jan 2-2	X	22 Nov 1-0	2 May 3-1	14 Feb 4-0	20 Dec 1-1	27 Sep 8-1	15 Nov 5-2	10 Jan 6-0
Morton	3 Jan 4-1	14 Feb 8-0	27 Sep 2-3	25 Oct 1-1	10 Jan 2-2	29 Nov 1-4	5 Nov 1-0	11 Oct 4-0	9 Aug 2-1	X	23 Aug 2-1	13 Dec 1-1	18 Oct 1-2	1 Nov 2-1	6 Sep 5-0	20 Sep 3-2
Motherwell	25 Apr 1-3	13 Sep 5-3	10 Jan 2-1	30 Aug 1-1	27 Sep 2-3	1 Nov 6-4	1 Jan 4-3	20 Dec 6-2	18 Oct 3-2	6 Dec 3-2	X	15 Nov 6-1	16 Aug 3-2	22 Nov 1-1	11 Oct 2-5	14 Feb 5-3
Partick Thistle	17 Jan 0-2	22 Nov 5-1	6 Apr 1-3	1 Jan 1-1	20 Dec 4-3	4 Oct 1-1	27 Sep 7-0	6 Dec 2-1	8 Nov 3-2	30 Aug 2-2	21 Feb 0-0	X	13 Sep 2-3	16 Aug 2-3	1 Nov 1-1	18 Oct 7-2
Queen's Park	27 Dec 2-2	11 Oct 2-0	13 Dec 1-1	1 Nov 1-3	15 Nov 1-2	23 Aug 3-1	10 Jan 3-1	14 Feb 4-1	20 Sep 1-2	31 Jan 2-0	29 Nov 3-1	3 Jan 2-2	X	21 Apr 1-2	9 Aug 1-2	1 Jan 4-1
Rangers	13 Dec 3-0	28 Apr 2-1	6 Sep 3-0	31 Jan 0-0	11 Oct 7-0	20 Sep 5-2	14 Feb 6-0	15 Nov 5-2	27 Dec 0-1	14 Apr 3-0	9 Aug 3-0	29 Nov 6-0	25 Oct 3-0	X	23 Aug 8-1	3 Jan 6-1
St Mirren	4 Oct 7-2	20 Dec 4-2	18 Oct 2-2	27 Sep 3-3	30 Aug 2-4	8 Nov 1-1	16 Aug 5-3	13 Sep 0-3	21 Feb 1-1	1 Jan 1-0	17 Jan 2-3	9 May 1-1	22 Nov 1-1	6 Dec 3-1	X	2 May 4-0
Third Lanark	21 Feb 2-0	27 Sep 3-4	7 Feb 1-1	6 Dec 5-3	16 Aug 4-3	17 Jan 0-3	22 Nov 3-1	30 Aug 6-4	4 Oct 4-2	20 Dec 4-4	8 Nov 0-4	31 Jan 3-2	6 Sep 4-1	13 Sep 0-2	25 Oct 3-1	X

		P	W	D	L	F	A	Pts
1	Rangers	30	22	4	4	97	35	48
2	Hibernian	30	18	4	8	85	46	40
3	Celtic	30	15	9	6	69	50	39
4	Motherwell	30	16	3	11	76	62	35
5	Clyde	30	13	6	11	79	75	32
6	Heart of Midlothian	30	14	4	12	85	72	32
7	Falkirk	30	13	4	13	60	72	30
8	Third Lanark	30	14	2	14	79	90	30
9	Morton	30	12	5	13	60	54	29
10	Queen's Park	30	11	5	14	55	56	27
11	St Mirren	30	10	7	13	60	82	27
12	Dumbarton	30	11	4	15	73	90	26
13	Partick Thistle	30	8	10	12	68	70	26
14	Airdrieonians	30	10	4	16	57	76	24
15	Albion Rovers	30	8	5	17	68	97	21
16	Hamilton Academical	30	5	4	21	56	100	14

The Scottish Southern Football League Cup 1941-42

Section 1	Dumbarton	Falkirk	Morton	St Mirren
Dumbarton	X	11 Apr 3-3	21 Mar 3-4	4 Apr 4-2
Falkirk	28 Mar 0-5	X	14 Mar 1-3	28 Feb 1-1
Morton	28 Feb 4-1	4 Apr 1-0	X	28 Mar 1-1
St Mirren	14 Mar 1-3	21 Mar 4-3	11 Apr 5-1	X

		P	W	D	L	F	A	Pts
1	Morton	6	4	1	1	14	11	9
2	Dumbarton	6	3	1	2	19	14	7
3	St Mirren	6	2	2	2	14	13	6
4	Falkirk	6	0	2	4	8	17	2

Section 2	Celtic	Hamilton A	Hibernian	Queen's Park
Celtic	X	14 Mar 1-0	7 Mar 4-1	21 Mar 6-2
Hamilton Academical	4 Apr 1-2	X	21 Mar 3-1	11 Apr 1-1
Hibernian	28 Mar 1-0	28 Feb 1-2	X	14 Mar 3-1
Queen's Park	28 Feb 1-2	28 Mar 2-1	4 Apr 0-1	X

		P	W	D	L	F	A	Pts
1	Celtic	6	5	0	1	15	6	10
2	Hibernian	6	3	0	3	8	10	6
3	Hamilton Acas	6	2	1	3	8	8	5
4	Queen's Park	6	1	1	4	7	14	3

Section 3	Airdrieonians	Albion Rovers	Clyde	Partick Th
Airdrieonians	X	28 Feb 3-1	14 Mar 1-1	28 Mar 2-3
Albion Rovers	21 Mar 1-1	X	11 Apr 4-3	4 Apr 1-1
Clyde	4 Apr 3-2	28 Mar 7-3	X	28 Feb 1-2
Partick Thistle	11 Apr 4-2	14 Mar 5-2	21 Mar 1-1	X

		P	W	D	L	F	A	Pts
1	Partick Th	6	4	2	0	16	9	10
2	Clyde	6	2	2	2	16	13	6
3	Airdrieonians	6	1	2	3	11	13	4
4	Albion Rov	6	1	2	3	12	20	4

Section 4	Hearts	Motherwell	Rangers	Third Lanark
Heart of Midlothian	X	21 Mar 5-1	11 Apr 0-2	4 Apr 3-0
Motherwell	28 Feb 2-3	X	14 Mar 1-3	28 Mar 2-1
Rangers	28 Mar 2-1	4 Apr 3-0	X	28 Feb 5-1
Third Lanark	14 Mar 3-5	11 Apr 0-1	21 Mar 2-5	X

		P	W	D	L	F	A	Pts
1	Rangers	6	6	0	0	20	5	12
2	Heart of Midlothian	6	4	0	2	17	10	8
3	Motherwell	6	2	0	4	7	15	4
4	Third Lanark	6	0	0	6	7	21	0

Semi-final
Played on 25 Apr, REPLAY on 29 Apr, both games at Ibrox Park, Glasgow
  Morton v Partick Thistle 1-1, 1-0
Played on 2 May at Hampden Park, Glasgow
  Rangers v Celtic 2-0

Final
Played on 9 May 1942 at Hampden Park, Glasgow
Att 45,000
Rangers 1 *(Gillick)*
Morton 0

Rangers: Dawson, Gray, Shaw, Little, Young, Thomson, Waddell, Gillick, McIntosh, Venters, Johnstone
Morton: McFeat, Maley, Fyfe, Campbell, Aird, Whyte, Cumner, Orr, Hunter, Steele, Kelly

The Scottish North Eastern Football League 1941-42

First series	Aberdeen	Dundee U	Dunfermline A	East Fife	Leith A	Raith R	Rangers	St Bernard's
Aberdeen	X	1 Nov 4-2	30 Aug 4-0	25 Oct 1-1	16 Aug 9-0	27 Sep 7-1	6 Sep 1-1	23 Sep 7-1
Dundee United	23 Aug 5-0	X	20 Sep 1-1	9 Aug 1-1	6 Sep 1-4	8 Nov 3-9	18 Oct 0-5	11 Oct 2-2
Dunfermline Athletic	18 Oct 3-1	25 Oct 7-2	X	11 Oct 1-1	23 Sep 2-1	6 Sep 4-4	23 Aug 1-4	9 Aug 7-3
East Fife	20 Sep 1-0	27 Sep 2-2	16 Aug 8-0	X	1 Nov 2-1	18 Oct 5-1	8 Nov 3-1	6 Sep 4-2
Leith Athletic	11 Oct 3-4	4 Oct 2-5	8 Nov 1-3	23 Aug 1-2	X	25 Oct 4-0	9 Aug 3-5	18 Oct 3-3
Raith Rovers	9 Aug 2-4	13 Sep 2-1	4 Oct 3-4	30 Aug 1-2	20 Sep 9-5	X	11 Oct 2-3	23 Aug 3-4
Rangers 'A'	4 Oct 1-1	30 Aug 5-3	1 Nov 6-2	23 Sep 3-1	27 Sep 7-0	16 Aug 8-1	X	25 Oct 0-2
St Bernard's	8 Nov 2-6	16 Aug 1-4	27 Sep 5-3	4 Oct 1-1	30 Aug 5-3	1 Nov 3-2	20 Sep 2-3	X

		P	W	D	L	F	A	Pts
1	Rangers 'A'	14	10	2	2	52	22	22
2	East Fife	14	8	5	1	34	16	21
3	Aberdeen	14	8	3	3	49	23	19
4	Dunfermline Athletic	14	6	3	5	38	44	15
5	St Bernard's	14	5	3	6	36	48	13
6	Dundee United	14	3	4	7	32	45	10
7	Raith Rovers	14	3	1	10	40	57	7
8	Leith Athletic	14	2	1	11	31	57	5

Second Series	Aberdeen	Dundee U	Dunfermline A	East Fife	Leith A	Raith R	Rangers	St Bernard's
Aberdeen	X	6 Jan 6-1	18 Apr 2-1	14 Mar 1-0	11 Apr 3-0	17 Jan 3-5	21 Feb 0-0	25 Apr 8-0
Dundee United	10 Jan 2-0	X	1 Jan 3-5	25 Apr 0-2	30 May 5-1	28 Mar 5-1	18 Apr 8-1	4 Apr 2-0
Dunfermline Athletic	21 Mar 1-2	21 Feb 0-2	X	22 Apr 1-3	10 Jan 5-1	3 Jan 3-2	4 Apr 2-3	28 Mar 2-2
East Fife	4 Apr 1-1	3 Jan 1-1	17 Jan 3-1	X	21 Mar 3-1	21 Feb 6-1	28 Mar 0-3	28 Feb 3-2
Leith Athletic	28 Mar 0-2	17 Jan 2-2	6 Jan 7-7	18 Apr 2-5	X	4 Apr 4-2	25 Apr 3-4	21 Feb 2-1
Raith Rovers	14 Feb 2-1	11 Apr 1-1	25 Apr 4-0	1 Jan 7-2	14 Mar 1-2	X	10 Jan 4-3	18 Apr 5-2
Rangers 'A'	1 Jan 1-3	21 Mar 4-2	14 Mar 7-0	11 Apr 4-0	3 Jan 4-3	28 Feb 6-3	X	17 Jan 3-0
St Bernard's	3 Jan 1-5	14 Mar 1-3	11 Apr 1-2	16 May 2-3	1 Jan 2-1	21 Mar 0-0	14 Feb 5-6	X

		P	W	D	L	F	A	BP	Pts
1	Aberdeen	14	9	2	3	37	15	6	26
2	Rangers 'A'	14	10	1	3	49	33	5	26
3	East Fife	14	8	2	4	32	27	4	22
4	Dundee United	14	7	3	4	37	25	4	21
5	Raith Rovers	14	6	2	6	38	38	3	17
6	Dunfermline Athletic	14	4	2	8	30	42	2	12
7	Leith Athletic	14	3	2	9	29	46	1	9
8	St Bernard's	14	1	2	11	19	45	0	4

BP - an extra point was awarded by having a better aggregate score over each opponent

The Scottish North Eastern Football League Cup 1941-42

First Series
First Round – 2 legs
First leg played on 15 Nov, second on 22 Nov
  Aberdeen v Dunfermline Athletic 3-2, 2-0
  Dundee United v St Bernard's 7-1, 3-3
  Leith Athletic v Rangers 'A' 4-5, 1-8
  Raith Rovers v East Fife 0-4, 2-5

Semi-final – 2 legs
First leg played on 29 Nov, second on 6 Dec
  Aberdeen v Rangers 'A' 3-0, 1-1
  Dundee United v East Fife 3-2, 1-1

Final – 2 legs
First leg, 13 Dec 1941 at Tannadice Park, Dundee
Att 8,000
Dundee United 4 *(Ross, Gardiner, Juliussen 2)*
Aberdeen 1 *(Donaldson)*

Dundee United: Brownlee, Sibley, Fordyce, Morgan, Simpson, Adamson, Ross, Gardiner, Juliussen, Gallacher, Cook
Aberdeen: Johnstone, Cooper, Dyer, Dunlop, Lyon, Taylor, Donaldson, Bain, Fleming, McCall, Williams

Second leg, 20 Dec 1941 at Pittodrie Park, Aberdeen
Att 10,000
Aberdeen 6 *(Williams, Donaldson 2, Anderson, Lyon (pen), Morgan (og))*
Dundee United 2 *(Watson (pen), Gallacher)*

Aberdeen: as first leg except Brown for Johnstone, Graham for Dyer, Hamilton for Bain, Anderson for Fleming
Dundee United: as first leg except Watson for Juliussen, Smart for Williams

Second Series
Semi-final – 2 legs
First leg played on 2 May, second on 9 May
  Dundee United v Rangers 'A' 2-1, 2-2
  East Fife v Aberdeen 1-1, 0-1

Final – 2 legs
First leg, 16 May 1942 at Tannadice Park, Dundee
Att 8,000
Dundee United 4 *(Low, Gardiner, Glassey 2)*
Aberdeen 3 *(Gourlay, Milne, Pattillo)*

Dundee United: Brownlee, Sibley, Fordyce, Melville, A Low, Adamson, D Low, Gardiner, Juliussen, Glassey, Nevins
Aberdeen: Johnstone, Cooper, Howe, Dunlop, Gavin, Taylor, Pattillo, Gourlay, Milne, Dyer, Dryden

Second leg, 23 May 1942 at Pittodrie Park, Aberdeen
Att 12,000
Aberdeen 3 *(Williams, Pattillo, Gourlay)*
Dundee United 1 *(Nevins)*
Aet, 90 mins 2-1
Aberdeen: as first leg except Gavin for Dryden
Dundee United: as first leg

NOTE this series was only open to the clubs that finished in the top four places of the Spring Series of the League.

Other Scottish Competitions 1941-42

SUMMER CUP

Semi-final
Played on 27 Jun
Hibernian v Motherwell 3-1 *(at Tynecastle Park, Edinburgh)*
Rangers v Albion Rovers 3-2 *(at Hampden Park, Glasgow)*

Final
4 Jul 1942 at Hampden Park, Glasgow
Att 60,000
Rangers 0
Hibernian 0
After extra time and 2 corners each, Rangers won on the toss of a coin

Rangers: Dawson, Gray, Shaw, Little, Young, Symon, Waddell, Thornton, Gillick, Venters, Johnstone
Hibernian: Crozier, Shaw, Hall, Busby, Baxter, Kean, Smith, Finnigan, Milne, Combe, Caskie

First round – 2 legs
First leg played on 30 May, second on 6 Jun
Albion Rovers v Queen's Park 2-0, 3-4
Celtic v Partick Thistle 2-1, 2-0
Dumbarton v Motherwell 1-0, 2-4
Falkirk v Morton 3-2, 0-1
(1-1 on corners – Falkirk won on toss of coin)
Hamilton Academical v Rangers 1-7, 3-2
Hibernian v Clyde 2-1, 2-0
St Mirren v Heart of Midlothian 3-3, 1-4
Third Lanark v Airdrieonians 4-3, 4-1

Second round – 2 legs
First leg played on 13 Jun, second on 20 Jun
Hibernian v Third Lanark 8-2, 5-1
Albion Rovers v Heart of Midlothian 3-0, 0-2
Celtic v Motherwell 1-2, 1-2
Falkirk v Rangers 1-0, 0-3

GLASGOW CUP

First round
Played on 20 Aug
Third Lanark v Clyde 3-6
Played on 27 Aug
Partick Thistle v Queen's Park 5-3

Semi-final
Played on 29 Sep
Rangers v Celtic 3-2 *(at Hampden Park, Glasgow)*
Partick Thistle v Clyde 0-3

Final
Played on 18 Oct at Hampden Park, Glasgow
Rangers v Clyde 6-0

GLASGOW CHARITY CUP

First round
Played on 25 Apr
Third Lanark v Celtic 0-2
Queen's Park v Rangers 0-1

Semi-final
Played on 12 May
Partick Thistle v Clyde 2-2 *(Clyde won on corners)*
Played on 13 May at Hampden Park, Glasgow
Rangers v Celtic 2-1

Final
Played on 16 May at Hampden Park, Glasgow
Rangers v Clyde 3-1

EAST OF SCOTLAND SHIELD

Semi-final
Played on 20 Apr
Hibernian v St Bernard's 7-1
Played on 9 May
Heart of Midlothian v Leith Athletic 10-3

Final
Played on 16 May at Tynecastle Park, Edinburgh
Heart of Midlothian v Hibernian 3-2

CITY CUP

First round
Played on 29 Nov
St Bernard's v Edinburgh City 7-1

COMPETITION ABANDONED

ROSEBERY CHARITY CUP

Played on 23 May at Tynecastle Park, Edinburgh
Heart of Midlothian v Hibernian 1-1
(Hearts won on the toss of a coin)

WILSON CUP

Played on 13 Aug at Easter Road, Edinburgh
Hibernian v Heart of Midlothian 0-1

RENFREWSHIRE CUP

Final
Played on 16 May at Cappielow Park, Greenock
Morton v St Mirren 5-1

Northern Ireland 1941-42

NORTHERN REGIONAL FOOTBALL LEAGUE

	Belfast Celtic	Cliftonville	Derry City	Distillery	Glentoran	Linfield
Belfast Celtic	X	8 Nov 3-1 3 Jan 9-0	20 Dec 1-0 14 Mar 10-1	6 Dec 5-2 14 Feb 1-1	29 Nov 4-0 7 Feb 2-1	0-0 28 Mar 0-3
Cliftonville	13 Dec 2-4 11 Apr 0-2	X	2-2 4 Apr 6-1	22 Nov 2-0 31 Jan 1-2	27 Dec 0-5 1-3	15 Nov 5-5 10 Jan 1-4
Derry City	15 Nov 0-0 10 Jan 1-4	29 Nov 1-0 7 Feb 2-1	X	13 Dec 2-0 1-4	1-1 28 Mar 0-2	6 Dec 2-2 14 Feb 1-2
Distillery	27 Dec 0-2 1-1	1-1 4-1	8 Nov 3-3 3 Jan 8-2	X	20 Dec 5-1 14 Mar 1-1	29 Nov 2-2 7 Feb 0-2
Glentoran	4-1 4 Apr 1-3	6 Dec 3-1 14 Feb 4-1	22 Nov 7-1 31 Jan 7-1	15 Nov 2-1 10 Jan 4-2	X	13 Dec 0-3 11 Apr 3-4
Linfield	22 Nov 2-2 31 Jan 3-3	20 Dec 3-1 14 Mar 6-2	27 Dec 9-1 28 Mar 4-1	1-2 4 Apr 3-2	8 Nov 3-7 3 Jan 3-3	X

		P	W	D	L	F	A	Pts
1	Belfast Celtic	20	12	6	2	57	23	30
2	Linfield	20	11	7	2	64	38	29
3	Glentoran	20	11	3	6	59	37	25
4	Distillery	20	6	6	8	41	38	18
5	Derry City	20	3	5	12	23	73	11
6	Cliftonville	20	2	3	15	29	64	7

SUBSTITUTE GOLD CUP

	Belfast Celtic	Cliftonville	Derry City	Distillery	Glentoran	Linfield
Belfast Celtic	X	27 Sep 8-0	4 Oct 5-2	25 Oct 2-1	18 Oct 1-3	30 Aug 1-1
Cliftonville	1 Nov 0-2	X	30 Aug 1-1	6 Sep 0-1	4 Oct 3-5	25 Oct 1-5
Derry City	23 Aug 0-0	11 Oct 2-0	X	27 Sep 0-1	20 Sep 0-3	18 Oct 4-0
Distillery	20 Sep 4-3	18 Oct 2-1	1 Nov 2-0	X	30 Aug 2-3	4 Oct 2-2
Glentoran	6 Sep 2-1	23 Aug 5-1	25 Oct 5-4	11 Oct 2-2	X	27 Sep 4-6
Linfield	11 Oct 2-1	20 Sep 6-2	6 Sep 2-2	23 Aug 2-3	1 Nov 1-3	X

		P	W	D	L	F	A	Pts
1	Glentoran	10	8	1	1	35	21	17
2	Distillery	10	6	2	2	20	15	14
3	Linfield	10	4	3	3	27	23	11
4	Belfast Celtic	10	4	2	4	24	15	10
5	Derry City	10	2	3	5	15	19	7
6	Cliftonville	10	0	1	9	9	37	1

Northern Ireland 1941-42

IRISH FA CUP

First round – 2 legs
First leg played on10 Jan, second on 17 Jan
Bangor reserves v Sirocco Works 6-0, 1-4
First leg played on 17 Jan, second on 24 Jan
Bangor v Ards 3-2, 0-4
Cliftonville v Royal Ulster Regiment 4-2, 7-2
Distillery v Belfast Celtic 1-0, 2-2
Linfield v Derry City 4-0, 2-1
Larne v Glentoran 1-3, 0-2

Second round – 2 legs
First leg played on 21 Feb, second on 28 Feb
Bangor reserves v Ards 1-4, 1-4
Cliftonville v Distillery 0-3, 0-4
Glentoran v Royal Irish Fusiliers 4-0, 0-2
Linfield v Royal Inniskillen Fusiliers 5-1, 4-1

Semi-final
Played on 21 Mar
Linfield v Distillery 6-0
Glentoran v Ards 2-0

Final
Played 18 Apr at Celtic Park, Belfast
Linfield v Glentoran 3-1

INTER CITY CUP

Derry City played all their home matches in Belfast
All League of Ireland clubs' home games were played at Dalymount Park, Dublin

First round – 2 legs
First leg played on 29 Apr, second on 6 May
Derry City v Shamrock Rovers 2-5, 1-5
First leg played on 29 Apr, second on 9 May
Bohemians v Cliftonville 4-1, 1-2
First leg played on 2 May, second on 4 May
Distillery v Cork United 3-0, 1-1
First leg played on 2 May, second on 9 May
St James' Gate v Linfield 6-1, 2-2
First leg played on 4 May, second on 9 May
Glentoran v Dundalk 1-5, 2-1
First leg played on 5 May, second on 11 May
Belfast Celtic v Shelbourne 2-1, 2-0

Second round - 2 legs
The first round winners were joined by the best Northern losers (Cliftonville) and Southern losers (Shelbourne were drawn from a hat over Cork United)
First leg played on 15 May, second on 19 May
St James' Gate v Cliftonville 3-0, 0-3 (Cliftonville won on corners)
First leg played on 16 May, second on 23 May
Bohemians v Belfast Celtic 5-2, 0-6
First leg played on 16 May, second on 19 May
Distillery v Dundalk 1-0, 1-2 (after Distillery refused to play extra-time, the tie was awarded to Dundalk)
First leg played on 17 May, second on 24 May
Shamrock Rovers v Shelbourne 6-3, 2-4

Semi-final - 2 legs
First leg played on 25 May, second on 27 May
Belfast Celtic v Dundalk 2-2, 0-1
Shamrock Rovers v Cliftonville 5-1, 2-0

Final
Played on 31 May at Dalymount Park, Dublin
Dundalk v Shamrock Rovers 1-0

1942-43

In England and Wales, three leagues would operate in this and the two subsequent seasons; North, West (which also included non-League sides) and South (in effect the London League which had been welcomed back into the fold). Again the North was subdivided into smaller groupings, each club playing nine others. The second half of the season saw the North and West clubs combined as the League North (Second Championship). The League Cup qualifying competition, results in the subsequent rounds and local cup ties also counted towards this.

Aston Villa competed in the non-League Birmingham & District League while Norwich City filled their season with friendly fixtures against services XIs.

The Scottish Southern League and North Eastern Football League were again also in operation.

A Northern Irish Northern Regional League also operated. A competition between clubs from the Home Nations, and from the Republic of Ireland was played too.

WINNERS OF THE PRINCIPAL COMPETITIONS

Football League North Cup	Blackpool
Football League South Cup	Arsenal
Football League West Cup	Swansea Town
Football League –	
North	Blackpool
North (Second Championship)	Liverpool
South	Arsenal
West	Lovell's Athletic
Scottish Southern League	Rangers
Scottish Southern League Cup	Rangers
Scottish North Eastern League –	
First Series	Aberdeen
Second Series	Aberdeen
North Eastern League Cup –	
First Series	Aberdeen
Second Series	Aberdeen
Irish FA Cup	Belfast Celtic
Northern Regional League	Linfield
Substitute Gold Cup	Linfield
Inter City Cup	Shamrock Rovers

The Football League 1942-43

NORTH

	Chester	Crewe Alex	Everton	Liverpool	Manchester City	Manchester United	Tranmere R	Wrexham
Chester	X		12 Dec 2-3	14 Nov 1-5	28 Nov 1-1	19 Sep 2-2	17 Oct 3-2	24 Oct 7-2
Crewe Alexandra		X	28 Nov 4-2		10 Oct 5-3		12 Sep 5-2	25 Dec 8-2
Everton	5 Dec 3-1	21 Nov 4-0	X	19 Sep 4-4	25 Dec 6-3	29 Aug 2-2	14 Nov 3-5	10 Oct 2-1
Liverpool	7 Nov 4-2		12 Sep 1-0	X	31 Oct 3-1	17 Oct 2-1	19 Dec 6-2	5 Sep 4-0
Manchester City	21 Nov 4-2	17 Oct 5-1	19 Dec 7-1	24 Oct 1-4	X	14 Nov 0-5	12 Dec 4-1	19 Sep 5-1
Manchester United	12 Sep 0-2		5 Sep 2-1	10 Oct 3-4	7 Nov 2-1	X	28 Nov 5-1	5 Dec 6-1
Tranmere Rovers	10 Oct 2-2	19 Sep 3-1	7 Nov 1-3	25 Dec 3-2	5 Dec 1-3	21 Nov 0-5	X	3 Oct 4-4
Wrexham	31 Oct 3-2	19 Dec 5-4	17 Oct 0-2	29 Aug 3-4	12 Sep 4-2	12 Dec 2-5	26 Sep 3-0	X

	Blackburn R	Blackpool	Bolton W	Burnley	Bury	Oldham Ath	Rochdale	Southport	Stockport Co
Blackburn Rovers	X	19 Dec 2-4	14 Nov 4-2	29 Aug 3-3	21 Nov 0-2	24 Oct 8-1	17 Oct 6-0	12 Dec 2-2	19 Sep 4-0
Blackpool	25 Dec 7-2	X	10 Oct 2-0	28 Nov 5-1	12 Sep 9-1	5 Dec 8-3	31 Oct 5-0	7 Nov 6-2	3 Oct 6-2
Bolton Wanderers	7 Nov 3-3	17 Oct 0-2	X	24 Oct 7-4	5 Sep 2-3	28 Nov 1-1	5 Dec 4-4	12 Sep 1-3	
Burnley	5 Sep 1-0	21 Nov 4-4	31 Oct 1-2	X		12 Sep 3-0	7 Nov 5-0		10 Oct 0-0
Bury	28 Nov 6-0	19 Sep 1-11	29 Aug 4-3		X	7 Nov 4-1	25 Dec 7-3	10 Oct 3-5	5 Dec 3-3
Oldham Athletic	31 Oct 0-1	12 Dec 1-4	21 Nov 3-1	19 Sep 1-3	14 Nov 3-3	X	3 Oct 1-0	25 Dec 6-0	
Rochdale	10 Oct 1-5	24 Oct 3-4	12 Dec 3-1	14 Nov 2-1	19 Dec 6-3	26 Sep 3-1	X	5 Sep 2-3	21 Nov 3-1
Southport	5 Dec 1-2	14 Nov 3-2	19 Sep 6-2		17 Oct 6-3	19 Dec 3-0	29 Aug 1-1	X	
Stockport County	12 Sep 3-2	26 Sep 0-6		17 Oct 4-1	12 Dec 4-1		28 Nov 3-2		X

There were no scheduled matches between the clubs that are blank in the above grids

The Football League 1942-43

NORTH

	Barnsley	Bradford	Bradford City	Gateshead	Huddersfield T	Leeds U	Middlesbrough	Newcastle U	Sunderland	York C
Barnsley	X	28 Nov 3-1	12 Sep 4-0		29 Aug 6-1					
Bradford	21 Nov 1-1	X	25 Dec 2-0	24 Oct 6-0		14 Nov 1-0	12 Sep 0-0	5 Sep 0-0	10 Oct 4-2	12 Dec 3-1
Bradford City	19 Sep 2-3	19 Dec 0-10	X	26 Sep 3-7	5 Dec 3-3		17 Oct 2-3	31 Oct 3-1	29 Aug 4-3	7 Nov 1-3
Gateshead		31 Oct 1-1	3 Oct 2-2	X	10 Oct 3-4	12 Sep 3-1	5 Dec 5-0	7 Nov 4-1 / 19 Dec 3-1	28 Nov 1-0	5 Sep 1-4
Huddersfield Town	5 Sep 3-3		12 Dec 3-2	17 Oct 2-1	X	19 Dec 4-1	31 Oct 4-1	12 Sep 4-0	3 Oct 2-2	
Leeds United		7 Nov 1-1		19 Sep 1-2	25 Dec 3-3	X	29 Aug 0-1	3 Oct 1-7	24 Oct 1-2	21 Nov 2-1
Middlesbrough		19 Sep 2-2	10 Oct 2-3	12 Dec 2-3	24 Oct 2-2	5 Sep 2-0	X	28 Nov 1-6	14 Nov 3-4 / 19 Dec 2-7	3 Oct 2-3
Newcastle United		29 Aug 1-4	24 Oct 1-0	14 Nov 7-4 / 25 Dec 6-6	19 Sep 0-4	26 Sep 3-5	21 Nov 3-0	X	12 Dec 3-3	17 Oct 3-3
Sunderland		17 Oct 2-1	5 Sep 3-1	21 Nov 3-4	26 Sep 1-3	31 Oct 4-1	7 Nov 4-1 / 25 Dec 0-4	5 Dec 3-5	X	12 Sep 0-0
York City		5 Dec 3-6	14 Nov 9-1	29 Aug 1-2		28 Nov 3-1	26 Sep 2-2	10 Oct 4-3	19 Sep 0-3	X

	Aston Villa	Birmingham	Coventry C	Derby Co	Leicester C	Northampton Town	Stoke C	Walsall	WBA	Wolves
Aston Villa	X	21 Nov 2-1	19 Sep 1-1	12 Dec 2-0	19 Dec 4-2	14 Nov 4-1	24 Oct 4-0	26 Sep 2-2	17 Oct 8-2	29 Aug 2-0
Birmingham	28 Nov 2-1	X	31 Oct 1-0	12 Sep 0-5	5 Sep 2-1	3 Oct 0-2	10 Oct 1-0	7 Nov 4-3	5 Dec 3-0	25 Dec 1-0
Coventry City	12 Sep 2-1	24 Oct 2-2	X		3 Oct 5-1	10 Oct 5-0 / 28 Nov 2-1		5 Sep 1-0 / 12 Dec 1-0	19 Dec 2-1	7 Nov 1-0
Derby County	5 Dec 4-2	19 Sep 3-1		X	14 Nov 5-3		3 Oct 0-1		24 Oct 4-0	28 Nov 3-1
Leicester City	25 Dec 2-5	29 Aug 0-1	26 Sep 0-0	7 Nov 2-3	X				19 Sep 0-0	12 Dec 5-0
Northampton Town	7 Nov 3-5	26 Sep 4-1	17 Oct 1-2 / 21 Nov 1-2					12 Sep 4-2 / 31 Oct 2-2	29 Aug 2-0	
Stoke City	31 Oct 1-0	17 Oct 1-3	X	26 Sep 5-2		X		19 Dec 7-1	14 Nov 5-1	19 Sep 1-0
Walsall	3 Oct 3-0	14 Nov 1-0	29 Aug 1-0 / 5 Dec 1-1			19 Sep 0-2 / 24 Oct 6-0	25 Dec 2-2	X	28 Nov 2-0	17 Oct 5-2
West Bromwich Albion	10 Oct 6-2	12 Dec 4-3	25 Dec 3-0	31 Oct 3-3	12 Sep 3-2	5 Sep 6-3	7 Nov 0-0	21 Nov 0-0	X	3 Oct 6-2
Wolverhampton Wanderers	5 Sep 1-2	19 Dec 1-1	14 Nov 1-1	21 Nov 8-1	5 Dec 0-2		12 Sep 3-2	10 Oct 3-2	26 Sep 2-0	X

There were no scheduled matches between the clubs that are blank in the above grids

The Football League 1942-43

NORTH

	Barnsley	Chesterfield	Doncaster R	Grimsby T	Lincoln C	Mansfield T	Rotherham U	Sheffield United	Sheffield Wednesday
Barnsley	X	19 Dec 3-1	5 Dec 1-1	26 Sep 1-3			7 Nov 2-3	17 Oct 2-1	31 Oct 0-3
Chesterfield	25 Dec 0-0	X	12 Sep 3-1			21 Nov 1-1	17 Oct 0-1	7 Nov 0-0	5 Dec 5-1
Doncaster Rovers	12 Dec 0-2	19 Sep 3-1	X	*NOT PLAYED*	26 Sep 0-2			24 Oct 2-4	29 Aug 1-3
Grimsby Town	3 Oct 1-1		19 Dec 3-2	X	12 Sep 5-2 / 7 Nov 2-2		12 Dec 4-1	28 Nov 4-3	
Lincoln City			3 Oct 3-0	19 Sep 2-2 / 14 Nov 2-2	X	10 Oct 7-1	21 Nov 1-1		
Mansfield Town		28 Nov 1-1		17 Oct 3-4		X	29 Aug 4-3	12 Dec 4-3	14 Nov 2-10
Rotherham United	14 Nov 1-5	10 Oct 3-3		5 Dec 1-6	28 Nov 3-0	5 Sep 0-0	X	26 Sep 1-1	19 Sep 2-2
Sheffield United	10 Oct 3-1	14 Nov 2-2	31 Oct 2-2	21 Nov 3-3		5 Dec 6-2	3 Oct 4-2	X	25 Dec 3-0
Sheffield Wednesday	24 Oct 5-1	12 Dec 6-0	5 Sep 3-2	17 Oct 2-0		7 Nov 9-1	12 Sep 4-1	19 Dec 4-0	X

There were no scheduled matches between the clubs that are blank in the above grids

Inter area matches

Played on 29 Aug
Manchester City v Blackpool 1-3
Chester v Oldham Athletic 5-1
Stoke City v Crewe Alexandra 4-1
Tranmere Rovers v Stockport County 4-2
Sheffield United v Halifax Town 3-1
Lincoln City v Nottingham Forest 3-3
Notts County v Derby County 1-6
Played on 5 Sep
Blackpool v Manchester City 5-2
Oldham Athletic v Chester 2-3
Stockport County v Tranmere Rovers 2-3
Crewe Alexandra v Stoke City 1-2
Halifax Town v Sheffield United 3-2
Derby County v Notts County 2-0
Nottingham Forest v Lincoln City 0-1
Played on 12 Sep
Rochdale v Halifax Town 1-3
Mansfield Town v Notts County 0-1
Nottingham Forest v Sheffield United 0-3
Played on 19 Sep
Halifax Town v Rochdale 3-0
Sheffield United v Nottingham Forest 2-2
Notts County v Mansfield Town 3-1
Played on 26 Sep
Blackburn Rovers v Manchester United 4-2
Manchester City v Bolton Wanderers 2-0
Bury v Liverpool 1-4
Chester v Halifax Town 4-1
Everton v Burnley 2-1
Southport v Crewe Alexandra 10-0
Sheffield Wednesday v Bradford 1-0
Mansfield Town v Nottingham Forest 0-1
Notts County v Chesterfield 2-0
Played on 3 Oct
Bolton Wanderers v Manchester City 2-1
Manchester United v Blackburn Rovers 5-2
Burnley v Everton 1-4
Halifax Town v Chester 3-1
Crewe Alexandra v Southport 2-4
Liverpool v Bury 5-2
Bradford v Sheffield Wednesday 3-3
Chesterfield v Notts County 6-1
Nottingham Forest v Mansfield Town 3-1

Played on 10 Oct
Oldham Athletic v Halifax Town 3-0
Leeds United v Doncaster Rovers 6-0
Leicester City v Notts County 1-3
Nottingham Forest v Derby County 5-1
Played on 17 Oct
Halifax Town v Oldham Athletic 4-1
Doncaster Rovers v Leeds United 2-2
Derby County v Nottingham Forest 3-2
Notts County v Leicester City 1-1
Played on 24 Oct
Stockport County v Manchester United 1-4
Crewe Alexandra v Wolverhampton W 4-1
Everton v Bury 9-2
Southport v Tranmere Rovers 8-0
York City v Grimsby Town 5-2
Chesterfield v Nottingham Forest 3-0
Halifax Town v Rotherham United 4-0
Notts County v Lincoln City 3-6
Mansfield Town v Leicester City 1-2
Played on 31 Oct
Manchester United v Stockport County 3-1
Wolverhampton W v Crewe Alexandra 3-2
Bury v Everton 4-1
Tranmere Rovers v Southport 2-2
Grimsby Town v York City 0-1
Nottingham Forest v Chesterfield 6-1
Rotherham United v Halifax Town 1-4
Leicester City v Mansfield Town 5-2
Lincoln City v Notts County 8-1
Played on 7 Nov
Wrexham v Stockport County 7-1
Crewe Alexandra v Huddersfield Town 1-1
Doncaster Rovers v Halifax Town 1-2
Nottingham Forest v Notts County 3-5
Played on 14 Nov
Stockport County v Wrexham 5-3
Huddersfield Town v Crewe Alexandra 4-0
Halifax Town v Doncaster Rovers 1-2
Notts County v Nottingham Forest 1-3

Played on 21 Nov
Wrexham v Stoke City 2-4
Southport v Liverpool 3-2
Doncaster Rovers v Bradford City 0-2
Halifax Town v Huddersfield Town 2-1
Notts County v Sheffield Wednesday 2-2
Leicester City v Nottingham Forest 2-1
(Played at Coalville)
Played on 28 Nov
Stoke City v Wrexham 2-0
Liverpool v Southport 6-2
Bradford City v Doncaster Rovers 1-4
Huddersfield Town v Halifax Town 4-1
Sheffield Wednesday v Notts County 3-1
Nottingham Forest v Leicester City 1-1
Played on 5 Dec
Crewe Alexandra v Stoke City 3-3
Burnley v Liverpool 3-1
Leeds United v Halifax Town 1-1
Northampton Town v Notts County 5-2
Nottingham Forest v Lincoln City 4-1
Played on 12 Dec
Stoke City v Crewe Alexandra 6-1
Liverpool v Burnley 9-2
Halifax Town v Leeds United 5-1
Lincoln City v Nottingham Forest 4-1
Notts County v Northampton Town 2-0
Played on 19 Dec
Bolton Wanderers v Manchester United 0-2
Chester v Stockport County 1-1
Halifax Town v Burnley 0-0
York City v Rotherham United 2-1
Mansfield Town v Derby County 1-1
Northampton Town v Nottingham Forest 5-2
Notts County v Lincoln City 4-2
Played on 25 Dec
Manchester United v Bolton Wanderers 4-0
Stockport County v Chester 1-2
Burnley v Halifax Town 1-1
Rotherham United v York City 3-2
Derby County v Mansfield Town 5-0
Lincoln City v Notts County 8-1
Nottingham Forest v Northampton Town 1-2

The Football League 1942-43

NORTH

Final Table

		P	W	D	L	F	A	Pts
1	Blackpool	18	16	1	1	93	28	33
2	Liverpool	18	14	1	3	70	34	29
3	Sheffield Wednesday	18	12	3	3	61	26	27
4	Manchester United	18	12	2	4	58	26	26
5	Huddersfield Town	18	10	6	2	52	32	26
6	Stoke City	18	11	3	4	46	25	25
7	Coventry City	18	10	5	3	28	16	25
8	Southport	18	11	3	4	64	42	25
9	Derby County	18	11	2	5	51	37	24
10	Bradford	18	8	7	3	46	21	23
11	Lincoln City	18	9	5	4	58	36	23
12	Halifax Town	18	10	3	5	39	27	23
13	Gateshead	18	10	3	5	52	45	23
14	Aston Villa	18	10	2	6	47	33	22
15	Everton	18	10	2	6	52	41	22
16	Grimsby Town	17	8	5	4	42	31	21
17	York City	18	9	3	6	47	36	21
18	Barnsley	18	8	5	5	39	30	21
19	Sheffield United	18	7	6	5	45	35	20
20	Birmingham	18	9	2	7	27	30	20
21	Blackburn Rovers	18	8	3	7	50	43	19
22	Sunderland	18	8	3	7	46	40	19
23	Chester	18	7	4	7	43	40	18
24	Walsall	18	6	5	7	33	31	17
25	Northampton Town	18	8	1	9	38	44	17
26	Newcastle United	18	6	4	8	51	52	16
27	Chesterfield	18	5	6	7	30	34	16
28	West Bromwich Albion	18	6	4	8	35	43	16
29	Bury	18	7	2	9	53	75	16
30	Notts County	18	7	2	9	34	57	16
31	Manchester City	18	7	1	10	46	47	15
32	Nottingham Forest	18	6	3	9	38	39	15
33	Burnley	18	5	5	8	35	45	15
34	Leicester City	18	5	4	9	32	37	14
35	Stockport County	18	5	3	10	34	55	13
36	Rotherham United	18	4	5	9	28	48	13
37	Tranmere Rovers	18	5	3	10	36	63	13
38	Wolverhampton Wanderers	18	5	2	11	28	41	12
39	Crewe Alexandra	18	5	2	11	43	64	12
40	Middlesbrough	18	4	4	10	30	50	12
41	Rochdale	18	5	2	11	34	57	12
42	Wrexham	18	5	1	12	43	67	11
43	Leeds United	18	3	4	11	28	45	10
44	Oldham Athletic	18	4	2	12	29	54	10
45	Bradford City	18	4	2	12	30	63	10
46	Bolton Wanderers	18	3	3	12	31	52	9
47	Doncaster Rovers	17	3	3	11	23	41	9
48	Mansfield Town	18	2	4	12	25	65	8

The Football League 1942-43

NORTH (SECOND CHAMPIONSHIP)
Including League North Cup and county cup matches

ABERAMAN ATHLETIC

LC	26 Dec	Lovell's Athletic	H	2-3
LC	2 Jan	Swansea T	A	0-2
LC	9 Jan	Cardiff C	A	1-0
LC	16 Jan	Cardiff C	H	3-1
LC	23 Jan	Bristol City	A	1-8
LC	30 Jan	Bristol City	H	2-1
LC	6 Feb	Bath City	A	2-3
LC	13 Feb	Bath City	H	4-2
LC	20 Feb	Lovell's Athletic	A	1-0
LC	27 Feb	Swansea T	H	6-2
LC	6 Mar	Bristol City	H	1-3
LC	13 Mar	Bristol City	A	2-0
	20 Mar	Swansea T	A	2-2
	27 Mar	Lovell's Athletic	A	3-1
WC	3 Apr	Bath City	A	5-2
WC	10 Apr	Cardiff C	A	3-2
WC	17 Apr	Lovell's Athletic	H	0-3
WC	24 Apr	Lovell's Athletic	A	1-6

13 Mar, aet 2-1

ASTON VILLA

LC	26 Dec	Wolverhampton W	H	1-0
LC	2 Jan	Wolverhampton W	A	4-0
LC	9 Jan	Stoke C	A	0-1
LC	16 Jan	Stoke C	H	3-0
LC	23 Jan	WBA	H	3-5
LC	30 Jan	WBA	A	1-2
LC	6 Feb	Northampton T	A	1-2
LC	13 Feb	Northampton T	H	2-1
LC	20 Feb	Walsall	H	2-1
LC	27 Feb	Walsall	A	4-1
LC	6 Mar	Wolverhampton W	H	5-2
LC	13 Mar	Wolverhampton W	A	5-3
LC	20 Mar	Stoke C	A	3-1
LC	27 Mar	Stoke C	H	2-0
LC	3 Apr	Bristol City	A	0-0
LC	10 Apr	Bristol City	H	2-1
LC	17 Apr	Blackpool	A	1-3
LC	24 Apr	Blackpool	H	2-1
	26 Apr	Birmingham	H	1-0
	1 May	WBA	H	2-6

BARNSLEY

LC	26 Dec	Leeds U	H	2-1
LC	2 Jan	Leeds U	A	3-1
LC	9 Jan	Doncaster R	A	2-1
LC	16 Jan	Doncaster R	H	1-1
LC	23 Jan	Huddersfield T	H	3-2
LC	30 Jan	Huddersfield T	A	0-4
LC	6 Feb	Bradford City	H	1-2
LC	13 Feb	Bradford City	A	3-2
LC	20 Feb	Sheffield United	H	2-4
LC	27 Feb	Sheffield United	A	2-2
LC	6 Mar	Sheffield United	H	1-4
LC	13 Mar	Sheffield United	A	0-3
	20 Mar	Huddersfield T	H	2-1
	27 Mar	Huddersfield T	A	0-5
SC	17 Apr	Sheffield United	H	4-1
	24 Apr	Sheffield United	A	1-2
	1 May	Rotherham U	H	7-1

BATH CITY

LC	26 Dec	Bristol City	A	2-4
LC	2 Jan	Cardiff C	H	2-1
LC	9 Jan	Lovell's Athletic	H	1-1
LC	16 Jan	Lovell's Athletic	A	2-4
LC	23 Jan	Swansea T	H	8-0
LC	30 Jan	Swansea T	A	3-5
LC	6 Feb	Aberaman Athletic	H	3-2
LC	13 Feb	Aberaman Athletic	A	2-4
LC	20 Feb	Bristol City	H	3-1
LC	27 Feb	Cardiff C	A	5-2
LC	6 Mar	Lovell's Athletic	A	2-1
LC	13 Mar	Lovell's Athletic	H	1-1
LC	20 Mar	Bristol City	H	2-2
LC	27 Mar	Bristol City	A	1-2
WC	3 Apr	Aberaman Athletic	H	2-5
WC	10 Apr	Lovell's Athletic	A	3-5
WC	17 Apr	Cardiff C	H	4-3
WC	24 Apr	Bristol City	H	3-3

BIRMINGHAM

LC	26 Dec	Northampton T	A	1-5
LC	2 Jan	Northampton T	H	2-4
LC	9 Jan	Leicester C	H	5-0
LC	16 Jan	Leicester C	A	1-2
LC	23 Jan	Walsall	A	1-1
LC	30 Jan	Walsall	H	1-0
LC	6 Feb	WBA	H	0-1
LC	13 Feb	WBA	A	1-2
LC	20 Feb	Coventry C	A	0-1
LC	27 Feb	Coventry C	H	3-1
	6 Mar	Walsall	A	2-1
	13 Mar	Walsall	H	2-1
	20 Mar	Coventry C	A	1-2
	27 Mar	Coventry C	H	1-2
	3 Apr	WBA	H	5-3
	10 Apr	WBA	A	4-0
	17 Apr	Northampton T	H	1-0
	24 Apr	Northampton T	A	0-1
	26 Apr	Aston Villa	A	0-1
	1 May	Chesterfield	A	1-1

BLACKBURN ROVERS

LC	26 Dec	Burnley	H	3-1
LC	2 Jan	Burnley	A	0-0
LC	9 Jan	Rochdale	A	0-4
LC	16 Jan	Rochdale	H	7-2
LC	23 Jan	Blackpool	H	3-3
LC	30 Jan	Blackpool	A	2-4
LC	6 Feb	Bolton W	A	1-3
LC	13 Feb	Bolton W	H	7-1
LC	20 Feb	Oldham Athletic	H	7-1
LC	27 Feb	Oldham Athletic	A	2-1
LC	6 Mar	Rochdale	A	2-1
LC	13 Mar	Rochdale	H	3-1
LC	20 Mar	Manchester City	H	2-0
LC	27 Mar	Manchester City	A	0-4
	3 Apr	Bolton W	H	1-3
	10 Apr	Bolton W	A	1-0
	17 Apr	Bury	A	2-2
	24 Apr	Bury	H	7-4

BLACKPOOL

LC	26 Dec	Southport	H	1-1
LC	2 Jan	Southport	A	3-2
LC	9 Jan	Manchester United	H	1-1
LC	16 Jan	Manchester United	A	3-5
LC	23 Jan	Blackburn R	A	3-3
LC	30 Jan	Blackburn R	H	4-2
LC	6 Feb	Oldham Athletic	H	4-0
LC	13 Feb	Oldham Athletic	A	1-1
LC	20 Feb	Bolton W	A	1-1
LC	27 Feb	Bolton W	H	5-0
LC	6 Mar	Everton	H	4-1
LC	13 Mar	Everton	A	3-4
LC	20 Mar	Liverpool	A	1-3
LC	27 Mar	Liverpool	H	5-0
LC	3 Apr	Manchester City	H	3-1
LC	10 Apr	Manchester City	A	1-1
LC	17 Apr	Aston Villa	A	1-2
LC	24 Apr	Aston Villa	A	1-2
LC	1 May	Sheffield Wed	H	2-2

BOLTON WANDERERS

LC	26 Dec	Manchester City	H	2-4
LC	2 Jan	Manchester City	A	0-2
LC	9 Jan	Oldham Athletic	A	3-3
LC	16 Jan	Oldham Athletic	H	5-0
LC	23 Jan	Burnley	H	4-1
LC	30 Jan	Burnley	A	1-0
LC	6 Feb	Blackburn R	H	3-1
LC	13 Feb	Blackburn R	A	1-7
LC	20 Feb	Blackpool	H	1-1
LC	27 Feb	Blackpool	A	0-5
	6 Mar	Burnley	H	4-1
	13 Mar	Burnley	A	1-4
	3 Apr	Blackburn R	A	3-1
	10 Apr	Blackburn R	H	0-1
	17 Apr	Chester	H	3-1
	24 Apr	Liverpool	H	3-6
	1 May	Liverpool	A	0-4

BRADFORD

LC	2 Jan	Huddersfield T	H	2-3
LC	9 Jan	Halifax T	H	5-1
LC	16 Jan	Halifax T	A	2-0
LC	23 Jan	Bradford City	A	1-2
LC	30 Jan	Bradford City	H	2-0
LC	6 Feb	Leeds U	H	2-1
LC	13 Feb	Leeds U	A	2-2
LC	20 Feb	Sunderland	A	1-1
LC	27 Feb	Sunderland	H	1-1
LC	6 Mar	Huddersfield T	H	0-0
LC	13 Mar	Huddersfield T	A	3-2
LC	20 Mar	York C	A	1-2
LC	27 Mar	York C	H	0-3
	3 Apr	Leeds U	A	0-2
	10 Apr	Leeds U	H	5-2
	17 Apr	Sunderland	H	0-1
	24 Apr	Sunderland	A	2-2
	26 Apr	Chesterfield	A	3-2
	1 May	Oldham Athletic	A	3-4

KEY: LC=League North Cup; WC=League West Cup; La=Lancashire Cup;
CC=Combined Counties Cup; Li=Liverpool Senior Cup; CB=Cheshire Bowl; SC=Sheffield Cup

The Football League 1942-43

NORTH (SECOND CHAMPIONSHIP)
Including League North Cup and county cup matches

BRADFORD CITY

LC	26 Dec	Halifax T	H	1-1
LC	2 Jan	Halifax T	A	2-3
LC	9 Jan	Gateshead	A	3-2
LC	16 Jan	Gateshead	H	2-3
LC	23 Jan	Bradford	H	2-1
LC	30 Jan	Bradford	A	0-2
LC	6 Feb	Barnsley	A	2-1
LC	13 Feb	Barnsley	H	2-3
LC	20 Feb	Leeds U	H	1-0
LC	27 Feb	Leeds U	A	5-1
LC	6 Mar	Sheffield Wed	A	0-1
LC	13 Mar	Sheffield Wed	H	1-1
	20 Mar	Halifax T	H	1-0
	27 Mar	Halifax T	A	1-3
	3 Apr	Sunderland	H	5-2
	10 Apr	Sunderland	A	1-5

BRISTOL CITY

LC	26 Dec	Bath C	H	4-2
LC	2 Jan	Lovell's Ath	A	0-8
LC	9 Jan	Swansea T	H	3-0
LC	16 Jan	Swansea T	H	4-3
LC	23 Jan	Aberaman Ath	H	8-1
LC	30 Jan	Aberaman Ath	H	1-2
LC	6 Feb	Cardiff C	A	3-0
LC	13 Feb	Cardiff C	H	1-1
LC	20 Feb	Bath C	A	1-3
LC	27 Feb	Lovell's Ath	H	1-1
LC	6 Mar	Aberaman Ath	A	3-1
LC	13 Mar	Aberaman Ath	H	0-2
LC	20 Mar	Bath C	A	2-2
LC	27 Mar	Bath C	H	2-1
LC	3 Apr	Aston Villa	H	0-0
LC	10 Apr	Aston Villa	A	1-2
WC	17 Apr	Swansea T	A	1-1
WC	24 Apr	Bath C	H	3-3
	1 May	Cardiff C	H	3-0

13 Mar, aet 1-2

BURNLEY

LC	26 Dec	Blackburn R	A	1-3
LC	2 Jan	Blackburn R	H	0-0
LC	9 Jan	Bury	H	0-0
LC	16 Jan	Bury	A	0-3
LC	23 Jan	Bolton W	A	1-4
LC	30 Jan	Bolton W	H	0-1
LC	6 Feb	Southport	H	5-4
LC	13 Feb	Southport	A	0-2
LC	20 Feb	Rochdale	A	2-4
LC	27 Feb	Rochdale	H	1-1
	6 Mar	Bolton W	A	1-4
	13 Mar	Bolton W	H	4-1
	3 Apr	Rochdale	A	0-4
	10 Apr	Rochdale	H	2-0

BURY

LC	26 Dec	Stoke C	H	10-0
LC	2 Jan	Stoke C	A	3-5
LC	9 Jan	Burnley	A	0-0
LC	16 Jan	Burnley	H	3-0
LC	23 Jan	Manchester City	H	2-3
LC	30 Jan	Manchester City	A	2-3
LC	6 Feb	Rochdale	A	2-3
LC	13 Feb	Rochdale	H	1-0
LC	20 Feb	Halifax T	H	4-0
LC	27 Feb	Halifax T	A	2-2
LC	6 Mar	Liverpool	A	3-1
LC	13 Mar	Liverpool	H	2-7
La	20 Mar	Manchester Utd	A	1-4
La	27 Mar	Manchester Utd	H	3-5
	17 Apr	Blackburn R	H	2-2
	24 Apr	Blackburn R	A	4-7

CARDIFF CITY

LC	26 Dec	Swansea T	H	2-2
LC	2 Jan	Bath C	A	1-2
LC	9 Jan	Aberaman Ath	H	0-1
LC	16 Jan	Aberaman Ath	A	1-3
LC	23 Jan	Lovell's Ath	H	0-4
LC	30 Jan	Lovell's Ath	A	1-4
LC	6 Feb	Bristol City	H	0-3
LC	13 Feb	Bristol City	A	1-1
LC	20 Feb	Swansea T	A	2-1
LC	27 Feb	Bath C	H	2-5
	6 Mar	Swansea T	H	2-0
	13 Mar	Swansea T	A	1-1
	20 Mar	Lovell's Ath	H	2-5
WC	10 Apr	Aberaman Ath	H	2-3
WC	17 Apr	Bath C	A	3-4
WC	24 Apr	Swansea T	H	2-5
	1 May	Bristol City	A	0-3

CHESTER

LC	26 Dec	Manchester Utd	A	0-3
LC	2 Jan	Manchester Utd	H	4-1
LC	9 Jan	Crewe Alex	H	0-0
LC	16 Jan	Crewe Alex	A	1-1
LC	23 Jan	Tranmere R	A	6-1
LC	30 Jan	Tranmere R	H	1-0
LC	6 Feb	Everton	A	5-4
LC	13 Feb	Everton	H	0-1
LC	20 Feb	Wrexham	H	3-0
LC	27 Feb	Wrexham	A	2-3
LC	6 Mar	Stoke C	H	2-3
LC	13 Mar	Stoke C	A	2-5
	20 Mar	Crewe Alex	H	1-3
	27 Mar	Crewe Alex	A	3-3
La	3 Apr	Liverpool	A	1-4
La	10 Apr	Liverpool	H	2-5
	17 Apr	Bolton W	A	1-3
	24 Apr	Wrexham	H	3-2
	26 Apr	Wrexham	A	1-3
	1 May	Southport	A	2-4

CHESTERFIELD

LC	26 Dec	Rotherham U	H	3-0
LC	2 Jan	Rotherham U	A	2-1
LC	9 Jan	Sheffield United	A	2-1
LC	16 Jan	Sheffield United	H	4-2
LC	23 Jan	Derby Co	H	0-2
LC	30 Jan	Derby Co	A	1-1
LC	6 Feb	Doncaster R	A	2-1
LC	13 Feb	Doncaster R	H	0-1
LC	20 Feb	Mansfield T	H	6-2
LC	27 Feb	Mansfield T	A	2-1
LC	6 Mar	Halifax T	A	1-2
LC	13 Mar	Halifax T	H	1-0
LC	20 Mar	WBA	A	3-2
LC	27 Mar	WBA	H	3-3
LC	3 Apr	York C	A	0-2
LC	10 Apr	York C	H	0-2
	17 Apr	Manchester City	H	1-2
	24 Apr	Manchester City	A	1-1
	26 Apr	Bradford	H	2-3
	1 May	Birmingham	H	1-1

13 Mar, aet 2-0

COVENTRY CITY

LC	26 Dec	Walsall	H	2-0
LC	2 Jan	Walsall	A	3-1
LC	9 Jan	WBA	A	3-2
LC	16 Jan	WBA	H	1-0
LC	23 Jan	Northampton T	A	2-0
LC	30 Jan	Northampton T	H	0-1
LC	6 Feb	Leicester C	A	2-0
LC	13 Feb	Leicester C	H	1-3
LC	20 Feb	Birmingham	H	1-0
LC	27 Feb	Birmingham	A	1-3
LC	6 Mar	WBA	H	1-1
LC	13 Mar	WBA	A	0-3
	20 Mar	Birmingham	A	2-1
	27 Mar	Birmingham	A	2-1
	3 Apr	Derby Co	A	1-1
	10 Apr	Derby Co	H	0-1
	17 Apr	Leicester C	A	3-1
	24 Apr	Leicester C	H	0-0
	26 Apr	Notts County	H	7-0
	1 May	Notts County	A	1-2

CREWE ALEXANDRA

LC	26 Dec	Stoke C	A	1-6
LC	2 Jan	Stoke C	H	1-3
LC	9 Jan	Chester	A	0-0
LC	16 Jan	Chester	H	1-1
LC	23 Jan	Wrexham	H	1-1
LC	30 Jan	Wrexham	A	1-0
LC	6 Feb	Wolverhampton	H	0-3
LC	13 Feb	Wolverhampton	A	1-6
LC	20 Feb	Manchester Utd	A	0-7
LC	27 Feb	Manchester Utd	H	2-3
	6 Mar	Stockport Co	A	3-2
	13 Mar	Stockport Co	H	8-3
	20 Mar	Chester	A	3-1
	27 Mar	Chester	H	3-3
	3 Apr	Manchester Utd	A	1-4
	10 Apr	Manchester Utd	H	0-6
	17 Apr	Wolverhampton	H	8-1
	24 Apr	Derby Co	H	0-4
	26 Apr	Derby Co	A	3-1
	1 May	Stockport Co	H	7-2

KEY: LC=League North Cup; WC=League West Cup; La=Lancashire Cup;
CC=Combined Counties Cup; Li=Liverpool Senior Cup; CB=Cheshire Bowl; SC=Sheffield Cup

The Football League 1942-43

NORTH (SECOND CHAMPIONSHIP)
Including League North Cup and county cup matches

DERBY COUNTY

LC	26 Dec	Notts County	A	3-2
LC	2 Jan	Notts County	H	1-2
LC	9 Jan	Mansfield T	H	10-0
LC	16 Jan	Mansfield T	A	1-1
LC	23 Jan	Chesterfield	A	2-0
LC	30 Jan	Chesterfield	H	1-1
LC	6 Feb	Nottingham F	A	1-4
LC	13 Feb	Nottingham F	H	3-1
LC	20 Feb	Stoke C	A	0-4
LC	27 Feb	Stoke C	H	0-1
LC	6 Mar	Notts County	H	1-3
LC	13 Mar	Notts County	A	2-2
	20 Mar	Leicester C	H	3-2
	27 Mar	Leicester C	A	1-3
	3 Apr	Coventry C	H	1-1
	10 Apr	Coventry C	A	1-0
	17 Apr	Stoke C	H	2-1
	24 Apr	Crewe Alex	A	4-0
	26 Apr	Crewe Alex	H	1-3
	1 May	Wolverhampton	H	3-3

DONCASTER ROVERS

LC	26 Dec	York C	A	3-3
LC	2 Jan	York C	H	3-5
LC	9 Jan	Barnsley	H	2-3
LC	16 Jan	Barnsley	A	1-1
LC	23 Jan	Grimsby T	A	2-5
LC	30 Jan	Grimsby T	H	1-0
LC	6 Feb	Chesterfield	H	1-2
LC	13 Feb	Chesterfield	A	0-1
LC	20 Feb	Huddersfield T	A	2-6
LC	27 Feb	Huddersfield	H	2-0
LC	6 Mar	Rotherham U	H	1-1
LC	13 Mar	Rotherham U	A	0-3
	27 Mar	Grimsby T	H	3-2
	3 Apr	Grimsby T	A	0-2
	10 Apr	Nottingham F	A	2-1
	17 Apr	Rotherham U	H	3-1
	24 Apr	Rotherham U	A	1-5

EVERTON

LC	26 Dec	Tranmere R	A	1-2
LC	2 Jan	Tranmere R	H	4-0
LC	9 Jan	Liverpool	H	1-3
LC	16 Jan	Liverpool	A	1-2
LC	23 Jan	Manchester Utd	A	4-1
LC	30 Jan	Manchester Utd	H	0-5
LC	6 Feb	Chester	H	4-5
LC	13 Feb	Chester	A	1-0
LC	20 Feb	Southport	A	8-3
LC	27 Feb	Southport	H	10-2
LC	6 Mar	Blackpool	A	1-4
LC	13 Mar	Blackpool	H	4-3
La	20 Mar	Southport	A	1-4
La	27 Mar	Southport	H	2-1
	3 Apr	Wrexham	A	1-4
	10 Apr	Tranmere R	H	4-1
	17 Apr	Tranmere R	A	2-1
Li	26 Apr	Liverpool	A	1-4
	1 May	Tranmere R	A	1-1

GATESHEAD

LC	26 Dec	Sunderland	A	1-7
LC	2 Jan	Sunderland	H	5-4
LC	9 Jan	Bradford City	H	2-3
LC	16 Jan	Bradford City	A	3-2
LC	23 Jan	Middlesbrough	A	3-2
LC	30 Jan	Middlesbrough	H	6-0
LC	6 Feb	York C	H	3-2
LC	13 Feb	York C	A	0-2
LC	20 Feb	Newcastle U	A	0-2
LC	27 Feb	Newcastle U	H	2-6
	6 Mar	Sunderland	A	2-1
	13 Mar	Sunderland	H	1-2
	26 Apr	Newcastle U	H	1-3

GRIMSBY TOWN

LC	26 Dec	Sheffield United	H	3-3
LC	2 Jan	Sheffield United	A	3-5
LC	9 Jan	Rotherham U	A	3-1
LC	16 Jan	Rotherham U	H	3-3
LC	23 Jan	Doncaster R	H	5-2
LC	30 Jan	Doncaster R	A	0-1
LC	6 Feb	Lincoln C	A	1-1
LC	13 Feb	Lincoln C	H	1-0
LC	20 Feb	Sheffield Wed	A	2-2
LC	27 Feb	Sheffield Wed	H	1-2
	27 Mar	Doncaster R	A	2-3
	3 Apr	Doncaster R	H	2-0
	26 Apr	Nottingham F	A	4-4

HALIFAX TOWN

LC	26 Dec	Bradford City	A	1-1
LC	2 Jan	Bradford City	H	3-2
LC	9 Jan	Bradford	A	1-5
LC	16 Jan	Bradford	H	0-2
LC	23 Jan	Oldham Ath	H	4-3
LC	30 Jan	Oldham Ath	A	1-0
LC	6 Feb	Rotherham U	A	3-2
LC	13 Feb	Rotherham U	H	5-0
LC	20 Feb	Bury	A	0-4
LC	27 Feb	Bury	H	2-2
LC	6 Mar	Chesterfield	H	2-1
LC	13 Mar	Chesterfield	A	0-1
	20 Mar	Bradford City	A	0-1
	27 Mar	Bradford City	H	3-1
	3 Apr	Huddersfield T	A	0-1
	10 Apr	Huddersfield T	H	0-2
	17 Apr	Middlesbrough	H	2-4
	24 Apr	Middlesbrough	A	3-7

13 Mar, aet 0-2

HUDDERSFIELD TOWN

LC	2 Jan	Bradford	A	3-2
LC	9 Jan	Leeds U	A	4-2
LC	16 Jan	Leeds U	H	4-1
LC	23 Jan	Barnsley	A	2-3
LC	30 Jan	Barnsley	H	4-0
LC	6 Feb	Middlesbrough	A	2-1
LC	13 Feb	Middlesbrough	H	5-0
LC	20 Feb	Doncaster R	H	6-2
LC	27 Feb	Doncaster R	A	1-3
LC	6 Mar	Bradford	A	0-0
LC	13 Mar	Bradford	H	2-3
LC	20 Mar	Barnsley	A	1-2
	27 Mar	Barnsley	H	5-0
CC	3 Apr	Halifax T	H	1-0
CC	10 Apr	Halifax T	A	2-0
CC	17 Apr	Newcastle U	H	1-0
CC	24 Apr	Newcastle U	A	2-2
	26 Apr	Manchester City	A	1-1
CC	1 May	Sunderland	A	2-6

LEEDS UNITED

LC	26 Dec	Barnsley	A	1-2
LC	2 Jan	Barnsley	H	1-3
LC	9 Jan	Huddersfield T	H	2-4
LC	16 Jan	Huddersfield T	A	1-4
LC	23 Jan	Newcastle U	A	0-9
LC	30 Jan	Newcastle U	H	7-2
LC	6 Feb	Bradford	A	1-2
LC	13 Feb	Bradford	H	2-2
LC	20 Feb	Bradford City	A	0-1
LC	27 Feb	Bradford City	H	1-5
	6 Mar	Middlesbrough	H	3-2
	13 Mar	Middlesbrough	A	3-2
	20 Mar	Newcastle U	H	1-3
	27 Mar	Newcastle U	A	5-4
CC	3 Apr	Bradford	H	2-0
CC	10 Apr	Bradford	A	2-5

LEICESTER CITY

LC	26 Dec	WBA	A	1-5
LC	2 Jan	WBA	H	9-0
LC	9 Jan	Birmingham	A	0-5
LC	16 Jan	Birmingham	H	2-1
LC	23 Jan	Nottingham F	A	5-0
LC	30 Jan	Nottingham F	H	0-4
LC	6 Feb	Coventry C	H	0-2
LC	13 Feb	Coventry C	A	3-1
LC	20 Feb	Northampton T	H	3-2
LC	27 Feb	Northampton T	H	4-2
LC	6 Mar	Nottingham F	A	1-0
LC	13 Mar	Nottingham F	H	0-1
	20 Mar	Derby Co	A	2-3
	27 Mar	Derby Co	H	3-1
	3 Apr	Northampton T	A	3-0
	10 Apr	Northampton T	A	2-2
	17 Apr	Coventry C	H	1-3
	24 Apr	Coventry C	A	0-0
	26 Apr	Stoke C	H	1-2
	1 May	Stoke C	A	0-3

13 Mar, aet 0-2

**KEY: LC=League North Cup; WC=League West Cup; La=Lancashire Cup;
CC=Combined Counties Cup; Li=Liverpool Senior Cup; CB=Cheshire Bowl; SC=Sheffield Cup**

The Football League 1942-43

NORTH (SECOND CHAMPIONSHIP)
Including League North Cup and county cup matches

LINCOLN CITY

LC	26 Dec	Sheffield Wed	A	3-4
LC	2 Jan	Sheffield Wed	H	0-3
LC	9 Jan	Notts County	H	0-2
LC	16 Jan	Notts County	A	2-1
LC	23 Jan	Mansfield T	A	3-2
LC	30 Jan	Mansfield T	H	8-1
LC	6 Feb	Grimsby T	H	1-1
LC	13 Feb	Grimsby T	A	0-1
LC	20 Feb	Nottingham F	H	4-0
LC	27 Feb	Nottingham F	A	2-3

LIVERPOOL

LC	26 Dec	Wrexham	H	2-2
LC	2 Jan	Wrexham	A	1-0
LC	9 Jan	Everton	A	3-1
LC	16 Jan	Everton	H	2-1
LC	23 Jan	Southport	H	8-1
LC	30 Jan	Southport	A	2-2
LC	6 Feb	Tranmere R	A	5-1
LC	13 Feb	Tranmere R	H	4-1
LC	20 Feb	Manchester City	H	4-2
LC	27 Feb	Manchester City	A	1-3
LC	6 Mar	Bury	H	1-3
LC	13 Mar	Bury	A	7-2
LC	20 Mar	Blackpool	H	3-1
LC	27 Mar	Blackpool	A	0-5
La	3 Apr	Chester	H	4-1
La	10 Apr	Chester	A	5-2
La	17 Apr	Southport	H	3-0
La	24 Apr	Bolton W	A	6-3
Li	26 Apr	Everton	H	4-1
La	1 May	Bolton W	H	4-0

LOVELL'S ATHLETIC

LC	26 Dec	Aberaman Ath	A	3-2
LC	2 Jan	Bristol City	H	8-0
LC	9 Jan	Bath C	A	1-1
LC	16 Jan	Bath C	H	4-2
LC	23 Jan	Cardiff C	A	4-0
LC	30 Jan	Cardiff C	H	4-1
LC	6 Feb	Swansea T	H	5-0
LC	13 Feb	Swansea T	A	2-2
LC	20 Feb	Aberaman Ath	H	0-1
LC	27 Feb	Bristol City	A	1-1
LC	6 Mar	Bath C	H	1-2
LC	13 Mar	Bath C	A	1-1
	20 Mar	Cardiff C	A	5-2
	27 Mar	Aberaman Ath	H	1-3
WC	3 Apr	Swansea T	A	3-3
WC	10 Apr	Bath C	H	5-3
WC	17 Apr	Aberaman Ath	A	3-0
WC	24 Apr	Aberaman Ath	H	6-1
WC	26 Apr	Swansea T	H	2-4
WC	1 May	Swansea T	A	4-3

MANCHESTER CITY

LC	26 Dec	Bolton W	A	4-2
LC	2 Jan	Bolton W	H	2-0
LC	9 Jan	Stockport Co	H	7-1
LC	16 Jan	Stockport Co	A	5-2
LC	23 Jan	Bury	A	3-2
LC	30 Jan	Bury	H	3-2
LC	6 Feb	Manchester Utd	H	0-0
LC	13 Feb	Manchester Utd	A	1-1
LC	20 Feb	Liverpool	A	2-4
LC	27 Feb	Liverpool	H	3-1
LC	6 Mar	Manchester Utd	A	1-0
LC	13 Mar	Manchester Utd	H	2-0
LC	20 Mar	Blackburn R	A	0-2
LC	27 Mar	Blackburn R	H	4-0
LC	3 Apr	Blackpool	A	1-3
LC	10 Apr	Blackpool	H	1-1
	17 Apr	Chesterfield	A	2-1
	24 Apr	Chesterfield	H	1-1
	26 Apr	Huddersfield T	H	1-1

MANCHESTER UNITED

LC	26 Dec	Chester	H	3-0
LC	2 Jan	Chester	A	1-4
LC	9 Jan	Blackpool	A	1-1
LC	16 Jan	Blackpool	H	5-3
LC	23 Jan	Everton	H	1-4
LC	30 Jan	Everton	A	5-0
LC	6 Feb	Manchester City	A	0-0
LC	13 Feb	Manchester City	H	1-1
LC	20 Feb	Crewe Alex	H	7-0
LC	27 Feb	Crewe Alex	A	3-2
LC	6 Mar	Manchester City	H	0-1
LC	13 Mar	Manchester City	A	0-2
La	20 Mar	Bury	H	4-1
La	27 Mar	Bury	A	5-3
	3 Apr	Crewe Alex	H	4-1
	10 Apr	Crewe Alex	A	6-0
La	17 Apr	Oldham Ath	H	3-0
La	24 Apr	Oldham Ath	A	1-3
	1 May	Sheffield United	H	2-0

MANSFIELD TOWN

LC	26 Dec	Nottingham F	A	1-3
LC	2 Jan	Nottingham F	A	1-3
LC	9 Jan	Derby Co	A	0-10
LC	16 Jan	Derby Co	H	1-1
LC	23 Jan	Lincoln C	H	2-3
LC	30 Jan	Lincoln C	A	1-8
LC	6 Feb	Notts County	H	2-4
LC	13 Feb	Notts County	A	0-2
LC	20 Feb	Chesterfield	A	2-6
LC	27 Feb	Chesterfield	H	2-1

MIDDLESBROUGH

LC	26 Dec	Newcastle U	A	2-3
LC	2 Jan	Newcastle U	H	3-7
LC	9 Jan	Sunderland	H	4-1
LC	16 Jan	Sunderland	A	0-7
LC	23 Jan	Gateshead	H	2-3
LC	30 Jan	Gateshead	A	0-6
LC	6 Feb	Huddersfield T	H	1-2
LC	13 Feb	Huddersfield T	A	0-5
LC	20 Feb	York C	H	1-5
LC	27 Feb	York C	A	0-6
	6 Mar	Leeds U	A	2-3
	13 Mar	Leeds U	H	2-3
	20 Mar	Sunderland	A	0-8
	27 Mar	Sunderland	H	1-0
CC	3 Apr	Newcastle U	H	2-1
CC	10 Apr	Newcastle U	A	0-4
	17 Apr	Halifax T	A	4-2
	24 Apr	Halifax T	H	7-3

NEWCASTLE UNITED

LC	26 Dec	Middlesbrough	H	3-2
LC	2 Jan	Middlesbrough	A	7-3
LC	16 Jan	York C	A	3-1
LC	23 Jan	Leeds U	H	9-0
LC	30 Jan	Leeds U	A	2-7
LC	6 Feb	Sunderland	A	3-3
LC	13 Feb	Sunderland	H	2-3
LC	20 Feb	Gateshead	H	2-0
LC	27 Feb	Gateshead	A	6-2
LC	6 Mar	York C	H	3-2
LC	13 Mar	York C	A	0-2
	20 Mar	Leeds U	A	3-1
	27 Mar	Leeds U	H	4-5
CC	3 Apr	Middlesbrough	A	1-2
CC	10 Apr	Middlesbrough	H	4-0
CC	17 Apr	Huddersfield T	A	0-1
CC	24 Apr	Huddersfield T	H	2-2
	26 Apr	Gateshead	H	3-1
	1 May	York C	A	5-5

NORTHAMPTON TOWN

LC	26 Dec	Birmingham	H	5-1
LC	2 Jan	Birmingham	A	4-2
LC	9 Jan	Walsall	H	2-2
LC	16 Jan	Walsall	A	0-2
LC	23 Jan	Coventry C	H	0-2
LC	30 Jan	Coventry C	A	1-0
LC	6 Feb	Aston Villa	H	2-1
LC	13 Feb	Aston Villa	A	1-2
LC	20 Feb	Leicester C	A	2-3
LC	27 Feb	Leicester C	A	2-4
	20 Mar	Walsall	H	2-4
	27 Mar	Walsall	A	5-2
	3 Apr	Leicester C	H	0-3
	10 Apr	Leicester C	A	2-2
	17 Apr	Birmingham	A	0-1
	24 Apr	Birmingham	H	1-0
	26 Apr	WBA	A	1-6

KEY: LC=League North Cup; WC=League West Cup; La=Lancashire Cup;
CC=Combined Counties Cup; Li=Liverpool Senior Cup; CB=Cheshire Bowl; SC=Sheffield Cup

The Football League 1942-43

NORTH (SECOND CHAMPIONSHIP)
Including League North Cup and county cup matches

NOTTINGHAM FOREST

LC	26 Dec	Mansfield T	A	3-1
LC	2 Jan	Mansfield T	H	3-1
LC	9 Jan	Sheffield Wed	H	1-1
LC	16 Jan	Sheffield Wed	A	1-1
LC	23 Jan	Leicester C	A	0-5
LC	30 Jan	Leicester C	H	4-0
LC	6 Feb	Derby Co	H	4-1
LC	13 Feb	Derby Co	A	1-3
LC	20 Feb	Lincoln C	A	0-4
LC	27 Feb	Lincoln C	H	3-2
LC	6 Mar	Leicester C	H	0-1
LC	13 Mar	Leicester C	A	1-0
LC	20 Mar	Sheffield Wed	H	1-0
LC	27 Mar	Sheffield Wed	A	1-5
	10 Apr	Doncaster R	H	1-2
	17 Apr	Notts County	H	1-1
	24 Apr	Notts County	A	1-2
	26 Apr	Grimsby T	H	2-4

13 Mar, aet 2-0

NOTTS COUNTY

LC	26 Dec	Derby Co	H	2-3
LC	2 Jan	Derby Co	H	2-1
LC	9 Jan	Lincoln C	A	2-0
LC	16 Jan	Lincoln C	H	1-2
LC	23 Jan	Sheffield Utd	H	1-1
LC	30 Jan	Sheffield Utd	A	2-3
LC	6 Feb	Mansfield T	A	4-2
LC	13 Feb	Mansfield T	H	2-0
LC	20 Feb	Rotherham U	H	4-0
LC	27 Feb	Rotherham U	A	2-2
LC	6 Mar	Derby Co	A	3-1
LC	13 Mar	Derby Co	H	2-2
LC	20 Mar	Sheffield Utd	A	1-4
LC	27 Mar	Sheffield Utd	H	2-1
	3 Apr	Stoke C	H	1-1
	10 Apr	Stoke C	A	1-1
	17 Apr	Nottingham F	A	1-1
	24 Apr	Nottingham F	H	2-1
	26 Apr	Coventry C	A	0-7
	1 May	Coventry C	H	2-1

OLDHAM ATHLETIC

LC	26 Dec	Rochdale	A	3-4
LC	2 Jan	Rochdale	H	2-3
LC	9 Jan	Bolton W	H	3-3
LC	16 Jan	Bolton W	A	0-5
LC	23 Jan	Halifax T	A	3-4
LC	30 Jan	Halifax T	H	0-1
LC	6 Feb	Blackpool	A	0-4
LC	13 Feb	Blackpool	H	1-1
LC	20 Feb	Blackburn R	A	1-7
LC	27 Feb	Blackburn R	H	1-2
	6 Mar	Southport	H	2-1
	13 Mar	Southport	A	1-2
	20 Mar	Rochdale	A	0-1
	27 Mar	Rochdale	H	3-1
La	17 Apr	Manchester Utd	A	0-3
La	24 Apr	Manchester Utd	H	3-1
	26 Apr	Stockport Co	A	1-1
	1 May	Bradford	H	4-3

ROCHDALE

LC	26 Dec	Oldham Ath	H	4-3
LC	2 Jan	Oldham Ath	A	3-2
LC	9 Jan	Blackburn R	H	4-0
LC	16 Jan	Blackburn R	A	2-2
LC	23 Jan	Stockport Co	A	4-3
LC	30 Jan	Stockport Co	H	6-0
LC	6 Feb	Bury	H	3-2
LC	13 Feb	Bury	A	0-1
LC	20 Feb	Burnley	H	4-2
LC	27 Feb	Burnley	A	1-1
LC	6 Mar	Blackburn R	H	1-2
LC	13 Mar	Blackburn R	A	1-3
	20 Mar	Oldham Ath	H	1-0
	27 Mar	Oldham Ath	A	1-3
	3 Apr	Burnley	H	4-0
	10 Apr	Burnley	A	0-2

ROTHERHAM UNITED

LC	26 Dec	Chesterfield	A	0-3
LC	2 Jan	Chesterfield	H	1-2
LC	9 Jan	Grimsby T	H	1-3
LC	16 Jan	Grimsby T	A	3-3
LC	23 Jan	Sheffield Wed	A	2-3
LC	30 Jan	Sheffield Wed	H	1-1
LC	6 Feb	Halifax T	H	2-3
LC	13 Feb	Halifax T	A	0-5
LC	20 Feb	Notts County	A	0-4
LC	27 Feb	Notts County	H	2-2
	6 Mar	Doncaster R	A	1-1
	13 Mar	Doncaster R	H	3-0
	3 Apr	Stockport Co	A	1-1
	10 Apr	Stockport Co	H	2-0
	17 Apr	Doncaster R	A	1-3
	24 Apr	Doncaster R	H	5-1
SC	26 Apr	Sheffield Wed	H	2-1
	1 May	Barnsley	A	1-7

SHEFFIELD UNITED

LC	26 Dec	Grimsby T	H	3-3
LC	2 Jan	Grimsby T	H	5-3
LC	9 Jan	Chesterfield	H	1-2
LC	16 Jan	Chesterfield	A	2-4
LC	23 Jan	Notts County	A	1-1
LC	30 Jan	Notts County	H	3-2
LC	6 Feb	Sheffield Wed	H	3-1
LC	13 Feb	Sheffield Wed	A	2-8
LC	20 Feb	Barnsley	A	4-2
LC	27 Feb	Barnsley	H	2-2
LC	6 Mar	Barnsley	A	4-1
LC	13 Mar	Barnsley	H	3-0
LC	20 Mar	Notts County	H	4-1
LC	27 Mar	Notts County	A	1-2
LC	3 Apr	Sheffield Wed	A	2-3
LC	10 Apr	Sheffield Wed	H	0-0
SC	17 Apr	Barnsley	A	1-4
SC	24 Apr	Barnsley	H	2-1
	1 May	Manchester Utd	A	0-2

SHEFFIELD WEDNESDAY

LC	26 Dec	Lincoln C	H	4-3
LC	2 Jan	Lincoln C	A	3-0
LC	9 Jan	Nottingham F	A	1-1
LC	16 Jan	Nottingham F	H	1-1
LC	23 Jan	Rotherham U	H	3-2
LC	30 Jan	Rotherham U	A	1-1
LC	6 Feb	Sheffield Utd	A	1-3
LC	13 Feb	Sheffield Utd	H	8-2
LC	20 Feb	Grimsby T	H	2-2
LC	27 Feb	Grimsby T	A	2-1
LC	6 Mar	Bradford City	H	1-0
LC	13 Mar	Bradford City	A	3-0
LC	20 Mar	Nottingham F	A	0-1
LC	27 Mar	Nottingham F	H	5-1
LC	3 Apr	Sheffield Utd	H	3-2
LC	10 Apr	Sheffield Utd	A	0-0
LC	17 Apr	York C	H	3-0
LC	24 Apr	York C	A	1-1
SC	26 Apr	Rotherham U	A	1-2
LC	1 May	Blackpool	A	2-2

SOUTHPORT

LC	26 Dec	Blackpool	A	1-1
LC	2 Jan	Blackpool	H	2-3
LC	9 Jan	Tranmere R	H	2-2
LC	16 Jan	Tranmere R	A	2-3
LC	23 Jan	Liverpool	A	1-3
LC	30 Jan	Liverpool	H	2-2
LC	6 Feb	Burnley	A	4-5
LC	13 Feb	Burnley	H	2-0
LC	20 Feb	Everton	H	3-8
LC	27 Feb	Everton	A	2-10
	6 Mar	Oldham Ath	A	1-2
	13 Mar	Oldham Ath	H	2-1
La	20 Mar	Everton	H	4-1
La	27 Mar	Everton	A	1-2
	3 Apr	Tranmere R	A	1-5
La	17 Apr	Liverpool	A	0-3
	24 Apr	Liverpool	H	4-5
	1 May	Chester	H	4-2

STOCKPORT COUNTY

LC	26 Dec	Bury	A	0-10
LC	2 Jan	Bury	H	5-3
LC	9 Jan	Manchester City	A	1-7
LC	16 Jan	Manchester City	H	2-5
LC	23 Jan	Rochdale	H	3-4
LC	30 Jan	Rochdale	A	0-6
LC	6 Feb	Wrexham	A	1-5
LC	13 Feb	Wrexham	H	5-2
LC	20 Feb	Tranmere R	H	4-3
LC	27 Feb	Tranmere R	A	1-1
	6 Mar	Crewe Alex	H	2-3
	13 Mar	Crewe Alex	A	3-8
CB	20 Mar	Tranmere R	A	1-1
CB	27 Mar	Tranmere R	H	2-1
	3 Apr	Rotherham U	H	1-1
	10 Apr	Rotherham U	A	0-2
	17 Apr	Wrexham	A	3-6
	26 Apr	Oldham Ath	H	1-1
CB	1 May	Crewe Alex	A	2-7

KEY: LC=League North Cup; WC=League West Cup; La=Lancashire Cup;
CC=Combined Counties Cup; Li=Liverpool Senior Cup; CB=Cheshire Bowl; SC=Sheffield Cup

The Football League 1942-43

NORTH (SECOND CHAMPIONSHIP)
Including League North Cup and county cup matches

STOKE CITY

	Date	Opponent	H/A	Score
LC	26 Dec	Crewe Alex	H	6-1
LC	2 Jan	Crew Alex	A	3-1
LC	9 Jan	Aston Villa	H	1-0
LC	16 Jan	Aston Villa	A	0-3
LC	23 Jan	Wolverhampton	A	4-4
LC	30 Jan	Wolverhampton	H	2-2
LC	6 Feb	Walsall	H	2-1
LC	13 Feb	Walsall	A	1-4
LC	20 Feb	Derby Co	H	4-0
LC	27 Feb	Derby Co	A	1-0
LC	6 Mar	Chester	A	3-2
LC	13 Mar	Chester	H	5-2
LC	20 Mar	Aston Villa	H	1-3
LC	27 Mar	Aston Villa	A	0-2
	3 Apr	Notts County	A	1-1
	10 Apr	Notts County	H	1-1
	17 Apr	Derby Co	A	1-2
	24 Apr	Wolverhampton	H	1-4
	26 Apr	Leicester C	A	2-1
	1 May	Leicester C	H	3-0

SUNDERLAND

	Date	Opponent	H/A	Score
LC	26 Dec	Gateshead	H	7-1
LC	2 Jan	Gateshead	A	4-5
LC	9 Jan	Middlesbrough	A	1-4
LC	16 Jan	Middlesbrough	H	7-0
LC	23 Jan	York C	A	0-4
LC	30 Jan	York C	H	4-5
LC	6 Feb	Newcastle U	H	3-3
LC	13 Feb	Newcastle U	A	3-2
LC	20 Feb	Bradford	H	1-1
LC	27 Feb	Bradford	A	1-1
	6 Mar	Gateshead	H	1-2
	13 Mar	Gateshead	A	2-1
	20 Mar	Middlesbrough	H	8-0
	27 Mar	Middlesbrough	A	0-1
CC	3 Apr	Bradford City	A	2-5
CC	10 Apr	Bradford City	H	5-1
CC	17 Apr	Bradford	A	1-0
CC	24 Apr	Bradford	H	2-2
CC	1 May	Huddersfield T	H	6-2

SWANSEA TOWN

	Date	Opponent	H/A	Score
LC	26 Dec	Cardiff C	A	2-2
LC	2 Jan	Aberaman Ath	H	2-0
LC	9 Jan	Bristol City	A	0-3
LC	16 Jan	Bristol City	H	3-4
LC	23 Jan	Bath C	A	0-8
LC	30 Jan	Bath C	H	5-3
LC	6 Feb	Lovell's Ath	A	0-5
LC	13 Feb	Lovell's Ath	H	2-2
LC	20 Feb	Cardiff C	H	1-2
LC	27 Feb	Aberaman Ath	A	2-6
	6 Mar	Cardiff C	A	0-2
	13 Mar	Cardiff C	H	1-1
	20 Mar	Aberaman Ath	H	2-2
WC	3 Apr	Lovell's Ath	H	3-3
WC	17 Apr	Bristol City	H	1-1
WC	24 Apr	Cardiff C	A	5-2
WC	26 Apr	Lovell's Ath	A	4-2
WC	1 May	Lovell's Ath	H	3-4

TRANMERE ROVERS

	Date	Opponent	H/A	Score
LC	26 Dec	Everton	H	2-1
LC	2 Jan	Everton	A	0-4
LC	9 Jan	Southport	A	2-2
LC	16 Jan	Southport	H	3-2
LC	23 Jan	Chester	H	1-6
LC	30 Jan	Chester	A	0-1
LC	6 Feb	Liverpool	H	1-5
LC	13 Feb	Liverpool	A	1-4
LC	20 Feb	Stockport Co	A	3-4
LC	27 Feb	Stockport Co	H	1-1
	6 Mar	Wrexham	H	4-0
	13 Mar	Wrexham	A	1-2
CB	20 Mar	Stockport Co	H	1-1
CB	27 Mar	Stockport Co	A	1-2
	3 Apr	Southport	H	5-1
	10 Apr	Everton	A	1-4
	17 Apr	Everton	H	1-2
	24 Apr	Southport	A	5-4
	26 Apr	Wolverhampton	H	3-1
	1 May	Everton	H	1-1

WALSALL

	Date	Opponent	H/A	Score
LC	26 Dec	Coventry C	A	0-2
LC	2 Jan	Coventry C	H	1-3
LC	9 Jan	Northampton T	A	2-2
LC	16 Jan	Northampton T	H	2-0
LC	23 Jan	Birmingham	H	1-1
LC	30 Jan	Birmingham	A	0-1
LC	6 Feb	Stoke C	A	1-2
LC	13 Feb	Stoke C	H	4-1
LC	20 Feb	Aston Villa	A	1-2
LC	27 Feb	Aston Villa	H	1-4
	6 Mar	Birmingham	H	1-2
	13 Mar	Birmingham	A	1-2
	20 Mar	Northampton T	A	4-2
	27 Mar	Northampton T	H	2-5
	17 Apr	WBA	A	0-4
	24 Apr	WBA	H	1-2

WEST BROMWICH ALBION

	Date	Opponent	H/A	Score
LC	26 Dec	Leicester C	H	5-1
LC	2 Jan	Leicester C	A	0-9
LC	9 Jan	Coventry C	H	2-3
LC	16 Jan	Coventry C	A	0-1
LC	23 Jan	Aston Villa	A	5-3
LC	30 Jan	Aston Villa	H	2-1
LC	6 Feb	Birmingham	A	1-0
LC	13 Feb	Birmingham	H	2-1
LC	20 Feb	WBA	A	0-1
LC	27 Feb	WBA	H	2-0
LC	6 Mar	Coventry C	A	1-1
LC	13 Mar	Coventry C	H	3-0
LC	20 Mar	Chesterfield	A	2-3
LC	27 Mar	Chesterfield	A	3-3
	3 Apr	Birmingham	A	3-5
	10 Apr	Birmingham	H	0-4
	17 Apr	Walsall	H	4-0
	24 Apr	Walsall	A	2-1
	26 Apr	Northampton T	H	6-1
	1 May	Aston Villa	A	6-2

WOLVERHAMPTON WANDERERS

	Date	Opponent	H/A	Score
LC	26 Dec	Aston Villa	A	0-1
LC	2 Jan	Aston Villa	H	0-4
LC	9 Jan	Wrexham	A	4-0
LC	16 Jan	Wrexham	A	3-3
LC	23 Jan	Stoke C	H	4-4
LC	30 Jan	Stoke C	A	2-2
LC	6 Feb	Crewe Alex	A	3-0
LC	13 Feb	Crewe Alex	H	6-1
LC	20 Feb	WBA	H	1-0
LC	27 Feb	WBA	A	0-2
LC	6 Mar	Aston Villa	A	2-5
LC	13 Mar	Aston Villa	H	3-5
	20 Mar	Wrexham	A	1-3
	17 Apr	Crewe Alex	A	1-8
	24 Apr	Stoke C	A	4-1
	26 Apr	Tranmere R	A	1-3
	1 May	Derby Co	A	3-3

WREXHAM

	Date	Opponent	H/A	Score
LC	26 Dec	Liverpool	A	2-2
LC	2 Jan	Liverpool	H	0-1
LC	9 Jan	Wolverhampton	A	0-4
LC	16 Jan	Wolverhampton	H	3-3
LC	23 Jan	Crewe Alex	A	1-1
LC	30 Jan	Crewe Alex	H	0-1
LC	6 Feb	Stockport Co	H	5-1
LC	13 Feb	Stockport Co	A	2-5
LC	20 Feb	Chester	A	0-3
LC	27 Feb	Chester	H	3-2
	6 Mar	Tranmere R	A	0-4
	13 Mar	Tranmere R	H	2-1
	20 Mar	Wolverhampton	H	3-1
	3 Apr	Everton	H	4-1
	17 Apr	Stockport Co	H	6-3
	24 Apr	Chester	A	2-3
	26 Apr	Chester	H	3-1

YORK CITY

	Date	Opponent	H/A	Score
LC	26 Dec	Doncaster R	H	3-3
LC	2 Jan	Doncaster R	A	5-3
LC	16 Jan	Newcastle U	A	1-3
LC	23 Jan	Sunderland	H	4-0
LC	30 Jan	Sunderland	A	5-4
LC	6 Feb	Gateshead	A	2-3
LC	13 Feb	Gateshead	H	2-0
LC	20 Feb	Middlesbrough	A	5-1
LC	27 Feb	Middlesbrough	H	6-0
LC	6 Mar	Newcastle U	A	2-3
LC	13 Mar	Newcastle U	H	2-0
LC	20 Mar	Bradford	H	2-1
LC	27 Mar	Bradford	A	3-0
LC	3 Apr	Chesterfield	H	2-0
LC	10 Apr	Chesterfield	A	2-0
LC	17 Apr	Sheffield Wed	A	0-3
LC	24 Apr	Sheffield Wed	H	1-1
	1 May	Newcastle U	H	5-5

KEY: LC=League North Cup; WC=League West Cup; La=Lancashire Cup;
CC=Combined Counties Cup; Li=Liverpool Senior Cup; CB=Cheshire Bowl; SC=Sheffield Cup

The Football League 1942-43

Final Table

		P	W	D	L	F	A	Pts
1	Liverpool	20	15	2	3	64	32	32
2	Lovell's Athletic	20	11	5	4	63	32	27
3	Manchester City	19	11	5	3	43	24	27
4	Aston Villa	20	13	1	6	44	30	27
5	Sheffield Wednesday	20	9	8	3	43	26	26
6	Manchester United	19	11	3	5	52	26	25
7	York City	18	11	3	4	52	30	25
8	Huddersfield Town	19	11	3	5	48	28	25
9	Coventry City	20	11	3	6	33	21	25
10	Stoke City	20	10	4	6	42	34	24
11	West Bromwich Albion	20	11	2	7	49	40	24
12	Notts County	20	9	6	5	37	34	24
13	Blackpool	19	8	7	4	49	31	23
14	Newcastle United	19	10	3	6	62	42	23
15	Blackburn Rovers	18	9	4	5	45	35	22
16	Bristol City	19	8	6	5	41	33	22
17	Chesterfield Town	20	9	4	7	35	30	22
18	Derby County	20	8	5	7	41	34	21
19	Aberaman Athletic	18	10	1	7	39	41	21
20	Sunderland	19	8	4	7	58	40	20
21	Rochdale	16	9	2	5	39	26	20
22	Leicester City	20	9	2	9	40	37	20
23	Sheffield United	19	8	4	7	43	42	20
24	Bradford	19	7	5	7	35	31	19
25	Everton	19	9	1	9	51	46	19
26	Bath City	18	7	4	7	49	46	18
27	Birmingham	20	8	2	10	32	29	18
28	Barnsley	17	8	2	7	34	37	18
29	Nottingham Forest	18	7	4	7	30	34	18
30	Crewe Alexandra	20	7	4	9	44	57	18
31	Wrexham	17	7	3	7	36	37	17
32	Bradford City	16	7	2	7	29	29	16
33	Bolton Wanderers	17	7	2	8	34	42	16
34	Tranmere Rovers	20	6	4	10	37	48	16
35	Halifax Town	18	7	2	9	30	39	16
36	Chester	20	6	3	11	40	49	15
37	Northampton Town	17	6	2	9	30	37	14
38	Wolverhampton Wanderers	17	5	4	8	38	45	14
39	Swansea Town	18	4	6	8	36	52	14
40	Grimsby Town	13	4	5	4	30	27	13
41	Bury	16	5	3	8	44	42	13
42	Doncaster Rovers	17	5	3	9	27	41	13
43	Rotherham United	18	4	5	9	28	43	13
44	Gateshead	13	6	0	7	29	36	12
45	Stockport County	19	4	4	11	37	76	12
46	Southport	18	4	3	11	38	58	11
47	Leeds United	16	5	1	10	32	50	11
48	Oldham Athletic	18	4	3	11	28	47	11
49	Middlesbrough	18	5	0	13	31	69	10
50	Lincoln City	10	4	1	5	23	18	9
51	Burnley	14	3	3	8	17	31	9
52	Walsall	16	3	2	11	22	35	8
53	Cardiff City	17	2	3	12	22	47	7
54	Mansfield Town	10	1	1	8	12	41	3

The Football League 1942-43

SOUTH

	Aldershot	Arsenal	Brentford	Brighton & HA	Charlton Ath	Chelsea	Clapton Orient	Crystal Palace	Fulham	Luton T	Millwall	Portsmouth	QPR	Reading	Southampton	Tottenham H	Watford	West Ham U
Aldershot	X	21 Nov 4-7	30 Jan 2-1	13 Feb 3-2	5 Sep 7-2	16 Jan 1-1		14 Nov 3-2		12 Dec 9-2	31 Oct 7-4	19 Dec 3-4		25 Dec 3-3	29 Aug 5-1	9 Jan 1-3	26 Sep 4-0	17 Oct 5-1
Arsenal	27 Feb 0-1	X	17 Oct 0-2		28 Nov 3-0	26 Dec 1-5	16 Jan 6-0	6 Feb 9-0	9 Jan 7-2	19 Sep 2-0	12 Dec 6-0	2 Jan 5-0	14 Nov 3-0	24 Oct 4-1	5 Sep 6-1	13 Feb 1-0		
Brentford	24 Oct 4-1	23 Jan 0-1	X	12 Sep 9-4	20 Feb 3-5	19 Sep 0-2	29 Aug 2-2		5 Dec 4-2	31 Oct 2-2	13 Feb 3-1		2 Jan 2-0	21 Nov 3-3		26 Dec 2-1	3 Oct 3-0	10 Oct 6-2
Brighton & HA	7 Nov 0-3		12 Dec 7-2	X	30 Jan 2-0	5 Sep 1-2	26 Dec 1-0	26 Sep 1-8		9 Jan 8-0	23 Jan 3-3	10 Oct 2-1	24 Oct 2-3	29 Aug 2-3	20 Feb 2-6		19 Dec 2-1	21 Nov 2-2
Charlton Athletic	5 Dec 6-4	29 Aug 2-6	14 Nov 1-4	31 Oct 1-3	X			19 Sep 1-2	3 Oct 4-4	23 Jan 2-0		30 Jan 3-0	13 Feb 4-3	21 Nov 3-2	2 Jan 3-1	12 Dec 0-3	10 Oct 7-0	26 Dec 4-4
Chelsea	10 Oct 1-3	25 Dec 5-2	19 Dec 2-4	5 Dec 0-0		X		7 Nov 0-2	24 Oct 4-1	26 Sep 4-2	21 Nov 4-2	12 Sep 2-1	29 Aug 1-1	20 Feb 2-0	23 Jan 3-1	30 Jan 0-1		9 Jan 1-3
Clapton Orient		10 Oct 1-4	28 Nov 2-0	25 Dec 3-1	19 Dec 4-2	13 Feb 3-1	X	5 Dec 1-2	21 Nov 4-2	30 Jan 4-2		14 Nov 3-2	12 Sep 0-4	31 Oct 1-2	9 Jan 2-0		23 Jan 4-3	26 Sep 0-5
Crystal Palace	20 Feb 5-2	31 Oct 1-7		2 Jan 1-4	9 Jan 0-2	30 Jan 0-2	5 Sep 5-3	X	10 Oct 2-4		26 Dec 2-2	23 Jan 1-2	19 Sep 0-1		21 Nov 2-1	28 Nov 0-0	13 Feb 0-2	12 Dec 0-0
Fulham		3 Oct 3-4	5 Sep 3-1		17 Oct 2-4	2 Jan 3-1	27 Feb 1-1	16 Jan 1-2	X	28 Nov 6-2	19 Sep 4-1	13 Feb 2-6	26 Dec 3-2	12 Dec 5-2	30 Jan 2-8		14 Nov 2-0	31 Oct 2-3
Luton Town	12 Sep 2-3	19 Dec 0-4	30 Jan 1-1	3 Oct 5-2			24 Oct 2-2		29 Aug 3-1	X	2 Jan 3-11	27 Feb 0-1	23 Jan 1-2	13 Feb 2-3	10 Oct 0-0	14 Nov 3-3	25 Dec 0-2	5 Dec 3-2
Millwall	30 Jan 4-1	12 Sep 1-2	7 Nov 1-2	17 Oct 2-4	24 Oct 2-2	27 Feb 3-0		25 Dec 2-1	19 Dec 1-6	26 Sep 5-1	X	5 Sep 1-2	9 Jan 1-2			16 Jan 0-3	28 Nov 3-3	20 Dec 3-3
Portsmouth	19 Sep 2-1	26 Sep 2-2		16 Jan 2-1		12 Dec 3-0	20 Feb 1-0	17 Oct 2-1	7 Nov 1-1	21 Nov 4-2	5 Dec 6-1	X		3 Oct 2-1	25 Dec 2-3	24 Oct 1-0	30 Jan 6-2	29 Aug 4-5
Queen's Park Rangers		20 Feb 3-2	26 Sep 4-1	30 Jan 3-4	27 Feb 2-0	28 Nov 4-1	12 Dec 3-1	19 Dec 3-0	25 Dec 2-1	17 Oct 2-2	3 Oct 3-2		X	16 Jan 3-2	31 Oct 3-1	5 Sep 0-1		7 Nov 5-2
Reading	26 Dec 3-4	30 Jan 4-5	27 Feb 7-1	28 Nov 5-1	26 Sep 0-1	14 Nov 1-4	30 Jan 0-0		12 Sep 4-1	7 Nov 2-1		9 Jan 2-2	10 Oct 1-2	X	19 Dec 2-7	17 Oct 2-6	5 Sep 3-2	
Southampton	28 Nov 2-1	5 Dec 1-3		14 Nov 2-2	7 Nov 4-0	17 Oct 1-2	3 Oct 5-2	27 Feb 5-1	24 Oct 4-2	16 Jan 11-0		26 Dec 0-2	30 Jan 4-2	19 Sep 2-2	X	2 Jan 2-1	12 Sep 4-1	
Tottenham Hotspur	3 Oct 4-0	7 Nov 1-0	25 Dec 1-1		12 Sep 6-1	31 Oct 1-1		29 Aug 1-3	X	20 Feb 4-1	10 Oct 2-1	30 Jan 5-2	5 Dec 6-0	23 Jan 2-2	26 Sep 1-1	X	21 Nov 6-0	19 Dec 2-0
Watford	2 Jan 5-3		9 Jan 2-0	19 Sep 1-1	16 Jan 3-5		17 Oct 2-3	7 Nov 5-3	20 Feb 1-4	26 Dec 1-2	29 Aug 3-4	31 Oct 4-2		5 Dec 2-5	12 Dec 3-4	27 Feb 0-3	X	30 Jan 3-2
West Ham United	23 Jan 6-3		16 Jan 4-1	27 Feb 2-1	25 Dec 1-3	3 Oct 0-1	2 Jan 10-3	12 Sep 2-2	30 Jan 2-1	5 Sep 3-1	14 Nov 7-5	28 Nov 2-1	13 Feb 1-3			19 Sep 3-1	24 Oct 3-0	X

There were no scheduled matches between the clubs that are blank in the above grid

The Football League 1942-43

SOUTH

Final Table

		P	W	D	L	F	A	Pts
1	Arsenal	28	21	1	6	102	40	43
2	Tottenham Hotspur	28	16	6	6	68	28	38
3	Queen's Park Rangers	28	18	2	8	64	49	38
4	Portsmouth	28	16	3	9	66	52	35
5	Southampton	28	14	5	9	86	58	33
6	West Ham United	28	14	5	9	80	66	33
7	Chelsea	28	14	4	10	52	45	32
8	Aldershot	28	14	2	12	87	77	30
9	Brentford	28	12	5	11	64	63	29
10	Charlton Athletic	28	13	3	12	68	75	29
11	Clapton Orient	28	11	5	12	54	72	27
12	Brighton & Hove Albion	28	10	5	13	65	73	25
13	Reading	28	9	6	13	67	74	24
14	Fulham	28	10	2	16	69	78	22
15	Crystal Palace	28	7	5	16	49	75	19
16	Millwall	28	6	5	17	66	88	17
17	Watford	28	7	2	19	51	88	16
18	Luton Town	28	4	6	18	43	100	14

WEST

	Aberaman Ath	Bath C	Bristol City	Cardiff C	Lovell's Ath	Swansea T
Aberaman Athletic	X	17 Oct 0-4 / 5 Dec 1-7	3 Oct 2-6 / 7 Nov 2-5	24 Oct 2-6 / 28 Nov 2-4	5 Sep 0-2	12 Sep 8-4 / 19 Dec 3-0
Bath City	10 Oct 7-3 / 12 Dec 5-0	X	31 Oct 5-2 / 25 Dec 5-2	29 Aug 3-0	12 Sep 1-2 / 28 Nov 2-1	26 Sep 5-1 / 7 Nov 4-3
Bristol City	26 Sep 7-1	24 Oct 2-3	X	12 Sep 9-1 / 12 Dec 5-0	10 Oct 2-3 / 19 Dec 2-2	5 Sep 6-1 / 28 Nov 4-0
Cardiff City	31 Oct 5-1 / 21 Nov 1-1	5 Sep 2-0 / 19 Dec 1-3	19 Sep 0-0 / 5 Dec 4-3	X	3 Oct 3-1 / 14 Nov 0-1	17 Oct 5-0
Lovell's Athletic	29 Aug 5-1 / 25 Dec 5-0	19 Sep 2-0 / 21 Nov 2-1	17 Oct 3-1	26 Sep 8-4 / 7 Nov 1-1	X	31 Oct 5-0 / 12 Dec 7-1
Swansea Town	19 Sep 3-2	3 Oct 0-7 / 14 Nov 2-4	29 Aug 2-2 / 21 Nov 3-1	10 Oct 2-4 / 25 Dec 3-1	24 Oct 2-3 / 5 Dec 0-6	X

		P	W	D	L	F	A	Pts
1	Lovell's Athletic	18	14	2	2	59	21	30
2	Bath City	18	14	0	4	66	26	28
3	Cardiff City	18	8	3	7	41	45	19
4	Bristol City	17	7	3	7	59	37	17
5	Swansea Town	18	3	1	14	27	77	7
6	Aberaman Athletic	17	2	1	14	29	75	5

Other English Competitions 1942-43

FOOTBALL LEAGUE (NORTH) CUP

Qualifying Round Final Table
See North (Second Championship) for results

		P	W	D	L	F	A	Pts
1	Manchester City	10	7	2	1	30	15	16
2	Rochdale	10	7	2	1	31	16	16
3	Liverpool	10	7	2	1	27	14	16
4	Lovell's Athletic	10	6	3	1	32	10	15
5	Chesterfield	10	7	1	2	22	12	15
6	Huddersfield Town	9	7	0	2	31	14	14
7	Sheffield Wednesday	10	5	4	1	26	16	14
8	Coventry City	10	7	0	3	16	10	14
9	Stoke City	10	6	2	2	24	16	14
10	York City	9	6	1	2	33	17	13
11	Manchester United	10	5	3	2	27	15	13
12	Newcastle United	9	6	1	2	37	21	13
13	Blackpool	10	4	5	1	26	16	13
14	Aston Villa	10	6	0	4	21	13	12
15	Chester	10	5	2	3	22	14	12
16	Notts County	10	5	2	3	22	14	12
17	Bristol City	10	5	2	3	26	21	12
18	Leicester City	10	6	0	4	27	22	12
19	Nottingham Forest	10	5	2	3	20	19	12
20	Aberaman Athletic	10	6	0	4	22	22	12
21	Halifax Town	10	5	2	3	20	21	12
22	Barnsley	10	5	2	3	19	20	12
23	West Bromwich Albion	10	6	0	4	19	22	12
24	Bradford	9	4	3	2	18	11	11
25	Wolverhampton Wanderers	10	4	3	3	23	17	11
26	Blackburn Rovers	10	4	3	3	27	20	11
27	Bath City	10	5	1	4	31	24	11
28	Bradford City	10	5	1	4	20	17	11
29	Sheffield United	10	4	3	3	26	28	11
30	Bury	10	4	2	4	29	16	10
31	Everton	10	5	0	5	34	23	10
32	Derby County	10	4	2	4	22	16	10
	All above qualified for the First round							
33	Grimsby Town	10	3	4	3	22	20	10
34	Bolton Wanderers	10	4	2	4	20	24	10
35	Gateshead	10	5	0	5	25	30	10
36	Lincoln City	10	4	1	5	23	18	9
37	Sunderland	10	3	3	4	31	26	9
38	Northampton Town	10	4	1	5	19	19	9
39	Birmingham	10	3	1	6	15	17	7
40	Wrexham	10	2	3	5	16	23	7
41	Stockport County	10	3	1	6	22	46	7
42	Walsall	10	2	2	6	13	18	6
43	Doncaster Rovers	10	2	2	6	17	26	6
44	Swansea Town	10	2	2	6	17	35	6
45	Tranmere Rovers	10	2	2	6	14	30	6
46	Southport	10	1	3	6	21	37	5
47	Burnley	10	1	3	6	10	22	5
48	Crewe Alexandra	10	1	3	6	8	30	5
49	Cardiff City	10	1	2	7	10	26	4
50	Leeds United	10	1	1	8	16	34	3
51	Rotherham United	10	0	3	7	12	29	3
52	Mansfield Town	10	1	1	8	12	41	3
53	Oldham Athletic	10	0	2	8	14	34	2
54	Middlesbrough	10	1	0	9	13	45	2

Other English Competitions 1942-43

FOOTBALL LEAGUE (NORTH) CUP

First round – 2 legs
First legs played on 6 Mar, second legs on 13 Mar
Aberaman Athletic v Bristol City 1-3, 2-1 (aet 90 mins 2-0)
Aston Villa v Wolverhampton Wanderers 5-2, 5-3
Barnsley v Sheffield United 1-4, 0-3
Blackpool v Everton 4-1, 3-4
Bradford v Huddersfield Town 0-0, 3-2
Chester v Stoke City 2-3, 2-5
Coventry City v West Bromwich Albion 1-1, 0-3
Derby County v Notts County 1-3, 2-2
Halifax Town v Chesterfield 2-1, 0-2 (aet 90 mins 0-1)
Liverpool v Bury 1-3, 7-2
Lovell's Athletic v Bath City 3-2, 1-1
Manchester City v Manchester United 0-1, 0-2
Newcastle United v York City 3-2, 0-2
Nottingham Forest v Leicester City 0-1, 2-0 (aet 90 mins 1-0)
Rochdale v Blackburn Rovers 1-2, 1-3
Sheffield Wednesday v Bradford City 2-0, 1-1

Second round – 2 legs
First legs played on 20 Mar, second legs on 27 Mar
Bath City v Bristol City 2-2, 1-2
Blackburn Rovers v Manchester City 2-0, 0-4
Liverpool v Blackpool 3-1, 0-5
Nottingham Forest v Sheffield Wednesday 1-0, 1-5
Sheffield United v Notts County 4-1, 1-2
Stoke City v Aston Villa 1-3, 0-2
West Bromwich Albion v Chesterfield 2-3, 3-3
York City v Bradford 2-1, 3-0

Third round – 2 legs
First legs played 3 Apr, second legs on 10 Apr
Blackpool v Manchester City 3-1, 1-1
Bristol City v Aston Villa 0-0, 1-2
Sheffield Wednesday v Sheffield United 3-2, 0-0
York City v Chesterfield 2-0, 2-0

Semi-final – 2 legs
First legs played on 17 Apr, second legs on 24 Apr
Blackpool v Aston Villa 3-1, 2-1
Sheffield Wednesday v York City 3-0, 1-1

Final – 2 legs
First leg, 23 May 1943 at Bloomfield Road, Blackpool
Att 28,000
Blackpool 2 *(Finan, Burbanks)*
Sheffield Wednesday 2 *(Cockroft, Robinson)*

Blackpool: Savage*, Pope*, S Jones, Farrow, Johnston, Powell*, Matthews*, Dix*, Dodds, Finan, Burbanks*
Sheffield Wednesday: Morton, Ashley, Catlin, Russell, Millership, Cockcoft*, Reynolds*, Robinson, Melling,   J Thompson, Swift

Second leg, 8 May 1943 at Hillsborough, Sheffield
Att 42,657
Sheffield Wednesday 1 *(Robinson)*
Blackpool 2 *(Dodds, Gardner)*

Sheffield Wednesday: as first leg except Gadsby* for Catlin
Blackpool: as first leg except Hubbick* for Jones, Hayward for Powell*, Gardner* for Matthews*

FOOTBALL LEAGUE (WEST) CUP

	Aberaman Ath	Bath City	Bristol City	Cardiff City	Lovell's Ath	Swansea T
Aberaman Athletic	X				17 Apr 0-3	
Bath City	3 Apr 2-5	X		17 Apr 4-3		
Bristol City		24 Apr 3-3	X			
Cardiff City	10 Apr 2-3			X		24 Apr 2-5
Lovell's Athletic	24 Apr 6-1	10 Apr 5-3			X	
Swansea Town			17 Apr 1-1		3 Apr 3-3	X

The remaining matches were unplayed and a final tie arranged between the two sides with the best record

Final – 2 legs
First leg played on 26 Apr, second leg on 1 May
Lovell's Athletic v Swansea Town 2-4, 4-3

COMBINED COUNTIES CUP

First round – 2 legs
First leg played on 3 Apr, second leg on 10 Apr
Huddersfield Town v Halifax Town 1-0, 2-0
Middlesbrough v Newcastle United 1-1, 0-4
Leeds United v Bradford 2-0, 2-5
Bradford City v Sunderland 5-2, 1-5

Semi-final – 2 legs
First leg played on 17 Apr, second leg on 24 Apr
Bradford v Sunderland 0-1, 2-2
Huddersfield Town v Newcastle United 1-0, 2-2

Final – 2 legs
First leg played on 1 May, second leg on 8 May
Sunderland v Huddersfield Town 6-2, 1-4

Other English Competitions 1942-43

FOOTBALL LEAGUE (SOUTH) CUP

Group 1	Arsenal	Brighton & HA	Watford	West Ham U
Arsenal	X	27 Mar 5-0	13 Mar 4-1	10 Apr 3-1
Brighton & HA	6 Mar 1-5	X	10 Apr 0-5	13 Mar 1-4
Watford	3 Apr 1-1	20 Mar 1-1	X	27 Mar 0-0
West Ham United	20 Mar 1-3	3 Apr 7-1	6 Mar 6-1	X

	P	W	D	L	F	A	Pts
Arsenal	6	5	1	0	21	5	11
West Ham United	6	3	1	2	19	9	7
Watford	6	1	3	2	9	12	5
Brighton & HA	6	0	1	5	4	27	1

Group 2	Brentford	Clapton Orient	QPR	Southampton
Brentford	X	3 Apr 3-2	6 Mar 1-2	20 Mar 1-6
Clapton Orient	13 Mar 1-1	X	20 Mar 1-1	27 Mar 1-0
Queen's Park Rangers	27 Mar 2-0	10 Apr 8-1	X	13 Mar 2-1
Southampton	10 Apr 2-1	6 Mar 1-0	3 Apr 4-1	X

	P	W	D	L	F	A	Pts
Queen's Park Rangers	6	4	1	1	16	8	9
Southampton	6	4	0	2	14	6	8
Clapton Orient	6	1	2	3	6	14	4
Brentford	6	1	1	4	7	15	3

Group 3	Chelsea	Millwall	Reading	Tottenham H
Chelsea	X	13 Mar 5-2	10 Apr 0-4	27 Mar 0-2
Millwall	3 Apr 1-2	X	6 Mar 1-5	10 Apr 0-1
Reading	20 Mar 7-2	27 Mar 5-0	X	13 Mar 1-1
Tottenham Hotspur	6 Mar 2-0	20 Mar 5-0	3 Apr 1-2	X

Group 4	Aldershot	Charlton Ath	Crystal Palace	Fulham	Luton Town	Portsmouth
Aldershot	X			13 Mar 4-1	10 Apr 1-4	27 Mar 1-2
Charlton Athletic		X	20 Mar 1-0	27 Mar 6-1	13 Mar 4-1	X
Crystal Palace		10 Apr 0-4	X		27 Mar 4-0	13 Mar 0-1
Fulham	3 Apr 2-2	6 Mar 3-1		X		20 Mar 2-2
Luton Town	20 Mar 0-1	3 Apr 0-4	6 Mar 0-0		X	
Portsmouth	6 Mar 2-3	X	3 Apr 3-3	10 Apr 1-3		X

	P	W	D	L	F	A	Pts
Reading	6	5	1	0	24	5	11
Tottenham Hotspur	6	4	1	1	12	3	9
Chelsea	6	2	0	4	9	18	4
Millwall	6	0	0	6	4	23	0

	P	W	D	L	F	A	Pts
Charlton Athletic	6	5	0	1	20	5	10
Aldershot	6	3	1	2	12	11	7
Portsmouth	6	2	2	2	11	12	6
Fulham	6	2	2	2	12	16	6
Crystal Palace	6	1	2	3	7	9	4
Luton Town	6	1	1	4	5	14	3

Semi-final
Played on 17 Apr at White Hart Lane, London
  Charlton Athletic v Reading 2-1
Played on 24 Apr at Stamford Bridge, London
  Arsenal v Queen's Park Rangers 4-1

Final
Played on 1 May 1943 at Wembley Stadium, London
Att 75,000
Arsenal 7 *(Lewis 4, Drake 2, D Compton)*
Charlton Athletic 1 *(Green)*

Arsenal: Marks, Scott, L Compston, Crayston, Joy, Male, Kirchen, Drake, Lewis, Bastin, D COmpton
Charlton A: Hobbins, Cann, Shreeve, Phipps, Oakes, Davies*, Green, Mason*, Welsh, Brown, Revell

LIVERPOOL SENIOR CUP
Final – 2 legs
First leg played on 26 Apr , second leg on 12 May
  Liverpool v Everton 4-1, 2-3

CHESHIRE BOWL
Semi-final -2 legs
First leg played on 20 Mar , second leg on 27 Mar
  Tranmere Rovers v Stockport County 1-1, 1-2
  Chester v Crewe Alexandra 1-3, 3-3

Final
Played on 1 May
  Crewe Alexandra v Stockport County 7-2

Other English Competitions 1942-43

LANCASHIRE CUP

First round – 2 legs
First leg played on 20 Mar , second leg on 27 Mar
Southport v Everton 4-1, 1-2
Blackpool Services v Burnley 3-1, 2-2
Manchester United v Bury 4-1, 5-3
First leg played on 3 Apr , second leg on 10 Apr
Liverpool v Chester 4-1, 5-2
Blackburn Rovers v Bolton Wanderers 1-3, 1-0
Oldham Athletic bye

Second round – 2 legs
One leg only, played on 17 Apr
Liverpool v Southport 3-0
First leg played on 3 Apr , second leg on 10 Apr
Oldham Athletic v Blackpool Services 3-3, 4-1
Manchester United bye
Bolton Wanderers bye

Semi-final -2 legs
First leg played on 17 Apr, second leg on 24 Apr
Manchester United v Oldham Athletic 3-0, 1-3
First leg played on 24 Apr , second leg on 1 May
Bolton Wanderers v Liverpool 3-6, 0-4

Final – 2 legs
First leg played on 8 May , second leg on 15 May
Liverpool v Manchester United 1-3, 3-3

SHEFFIELD COUNTY CUP

Semi-final
First leg played on 17 Apr , second leg on 24 Apr
Barnsley v Sheffield United 4-1, 1-2
Played on 26 Apr
Rotherham United v Sheffield Wednesday 2-1

Final
Played on 15 May
Rotherham United v Barnsley 5-3

CUP WINNERS MATCH
Played between the winners of the League North Cup and League South Cup

Played on 15 May 1943 at Stamford Bridge, London
Att 55,195
Blackpool 4 *(Dix, Burbanks, Dodds, Finan)*
Arsenal 2 *(Lewis, D Compton)*

Blackpool: Savage*, Pope*, Hubbick*, Farrow, Hayward, Johnston, Matthews*, Dix*, Dodds, Finan, Burbanks*
Arsenal: Marks, Scott, L Compston, Crayston, Joy, Male, Kirchen, Drake, Lewis, Bastin, D COmpton

The Scottish Southern Football League 1942-43

	Airdrieonians	Albion Rovers	Celtic	Clyde	Dumbarton	Falkirk	Hamilton Ac	Heart of Midlothian	Hibernian	Morton	Motherwell	Partick Thistle	Queen's Park	Rangers	St Mirren	Third Lanark
Airdrieonians	X	5 Sep 4-4	24 Oct 1-5	22 Aug 0-1	7 Nov 1-0	10 Apr 3-1	8 Aug 1-2	20 Feb 2-4	17 Oct 0-5	12 Dec 2-5	16 Jan 3-1	9 Jan 3-5	26 Dec 3-4	28 Nov 1-7	19 Sep 3-1	6 Feb 4-0
Albion Rovers	1 Jan 5-3	X	14 Nov 4-4	31 Oct 1-5	3 Oct 3-4	15 Aug 1-4	10 Oct 3-1	23 Jan 1-3	21 Nov 1-4	30 Jan 1-5	29 Aug 1-2	13 Feb 1-5	26 Sep 3-1	19 Dec 0-4	5 Dec 5-1	12 Sep 2-2
Celtic	30 Jan 2-1	20 Feb 4-0	X	12 Dec 1-1	8 Aug 2-2	31 Oct 2-2	22 Aug 2-2	7 Nov 3-0	26 Sep 0-3	26 Dec 0-2	19 Dec 3-2	2 Jan 3-3	28 Nov 2-1	10 Apr 2-2	10 Oct 3-2	23 Jan 3-2
Clyde	5 Dec 3-2	6 Feb 5-0	29 Aug 1-3	X	24 Oct 6-2	13 Feb 1-0	9 Jan 2-0	19 Sep 2-2	14 Nov 7-2	3 Oct 2-3	15 Aug 1-3	1 Jan 4-1	17 Oct 2-5	16 Jan 1-3	12 Sep 4-2	21 Nov 2-0
Dumbarton	13 Feb 3-3	2 Jan 6-1	21 Nov 4-2	30 Jan 6-2	X	1 Jan 2-2	23 Jan 2-2	10 Oct 2-2	29 Aug 1-4	19 Dec 0-3	12 Sep 5-3	5 Dec 4-1	31 Oct 3-3	26 Sep 1-2	15 Aug 4-0	14 Nov 5-3
Falkirk	3 Oct 5-0	28 Nov 7-2	6 Dec 6-0	7 Nov 1-2	5 Sep 5-4	X	12 Dec 0-4	26 Dec 2-2	16 Jan 3-1	20 Feb 4-1	17 Oct 7-0	19 Sep 2-1	8 Aug 2-1	22 Aug 0-5	24 Oct 1-1	9 Jan 2-1
Hamilton Academical	21 Nov 2-1	16 Jan 3-2	5 Dec 2-1	26 Sep 3-3	17 Oct 2-1	29 Aug 3-2	X	3 Oct 3-2	15 Aug 1-3	31 Oct 0-2	1 Jan 3-2	12 Sep 2-2	19 Dec 3-1	30 Jan 0-3	14 Nov 3-2	13 Feb 4-2
Heart Of Midlothian	14 Nov 5-2	17 Oct 5-1	13 Feb 5-3	19 Dec 1-3	16 Jan 0-1	12 Sep 3-2	10 Apr 4-0	X	1 Jan 1-4	26 Sep 5-2	5 Dec 1-6	21 Nov 3-3	30 Jan 1-0	31 Oct 0-3	29 Aug 4-2	15 Aug 3-1
Hibernian	23 Jan 7-1	8 Aug 3-1	9 Jan 4-0	20 Feb 2-2	12 Dec 4-1	10 Oct 4-0	28 Nov 3-1	5 Sep 2-2	X	7 Nov 2-2	3 Oct 2-1	24 Oct 0-0	22 Aug 4-0	26 Dec 1-1	6 Feb 3-2	19 Sep 5-1
Morton	29 Aug 3-3	24 Oct 2-1	12 Sep 4-0	2 Jan 3-1	19 Sep 1-3	14 Nov 3-1	6 Feb 3-2	9 Jan 2-0	13 Feb 1-0	X	21 Nov 1-2	15 Aug 2-1	10 Oct 3-1	23 Jan 1-1	1 Jan 8-0	5 Dec 6-2
Motherwell	10 Oct 4-0	12 Dec 1-0	19 Sep 2-1	28 Nov 2-2	26 Dec 0-2	23 Jan 3-0	5 Sep 5-2	22 Aug 3-2	2 Jan 2-1	8 Aug 1-4	X	6 Feb 1-1	20 Feb 1-1	7 Nov 0-2	10 Apr 1-0	24 Oct 5-2
Partick Thistle	26 Sep 2-0	7 Nov 6-2	3 Oct 2-3	10 Oct 1-3	22 Aug 2-1	19 Dec 0-3	26 Dec 4-4	8 Aug 2-2	30 Jan 1-5	28 Nov 1-3	31 Oct 1-2	X	12 Dec 2-1	20 Feb 0-2	23 Jan 8-1	16 Jan 2-1
Queen's Park	12 Sep 3-5	9 Jan 1-4	15 Aug 2-2	23 Jan 3-5	6 Feb 4-2	21 Nov 1-0	19 Sep 0-2	24 Oct 3-2	5 Dec 2-3	16 Jan 2-2	14 Nov 0-2	29 Aug 2-3	X	3 Oct 1-0	13 Feb 0-2	1 Jan 6-2
Rangers	15 Aug 4-1	19 Sep 3-0	1 Jan 8-1	26 Apr 0-1	9 Jan 1-0	5 Dec 1-1	24 Oct 4-2	6 Feb 1-1	12 Sep 1-1	17 Oct 7-0	13 Feb 2-1	14 Nov 4-1	2 Jan 5-2	X	21 Nov 5-1	29 Aug 4-2
St Mirren	19 Dec 3-0	22 Aug 0-0	16 Jan 0-2	26 Dec 1-3	28 Nov 5-2	30 Jan 2-2	20 Feb 4-1	12 Dec 2-1	31 Oct 1-2	5 Sep 1-2	26 Sep 2-2	17 Oct 2-1	7 Nov 3-2	8 Aug 0-1	X	3 Oct 2-2
Third Lanark	31 Oct 1-0	26 Dec 1-3	17 Oct 4-2	8 Aug 2-1	20 Feb 7-3	26 Sep 4-1	7 Nov 1-2	28 Nov 1-2	19 Dec 3-2	22 Aug 2-2	30 Jan 2-0	10 Apr 1-1	5 Sep 3-2	12 Dec 0-3	2 Jan 3-4	X

		P	W	D	L	F	A	Pts
1	Rangers	30	22	6	2	89	23	50
2	Morton	30	20	5	5	81	48	45
3	Hibernian	30	19	6	5	86	40	44
4	Clyde	30	17	5	8	78	55	39
5	Motherwell	30	15	4	11	60	54	34
6	Hamilton Academical	30	14	5	11	61	67	33
7	Heart of Midlothian	30	12	7	11	68	64	31
8	Falkirk	30	12	6	12	68	58	30
9	Celtic	30	10	8	12	61	76	28
10	Dumbarton	30	11	6	13	76	76	28
11	Partick Thistle	30	9	8	13	63	67	26
12	St Mirren	30	8	5	17	49	78	21
13	Third Lanark	30	8	4	18	58	83	20
14	Queen's Park	30	7	4	19	55	76	18
15	Airdrieonians	30	7	3	20	55	97	17
16	Albion Rovers	30	6	4	20	53	99	16

The Scottish Southern Football League Cup 1942-43

Section A	Albion Rovers	Dumbarton	Falkirk	Morton
Albion Rovers	X	27 Feb 2-1	27 Mar 5-1	3 Apr 1-1
Dumbarton	20 Mar 1-2	X	3 Apr 1-3	6 Mar 3-3
Falkirk	6 Mar 1-0	13 Mar 7-2	X	20 Mar 3-2
Morton	13 Mar 1-1	27 Mar 5-2	27 Feb 0-0	X

		P	W	D	L	F	A	Pts
1	Falkirk	6	4	1	1	15	10	9
2	Albion Rovers	6	3	2	1	11	6	8
3	Morton	6	1	4	1	12	10	6
4	Dumbarton	6	0	1	5	10	22	1

Section B	Airdrieonians	Motherwell	Partick Thistle	Third Lanark
Airdrieonians	X	6 Mar 5-0	20 Mar 0-2	13 Mar 1-3
Motherwell	27 Mar 5-1	X	3 Apr 0-3	27 Feb 2-2
Partick Thistle	27 Feb 3-0	13 Mar 5-1	X	27 Mar 1-1
Third Lanark	3 Apr 5-1	20 Mar 2-0	6 Mar 3-2	X

		P	W	D	L	F	A	Pts
1	Third Lanark	6	4	2	0	16	7	10
2	Partick Thistle	6	4	1	1	16	5	9
3	Motherwell	6	1	1	4	8	18	3
4	Airdrieonians	6	1	0	5	8	18	2

Section C	Clyde	Hamilton A	Hearts	Queen's Park
Clyde	X	3 Apr 2-3	6 Mar 1-0	20 Mar 3-2
Hamilton Academical	13 Mar 3-1	X	20 Mar 5-0	6 Mar 4-4
Heart of Midlothian	27 Mar 1-1	27 Feb 1-4	X	3 Apr 4-2
Queen's Park	27 Feb 0-1	27 Mar 1-4	13 Mar 0-0	X

		P	W	D	L	F	A	Pts
1	Hamilton Academical	6	5	1	0	23	9	11
2	Clyde	6	3	1	2	9	9	·7
3	Heart of Midlothian	6	1	2	3	6	13	4
4	Queen's Park	6	0	2	4	9	16	2

Section D	Celtic	Hibernian	Rangers	St Mirren
Celtic	X	27 Feb 2-1	27 Mar 0-2	13 Mar 2-0
Hibernian	20 Mar 2-1	X	13 Mar 0-2	6 Mar 2-1
Rangers	6 Mar 3-0	3 Apr 1-0	X	20 Mar 3-1
St Mirren	3 Apr 5-1	27 Mar 1-3	27 Feb 0-3	X

		P	W	D	L	F	A	Pts
1	Rangers	6	6	0	0	14	1	12
2	Hibernian	6	3	0	3	8	8	6
3	Celtic	6	2	0	4	6	13	4
4	St Mirren	6	1	0	5	8	14	2

Semi-final
Played on 24 Apr
  Falkirk v Third Lanark 3-1 *(at Ibrox Park, Glasgow)*
  Rangers v Hamilton Academical 3-0 *(at Hampden Park, Glasgow)*

Final
Played on 8 May 1943 at Hampden Park, Glasgow
Att 20,000
Rangers 1 *(Gillick)*
Falkirk 1 *(Campbell)*
Rangers won 11-3 on corner kicks

Rangers: Dawson, Gray, Shaw, Little, Young, Symon, Waddell, Duncanson, Gillick, Venters, Johnstone
Falkirk: Matthews, White, Peak, Pinkerton, Shankly, Busby, Ogilvie, Campbell, Inglis, Fitzsimmons, Dawson

The Scottish North Eastern Football League 1942-43

First series	Aberdeen	Dundee U	Dunfermline A	East Fife	Hearts 'A'	Hibernian 'A'	Raith R	Rangers
Aberdeen	X	24 Oct 1-0	15 Aug 5-0	31 Oct 1-1	29 Aug 4-0	5 Sep 6-3	10 Oct 8-1	26 Sep 4-2
Dundee United	12 Sep 0-4	X	29 Aug 3-1	17 Oct 0-1	26 Sep 3-1	19 Sep 3-1	15 Aug 3-2	10 Oct 3-2
Dunfermline Athletic	3 Oct 1-3	7 Nov 5-3	X	8 Aug 3-1	17 Oct 2-0	22 Aug 2-0	19 Sep 2-1	12 Sep 0-1
East Fife	19 Sep 0-1	5 Sep 3-0	10 Oct 2-3	X	15 Aug 4-0	24 Oct 1-0	26 Sep 4-1	29 Aug 2-1
Heart of Midlothian 'A'	7 Nov 5-3	22 Aug 3-1	5 Sep 0-1	3 Oct 3-1	X	8 Aug 4-2	24 Oct 2-3	19 Sep 2-1
Hibernian 'A'	17 Oct 0-7	31 Oct 6-4	26 Sep 3-0	12 Sep 2-3	21 Sep 2-3	X	29 Aug 3-2	15 Aug 4-3
Raith Rovers	8 Aug 1-3	3 Oct 4-0	31 Oct 1-4	22 Aug 0-2	12 Sep 2-1	7 Nov 1-1	X	5 Sep 3-1
Rangers 'A'	22 Aug 2-1	8 Aug 2-1	24 Oct 1-3	7 Nov 4-2	31 Oct 3-2	3 Oct 5-2	17 Oct 3-1	X

Both Dunfermline Athletic v Rangers 'A' games were played at East End Park, Dunfermline

		P	W	D	L	F	A	Pts
1	Aberdeen	14	11	1	2	51	16	23
2	Dunfermline Athletic	14	9	0	5	27	24	18
3	East Fife	14	8	1	5	27	19	17
4	Rangers 'A'	14	7	0	7	31	33	14
5	Heart of Midlothian 'A'	14	6	0	8	26	32	12
6	Dundee United	14	5	0	9	24	36	10
7	Hibernian 'A'	14	4	1	9	29	44	9
8	Raith Rovers	14	4	1	9	23	37	9

Second Series	Aberdeen	Dundee U	Dunfermline A	East Fife	Hearts 'A'	Hibernian 'A'	Raith R	Rangers
Aberdeen	X	13 Feb 3-0	23 Jan 4-1	6 Mar 4-1	27 Feb 8-3	20 Mar 2-0	9 Jan 2-0	2 Jan 2-1
Dundee United	1 Jan 1-0	X	20 Mar 4-2	2 Jan 1-2	16 Jan 2-2	6 Mar 2-0	27 Mar 3-4	6 Feb 2-1
Dunfermline Athletic	27 Mar 0-0	17 Apr 3-1	X	13 Mar 2-2	30 Jan 3-3	20 Feb 4-1	13 Feb 3-0	1 Jan 3-1
East Fife	30 Jan 1-0	27 Feb 5-1	6 Feb 4-1	X	13 Feb 2-1	9 Jan 7-1	1 Jan 2-3	20 Mar 1-1
Heart of Midlothian 'A'	6 Feb 2-6	20 Feb 1-4	6 Mar 2-1	23 Jan 2-3	X	13 Mar 7-1	20 Mar 2-6	17 Apr 0-0
Hibernian 'A'	16 Jan 0-5	30 Jan 3-2	2 Jan 1-3	27 Mar 3-6	1 Jan 2-6	X	27 Feb 2-3	13 Feb 2-8
Raith Rovers	13 Mar 1-1	23 Jan 3-1	16 Jan 5-3	20 Feb 2-0	2 Jan 3-5	6 Feb 5-3	X	6 Mar 3-2
Rangers 'A'	20 Feb 1-2	13 Mar 3-1	27 Feb 0-1	16 Jan 1-2	27 Mar 4-0	23 Jan 4-0	30 Jan 5-4	X

		P	W	D	L	F	A	BP	Pts
1	Aberdeen	14	10	2	2	39	12	7	29
2	East Fife	14	9	2	3	38	23	5	25
3	Raith Rovers	14	9	1	4	42	34	4	23
4	Dunfermline Athletic	14	6	3	5	30	28	3	18
5	Rangers 'A'	14	5	2	7	32	23	3	15
6	Dundee United	14	5	1	8	25	32	2	13
7	Heart of Midlothian 'A'	14	4	3	7	36	45	2	13
8	Hibernian 'A'	14	1	0	13	19	64	0	2

BP = an extra point was awarded by having a better aggregate score over each opponent

Other Scottish Competitions 1942-43

SCOTTISH NORTH EASTERN LEAGUE CUP

First Series
First Round - 2 legs
First leg played on 21 Nov, second on 28 Nov
  Hibernian 'A' v Dunfermline Athletic 2-1, 1-4
  Dundee United v Rangers 'A' 0-0, 1-2
  East Fife v Raith Rovers 1-4, 2-1
  Aberdeen v Heart of Midlothian 'A' 9-1, 6-0

Semi-final - 2 legs
First leg played on 5 Dec, second on 12 Dec
  Dunfermline v Rangers 'A' 5-2, 0-1
  Raith Rovers v Aberdeen 2-6, 2-5

Final - 2 legs
First leg, 19 Dec 1942 at East End Park, Dunfermline
Att 3,500
Dunfermline Athletic 2 *(Neill 2)*
Aberdeen 3 *(Gourlay 3)*

Dunfermline Athletic: Wallace, Hogg, O'Neil, Walker,
Hart, Forbes, Fougan, Logie, Neill, McGillivray, Harrower
Aberdeen: Johnstone, Cooper, Dyer, Dunlop, Gavin,
Taylor, Ancell, Gourlay, Pattillo, Ferguson, Dryden

Second leg, 26 Dec at Pittodrie Park, Aberdeen
Att 12,000
Aberdeen 6 *(Gourlay, Pattillo 3, Ancell 2)*
Dunfermline AThletic 1 *(Walker)*

Aberdeen: as first leg
Dunfermline Athletic: Wallace, Hogg, Cameron, O'Neil,
Hart, Forbes, Harrower, McGillivray, Neill, Walker, Dougan

Second Series
First Round - 2 legs
First leg played on 3 Apr, second on 10 Apr
  East Fife v Rangers 'A' 1-2, 3-1 *(aet, 90 mins 1-2)*
  Raith Rovers v Dundee United 5-0, 3-4
  Hibernian 'A' v Heart of Midlothian 'A' 3-1 *(one leg played)*
  Dunfermline Athletic v Aberdeen 1-2, 2-3

Semi-final - 2 legs
First leg played on 24 Apr, second on 3 May
  East Fife v Raith Rovers 2-3, 1-2
  Hibernian 'A' v Aberdeen 1-1, 1-2

Final - 2 legs
First leg, 8 May 1943 at Stark's Park, Kirkcaldy
Att 8,000
Raith Rovers 0
Aberdeen 0
Abandoned after 46 minutes due to the referee taking ill

Raith Rovers: Moodie, Dutch, Cook, Phypers, Low, Aird,
Stewart, Hurrell, Payne, Glassey, Penman
Aberdeen: Johnstone, Ancell, Dyer, Dunlop, Gavin,
Taylor, McSpadyen, Anderson, Newman, Ferguson,
Deakin

First leg REPLAY, 15 May 1943 at Stark's Park, Kirkcaldy
Att 10,000
Raith Rovers 1 *(Glassey)*
Aberdeen 1 *(Ferguson)*

Raith Rovers: Moodie, Donald, Cook* (Everton), Dutch,
Low, Aird, Stewart, Hurrell, Inglis*, Glassey, Cook* (Clyde)
Aberdeen: Johnstone, Ancell, Dyer, Dunlop, Gavin,
Taylor, McSpadyen, Anderson, Newman, Ferguson,
Cruikshank*

Second leg, 29 May 1943 at Pittodrie Park, Aberdeen
Att 14,000
Aberdeen 6 *(Dryden, Mortensen, McSpadyen, Dyer (pen),
Pattillo 2)*
Raith Rovers 2 *(Payne, Low (pen)*

Aberdeen: as first leg replay except Mutch for Anderson,
Pattillo for Newman, Mortensen for Ferguson, Dryden for
Cruikshank
Raith Rovers: as first leg replay except Harvey for Aird,
Payne for Inglis, Penman for Cook (Clyde)

SUMMER CUP

First round – 2 legs
First leg played on 29 May, second on 5 Jun
  St Mirren v Third Lanark 6-3, 3-1
  Dumbarton v Hamilton Academical 6-2, 1-2
  Clyde v Morton 1-1, 3-8
  Albion Rovers v Falkirk 0-1, 0-4
  Motherwell v Celtic 2-2, 2-3
  Rangers v Heart of Midlothian 2-0, 2-1
  Queen's Park v Airdrieonians 3-2, 4-1
  Hibernian v Partick Thistle 7-0, 5-2

Second Round - 2 legs
First leg played on 12 Jun, second on 19 Jun
  St Mirren v Dumbarton 6-3, 1-1
  Morton v Falkirk 3-0, 4-1
  Celtic v Rangers 0-4, 1-4
  Queen's Park v Hibernian 1-2, 0-4

Semi-final
Played on 26 Jun
  Rangers v Hibernian 3-1 *(at Hampden Park, Glasgow)*
Played on 26 Jun, REPLAY on 3 Jul
  St Mirren v Morton 3-3 *(at Ibrox Park, Glasgow)*
  St Mirren v Morton 3-2 *(at Hampden Park, Glasgow)*

Final
10 Jul 1943 at Hampden Park, Glasgow
Att 45,000
St Mirren 1 *(Linwood)*
Rangers 0

St Mirren: Wears, Drinkwater, McLatchie, Housam, Kelly,
Colquhoun, Jess, Stenhouse, Linwood, Deakin, McGarry
Rangers: Dawson, Gray, Shaw, Little, Young, Symon, Waddell,
Duncanson, Gillick, Venters, Johnstone

Other Scottish Competitions 1942-43

GLASGOW CUP

First round
Played on 5 Sep
  Rangers v Celtic 2-1
  Partick Thistle v Clyde 3-1

Semi-final
Played on 28 Sep
  Third Lanark v Queen's Park 3-2
  Partick Thistle v Rangers 0-2

Final
Played on 10 Oct at Hampden Park, Glasgow
  Rangers v Third Lanark 5-2

GLASGOW CHARITY CUP

First round
Played on 1 May
  Celtic v Queen's Park 3-0
  Rangers v Clyde 1-2

Semi-final
Played on 15 May
  Partick Thistle v Third Lanark 2-3
  Celtic v Clyde 3-1

Final
Played on 22 May at Hampden Park, Glasgow
  Celtic v Third Lanark 3-0

ROSEBERY CHARITY CUP

Played on 22 May at Easter Road, Edinburgh
  Hibernian v Heart of Midlothian 1-1 (Hearts won on the toss of a coin)

EAST OF SCOTLAND SHIELD

Semi-final
Played on 1 May
  Heart of Midlothian v Edinburgh City 2-0

Final
Played on 8 May, REPLAY on 15 May, both games at Easter Road, Edinburgh
  Hibernian v Heart of Midlothian 1-1 abandoned after 30 mins), 3-2

RENFREWSHIRE CUP

2 legs, first leg played on 1 May, second on 5 May
  St Mirren v Morton 2-4, 5-6

Northern Ireland 1942-43

NORTHERN REGIONAL FOOTBALL LEAGUE

	Belfast Celtic	Cliftonville	Derry City	Distillery	Glentoran	Linfield
Belfast Celtic	X	30 Jan 4-0 / 14 Nov 6-1	2 Jan 4-0 / 24 Apr 4-0	26 Dec 5-1 / 10 Apr 1-1	12 Dec 3-0 / 13 Mar 2-1	6 Feb 2-1 / 21 Nov 1-4
Cliftonville	19 Dec 1-4 / 3 / 20 Mar 0-2	X	6 Feb 1-2 3-0 / 21 Nov 1-1	7 Nov 0-4 / 9 Jan 2-1	2 Jan 4-2 / 24 Apr 2-2	26 Dec 0-4 / 10 Apr 0-1
Derry City	5 Dec 0-1 / 6 Mar 0-0	4-2 / 3 Apr 1-1	X	14 Nov 3-2 / 30 Jan 2-0	28 Nov 4-2 / 13 Feb 2-6	12 Dec 1-4 / 13 Mar 0-2
Distillery	28 Nov 3-2 / 13 Feb 1-2	12 Dec 4-2 / 13 Mar 4-1	19 Dec 3-2 / 20 Mar 1-2	X	6 Feb 5-2 / 21 Nov 2-1	2 Jan 2-0 / 24 Apr 0-0
Glentoran	7 Nov 3-4 / 9 Jan 2-1	5 Dec 9-3 / 6 Mar 6-2	26 Dec 3-3 / 10 Apr 3-2	2-1 / 3 Apr 1-3	X	14 Nov 2-1 / 30 Jan 1-3
Linfield	2-2 / 3 Apr 1-0	28 Nov 5-1 / 13 Feb 5-0	7 Nov 6-2 / 9 Jan 3-2	5 Dec 2-0 / 6 Mar 2-4	19 Dec 4-3 / 20 Mar 5-3	X

		P	W	D	L	F	A	Pts
1	Linfield	20	14	2	4	55	26	30
2	Belfast Celtic	20	13	3	4	50	22	29
3	Distillery	20	10	2	8	42	34	22
4	Glentoran	20	7	2	11	54	56	16
5	Derry City	20	6	3	11	32	51	15
6	Cliftonville	20	3	2	15	26	70	8

SUBSTITUTE GOLD CUP

	Belfast Celtic	Cliftonville	Derry City	Distillery	Glentoran	Linfield
Belfast Celtic	X	29 Aug 6-0	17 Oct 5-1	22 Aug 5-0	19 Sep 2-4	31 Oct 3-3
Cliftonville	10 Oct 0-2	X	24 Oct 3-1	26 Sep 1-4	3 Oct 3-1	5 Sep 0-2
Derry City	5 Sep 1-0	19 Sep 3-2	X	10 Oct 1-1	31 Oct 4-2	22 Aug 0-3
Distillery	3 Oct 1-2	31 Oct 1-0	29 Aug 2-1	X	17 Oct 1-3	19 Sep 2-7
Glentoran	24 Oct 1-2	22 Aug 4-1	26 Sep 4-2	5 Sep 2-2	X	10 Oct 1-4
Linfield	26 Sep 2-1	17 Oct 4-2	3 Oct 5-4	24 Oct 1-0	29 Aug 6-1	X

		P	W	D	L	F	A	Pts
1	Linfield	10	9	1	0	37	14	19
2	Belfast Celtic	10	6	1	3	28	13	13
3	Glentoran	10	4	1	5	23	27	9
4	Distillery	10	3	2	5	14	23	8
5	Derry City	10	3	1	6	18	27	7
6	Cliftonville	10	2	0	8	12	28	4

IRISH FA CUP

First round – 2 legs
First leg played on16 Jan, second on 23 Jan
 Bangor v Glentoran 2-3, 2-8
 Cliftonville v Alexandra Works 0-1, 2-4
 Derry City v Belfast Celtic 2-2, 0-3
 Distillery v Linfield 4-5, 1-0

Second round – 2 legs
First leg played on 20 Feb, second on 27 Feb
 Alexandra Works v Belfast Celtic 1-2, 2-3
 Glentoran v Royal Irish Fusiliers 7-2, 8-0
 Infantry Training Centre v Ards 1-2, 0-5

Semi-final
Played on 27 Mar
 Larne v Belfast Celtic 2-4
 Glentoran v Ards 4-2

Final
Played on 17 Apr at Windsor Park, Belfast
 Belfast Celtic v Glentoran 1-0

INTER CITY CUP

Derry City played all their home matches in Belfast
All League of Ireland clubs' home games were played
at Dalymount Park, Dublin

First round – 2 legs
First leg played on 28 Apr, second on 30 Apr
 St James' Gate v Derry City 3-1, 0-4
First leg played on 30 Apr, second on 8 May
 Shamrock Rovers v Linfield 3-2, 4-2
First leg played on 1 May, second on 7 May
 Shelbourne v Glentoran 1-0, 2-0
First leg played on 1 May, second on 3 May
 Belfast Celtic v Cork United 5-1, 0-1
First leg played on 3 May, second on 10 May
 Cliftonville v Dundalk 2-1, 1-3
First leg played on 8 May, second on 10 May
 Bohemians v Distillery 1-0, 0-1

Second round - 2 legs
The first round winners were joined by Distillery and
Bohemians who finished level on aggregate

First leg played on 15 May, second on 18 May
 Shelbourne v Belfast Celtic 1-4, 1-3
First leg played on 15 May, second on 19 May
 Distillery v Dundalk 5-2, 5-3
First leg played on 17 May, second on 22 May
 Bohemians v Derry City 4-2, 3-1
 Cliftonville v Shamrock Rovers 1-1, 1-3

Semi-final - 2 legs
First leg played on 24 May, second on 26 May
 Bohemians v Belfast Celtic 2-2, 1-0
 Distillery v Shamrock Rovers 0-2, 2-4

Final - 2 legs
First leg played on 29 May, second on 30 May
 Bohemians v Shamrock Rovers 2-0, 0-2 (Shamrock won
on corners)

NOTE first leg was played at Windsor Park, Belfast,
second leg at Daymount Park, Dublin

1943-44

In England and Wales, three leagues would again operate North, West (which also included non-League sides) and South. Again the North was subdivided into smaller groupings, each club playing nine others. The second half of the season saw the North and West clubs combined as the League North (Second Championship). The League Cup qualifying competition, results in the subsequent rounds and local cup ties also counted towards this.

Norwich City again filled their season with friendly fixtures against services XIs.

The Scottish Southern League was joined by the North Eastern Football League. Because of its size, it was played over Autumn and Spring series, with bonus points being awarded in the latter.

The Northern Irish Northern Regional League also operated. There was also an international competition involving clubs from the Republic of Ireland.

WINNERS OF THE PRINCIPAL COMPETITIONS

Football League North Cup	Aston Villa
Football League South Cup	Charlton Athletic
Football League West Cup	Bath City
Football League –	
North	Blackpool
North (Second Championship)	Bath City
South	Tottenham Hotspur
West	Lovell's Athletic
Scottish Southern League	Rangers
Scottish Southern League Cup	Hibernian
Scottish North Eastern League –	
First Series	Raith Rovers
Second Series	Aberdeen
North Eastern League Cup –	
First Series	Rangers 'A'
Second Series	Rangers 'A'
Irish FA Cup	Belfast Celtic
Northern Regional League	Belfast Celtic
Substitute Gold Cup	Belfast Celtic
Inter City Cup	Glentoran

The Football League 1943-44

NORTH

	Chester	Crewe A	Everton	Liverpool	Man City	Man Utd	Tranmere	Wrexham
Chester	X		4 Dec 1-0	6 Nov 3-1	20 Nov 1-2	16 Oct 5-4	23 Oct 3-2	4 Sep 3-3
Crewe Alexandra		X	20 Nov 0-8		30 Oct 0-2		16 Oct 2-3	18 Dec 5-3
Everton	11 Dec 0-1	27 Nov 5-5	X	9 Oct 4-6	18 Dec 4-0	18 Sep 6-1	6 Nov 9-2	30 Oct 4-2
Liverpool	13 Nov 9-0		16 Oct 5-2	X	28 Aug 4-1	23 Oct 3-4	25 Dec 2-1	11 Sep 8-0
Manchester City	27 Nov 3-0	23 Oct 2-0	25 Dec 3-5	4 Sep 2-1	X	6 Nov 2-2	4 Dec 2-2	16 Oct 4-1
Manchester United	9 Oct 3-1		11 Sep 4-1	30 Oct 1-0	13 Nov 3-0	X	20 Nov 6-3	11 Dec 5-0
Tranmere Rovers	30 Oct 3-1	9 Oct 5-1	13 Nov 2-6	18 Dec 2-9	11 Dec 0-6	27 Nov 0-1	X	2 Oct 6-0
Wrexham	28 Aug 8-4	25 Dec 2-1	23 Oct 1-3	18 Sep 2-5	9 Oct 0-1	4 Dec 1-4	25 Sep 9-0	X

On 16 Oct, Manchester City v Wrexham was played at The Racecourse, Wrexham because Maine Road was being used for an international match

	Aston Villa	Birmingham	Coventry C	Derby Co	Leicester C	Mansfield T	Northampton Town	Stoke C	Walsall	WBA	Wolverhampton Wanderers
Aston Villa	X	27 Nov 3-0	9 Oct 0-0	4 Dec 0-1	25 Dec 3-1		6 Nov 4-0	4 Sep 2-1	2 Oct 4-4	23 Oct 3-1	18 Sep 4-1
Birmingham	20 Nov 2-1	X	28 Aug 0-0	16 Oct 3-3	11 Sep 3-0		25 Sep 1-3	30 Oct 2-0	13 Nov 5-1	11 Dec 3-0	18 Dec 4-2
Coventry City	16 Oct 0-1	4 Sep 2-1	X		25 Sep 0-1		30 Oct 4-1 / 20 Nov 0-1		11 Sep 3-3 / 4 Dec 1-3	25 Dec 8-0	13 Nov 1-1
Derby County	11 Dec 3-3	9 Oct 5-3		X	13 Nov 3-2	25 Dec 4-3		2 Oct 2-2		4 Sep 1-5	27 Nov 2-2
Leicester City	18 Dec 1-3	18 Sep 2-2	2 Oct 1-0	6 Nov 0-1	X	28 Aug 4-1				9 Oct 0-3	4 Dec 1-0
Mansfield Town				18 Dec 3-1	4 Sep 0-0	X					
Northampton Town	13 Nov 5-0	2 Oct 2-1	23 Oct 0-3 / 27 Nov 4-1				X		28 Aug 2-0 / 9 Oct 2-0	18 Sep 2-1	
Stoke City	28 Aug 0-2	23 Oct 1-1		25 Sep 5-1				X	25 Dec 0-1	6 Nov 3-3	9 Oct 5-0
Walsall	25 Sep 0-2	6 Nov 2-4	18 Sep 1-1 / 11 Dec 0-0				4 Sep 0-0 / 16 Oct 0-0	18 Dec 4-2	X	20 Nov 2-0	23 Oct 1-3
West Bromwich Albion	30 Oct 5-4	4 Dec 1-3	18 Dec 3-0	28 Aug 3-2	16 Oct 2-2		11 Sep 4-4	13 Nov 3-0	27 Nov 1-4	X	25 Sep 4-1
Wolverhampton Wanderers	11 Sep 2-4	25 Dec 3-0	6 Nov 2-1	20 Nov 1-3	11 Dec 4-1			16 Oct 1-2	30 Oct 1-1	2 Oct 2-3	X

There were no scheduled matches between the clubs that are blank in the above grids

The Football League 1943-44

NORTH

	Chesterfield	Doncaster R	Grimsby T	Lincoln C	Mansfield T	Nottingham Forest	Notts Co	Rotherham U	Sheffield United	Sheffield Wednesday
Chesterfield	X	16 Oct 2-3	18 Sep 1-2		27 Nov 2-3	4 Sep 3-1	25 Sep 3-0	23 Oct 7-1	13 Nov 0-2	11 Dec 3-1
Doncaster Rovers	9 Oct 4-0	X	18 Dec 2-1	2 Oct 3-1					4 Sep 2-1	18 Sep 3-1
Grimsby Town	11 Sep 0-0	25 Dec 1-3	X	16 Oct 3-2 / 13 Nov 3-2				4 Dec 4-1	20 Nov 4-2	30 Oct 1-3
Lincoln City		25 Sep 2-1	9 Oct 2-2 / 6 Nov 4-0	X	30 Oct 7-2	11 Sep 3-0 / 4 Dec 2-2	28 Aug 4-5 / 18 Dec 8-5	27 Nov 5-1		
Mansfield Town	20 Nov 2-0			23 Oct 1-0	X	2 Oct 0-1	16 Oct 4-0	18 Sep 3-2	4 Dec 0-0	6 Nov 0-2
Nottingham Forest	28 Aug 1-2			18 Sep 8-1 / 11 Dec 1-1	25 Sep 1-2	X	13 Nov 0-4		16 Oct 4-0	
Notts County	2 Oct 1-0			4 Sep 0-0 / 25 Dec 2-5	9 Oct 0-2	6 Nov 0-1	X			27 Nov 0-0
Rotherham United	30 Oct 2-0		11 Dec 4-3	20 Nov 1-2	11 Sep 3-1			X	2 Oct 2-3	9 Oct 5-1
Sheffield United	6 Nov 1-0	28 Aug 2-3	27 Nov 1-1		11 Dec 4-2	9 Oct 1-1		25 Sep 3-1	X	25 Dec 1-1
Sheffield Wednesday	4 Dec 5-0	11 Sep 2-2	23 Oct 2-3		13 Nov 2-3		20 Nov 1-0	16 Oct 1-1	18 Dec 0-2	X

	Blackburn R	Blackpool	Bolton W	Burnley	Bury	Oldham A	Rochdale	Southport	Stockport Co
Blackburn Rovers	X	6 Nov 1-1	18 Sep 3-1		27 Nov 5-1	25 Dec 5-2	23 Oct 6-1	4 Dec 3-0	16 Oct 8-2
Blackpool	13 Nov 8-0	X	30 Oct 1-2	20 Nov 3-0	16 Oct 3-1	11 Dec 3-1	28 Aug 6-1	25 Dec 5-0	25 Sep 3-2
Bolton Wanderers	11 Sep 1-4	23 Oct 1-2	X	4 Sep 0-2	13 Nov 2-4	20 Nov 3-0		9 Oct 3-1	
Burnley		27 Nov 3-5	28 Aug 4-0	X	11 Sep 5-1	16 Oct 1-0	13 Nov 2-0		30 Oct 0-0
Bury	20 Nov 1-0	9 Oct 1-0	6 Nov 2-3	18 Sep 1-1	X	28 Aug 3-1	18 Dec 1-4	30 Oct 5-1	11 Dec 4-0
Oldham Athletic	18 Dec 2-4	4 Dec 1-1	27 Nov 4-2	9 Oct 4-2	4 Sep 3-2	X	25 Sep 2-0	13 Nov 2-1	
Rochdale	30 Oct 2-1	4 Sep 2-6		6 Nov 3-1	25 Dec 5-0	2 Oct 2-1	X	11 Sep 6-1	27 Nov 2-0
Southport	11 Dec 3-1	18 Dec 1-1	16 Oct 2-0		23 Oct 4-1	6 Nov 0-1	18 Sep 4-4	X	
Stockport County	9 Oct 1-2	2 Oct 0-0		23 Oct 1-1	4 Dec 2-1		20 Nov 1-3		X

There were no scheduled matches between the clubs that are blank in the above grids

The Football League 1943-44

NORTH

	Barnsley	Bradford	Bradford City	Darlington	Gateshead	Hartlepools U	Huddersfield Town	Leeds U	Middlesbrough	Newcastle U	Sunderland	York City
Barnsley	X	20 Nov 1-5	16 Oct 3-0				18 Sep 1-2					
Bradford	27 Nov 5-3	X	18 Dec 8-0				4 Sep 1-2	6 Nov 6-1	16 Oct 1-1	11 Sep 1-0	30 Oct 0-0	4 Dec 6-1
Bradford City	9 Oct 2-1	25 Dec 1-6	X	2 Oct 1-1	13 Nov 1-4		23 Oct 1-3	18 Sep 3-3		28 Aug 2-1		
Darlington			25 Sep 3-1	X	4 Sep 2-2 / 11 Dec 7-1	13 Nov 2-2 / 25 Dec 1-5			18 Sep 3-3	20 Nov 4-1	9 Oct 1-2	23 Oct 4-2
Gateshead			6 Nov 2-1	28 Aug 4-3 / 4 Dec 2-1	X	25 Sep 3-3		16 Oct 3-4	30 Oct 5-3	18 Dec 1-3	20 Nov 2-3	11 Sep 3-0
Hartlepools United				6 Nov 2-1 / 18 Dec 5-1	2 Oct 5-0	X			28 Aug 1-0 / 27 Nov 3-4	30 Oct 5-4	11 Sep 0-3 / 11 Dec 1-1	16 Oct 4-1
Huddersfield Town	11 Sep 1-4	28 Aug 7-4	30 Oct 2-1				X	25 Dec 3-0		16 Oct 1-1	25 Sep 4-0	
Leeds United		13 Nov 2-2	11 Sep 1-5		9 Oct 5-2		18 Dec 0-3	X	25 Sep 3-0		4 Sep 1-5	27 Nov 1-0
Middlesbrough		9 Oct 1-8		11 Sep 2-6	23 Oct 3-0	4 Sep 3-2 / 20 Nov 1-3		2 Oct 3-3	X	4 Dec 1-1	25 Dec 4-0	6 Nov 1-1
Newcastle United		18 Sep 2-1	4 Sep 3-2	27 Nov 4-5	25 Dec 0-2	23 Oct 0-1	9 Oct 5-2		11 Dec 1-1	X	13 Nov 3-1	2 Oct 1-1
Sunderland		23 Oct 1-1		16 Oct 4-2	27 Nov 2-3	18 Sep 3-0 / 4 Dec 1-2	2 Oct 3-2	28 Aug 7-1	18 Dec 6-1	6 Nov 4-2	X	
York City		11 Dec 2-4		30 Oct 5-2	18 Sep 5-1	9 Oct 2-0		20 Nov 1-3	13 Nov 5-3	25 Sep 2-0		X

There were no scheduled matches between the clubs that are blank in the above grid

The Football League 1943-44

NORTH

Inter area matches

Played on 28 Aug
Barnsley v Sheffield Wednesday 3-1
Blackburn Rovers v Everton 1-3
Grimsby Town v York City 3-2
Manchester United v Stockport County 6-0
Rotherham United v Halifax Town 3-0
Tranmere Rovers v Southport 2-3
Wolverhampton Wanderers v Crewe Alexandra 2-4

Played on 4 Sep
Crewe Alexandra v Wolverhampton Wanderers 1-2
Everton v Blackburn Rovers 0-0
Halifax Town v Rotherham United 2-1
Sheffield Wednesday v Barnsley 3-1
Southport v Tranmere Rovers 3-1
Stockport County v Manchester United 3-3
York City v Grimsby Town 2-0

Played on 11 Sep
Blackpool v Manchester City 6-2
Crewe Alexandra v Stoke City 2-1
Halifax Town v Sheffield United 2-2
Notts County v Derby County 3-1
Oldham Athletic v Chester 0-3
Stockport County v Tranmere Rovers 5-3

Played on 18 Sep
Chester v Oldham Athletic 6-1
Derby County v Notts County 4-2
Manchester City v Blackpool 1-2
Sheffield United v Halifax Town 2-0
Stoke City v Crewe Alexandra 4-2
Tranmere Rovers v Stockport County 2-3

Played on 25 Sep
Bolton Wanderers v Manchester City 4-1
Bradford v Sheffield Wednesday 3-1
Burnley v Everton 0-0
Crewe Alexandra v Southport 2-5
Grimsby Town v Barnsley 1-0
Halifax Town v Chester 1-4
Liverpool v Bury 3-1
Manchester United v Blackburn Rovers 2-1

Played on 2 Oct
Barnsley v Grimsby Town 3-0
Blackburn Rovers v Manchester United 2-1
Bury v Liverpool 1-2
Chester v Halifax Town 3-1
Everton v Burnley 0-0
Manchester City v Bolton Wanderers 4-0
Sheffield Wednesday v Bradford 2-3
Southport v Crewe Alexandra 3-2

Played on 9 Oct
Halifax Town v Rochdale 2-2

Played on 16 Oct
Rochdale v Halifax Town 4-3

Played on 23 Oct
Barnsley v Sheffield United 3-2
Leicester City v Notts County 5-0
Doncaster Rovers v Leeds United 3-3
Halifax Town v Oldham Athletic 1-5
Nottingham Forest v Derby County 4-3

Played on 30 Oct
Derby County v Nottingham Forest 3-1
Leeds United v Doncaster Rovers 2-2
Notts County v Leicester City 1-9
Oldham Athletic v Halifax Town 0-5
Sheffield United v Barnsley 1-0

Played on 6 Nov
Halifax Town v Doncaster Rovers 1-0
Huddersfield Town v Crewe Alexandra 8-0
Rotherham United v Barnsley 3-1
Stockport County v Wrexham 1-0

Played on 13 Nov
Barnsley v Rotherham United 3-3
Crewe Alexandra v Huddersfield Town 0-1
Doncaster Rovers v Halifax Town 3-1
Wrexham v Stockport County 4-1

Played on 20 Nov
Bradford City v Doncaster Rovers 1-1
Huddersfield Town v Halifax Town 0-0
Liverpool v Southport 9-0
Nottingham Forest Leicester City 1-0
Wrexham v Stoke City 4-1

Played on 27 Nov
Doncaster Rovers v Bradford City 3-1
Halifax Town v Huddersfield Town 4-1
Leicester City v Nottingham Forest 3-3
Southport v Liverpool 1-3
Stoke City v Wrexham 7-3

Played on 4 Dec
Burnley v Liverpool 0-1
Doncaster Rovers v Barnsley 3-3
Halifax Town v Leeds United 2-1
Huddersfield Town v Bolton Wanderers 2-0
Notts County v Northampton Town 2-5
Rochdale v Bradford City 2-1
Stoke City v Crewe Alexandra 5-0

Played on 11 Dec
Barnsley v Doncaster Rovers 0-4
Bolton Wanderers v Huddersfield Town 0-4
Bradford City v Rochdale 3-0
Crewe Alexandra v Stoke City 2-1
Leeds United v Halifax Town 4-0
Liverpool v Burnley 1-1
Northampton Town v Notts County 1-1

Played on 18 Dec
Chesterfield v Barnsley 2-0
Halifax Town v Burnley 1-1
Manchester United v Bolton Wanderers 3-1
Nottingham Forest v Northampton Town 2-2
Rotherham United v York City 3-1
Stockport County v Chester 1-0

Played on 25 Dec
Barnsley v Chesterfield 2-4
Bolton Wanderers v Manchester United 1-3
Burnley v Halifax Town 0-1
Chester v Stockport County 1-1
Northampton Town v Nottingham Forest 9-1
York City v Rotherham United 2-1

The Football League 1943-44

NORTH

Final Table

		P	W	D	L	F	A	Pts
1	Blackpool	18	12	4	2	56	20	28
2	Manchester United	18	13	2	3	56	30	28
3	Liverpool	18	13	1	4	72	26	27
4	Doncaster Rovers	18	11	5	2	45	25	27
5	Bradford	18	11	4	3	65	28	26
6	Huddersfield Town	18	12	2	4	48	25	26
7	Northampton Town	18	10	5	3	43	25	25
8	Aston Villa	18	11	3	4	43	27	25
9	Sunderland	18	10	3	5	46	30	23
10	Hartlepools United	18	10	3	5	44	31	23
11	Everton	18	9	4	5	60	34	22
12	Blackburn Rovers	18	10	2	6	47	32	22
13	Rochdale	18	10	2	6	43	41	22
14	Sheffield United	18	8	5	5	30	26	21
15	Lincoln City	18	8	4	6	51	40	20
16	Birmingham	18	8	4	6	38	31	20
17	Manchester City	18	9	2	7	38	35	20
18	Mansfield Town	18	9	2	7	32	33	20
19	Derby County	18	8	4	6	43	45	20
20	Chester	18	9	2	7	40	43	20
21	Grimsby Town	18	8	3	7	32	36	19
22	West Bromwich Albion	18	8	3	7	42	44	19
23	Gateshead	18	8	2	8	40	51	18
24	Burnley	18	5	7	6	24	22	17
25	Walsall	18	5	7	6	27	31	17
26	Nottingham Forest	18	6	5	7	33	39	17
27	Leeds United	18	6	5	7	38	50	17
28	Leicester City	18	6	4	8	33	30	16
29	Darlington	18	6	4	8	49	48	16
30	Rotherham United	18	7	2	9	38	42	16
31	York City	18	7	2	9	35	40	16
32	Halifax Town	18	6	4	8	27	36	16
33	Southport	18	7	2	9	33	51	16
34	Stoke City	18	6	3	9	40	35	15
35	Chesterfield Town	18	7	1	10	29	31	15
36	Oldham Athletic	18	7	1	10	30	44	15
37	Stockport County	18	5	5	8	24	43	15
38	Coventry City	18	4	6	8	25	23	14
39	Newcastle United	18	5	4	9	32	37	14
40	Sheffield Wednesday	18	5	4	9	29	34	14
41	Middlesbrough	18	4	6	8	35	52	14
42	Wolverhampton Wanderers	18	5	3	10	30	42	13
43	Bury	18	6	1	11	31	44	13
44	Barnsley	18	5	2	11	32	42	12
45	Bradford City	18	4	3	11	27	47	11
46	Wrexham	18	5	1	12	43	63	11
47	Notts County	18	4	3	11	26	53	11
48	Bolton Wanderers	18	5	0	13	24	46	10
49	Tranmere Rovers	18	4	1	13	39	71	9
50	Crewe Alexandra	18	4	1	13	29	62	9

The Football League 1943-44

NORTH (SECOND CHAMPIONSHIP)
Including League Cup and county cup matches

ABERAMAN ATHLETIC				
LC	26 Dec	Lovell's Ath	A	1-4
LC	1 Jan	Lovell's Ath	H	0-5
LC	8 Jan	Bath C	H	1-2
LC	15 Jan	Bath C	A	0-5
LC	22 Jan	Cardiff C	H	1-2
LC	29 Jan	Cardiff C	A	1-4
LC	5 Feb	Swansea T	A	1-6
LC	12 Feb	Swansea T	A	2-4
LC	19 Feb	Bristol City	A	0-2
LC	26 Feb	Bristol City	H	4-4
WC	4 Mar	Swansea T	A	0-4
WC	11 Mar	Swansea T	H	2-3
WC	18 Mar	Cardiff C	A	0-6
WC	25 Mar	Cardiff C	H	0-5
WC	10 Apr	Bristol City	A	0-5
WC	15 Apr	Bristol City	H	3-1
WC	22 Apr	Bath C	A	3-16
WC	29 Apr	Bath C	H	1-8

ASTON VILLA				
LC	26 Dec	Northampton T	H	2-1
LC	1 Jan	Northampton T	A	2-1
LC	8 Jan	Stoke C	A	3-6
LC	15 Jan	Stoke C	H	0-2
LC	22 Jan	Wolverhampton	A	4-0
LC	29 Jan	Wolverhampton	A	2-2
LC	5 Feb	Coventry C	H	4-0
LC	12 Feb	Coventry C	A	0-2
LC	19 Feb	Birmingham	A	1-1
LC	26 Feb	Birmingham	H	1-2
LC	4 Mar	Stoke C	A	5-4
LC	11 Mar	Stoke C	H	3-0
LC	18 Mar	Coventry C	A	2-1
LC	25 Mar	Coventry C	H	2-1
LC	1 Apr	Bath C	H	1-0
LC	8 Apr	Bath C	A	3-3
	10 Apr	WBA	H	4-1
LC	15 Apr	Sheffield United	H	3-2
LC	22 Apr	Sheffield United	A	2-2
LC	29 Apr	Blackpool	A	1-2
LC	6 May	Blackpool	H	4-2

BARNSLEY				
LC	26 Dec	Bradford City	H	4-0
LC	1 Jan	Bradford City	A	1-0
LC	8 Jan	Leeds U	A	0-2
LC	15 Jan	Leeds U	H	3-2
LC	22 Jan	York C	H	2-1
LC	29 Jan	York C	A	0-2
LC	5 Feb	Huddersfield T	A	2-2
LC	12 Feb	Huddersfield T	H	4-1
LC	19 Feb	Bradford	A	3-3
LC	26 Feb	Bradford	H	3-3
LC	4 Mar	York C	A	1-4
LC	11 Mar	York C	H	3-1
SC	18 Mar	Doncaster R	A	1-1
SC	25 Mar	Doncaster R	H	1-0
	1 Apr	Rotherham U	H	1-4
	8 Apr	Rotherham U	A	0-3
	10 Apr	Sheffield United	H	5-1

BATH CITY				
LC	26 Dec	Cardiff C	H	3-2
LC	1 Jan	Cardiff C	A	2-1
LC	8 Jan	Aberaman Ath	A	2-1
LC	15 Jan	Aberaman Ath	H	5-0
LC	22 Jan	Bristol City	H	3-0
LC	29 Jan	Bristol City	A	2-2
LC	5 Feb	Lovell's Ath	H	5-1
LC	12 Feb	Lovell's Ath	A	0-2
LC	19 Feb	Swansea T	H	3-0
LC	26 Feb	Swansea T	A	5-2
LC	4 Mar	Bristol City	H	2-1
LC	11 Mar	Bristol City	A	2-1
LC	18 Mar	Lovell's Ath	A	3-1
LC	25 Mar	Lovell's Ath	H	3-0
LC	1 Apr	Aston Villa	A	01
LC	8 Apr	Aston Villa	H	3-3
WC	10 Apr	Swansea T	A	1-2
WC	15 Apr	Swansea T	H	6-0
WC	22 Apr	Aberaman Ath	H	16-3
WC	29 Apr	Aberaman Ath	A	8-1
WC	6 May	Cardiff C	H	4-2

BIRMINGHAM				
LC	26 Dec	WBA	A	1-1
LC	1 Jan	WBA	H	4-0
LC	8 Jan	Northampton T	H	5-1
LC	22 Jan	Stoke C	H	4-1
LC	29 Jan	Stoke C	A	1-4
LC	5 Feb	Wolverhampton	A	2-0
LC	12 Feb	Wolverhampton	H	2-1
LC	19 Feb	Aston Villa	H	1-1
LC	26 Feb	Aston Vila	A	2-1
LC	4 Mar	Leicester C	H	3-1
LC	11 Mar	Leicester C	A	0-2
LC	18 Mar	Manchester Utd	H	3-1
LC	25 Mar	Manchester Utd	A	1-1
LC	1 Apr	Manchester City	A	0-1
LC	8 Apr	Manchester City	H	0-0
	10 Apr	Coventry C	A	3-0
	15 Apr	Walsall	A	2-2
	22 Apr	Walsall	H	5-0
	29 Apr	Northampton T	H	3-1
	6 May	Northampton T	A	5-0

11 Mar, aet 1-2

BLACKBURN ROVERS				
LC	26 Dec	Blackpool	A	2-2
LC	1 Jan	Blackpool	H	3-1
LC	8 Jan	Rochdale	H	3-1
LC	15 Jan	Rochdale	A	0-4
LC	22 Jan	Southport	A	2-1
LC	29 Jan	Southport	H	5-0
LC	5 Feb	Bolton W	H	2-0
LC	12 Feb	Bolton W	A	1-4
LC	19 Feb	Burnley	A	1-5
LC	26 Feb	Burnley	H	2-0
LC	4 Mar	Manchester City	A	0-3
LC	11 Mar	Manchester City	H	3-0
La	18 Mar	Burnley	H	2-1
La	25 Mar	Burnley	A	2-2
	29 Apr	Liverpool	H	0-1
	6 May	Bury	H	2-2

11 Mar, aet 4-2

KEY: LC=League Cup; WC=League West Cup; La=Lancashire Cup; MC=Midland Cup;
CC=Combined Counties Cup; Li=Liverpool Senior Cup; TT=Tyne, Tees & Wear Cup; CB=Cheshire Bowl

The Football League 1943-44

NORTH (SECOND CHAMPIONSHIP)
Including League Cup and county cup matches

BLACKPOOL

LC	26 Dec	Blackburn R	H	2-2
LC	1 Jan	Blackburn R	A	1-3
LC	8 Jan	Southport	A	4-1
LC	15 Jan	Southport	H	2-1
LC	22 Jan	Bolton W	H	6-0
LC	29 Jan	Bolton W	A	2-1
LC	5 Feb	Burnley	A	1-2
LC	12 Feb	Burnley	H	1-3
LC	19 Feb	Rochdale	H	2-0
LC	26 Feb	Rochdale	A	2-0
LC	4 Mar	Everton	H	7-1
LC	11 Mar	Everton	A	3-1
LC	18 Mar	Rochdale	H	8-0
LC	25 Mar	Rochdale	A	1-2
LC	1 Apr	Bradford	H	2-2
LC	8 Apr	Bradford	A	2-1
LC	15 Apr	Manchester City	H	1-1
LC	22 Apr	Manchester City	A	2-1
LC	29 Apr	Aston Villa	H	2-1
LC	6 May	Aston Villa	A	2-4

BOLTON WANDERERS

LC	26 Dec	Rochdale	A	0-5
LC	1 Jan	Rochdale	H	2-2
LC	8 Jan	Burnley	H	2-1
LC	15 Jan	Burnley	A	1-5
LC	22 Jan	Blackpool	A	0-6
LC	29 Jan	Blackpool	H	1-2
LC	5 Feb	Blackburn R	A	0-2
LC	12 Feb	Blackburn R	H	4-1
LC	19 Feb	Southport	H	5-1
LC	26 Feb	Southport	A	0-2
	4 Mar	Bury	H	6-1
	11 Mar	Bury	A	2-5
	18 Mar	Wrexham	A	3-3
	25 Mar	Wrexham	H	1-1
La	1 Apr	Manchester Utd	H	3-0
La	8 Apr	Manchester Utd	A	2-3
La	10 Apr	Bury	H	3-2
La	15 Apr	Bury	A	0-1
La	22 Apr	Stockport Co	H	4-2
La	29 Apr	Stockport Co	A	2-1
La	6 May	Liverpool	A	1-3

15 Apr, aet 1-1

BRADFORD

LC	26 Dec	Leeds U	H	2-1
LC	1 Jan	Leeds U	A	1-3
LC	8 Jan	Huddersfield T	A	2-1
LC	15 Jan	Huddersfield T	H	1-1
LC	22 Jan	Bradford City	H	1-0
LC	29 Jan	Bradford City	A	5-1
LC	5 Feb	York C	A	1-0
LC	12 Feb	York C	H	4-1
LC	19 Feb	Barnsley	H	3-3
LC	26 Feb	Barnsley	A	3-3
LC	4 Mar	Sheffield Wed	H	5-0
LC	11 Mar	Sheffield Wed	A	2-1
LC	18 Mar	York C	A	5-1
LC	25 Mar	York C	H	2-1
LC	1 Apr	Blackpool	A	2-2
LC	8 Apr	Blackpool	H	1-2
	15 Apr	Doncaster R	H	3-4
	22 Apr	Doncaster R	A	1-3
	29 Apr	Doncaster R	H	5-0
	6 May	Manchester City	A	1-2

BRADFORD CITY

LC	26 Dec	Barnsley	A	0-4
LC	1 Jan	Barnsley	H	0-1
LC	8 Jan	York C	H	4-1
LC	15 Jan	York C	A	1-3
LC	22 Jan	Bradford	A	0-1
LC	29 Jan	Bradford	H	1-5
LC	5 Feb	Leeds U	H	3-3
LC	12 Feb	Leeds U	A	0-2
LC	19 Feb	Huddersfield T	A	0-2
LC	26 Feb	Huddersfield T	H	2-4
	4 Mar	Halifax T	A	2-4
	11 Mar	Halifax T	H	1-3
	18 Mar	Chesterfield	H	3-3
	25 Mar	Chesterfield	A	3-4
	1 Apr	Huddersfield T	H	3-0
	8 Apr	Huddersfield T	A	0-5
	15 Apr	Lincoln C	A	1-0
	22 Apr	Lincoln C	H	3-2

BRISTOL CITY

LC	26 Dec	Swansea T	A	1-1
LC	1 Jan	Swansea T	H	2-1
LC	8 Jan	Lovell's Ath	A	3-3
LC	15 Jan	Lovell's Ath	H	1-0
LC	22 Jan	Bath C	A	0-3
LC	29 Jan	Bath C	H	2-2
LC	5 Feb	Cardiff C	A	0-2
LC	12 Feb	Cardiff C	H	2-0
LC	19 Feb	Aberaman Ath	H	2-0
LC	26 Feb	Aberaman Ath	A	4-4
LC	4 Mar	Bath C	A	1-2
LC	11 Mar	Bath C	H	1-2
WC	18 Mar	Swansea T	A	4-5
WC	25 Mar	Swansea T	H	3-3
WC	1 Apr	Cardiff C	A	2-6
WC	8 Apr	Cardiff C	H	1-2
WC	10 Apr	Aberaman Ath	H	5-0
WC	15 Apr	Aberaman Ath	A	1-3
WC	22 Apr	Lovell's Ath	H	2-1
WC	29 Apr	Lovell's Ath	A	1-2

BURNLEY

LC	26 Dec	Southport	H	2-2
LC	1 Jan	Southport	A	1-4
LC	8 Jan	Bolton W	A	1-2
LC	15 Jan	Bolton W	H	5-1
LC	22 Jan	Rochdale	H	2-2
LC	29 Jan	Rochdale	A	1-3
LC	5 Feb	Blackpool	H	2-1
LC	12 Feb	Blackpool	A	3-1
LC	19 Feb	Blackburn R	H	5-1
LC	26 Feb	Blackburn R	A	0-2
LC	4 Mar	Rochdale	H	3-3
LC	11 Mar	Rochdale	A	1-1
La	18 Mar	Blackburn R	A	1-2
La	25 Mar	Blackburn R	H	2-2
	1 Apr	Bury	A	4-2
	8 Apr	Bury	H	3-1
	15 Apr	Manchester United	A	0-9
	22 Apr	Manchester United	H	3-3

11 Mar, aet 1-2

**KEY: LC=League Cup; WC=League West Cup; La=Lancashire Cup; MC=Midland Cup;
CC=Combined Counties Cup; Li=Liverpool Senior Cup; TT=Tyne, Tees & Wear Cup; CB=Cheshire Bowl**

The Football League 1943-44

NORTH (SECOND CHAMPIONSHIP)
Including League Cup and county cup matches

BURY						CARDIFF CITY						CHESTER				
LC	26 Dec	Manchester City	H	0-4		LC	26 Dec	Bath C	A	2-3		LC	26 Dec	Everton	H	3-5
LC	1 Jan	Manchester City	A	7-1		LC	1 Jan	Bath C	H	1-2		LC	1 Jan	Everton	A	0-7
LC	8 Jan	Halifax T	A	0-2		LC	8 Jan	Swansea T	A	7-1		LC	8 Jan	Wrexham	A	0-3
LC	15 Jan	Halifax T	H	0-0		LC	15 Jan	Swansea T	A	2-1		LC	15 Jan	Wrexham	H	1-3
LC	22 Jan	Oldham Ath	H	3-7		LC	22 Jan	Aberaman Ath	A	2-1		LC	22 Jan	Crewe Alex	A	4-6
LC	29 Jan	Oldham Ath	A	0-3		LC	29 Jan	Aberaman Ath	H	4-1		LC	29 Jan	Crewe Alex	H	6-1
LC	5 Feb	Manchester United	H	0-3		LC	5 Feb	Bristol City	H	2-0		LC	5 Feb	Tranmere R	H	6-2
LC	12 Feb	Manchester United	A	3-3		LC	12 Feb	Bristol City	A	0-2		LC	12 Feb	Tranmere R	A	3-2
LC	19 Feb	Southport	A	1-5		LC	19 Feb	Lovell's Ath	H	2-0		LC	19 Feb	Liverpool	A	2-4
LC	26 Feb	Southport	H	4-2		LC	26 Feb	Lovell's Ath	A	2-1		LC	26 Feb	Liverpool	H	6-0
	4 Mar	Bolton W	A	1-6		LC	4 Mar	Lovell's Ath	A	0-2		CB	4 Mar	Crewe Alex	A	9-5
	11 Mar	Bolton W	H	5-2		LC	11 Mar	Lovell's Ath	H	1-0		CB	11 Mar	Crewe Alex	H	4-1
	18 Mar	Southport	H	3-1		WC	18 Mar	Aberaman Ath	H	4-0		La	18 Mar	Everton	A	2-5
	25 Mar	Southport	A	2-4		WC	25 Mar	Aberaman Ath	A	5-0		La	25 Mar	Everton	H	2-9
	1 Apr	Burnley	H	2-4		WC	1 Apr	Bristol City	H	6-2			8 Apr	Wrexham	A	0-5
	8 Apr	Burnley	A	2-3		WC	8 Apr	Bristol City	A	2-1			10 Apr	Wrexham	H	2-2
La	10 Apr	Bolton W	A	2-3		WC	10 Apr	Lovell's Ath	H	1-1			15 Apr	Wolverhampton	H	1-3
La	15 Apr	Bolton W	H	1-0		WC	15 Apr	Lovell's Ath	A	0-2			22 Apr	Wolverhampton	A	4-0
	29 Apr	Everton	H	1-0		WC	22 Apr	Swansea T	A	4-2			29 Apr	Southport	A	4-3
	6 May	Blackburn R	A	2-2		WC	29 Apr	Swansea T	H	3-1		CB	6 May	Stockport Co	H	6-1
						WC	6 May	Bath C	A	2-4						

15 Apr, aet 1-1

CHESTERFIELD						COVENTRY CITY						CREWE ALEXANDRA				
LC	26 Dec	Sheffield Wed	H	0-2		LC	26 Dec	Walsall	H	3-0		LC	26 Dec	Tranmere R	H	6-1
LC	1 Jan	Sheffield Wed	A	1-3		LC	1 Jan	Walsall	A	0-3		LC	1 Jan	Tranmere R	A	4-3
LC	8 Jan	Rotherham U	A	1-1		LC	8 Jan	Wolverhampton	H	3-2		LC	8 Jan	Everton	A	1-9
LC	15 Jan	Rotherham U	H	1-2		LC	15 Jan	Wolverhampton	A	2-2		LC	15 Jan	Everton	H	2-6
LC	22 Jan	Sheffield United	H	1-4		LC	22 Jan	WBA	A	2-2		LC	22 Jan	Chester	H	4-4
LC	29 Jan	Sheffield United	A	1-5		LC	29 Jan	WBA	H	3-3		LC	29 Jan	Chester	A	1-6
LC	5 Feb	Doncaster R	H	4-0		LC	5 Feb	Aston Villa	A	0-4		LC	5 Feb	Liverpool	H	1-3
LC	12 Feb	Doncaster R	A	2-3		LC	12 Feb	Aston Villa	H	2-0		LC	12 Feb	Liverpool	A	0-8
LC	19 Feb	Grimsby T	H	5-1		LC	19 Feb	Northampton T	H	2-0		LC	19 Feb	Wrexham	A	2-5
LC	26 Feb	Grimsby T	A	1-4		LC	26 Feb	Northampton T	A	2-1		LC	26 Feb	Wrexham	H	0-1
	4 Mar	Huddersfield T	A	0-4		LC	4 Mar	Derby Co	A	1-2		CB	4 Mar	Chester	H	5-9
	11 Mar	Huddersfield T	H	2-0		LC	11 Mar	Derby Co	H	3-0		CB	11 Mar	Chester	A	1-4
	18 Mar	Bradford City	A	3-3		LC	18 Mar	Aston Villa	H	1-2			25 Mar	Derby Co	A	0-4
	25 Mar	Bradford City	H	4-3		LC	25 Mar	Aston Villa	A	1-2			1 Apr	Stockport Co	A	1-3
	1 Apr	Leeds U	H	1-3		MC	1 Apr	Nottingham F	A	1-4			8 Apr	Stockport Co	H	1-2
	8 Apr	Leeds U	A	0-1		MC	8 Apr	Nottingham F	H	3-1			10 Apr	Stoke C	H	1-6
	10 Apr	Doncaster R	A	1-1			10 Apr	Birmingham	H	0-3			29 Apr	Wrexham	A	0-4
	15 Apr	York C	H	2-0			15 Apr	Leicester C	A	1-1			6 May	Wrexham	H	1-5
	22 Apr	York C	A	1-1			22 Apr	Leicester C	H	6-2						
							29 Apr	Notts County	A	4-1						
							6 May	Notts County	H	8-2						

KEY: LC=League Cup; WC=League West Cup; La=Lancashire Cup; MC=Midland Cup;
CC=Combined Counties Cup; Li=Liverpool Senior Cup; TT=Tyne, Wear & Tees Cup; CB=Cheshire Bowl

The Football League 1943-44

NORTH (SECOND CHAMPIONSHIP)
Including League Cup and county cup matches

DARLINGTON

LC	26 Dec	Gateshead	H	5-0
LC	1 Jan	Gateshead	A	1-2
LC	8 Jan	Sunderland	H	5-1
LC	15 Jan	Sunderland	A	5-1
LC	22 Jan	Middlesbrough	A	1-0
LC	29 Jan	Middlesbrough	H	0-0
LC	5 Feb	Hartlepools U	A	1-2
LC	12 Feb	Hartlepools U	H	2-4
LC	19 Feb	Newcastle U	A	0-2
LC	26 Feb	Newcastle U	H	8-2
LC	4 Mar	Gateshead	A	2-1
LC	11 Mar	Gateshead	H	1-1
LC	18 Mar	Newcastle U	H	2-0
LC	25 Mar	Newcastle U	A	1-4
	1 Apr	Middlesbrough	H	2-3
TT	8 Apr	Middlesbrough	A	4-1
TT	10 Apr	Middlesbrough	A	3-2
TT	15 Apr	Gateshead	A	0-1
TT	22 Apr	Gateshead	H	4-0
TT	29 Apr	Newcastle U	H	2-3
TT	6 May	Newcastle U	A	0-1

6 May, aet 1-1

DERBY COUNTY

LC	26 Dec	Nottingham F	H	2-1
LC	1 Jan	Nottingham F	A	1-1
LC	8 Jan	Leicester C	H	0-1
LC	15 Jan	Leicester C	A	0-1
LC	22 Jan	Sheffield Wed	A	1-3
LC	29 Jan	Sheffield Wed	H	4-1
LC	5 Feb	Notts County	A	2-0
LC	12 Feb	Notts County	H	7-3
LC	19 Feb	Mansfield T	H	0-1
LC	26 Feb	Mansfield T	A	3-2
LC	4 Mar	Coventry C	H	2-1
LC	11 Mar	Coventry C	A	0-3
	18 Mar	Leeds U	H	2-2
	25 Mar	Crewe Alex	H	4-0
MC	1 Apr	Stoke C	H	1-3
MC	8 Apr	Stoke C	A	1-1
	10 Apr	Chesterfield	H	1-1
	15 Apr	Rotherham U	A	2-0
	22 Apr	Rotherham U	H	0-0
	29 Apr	Leicester C	H	0-2
	6 May	Leicester C	A	0-1

DONCASTER ROVERS

LC	26 Dec	Grimsby T	H	1-0
LC	1 Jan	Grimsby T	A	1-1
LC	8 Jan	Lincoln C	A	5-4
LC	22 Jan	Rotherham U	H	1-2
LC	29 Jan	Rotherham U	A	2-2
LC	5 Feb	Chesterfield	A	0-4
LC	12 Feb	Chesterfield	H	3-2
LC	19 Feb	Sheffield Utd	H	1-2
LC	26 Feb	Sheffield Utd	A	0-7
	4 Mar	Lincoln C	H	6-1
	11 Mar	Lincoln C	A	7-2
SC	18 Mar	Barnsley	H	1-1
SC	25 Mar	Barnsley	A	0-1
	1 Apr	Notts County	H	6-0
	8 Apr	Notts County	A	1-0
	15 Apr	Bradford	A	4-3
	22 Apr	Bradford	H	3-1

EVERTON

LC	26 Dec	Chester	A	5-3
LC	1 Jan	Chester	H	7-0
LC	8 Jan	Crewe Alex	A	9-1
LC	15 Jan	Crewe Alex	H	6-2
LC	22 Jan	Liverpool	A	4-1
LC	29 Jan	Liverpool	H	2-3
LC	5 Feb	Wrexham	H	2-3
LC	12 Feb	Wrexham	A	1-2
LC	19 Feb	Tranmere R	A	1-0
LC	26 Feb	Tranmere R	H	5-1
LC	4 Mar	Blackpool	A	1-7
LC	11 Mar	Blackpool	H	1-3
La	18 Mar	Chester	H	5-2
La	25 Mar	Chester	A	9-2
Li	1 Apr	Tranmere R	A	5-0
Li	8 Apr	Tranmere R	H	4-0
La	10 Apr	Liverpool	H	3-0
La	15 Apr	Liverpool	A	0-3
La	22 Apr	Liverpool	A	2-4
	29 Apr	Bury	A	0-1
Li	6 May	Southport	A	1-1

GATESHEAD

LC	26 Dec	Darlington	A	0-5
LC	1 Jan	Darlington	H	2-1
LC	8 Jan	Middlesbrough	H	2-1
LC	15 Jan	Middlesbrough	A	2-4
LC	22 Jan	Newcastle U	A	1-2
LC	29 Jan	Newcastle U	H	1-3
LC	5 Feb	Sunderland	H	7-4
LC	12 Feb	Sunderland	A	4-1
LC	19 Feb	Hartlepools U	A	6-5
LC	26 Feb	Hartlepools U	H	2-2
	4 Mar	Darlington	H	1-2
	11 Mar	Darlington	A	1-1
	18 Mar	Middlesbrough	H	2-1
	25 Mar	Middlesbrough	A	1-4
TT	1 Apr	Hartlepools U	H	3-2
TT	8 Apr	Hartlepools U	A	3-3
	10 Apr	Sunderland	A	1-1
TT	15 Apr	Darlington	H	1-0
TT	22 Apr	Darlington	A	0-4
	29 Apr	Halifax T	H	3-1
	6 May	Halifax T	A	2-6

GRIMSBY TOWN

LC	26 Dec	Doncaster R	A	0-1
LC	1 Jan	Doncaster R	H	1-1
LC	8 Jan	Sheffield Utd	H	2-0
LC	15 Jan	Sheffield Utd	A	1-3
LC	22 Jan	Lincoln C	A	3-1
LC	29 Jan	Lincoln C	H	3-0
LC	5 Feb	Rotherham U	H	2-1
LC	12 Feb	Rotherham U	A	1-6
LC	19 Feb	Chesterfield	A	1-5
LC	26 Feb	Chesterfield	H	4-1
LC	4 Mar	Rotherham U	A	2-2
LC	11 Mar	Rotherham U	H	2-1
LC	18 Mar	Sheffield Utd	A	0-4
LC	25 Mar	Sheffield Utd	H	0-1
	10 Apr	Lincoln C	A	1-1

**KEY: LC=League Cup; WC=League West Cup; La=Lancashire Cup; MC=Midland Cup;
CC=Combined Counties Cup; Li=Liverpool Senior Cup; TT=Tyne, Wear & Tees Cup; CB=Cheshire Bowl**

The Football League 1943-44

NORTH (SECOND CHAMPIONSHIP)
Including League Cup and county cup matches

HALIFAX TOWN

LC	26 Dec	Manchester Utd	A	2-6
LC	1 Jan	Manchester Utd	H	1-1
LC	8 Jan	Bury	H	2-0
LC	15 Jan	Bury	A	0-0
LC	22 Jan	Stockport Co	H	0-1
LC	29 Jan	Stockport Co	A	3-4
LC	5 Feb	Oldham Ath	A	3-1
LC	12 Feb	Oldham Ath	H	0-3
LC	19 Feb	Manchester City	H	3-5
LC	26 Feb	Manchester City	A	0-4
	4 Mar	Bradford City	H	4-2
	11 Mar	Bradford City	A	3-1
	18 Mar	Huddersfield T	A	1-2
	25 Mar	Huddersfield T	H	4-1
CC	1 Apr	York C	H	4-1
CC	8 Apr	York C	A	1-1
CC	15 Apr	Leeds U	A	2-2
CC	22 Apr	Leeds U	H	5-2
CC	29 Apr	Huddersfield T	A	4-1
CC	6 May	Huddersfield T	H	2-4

HARTLEPOOLS UNITED

LC	26 Dec	Middlesbrough	A	1-1
LC	1 Jan	Middlesbrough	H	1-1
LC	8 Jan	Newcastle U	H	1-2
LC	15 Jan	Newcastle U	A	1-5
LC	22 Jan	Sunderland	A	4-3
LC	29 Jan	Sunderland	H	4-2
LC	5 Feb	Darlington	H	2-1
LC	12 Feb	Darlington	A	4-2
LC	19 Feb	Gateshead	H	5-6
LC	26 Feb	Gateshead	A	2-2
LC	4 Mar	Newcastle U	H	3-1
LC	11 Mar	Newcastle U	A	0-3
	18 Mar	Sunderland	A	0-3
	25 Mar	Sunderland	H	2-1
TT	1 Apr	Gateshead	A	2-3
TT	8 Apr	Gateshead	H	3-3
	15 Apr	Middlesbrough	H	5-6
	22 Apr	Middlesbrough	A	5-0
	29 Apr	Gateshead	A	1-3
	6 May	Gateshead	H	6-2

HUDDERSFIELD TOWN

LC	26 Dec	York C	A	1-2
LC	1 Jan	York C	H	0-3
LC	8 Jan	Bradford	H	1-2
LC	15 Jan	Bradford	A	1-1
LC	22 Jan	Leeds U	H	4-1
LC	29 Jan	Leeds U	A	0-2
LC	5 Feb	Barnsley	H	2-2
LC	12 Feb	Barnsley	A	1-4
LC	19 Feb	Bradford City	H	2-0
LC	26 Feb	Bradford City	A	4-2
LC	4 Mar	Chesterfield	H	4-0
LC	11 Mar	Chesterfield	A	0-2
	18 Mar	Halifax T	H	2-1
	25 Mar	Halifax T	A	1-4
CC	1 Apr	Bradford City	A	0-3
CC	8 Apr	Bradford City	H	5-0
	10 Apr	Sheffield Wed	A	2-2
CC	15 Apr	Sheffield Wed	A	1-2
CC	22 Apr	Sheffield Wed	H	5-1
CC	29 Apr	Halifax T	H	1-4
CC	6 May	Halifax T	A	4-2

LEEDS UNITED

LC	26 Dec	Bradford	A	1-2
LC	1 Jan	Bradford	H	2-1
LC	8 Jan	Barnsley	H	2-0
LC	15 Jan	Barnsley	A	2-3
LC	22 Jan	Huddersfield T	A	1-4
LC	29 Jan	Huddersfield T	H	2-0
LC	5 Feb	Bradford City	A	3-3
LC	12 Feb	Bradford City	H	2-0
LC	19 Feb	York C	H	2-1
LC	26 Feb	York C	A	1-8
LC	4 Mar	Sheffield Utd	A	1-3
LC	11 Mar	Sheffield Utd	H	1-0
	18 Mar	Derby Co	H	2-2
CC	1 Apr	Chesterfield	A	3-1
CC	8 Apr	Chesterfield	H	1-0
	10 Apr	Rotherham U	A	3-5
CC	15 Apr	Halifax T	H	2-2
CC	22 Apr	Halifax T	A	2-5

LEICESTER CITY

LC	26 Dec	Notts County	A	2-1
LC	1 Jan	Notts County	H	7-2
LC	8 Jan	Derby Co	A	1-0
LC	15 Jan	Derby Co	H	1-0
LC	22 Jan	Mansfield T	H	5-2
LC	29 Jan	Mansfield T	A	1-1
LC	5 Feb	Sheffield Wed	H	1-1
LC	12 Feb	Sheffield Wed	A	3-0
LC	19 Feb	Nottingham F	A	0-1
LC	26 Feb	Nottingham F	H	1-1
LC	4 Mar	Birmingham	A	1-3
LC	11 Mar	Birmingham	H	2-0
	18 Mar	Stoke C	A	5-2
	25 Mar	Stoke C	A	2-2
MC	1 Apr	Northampton T	H	0-2
MC	8 Apr	Northampton T	A	1-3
	10 Apr	Wolverhampton	A	1-4
	15 Apr	Coventry C	H	1-1
	22 Apr	Coventry C	A	2-6
	29 Apr	Derby Co	A	2-0
	6 May	Derby Co	H	1-0

11 Mar, aet 2-1

LINCOLN CITY

LC	26 Dec	Mansfield T	A	1-2
LC	1 Jan	Mansfield T	H	3-2
LC	8 Jan	Doncaster R	H	4-5
LC	22 Jan	Grimsby T	H	1-3
LC	29 Jan	Grimsby T	A	0-3
LC	5 Feb	Sheffield Utd	A	2-6
LC	12 Feb	Sheffield Utd	H	0-0
LC	19 Feb	Rotherham U	H	2-4
LC	26 Feb	Rotherham U	A	1-6
	4 Mar	Doncaster R	A	1-6
	11 Mar	Doncaster R	H	2-7
	18 Mar	Mansfield T	A	0-4
	25 Mar	Mansfield T	H	3-0
	1 Apr	Sheffield Wed	H	2-1
	8 Apr	Sheffield Wed	A	0-2
	10 Apr	Grimsby T	H	1-1
	15 Apr	Bradford City	H	0-1
	22 Apr	Bradford City	A	2-3

KEY: LC=League Cup; WC=League West Cup; La=Lancashire Cup; MC=Midland Cup;
CC=Combined Counties Cup; Li=Liverpool Senior Cup; TT=Tyne, Wear & Tees Cup; CB=Cheshire Bowl

The Football League 1943-44

LIVERPOOL

LC	26 Dec	Wrexham	H	4-0
LC	1 Jan	Wrexham	A	2-4
LC	8 Jan	Tranmere R	A	6-1
LC	15 Jan	Tranmere R	H	5-1
LC	22 Jan	Everton	H	1-4
LC	29 Jan	Everton	A	3-2
LC	5 Feb	Crewe Alex	A	3-1
LC	12 Feb	Crewe Alex	H	8-0
LC	19 Feb	Chester	H	4-2
LC	26 Feb	Chester	A	0-6
LC	4 Mar	Oldham Ath	H	8-1
LC	11 Mar	Oldham Ath	A	0-1
LC	18 Mar	Manchester City	A	1-1
LC	25 Mar	Manchester City	H	2-2
La	1 Apr	Southport	H	6-2
La	8 Apr	Southport	A	7-4
La	10 Apr	Everton	A	0-3
La	15 Apr	Everton	H	3-0
La	22 Apr	Everton	H	4-2
La	29 Apr	Blackburn R	H	1-0
La	6 May	Bolton W	H	3-1

25 Mar, aet 2-3

LOVELL'S ATHLETIC

LC	26 Dec	Aberaman Ath	H	4-1
LC	1 Jan	Aberaman Ath	A	5-0
LC	8 Jan	Bristol City	H	3-3
LC	15 Jan	Bristol City	A	0-1
LC	22 Jan	Swansea T	H	11-2
LC	29 Jan	Swansea T	A	4-1
LC	5 Feb	Bath C	A	1-5
LC	12 Feb	Bath C	H	2-0
LC	19 Feb	Cardiff C	A	0-2
LC	26 Feb	Cardiff C	H	2-1
LC	4 Mar	Cardiff C	H	2-0
LC	11 Mar	Cardiff C	A	0-1
LC	18 Mar	Bath C	H	1-3
LC	25 Mar	Bath C	A	0-3
WC	1 Apr	Swansea T	A	1-2
WC	8 Apr	Swansea T	H	5-1
WC	10 Apr	Cardiff C	A	1-1
WC	15 Apr	Cardiff C	H	2-0
WC	22 Apr	Bristol City	A	1-2
WC	29 Apr	Bristol City	H	2-1

MANCHESTER CITY

LC	26 Dec	Bury	A	4-0
LC	1 Jan	Bury	H	1-7
LC	8 Jan	Oldham Ath	H	0-0
LC	15 Jan	Oldham Ath	A	1-1
LC	22 Jan	Manchester Utd	A	3-1
LC	29 Jan	Manchester Utd	H	2-3
LC	5 Feb	Stockport Co	H	4-0
LC	12 Feb	Stockport Co	A	3-4
LC	19 Feb	Halifax T	A	5-2
LC	26 Feb	Halifax T	H	4-0
LC	4 Mar	Blackburn R	H	3-0
LC	11 Mar	Blackburn R	A	0-3
LC	18 Mar	Liverpool	H	1-1
LC	25 Mar	Liverpool	A	2-2
LC	1 Apr	Birmingham	H	1-0
LC	8 Apr	Birmingham	A	0-0
	10 Apr	Manchester Utd	H	4-1
LC	15 Apr	Blackpool	A	1-1
LC	22 Apr	Blackpool	H	1-2
	29 Apr	Bradford	A	0-5
	6 May	Bradford	H	2-1

11 Mar, aet 2-4
25 Mar, aet 3-2

MANCHESTER UNITED

LC	26 Dec	Halifax T	H	6-2
LC	1 Jan	Halifax T	A	1-1
LC	8 Jan	Stockport Co	A	3-2
LC	15 Jan	Stockport Co	H	4-2
LC	22 Jan	Manchester City	H	1-3
LC	29 Jan	Manchester City	A	3-2
LC	5 Feb	Bury	A	3-0
LC	12 Feb	Bury	H	3-3
LC	19 Feb	Oldham Ath	H	3-2
LC	26 Feb	Oldham Ath	A	1-1
	4 Mar	Wrexham	A	4-1
	11 Mar	Wrexham	H	2-2
	18 Mar	Birmingham	A	1-3
	25 Mar	Birmingham	H	1-1
La	1 Apr	Bolton W	A	0-3
La	8 Apr	Bolton W	H	3-2
	10 Apr	Manchester City	A	1-4
	15 Apr	Burnley	H	9-0
	22 Apr	Burnley	A	3-3
	29 Apr	Oldham Ath	A	0-0
	6 May	Oldham Ath	A	3-1

MANSFIELD TOWN

LC	26 Dec	Lincoln C	H	2-1
LC	1 Jan	Lincoln C	A	2-3
LC	8 Jan	Notts County	A	0-5
LC	15 Jan	Notts County	H	1-0
LC	22 Jan	Leicester C	A	2-5
LC	29 Jan	Leicester C	H	1-1
LC	5 Feb	Nottingham F	H	0-1
LC	12 Feb	Nottingham F	A	1-0
LC	19 Feb	Derby Co	A	1-0
LC	26 Feb	Derby Co	H	2-3
	18 Mar	Lincoln C	H	4-0
	25 Mar	Lincoln C	A	0-3
	15 Apr	Notts County	H	5-0
	22 Apr	Notts County	A	2-3

MIDDLESBROUGH

LC	26 Dec	Hartlepools U	H	1-1
LC	1 Jan	Hartlepools U	A	1-1
LC	8 Jan	Gateshead	A	1-2
LC	15 Jan	Gateshead	H	4-2
LC	22 Jan	Darlington	A	0-1
LC	29 Jan	Darlington	H	0-0
LC	5 Feb	Newcastle U	H	2-1
LC	12 Feb	Newcastle U	A	1-4
LC	19 Feb	Sunderland	A	0-3
LC	26 Feb	Sunderland	H	4-5
	4 Mar	Sunderland	A	1-4
	11 Mar	Sunderland	H	2-3
	18 Mar	Gateshead	A	1-2
	25 Mar	Gateshead	H	4-1
TT	1 Apr	Darlington	A	3-2
TT	8 Apr	Darlington	H	1-4
	15 Apr	Hartlepools U	A	6-2
	22 Apr	Hartlepools U	H	0-5
	29 Apr	Sunderland	A	3-3
	6 May	Sunderland	H	4-2

KEY: LC=League Cup; WC=League West Cup; La=Lancashire Cup; MC=Midland Cup;
CC=Combined Counties Cup; Li=Liverpool Senior Cup; TT=Tyne, Wear & Tees Cup; CB=Cheshire Bowl

The Football League 1943-44

NORTH (SECOND CHAMPIONSHIP)
Including League Cup and county cup matches

NEWCASTLE UNITED

LC	26 Dec	Sunderland	H	4-2
LC	1 Jan	Sunderland	A	0-3
LC	8 Jan	Hartlepools U	A	2-1
LC	15 Jan	Hartlepools U	H	5-1
LC	22 Jan	Gateshead	H	2-1
LC	29 Jan	Gateshead	A	3-1
LC	5 Feb	Middlesbrough	A	1-2
LC	12 Feb	Middlesbrough	H	4-1
LC	19 Feb	Darlington	H	2-0
LC	26 Feb	Darlington	A	2-8
LC	4 Mar	Hartlepools U	A	1-3
LC	11 Mar	Hartlepools U	H	3-0
LC	18 Mar	Darlington	A	0-2
LC	25 Mar	Darlington	H	4-1
	1 Apr	Sheffield Utd	A	0-4
	8 Apr	Sheffield Utd	H	3-1
TT	15 Apr	Sunderland	A	3-0
TT	22 Apr	Sunderland	H	5-2
TT	29 Apr	Darlington	A	3-2
TT	6 May	Darlington	H	0-1

6 May, aet 1-1

NORTHAMPTON TOWN

LC	26 Dec	Aston Villa	A	1-2
LC	1 Jan	Aston Villa	H	1-2
LC	8 Jan	Birmingham	A	1-5
LC	22 Jan	Walsall	A	0-3
LC	29 Jan	Walsall	H	2-0
LC	5 Feb	WBA	H	2-0
LC	12 Feb	WBA	A	1-3
LC	19 Feb	Coventry C	A	0-2
LC	26 Feb	Coventry C	H	1-2
	4 Mar	Wolverhampton	A	4-1
	11 Mar	Wolverhampton	H	1-2
MC	18 Mar	Notts County	A	4-1
MC	25 Mar	Notts County	H	4-1
MC	1 Apr	Leicester C	A	2-0
MC	8 Apr	Leicester C	H	3-1
MC	15 Apr	Nottingham F	A	0-5
MC	22 Apr	Nottingham F	H	3-1
	29 Apr	Birmingham	A	1-3
	6 May	Birmingham	H	0-5

NOTTINGHAM FOREST

LC	26 Dec	Derby Co	A	1-2
LC	1 Jan	Derby Co	H	1-1
LC	8 Jan	Sheffield Wed	A	0-0
LC	22 Jan	Notts County	H	0-2
LC	29 Jan	Notts County	A	3-0
LC	5 Feb	Mansfield T	A	1-0
LC	12 Feb	Mansfield T	H	0-1
LC	19 Feb	Leicester C	H	1-0
LC	26 Feb	Leicester C	A	1-1
	4 Mar	WBA	A	1-0
	11 Mar	WBA	H	3-2
	18 Mar	Walsall	A	0-0
	25 Mar	Walsall	H	2-0
MC	1 Apr	Coventry C	A	4-1
MC	8 Apr	Coventry C	A	1-3
	10 Apr	Notts County	H	3-0
MC	15 Apr	Northampton T	H	5-0
MC	22 Apr	Northampton T	A	1-3
MC	29 Apr	WBA	A	2-2
MC	6 May	WBA	H	2-2

6 May, aet 3-4

NOTTS COUNTY

LC	26 Dec	Leicester C	H	1-2
LC	1 Jan	Leicester C	A	2-7
LC	8 Jan	Mansfield T	H	5-0
LC	15 Jan	Mansfield T	A	0-1
LC	22 Jan	Nottingham F	A	2-0
LC	29 Jan	Nottingham F	A	0-3
LC	5 Feb	Derby Co	H	0-2
LC	12 Feb	Derby Co	A	3-7
LC	19 Feb	Sheffield Wed	A	0-2
LC	26 Feb	Sheffield Wed	H	1-5
LC	11 Mar	Walsall	A	1-2
MC	18 Mar	Northampton T	H	1-4
MC	25 Mar	Northampton T	A	1-4
	1 Apr	Doncaster R	A	0-6
	8 Apr	Doncaster R	H	0-1
	10 Apr	Nottingham F	A	0-3
	15 Apr	Mansfield T	A	0-5
	22 Apr	Mansfield T	H	3-2
	29 Apr	Coventry C	H	1-4
	6 May	Coventry C	A	2-8

OLDHAM ATHLETIC

LC	26 Dec	Stoke C	A	1-2
LC	1 Jan	Stoke C	A	5-1
LC	8 Jan	Manchester City	A	0-0
LC	15 Jan	Manchester City	H	1-1
LC	22 Jan	Bury	A	7-3
LC	29 Jan	Bury	H	3-0
LC	5 Feb	Halifax T	H	1-3
LC	12 Feb	Halifax T	A	3-0
LC	19 Feb	Manchester Utd	A	2-3
LC	26 Feb	Manchester Utd	H	1-1
LC	4 Mar	Liverpool	A	1-8
LC	11 Mar	Liverpool	H	1-0
La	1 Apr	Rochdale	A	0-4
La	8 Apr	Rochdale	H	0-2
	10 Apr	Tranmere R	H	0-3
	15 Apr	Tranmere R	A	1-2
	29 Apr	Manchester Utd	A	0-0
	6 May	Manchester Utd	H	1-3

ROCHDALE

LC	26 Dec	Bolton W	H	5-0
LC	1 Jan	Bolton W	A	2-2
LC	8 Jan	Blackburn R	A	1-3
LC	15 Jan	Blackburn R	H	4-0
LC	22 Jan	Burnley	A	2-2
LC	29 Jan	Burnley	H	3-1
LC	5 Feb	Southport	H	0-0
LC	12 Feb	Southport	A	4-2
LC	19 Feb	Blackpool	A	0-2
LC	26 Feb	Blackpool	H	0-2
LC	4 Mar	Burnley	A	3-3
LC	11 Mar	Burnley	H	1-1
LC	18 Mar	Blackpool	A	0-8
LC	25 Mar	Blackpool	H	2-1
La	1 Apr	Oldham Ath	H	4-0
La	8 Apr	Oldham Ath	A	2-0
La	10 Apr	Stockport Co	H	1-4
La	15 Apr	Stockport Co	A	2-3
	22 Apr	Tranmere R	A	0-1
	29 Apr	Tranmere R	H	4-1

11 Mar, aet 2-1

KEY: LC=League Cup; WC=League West Cup; La=Lancashire Cup; MC=Midland Cup;
CC=Combined Counties Cup; Li=Liverpool Senior Cup; TT=Tyne, Wear & Tees Cup; CB=Cheshire Bowl

The Football League 1943-44

NORTH (SECOND CHAMPIONSHIP)
Including League Cup and county cup matches

ROTHERHAM UNITED

LC	26 Dec	Sheffield Utd	A	1-4
LC	1 Jan	Sheffield Utd	H	7-2
LC	8 Jan	Chesterfield	H	1-1
LC	15 Jan	Chesterfield	A	2-1
LC	22 Jan	Doncaster R	A	2-1
LC	29 Jan	Doncaster R	H	2-2
LC	5 Feb	Grimsby T	A	1-2
LC	12 Feb	Grimsby T	H	6-1
LC	19 Feb	Lincoln C	A	4-2
LC	26 Feb	Lincoln C	H	6-1
	4 Mar	Grimsby T	H	2-2
	11 Mar	Grimsby T	A	1-2
	18 Mar	Sheffield Wed	H	3-1
	25 Mar	Sheffield Wed	A	0-0
SC	1 Apr	Barnsley	A	4-1
SC	8 Apr	Barnsley	H	3-0
	10 Apr	Leeds U	H	5-3
	15 Apr	Derby Co	H	02
	22 Apr	Derby Co	A	0-0
SC	29 Apr	Sheffield Utd	H	1-1
SC	6 May	Sheffield Utd	A	3-2

SHEFFIELD UNITED

LC	26 Dec	Rotherham U	H	4-1
LC	1 Jan	Rotherham U	A	2-7
LC	8 Jan	Grimsby T	A	0-2
LC	15 Jan	Grimsby T	H	3-1
LC	22 Jan	Chesterfield	A	4-1
LC	29 Jan	Chesterfield	H	5-1
LC	5 Feb	Lincoln C	H	6-2
LC	12 Feb	Lincoln C	A	0-0
LC	19 Feb	Doncaster R	A	2-1
LC	26 Feb	Doncaster R	H	7-0
LC	4 Mar	Leeds U	H	3-1
LC	11 Mar	Leeds U	A	0-1
LC	18 Mar	Grimsby T	H	4-0
LC	25 Mar	Grimsby T	A	1-0
LC	1 Apr	Newcastle U	H	4-0
LC	8 Apr	Newcastle U	A	1-3
	10 Apr	Barnsley	A	1-5
LC	15 Apr	Aston Villa	A	2-3
LC	22 Apr	Aston Villa	H	2-2
SC	29 Apr	Rotherham U	A	0-1
SC	6 May	Rotherham U	H	2-3

SHEFFIELD WEDNESDAY

LC	26 Dec	Chesterfield	A	2-0
LC	1 Jan	Chesterfield	H	3-1
LC	8 Jan	Nottingham F	H	0-0
LC	22 Jan	Derby Co	H	3-1
LC	29 Jan	Derby Co	A	1-4
LC	5 Feb	Leicester C	A	1-1
LC	12 Feb	Leicester C	H	0-3
LC	19 Feb	Notts County	H	2-0
LC	26 Feb	Notts County	A	5-1
LC	4 Mar	Bradford	A	0-5
LC	11 Mar	Bradford	H	1-2
	18 Mar	Rotherham U	A	1-3
	25 Mar	Rotherham U	H	0-0
	1 Apr	Lincoln C	A	1-2
	8 Apr	Lincoln C	H	2-0
	10 Apr	Huddersfield T	H	2-2
CC	15 Apr	Huddersfield T	H	2-1
CC	22 Apr	Huddersfield T	A	1-5
	29 Apr	York C	H	2-1
	6 May	York C	A	3-4

SOUTHPORT

LC	26 Dec	Burnley	A	2-2
LC	1 Jan	Burnley	H	4-1
LC	8 Jan	Blackpool	H	1-4
LC	15 Jan	Blackpool	A	1-2
LC	22 Jan	Blackburn R	H	1-2
LC	29 Jan	Blackburn R	A	0-5
LC	5 Feb	Rochdale	A	0-0
LC	12 Feb	Rochdale	H	2-4
LC	19 Feb	Bolton W	A	1-5
LC	26 Feb	Bolton W	H	2-0
	4 Mar	Tranmere R	A	0-4
	11 Mar	Tranmere R	H	2-3
	18 Mar	Bury	A	1-3
	25 Mar	Bury	H	4-2
La	1 Apr	Liverpool	A	2-6
La	8 Apr	Liverpool	H	4-7
	15 Apr	Wrexham	A	3-8
	22 Apr	Wrexham	H	1-4
	29 Apr	Chester	H	3-4
	6 May	Everton	H	1-1

STOCKPORT COUNTY

LC	26 Dec	Oldham Ath	A	2-1
LC	1 Jan	Oldham Ath	H	1-5
LC	8 Jan	Manchester Utd	H	2-3
LC	15 Jan	Manchester Utd	A	2-4
LC	22 Jan	Halifax T	A	1-0
LC	29 Jan	Halifax T	H	4-3
LC	5 Feb	Manchester City	A	0-4
LC	12 Feb	Manchester City	H	4-3
LC	19 Feb	Bury	H	5-1
LC	26 Feb	Bury	A	2-4
CB	18 Mar	Tranmere R	H	4-0
CB	25 Mar	Tranmere R	A	1-4
	1 Apr	Crewe Alex	H	3-1
	8 Apr	Crewe Alex	A	2-1
La	10 Apr	Rochdale	A	4-1
La	15 Apr	Rochdale	H	3-2
La	22 Apr	Bolton W	A	2-4
La	29 Apr	Bolton W	H	1-2
CB	6 May	Chester	A	1-6

SUNDERLAND

LC	26 Dec	Newcastle U	A	2-4
LC	1 Jan	Newcastle U	H	3-0
LC	8 Jan	Darlington	A	1-5
LC	15 Jan	Darlington	H	1-5
LC	22 Jan	Hartlepools U	H	3-4
LC	29 Jan	Hartlepools U	A	2-4
LC	5 Feb	Gateshead	A	4-7
LC	12 Feb	Gateshead	H	1-4
LC	19 Feb	Middlesbrough	H	3-0
LC	26 Feb	Middlesbrough	A	5-4
	4 Mar	Middlesbrough	H	4-1
	11 Mar	Middlesbrough	A	3-2
	18 Mar	Hartlepools U	H	3-0
	25 Mar	Hartlepools U	A	1-2
	10 Apr	Gateshead	H	1-1
TT	15 Apr	Newcastle U	H	0-3
TT	22 Apr	Newcastle U	A	2-5
	29 Apr	Middlesbrough	H	3-3
	6 May	Middlesbrough	A	2-4

KEY: LC=League Cup; WC=League West Cup; La=Lancashire Cup; MC=Midland Cup;
CC=Combined Counties Cup; Li=Liverpool Senior Cup; TT=Tyne, Wear & Tees Cup; CB=Cheshire Bowl

The Football League 1943-44

NORTH (SECOND CHAMPIONSHIP)
Including League Cup and county cup matches

		SWANSEA TOWN		
LC	26 Dec	Bristol City	H	1-1
LC	1 Jan	Bristol City	A	1-2
LC	8 Jan	Cardiff City	A	1-7
LC	15 Jan	Cardiff City	H	1-2
LC	22 Jan	Lovell's Ath	A	2-11
LC	29 Jan	Lovell's Ath	H	1-4
LC	5 Feb	Aberaman Ath	H	6-1
LC	12 Feb	Aberaman Ath	A	4-2
LC	19 Feb	Bath C	A	0-3
LC	26 Feb	Bath C	H	2-5
WC	4 Mar	Aberaman Ath	H	4-0
WC	11 Mar	Aberaman Ath	A	3-2
WC	18 Mar	Bristol City	H	5-4
WC	25 Mar	Bristol City	A	3-3
WC	1 Apr	Lovell's Ath	H	2-1
WC	8 Apr	Lovell's Ath	A	1-5
WC	10 Apr	Bath C	H	2-1
WC	15 Apr	Bath C	A	0-6
WC	22 Apr	Cardiff C	H	2-4
WC	29 Apr	Cardiff C	A	1-3

		TRANMERE ROVERS		
LC	26 Dec	Crewe Alex	A	1-6
LC	1 Jan	Crewe Alex	H	3-4
LC	8 Jan	Liverpool	H	1-6
LC	15 Jan	Liverpool	A	1-5
LC	22 Jan	Wrexham	H	0-3
LC	29 Jan	Wrexham	A	0-2
LC	5 Feb	Chester	A	2-6
LC	12 Feb	Chester	H	2-3
LC	19 Feb	Everton	H	0-1
LC	26 Feb	Everton	A	1-5
	4 Mar	Southport	H	4-0
	11 Mar	Southport	A	3-2
CB	18 Mar	Stockport Co	A	0-4
CB	25 Mar	Stockport Co	H	4-1
	1 Apr	Everton	H	0-5
	8 Apr	Everton	A	0-4
	10 Apr	Oldham Ath	A	3-0
	15 Apr	Oldham Ath	H	2-1
	22 Apr	Rochdale	H	1-0
	29 Apr	Rochdale	A	1-4

		WALSALL		
LC	26 Dec	Coventry C	A	0-3
LC	1 Jan	Coventry C	H	3-0
LC	8 Jan	WBA	H	2-2
LC	15 Jan	WBA	A	1-7
LC	22 Jan	Northampton T	H	3-0
LC	29 Jan	Northampton T	A	0-2
LC	5 Feb	Stoke C	A	1-5
LC	12 Feb	Stoke C	H	0-2
LC	19 Feb	Wolverhampton	H	0-0
LC	26 Feb	Wolverhampton	A	1-1
	11 Mar	Notts County	A	2-1
MC	18 Mar	Nottingham F	H	0-0
MC	25 Mar	Nottingham F	A	0-2
	1 Apr	WBA	H	2-2
	8 Apr	WBA	A	0-1
	15 Apr	Birmingham	H	2-2
	22 Apr	Birmingham	A	0-5

		WEST BROMWICH ALBION		
LC	26 Dec	Birmingham	H	1-1
LC	1 Jan	Birmingham	A	0-4
LC	8 Jan	Walsall	A	2-2
LC	15 Jan	Walsall	H	7-1
LC	22 Jan	Coventry C	H	2-2
LC	29 Jan	Coventry C	A	3-3
LC	5 Feb	Northampton T	A	0-2
LC	12 Feb	Northampton T	H	3-1
LC	19 Feb	Stoke C	H	2-8
LC	26 Feb	Stoke C	A	4-5
LC	4 Mar	Nottingham F	H	0-1
LC	11 Mar	Nottingham F	A	2-3
MC	18 Mar	Wolverhampton	H	5-0
MC	25 Mar	Wolverhampton	A	3-3
	1 Apr	Walsall	A	2-2
	8 Apr	Walsall	H	1-0
	10 Apr	Aston Villa	A	1-4
MC	15 Apr	Stoke C	A	1-1
MC	22 Apr	Stoke C	H	3-1
MC	29 Apr	Nottingham F	H	2-2
MC	6 May	Nottingham F	A	2-2

6 May, aet 4-3

		WOLVERHAMPTON WANDERERS		
LC	26 Dec	Stoke C	H	1-1
LC	1 Jan	Stoke C	A	3-9
LC	8 Jan	Coventry C	A	2-3
LC	15 Jan	Coventry C	H	2-2
LC	22 Jan	Aston Villa	H	0-4
LC	29 Jan	Aston Villa	A	1-3
LC	5 Feb	Birmingham	H	0-2
LC	12 Feb	Birmingham	A	1-2
LC	19 Feb	Walsall	A	0-0
LC	26 Feb	Walsall	H	1-1
	4 Mar	Northampton T	H	1-4
	11 Mar	Northampton T	A	2-7
MC	18 Mar	WBA	A	0-5
MC	25 Mar	WBA	H	3-3
	1 Apr	Wrexham	H	0-1
	10 Apr	Leicester C	H	4-1
	15 Apr	Chester	A	3-1
	22 Apr	Chester	H	0-4
	29 Apr	Stoke C	A	2-2
	6 May	Stoke C	H	2-1

		WREXHAM		
LC	26 Dec	Liverpool	A	0-4
LC	1 Jan	Liverpool	H	4-2
LC	8 Jan	Chester	H	3-0
LC	15 Jan	Chester	A	3-1
LC	22 Jan	Tranmere R	A	3-0
LC	29 Jan	Tranmere R	H	2-0
LC	5 Feb	Everton	A	3-2
LC	12 Feb	Everton	H	2-1
LC	19 Feb	Crewe Alex	H	5-2
LC	26 Feb	Crewe Alex	A	1-0
LC	4 Mar	Manchester Utd	H	1-4
LC	11 Mar	Manchester Utd	A	2-2
	18 Mar	Bolton W	H	3-3
	25 Mar	Bolton W	A	1-1
	1 Apr	Wolverhampton	A	1-0
	8 Apr	Chester	H	5-0
	10 Apr	Chester A	A	2-2
	15 Apr	Southport	H	8-3
	22 Apr	Southport	A	4-1
	29 Apr	Crewe Alex	H	4-0
	6 May	Crewe Alex	A	5-1

		YORK CITY		
LC	26 Dec	Huddersfield T	H	2-1
LC	1 Jan	Huddersfield t	A	3-0
LC	8 Jan	Bradford City	A	1-4
LC	15 Jan	Bradford City	H	3-1
LC	22 Jan	Barnsley	A	1-2
LC	29 Jan	Barnsley	H	2-0
LC	5 Feb	Bradford	H	0-1
LC	12 Feb	Bradford	A	1-4
LC	19 Feb	Leeds U	A	1-2
LC	26 Feb	Leeds U	H	8-1
LC	4 Mar	Barnsley	H	4-1
LC	11 Mar	Barnsley	A	1-3
LC	18 Mar	Bradford	H	1-5
LC	25 Mar	Bradford	A	1-2
CC	1 Apr	Halifax T	A	1-4
CC	8 Apr	Halifax T	H	1-1
	15 Apr	Chesterfield	A	0-2
	22 Apr	Chesterfield	H	1-1
	29 Apr	Sheffield Wed	A	1-2
	6 May	Sheffield Wed	H	4-3

KEY: LC=League Cup; WC=League West Cup; La=Lancashire Cup; MC=Midland Cup;
CC=Combined Counties Cup; Li=Liverpool Senior Cup; TT=Tyne, Wear & Tees Cup; CB=Cheshire Bowl

The Football League 1943-44

NORTH (SECOND CHAMPIONSHIP)

Final Table

		P	W	D	L	F	A	Pts
1	Bath City	21	16	2	3	78	26	34
2	Wrexham	21	15	4	2	62	29	34
3	Liverpool	21	14	2	5	71	38	30
4	Birmingham	20	12	5	3	47	19	29
5	Rotherham United	21	12	5	4	54	30	29
6	Aston Villa	21	13	3	5	50	34	29
7	Blackpool	20	12	3	5	53	27	27
8	Cardiff City	21	13	1	7	53	28	27
9	Manchester United	21	10	7	4	55	38	27
10	Bradford	20	11	4	5	50	30	26
11	Newcastle United	20	13	0	7	47	36	26
12	Everton	21	12	1	8	73	39	25
13	Stoke City	21	10	5	6	66	45	25
14	Leicester City	21	10	5	6	40	32	25
15	Darlington	21	11	2	8	50	30	24
16	Nottingham Forest	20	9	6	5	32	20	24
17	Sheffield United	21	11	2	8	53	35	24
18	Coventry City	21	10	4	7	48	37	24
19	Manchester City	21	9	6	6	42	35	24
20	Lovell's Athletic	20	10	2	8	48	30	22
21	Gateshead	21	9	4	8	45	53	22
22	Doncaster Rovers	17	9	3	5	42	33	21
23	Derby County	21	8	5	8	33	28	21
24	Rochdale	20	8	5	7	40	36	21
25	Barnsley	17	8	4	5	34	30	20
26	Halifax Town	20	8	4	8	44	42	20
27	Chester	20	9	2	9	65	65	20
28	Hartlepool	20	8	4	8	49	50	20
29	Stockport County	19	10	0	9	44	49	20
30	Sheffield Wednesday	20	8	4	8	32	36	20
31	Blackburn Rovers	16	8	3	5	30	27	19
32	Huddersfield Town	21	8	3	10	41	40	19
33	West Bromwich Albion	21	5	9	7	46	48	19
34	Bolton Wanderers	21	8	3	10	42	49	19
35	Leeds United	18	8	3	7	34	40	19
36	Northampton Town	19	9	0	10	37	39	18
37	Burnley	18	6	6	6	39	42	18
38	Bristol City	20	6	5	9	38	42	17
39	York City	20	7	2	11	37	40	16
40	Middlesbrough	21	6	4	11	41	51	16
41	Swansea Town	20	7	2	11	42	67	16
42	Grimsby Town	15	6	3	6	23	28	15
43	Bury	20	6	3	11	38	55	15
44	Oldham Athletic	18	5	4	9	28	36	14
45	Sunderland	19	6	2	11	44	58	14
46	Chesterfield	19	5	4	10	31	41	14
47	Mansfield Town	14	6	1	7	23	25	13
48	Wolverhampton Wanderers	20	3	6	11	28	56	12
49	Walsall	17	3	6	8	17	35	12
50	Tranmere Rovers	20	6	0	14	29	62	12
51	Bradford City	18	4	2	12	27	47	10
52	Southport	20	3	3	14	35	67	9
53	Lincoln City	18	3	2	13	25	56	8
54	Notts County	20	3	0	17	23	68	6
55	Crewe Alexandra	18	2	1	15	31	83	5
56	Aberaman Athletic	18	1	1	16	20	87	3

The Football League 1943-44

SOUTH

	Aldershot	Arsenal	Brentford	Brighton	Charlton A	Chelsea	Clapton O	C Palace	Fulham	Luton T	Millwall	Portsmouth	QPR	Reading	Southampton	Tottenham H	Watford	West Ham U
Aldershot	X	1 Apr 0-3	12 Feb 4-2		4 Dec 2-1	9 Oct 1-3	22 Apr 0-3	29 Apr 0-6	11 Apr 2-2	1 Sep 3-1	1 Jan 3-1	30 Oct 1-1	8 Jan 3-2	5 Feb 1-3	26 Dec 2-1	27 Nov 10-1	22 Jan 0-1	25 Sep 3-3
Arsenal	6 May 3-1	X	16 Oct 3-3	10 Apr 3-1	27 Nov 6-2	6 Nov 6-0	29 Jan 1-0	8 Apr 5-2	22 Jan 1-1		26 Dec 1-1	18 Sep 1-2	13 Nov 5-0		4 Sep 4-1	22 Apr 3-3	23 Oct 4-2	11 Dec 1-1
Brentford	23 Oct 2-4	5 Feb 4-1	X	11 Sep 2-3		18 Sep 3-1	28 Aug 4-2	10 Apr 2-0	4 Dec 1-1	1 Apr 2-0		13 Nov 2-0	25 Dec 2-5	15 Apr 1-0	18 Dec 7-2	6 Nov 0-2	2 Oct 4-1	29 Jan 2-1
Brighton & HA		25 Sep 1-1	11 Dec 0-2	X	8 Apr 3-3	4 Sep 1-3	18 Sep 2-0	25 Dec 1-3	8 Jan 3-6	22 Jan 8-0	16 Oct 1-2	22 Apr 0-3	23 Oct 3-1	28 Aug 0-4	13 Nov 2-4	29 Jan 0-2		20 Nov 1-2
Charlton Athletic	4 Sep 0-4	28 Aug 1-0		30 Oct 1-4	X	2 Oct 0-1	26 Dec 1-0	X	16 Oct 1-1	13 Nov 8-2	8 Jan 3-5	23 Oct 1-5	20 Nov 1-0	10 Apr 3-1	1 Jan 2-2	11 Dec 0-2	29 Jan 1-1	4 Apr 1-1
Chelsea	29 Jan 8-0	8 Jan 2-0	1 Jan 0-3	4 Dec 0-1	22 Jan 5-2	X		23 Oct 2-1	25 Sep 3-0	16 Oct 6-0	20 Nov 0-1	11 Sep 6-2	28 Aug 1-3	29 Apr 3-1		8 Apr 1-1	22 Apr 2-1	25 Dec 3-3
Clapton Orient	18 Dec 1-3	9 Oct 1-1	27 Nov 1-4	1 Jan 3-0	25 Dec 1-7		X	4 Dec 1-6	20 Nov 1-3	8 Jan 2-1	23 Oct 0-1	2 Oct 1-1	11 Sep 2-3	8 Apr 1-0		13 Nov 0-4	5 Feb 0-0	25 Sep 0-4
Crystal Palace	13 Nov 4-1	30 Oct 1-1	25 Sep 1-1	26 Dec 6-2		12 Feb 1-0	4 Sep 5-2	X	29 Jan 6-2	11 Dec 5-0	22 Apr 2-0	16 Oct 2-3		18 Sep 1-5	6 May 0-0	27 Nov 3-0	8 Jan 1-0	2 Oct 1-6
Fulham	11 Dec 2-2	2 Oct 3-4	4 Sep 4-3	6 Nov 6-2	5 Feb 5-1	10 Apr 2-3	6 May 3-1	9 Oct 4-5	X		27 Nov 4-1	18 Sep 4-1		18 Dec 2-2	12 Feb 6-2	26 Dec 0-2	13 Nov 0-0	30 Oct 2-6
Luton Town	18 Sep 0-2		30 Oct 2-2	2 Oct 2-4	29 Apr 2-5	5 Feb 3-5	6 Nov 2-1	11 Sep 1-2	28 Aug 2-2	X	15 Jan 1-1	6 May 1-1		22 Apr 2-4	9 Apr 2-3	23 Oct 4-2	25 Dec 2-3	4 Dec 0-1
Millwall	8 Apr 2-3	25 Dec 1-5		5 Feb 7-4	6 Nov 5-2	6 May 4-2	12 Feb 5-1	18 Feb 5-1	1 Jan 5-1	25 Sep 2-2	X	4 Dec 1-3	29 Jan 3-4	11 Sep 2-3	22 Jan 1-5		27 Nov 4-3	29 Apr 1-3
Portsmouth	6 Nov 4-1	1 Jan 2-1	29 Apr 3-2	18 Dec 2-3	12 Feb 4-0	11 Dec 1-5	22 Jan 2-1	5 Feb 1-0		20 Nov 4-2	4 Sep 1-5	X	25 Sep 1-1	9 Oct 1-1	26 Dec 4-2		30 Oct 2-3	28 Aug 2-0
Queen's Park Rangers	16 Oct 2-2	29 Apr 1-1	26 Dec 3-2	12 Feb 1-0	6 May 3-3	27 Nov 2-11	11 Dec 6-2		22 Apr 3-3		9 Oct 2-0	10 Apr 1-1	X		22 Jan 2-0	30 Oct 7-0	4 Sep 1-0	8 Jan 3-0
Reading	25 Dec 3-4		6 May 0-3	27 Nov 2-3	25 Sep 1-0	13 Nov 3-2	30 Oct 8-2	1 Jan 0-3		18 Dec 7-2	11 Dec 3-0	29 Jan 1-4	2 Oct 0-0	X	8 Jan 2-3	16 Oct 2-3	4 Sep 8-2	12 Feb 3-2
Southampton	28 Aug 2-2	4 Dec 1-2	22 Apr 2-2	29 Apr 3-0	18 Sep 1-2			20 Nov 2-2	23 Oct 2-3	29 Jan 3-0	2 Oct 1-0	25 Dec 6-3	1 Apr 2-2	6 Nov 5-3	X	15 Jan 2-3	11 Dec 4-1	16 Oct 2-4
Tottenham Hotspur	2 Oct 5-2	18 Dec 2-1	8 Jan 1-0	9 Oct 2-0	11 Sep 4-2	30 Oct 5-1	29 Apr 1-0	28 Aug 1-1	25 Dec 2-0	12 Feb 8-1			4 Dec 2-2	5 Feb 2-2	25 Sep 2-2	X	20 Nov 4-2	1 Jan 1-0
Watford	10 Apr 2-1	12 Feb 0-2	22 Jan 4-4		9 Oct 2-2	18 Dec 1-0	16 Oct 6-1	6 Nov 2-4	29 Apr 3-6	26 Dec 1-2	28 Aug 1-4	1 Apr 1-3	1 Jan 2-2	4 Dec 3-5	11 Sep 6-1	6 May 1-1	X	
West Ham United		11 Sep 2-2	9 Oct 0-0	6 May 6-2	18 Dec 0-1	26 Dec 3-0	10 Apr 3-1	22 Jan 3-0	1 Apr 3-2	4 Sep 3-2	13 Nov 3-0	27 Nov 5-1	6 Nov 1-1	23 Oct 1-0	5 Feb 4-1	18 Sep 3-3		X

Chelsea v Reading on 29 April was played at Reading

Brentford v Reading (0-1), and Aldershot v Arsenal (3-2) on 20 November were both abandoned and replayed at a later date

Charlton Athletic v Reading (2-0) on 15 January was abandoned and replayed at a later date

There were no scheduled matches between the clubs that are blank in the above grid

The Football League 1943-44

SOUTH

Final Table

		P	W	D	L	F	A	Pts
1	Tottenham Hotspur	30	19	8	3	71	36	46
2	West Ham United	30	17	7	6	74	39	41
3	Queen's Park Rangers	30	14	12	4	69	54	40
4	Arsenal	30	14	10	6	72	42	38
5	Crystal Palace	30	16	5	9	75	53	37
6	Portsmouth	30	16	5	9	68	59	37
7	Brentford	30	14	7	9	71	51	35
8	Chelsea	30	16	2	12	79	55	34
9	Fulham	30	11	9	10	80	73	31
10	Millwall	30	13	4	13	70	66	30
11	Aldershot	30	12	6	12	64	73	30
12	Reading	30	12	3	15	73	62	27
13	Southampton	30	10	7	13	67	88	27
14	Charlton Athletic	30	9	7	14	57	73	25
15	Watford	30	6	8	16	58	80	20
16	Brighton & Hove Albion	30	9	2	19	55	82	20
17	Luton Town	30	3	5	22	42	104	11
18	Clapton Orient	30	4	3	23	32	87	11

WEST

	Aberaman Ath	Bath City	Bristol City	Cardiff City	Lovell's Ath	Swansea T
Aberaman Athletic	X	28 Aug 3-2 / 13 Nov 4-3	30 Oct 2-0 / 4 Dec 2-1	16 Oct 1-2	11 Sep 0-1 / 20 Nov 2-4	25 Sep 2-2 / 18 Dec 2-1
Bath City	4 Sep 0-0 / 6 Nov 2-3	X	16 Oct 1-0 / 18 Dec 3-2	2 Oct 3-1 / 27 Nov 2-1	23 Oct 3-1 / 4 Dec 1-0	18 Sep 5-2
Bristol City	23 Oct 2-1 / 11 Dec 3-1	9 Oct 2-4 / 25 Dec 3-1	X	18 Sep 2-1 / 13 Nov 1-1	25 Sep 3-2	4 Sep 6-0 / 20 Nov 3-2
Cardiff City	9 Oct 3-2	25 Sep 7-2 / 20 Nov 3-1	11 Sep 4-1 / 6 Nov 1-0	X	28 Aug 1-2 / 25 Dec 5-1	23 Oct 5-0 / 4 Dec 1-0
Lovell's Athletic	18 Sep 2-3 / 27 Nov 4-1	30 Oct 5-0 / 11 Dec 4-2	2 Oct 6-0	4 Sep 3-1 / 18 Dec 4-1	X	9 Oct 9-0 / 13 Nov 5-2
Swansea Town	2 Oct 1-3 / 25 Dec 2-0	11 Sep 1-6	28 Aug 1-3 / 27 Nov 3-0	30 Oct 1-3 / 11 Dec 2-4	16 Oct 4-2 / 6 Nov 1-7	X

		P	W	D	L	F	A	Pts
1	Lovell's Athletic	18	12	0	6	62	30	24
2	Cardiff City	18	11	1	6	45	28	23
3	Bath City	18	9	1	8	41	42	19
4	Aberaman Athletic	18	8	2	8	32	35	18
5	Bristol City	18	8	1	9	32	36	17
6	Swansea Town	18	3	1	14	25	66	7

Other English Competitions 1943-44

LEAGUE NORTH (WAR) CUP

Qualifying Round Final Table
See League North (Second Championship) for results

		P	W	D	L	F	A	Pts
1	Wrexham	10	9	0	1	26	12	18
2	Bath City	10	8	1	1	30	11	17
3	Stoke City	10	8	1	1	43	19	17
4	Leicester City	10	6	3	1	22	9	15
5	Sheffield United	10	7	1	2	33	16	15
6	Bradford	10	6	3	1	23	14	15
7	Manchester United	10	6	3	1	28	18	15
8	Everton	10	7	0	3	42	16	14
9	Birmingham	9	6	2	1	22	10	14
10	Rotherham United	10	6	2	2	32	17	14
11	Liverpool	10	7	0	3	36	21	14
12	Newcastle United	10	7	0	3	25	20	14
13	Lovell's Athletic	10	6	1	3	33	16	13
14	Blackpool	10	6	1	3	23	13	13
15	Barnsley	10	5	3	2	22	16	13
16	Coventry City	10	5	3	2	19	17	13
17	Blackburn Rovers	10	6	1	3	21	18	13
18	Cardiff City	10	6	0	4	23	13	12
19	Sheffield Wednesday	9	5	2	2	17	11	12
20	Manchester City	10	5	2	3	27	19	12
21	Bristol City	10	4	4	2	17	16	12
22	Darlington	10	5	1	4	28	14	11
23	Oldham Athletic	10	4	3	3	24	14	11
24	Rochdale	10	4	3	3	21	14	11
25	Derby County	10	5	1	4	20	14	11
26	Aston Villa	10	5	1	4	20	16	11
27	Hartlepool	10	4	3	3	25	25	11
28	Gateshead	10	5	1	4	27	28	11
29	Grimsby Town	10	5	1	4	18	19	11
30	Leeds United	10	5	1	4	19	22	11
31	York City	10	5	0	5	22	16	10
32	Burnley	10	4	2	4	22	19	10

All above qualified for the First Round

		P	W	D	L	F	A	Pts
33	Stockport County	10	5	0	5	23	28	10
34	Nottingham Forest	9	3	3	3	8	7	9
35	Chester	10	4	1	5	31	31	9
36	Mansfield Town	10	4	1	5	12	19	9
37	Huddersfield Town	10	3	2	5	16	19	8
38	West Bromwich Albion	10	2	4	4	24	29	8
39	Doncaster Rovers	9	3	2	4	14	24	8
40	Middlesbrough	10	2	3	5	14	20	7
41	Bolton Wanderers	10	3	1	6	15	27	7
42	Walsall	10	2	3	5	11	22	7
43	Sunderland	10	3	0	7	25	37	6
44	Bury	10	2	2	6	18	30	6
45	Halifax Town	10	2	2	6	14	25	6
46	Southport	10	2	2	6	14	25	6
47	Chesterfield	10	2	1	7	17	25	5
48	Swansea Town	10	2	1	7	19	38	5
49	Crewe Alexandra	10	2	1	7	21	46	5
50	Notts County	10	2	0	8	14	29	4
51	Northampton Town	9	2	0	7	9	19	4
52	Wolverhampton Wanderers	10	0	4	6	11	27	4
53	Lincoln City	9	1	1	7	14	31	3
54	Bradford City	10	1	1	8	11	26	3
55	Aberaman Athletic	10	0	1	9	11	39	1
56	Tranmere Rovers	10	0	0	10	11	41	0

Other English Competitions 1943-44

LEAGUE NORTH (WAR) CUP

First round – 2 legs
First legs played on 4 Mar, second legs on 11 Mar
Bath City v Bristol City 2-1, 2-1
Birmingham v Leicester City 3-1, 1-2 *(aet, 90 mins 0-2)*
Blackpool v Everton 7-1,, 3-1
Bradford v Sheffield Wednesday 5-0, 2-1
Burnley v Rochdale 3-3, 1-2 *(aet, 90 mins 1-1)*
Derby County v Coventry City 2-1, 0-3
Gateshead v Darlington 1-2, 1-1
Hartlepools United v Newcastle United 3-1, 0-3
Liverpool v Oldham Athletic 8-1, 0-1
Lovell's Athletic v Cardiff City 2-0, 0-1
Manchester City v Blackburn Rovers 3-0, 2-4
(aet, 90 mins 0-3)
Rotherham United v Grimsby Town 2-2, 1-2
Sheffield United v Leeds United 3-1, 0-1
Stoke City v Aston Villa 4-5, 0-3
Wrexham v Manchester United 1-4, 2-2
York City v Barnsley 4-1, 1-3

Second round – 2 legs
First legs played on 18 Mar, second legs on 25 Mar
Birmingham v Manchester United 3-1, 1-1
Blackpool v Rochdale 8-0, 1-2
Coventry City v Aston Villa 1-2, 1-2
Darlington v Newcastle United 2-0, 1-4
Lovell's Athletic v Batch City 1-3, 0-3
Manchester City v Liverpool 1-1, 3-2 *(aet, 90 mins 2-2)*
Sheffield United v Grimsby Town 4-0, 1-0
York City v Bradford 1-5, 1-2

Third round – 2 legs
First legs played 1 Apr, second legs on 8 Apr
Aston Villa v Bath City 1-0, 3-3
Blackpool v Bradford 2-2, 2-1
Manchester City v Birmingham 1-0, 0-0
Sheffield United v Newcastle United 4-0, 1-3

Semi-final – 2 legs
First legs played on 15 Apr, second legs on 22 Apr
Aston Villa v Sheffield United 3-2, 2-2
Blackpool v Manchester City 1-1, 2-1

Final – 2 legs
First leg, 29 Apr 1944 at Bloomfield Road, Blackpool
Att 28,000
Blackpool 2 *(Dodds 2)*
Aston Villa 1 *(Goffin)*

Blackpool: Savage*, Pope*, Kinsell*, Johnston, Hayward*, S Jones, Matthews*, Dix*, Dodds, Finan, Pearson*
Aston Villa: Wakeman, Potts*, Cummings, Massie, Callaghan, Iverson, Broome, Edwards, Parkes, Starling, Goffin

Second leg, 6 May 1944 at Villa Park, Birmingham
Att 54,824
Aston Villa 4 *(Broome 2, Edwards, Iverson)*
Blackpool 2 *(Dix, Pearson)*

Aston Villa: as first leg except Houghton for Goffin
Blackpool: as first leg

LEAGUE WEST (WAR) CUP

	Aberaman Athletic	Bath C	Bristol City	Cardiff City	Lovell's Athletic	Swansea Town
Aberaman Athletic	X	29 Apr 1-8	15 Apr 3-1	25 Mar 0-5	X	11 Mar 2-3
Bath City	22 Apr 16-3	X	4 Mar 2-1	X	25 Mar 3-0	15 Apr 6-0
Bristol City	10 Apr 5-0	11 Mar 1-2	X	8 Apr 1-2	22 Apr 2-1	25 Mar 3-3
Cardiff City	18 Mar 6-0	X	1 Apr 6-2	X	10 Apr 1-1	29 Apr 3-1
Lovell's Athletic	X	18 Mar 1-3	29 Apr 2-1	15 Apr 2-0	X	8 Apr 5-1
Swansea Town	4 Mar 4-0	10 Apr 2-1	18 Mar 5-4	22 Apr 2-4	1 Apr 2-1	X

		P	W	D	L	F	A	Pts
1	Bath City	8	7	0	1	41	9	14
2	Cardiff City	8	6	1	1	27	9	13
3	Swansea Town	10	5	1	4	23	29	11
4	Lovell's Athletic	8	3	1	4	13	13	7
5	Bristol City	10	2	1	7	21	26	5
6	Aberaman Athletic	8	1	0	7	9	48	2

Final – 2 legs
First leg played on 6 May, second leg on 13 May
Bath City v Cardiff City 4-2, 0-0

Other English Competitions 1943-44

COMBINED COUNTIES CUP

First round – 2 legs
First leg played on 1 Apr, second leg on 8 Apr
Bradford City v Huddersfield Town 3-0, 0-5
Chesterfield v Leeds United 1-3, 0-1
Halifax Town v York City 4-1, 1-1
Sheffield Wednesday bye

Semi-final – 2 legs
First leg played on 15 Apr, second leg on 22 Apr
Leeds United v Halifax Town 2-2, 2-5
Sheffield Wednesday v Huddersfield Town 2-1, 1-5

Final – 2 legs
First leg played on 26 Apr, second leg on 6 May
Huddersfield Town v Halifax Town 1-4, 4-2

LANCASHIRE CUP

First round – 2 legs
First leg played on 4 Mar, second leg on 11 Mar
Bolton Wanderers v Bury 6-1, 2-5
First leg played on 18 Mar, second leg on 25 Mar
Everton v Chester 5-2, 9-2
Blackburn Rovers v Burnley 2-1, 2-2
First leg played on 1 Apr, second leg on 8 Apr
Liverpool v Southport 6-2, 7-4
Rochdale v Oldham Athletic 4-0, 2-0
Blackpool Services bye
Stockport County bye

Second round – 2 legs
First leg played on 1 Apr, second leg on 8 Apr
Blackburn Rovers v Blackpool Services 3-0, 2-1
Bolton Wanderers v Manchester United 3-0, 2-3
First leg played on 10 Apr, second leg on 15 Apr
Rochdale v Stockport County 1-4, 2-3
Everton v Liverpool 3-0, 0-3
REPLAY on 22 Apr
Liverpool v Everton 4-2

Semi-final
2 legs, first leg played on 22 Apr, second leg on 29 Apr
Bolton Wanderers v Stockport County 4-2, 2-1
1 leg, played on 29 Apr
Liverpool v Blackburn Rovers 1-0

Final – 2 legs
First leg played on 6 May, second leg on 13 May
Liverpool v Bolton Wanderers 3-1, 2-3

LIVERPOOL SENIOR CUP

Semi-final – 2 legs
First leg played on 1 Apr, second leg on 8 Apr
Tranmere Rovers v Everton 0-5, 0-4

Final – 2 legs
First leg played on 6 May, second leg on 13 May
Southport v Everton 1-1, 1-0

CHESHIRE BOWL

Semi-final – 2 legs
First leg played on 4 Mar, second leg on 11 Mar
Crewe Alexandra v Chester 5-9, 1-4
First leg played on 18 Mar, second leg on 23 Mar
Stockport County v Tranmere Rovers 4-0, 1-4

Final
Played on 6 May
Chester v Stockport County 6-1

TYNE, WEAR & TEES CUP

First round – 2 legs
First leg played on 1 Apr, second leg on 8 Apr
Darlington v Middlesbrough 2-3, 4-1
Gateshead v Hartlepools United 3-2, 7-3

Semi-final – 2 legs
First leg played on 15 Apr, second leg on 22 Apr
Gateshead v Darlington 1-0, 0-4
Sunderland v Newcastle United 0-3, 2-5

Final – 2 legs
First leg played on 29 Apr, second leg on 6 May
Darlington v Newcastle United 2-3, 1-1 (aet, 90 mins 1-0)

MIDLAND CUP

First round – 2 legs
First leg played on 18 Mar, second leg on 25 Mar
Walsall v Nottingham Forest 0-0, 0-2
Notts County v Northampton Town 1-4, 1-4

Second round – 2 legs
First leg played on 18 Mar, second leg on 25 Mar
West Bromwich Albion v Wolverhampton Wanderers 5-0, 3-3
First leg played on 1 Apr, second leg on 8 Apr
Nottingham Forest v Coventry City 4-1, 3-3
Leicester City v Northampton Town 0-2, 1-3
Derby County v Stoke City 1-3, 1-1

Semi-final – 2 legs
First leg played on 15 Apr, second leg on 22 Apr
Nottingham Forest v Northampton Town 5-0,
Stoke City v West Bromwich Albion 1-1, 1-3

Final – 2 legs
First leg played on 29 Apr, second leg on 6 May
West Bromwich Albion v Nottingham Forest 2-2, 4-3 (aet, 90 mins 2-2)

SHEFFIELD COUNTY CUP

Semi-final – 2 legs
First leg played on 1 Apr, second leg on 8 Apr
Barnsley v Rotherham United 1-4, 0-3

Final – 2 legs
First leg played on 29 Apr, second leg on 6 May
Rotherham United v Sheffield United 1-0, 3-2

Other English Competitions 1943-44

LEAGUE SOUTH (WAR) CUP

Group 1	Brentford	Brighton & HA	Charlton Athletic	Crystal Palace
Brentford	X	4 Mar 8-0	18 Mar 2-2	19 Feb 3-4
Brighton & HA	25 Mar 5-0	X	19 Feb 1-2	18 Mar 2-4
Charlton Athletic	26 Feb 5-3	11 Mar 2-0	X	25 Mar 0-0
Crystal Palace	11 Mar 1-2	26 Feb 2-3	4 Mar 5-1	X

	P	W	D	L	F	A	Pts
Charlton Athletic	6	3	2	1	12	11	8
Crystal Palace	6	3	1	2	16	11	7
Brentford	6	2	1	3	18	17	5
Brighton & Hove Albion	6	2	0	4	11	18	4

Group 2	Chelsea	Southampton	Watford	West Ham U
Chelsea	X	19 Feb 3-2	18 Mar 1-1	4 Mar 4-0
Southampton	11 Mar 1-5	X	4 Mar 3-1	26 Feb 1-2
Watford	26 Feb 0-3	25 Mar 1-4	X	11 Mar 2-1
West Ham United	25 Mar 6-1	18 Mar 5-1	19 Feb 1-2	X

	P	W	D	L	F	A	Pts
Chelsea	6	4	1	1	17	10	9
West Ham United	6	3	0	3	15	11	6
Watford	6	2	1	3	7	13	5
Southampton	6	2	0	4	12	17	4

Group 3	Aldershot	Millwall	Portsmouth	Tottenham H
Aldershot	X	26 Feb 7-1	11 Mar 1-1	4 Mar 2-1
Millwall	18 Mar 0-5	X	4 Mar 5-0	19 Feb 0-1
Portsmouth	19 Feb 0-2	25 Mar 1-1	X	18 Mar 1-2
Tottenham Hotspur	25 Mar 2-0	11 Mar 1-0	26 Feb 1-0	X

	P	W	D	L	F	A	Pts
Tottenham Hotspur	6	5	0	1	8	3	10
Aldershot	6	4	1	1	17	5	9
Millwall	6	1	1	4	7	15	3
Portsmouth	6	0	2	4	3	12	2

Group 4	Arsenal	Clapton Orient	Fulham	Luton Town	QPR	Reading
Arsenal	X			19 Feb 7-1	18 Mar 1-4	4 Mar 2-3
Clapton Orient		X	4 Mar 0-4		19 Feb 2-5	18 Mar 0-5
Fulham		25 Mar 4-5	X	26 Feb 2-0		11 Mar 3-4
Luton Town	11 Mar 1-1		18 Mar 3-2	X	4 Mar 3-4	
QPR	26 Feb 1-1	11 Mar 6-0		25 Mar 5-0	X	
Reading	25 Mar 5-1	26 Feb 3-0	19 Feb 3-0			X

	P	W	D	L	F	A	Pts
Reading	6	6	0	0	23	6	12
Queen's Park Rangers	6	5	1	0	25	7	11
Arsenal	6	1	2	3	13	15	4
Fulham	6	2	0	4	15	15	4
Luton Town	6	1	1	4	8	21	3
Clapton Orient	6	1	0	5	7	27	2

Semi-final
Played on 1 Apr
  Chelsea v Reading 3-2 *(aet, 90 mins 1-1, at White Hart Lane)*
  Tottenham Hotspur v Charlton Athletic 0-3 *(at Stamford Bridge)*

Final
15 Apr 1944 at Wembley Stadium, London
Att 85,000
Charlton Athletic 3 *(Revell 2, Welsh)*
Chelsea 1 *(Payne (pen))*

Charlton A: Bartram, Shreeve, Jobling, Smith, Oakes, Chilton*, Robinson, Brown, Revell, Welsh, Duffy*
Chelsea: Woodley, Hardwick*, Westwood*, Russell*, Harris*, Foss, Ashcroft*, Fagan*, Payne, Bowie, Mitten*

CUP WINNERS MATCH
Played between the winners of the League North (War) Cup and the League South (War) Cup

Played on 20 May 1944 at Stamford Bridge, London
Att 38,540
Aston Villa 1 *(Houghton)*
Charlton Athletic 1 *(Revell)*

Aston Villa: Wakeman, Potts*, Cummings, Massie, Callaghan, Starling, Broome, Edwards, Parkes, Iverson, Houghton
Charlton A: Bartram, Shreeve, Jobling, Smith, Oakes, Chilton*, Robinson, Brown, Revell, Welsh, Duffy*

Scottish Southern Football League 1943-44

	Airdrieonians	Albion Rovers	Celtic	Clyde	Dumbarton	Falkirk	Hamilton Ac	Heart of Midlothian	Hibernian	Morton	Motherwell	Partick Thistle	Queen's Park	Rangers	St Mirren	Third Lanark
Airdrieonians	X	1 Jan 4-2	16 Oct 1-3	18 Sep 1-5	27 Nov 1-3	26 Feb 0-0	8 Jan 6-2	2 Oct 1-3	20 Nov 2-5	11 Dec 1-4	9 Oct 1-3	5 Feb 5-0	21 Aug 4-2	4 Sep 1-3	30 Oct 2-0	19 Feb 2-0
Albion Rovers	11 Sep 2-1	X	15 Jan 2-1	29 Jan 2-0	23 Oct 0-1	28 Aug 2-1	22 Jan 2-4	13 Nov 1-2	4 Dec 2-4	3 Jan 4-1	18 Dec 2-2	25 Dec 2-1	12 Feb 0-5	6 Nov 1-5	25 Sep 3-3	14 Aug 1-3
Celtic	29 Jan 3-1	2 Oct 3-2	X	27 Nov 4-0	4 Sep 1-4	23 Oct 3-2	18 Sep 1-0	8 Jan 4-0	12 Feb 2-2	21 Aug 2-1	6 Nov 2-1	9 Oct 4-5	11 Jan 2-0	1 Jan 1-3	13 Nov 5-0	3 Jan 4-0
Clyde	25 Dec 2-2	16 Oct 0-2	14 Aug 1-2	X	26 Feb 4-1	18 Dec 3-1	5 Feb 5-0	30 Oct 2-0	25 Sep 2-1	19 Feb 0-3	15 Jan 1-0	11 Sep 5-0	20 Nov 1-1	22 Jan 0-3	4 Dec 3-0	10 Apr 3-3
Dumbarton	14 Aug 3-1	5 Feb 2-2	18 Dec 1-1	13 Nov 1-0	X	11 Sep 2-3	16 Oct 3-2	19 Feb 2-1	25 Dec 1-1	30 Oct 1-4	25 Sep 4-2	15 Jan 2-2	9 Oct 2-1	3 Jan 1-1	28 Aug 2-1	4 Dec 2-3
Falkirk	13 Nov 3-3	11 Dec 4-1	5 Feb 3-2	4 Sep 6-3	1 Jan 4-0	X	27 Nov 8-4	21 Aug 2-3	9 Oct 3-5	18 Sep 2-0	3 Jan 1-1	16 Oct 4-3	2 Oct 2-3	8 Jan 0-2	19 Feb 3-0	30 Oct 5-6
Hamilton Academical	25 Sep 2-1	9 Oct 7-1	25 Dec 3-3	23 Oct 1-2	29 Jan 0-1	14 Aug 6-4	X	3 Jan 2-1	28 Aug 1-2	13 Nov 2-2	11 Sep 1-0	4 Dec 3-1	6 Feb 4-2	12 Dec 1-4	18 Dec 4-2	15 Jan 6-2
Heart Of Midlothian	15 Jan 1-1	26 Feb 1-0	25 Sep 0-0	12 Feb 2-2	6 Nov 3-0	4 Dec 1-1	20 Nov 5-6	X	11 Sep 0-1	9 Oct 1-1	28 Aug 3-1	14 Aug 2-3	23 Oct 9-0	29 Jan 1-3	25 Dec 5-2	18 Dec 6-3
Hibernian	3 Jan 1-2	21 Aug 3-0	30 Oct 2-2	8 Jan 3-1	18 Sep 4-3	22 Jan 4-3	11 Dec 3-5	1 Jan 0-1	X	2 Oct 2-0	13 Nov 3-3	19 Feb 2-0	4 Sep 2-1	27 Nov 3-4	16 Oct 4-1	5 Feb 6-0
Morton	28 Aug 2-1	20 Nov 6-2	4 Dec 1-1	6 Nov 2-4	12 Feb 3-2	25 Dec 3-2	26 Feb 5-4	22 Jan 1-3	15 Jan 3-1	X	14 Aug 1-1	18 Dec 1-2	29 Jan 2-4	23 Oct 1-1	11 Sep 3-3	25 Sep 2-1
Motherwell	22 Jan 3-0	4 Sep 2-1	19 Feb 1-2	2 Oct 1-3	8 Jan 2-0	20 Nov 5-3	1 Jan 6-1	11 Dec 2-2	15 Apr 0-1	27 Nov 3-0	X	30 Oct 2-2	18 Sep 6-0	21 Aug 0-5	5 Feb 2-2	16 Oct 5-2
Partick Thistle	23 Oct 6-1	18 Sep 4-0	22 Jan 1-2	1 Jan 3-2	2 Oct 2-6	29 Jan 3-2	21 Aug 2-2	27 Nov 0-1	6 Nov 3-1	4 Sep 0-1	12 Feb 2-2	X	8 Jan 1-0	11 Dec 1-2	3 Jan 1-2	13 Nov 6-1
Queen's Park	4 Dec 2-2	30 Oct 3-1	10 Apr 1-4	3 Jan 2-3	22 Jan 0-0	15 Jan 6-2	19 Feb 2-3	5 Feb 2-2	18 Dec 4-2	16 Oct 4-1	25 Dec 1-6	25 Sep 3-1	X	13 Nov 1-4	14 Aug 1-3	1 Jan 4-1
Rangers	18 Dec 3-0	19 Feb 5-0	11 Sep 0-1	28 Aug 3-2	20 Nov 2-0	25 Sep 2-0	30 Oct 6-0	16 Oct 1-3	14 Aug 4-0	5 Feb 4-1	4 Dec 2-0	10 Apr 3-3	26 Feb 1-1	X	15 Jan 1-2	25 Dec 3-1
St Mirren	12 Feb 2-3	8 Jan 4-1	26 Feb 2-2	21 Aug 1-1	11 Dec 5-2	6 Nov 3-3	4 Sep 3-2	18 Sep 5-3	29 Jan 1-2	1 Jan 1-5	23 Oct 2-3	20 Nov 3-1	27 Nov 1-4	2 Oct 1-4	X	9 Oct 2-1
Third Lanark	6 Nov 2-3	27 Nov 3-2	20 Nov 3-4	11 Dec 7-2	21 Aug 2-3	12 Feb 1-3	2 Oct 3-2	4 Sep 1-2	23 Oct 0-2	8 Jan 4-3	29 Jan 3-4	26 Feb 0-3	11 Sep 3-3	18 Sep 0-6	22 Jan 1-1	X

		P	W	D	L	F	A	Pts
1	Rangers	30	23	4	3	90	27	50
2	Celtic	30	18	7	5	71	43	43
3	Hibernian	30	17	4	9	72	54	38
4	Heart of Midlothian	30	14	7	9	67	50	35
5	Dumbarton	30	13	6	11	54	58	32
6	Motherwell	30	12	8	10	69	53	32
7	Clyde	30	13	5	12	62	58	31
8	Morton	30	12	6	12	63	61	30
9	Hamilton Academical	30	13	3	14	80	88	29
10	Partick Thistle	30	11	5	14	62	66	27
11	Queen's Park	30	10	6	14	64	75	26
12	Falkirk	30	10	5	15	79	80	25
13	St Mirren	30	9	7	14	58	78	25
14	Airdrieonians	30	9	5	16	54	72	23
15	Albion Rovers	30	7	3	20	43	85	17
16	Third Lanark	30	7	3	20	60	100	17

Scottish Southern Football League Cup 1943-44

Section A

Section A	Airdrieonians	Hearts	Motherwell	Rangers
Airdrieonians	X	11 Mar 2-3	25 Mar 1-2	18 Mar 0-1
Heart of Midlothian	15 Apr 3-0	X	18 Mar 4-0	4 Mar 2-4
Motherwell	4 Mar 3-3	8 Apr 3-1	X	1 Apr 2-3
Rangers	8 Apr 4-0	25 Mar 2-0	11 Mar 0-1	X

		P	W	D	L	F	A	Pts
1	Rangers	6	5	0	1	14	5	10
2	Motherwell	6	3	1	2	11	12	7
3	Hearts	6	3	0	3	13	11	6
4	Airdrieonians	6	0	1	5	6	16	1

Section B

Section B	Celtic	Falkirk	Hamilton Ac	Partick Th
Celtic	X	1 Apr 3-0	4 Mar 8-1	8 Apr 6-0
Falkirk	11 Mar 1-3	X	8 Apr 2-3	25 Mar 3-0
Hamilton Academical	25 Mar 0-3	18 Mar 1-1	X	11 Mar 1-3
Partick Thistle	18 Mar 0-1	4 Mar 2-1	1 Apr 4-2	X

		P	W	D	L	F	A	Pts
1	Celtic	6	6	0	0	24	2	12
2	Partick Thistle	6	3	0	3	9	14	6
3	Falkirk	6	1	1	4	8	12	3
4	Hamilton Academical	6	1	1	4	8	21	3

Section C

Section C	Albion R	Hibernian	Morton	Third Lanark
Albion Rovers	X	1 Apr 0-2	4 Mar 3-3	8 Apr 4-2
Hibernian	11 Mar 2-1	X	8 Apr 6-3	25 Mar 4-0
Morton	25 Mar 4-1	18 Mar 2-2	X	11 Mar 2-1
Third Lanark	18 Mar 2-2	4 Mar 0-4	1 Apr 0-5	X

		P	W	D	L	F	A	Pts
1	Hibernian	6	5	1	0	20	6	11
2	Morton	6	3	2	1	19	13	8
3	Albion Rovers	6	1	2	3	11	15	4
4	Third Lanark	6	0	1	5	5	21	1

Section D

Section D	Clyde	Dumbarton	Queen's Park	St Mirren
Clyde	X	11 Mar 0-1	18 Mar 0-0	25 Mar 2-1
Dumbarton	1 Apr 1-3	X	4 Mar 1-4	8 Apr 2-1
Queen's Park	8 Apr 0-6	25 Mar 0-2	X	11 Mar 1-2
St Mirren	15 Apr 1-1	18 Mar 2-2	1 Apr 1-2	X

		P	W	D	L	F	A	Pts
1	Clyde	6	3	2	1	12	4	8
2	Dumbarton	6	3	1	2	9	10	7
3	Queen's Park	6	2	1	3	7	12	5
4	St Mirren	6	1	2	4	8	10	4

Semi-final
Played on 29 Apr at Hampden Park, Glasgow
  Falkirk v Celtic 4-2
Played on 6 May at Hampden Park, Glasgow
  Hibernian v Clyde 5-2

Final
20 May 1944 at Hampden Park, Glasgow
Att 50,000
Hibernian 0
Rangers 0
Hibernian won 6-5 on corner kicks

Hibernian: Downie, Fraser, Hall, Finnigan, Baxter, Kean, G Smith, Bogan, Nelson, Woodburn, Caskie
Rangers: Dawson, Gray, Shaw, Little, Young, Symon, Waddell, Gillick, Smith, Duncanson, Johnstone

Scottish North Eastern Football League 1943-44

First series	Aberdeen	Dundee U	Dunfermline A	East Fife	Falkirk 'A'	Hearts 'A'	Raith R	Rangers
Aberdeen	X	6 Nov 5-1	14 Aug 7-2	25 Sep 2-0	18 Sep 3-0	9 Oct 3-0	16 Oct 4-1	28 Aug 4-1
Dundee United	11 Sep 2-0	X	16 Oct 1-3	20 Nov 4-3	9 Oct 7-1	14 Aug 6-3	28 Aug 2-1	25 Sep 4-1
Dunfermline Athletic	2 Oct 3-1	4 Sep 5-0	X	6 Nov 5-0	21 Aug 3-0	11 Sep 1-2	9 Oct 2-1	30 Oct 1-1
East Fife	30 Oct 1-1	18 Sep 3-1	28 Aug 0-2	X	16 Oct 6-0	23 Oct 1-3	14 Aug 2-3	9 Oct 1-0
Falkirk 'A'	20 Nov 2-2	13 Nov 3-6	23 Oct 3-2	11 Sep 1-0	X	28 Aug 1-5	6 Nov 3-5	14 Aug 0-3
Heart of Midlothian 'A'	4 Sep 2-2	2 Oct 4-2	13 Nov 2-1	21 Aug 5-2	30 Oct 4-1	X	18 Sep 2-3	16 Oct 1-0
Raith Rovers	21 Aug 3-2	23 Oct 3-0	25 Sep 4-2	2 Oct 4-2	4 Sep 6-0	20 Nov 3-0	X	11 Sep 3-2
Rangers 'A'	23 Oct 4-0	21 Aug 8-0	18 Sep 0-3	4 Sep 0-1	2 Oct 2-0	6 Nov 1-2	13 Nov 1-2	X

		P	W	D	L	F	A	Pts
1	Raith Rovers	14	11	0	3	42	24	22
2	Heart of Midlothian 'A'	14	9	1	4	35	27	19
3	Aberdeen	14	7	3	4	36	22	17
4	Dunfermline Athletic	14	8	1	5	35	22	17
5	Dundee United	14	7	0	7	36	43	14
6	East Fife	14	4	1	9	22	31	9
7	Rangers 'A'	14	4	1	9	24	22	9
8	Falkirk 'A'	14	2	1	11	15	54	5

Second Series	Aberdeen	Dundee U	Dunfermline A	East Fife	Falkirk 'A'	Hearts 'A'	Raith R	Rangers
Aberdeen	X	1 Jan 1-1	25 Mar 3-2	3 Jan 0-0	5 Feb 3-1	15 Jan 5-2	11 Mar 1-0	22 Apr 3-0
Dundee United	29 Jan 1-7	X	18 Mar 2-0	19 Feb 3-1	25 Mar 3-0	26 Feb 3-6	3 Jan 3-1	15 Jan 6-2
Dunfermline Athletic	8 Jan 1-2	11 Mar 2-1	X	29 Jan 1-0	22 Apr 3-4	3 Jan 3-1	12 Feb 1-1	19 Feb 1-3
East Fife	22 Jan 2-1	8 Jan 1-2	4 Mar 4-0	X	11 Mar 4-0	12 Feb 3-3	22 Apr 4-0	5 Feb 2-1
Falkirk 'A'	4 Mar 2-10	12 Feb 6-3	22 Jan 2-6	15 Jan 0-0	X	18 Mar 2-0	29 Jan 4-3	26 Feb 2-4
Heart of Midlothian 'A'	19 Feb 1-2	22 Jan 4-1	5 Feb 3-2	25 Mar 1-0	1 Jan 4-1	X	8 Jan 2-2	11 Mar 1-4
Raith Rovers	18 Mar 2-0	5 Feb 2-0	15 Jan 1-4	1 Jan 0-4	19 Feb 3-1	4 Mar 1-0	X	25 Mar 2-2
Rangers 'A'	12 Feb 3-2	27 May 6-1	1 Jan 6-1	18 Mar 2-1	8 Jan 2-2	29 Jan 4-0	22 Jan 3-1	X

		P	HW	AW	HD	AD	L	F	A	Pts
1	Aberdeen	14	5	4	2	0	3	40	18	24
2	Rangers 'A'	14	6	3	1	1	3	42	25	24
3	East Fife	14	5	1	1	2	5	26	14	18
4	Dundee United	14	4	2	1	0	7	30	39	15
5	Heart of Midlothian 'A'	14	4	1	1	1	7	28	33	14
6	Dunfermline Athletic	14	3	2	1	0	8	27	33	13
7	Raith Rovers	14	4	0	1	2	7	19	29	13
8	Falkirk 'A'	14	3	1	1	1	8	27	48	12

3 points were awarded for an away win, 2 points for an away draw

Other Scottish Competitions 1943-44

SCOTTISH NORTH EASTERN LEAGUE CUP

First Series
First Round - 2 legs
First leg played on 27 Nov, second on 4 Dec
  Aberdeen v Raith Rovers 6-1, 1-2
  Dunfermline Athletic v Falkirk 'A' 1-5, 2-5
  Heart of Midlothian 'A' v Dundee United 6-2, 4-5
  Rangers 'A' v East Fife 2-2, 2-0

Semi-final - 2 legs
First leg played on 11 Dec , second on 18 Dec
  Heart of Midlothian 'A' v Falkirk 'A' 2-3, 1-2
  Rangers 'A' v Aberdeen 2-0 , 2-0

Final - 2 legs
First leg, 25 Dec 43 at Brockville Park, Falkirk
Att 7,000
Falkirk 1 *(Calder)*
Rangers 3 *(McKinlay 2, Venters)*

Falkirk: Nimmo, Neil, Stewart, Carrick, Brown, Mather, Ogilvie, Dougal, Rooney, Campbell, Calder
Rangers: Jenkins, McKillop, Craven, Stewart, Woodburn, Watkins, McKinnon, Cargill, Mackay, Venters, McCormack

Second leg, 3 Jan 1944 at Ibrox Park, Glasgow
Att
Rangers 1 *(Mackay)*
Falkirk 0

Rangers:

Falkirk: Pidgeon, Neil, Stewart, Rice, Brown, Mather, Rooney, Dougal, Inglis, Murray, Calder

Second Series
First Round - 2 legs
First leg played on 1 Apr, second on 8 Apr
  Aberdeen 'A' v Dunfermline Athletic 3-2, 2-1
  Dundee United v East Fife 2-1, 0-3
  Falkirk 'A' v Raith Rovers 2-4, 4-3
  Rangers 'A' v Heart of Midlothian 'A' 7-1, 3-0

Semi-final - 2 legs
First leg played on 15 Apr, second on 29 Apr
  Aberdeen v Raith Rovers 2-2, 1-2
  Rangers 'A' v East Fife 4-0, 1-3

Final - 2 legs
First leg, 6 May 1944 at Ibrox Park, Glasgow
Att 10,000
Rangers 3 *(McIntosh 2, McCormack)*
Raith Rovers 2 *(Penman, Stewart)*

Rangers: Jenkins, Watkins, Woodburn, Dougal, ____, McIntosh, Waddell, Duncanson, McCormack, Venters
Raith Rovers: Bruce, _____, Donald, ____, Low, ____, Stewart, ____, _____, _____, Penman

Second leg, 13 May 1944 at Stark's Park, Kirkcaldy
Att 12,000
Raith Rovers 2 *(Waldon (pen), Penman)*
Rangers 3 *(Venters 2, Rutherford)*

Rangers: Jenkins, Frew, Craven, Watkins, Woodburn, Dougal, Rutherford, Cargill, McIntosh, Venters, McCormack
Raith Rovers: Bruce, Shufflebotham, Donald, Dutch, Low, Kelly, Stewart, Ventre, Waldron, Hendry, Penman

GLASGOW CUP

First round
Played on 28 Aug
  Third Lanark v Queen's Park 4-3
  Celtic v Partick Thistle 1-3

Semi-final
Played on 27 Sep
  Third Lanark v Clyde 02
  Partick Thistle v Rangers 0-3

Final
Played on 9 Oct at Hampden Park, Glasgow
  Rangers v Clyde 2-0

GLASGOW CHARITY CUP

First round
Played on 15 Apr
  Queen's Park v Celtic 1-4
  Partick Thistle v Third Lanark 4-2

Semi-final
Played on 13 May
  Rangers v Partick Thistle 3-0
  Celtic v Clyde 1-4

Final
Played on 27 May at Hampden Park, Glasgow
  Rangers v Clyde 2-1

EAST OF SCOTLAND SHIELD

Semi-final
Played on 29 Apr
  Heart of Midlothian v Edinburgh City 6-1

Final
Played on 13 May at Tynecastle Park, Edinburgh
  Heart of Midlothian v Hibernian 2-1

ROSEBERY CHARITY CUP
Played on 27 May at Tynecastle Park, Edinburgh
  Heart of Midlothian v Hibernian 1-4

WILSON CUP
Played on 20 Sep at Tynecastle Park, Edinburgh
  Heart of Midlothian v Hibernian 2-1

RENFREWSHIRE CUP
Played on 13 May at St Mirren Park, Paisley
  St Mirren v Morton 3-1

Summer Cup 1943-44

First Round - 2 legs
First leg played on 3 Jun, second on 10 Jun
Airdrieonians v Hibernian 2-4. 0-3
Dumbarton v Clyde 2-4, 0-6
Falkirk v Dundee United 4-0, 2-0
Hamilton Academical v Motherwell 2-1, 0-8
Heart of Midlothian v Albion Rovers 5-1, 3-2
Partick Thistle v Third Lanark 3-1, 3-2
Queen's Park v St Mirren 2-2, 1-2
Raith Roversv Morton 1-2, 3-3

Second Round - 2 legs
First leg played on 17 Jun, second on 24 Jun
Heart of Midlothian v Falkirk 1-4, 0-2
Morton v Hibernian 1-1, 2-0
Partick Thistle v Clyde 1-3, 1-6
St Mirren v Motherwell 2-3, 0-4

Semi-final
Played on 1 Jul
Clyde v Morton 3-3 *(aet 90 mins 3-3, at Hampden Park, Glasgow)*
(After corner count of 15 each, Clyde were awarded the tie on better Cup goal average)
Motherwell v Falkirk 3-1 *(at Firhill Park, Glasgow)*

Final
8 Jul 1944 at Hampden Park, Glasgow
Att 35,000
Motherwell 1 *(Gibson)*
Clyde 0

Motherwell: Johnstone, Kilmarnock, Shaw, Ross, Paton, Russell, Gibson, Watson, Mathie, Gillan, McGowan
Clyde: Sweeney, Gibson, Hickie, Douglas, Weir, Long, Galletley, Gordon, Wallace, Johnstone, Gillies

Northern Ireland 1943-44

NORTHERN REGIONAL FOOTBALL LEAGUE

	Belfast Celtic	Cliftonville	Derry City	Distillery	Glentoran	Linfield
Belfast Celtic	X	25 Dec 3-0 / 1 Apr 7-1	9-0 29 Jan 4-0	1 Jan 4-3 / 15 Apr 1-1	11 Dec 3-1 / 11 Mar 5-3	3-1 8 Apr 0-2
Cliftonville	5 Feb 1-1 / 0-5	X	4 Dec 2-1 / 4 Mar 7-0	6 Nov 3-1 / 8 Apr 0-5	13 Nov 4-2 / 29 Jan 3-5	11 Dec 0-2 / 11 Mar 0-3
Derry City	18 Dec 0-0 / 18 Mar 1-2	1 Jan 2-1 / 1-0	X	27 Nov 3-5 / 8 Jan 3-4	6 Nov 2-1 / 4-2	NOT PLAYED 5 Feb 2-6
Distillery	4 Dec 1-1 / 4 Mar 3-2	1-0 26 Feb 0-2	11 Dec 5-3 / 11 Mar 3-1	X	20 Nov 1-3 / 25 Dec 3-1	2-2 29 Jan 6-1
Glentoran	8 Jan 0-1 / 0-1	18 Dec 1-2 / 18 Mar 3-1	12 Feb 5-0 / 8 Apr 5-4	5 Feb 3-1 / 1 Apr 4-2	X	1 Jan 2-2 / 1-3
Linfield	NOT PLAYED / 2-2	8 Jan 4-2 / 2-1	25 Dec 5-2 / 1 Apr 3-5	18 Dec 0-0 / 18 Mar 2-4	4 Dec 4-1 / 4 Mar 5-5	X

		P	W	D	L	F	A	Pts
1	Belfast Celtic	19	12	5	2	55	21	29
2	Linfield	18	11	3	4	57	38	25
3	Distillery	20	10	3	7	52	47	23
4	Glentoran	20	8	1	11	49	50	17
5	Cliftonville	20	5	1	14	29	51	11
6	Derry City	19	5	1	13	35	70	11

Linfield v Belfast Celtic was played on 6 November, Celtic winning 5-1. However this was played as a friendly by both clubs as they had wanted the tie played on Christmas Day, which was vetoed by the other clubs.

SUBSTITUTE GOLD CUP

	Belfast Celtic	Cliftonville	Derry City	Distillery	Glentoran	Linfield
Belfast Celtic	X	18 Sep 1-2	21 Aug 11-1	16 Oct 3-0	9 Oct 5-1	25 Sep 3-1
Cliftonville	23 Oct 0-3	X	25 Sep 2-5	2 Oct 2-3	4 Sep 1-3	28 Aug 1-2
Derry City	2 Oct 0-2	30 Oct 1-3	X	28 Aug 2-1	23 Oct 1-2	4 Sep 1-0
Distillery	4 Sep 2-2	21 Aug 2-1	9 Oct 6-2	X	30 Oct 0-0	23 Oct 4-1
Glentoran	28 Aug 1-0	16 Oct 2-0	18 Sep 6-2	25 Sep 2-3	X	2 Oct 1-1
Linfield	30 Oct 1-2	9 Oct 8-0	16 Oct 2-0	18 Sep 2-1	21 Aug 3-1	X

		P	W	D	L	F	A	Pts
1	Belfast Celtic	10	7	1	2	32	9	15
2	Distillery	10	5	2	3	24	17	12
3	Glentoran	10	5	2	3	19	16	12
4	Linfield	10	5	1	4	21	14	11
5	Derry City	10	3	0	7	15	37	6
6	Cliftonville	10	2	0	8	12	30	4

IRISH FA CUP

First round – 2 legs
First leg played on 15 Jan, second on 22 Jan
Bangor v Ards 3-2, 0-3
Cliftonville v Derry City 3-0. 0-2
Coleraine v Distillery 0-3, 1-6
Glentoran v Belfast Celtic 1-7, 2-9
Victoria Works United v Bangor reserves 1-4, 3-3

Second round – 2 legs
First leg played on 12 Feb, second on 19 Feb
Bangor reserves v Infantry Training Centre 0-1, 2-2
Belfast Celtic v Distillery 2-0, 4-1
Cliftonville v Ards 2-2, 3-0
Linfield v Larne 4-2, 5-1

Semi-final
Played on 25 Mar at Solitude, Belfast
Belfast Celtic v Infantry Training Centre 3-0
Played on 25 Mar, REPLAY on 27 Mar, both at Grosvenor Park, Belfast
Linfield v Cliftonville 0-0, 2-0

Final
Played on 17 Apr at Windsor Park, Belfast
Belfast Celtic v Linfield 3-1

Northern Ireland 1943-44

Derry City played all their home matches in Belfast
All League of Ireland clubs' home games were played at Dalymount Park, Dublin

First round – 2 legs
First leg played on 26 Apr, second on 1 May
  Dundalk v Derry City 1-0, 0-2
First leg played on 28 Apr, second on 8 May
  St James' Gate v Glentoran 1-2, 1-5
First leg played on 29 Apr, second on 6 May
  Shamrock Rovers v Belfast Celtic 1-1, 3-4
First leg played on 29 Apr, second on 1 May
  Distillery v Cork United 1-0, 0-0
First leg played on 6 May, second on 10 May
  Shelbourne v Cliftonville 3-0, 1-0
  Linfield v Bohemians 0-4, 3-1

Second round - 2 legs
The first round winners were joined by the best losers (Dundalk and Shamrock Rovers)

First leg played on 13 May, second on 20 May
  Shamrock Rovers v Belfast Celtic 1-4, 3-4
First leg played on 13 May, second on 17 May
  Derry City v Bohemians 0-2, 2-3
First leg played on 13 May, second on 19 May
  Distillery v Dundalk 4-1, 1-1
First leg played on 15 May, second on 20 May
  Glentoran v Shelbourne 2-2, 0-0 *(Glentoran won on corners)*

Semi-final - 2 legs
First leg played on 22 May, second on 24 May
  Distillery v Glentoran 2-1, 1-6
NOTE First leg played at Dalymount Park, Dublin
  Belfast Celtic v Bohemians 1-0, 1-1

Final - 2 legs
First leg played on 27 May, second on 29 May
  Glentoran v Belfast Celtic 3-3, 2-1
NOTE First leg played at Windsor Park, Belfast, second leg at Dalymount Park, Dublin

1944-45

In England and Wales, three leagues would again operate; North, West (which also included non-League sides) and South. Again the North was subdivided into smaller groupings, each club playing nine others. The second half of the season saw the North and West clubs combined as the League North (Second Championship). The League Cup qualifying competition, results in the subsequent rounds and local cup ties also counted towards this.
Norwich City again filled their season with friendly fixtures against services XIs.

The Scottish Southern League and North Eastern Football League continued as in previous seasons.
Kilmarnock re-appeared and fielded their first XI in the Glasgow & District Reserve League.

The Northern Irish Northern Regional League also operated. There was also an international competition involving clubs from the Republic of Ireland.

WINNERS OF THE PRINCIPAL COMPETITIONS

Football League North Cup	Bolton Wanderers
Football League South Cup	Chelsea
Football League West Cup	Bath City
Football League –	
North	Huddersfield Town
North (Second Championship)	Derby County
South	Tottenham Hotspur
West	Cardiff City
Scottish Southern League	Rangers
Scottish Southern League Cup	Rangers
Scottish North Eastern League –	
First Series	Dundee
Second Series	Aberdeen
North Eastern League Cup –	
First Series	Aberdeen
Second Series	Aberdeen
Irish FA Cup	Linfield
Northern Regional League	Linfield
Substitute Gold Cup	Linfield
Inter City Cup	Bohemians

The Football League 1944-45

NORTH

	Bury	Chester	Crewe Alex	Everton	Liverpool	Manchester City	Manchester United	Stockport Co	Tranmere R	Wrexham
Bury	X	21 Oct 2-4	16 Oct 2-5	9 Sep 1-2	18 Nov 2-0	9 Oct 2-1	30 Sep 4-2	7 Oct 2-1	11 Nov 3-2	2 Sep 1-3
Chester	28 Oct 1-1	X	2 Sep 4-0	30 Sep 2-6	9 Oct 3-2	16 Oct 5-2	7 Oct 2-0	4 Nov 5-2	18 Nov 2-2	9 Sep 3-1
Crewe Alexandra	23 Dec 4-1	26 Aug 2-4	X	25 Nov 1-5	23 Sep 4-1	14 Oct 1-6	2 Dec 1-4	28 Oct 5-1	16 Sep 0-1	4 Nov 0-1
Everton	16 Sep 4-1	23 Sep 6-2	18 Nov 3-5	X	21 Oct 0-2	11 Nov 4-1	26 Aug 1-2	16 Dec 6-1	14 Oct 2-1	9 Dec 2-2
Liverpool	25 Nov 3-1	2 Dec 6-0	30 Sep 1-4	28 Oct 0-0	X	9 Sep 2-2	4 Nov 3-2	2 Sep 2-0	23 Dec 3-0	7 Oct 0-3
Manchester City	2 Dec 4-0	23 Dec 6-0	7 Oct 1-1	4 Nov 1-3	16 Sep 2-2	X	25 Nov 4-0	30 Sep 5-1	26 Aug 4-1	28 Oct 2-1
Manchester United	23 Sep 2-2	14 Oct 1-0	9 Dec 2-0	2 Sep 1-3	11 Nov 2-5	18 Nov 3-2	X	9 Sep 3-4	21 Oct 6-1	16 Dec 1-0
Stockport County	14 Oct 3-2	11 Nov 4-2	21 Oct 2-4	23 Dec 0-7	26 Aug 2-3	23 Sep 2-6	16 Sep 4-4	X	9 Dec 2-1	25 Nov 0-3
Tranmere Rovers	4 Nov 2-1	25 Nov 2-3	9 Sep 0-2	7 Oct 1-4	16 Dec 1-5	2 Sep 0-4	28 Oct 2-4	2 Dec 2-4	X	30 Sep 1-3
Wrexham	26 Aug 5-0	16 Sep 1-1	11 Nov 2-4	2 Dec 1-0	14 Oct 2-1	21 Oct 1-1	23 Dec 2-1	18 Nov 8-0	23 Sep 1-0	X

Everton v Bury on 16 Sep was played at Bury

	Aston Villa	Birmingham	Coventry C	Leicester C	Northampton Town	Port Vale	Stoke C	Walsall	WBA	Wolverhampton Wanderers
Aston Villa	X	14 Oct 1-1	18 Nov 4-0	9 Dec 5-0	16 Dec 5-2	11 Nov 4-0	26 Aug 4-0	23 Sep 1-1	21 Oct 2-2	16 Sep 3-1
Birmingham	7 Oct 3-2	X	9 Sep 1-2	30 Sep 3-3	2 Dec 0-0	2 Sep 4-0	28 Oct 1-1	25 Nov 2-2	16 Nov 2-0	4 Nov 1-0
Coventry City	25 Nov 0-6	16 Sep 0-1	X	11 Nov 3-1	28 Oct 3-1	14 Oct 4-3	2 Dec 0-1	2 Sep 2-1	23 Sep 1-1	23 Dec 1-2
Leicester City	2 Dec 0-3	23 Sep 0-1	4 Nov 2-1	X	25 Nov 2-2	21 Oct 4-1	23 Dec 1-5	9 Sep 2-3	14 Oct 0-2	26 Aug 2-2
Northampton Town	23 Dec 2-3	9 Dec 2-1	21 Oct 4-1	18 Nov 3-1	X	23 Sep 3-1	16 Sep 1-1	4 Nov 1-1	26 Aug 1-4	14 Oct 1-1
Port Vale	4 Nov 2-1	26 Aug 3-0	7 Oct 2-0	28 Oct 2-1	30 Sep 1-2	X	25 Nov 3-0	23 Dec 1-2	16 Sep 0-0	2 Dec 0-3
Stoke City	2 Sep 3-1	21 Oct 0-0	9nDec 5-0	16 Dec 5-2	9 Sep 5-0	18 Nov 2-0	X	14 Oct 0-2	11 Nov 2-3	23 Sep 2-0
Walsall	30 Sep 0-2	18 Nov 4-1	26 Aug 2-3	16 Sep 0-1	11 Nov 3-2	16 Dec 2-2	7 Oct 1-1	X	9 Dec 1-2	28 Oct 1-2
West Bromwich Albion	28 Oct 1-5	23 Dec 1-4	30 Sep 4-1	7 Oct 1-1	2 Sep 3-1	9 Sep 2-1	4 Nov 2-3	2 Dec 3-0	X	25 Nov 3-2
Wolverhampton Wanderers	9 Sep 1-2	11 Nov 0-4	16 Dec 1-1	2 Sep 4-0	7 Oct 2-2	9 Dec 2-0	30 Sep 4-1	21 Oct 1-1	18 Nov 3-2	X

Inter area matches

Played on 26 Aug
 Barnsley v Huddersfield Town 1-2
 Hull City v Doncaster Rovers 1-8
Played on 2 Sep
 Huddersfield Town v Barnsley 2-1
 Doncaster Rovers v Hull City 2-1
Played on 9 Sep
 Bradford City v Accrington Stanley 4-0
 Halifax Town v Hull City 1-1

Played on 16 Sep
 Accrington Stanley v Bradford City 2-3
 Hull City v Halifax Town 2-0
Played on 2 Dec
 Bradford City v Doncaster Rover 2-3
 Hull City v Grimsby Town 4-3
Played on 9 Dec
 Doncaster Rovers v Bradford City 4-1
 Grimsby Town v Hull City 0-0

The Football League 1944-45

NORTH

	Bradford	Bradford City	Darlington	Gateshead	Hartlepools U	Huddersfield Town	Hull City	Leeds U	Middlesbrough	Newcastle U	Sunderland	York City
Bradford	X	23 Sep 4-1	18 Nov 0-3	9 Dec 1-4	14 Oct 4-1	21 Oct 2-2	23 Dec 6-1	26 Aug 4-3		16 Sep 1-0		11 Nov 5-3
Bradford City	30 Sep 1-3	X	2 Sep 3-2		16 Dec 2-4			4 Nov 2-6	28 Oct 2-0	25 Nov 5-2	7 Oct 1-1	
Darlington	25 Nov 3-2	26 Aug 6-0	X	4 Nov 1-6	16 Sep 2-1	23 Sep 2-3	28 Oct 7-1		23 Dec 5-2		2 Dec 1-3	14 Oct 6-4
Gateshead	2 Dec 1-2		11 Nov 1-3	X	23 Sep 1-3	14 Oct 2-6	25 Nov 5-2		16 Sep 5-5	26 Aug 2-2	23 Dec 1-0	21 Oct 4-2
Hartlepools United	7 Oct 0-0	23 Dec 4-3	9 Sep 4-2	30 Sep 2-5	X			25 Nov 3-0	4 Nov 2-3	2 Dec 2-3	21 Oct 2-6	2 Sep 5-0
Huddersfield Town	28 Oct 1-1		30 Sep 1-2	7 Oct 4-0		X		2 Dec 4-2	25 Nov 5-1	23 Dec 4-1	4 Nov 3-0	9 Sep 2-1
Hull City	16 Dec 0-4		21 Oct 3-2	18 Nov 1-3			X	14 Oct 0-0		11 Nov 3-6		23 Dec 1-0
Leeds United	2 Sep 3-3	11 Nov 4-1	X	X	18 Nov 6-2	9 Dec 2-3	7 Oct 5-2	X	30 Sep 4-2	21 Oct 2-1	9 Sep 0-1	16 Dec 3-1
Middlesbrough		21 Oct 2-3	16 Dec 3-3	9 Sep 4-1	11 Nov 0-3	18 Nov 0-1		23 Sep 3-2	X	14 Oct 2-8	2 Sep 1-5	16 Dec 3-1
Newcastle United	9 Sep 0-2	18 Nov 11-0		2 Sep 3-1	9 Dec 3-0	16 Dec 1-2	4 Nov 7-0	28 Oct 2-4	7 Oct 0-1	X	30 Sep 1-5	
Sunderland		14 Oct 2-1	9 Dec 6-2	16 Dec 2-1	28 Oct 4-2	11 Nov 2-2		16 Sep 5-1	26 Aug 0-0	23 Sep 2-0	X	25 Nov 3-3
York City	4 Nov 4-1		7 Oct 2-0	28 Oct 10-2	26 Aug 3-1	16 Sep 1-3	30 Sep 1-0	23 Dec 3-6	2 Dec 5-1		18 Nov 3-5	X

Hull City v Newcastle United on 11 Nov and Bradford v Gateshead on 9 Dec were both played at York

	Barnsley	Chesterfield	Derby Co	Doncaster R	Grimsby T	Lincoln C	Mansfield T	Nottingham Forest	Notts Co	Rotherham U	Sheffield United	Sheffield Wednesday
Barnsley	X	21 Oct 3-1	16 Sep 2-0			9 Dec 5-3	11 Nov 3-2		14 Oct 6-2	18 Nov 6-5	23 Sep 2-1	16 Dec 2-3
Chesterfield	28 Oct 0-0	X	25 Nov 0-1	4 Nov 1-2		9 Sep 3-1		7 Oct 0-1	23 Dec 8-0	2 Dec 0-0	2 Sep 1-1	30 Sep 5-2
Derby County	9 Sep 1-2	18 Nov 3-1	X	30 Sep 4-1	7 Oct 3-2		9 Dec 7-1	2 Sep 5-0	11 Nov 6-3	16 Dec 4-0	21 Oct 4-2	
Doncaster Rovers		11 Nov 0-1	23 Sep 1-4	X	9 Sep 1-3	16 Dec 9-2	18 Nov 2-1		21 Oct 3-1		14 Oct 3-0	
Grimsby Town			14 Oct 3-1	16 Sep 2-1	X	21 Oct 4-0	26 Aug 5-1	16 Dec 3-1		23 Sep 1-1	11 Nov 1-0	18 Nov 1-2
Lincoln City	2 Dec 2-5	16 Sep 0-1		23 Dec 0-3	28 Oct 5-2	X	23 Sep 3-1	25 Nov 2-2	26 Aug 4-2	14 Oct 2-6		4 Nov 0-3
Mansfield Town	4 Nov 1-1		2 Dec 0-4	25 Nov 0-2	2 Sep 1-1	30 Sep 1-0	X	28 Oct 4-2		9 Sep 1-2	23 Dec 4-1	7 Oct 2-0
Nottingham Forest		14 Oct 2-1	26 Aug 0-0		23 Dec 1-2	18 Nov 2-2	21 Oct 2-5	X	23 Sep 2-1	11 Nov 1-2	16 Sep 2-2	9 Dec 1-0
Notts County	7 Oct 0-3	16 Dec 0-3	4 Nov 1-4	28 Oct 0-2		2 Sep 4-5		30 Sep 0-0	X	2 Dec 0-2	25 Nov 1-0	9 Sep 2-0
Rotherham United	25 Nov 1-0	26 Aug 3-2	23 Dec 0-1		30 Sep 2-0	7 Oct 1-0	16 Sep 0-0	4 Nov 1-2	9 Dec 2-1	X		28 Oct 3-3
Sheffield United	30 Sep 1-0	9 Dec 0-1	28 Oct 0-2	7 Oct 3-1	4 Nov 3-1		16 Dec 4-0	9 Sep 2-0	18 Nov 6-0		X	2 Sep 0-1
Sheffield Wednesday	23 Dec 5-0	23 Sep 0-1		25 Nov 2-3	11 Nov 2-1	14 Oct 1-6	2 Dec 2-1	16 Sep 6-1	21 Oct 1-0	26 Aug 1-1		X

Rotherham United v Barnsley on 25 Nov was played at Doncaster

There were no scheduled matches between the clubs that are blank in the above grids

The Football League 1944-45

NORTH

	Accrington S	Blackburn R	Blackpool	Bolton W	Burnley	Halifax Town	Oldham Ath	Preston NE	Rochdale	Southport
Accrington Stanley	X	14 Oct 1-4	23 Sep 3-4	11 Nov 2-3	25 Nov 0-5		26 Aug 5-1	2 Dec 0-3	21 Oct 1-2	23 Dec 4-1
Blackburn Rovers	7 Oct 1-2	X	23 Dec 2-2	30 Sep 2-1	2 Sep 0-2	2 Dec 4-0	25 Nov 1-1	28 Oct 2-1	9 Sep 3-0	4 Nov 4-2
Blackpool	30 Sep 6-0	16 Dec 2-1	X	9 Sep 1-2	2 Dec 0-2	25 Nov 4-2	4 Nov 1-3	7 Oct 1-1	2 Sep 3-2	28 Oct 10-2
Bolton Wanderers	4 Nov 3-3	23 Sep 0-0	16 Sep 1-0	X	28 Oct 4-0	26 Aug 0-0	23 Dec 2-1	25 Nov 0-0	14 Oct 0-0	2 Dec 3-1
Burnley	18 Nov 0-0	26 Aug 1-1	9 Dec 5-1	21 Oct 6-3	X	11 Nov 1-2	14 Oct 1-0	23 Dec 5-1	23 Sep 2-2	16 Sep 3-1
Halifax Town		9 Dec 2-1	18 Nov 4-3	2 Sep 2-0	4 Nov 2-1	X	28 Oct 5-1	30 Sep 1-1	16 Dec 4-2	7 Oct 2-2
Oldham Athletic	2 Sep 2-1	18 Nov 3-0	11 Nov 2-3	16 Dec 0-5	7 Oct 3-1	21 Oct 0-1	X	9 Sep 0-1	9 Dec 0-2	30 Sep 2-0
Preston North End	9 Dec 1-3	21 Oct 0-2	14 Oct 1-0	18 Nov 2-3	16 Dec 1-1	23 Sep 1-0	16 Sep 4-1	X	11 Nov 2-1	26 Aug 3-0
Rochdale	28 Oct 3-0	16 Sep 2-0	26 Aug 3-7	7 Oct 2-2	30 Sep 3-1	23 Dec 3-0	2 Dec 2-3	4 Nov 5-2	X	25 Nov 1-1
Southport	16 Dec 0-2	11 Nov 7-2	21 Oct 4-5	9 Dec 0-2	9 Sep 3-2	14 Oct 2-2	23 Sep 1-5	2 Sep 3-1	18 Nov 2-2	X

There were no scheduled matches between the clubs that are blank in the above grid

The Football League 1944-45

NORTH

Final Table

		P	W	D	L	F	A	Pts
1	Huddersfield Town	18	14	3	1	50	22	31
2	Derby County	18	14	1	3	54	19	29
3	Sunderland	18	12	4	2	52	25	28
4	Aston Villa	18	12	3	3	54	19	27
5	Everton	18	12	2	4	58	25	26
6	Wrexham	18	11	3	4	40	18	25
7	Doncaster Rovers	18	12	0	6	48	27	24
8	Bradford	18	10	4	4	45	31	24
9	Bolton Wanderers	18	9	6	3	34	22	24
10	Manchester City	18	9	4	5	53	31	22
11	Stoke City	18	9	4	5	37	25	22
12	Birmingham	18	8	6	4	30	21	22
13	Barnsley	18	10	2	6	42	32	22
14	Rotherham United	18	9	4	5	31	25	22
15	West Bromwich Albion	18	9	4	5	36	30	22
16	Liverpool	18	9	3	6	41	30	21
17	Grimsby Town	18	9	3	6	37	29	21
18	Halifax Town	18	8	5	5	30	29	21
19	Chester	18	9	3	6	45	45	21
20	Blackpool	18	9	2	7	53	38	20
21	Burnley	18	8	4	6	39	27	20
22	Leeds United	18	9	2	7	53	42	20
23	Sheffield Wednesday	18	9	2	7	34	30	20
24	Chesterfield	18	8	3	7	30	19	19
25	Darlington	18	9	1	8	52	45	19
26	Wolverhampton Wanderers	18	7	5	6	31	27	19
27	Rochdale	18	7	5	6	35	33	19
28	Crewe Alexandra	18	9	1	8	43	41	19
29	Blackburn Rovers	18	7	4	7	30	29	18
30	Manchester United	18	8	2	8	40	40	18
31	Preston North End	18	7	4	7	26	28	18
32	Walsall	18	5	6	7	27	29	16
33	Gateshead	18	7	2	9	45	53	16
34	Northampton Town	18	5	6	7	30	38	16
35	Newcastle United	18	7	1	10	51	38	15
36	Sheffield United	18	6	3	9	27	25	15
37	Hartlepools United	18	7	1	10	41	47	15
38	Oldham Athletic	18	7	1	10	28	36	15
39	Mansfield Town	18	6	3	9	31	40	15
40	Nottingham Forest	18	5	5	8	22	34	15
41	Coventry City	18	6	2	10	23	42	14
42	York City	18	6	1	11	49	52	13
43	Middlesbrough	18	5	3	10	34	57	13
44	Bradford City	18	6	1	11	35	60	13
45	Accrington Stanley	18	5	2	11	29	46	12
46	Port Vale	18	5	2	11	22	36	12
47	Bury	18	5	2	11	28	48	12
48	Stockport County	18	5	1	12	33	70	11
49	Hull City	18	4	3	11	23	60	11
50	Southport	18	3	4	11	32	55	10
51	Lincoln City	18	4	2	12	32	56	10
52	Leicester City	18	3	4	11	23	46	10
53	Tranmere Rovers	18	2	1	15	20	53	5
54	Notts County	18	2	1	15	19	62	5

The Football League 1944-45

NORTH (SECOND CHAMPIONSHIP)
Including League Cup and county cup matches

ABERAMAN ATHLETIC
LC	25 Dec	Lovell's Ath	A	1-6
LC	26 Dec	Lovell's Ath	H	1-2
LC	6 Jan	Bath C	A	6-4
LC	13 Jan	Bath C	H	3-4
LC	20 Jan	Bristol City	A	0-10
LC	3 Feb	Cardiff C	H	2-5
LC	10 Feb	Cardiff C	A	0-0
LC	17 Feb	Swansea T	A	2-5
LC	24 Feb	Swansea T	H	2-8
LC	3 Mar	Bristol City	H	0-2
WC	10 Mar	Lovell's Ath	H	2-3
WC	17 Mar	Lovell's Ath	A	4-4
WC	2 Apr	Swansea T	A	3-4
WC	7 Apr	Swansea T	H	8-1
WC	21 Apr	Bristol City	A	1-2
WC	28 Apr	Bath C	A	1-5
WC	5 May	Bath C	H	0-4

ACCRINGTON STANLEY
LC	25 Dec	Rochdale	H	0-1
LC	30 Dec	Rochdale	A	1-1
LC	6 Jan	Preston NE	A	2-1
LC	13 Jan	Preston NE	H	2-1
LC	20 Jan	Burnley	H	0-4
LC	27 Jan	Burnley	A	0-3
LC	3 Feb	Blackpool	A	3-0
LC	10 Feb	Blackpool	H	4-2
LC	17 Feb	Blackburn R	H	3-2
LC	24 Feb	Blackburn R	A	0-3
LC	3 Mar	Blackpool	H	4-1
La	10 Mar	Blackpool	A	2-1
La	17 Mar	Southport	A	2-2
	24 Mar	Bolton W	A	0-0
	31 Mar	Bolton W	H	0-4
	2 Apr	Blackburn R	A	4-4
La	7 Apr	Burnley	A	0-1
La	14 Apr	Burnley	H	4-0
	21 Apr	Bury	H	0-1
	28 Apr	Bury	A	2-2
La	5 May	Everton	H	1-1
La	12 May	Everton	A	2-0
La	19 May	Blackburn R	A	0-2
La	26 May	Blackburn R	H	3-4

ASTON VILLA
	26 Dec	WBA	H	3-4
LC	30 Dec	Northampton T	A	0-2
LC	6 Jan	WBA	A	3-1
LC	13 Jan	WBA	H	6-2
LC	20 Jan	Birmingham	H	3-1
LC	27 Jan	Birmingham	A	1-0
LC	3 Feb	Coventry C	A	3-2
LC	10 Feb	Coventry C	H	5-2
LC	17 Feb	Walsall	H	6-1
LC	24 Feb	Walsall	A	2-0
LC	3 Mar	Northampton T	H	2-2
	10 Mar	Birmingham	H	5-0
	17 Mar	Birmingham	A	3-0
LC	24 Mar	Wolverhampton	A	0-1
LC	31 Mar	Wolverhampton	A	0-1
	2 Apr	WBA	A	4-2
	7 Apr	Leicester C	A	0-2
	14 Apr	Leicester C	H	7-2
MC	21 Apr	Stoke C	A	0-1
MC	28 Apr	Stoke C	H	2-0
MC	5 May	Coventry C	H	9-2
MC	12 May	Coventry C	A	1-3
MC	19 May	Derby Co	H	0-3
	21 May	Wolverhampton	H	4-4
MC	26 May	Derby Co	A	0-6

26 Dec, abandoned after 80 mins, result stood

BARNSLEY
LC	25 Dec	Bradford	A	1-3
	26 Dec	Huddersfield T	H	0-1
LC	30 Dec	Bradford	H	2-1
LC	6 Jan	Leeds U	A	1-0
LC	13 Jan	Leeds U	H	5-0
LC	20 Jan	Bradford City	A	1-0
LC	27 Jan	Bradford City	H	2-1
LC	3 Feb	York C	H	2-1
LC	10 Feb	York C	A	1-5
LC	17 Feb	Hull C	A	0-3
LC	24 Feb	Hull C	H	3-0
	3 Mar	Burnley	A	0-4
	10 Mar	Burnley	H	2-0
	17 Mar	Blackpool	A	2-0
LC	24 Mar	Rotherham U	A	1-2
LC	31 Mar	Rotherham U	H	3-0
LC	7 Apr	Chesterfield	H	2-2
LC	14 Apr	Chesterfield	A	0-2
	21 Apr	Leeds U	H	1-3
	28 Apr	Leeds U	A	3-1
SC	5 May	Sheffield Wed	H	3-3
	8 May	Huddersfield T	H	2-4
V	9 May	Huddersfield T	A	1-2
SC	12 May	Sheffield Wed	A	1-4

BATH CITY
LC	25 Dec	Bristol City	A	1-2
LC	30 Dec	Bristol City	H	0-2
LC	6 Jan	Aberaman Ath	H	4-6
LC	13 Jan	Aberaman Ath	A	4-3
LC	20 Jan	Cardiff C	A	2-4
LC	3 Feb	Swansea T	H	7-4
LC	10 Feb	Swansea T	A	6-2
LC	17 Feb	Lovell's Ath	A	2-4
LC	24 Feb	Lovell's Ath	H	1-3
LC	3 Mar	Cardiff C	H	1-4
WC	10 Mar	Bristol City	A	1-4
WC	17 Mar	Bristol City	H	1-0
WC	24 Mar	Swansea T	H	2-1
WC	31 Mar	Swansea T	A	0-1
WC	14 Apr	Lovell's Ath	H	4-2
WC	21 Apr	Lovell's Ath	A	0-2
WC	28 Apr	Aberaman Ath	H	5-1
WC	5 May	Aberaman Ath	A	4-0
WC	19 May	Bristol City	H	1-0
WC	26 May	Bristol City	A	4-3

BIRMINGHAM
	26 Dec	Coventry C	H	0-0
LC	30 Dec	Walsall	H	3-1
LC	6 Jan	Coventry C	H	5-1
LC	13 Jan	Coventry C	A	2-1
LC	20 Jan	Aston Villa	A	1-3
LC	27 Jan	Aston Villa	H	0-1
LC	3 Feb	Northampton T	H	4-0
LC	10 Feb	Northampton T	A	1-2
LC	17 Feb	WBA	A	0-4
LC	24 Feb	WBA	H	1-1
LC	3 Mar	Walsall	A	2-0
	10 Mar	Aston Villa	A	0-5
	17 Mar	Aston Villa	H	0-3
LC	24 Mar	Northampton T	A	2-0
LC	31 Mar	Northampton T	H	2-2
	2 Apr	Wolverhampton	A	1-2
LC	7 Apr	Wolverhampton	H	0-0
LC	14 Apr	Wolverhampton	A	0-0
MC	21 Apr	Coventry C	H	1-2
MC	28 Apr	Coventry C	A	2-2
	5 May	WBA	H	4-1
	12 May	WBA	A	3-2
	19 May	Nottingham F	H	4-1
	26 May	Nottingham F	A	0-0

14 Apr, aet 0-1

KEY: LC=League Cup; WC=League West Cup; La=Lancashire Cup; MC=Midland Cup;
CB=Cheshire Bowl; Li=Liverpool Senior Cup; TT=Tyne, Wear & Tees Cup; SC=Sheffield County Cup

The Football League 1944-45

NORTH (SECOND CHAMPIONSHIP)
Including League Cup and county cup matches

BLACKBURN ROVERS

LC	25 Dec	Burnley	H	2-4
	26 Dec	Preston NE	A	2-3
LC	30 Dec	Burnley	A	1-4
LC	13 Jan	Rochdale	H	3-2
LC	20 Jan	Blackpool	H	7-4
LC	27 Jan	Blackpool	A	1-3
LC	3 Feb	Preston NE	A	1-3
LC	10 Feb	Preston NE	H	3-2
LC	17 Feb	Accrington S	A	2-3
LC	24 Feb	Accrington S	H	3-0
LC	3 Mar	Rochdale	A	8-0
La	10 Mar	Rochdale	A	1-0
La	17 Mar	Rochdale	H	4-0
	24 Mar	Sheffield Wed	H	2-2
	31 Mar	Sheffield Wed	A	0-2
	2 Apr	Accrington S	H	4-4
La	7 Apr	Bury	A	3-2
La	14 Apr	Bury	H	4-2
	21 Apr	Preston NE	A	0-5
	28 Apr	Preston NE	H	1-0
La	5 May	Crewe Alex	H	2-0
V	9 May	Burnley	A	2-3
La	12 May	Crewe Alex	A	2-3
La	19 May	Accrington S	H	2-0
La	26 May	Accrington S	A	4-3

BLACKPOOL

	25 Dec	Preston NE	A	1-1
LC	26 Dec	Preston NE	A	3-1
LC	30 Dec	Preston NE	H	1-1
LC	6 Jan	Burnley	A	0-2
LC	13 Jan	Burnley	H	4-0
LC	20 Jan	Blackburn R	A	4-7
LC	27 Jan	Blackburn R	H	3-1
LC	3 Feb	Accrington S	H	0-3
LC	10 Feb	Accrington S	A	2-4
LC	17 Feb	Rochdale	H	6-3
LC	24 Feb	Rochdale	H	4-0
La	3 Mar	Accrington S	A	1-4
La	10 Mar	Accrington S	H	1-2
	17 Mar	Barnsley	H	0-2
LC	24 Mar	Wrexham	H	2-0
LC	31 Mar	Wrexham	A	2-2
	2 Apr	Manchester Utd	H	4-1
LC	7 Apr	Bolton W	H	1-4
LC	14 Apr	Bolton W	A	2-1
	21 Apr	Manchester City	A	1-0
	28 Apr	Manchester City	H	4-0
	5 May	Preston NE	H	8-1
	12 May	Preston NE	A	4-0
	19 May	Liverpool	A	0-2

BOLTON WANDERERS

LC	26 Dec	Stockport Co	H	2-0
LC	30 Dec	Stockport Co	A	0-2
LC	6 Jan	Everton	A	1-2
LC	13 Jan	Everton	H	1-3
LC	27 Jan	Southport	A	4-3
LC	3 Feb	Tranmere R	A	4-1
LC	10 Feb	Tranmere R	H	6-1
LC	17 Feb	Liverpool	H	2-1
LC	24 Feb	Liverpool	A	1-1
	3 Mar	Crewe Alex	A	1-4
LC	10 Mar	Southport	H	6-1
La	17 Mar	Bury	H	3-3
LC	24 Mar	Accrington S	H	0-0
LC	31 Mar	Accrington S	A	4-0
La	2 Apr	Bury	A	0-1
LC	7 Apr	Blackpool	A	4-1
LC	14 Apr	Blackpool	H	1-2
LC	21 Apr	Newcastle U	H	3-0
LC	28 Apr	Newcastle U	A	1-4
LC	5 May	Wolverhampton	A	2-2
LC	12 May	Wolverhampton	H	2-1
LC	19 May	Manchester Utd	H	1-0
LC	26 May	Manchester Utd	A	2-2

28 Apr, aet 2-4

BRADFORD

LC	25 Dec	Barnsley	H	3-1
	26 Dec	Burnley	A	2-4
LC	30 Dec	Barnsley	A	1-2
LC	6 Jan	York C	H	4-2
LC	27 Jan	Hull C	H	2-1
LC	3 Feb	Bradford City	H	2-2
LC	10 Feb	Bradford City	A	1-3
LC	17 Feb	Leeds U	H	5-2
LC	24 Feb	Leeds U	A	2-0
LC	3 Mar	York C	A	1-6
LC	10 Mar	Hull C	A	2-0
	17 Mar	Huddersfield T	H	5-0
LC	24 Mar	Doncaster r	H	1-1
LC	31 Mar	Doncaster R	A	0-2
	2 Apr	Preston NE	H	6-1
	7 Apr	Middlesbrough	H	3-1
	14 Apr	Middlesbrough	A	0-1
	21 Apr	Sheffield Wed	A	1-3
	28 Apr	Sheffield Wed	H	5-2
	5 May	Burnley	A	1-1
	19 May	Chesterfield	H	2-2
	26 May	Chesterfield	A	0-1

BRADFORD CITY

LC	26 Dec	Leeds U	A	1-9
LC	30 Dec	Leeds U	H	6-2
LC	6 Jan	Hull C	A	3-1
LC	13 Jan	Hull C	H	2-1
LC	20 Jan	Barnsley	H	0-1
LC	27 Jan	Barnsley	A	1-2
LC	3 Feb	Bradford	A	2-2
LC	10 Feb	Bradford	H	3-1
LC	17 Feb	York C	A	2-2
LC	24 Feb	York C	H	3-0
LC	3 Mar	Rotherham U	H	5-3
	10 Mar	Grimsby T	A	2-3
	17 Mar	Rotherham U	A	0-2
LC	24 Mar	Sheffield Utd	A	2-2
LC	31 Mar	Sheffield Utd	H	4-3
	2 Apr	Hull C	A	1-3
LC	7 Apr	Newcastle U	A	2-6
LC	14 Apr	Newcastle U	H	0-1
	21 Apr	Halifax T	H	4-0
	28 Apr	Halifax T	A	0-2

BRISTOL CITY

LC	25 Dec	Bath C	H	2-1
LC	30 Dec	Bath C	A	2-0
LC	6 Jan	Swansea T	A	2-1
LC	13 Jan	Swansea T	H	3-1
LC	20 Jan	Aberaman Ath	H	10-0
LC	3 Feb	Lovell's Ath	H	2-1
LC	10 Feb	Lovell's Ath	A	1-2
LC	17 Feb	Cardiff C	A	2-4
LC	24 Feb	Cardiff C	H	1-0
LC	3 Mar	Aberaman Ath	A	2-0
WC	10 Mar	Bath C	H	4-1
WC	17 Mar	Bath C	A	0-1
LC	24 Mar	WBA	H	5-2
LC	31 Mar	WBA	A	3-3
WC	2 Apr	Cardiff C	A	2-3
LC	7 Apr	Cardiff C	H	1-2
LC	14 Apr	Cardiff C	A	2-1
WC	21 Apr	Aberaman Ath	A	2-1
WC	28 Apr	Swansea T	A	2-2
WC	5 May	Swansea T	H	4-2
WC	19 May	Bath C	A	0-1
WC	26 May	Bath C	H	3-4

14 Apr, aet 2-2

**KEY: LC=League Cup; WC=League West Cup; La=Lancashire Cup; MC=Midland Cup;
CB=Cheshire Bowl; Li=Liverpool Senior Cup; TT=Tyne, Wear & Tees Cup; SC=Sheffield County Cup**

The Football League 1944-45

NORTH (SECOND CHAMPIONSHIP)
Including League Cup and county cup matches

BURNLEY

LC	25 Dec	Blackburn R	A	4-2
	26 Dec	Bradford	H	4-2
LC	30 Dec	Blackburn R	H	4-1
LC	6 Jan	Blackpool	H	2-0
LC	13 Jan	Blackpool	A	0-4
LC	20 Jan	Accrington S	A	4-0
LC	27 Jan	Accrington S	H	3-0
LC	3 Feb	Rochdale	H	2-0
LC	10 Feb	Rochdale	A	4-0
LC	17 Feb	Preston NE	A	1-2
LC	24 Feb	Preston NE	H	1-1
	3 Mar	Barnsley	H	4-0
	10 Mar	Barnsley	A	0-2
La	17 Mar	Oldham Ath	A	2-1
LC	24 Mar	Manchester Utd	H	2-3
LC	31 Mar	Manchester Utd	A	0-4
La	2 Apr	Oldham Ath	H	3-1
La	7 Apr	Accrington S	H	1-0
La	14 Apr	Accrington S	A	0-4
	21 Apr	Sheffield Utd	H	2-0
	28 Apr	Sheffield Utd	A	1-1
	5 May	Bradford	H	1-1
V	9 May	Blackburn R	H	3-2
	12 May	Tranmere R	A	2-3
	19 May	Tranmere R	H	5-1
	26 May	Preston NE	A	1-2

BURY

	26 Dec	Oldham Ath	A	2-2
	30 Dec	Manchester City	A	2-3
LC	6 Jan	Oldham Ath	H	3-1
LC	13 Jan	Oldham Ath	A	0-2
LC	20 Jan	Huddersfield T	A	1-2
LC	27 Jan	Huddersfield T	H	4-3
LC	3 Feb	Halifax T	H	2-1
LC	10 Feb	Halifax T	A	2-2
LC	17 Feb	Manchester Utd	A	0-2
LC	24 Feb	Manchester Utd	H	3-1
LC	3 Mar	Manchester City	H	4-2
La	17 Mar	Bolton W	A	3-3
	24 Mar	Stockport Co	H	3-2
	31 Mar	Stockport Co	A	0-3
La	2 Apr	Bolton W	H	1-0
La	7 Apr	Blackburn R	H	2-3
La	14 Apr	Blackburn R	A	2-4
	21 Apr	Accrington S	A	1-0
	28 Apr	Accrington S	H	2-2
	5 May	Rotherham U	A	1-5

CARDIFF CITY

LC	25 Dec	Swansea T	H	3-1
LC	30 Dec	Swansea T	A	3-1
LC	6 Jan	Lovell's Ath	A	0-1
LC	13 Jan	Lovell's Ath	H	3-0
LC	20 Jan	Bath C	H	4-2
LC	3 Feb	Aberaman Ath	A	5-2
LC	10 Feb	Aberaman Ath	H	0-0
LC	17 Feb	Bristol City	H	4-2
LC	24 Feb	Bristol City	A	0-1
LC	3 Mar	Bath C	A	4-1
LC	10 Mar	Swansea T	A	0-1
LC	17 Mar	Swansea T	H	6-2
LC	24 Mar	Lovell's Ath	H	1-0
LC	31 Mar	Lovell's Ath	A	0-0
WC	2 Apr	Bristol City	H	3-2
LC	7 Apr	Bristol City	A	2-1
LC	14 Apr	Bristol City	H	1-2
LC	21 Apr	Wolverhampton	A	0-3
LC	28 Apr	Wolverhampton	H	2-1
WC	12 May	Lovell's Ath	H	0-4

14 Apr, aet 2-2

CHESTER

LC	25 Dec	Wrexham	A	2-4
LC	30 Dec	Wrexham	H	2-5
LC	6 Jan	Port Vale	H	2-3
LC	13 Jan	Port Vale	A	2-0
LC	20 Jan	Wolverhampton	A	1-6
LC	3 Feb	Stoke C	H	2-3
LC	10 Feb	Stoke C	A	0-7
LC	17 Feb	Crewe Alex	H	3-3
LC	24 Feb	Crewe Alex	A	0-4
La	3 Mar	Everton	A	1-4
La	10 Mar	Everton	H	6-3
LC	17 Mar	Wolverhampton	H	0-4
	24 Mar	Preston NE	A	2-3
	31 Mar	Preston NE	H	4-1
	2 Apr	Rochdale	H	3-0
	7 Apr	Southport	A	2-1
	14 Apr	Southport	H	5-3
	21 Apr	Wrexham	A	2-2
	28 Apr	Wrexham	H	2-1
	5 May	Rochdale	A	1-2
CB	19 May	Crewe Alex	A	3-0
CB	26 May	Crewe Alex	H	4-2

10 Mar, aet 6-4

CHESTERFIELD

LC	25 Dec	Derby Co	A	2-2
LC	30 Dec	Derby Co	H	0-1
LC	6 Jan	Notts County	H	3-1
LC	13 Jan	Notts County	A	3-1
LC	20 Jan	Leicester C	H	1-0
LC	27 Jan	Leicester C	A	2-2
LC	3 Feb	Nottingham F	H	0-1
LC	10 Feb	Nottingham F	A	1-1
LC	17 Feb	Mansfield T	A	3-4
LC	24 Feb	Mansfield T	H	3-0
	3 Mar	Doncaster R	A	1-2
	17 Mar	Doncaster R	H	2-0
LC	24 Mar	Halifax T	A	1-1
LC	31 Mar	Halifax T	H	1-1
	2 Apr	Leeds U	A	2-0
LC	7 Apr	Barnsley	A	2-2
LC	14 Apr	Barnsley	H	2-0
LC	21 Apr	Liverpool	A	0-0
LC	28 Apr	Liverpool	H	1-0
LC	5 May	Manchester Utd	A	1-1
LC	12 May	Manchester Utd	H	0-1
	19 May	Bradford	A	2-2
	21 May	Leeds U	H	6-1
	26 May	Bradford	H	1-0

COVENTRY CITY

	26 Dec	Birmingham	A	0-0
	30 Dec	WBA	A	1-1
LC	6 Jan	Birmingham	A	1-5
LC	13 Jan	Birmingham	H	1-2
LC	20 Jan	Walsall	A	5-6
LC	27 Jan	Walsall	H	0-2
LC	3 Feb	Aston Villa	H	2-3
LC	10 Feb	Aston Villa	A	2-5
LC	17 Feb	Northampton T	A	1-8
LC	24 Feb	Northampton T	H	3-0
LC	3 Mar	WBA	H	0-3
	10 Mar	Notts County	H	4-0
	17 Mar	Leicester C	A	2-2
	24 Mar	Notts County	H	1-0
	31 Mar	Notts County	A	2-1
	7 Apr	Nottingham F	A	1-1
	14 Apr	Nottingham F	H	1-1
MC	21 Apr	Birmingham	A	2-1
MC	28 Apr	Birmingham	H	2-2
MC	5 May	Aston Villa	A	2-9
MC	12 May	Aston Villa	H	3-1

KEY: LC=League Cup; WC=League West Cup; La=Lancashire Cup; MC=Midland Cup; CB=Cheshire Bowl; Li=Liverpool Senior Cup; TT=Tyne, Wear & Tees Cup; SC=Sheffield County Cup

The Football League 1944-45

NORTH (SECOND CHAMPIONSHIP)
Including League Cup and county cup matches

CREWE ALEXANDRA

LC	25 Dec	Port Vale	A	3-1
LC	30 Dec	Port Vale	H	2-1
LC	6 Jan	Wolverhampton	H	2-3
LC	13 Jan	Wolverhampton	A	1-3
LC	3 Feb	Wrexham	H	3-3
LC	10 Feb	Wrexham	A	1-6
LC	17 Feb	Chester	A	3-3
LC	24 Feb	Chester	H	4-0
	3 Mar	Bolton W	H	4-1
LC	10 Mar	Stoke C	A	2-1
LC	17 Mar	Stoke C	H	2-2
LC	24 Mar	Manchester City	A	1-5
LC	31 Mar	Manchester City	H	2-0
	2 Apr	Halifax T	H	4-1
	7 Apr	Preston NE	A	1-4
	14 Apr	Preston NE	H	0-3
CB/La	21 Apr	Stockport Co	A	1-0
CB/La	28 Apr	Stockport Co	H	6-0
La	5 May	Blackburn R	A	0-2
La	12 May	Blackburn R	H	3-2
CB	19 May	Chester	H	0-3
CB	21 May	Stoke C	H	3-2
	26 May	Chester	A	2-4

DARLINGTON

LC	25 Dec	Gateshead	H	1-1
LC	30 Dec	Gateshead	A	1-2
LC	6 Jan	Sunderland	A	1-1
LC	13 Jan	Sunderland	H	3-2
LC	20 Jan	Hartlepools U	H	3-2
LC	3 Feb	Middlesbrough	A	1-0
LC	10 Feb	Middlesbrough	H	6-4
LC	17 Feb	Newcastle U	A	1-3
LC	24 Feb	Newcastle U	H	2-3
	3 Mar	Middlesbrough	H	1-0
	10 Mar	Sunderland	A	5-1
LC	17 Mar	Hartlepools U	A	3-0
LC	24 Mar	Newcastle U	A	1-2
LC	31 Mar	Newcastle U	H	0-3
	2 Apr	York C	H	7-3
	7 Apr	Gateshead	H	2-4
	14 Apr	Gateshead	A	4-3
TT	21 Apr	York C	A	0-2
TT	28 Apr	York C	H	2-2
	5 May	Hartlepools U	A	0-2
V	9 May	Middlesbrough	H	5-3
	12 May	Hartlepools U	H	3-0
	19 May	York C	H	4-2
	21 May	Hartlepools U	A	5-0

DERBY COUNTY

LC	25 Dec	Chesterfield	H	2-2
	26 Dec	Stoke C	A	2-4
LC	30 Dec	Chesterfield	A	1-0
LC	6 Jan	Nottingham F	A	1-1
LC	13 Jan	Nottingham F	H	3-0
LC	20 Jan	Notts County	H	7-0
LC	27 Jan	Notts County	A	4-2
LC	3 Feb	Mansfield T	A	8-1
LC	10 Feb	Mansfield T	H	7-1
LC	17 Feb	Leicester C	A	2-2
LC	24 Feb	Leicester C	H	3-0
	3 Mar	Huddersfield T	A	4-0
	10 Mar	Huddersfield T	H	2-1
	17 Mar	Sheffield Utd	H	3-2
LC	24 Mar	Leicester C	A	1-2
LC	31 Mar	Leicester C	H	2-0
	2 Apr	Stoke C	H	2-1
LC	7 Apr	Doncaster R	A	2-1
LC	14 Apr	Doncaster R	H	1-4
MC	21 Apr	Northampton T	A	1-2
MC	28 Apr	Northampton T	H	5-0
MC	5 May	Leicester C	H	3-1
MC	12 May	Leicester C	A	2-1
MC	19 May	Aston Villa	A	3-0
	21 May	Liverpool	H	1-0
MC	26 May	Aston Villa	H	6-0

DONCASTER ROVERS

LC	26 Dec	Rotherham U	H	0-0
LC	30 Dec	Rotherham U	A	0-3
LC	6 Jan	Lincoln C	H	6-1
LC	13 Jan	Lincoln C	A	3-1
LC	20 Jan	Grimsby T	A	2-1
LC	27 Jan	Grimsby T	H	5-1
LC	3 Feb	Sheffield Wed	H	1-3
LC	10 Feb	Sheffield Wed	A	6-1
LC	17 Feb	Sheffield Utd	A	4-0
LC	24 Feb	Sheffield Utd	H	3-2
	3 Mar	Chesterfield	H	2-1
	10 Mar	Sheffield Wed	A	0-1
	17 Mar	Chesterfield	A	0-2
LC	24 Mar	Bradford	A	1-1
LC	31 Mar	Bradford	H	2-0
	2 Apr	Rotherham U	A	2-0
LC	7 Apr	Derby Co	H	1-2
LC	14 Apr	Derby Co	A	4-1
LC	21 Apr	Manchester Utd	H	1-2
LC	28 Apr	Manchester Utd	A	1-3

EVERTON

LC	25 Dec	Tranmere R	H	2-4
Li	26 Dec	Liverpool	H	2-2
LC	30 Dec	Tranmere R	A	4-0
LC	6 Jan	Bolton W	H	2-1
LC	13 Jan	Bolton W	A	3-1
LC	20 Jan	Stockport Co	A	3-0
LC	27 Jan	Stockport Co	H	9-2
LC	3 Feb	Liverpool	H	4-1
LC	10 Feb	Liverpool	A	1-3
LC	17 Feb	Southport	H	6-0
LC	24 Feb	Southport	A	5-3
La	3 Mar	Chester	H	4-1
La	10 Mar	Chester	A	3-6
	17 Mar	Preston NE	H	3-0
LC	24 Mar	Liverpool	A	0-1
LC	31 Mar	Liverpool	H	0-1
Li	2 Apr	Liverpool	A	3-1
	7 Apr	Wrexham	A	2-1
	14 Apr	Wrexham	H	5-3
La	21 Apr	Southport	A	5-0
La	28 Apr	Southport	H	1-1
La	5 May	Accrington S	A	1-1
Li	9 May	Tranmere R	A	3-0
La	12 May	Accrington S	H	0-2
	19 May	Stoke C	A	1-5
Li	21 May	Tranmere R	H	4-1
	26 May	Stoke C	H	3-2

10 Mar, aet 4-6

GATESHEAD

LC	25 Dec	Darlington	A	1-1
LC	30 Dec	Darlington	H	2-1
LC	6 Jan	Hartlepools U	H	1-2
LC	13 Jan	Hartlepools U	A	1-1
LC	20 Jan	Newcastle U	A	4-2
LC	3 Feb	Sunderland	H	2-1
LC	10 Feb	Sunderland	A	0-3
LC	17 Feb	Middlesbrough	A	3-2
LC	24 Feb	Middlesbrough	H	1-2
	3 Mar	Sunderland	A	2-0
LC	17 Mar	Newcastle U	H	0-3
	24 Mar	Sunderland	A	2-2
	31 Mar	Sunderland	H	4-2
	2 Apr	Middlesbrough	A	1-3
	7 Apr	Darlington	A	4-2
	14 Apr	Darlington	H	3-4
TT	5 May	Huddersfield T	H	3-3
TT	12 May	Huddersfield T	A	2-2
	19 May	Newcastle U	H	3-0
	21 May	Newcastle U	A	1-3
TT	26 May	Sunderland	H	6-3

12 May, aet 3-2

KEY: LC=League Cup; WC=League West Cup; La=Lancashire Cup; MC=Midland Cup;
CB=Cheshire Bowl; Li=Liverpool Senior Cup; TT=Tyne, Wear & Tees Cup; SC=Sheffield County Cup

The Football League 1944-45

NORTH (SECOND CHAMPIONSHIP)
Including League Cup and county cup matches

GRIMSBY TOWN

LC	25 Dec	Lincoln C	H	2-2
LC	30 Dec	Lincoln C	A	0-2
LC	6 Jan	Sheffield Wed	H	4-1
LC	13 Jan	Sheffield Wed	A	2-2
LC	20 Jan	Doncaster R	H	1-2
LC	27 Jan	Doncaster R	A	1-5
LC	3 Feb	Sheffield Utd	A	2-2
LC	10 Feb	Sheffield Utd	H	1-2
LC	17 Feb	Rotherham Utd	H	5-0
LC	24 Feb	Rotherham Utd	A	0-3
	3 Mar	Hull C	A	1-3
	10 Mar	Bradford City	H	3-2
	17 Mar	Hull C	H	4-0
	24 Mar	Leeds U	A	1-1
	31 Mar	Lincoln C	`H	4-2
	2 Apr	Lincoln C	A	3-3
	7 Apr	Leeds U	H	3-0
	14 Apr	Lincoln C	H	4-3
	21 Apr	Lincoln C	A	2-2
	5 May	Notts County	H	3-1
	12 May	Notts County	A	3-1

HALIFAX TOWN

LC	25 Dec	Huddersfield T	A	0-0
LC	30 Dec	Huddersfield T	H	4-2
LC	6 Jan	Manchester City	H	1-1
LC	13 Jan	Manchester City	A	3-2
LC	3 Feb	Bury	A	1-2
LC	10 Feb	Bury	H	2-2
LC	17 Feb	Oldham Ath	H	0-2
LC	24 Feb	Oldham Ath	A	2-1
	3 Mar	Preston NE	A	0-2
LC	10 Mar	Manchester Utd	H	1-0
LC	17 Mar	Manchester Utd	A	0-2
LC	24 Mar	Chesterfield	H	1-1
LC	31 Mar	Chesterfield	A	1-1
	2 Apr	Crewe Alex	A	1-4
	7 Apr	Sheffield Wed	H	3-2
	14 Apr	Sheffield Wed	A	0-7
	21 Apr	Bradford City	A	0-4
	28 Apr	Bradford City	H	2-0

31 Mar, aet 1-3

HARTLEPOOLS UNITED

LC	26 Dec	Middlesbrough	A	0-0
LC	30 Dec	Middlesbrough	H	6-4
LC	6 Jan	Gateshead	A	2-1
LC	13 Jan	Gateshead	A	1-1
LC	20 Jan	Darlington	A	2-3
LC	10 Feb	Newcastle U	A	1-4
LC	17 Feb	Sunderland	A	2-6
LC	24 Feb	Sunderland	H	3-1
LC	3 Mar	Newcastle U	H	2-1
	10 Mar	York C	H	1-1
LC	17 Mar	Darlington	H	0-3
	24 Mar	Middlesbrough	H	3-0
	31 Mar	Middlesbrough	A	3-1
	7 Apr	Huddersfield T	H	1-6
	14 Apr	Huddersfield T	A	3-6
TT	21 Apr	Sunderland	A	0-5
TT	28 Apr	Sunderland	H	0-2
	5 May	Darlington	H	2-0
	12 May	Darlington	A	0-3
	19 May	Middlesbrough	A	2-1
	21 May	Darlington	H	0-5

HUDDERSFIELD TOWN

LC	25 Dec	Halifax T	H	0-0
	26 Dec	Barnsley	A	1-0
LC	30 Dec	Halifax T	A	2-4
LC	6 Jan	Manchester Utd	A	0-1
LC	13 Jan	Manchester Utd	H	2-2
LC	20 Jan	Bury	H	2-1
LC	27 Jan	Bury	A	3-4
LC	3 Feb	Oldham Ath	A	3-2
LC	10 Feb	Oldham Ath	H	6-1
LC	17 Feb	Manchester City	H	3-1
LC	24 Feb	Manchester City	A	0-2
	3 Mar	Derby Co	H	0-4
	10 Mar	Derby Co	A	1-2
	17 Mar	Bradford	A	0-5
	24 Mar	York C	A	0-1
	31 Mar	York C	H	1-0
	2 Apr	Sheffield Utd	A	1-3
	7 Apr	Hartlepools U	A	6-1
	14 Apr	Hartlepools U	H	6-3
TT	21 Apr	Middlesbrough	A	1-2
TT	28 Apr	Middlesbrough	H	1-0
TT	5 May	Gateshead	A	3-3
	8 May	Barnsley	A	4-2
V	9 May	Barnsley	H	2-1
TT	12 May	Gateshead	H	2-2
	19 May	Sunderland	H	1-0
	21 May	Sunderland	A	0-2

28 Apr, aet 2-0
12 May, aet 2-3

HULL CITY

LC	25 Dec	York C	A	1-5
LC	30 Dec	York C	H	4-2
LC	6 Jan	Bradford City	H	1-3
LC	13 Jan	Bradford City	A	1-2
LC	27 Jan	Bradford	A	1-2
LC	3 Feb	Leeds U	A	1-6
LC	10 Feb	Leeds U	H	1-1
LC	17 Feb	Barnsley	H	3-0
LC	24 Feb	Barnsley	A	0-3
	3 Mar	Grimsby T	H	3-1
LC	10 Mar	Bradford	H	0-2
	17 Mar	Grimsby T	A	0-4
	24 Mar	Lincoln C	H	1-4
	2 Apr	Bradford City	H	3-1
	7 Apr	Lincoln C	A	2-4
	14 Apr	Leeds U	A	2-6
	21 Apr	Rotherham U	H	2-8
	28 Apr	Rotherham U	A	2-1

LEEDS UNITED

LC	26 Dec	Bradford City	H	9-1
LC	30 Dec	Bradford City	A	2-6
LC	6 Jan	Barnsley	H	0-1
LC	13 Jan	Barnsley	A	0-5
LC	20 Jan	York C	A	5-0
LC	27 Jan	York C	H	4-3
LC	3 Feb	Hull C	H	6-1
LC	10 Feb	Hull C	A	1-1
LC	17 Feb	Bradford	A	2-5
LC	24 Feb	Bradford	H	0-2
	3 Mar	Sheffield Wed	H	4-3
	10 Mar	Preston NE	H	3-1
	17 Mar	Sheffield Wed	A	1-1
	24 Mar	Grimsby T	H	1-1
	2 Apr	Chesterfield	H	0-2
	7 Apr	Grimsby T	A	0-3
	14 Apr	Hull C	H	6-2
	21 Apr	Barnsley	A	3-1
	28 Apr	Barnsley	H	1-3
	5 May	Sheffield Utd	A	0-6
	12 May	Sheffield Utd	H	4-1
	21 May	Chesterfield	A	1-6

KEY: LC=League Cup; WC=League West Cup; La=Lancashire Cup; MC=Midland Cup;
CB=Cheshire Bowl; Li=Liverpool Senior Cup; TT=Tyne, Wear & Tees Cup; SC=Sheffield County Cup

The Football League 1944-45

NORTH (SECOND CHAMPIONSHIP)
Including League Cup and county cup matches

LEICESTER CITY

LC	30 Dec	Nottingham F	A	0-0
LC	6 Jan	Mansfield T	A	2-2
LC	13 Jan	Mansfield T	H	8-3
LC	20 Jan	Chesterfield	A	0-1
LC	27 Jan	Chesterfield	H	2-2
LC	3 Feb	Notts County	A	4-1
LC	10 Feb	Notts County	A	4-1
LC	17 Feb	Derby Co	H	2-2
LC	24 Feb	Derby Co	A	0-3
LC	3 Mar	Nottingham F	H	1-1
	10 Mar	Wolverhampton	A	2-3
	17 Mar	Coventry C	H	2-2
LC	24 Mar	Derby Co	H	2-1
LC	31 Mar	Derby Co	A	0-2
	2 Apr	Sheffield Wed	H	2-1
	7 Apr	Aston Villa	H	2-0
	14 Apr	Aston Villa	A	2-7
MC	21 Apr	WBA	A	0-1
MC	28 Apr	WBA	H	3-0
MC	5 May	Derby Co	A	1-3
MC	12 May	Derby Co	H	1-2

LINCOLN CITY

LC	25 Dec	Grimsby T	A	2-2
LC	30 Dec	Grimsby T	H	0-2
LC	6 Jan	Doncaster R	A	1-6
LC	13 Jan	Doncaster R	H	1-3
LC	27 Jan	Sheffield Utd	A	2-10
LC	3 Feb	Rotherham U	A	2-3
LC	10 Feb	Rotherham U	H	2-2
LC	17 Feb	Sheffield Wed	H	5-3
LC	24 Feb	Sheffield Wed	A	3-1
	3 Mar	Notts County	H	3-2
LC	10 Mar	Sheffield Utd	H	3-1
	24 Mar	Hull C	A	4-1
	31 Mar	Grimsby T	A	2-4
	2 Apr	Grimsby T	H	3-3
	7 Apr	Hull C	H	4-2
	14 Apr	Grimsby T	A	3-4
	21 Apr	Grimsby T	H	2-2

20 Jan, League Cup match with Sheffield U was
abandoned at 0-0 because of the weather

LIVERPOOL

LC	25 Dec	Southport	A	4-1
Li	26 Dec	Everton	A	2-2
LC	30 Dec	Southport	H	12-1
LC	6 Jan	Stockport Co	A	3-2
LC	13 Jan	Stockport Co	H	4-1
LC	3 Feb	Everton	A	1-4
LC	10 Feb	Everton	H	3-1
LC	17 Feb	Bolton W	A	1-2
LC	24 Feb	Bolton W	H	1-1
	3 Mar	Southport	A	5-0
LC	10 Mar	Tranmere R	H	3-1
LC	17 Mar	Tranmere R	A	2-1
LC	24 Mar	Everton	H	1-0
LC	31 Mar	Everton	A	1-0
Li	2 Apr	Everton	H	1-3
LC	7 Apr	Manchester City	H	3-0
LC	14 Apr	Manchester City	A	3-1
LC	21 Apr	Chesterfield	H	0-0
LC	28 Apr	Chesterfield	A	0-1
	5 May	Oldham Ath	H	3-2
V	9 May	Preston NE	H	5-1
	12 May	Oldham Ath	A	7-0
	19 May	Blackpool	H	2-0
	21 May	Derby Co	A	0-1

LOVELL'S ATHLETIC

LC	25 Dec	Aberaman Ath	H	6-1
LC	30 Dec	Aberaman Ath	H	2-1
LC	6 Jan	Cardiff C	H	1-0
LC	13 Jan	Cardiff C	A	0-3
LC	20 Jan	Swansea T	A	1-4
LC	3 Feb	Bristol City	A	1-2
LC	10 Feb	Bristol City	H	2-1
LC	17 Feb	Bath C	H	4-2
LC	24 Feb	Bath C	A	3-1
LC	3 Mar	Swansea T	H	4-0
WC	10 Mar	Aberaman Ath	A	3-2
WC	17 Mar	Aberaman Ath	H	4-4
LC	24 Mar	Cardiff C	A	0-1
LC	31 Mar	Cardiff C	H	0-0
WC	14 Apr	Bath C	A	2-4
WC	21 Apr	Bath C	H	2-0
WC	12 May	Cardiff C	A	4-0
	19 May	Swansea T	H	3-0
	26 May	Swansea T	A	2-1

MANCHESTER CITY

	26 Dec	Blackpool	H	1-1
LC	30 Dec	Bury	H	3-2
LC	6 Jan	Halifax T	A	1-1
LC	13 Jan	Halifax T	H	2-3
LC	27 Jan	Oldham Ath	A	4-3
LC	3 Feb	Manchester Utd	A	3-1
LC	10 Feb	Manchester Utd	H	2-0
LC	17 Feb	Huddersfield T	A	1-3
LC	24 Feb	Huddersfield T	H	2-0
LC	3 Mar	Bury	A	2-4
LC	10 Mar	Oldham Ath	H	3-2
La	17 Mar	Stockport Co	A	1-4
LC	24 Mar	Crewe Alex	H	5-1
LC	31 Mar	Crewe Alex	A	0-2
La	2 Apr	Stockport Co	H	1-5
LC	7 Apr	Liverpool	A	0-3
LC	14 Apr	Liverpool	H	1-3
	21 Apr	Blackpool	H	0-1
	28 Apr	Blackpool	A	0-4

MANCHESTER UNITED

	26 Dec	Sheffield Utd	A	4-3
LC	30 Dec	Oldham Ath	A	4-3
LC	6 Jan	Huddersfield T	H	1-0
LC	13 Jan	Huddersfield T	A	2-2
LC	3 Feb	Manchester City	H	1-3
LC	10 Feb	Manchester City	A	0-2
LC	17 Feb	Bury	H	2-0
LC	24 Feb	Bury	A	1-3
LC	3 Mar	Oldham Ath	H	3-2
LC	10 Mar	Halifax T	A	0-1
LC	17 Mar	Halifax T	H	2-0
LC	24 Mar	Burnley	A	3-2
LC	31 Mar	Burnley	H	4-0
	2 Apr	Blackpool	A	1-4
LC	7 Apr	Stoke C	H	6-1
LC	14 Apr	Stoke C	A	4-1
LC	21 Apr	Doncaster R	A	2-1
LC	28 Apr	Doncaster R	H	3-1
LC	5 May	Chesterfield	H	1-1
LC	12 May	Chesterfield	A	1-0
LC	19 May	Bolton W	A	0-1
LC	26 May	Bolton W	H	2-2

25 Dec, League Cup match with Oldham Ath was
abandoned after 23 mins at 1-1 because
of the weather

KEY: LC=League Cup; WC=League West Cup; La=Lancashire Cup; MC=Midland Cup;
CB=Cheshire Bowl; Li=Liverpool Senior Cup; TT=Tyne, Wear & Tees Cup; SC=Sheffield County Cup

The Football League 1944-45

NORTH (SECOND CHAMPIONSHIP)
Including League Cup and county cup matches

MANSFIELD TOWN

LC	26 Dec	Notts County	A	2-0
LC	30 Dec	Notts County	H	3-1
LC	6 Jan	Leicester C	H	2-2
LC	13 Jan	Leicester C	A	3-8
LC	3 Feb	Derby Co	H	1-8
LC	10 Feb	Derby Co	A	1-7
LC	17 Feb	Chesterfield	H	4-3
LC	24 Feb	Chesterfield	A	0-3
LC	10 Mar	Nottingham F	A	1-2
LC	17 Mar	Nottingham F	H	1-0
	2 Apr	Walsall	H	2-0
	5 May	Walsall	A	2-4

MIDDLESBROUGH

LC	26 Dec	Hartlepools U	H	0-0
LC	30 Dec	Hartlepools U	A	4-6
LC	6 Jan	Newcastle U	A	1-5
LC	13 Jan	Newcastle U	H	5-3
LC	20 Feb	Sunderland	A	3-4
LC	3 Feb	Darlington	H	0-1
LC	10 Feb	Darlington	A	4-6
LC	17 Feb	Gateshead	H	2-3
LC	24 Feb	Gateshead	A	2-1
	3 Mar	Darlington	A	0-1
	10 Mar	Newcastle U	H	1-5
LC	17 Mar	Sunderland	H	2-1
	24 Mar	Hartlepools U	A	0-3
	31 Mar	Hartlepools U	H	1-3
	2 Apr	Gateshead	H	3-1
	7 Apr	Bradford	A	1-3
	14 Apr	Bradford	H	1-0
TT	21 Apr	Huddersfield T	H	2-1
TT	28 Apr	Huddersfield T	A	0-1
	5 May	Newcastle U	H	1-1
V	9 May	Darlington	A	3-5
	12 May	Newcastle U	A	0-11
	19 May	Hartlepools U	H	1-2
	21 May	York C	A	3-5

28 Apr, aet 0-2

NEWCASTLE UNITED

LC	26 Dec	Sunderland	H	3-1
LC	30 Dec	Sunderland	A	3-4
LC	6 Jan	Middlesbrough	H	5-1
LC	13 Jan	Middlesbrough	A	3-5
LC	20 Feb	Gateshead	H	2-4
LC	10 Feb	Hartlepools U	H	4-1
LC	17 Feb	Darlington	H	3-1
LC	24 Feb	Darlington	A	3-2
LC	3 Mar	Hartlepools U	A	1-2
	10 Mar	Middlesbrough	A	3-1
LC	17 Mar	Gateshead	A	3-0
LC	24 Mar	Darlington	H	2-1
LC	31 Mar	Darlington	A	3-0
	2 Apr	Sunderland	H	0-3
LC	7 Apr	Bradford City	H	6-2
LC	14 Apr	Bradford City	A	1-0
LC	21 Apr	Bolton W	A	0-3
LC	28 Apr	Bolton W	H	4-1
	5 May	Middlesbrough	A	1-1
	9 May	Sunderland	H	5-0
	12 May	Middlesbrough	H	11-0
	19 May	Gateshead	A	0-3
	21 May	Gateshead	H	3-1

28 Apr, aet 4-2

NORTHAMPTON TOWN

LC	30 Dec	Aston Villa	H	2-0
LC	6 Jan	Walsall	H	2-1
LC	13 Jan	Walsall	A	1-0
LC	20 Jan	Birmingham	A	0-4
LC	10 Feb	Birmingham	H	2-1
LC	17 Feb	Coventry C	H	8-1
LC	24 Feb	Coventry C	A	0-3
LC	3 Mar	Aston Villa	A	2-2
LC	10 Mar	WBA	H	2-2
LC	17 Mar	WBA	A	0-6
LC	24 Mar	Birmingham	H	0-2
LC	31 Mar	Birmingham	A	2-2
MC	21 Apr	Derby Co	H	2-1
MC	28 Apr	Derby Co	A	0-5

NOTTINGHAM FOREST

LC	30 Dec	Leicester C	H	0-0
LC	6 Jan	Derby Co	H	1-1
LC	13 Jan	Derby Co	A	0-3
LC	3 Feb	Chesterfield	A	1-0
LC	10 Feb	Chesterfield	H	1-1
LC	17 Feb	Notts Co	H	1-4
LC	24 Feb	Notts Co	A	2-1
LC	3 Mar	Leicester C	A	1-1
LC	10 Mar	Mansfield T	H	2-1
LC	17 Mar	Mansfield T	A	0-1
	2 Apr	Notts Co	H	6-0
	7 Apr	Coventry C	H	1-1
	14 Apr	Coventry C	A	1-1
	21 Apr	Notts Co	A	3-1
	28 Apr	Notts Co	H	2-5
	19 May	Birmingham	A	1-4
	26 May	Birmingham	H	0-0

NOTTS COUNTY

LC	26 Dec	Mansfield T	H	0-2
LC	30 Dec	Mansfield T	A	1-3
LC	6 Jan	Chesterfield	A	1-3
LC	13 Jan	Chesterfield	H	1-3
LC	20 Jan	Derby Co	A	0-7
LC	27 Jan	Derby Co	H	2-4
LC	3 Feb	Leicester C	H	1-4
LC	10 Feb	Leicester C	A	1-4
LC	17 Feb	Nottingham F	A	4-1
LC	24 Feb	Nottingham F	H	1-2
	3 Mar	Lincoln C	A	2-3
	10 Mar	Coventry C	A	0-4
	24 Mar	Coventry C	A	0-1
	31 Mar	Coventry C	H	1-2
	2 Apr	Nottingham F	A	0-6
	7 Apr	Port Vale	A	4-1
	14 Apr	Port Vale	H	2-1
	21 Apr	Nottingham F	H	1-3
	28 Apr	Nottingham F	A	5-2
	5 May	Grimsby T	A	1-3
	12 May	Grimsby T	H	1-3

KEY: LC=League Cup; WC=League West Cup; La=Lancashire Cup; MC=Midland Cup;
CB=Cheshire Bowl; Li=Liverpool Senior Cup; TT=Tyne, Wear & Tees Cup; SC=Sheffield County Cup

The Football League 1944-45

NORTH (SECOND CHAMPIONSHIP)
Including League Cup and county cup matches

OLDHAM ATHLETIC

	Date	Opponent		Score
	26 Dec	Bury	H	2-2
LC	30 Dec	Manchester Utd	H	3-4
LC	6 Jan	Bury	A	1-3
LC	13 Jan	Bury	H	2-0
LC	27 Jan	Manchester City	H	3-4
LC	3 Feb	Huddersfield T	H	2-3
LC	10 Feb	Huddersfield T	A	1-6
LC	17 Feb	Halifax T	A	2-0
LC	24 Feb	Halifax T	H	1-2
LC	3 Mar	Manchester Utd	A	2-3
LC	10 Mar	Manchester City	A	2-3
La	17 Mar	Burnley	H	1-2
	24 Mar	Southport	A	5-2
	31 Mar	Southport	H	2-0
La	2 Apr	Burnley	A	1-3
	7 Apr	Tranmere R	A	1-7
	14 Apr	Tranmere R	H	2-1
	21 Apr	Rochdale	A	2-1
	28 Apr	Rochdale	H	2-0
	5 May	Liverpool	A	2-3
	12 May	Liverpool	H	0-7

25 Dec, League Cup match at Man United was
abandoned after 23 mins at 1-1 because
of the weather

PORT VALE

	Date	Opponent		Score
LC	25 Dec	Crewe Alex	H	1-3
	26 Dec	Wrexham	A	0-4
LC	30 Dec	Crewe Alex	A	1-2
LC	6 Jan	Chester	A	3-2
LC	13 Jan	Chester	H	0-2
LC	20 Jan	Wrexham	A	0-5
LC	3 Feb	Wolverhampton	H	2-0
LC	10 Feb	Wolverhampton	A	2-1
LC	17 Feb	Stoke C	A	1-8
LC	24 Feb	Stoke C	H	2-6
	3 Mar	Stockport Co	H	5-0
	10 Mar	Stockport Co	A	0-3
LC	17 Mar	Wrexham	H	1-1
	24 Mar	Walsall	H	3-2
	31 Mar	Walsall	A	0-2
	2 Apr	Wrexham	H	2-2
	7 Apr	Notts County	H	1-4
	14 Apr	Notts County	A	1-2
	28 Apr	Tranmere R	H	0-1
	5 May	Stoke C	A	0-6
V	9 May	Stoke C	H	2-4

PRESTON NORTH END

	Date	Opponent		Score
LC	25 Dec	Blackpool	H	1-3
	26 Dec	Blackburn R	H	3-2
LC	30 Dec	Blackpool	A	1-1
LC	6 Jan	Accrington S	H	1-2
LC	13 Jan	Accrington S	A	1-2
LC	20 Jan	Rochdale	A	1-1
LC	27 Jan	Rochdale	H	1-1
LC	3 Feb	Blackburn R	H	3-1
LC	10 Feb	Blackburn R	A	2-3
LC	17 Feb	Burnley	H	2-1
LC	24 Feb	Burnley	A	1-1
	3 Mar	Halifax T	H	2-0
	10 Mar	Leeds U	A	1-3
	17 Mar	Everton	A	0-3
	24 Mar	Chester	H	3-2
	31 Mar	Chester	A	1-4
	2 Apr	Bradford	A	1-6
	7 Apr	Crewe Alex	H	4-1
	14 Apr	Crewe Alex	A	3-0
	21 Apr	Blackburn R	H	5-0
	28 Apr	Blackburn R	A	0-1
	5 May	Blackpool	A	1-8
V	9 May	Liverpool	A	1-5
	12 May	Blackpool	A	0-4
	26 May	Burnley	H	2-1

ROCHDALE

	Date	Opponent		Score
LC	25 Dec	Accrington S	A	1-0
LC	30 Dec	Accrington S	H	1-1
LC	13 Jan	Blackburn R	A	2-3
LC	20 Jan	Preston NE	H	1-1
LC	27 Jan	Preston NE	A	1-1
LC	3 Feb	Burnley	A	0-2
LC	10 Feb	Burnley	H	0-4
LC	17 Feb	Blackpool	H	3-6
LC	24 Feb	Blackpool	A	0-4
LC	3 Mar	Blackburn R	H	0-8
La	10 Mar	Blackburn R	H	0-1
La	17 Mar	Blackburn R	A	0-4
	24 Mar	Tranmere R	A	1-0
	31 Mar	Tranmere R	H	4-1
	2 Apr	Chester	A	0-3
	7 Apr	Stockport Co	H	0-3
	14 Apr	Stockport Co	A	0-2
	21 Apr	Oldham Ath	H	1-2
	28 Apr	Oldham Ath	A	0-2
	5 May	Chester	H	2-1

ROTHERHAM UNITED

	Date	Opponent		Score
LC	26 Dec	Doncaster R	A	0-0
LC	30 Dec	Doncaster R	H	3-0
LC	6 Jan	Sheffield Utd	A	1-0
LC	13 Jan	Sheffield Utd	H	1-4
LC	20 Jan	Sheffield Wed	A	4-1
LC	27 Jan	Sheffield Wed	H	1-1
LC	3 Feb	Lincoln C	H	3-2
LC	10 Feb	Lincoln C	A	2-2
LC	17 Feb	Grimsby T	A	0-5
LC	24 Feb	Grimsby T	H	3-0
	3 Mar	Bradford City	A	3-5
	17 Mar	Bradford City	H	2-0
LC	24 Mar	Barnsley	H	2-1
LC	31 Mar	Barnsley	A	0-3
	2 Apr	Doncaster R	H	0-2
SC	7 Apr	Sheffield Utd	A	1-6
SC	14 Apr	Sheffield Utd	H	1-0
	21 Apr	Hull C	A	8-2
	28 Apr	Hull C	H	1-2
	5 May	Bury	H	5-1

SHEFFIELD UNITED

	Date	Opponent		Score
LC	25 Dec	Sheffield Wed	A	2-1
	26 Dec	Manchester Utd	H	3-4
LC	30 Dec	Sheffield Wed	H	1-0
LC	6 Jan	Rotherham U	H	0-1
LC	13 Jan	Rotherham U	A	4-1
LC	27 Jan	Lincoln C	H	10-2
LC	3 Feb	Grimsby T	H	2-2
LC	10 Feb	Grimsby T	A	2-1
LC	17 Feb	Doncaster R	H	0-4
LC	24 Feb	Doncaster R	A	2-3
LC	10 Mar	Lincoln C	A	1-3
	17 Mar	Derby Co	A	2-3
LC	24 Mar	Bradford City	H	2-2
LC	31 Mar	Bradford City	A	3-4
	2 Apr	Huddersfield T	H	3-1
	7 Apr	Rotherham U	H	6-1
	14 Apr	Rotherham U	A	0-1
	21 Apr	Burnley	A	0-2
	28 Apr	Burnley	H	1-1
	5 May	Leeds U	H	6-0
V	9 May	Sheffield Wed	H	2-0
	12 May	Leeds U	A	1-4
SC	19 May	Sheffield Wed	H	1-3
SC	26 May	Sheffield Wed	A	2-4

20 Jan, League Cup match at Lincoln C was
abandoned at 0-0 because of the weather

KEY: LC=League Cup; WC=League West Cup; La=Lancashire Cup; MC=Midland Cup;
CB=Cheshire Bowl; Li=Liverpool Senior Cup; TT=Tyne, Wear & Tees Cup; SC=Sheffield County Cup

The Football League 1944-45

NORTH (SECOND CHAMPIONSHIP)
Including League Cup and county cup matches

SHEFFIELD WEDNESDAY

LC	25 Dec	Sheffield Utd	H	1-2
LC	30 Dec	Sheffield Utd	A	0-1
LC	6 Jan	Grimsby T	A	1-4
LC	13 Jan	Grimsby T	H	2-2
LC	20 Jan	Rotherham U	H	1-4
LC	27 Jan	Rotherham U	A	1-1
LC	3 Feb	Doncaster R	A	3-1
LC	10 Feb	Doncaster R	H	1-6
LC	17 Feb	Lincoln C	A	3-5
LC	24 Feb	Lincoln C	H	1-3
	3 Mar	Leeds U	A	3-4
	10 Mar	Doncaster R	H	1-0
	17 Mar	Leeds U	H	1-1
	24 Mar	Blackburn R	A	2-2
	31 Mar	Blackburn R	H	2-0
	2 Apr	Leicester C	A	1-2
	7 Apr	Halifax T	A	2-3
	14 Apr	Halifax T	H	7-0
	21 Apr	Bradford	H	3-1
	28 Apr	Bradford	A	3-5
	5 May	Barnsley	A	3-3
V	9 May	Sheffield Utd	A	0-2
	12 May	Barnsley	H	4-1
SC	19 May	Sheffield Utd	A	3-1
SC	26 May	Sheffield Utd	H	4-2

SOUTHPORT

LC	25 Dec	Liverpool	H	1-4
	26 Dec	Tranmere R	A	2-5
LC	30 Dec	Liverpool	A	1-12
LC	6 Jan	Tranmere R	H	0-0
LC	13 Jan	Tranmere R	A	3-0
LC	27 Jan	Bolton W	H	3-4
LC	3 Feb	Stockport Co	H	2-1
LC	10 Feb	Stockport Co	A	5-2
LC	17 Feb	Everton	A	0-6
LC	24 Feb	Everton	H	3-5
La	3 Mar	Liverpool	H	0-5
LC	10 Mar	Bolton W	A	1-6
	17 Mar	Accrington S	H	2-2
	24 Mar	Oldham Ath	A	2-5
	31 Mar	Oldham Ath	A	0-2
	2 Apr	Tranmere R	H	2-3
	7 Apr	Chester	H	1-2
	14 Apr	Chester	A	3-5
La	21 Apr	Everton	H	0-5
La	28 Apr	Everton	A	1-1
	5 May	Wrexham	A	0-2
	12 May	Wrexham	H	1-5

STOCKPORT COUNTY

LC	26 Dec	Bolton W	A	0-2
LC	30 Dec	Bolton W	H	2-0
LC	6 Jan	Liverpool	H	2-3
LC	13 Jan	Liverpool	A	1-4
LC	20 Jan	Everton	H	0-3
LC	27 Jan	Everton	H	2-9
LC	3 Feb	Southport	A	1-2
LC	10 Feb	Southport	H	2-5
LC	17 Feb	Tranmere R	H	4-3
LC	24 Feb	Tranmere R	A	0-4
	3 Mar	Port Vale	A	0-5
	10 Mar	Port Vale	H	3-0
La	17 Mar	Manchester City	H	4-1
La	2 Apr	Manchester City	A	5-1
	7 Apr	Rotherham U	A	3-0
	14 Apr	Rotherham U	H	2-0
La/CB	21 Apr	Crewe Alex	H	0-1
La/CB	28 Apr	Crewe Alex	A	0-6
	5 May	Tranmere R	A	0-1

STOKE CITY

	26 Dec	Derby Co	H	4-2
LC	30 Dec	Wolverhampton	H	2-0
LC	6 Jan	Wrexham	H	2-2
LC	13 Jan	Wrexham	A	1-2
LC	3 Feb	Chester	A	3-2
LC	10 Feb	Chester	H	7-0
LC	17 Feb	Port Vale	H	8-1
LC	24 Feb	Port Vale	A	6-2
LC	3 Mar	Wolverhampton	A	3-1
LC	10 Mar	Crewe Alex	H	1-2
LC	17 Mar	Crewe Alex	A	2-2
LC	24 Mar	Bury	A	2-3
LC	31 Mar	Bury	H	3-0
	2 Apr	Derby Co	A	1-2
LC	7 Apr	Manchester Utd	A	1-6
LC	14 Apr	Manchester Utd	H	1-4
La	21 Apr	Aston Villa	H	1-0
La	28 Apr	Aston Villa	A	0-2
	5 May	Port Vale	H	6-0
V	9 May	Port Vale	A	4-2
	19 May	Everton	H	5-1
	21 May	Crewe Alex	A	2-3
	26 May	Everton	A	2-3

SUNDERLAND

LC	26 Dec	Newcastle U	A	1-3
LC	30 Dec	Newcastle U	H	4-3
LC	6 Jan	Darlington	H	1-1
LC	13 Jan	Darlington	A	2-3
LC	20 Jan	Middlesbrough	H	4-3
LC	3 Feb	Gateshead	A	1-2
LC	10 Feb	Gateshead	H	3-0
LC	17 Feb	Hartlepools U	H	6-2
LC	24 Feb	Hartlepools U	A	1-3
	3 Mar	Gateshead	H	0-2
	10 Mar	Darlington	H	1-5
LC	17 Mar	Middlesbrough	A	1-2
	24 Mar	Gateshead	H	2-2
	31 Mar	Gateshead	H	2-4
	2 Apr	Newcastle U	A	3-0
	7 Apr	York C	H	0-0
	14 Apr	York C	A	2-4
TT	21 Apr	Hartlepools U	H	5-0
TT	28 Apr	Hartlepools U	A	2-0
TT	5 May	York C	A	1-2
	9 May	Newcastle U	A	0-5
TT	12 May	York C	H	6-1
	19 May	Huddersfield T	A	0-1
	21 May	Huddersfield T	H	2-0
TT	26 May	Gateshead	N	3-6

SWANSEA TOWN

LC	25 Dec	Cardiff C	A	1-3
LC	30 Dec	Cardiff C	H	1-3
LC	6 Jan	Bristol City	H	1-2
LC	13 Jan	Bristol City	A	1-3
LC	20 Jan	Lovell's Ath	H	4-1
LC	3 Feb	Bath C	A	4-7
LC	10 Feb	Bath C	H	2-6
LC	17 Feb	Aberaman Ath	H	5-2
LC	24 Feb	Aberaman Ath	A	8-2
LC	3 Mar	Lovell's Ath	A	0-4
WC	10 Mar	Cardiff C	H	1-0
LC	17 Mar	Cardiff C	A	2-6
WC	24 Mar	Bath C	A	1-2
WC	31 Mar	Bath C	H	1-0
WC	2 Apr	Aberaman Ath	H	4-3
WC	7 Apr	Aberaman Ath	A	1-8
WC	28 Apr	Bristol City	H	2-2
WC	5 May	Bristol City	A	2-4
WC	19 May	Lovell's Ath	A	0-3
WC	26 May	Lovell's Ath	H	1-2

KEY: LC=League Cup; WC=League West Cup; La=Lancashire Cup; MC=Midland Cup;
CB=Cheshire Bowl; Li=Liverpool Senior Cup; TT=Tyne, Wear & Tees Cup; SC=Sheffield County Cup

The Football League 1944-45

NORTH (SECOND CHAMPIONSHIP)
Including League Cup and county cup matches

TRANMERE ROVERS

	Date	Opponent		Score
LC	26 Dec	Everton	A	4-2
	26 Dec	Southport	H	5-2
LC	30 Dec	Everton	H	0-4
LC	6 Jan	Southport	A	0-0
LC	13 Jan	Southport	H	0-3
LC	3 Feb	Bolton W	H	1-4
LC	10 Feb	Bolton W	A	1-6
LC	17 Feb	Stockport Co	A	3-4
LC	24 Feb	Stockport Co	H	4-0
	3 Mar	Wrexham	A	1-2
LC	10 Mar	Liverpool	A	1-3
LC	17 Mar	Liverpool	H	1-2
	24 Mar	Rochdale	H	0-1
	31 Mar	Rochdale	A	1-4
	2 Apr	Southport	A	3-2
	7 Apr	Oldham Ath	H	7-1
	14 Apr	Oldham Ath	A	1-2
	28 Apr	Port Vale	A	1-0
	5 May	Stockport Co	H	1-0
Li	9 May	Everton	H	0-3
	12 May	Burnley	H	3-2
	19 May	Burnley	A	1-5
Li	21 May	Everton	A	1-4

WALSALL

	Date	Opponent		Score
	26 Dec	Wolverhampton	A	1-1
LC	30 Dec	Birmingham	A	1-3
LC	6 Jan	Northampton T	A	1-2
LC	13 Jan	Northampton t	H	0-1
LC	20 Jan	Coventry C	H	6-5
LC	27 Jan	Coventry C	A	2-0
LC	3 Feb	WBA	A	2-0
LC	10 Feb	WBA	H	0-0
LC	17 Feb	Aston Villa	A	1-6
LC	24 Feb	Aston Villa	H	0-2
LC	3 Mar	Birmingham	H	0-2
	10 Mar	Wrexham	A	0-1
	24 Mar	Port Vale	A	2-3
	31 Mar	Port Vale	H	2-0
	2 Apr	Mansfield T	A	0-2
	7 Apr	WBA	A	1-1
	14 Apr	WBA	H	1-2
	5 May	Mansfield T	H	4-2

WEST BROMWICH ALBION

	Date	Opponent		Score
	26 Dec	Aston Villa	A	4-3
LC	30 Dec	Coventry C	H	1-1
LC	6 Jan	Aston Villa	H	1-3
LC	13 Jan	Aston Villa	A	2-6
LC	3 Feb	Walsall	H	0-2
LC	10 Feb	Walsall	A	0-0
LC	17 Feb	Birmingham	H	4-0
LC	24 Feb	Birmingham	A	1-1
LC	3 Mar	Coventry C	A	3-0
LC	10 Mar	Northampton T	A	2-2
LC	17 Mar	Northampton T	H	6-0
LC	24 Mar	Bristol City	A	2-5
LC	31 Mar	Bristol City	H	3-3
	2 Apr	Aston Villa	H	2-4
	7 Apr	Walsall	H	1-1
	14 Apr	Walsall	A	2-1
MC	21 Apr	Leicester C	H	1-0
MC	28 Apr	Leicester C	A	0-3
	5 May	Birmingham	A	1-4
	12 May	Birmingham	H	2-3
	19 May	Wolverhampton	A	0-1
	26 May	Wolverhampton	H	1-1

WOLVERHAMPTON WANDERERS

	Date	Opponent		Score
	26 Dec	Walsall	H	1-1
LC	30 Dec	Stoke C	A	0-2
LC	6 Jan	Crewe Alex	A	3-2
LC	13 Jan	Crewe Alex	A	3-1
LC	20 Jan	Chester	H	6-1
LC	3 Feb	Port Vale	A	0-2
LC	10 Feb	Port Vale	H	1-2
LC	17 Feb	Wrexham	H	4-1
LC	24 Feb	Wrexham	A	1-1
LC	3 Mar	Stoke C	H	1-3
	10 Mar	Leicester C	H	3-2
LC	17 Mar	Chester	A	4-0
LC	24 Mar	Aston Villa	A	2-1
LC	31 Mar	Aston Villa	H	1-0
	2 Apr	Birmingham	A	2-1
LC	7 Apr	Birmingham	A	0-0
LC	14 Apr	Birmingham	H	0-0
LC	21 Apr	Cardiff C	H	3-0
	28 Apr	Cardiff C	A	1-2
LC	5 May	Bolton W	H	2-2
LC	12 May	Bolton W	A	1-2
	19 May	WBA	H	1-0
	21 May	Aston Villa	A	4-4
	26 May	WBA	A	1-1

14 Apr, aet 1-0

WREXHAM

	Date	Opponent		Score
LC	25 Dec	Chester	H	4-2
	26 Dec	Port Vale	H	4-0
LC	30 Dec	Chester	A	5-2
LC	6 Jan	Stoke C	A	2-2
LC	13 Jan	Stoke C	H	2-1
LC	20 Jan	Port Vale	H	5-0
LC	3 Feb	Crewe Alex	A	3-3
LC	10 Feb	Crewe Alex	H	6-1
LC	17 Feb	Wolverhampton	A	1-4
LC	24 Feb	Wolverhampton	H	1-1
	3 Mar	Tranmere R	H	2-1
	10 Mar	Walsall	H	1-0
LC	17 Mar	Port Vale	A	1-1
LC	24 Mar	Blackpool	A	0-2
LC	31 Mar	Blackpool	H	2-2
	2 Apr	Port Vale	A	2-2
	7 Apr	Everton	H	1-2
	14 Apr	Everton	A	3-5
	21 Apr	Chester	H	2-2
	28 Apr	Chester	A	1-2
	5 May	Southport	H	2-0
	12 May	Southport	A	5-1

YORK CITY

	Date	Opponent		Score
LC	25 Dec	Hull C	H	5-1
LC	30 Dec	Hull C	A	1-6
LC	6 Jan	Bradford	A	2-4
LC	20 Jan	Leeds U	H	0-5
LC	27 Jan	Leeds U	A	3-4
LC	3 Feb	Barnsley	A	1-2
LC	10 Feb	Barnsley	H	5-1
LC	17 Feb	Bradford City	H	2-2
LC	24 Feb	Bradford City	A	0-3
LC	3 Mar	Bradford	H	6-1
	10 Mar	Hartlepools U	A	1-1
	24 Mar	Huddersfield T	H	1-0
	31 Mar	Huddersfield T	A	0-1
	2 Apr	Darlington	A	3-7
	7 Apr	Sunderland	A	0-0
	14 Apr	Sunderland	H	4-2
TT	21 Apr	Darlington	H	2-0
TT	28 Apr	Darlington	A	2-2
TT	5 May	Sunderland	H	2-1
TT	12 May	Sunderland	A	1-6
	19 May	Darlington	A	2-4
	21 May	Middlesbrough	H	5-3

**KEY: LC=League Cup; WC=League West Cup; La=Lancashire Cup; MC=Midland Cup;
CB=Cheshire Bowl; Li=Liverpool Senior Cup; TT=Tyne, Wear & Tees Cup; SC=Sheffield County Cup**

The Football League 1944-45

NORTH (SECOND CHAMPIONSHIP)

Final Table

		P	W	D	L	F	A	Pts
1	Derby County	26	19	3	4	78	28	41
2	Everton	27	17	3	7	79	43	37
3	Liverpool	24	16	3	5	66	26	35
4	Burnley	26	15	3	8	56	36	33
5	Newcastle United	23	15	1	7	69	37	31
6	Aston Villa	25	14	2	9	70	45	30
7	Chesterfield	24	10	9	5	40	24	29
8	Wolverhampton Wanderers	24	11	7	6	45	31	29
9	Manchester United	22	13	3	6	47	33	29
10	Darlington	24	13	3	8	61	45	29
11	Bristol City	22	13	2	7	55	33	28
12	Blackburn Rovers	25	13	2	10	62	51	28
13	Huddersfield Town	27	12	4	11	51	49	28
14	Wrexham	22	10	7	5	55	36	27
15	Bolton Wanderers	23	11	5	7	51	35	27
16	Blackpool	24	12	3	9	58	42	27
17	Stoke City	23	12	2	9	67	42	26
18	Lovell's Athletic	19	12	2	5	44	27	26
19	Cardiff City	20	12	2	6	41	27	26
20	Grimsby Town	21	10	6	5	51	37	26
21	Birmingham	24	9	7	8	38	34	25
22	Crewe Alexandra	23	11	3	9	50	50	25
23	Doncaster Rovers	20	11	2	7	44	26	24
24	Bradford	22	10	4	8	49	39	24
25	Accrington Stanley	24	9	6	9	39	41	24
26	Barnsley	24	11	2	11	39	42	24
27	Rotherham United	20	10	3	7	41	37	23
28	Gateshead	21	9	5	7	46	42	23
29	Preston North End	25	9	4	12	41	56	22
30	Sheffield United	24	9	3	12	56	48	21
31	Sunderland	25	9	3	13	53	54	21
32	Leeds United	22	9	3	10	53	55	21
33	Sheffield Wednesday	25	8	5	12	53	56	21
34	Leicester City	21	7	6	8	40	38	20
35	Bath City	20	10	0	10	50	48	20
36	Bury	20	8	4	8	38	43	20
37	York City	22	8	4	10	48	56	20
38	Chester	22	9	2	11	49	61	20
39	Bradford City	20	8	3	9	43	46	19
40	West Bromwich Albion	22	6	7	9	39	44	19
41	Hartlepools United	21	8	3	10	34	54	19
42	Coventry City	21	6	6	9	36	53	18
43	Nottingham Forest	17	5	7	5	23	25	17
44	Tranmere Rovers	23	8	1	14	40	56	17
45	Halifax Town	18	6	5	7	22	35	17
46	Lincoln City	17	6	4	7	41	51	16
47	Manchester City	19	7	2	10	32	43	16
48	Northampton Town	14	6	3	5	23	30	15
49	Oldham Athletic	21	7	1	13	39	56	15
50	Stockport County	19	7	0	12	31	50	14
51	Middlesbrough	24	6	2	16	40	70	14
52	Walsall	18	5	3	10	24	33	13
53	Swansea Town	20	6	1	13	42	63	13
54	Port Vale	21	5	2	14	27	60	12
55	Mansfield Town	12	5	1	6	22	38	11
56	Hull City	18	5	1	12	30	54	11
57	Rochdale	20	4	3	13	17	49	11
58	Southport	22	3	3	16	33	82	9
59	Notts County	21	4	0	17	29	62	8
60	Aberaman Athletic	17	2	2	13	36	69	6

The Football League 1944-45

SOUTH

	Aldershot	Arsenal	Brentford	Brighton & HA	Charlton A	Chelsea	Clapton Orient	Crystal Palace	Fulham	Luton T	Millwall	Portsmouth	QPR	Reading	Southampton	Tottenham H	Watford	West Ham U
Aldershot	X	16 Dec 2-3	13 Jan 0-1	14 Oct 3-1		9 Dec 3-4	16 Sep 1-0	21 Oct 0-4		18 Nov 3-2	26 Aug 6-3	24 Mar 1-2	11 Nov 1-1	2 Apr 0-2	28 Apr 3-5	31 Mar 1-2	23 Sep 1-0	7 Oct 2-3
Arsenal	9 Sep 1-0	X	23 Dec 5-2	7 Oct 6-3	11 Nov 4-3	28 Apr 3-0		24 Mar 1-0	27 Jan 8-3	2 Dec 9-3	13 Jan 4-1		23 Sep 2-0	31 Mar 0-2	30 Dec 2-4	9 Dec 2-3	18 Nov 4-0	21 Oct 0-3
Brentford	30 Sep 5-2	2 Apr 3-1	X	26 Aug 6-2	20 Jan 3-1	9 Sep 0-5		18 Nov 1-2	31 Mar 2-3	30 Dec 6-0	23 Sep 4-1	9 Dec 7-1	21 Oct 3-1	28 Apr 7-2	11 Nov 0-1	24 Mar 0-2	14 Oct 4-1	
Brighton & HA	5 May 5-0	20 Jan 3-0	2 Dec 2-7	X	4 Nov 1-7	18 Nov 3-5	2 Sep 3-1	16 Dec 0-3	16 Sep 1-7	6 Jan 3-2		28 Apr 8-0	24 Mar 1-1	21 Oct 3-9	26 Dec 2-0		14 Apr 3-2	30 Sep 0-1
Charlton Athletic		14 Apr 5-0	7 Oct 0-4	31 Mar 2-1	X	23 Sep 0-3	25 Dec 4-0		21 Oct 1-3	28 Oct 9-4	30 Dec 1-4	16 Dec 1-0	18 Nov 1-2	26 Aug 2-8	27 Jan 3-5	13 Jan 1-2	28 Apr 3-3	2 Sep 3-2
Chelsea	2 Sep 1-1	25 Nov 2-1	16 Dec 0-2	21 Apr 0-2	4 Jan 4-0	X	30 Sep 5-0	16 Sep 8-2	2 Dec 2-0	11 Nov 7-1	21 Oct 7-0	20 Jan 1-1			31 Mar 3-4	27 Jan 1-2	5 May 3-4	2 Apr 3-4
Clapton Orient	30 Dec 1-1			9 Dec 2-2	23 Dec 1-3	13 Jan 2-6	X	14 Apr 1-1	24 May 0-0	9 Sep 3-3	25 Nov 3-2	2 Dec 2-1	14 Oct 0-3	23 Sep 2-1	17 Mar 1-0	18 Nov 0-2	7 Oct 4-4	4 Nov 0-3
Crystal Palace	17 Mar 3-1	28 Oct 4-3	21 Apr 6-1	9 Sep 5-2		30 Dec 3-3	11 Nov 6-1	X	6 Jan 0-2	30 Sep 1-1	31 Mar 2-1	23 Dec 1-0	26 Aug 7-4	27 Jan 4-1		7 Oct 1-3	9 Dec 2-3	25 Nov 3-0
Fulham		14 Oct. 4-4	4 Nov 0-2	30 Dec 2-3	5 May 5-3	26 Aug 7-4	28 Oct 5-2	23 Sep 6-2	X	23 Dec 3-2		18 Nov 0-2	9 Sep 2-2	9 Dec 2-3	7 Oct 4-3	28 Apr 2-4	13 Jan 0-2	11 Nov 4-7
Luton Town	21 Apr 1-2	26 Aug 2-2	16 Sep 1-3	23 Sep 4-2	24 Mar 2-3	14 Apr 1-1	16 Dec 4-2	2 Apr 3-3	26 Dec 3-1	X	2 Sep 0-0		28 Apr 2-1	7 Oct 0-4		21 Oct 1-9	4 Nov 2-3	14 Oct 3-4
Millwall	2 Dec 2-2	30 Sep 1-4	6 Jan 0-0		16 Sep 1-3	26 May 1-2	28 Apr 4-1	4 Nov 1-2		9 Dec 2-3	X	14 Oct 0-0	20 Jan 3-3	21 Apr 3-2	9 Sep 1-4	11 Nov 3-4	23 Dec 3-3	28 Oct 0-3
Portsmouth	28 Oct 3-0		2 Sep 2-4	25 Nov 0-1	9 Sep 5-1	7 Oct 1-5	26 Aug 5-1	26 Dec 9-1	21 Apr 3-1		2 Apr 2-4	X	4 Nov 4-1	11 Nov 3-1	30 Sep 3-1	30 Dec 0-0	17 Mar 3-4	23 Sep 1-3
Queen's Park Rangers	14 Apr 3-0	6 Jan 3-2	17 Mar 1-1	28 Oct 6-0	21 Apr 2-3		27 Jan 3-3	2 Dec 0-0	16 Dec 4-4	25 Nov 7-1	7 Oct 4-1	31 Mar 1-0	X	13 Jan 5-1	2 Sep 4-5	23 Dec 0-0		16 Sep 0-1
Reading	25 Dec 4-2	4 Nov 3-1	21 Nov 4-4	17 Mar 3-2	2 Dec 2-3		6 Jan 3-1	14 Oct 4-1	2 Sep 5-4	20 Jan 0-3	18 Nov 2-2	14 Apr 1-0	30 Sep 1-1	X	28 Oct 1-5	9 Sep 0-0	30 Dec 4-2	
Southampton	25 Nov 7-2	16 Sep 0-2	14 Apr 4-2	23 Dec 3-2	14 Oct 3-3	4 Nov 3-3	21 Oct 6-2		20 Jan 3-0		16 Dec 5-3	13 Jan 2-4	9 Dec 4-5	24 Mar 1-1	X	23 Sep 1-3	26 Aug 9-0	18 Nov 2-1
Tottenham Hotspur	4 Nov 7-0	2 Sep 4-0	28 Oct 2-2		30 Sep 2-1	14 Oct 1-5	21 Apr 4-0	20 Jan 3-1	25 Nov 2-1	5 May 1-0	14 Apr 4-0	16 Sep 1-1	25 Dec 3-2	16 Dec 3-2	6 Jan 4-0	X		26 Aug 2-2
Watford	6 Jan 1-3	21 Apr 3-2	19 May 5-1	11 Nov 5-1	25 Nov 3-2	28 Oct 1-6	20 Jan 0-3	2 Sep 2-4	30 Sep 1-2	31 Mar 1-1	12 May 1-2	21 Oct 3-0		16 Sep 2-2	2 Dec 2-1		X	9 Sep 3-3
West Ham United	20 Jan 8-1	5 May 1-1		13 Jan 5-4	9 Dec 2-0	19 May 2-1	31 Mar 1-0	28 Apr 5-0	14 Apr 3-2	12 May 9-1	24 Mar 3-1	6 Jan 4-0	30 Dec 4-2		21 Apr 3-5	2 Dec 0-1	16 Dec 6-2	X

On 25 Dec, Brentford v Arsenal (1-1 after 28 mins) was abandoned and played at a later date.
On 26 Dec, Aldershot v Reading (1-3 after 37 mins) and Watford v Millwall (0-3 after 60 mins) were both abandoned and played at a later date.

There were no scheduled matches between the clubs that are blank in the above grid

The Football League 1944-45

Final Table

		P	W	D	L	F	A	Pts
1	Tottenham Hotspur	30	23	6	1	81	30	52
2	West Ham United	30	22	3	5	96	47	47
3	Brentford	30	17	4	9	87	57	38
4	Chelsea	30	16	5	9	100	55	37
5	Southampton	30	17	3	10	96	69	37
6	Crystal Palace	30	15	5	10	74	70	35
7	Reading	30	14	6	10	78	68	34
8	Arsenal	30	14	3	13	77	67	31
9	Queen's Park Rangers	30	10	10	10	70	61	30
10	Watford	30	11	6	13	66	84	28
11	Fulham	30	11	4	15	79	83	26
12	Portsmouth	30	11	4	15	56	61	26
13	Charlton Athletic	30	12	2	16	72	81	26
14	Brighton and Hove Albion	30	10	2	18	66	95	22
15	Luton Town	30	6	7	17	56	104	19
16	Aldershot	30	7	4	19	44	85	18
17	Millwall	30	5	7	18	50	84	17
18	Clapton Orient	30	5	7	18	39	86	17

WEST

	Aberaman Ath	Bath City	Bristol City	Cardiff City	Lovell's Ath	Swansea T
Aberaman Athletic	X	7 Oct 1-0 / 9 Dec 5-6	16 Sep 0-4 / 18 Nov 1-5	30 Sep 0-6 / 4 Nov 0-3	28 Oct 4-2	2 Sep 4-6 / 16 Dec 5-2
Bath City	14 Oct 5-2 / 2 Dec 3-2	X	28 Oct 2-2 / 16 Dec 1-5	16 Sep 2-2 / 18 Nov 4-2	26 Aug 3-1 / 11 Nov 1-2	30 Sep 3-1
Bristol City	9 Sep 5-2 / 25 Nov 4-2	21 Oct 2-0 / 23 Dec 4-3	X	2 Sep 3-0	23 Sep 1-3 / 9 Dec 5-1	7 Oct 6-1 / 4 Nov 4-2
Cardiff City	23 Sep 8-2 / 11 Nov 3-0	9 Sep 2-1 / 25 Nov 6-2	26 Aug 4-1	X	7 Oct 1-1 / 23 Dec 0-1	21 Oct 3-2 / 9 Dec 3-1
Lovell's Athletic	21 Oct 4-1	2 Sep 1-2 / 4 Nov 3-3	30 Sep 2-0 / 2 Dec 3-2	14 Oct 1-1 / 16 Dec 2-3	X	16 Sep 5-0 / 25 Nov 2-1
Swansea Town	26 Aug 3-0 / 23 Dec 3-3	23 Sep 3-6	14 Oct 0-2 / 11 Nov 3-4	28 Oct 0-4 / 2 Dec 1-3	9 Sep 2-4 / 18 Nov 1-2	X

		P	W	D	L	F	A	Pts
1	Cardiff City	18	12	3	3	54	24	27
2	Bristol City	18	13	1	4	59	10	27
3	Lovell's Athletic	18	10	3	5	40	31	23
4	Bath City	18	8	3	7	47	46	19
5	Aberaman Athletic	18	3	1	14	34	72	7
6	Swansea Town	18	2	1	15	32	63	5

Other English Competitions 1944-45

LEAGUE NORTH (WAR) CUP

Qualifying Round Final Table
See League North (Second Championship) for results

		P	W	D	L	F	A	Pts
1	Derby County	10	7	3	0	38	9	17
2	Aston Villa	10	8	1	1	31	13	17
3	Bristol City	10	8	0	2	27	10	16
4	Everton	10	8	0	2	39	15	16
5	Burnley	10	7	1	2	25	10	15
6	Cardiff City	10	7	1	2	26	11	15
7	Doncaster Rovers	10	7	1	2	30	13	15
8	Liverpool	10	7	1	2	34	15	15
9	Stoke City	10	6	2	2	35	14	14
10	Lovell's Athletic	10	7	0	3	24	15	14
11	Barnsley	10	7	0	3	18	14	14
12	Wrexham	10	5	4	1	30	17	14
13	Bolton Wanderers	10	6	1	3	27	15	13
14	Bradford	10	6	1	3	23	19	13
15	Manchester City	10	6	1	3	23	19	13
16	Rotherham United	10	5	3	2	18	15	13
17	Newcastle United	10	6	0	4	30	21	12
18	Darlington	10	5	2	3	22	18	12
19	Bradford City	10	5	2	3	23	21	12
20	Northampton Town	10	5	2	3	19	20	12
21	Wolverhampton Wanderers	10	5	1	4	23	15	11
22	Leicester City	10	3	5	2	23	16	11
23	Chesterfield Town	10	4	3	3	18	13	11
24	Birmingham	10	5	1	4	19	14	11
25	Sheffield United	10	5	1	4	24	18	11
26	Blackpool	10	5	1	4	27	22	11
27	Bury	10	5	1	4	21	19	11
28	Crewe Alexandra	10	4	3	3	23	23	11
29	Halifax Town	10	4	3	3	14	14	11
30	Manchester United	10	5	1	4	16	16	11
31	Accrington Stanley	10	5	1	4	15	18	11
32	West Bromwich Albion	10	3	4	3	20	15	10

All above qualified for the First Round

		P	W	D	L	F	A	Pts
33	Blackburn Rovers	10	5	0	5	31	25	10
34	Huddersfield Town	10	4	2	4	21	18	10
35	Gateshead	10	4	2	4	15	18	10
36	Hartlepool	10	4	2	4	19	24	10
37	Nottingham Forest	10	3	4	3	9	13	10
38	Leeds United	10	4	1	5	29	25	9
39	Sunderland	10	4	1	5	24	22	9
40	Grimsby Town	10	3	3	4	20	19	9
41	Mansfield Town	10	4	1	5	18	34	9
42	Preston North End	10	2	4	4	14	16	8
43	Lincoln City	10	3	2	5	21	33	8
44	York City	10	3	1	6	25	29	7
45	Middlesbrough	10	3	1	6	23	30	7
46	Walsall	10	3	1	6	13	21	7
47	Southport	10	3	1	6	19	40	7
48	Port Vale	10	3	1	6	13	30	7
49	Bath City	10	3	0	7	28	34	6
50	Swansea Town	10	3	0	7	27	33	6
51	Hull City	10	2	1	7	15	25	5
52	Tranmere Rovers	10	2	1	7	15	28	5
53	Rochdale	10	1	3	6	9	30	5
54	Oldham Athletic	10	2	0	8	19	28	4
55	Sheffield Wednesday	10	1	2	7	14	29	4
56	Stockport County	10	2	0	8	14	35	4
57	Coventry City	10	1	1	8	16	35	3
58	Aberaman Athletic	10	1	1	8	17	46	3
59	Chester	10	1	1	8	14	39	3
60	Notts County	10	1	0	9	12	33	2

Other English Competitions 1944-45

LEAGUE NORTH (WAR) CUP

First round – 2 legs
First legs played on 24 Mar, second legs on 31 Mar
Aston Villa v Wolverhampton Wanderers 1-2, 0-1
Blackpool v Wrexham 2-0, 2-2
Bolton Wanderers v Accrington Stanley 0-0, 4-0
Bradford v Doncaster Rovers 1-1, 0-2
Bristol City v West Bromwich Albion 5-2, 3-3
Burnley v Manchester United 2-3, 0-4
Bury v Stoke City 3-2, 0-3
Cardiff City v Lovell's Athletic 1-0, 0-0
Halifax Town v Chesterfield 1-1, 1-3 *(aet, 90 mins 0-0)*
Leicester City v Derby County 2-1, 0-2
Liverpool v Everton 1-0, 1-0
Manchester City v Crewe Alexandra 5-1, 0-2
Newcastle United v Darlington 2-1, 3-0
Northampton Town v Birmingham 0-2, 2-2
Rotherham United v Barnsley 2-1, 0-3
Sheffield United v Bradford City 2-2, 3-4

Second round – 2 legs
First legs played on 7 Apr, second legs on 14 Apr
Barnsley v Chesterfield 2-2, 0-2
Birmingham v Wolverhampton Wanderers 0-0, 0-1 *(aet, 90 mins 0-0)*
Blackpool v Bolton Wanderers 1-4, 2-1
Bristol City v Cardiff City 1-2, 2-2 *(aet, 90 mins 2-1)*
Doncaster Rovers v Derby County 1-2, 4-1
Liverpool v Manchester City 3-0, 3-1
Manchester United v Stoke City 6-1, 4-1
Newcastle United v Bradford City 6-2, 1-0

Third round – 2 legs
First legs played on 21 Apr, second legs on 28 Apr
Bolton Wanderers v Newcastle United 3-0, 2-4 *(aet, 90 mins 1-4)*
Doncaster Rovers v Manchester United 1-2, 1-3
Liverpool v Chesterfield 0-0, 0-1
Wolverhampton Wanderers v Cardiff City 3-0, 1-2

Semi-final – 2 legs
First legs played on 5 May, second legs on 12 May
Manchester United v Chesterfield 1-1, 1-0
Wolverhampton Wanderers v Bolton Wanderers 2-2, 1-2

Final – 2 legs
First leg, 19 May 1945 at Burnden Park, Bolton
Att 40,000
Bolton Wanderers 1 *(Lofthouse)*
Manchester United 0

Bolton W: Fielding, Threfall, Hubbick, Taylor, Hamlett, Murphy, Woodward, Hunt, Lofthouse, Barrass, Butler
Manchester United: Crompton, Walton, Roughton, Warner, Whalley. Chilton, Chadwick, White*, Bryant, Sloan*, Wrigglesworth

Second leg, 26 May 1945 at Maine Road, Manchester
Att 57,395
Manchester United 2 *(Wrigglesworth, Bryant)*
Bolton Wanderers 2 *(Barrass 2)*

Manchester United: as first leg except Astbury* for Chilton, Glidden* for Chadwick
Bolton W: as first leg

LEAGUE WEST (WAR) CUP

	Aberaman Athletic	Bath C	Bristol City	Cardiff City	Lovell's Athletic	Plymouth Argyle	Swansea Town
Aberaman Athletic	X	5 May 0-4			3 Mar 2-3	31 Mar 1-1	7 Apr 8-1
Bath City	28 Apr 5-1	X	17 Mar 1-0		14 Apr 4-2	2 Apr 5-1	24 Mar 2-1
Bristol City	21 Apr 2-1	10 Mar 4-1	X			12 May 3-1	5 May 4-2
Cardiff City			2 Apr 3-2	X	12 May 0-4		
Lovell's Athletic	10 Mar 4-4	21 Apr 2-0			X	28 Apr 2-5	
Plymouth Argyle	24 Mar 2-1	7 Apr 1-3			5 May 3-1	X	21 Apr 3-1
Swansea Town	2 Apr 4-3	31 Mar 1-0	28 Apr 2-2			14 Apr 3-2	X

		P	W	D	L	F	A	Pts
1	Bath City	10	7	0	3	25	13	14
2	Bristol City	7	4	1	2	17	11	9
3	Plymouth Argyle	9	4	1	4	19	20	9
4	Lovell's Athletic	7	3	1	3	18	18	7
5	Swansea Town	8	3	1	4	15	24	7
6	Aberaman Athletic	9	1	2	6	21	26	4
7	Cardiff City	2	1	0	1	3	6	2

Final – 2 legs
First leg played on 19 May, second leg on 26 May
Bath City v Bristol City 1-0, 4-3

The remaining fixtures were left incomplete

CUP WINNERS MATCH
Played between the winners of the League North (War) Cup and the League South (War) Cup

2 June 1945 at Stamford Bridge, London
Att 35,000
Bolton Wanderers 2 *(Hunt, Hamlett)*
Chelsea 1 *(Rooke)*

Bolton W: Fielding, Threfall, Hubbick, Taylor, Hamlett, Murphy, Woodward, Hunt, Lofthouse, Barrass, Moir
Chelsea: Black*, Cowan*, Hardwick*, Russell, Harris*, Foss, Wardle*, Mackin, Rooke*, Goulden*, Bain

The Football League South (War) Cup 1944-45

Group 1	Arsenal	Clapton Orient	Portsmouth	Reading
Arsenal	X	10 Feb 5-0	10 Mar 2-4	24 Feb 3-0
Clapton Orient	3 Mar 1-3	X	3 Feb 0-1	10 Mar 1-1
Portsmouth	17 Feb 2-4	24 Feb 4-1	X	10 Feb 5-0
Reading	3 Feb 1-3	17 Feb 2-2	3 Mar 1-0	X

	P	W	D	L	F	A	Pts
Arsenal	6	5	0	1	20	8	10
Portsmouth	6	4	0	2	16	8	8
Reading	6	1	2	3	5	14	4
Clapton Orient	6	0	2	4	5	16	2

Group 2	Brentford	Brighton & HA	Fulham	Millwall
Brentford	X	3 Feb 3-5	10 Mar 2-5	3 Mar 2-2
Brighton & HA	24 Feb 2-4	X	10 Feb 1-3	17 Feb 6-2
Fulham	17 Feb 1-0	3 Mar 5-2	X	3 Feb 1-3
Millwall	10 Feb 3-2	10 Mar 1-0	24 Feb 1-0	X

	P	W	D	L	F	A	Pts
Millwall	6	4	1	1	12	11	9
Fulham	6	4	0	2	15	9	8
Brighton & HA	6	2	0	4	16	18	4
Brentford	6	1	1	4	13	18	3

Group 3	Aldershot	QPR	Tottenham H	West Ham U
Aldershot	X	3 Mar 0-2	10 Mar 0-2	3 Feb 1-3
Queen's Park Rangers	10 Feb 2-1	X	24 Feb 1-0	17 Feb 1-1
Tottenham Hotspur	17 Feb 6-1	3 Feb 1-1	X	3 Mar 4-0
West Ham United	24 Feb 4-0	10 Mar 5-0	10 Feb 1-0	X

	P	W	D	L	F	A	Pts
West Ham U	6	4	1	1	14	6	9
QPR	6	3	2	1	7	8	8
Tottenham H	6	3	1	2	13	4	7
Aldershot	6	0	0	6	3	19	0

Group 4	Charlton Ath	Chelsea	Crystal Palace	Luton Town	Southampton	Watford
Charlton Athletic	X		3 Mar 1-0	17 Feb 6-1		3 Feb 1-1
Chelsea		X	10 Mar 2-0	24 Feb 4-1		10 Feb 3-1
Crystal Palace	10 Feb 0-2	17 Feb 1-1	X		24 Feb 3-3	
Luton Town	10 Mar 1-0	3 Feb 0-1		X	10 Feb 2-2	
Southampton		3 Feb 4-1	3 Mar 12-3		X	10 Mar 2-1
Watford	24 Feb 2-6	3 Mar 0-2		17 Feb 1-6 or 5		X

	P	W	D	L	F	A	Pts
Chelsea	6	5	1	0	13	3	11
Southampton	6	4	2	0	29	11	10
Charlton Ath	6	4	1	1	16	5	9
Luton Town	6	1	1	4	8	25	3
Crystal Palace	6	0	2	4	5	13	2
Watford	6	0	1	5	6	20	1

Semi-final
Played on 17 Mar
  Arsenal v Millwall 0-1 (at Stamford Bridge)
  West Ham United v Chelsea 1-2 (at White Hart Lane)

Final
7 Apr 1945 at Wembley Stadium, London
Att 90,000
Chelsea 2 *(McDonald, Wardle)*
Millwall 0

Chelsea: Black*, Winter*, Hardwick*, Russell, Harris*, Foss, Wardle*, L Smith*, Payne, Goulden*, McDonald*
Millwall: Bartram*, Dudley, G Fisher, Ludford*, E Smith, Tyler, Rawlings, R Brown*, Jinks, T Brown, Williams*

Other English Competitions 1944-45

LANCASHIRE CUP

First round – 2 legs
First leg played on 3 Mar , second leg on 10 Mar
Everton v Chester 4-1, 4-6 *(aet, 90 mins 3-6)*
Accrington Stanley v Blackpool 4-1, 2-1
Rochdale v Blackburn Rovers 0-1, 0-4
Southport v Liverpool 0-5 *(Liverpool scratched)*
First leg played on 17 Mar , second leg on 2 Apr
Oldham Athletic v Burnley 2-1, 1-3
Stockport County v Manchester City 4-1, 5-1
Bolton Wanderers v Bury 3-3, 0-1

Manchester United v Crewe Alexandra (Manchester United withdrew due to their involvement in the League North (War) Cup)

Second round – 2 legs
First leg played on 21 Apr , second leg on 28 Apr
Southport v Everton 0-5, 1-1
Stockport County v Crewe Alexandra 0-1, 0-6
(NOTE this was also a Cheshire Bowl tie)
First leg played on 7 Apr , second leg on 14 Apr
Burnley v Accrington Stanley 1-0, 0-4
Bury v Blackburn Rovers 2-3, 2-4

Semi-final – 2 legs
First leg played on 5 May, second leg on 12 May
Accrington Stanley v Everton 1-1, 2-0
Blackburn Rovers v Crewe Alexandra 2-0, 2-3

Final – 2 legs
First leg played on 19 May , second leg on 26 May
Blackburn Rovers v Accrington Stanley 2-0, 4-3

LIVERPOOL SENIOR CUP

Semi-final – 2 legs
First leg played on 26 Dec, second leg on 2 Apr
Everton v Liverpool 2-2 3-1

Final – 2 legs
First leg played on 9 May , second leg on 21 May
Tranmere Rovers v Everton 0-3, 1-4

CHESHIRE BOWL

Semi-final – 2 legs
First leg played on 21 Apr, second leg on 28 Apr
Stockport County v Crewe Alexandra 0-1, 0-6
(NOTE this was also a Lancashire Cup tie)

Final – 2 legs
First leg played on 19 May, second leg on 26 May
Crewe Alexandra v Chester 0-3, 2-4

TYNE, WEAR & TEES CUP

First round – 2 legs
First leg played on 21 Apr , second leg on 28 Apr
Sunderland v Hartlepools United 5-0, 2-0
Middlesbrough v Huddersfield Town 2-1, 0-2 *(aet, 90 mins 0-1)*
York City v Darlington 2-0, 2-2

Semi-final – 2 legs
First leg played on 5 May , second leg on 12 May
York City v Sunderland 2-1, 1-6
Gateshead v Huddersfield Town 3-3, 3-2 *(aet, 90 mins 2-2)*

Final
Played on 26 May at St James' Park, Newcastle
Sunderland v Gateshead 3-6

MIDLAND CUP

First round – 2 legs
First leg played on 21 Apr , second leg on 28 Apr
Birmingham v Coventry City 1-2, 2-2
Northampton Town v Derby County 2-1, 0-5
West Bromwich Albion v Leicester City 1-0, 0-3
Stoke City v Aston Villa 1-0, 0-2

Semi-final – 2 legs
First leg played on 5 May, second leg on 12 May
Aston Villa v Coventry City 9-2, 3-1
Derby County v Leicester City 3-1, 2-1

Final – 2 legs
First leg played on 19 May , second leg on 26 May
Aston Villa v Derby County 0-3, 0-6

SHEFFIELD COUNTY CUP

Semi-final – 2 legs
First leg played on 7 Apr , second leg on 14 Apr
Sheffield United v Rotherham United 6-1, 0-1
First leg played on 5 May , second leg on 12 May
Barnsley v Sheffield Wednesday 3-3, 1-4

Final – 2 legs
First leg played on 19 May , second leg on 26 May
Sheffield United v Sheffield Wednesday 1-3, 2-4

The Scottish Southern Football League 1944-45

	Airdrieonians	Albion Rovers	Celtic	Clyde	Dumbarton	Falkirk	Hamilton Ac	Heart of Midlothian	Hibernian	Morton	Motherwell	Partick Thistle	Queen's Park	Rangers	St Mirren	Third Lanark
Airdrieonians	X	9 Sep 4-0	3 Feb 1-2	16 Dec 1-2	23 Sep 2-1	21 Oct 2-2	12 Aug 0-2	2 Dec 1-1	17 Feb 1-1	26 Aug 2-3	7 Oct 1-1	4 Nov 0-3	6 Jan 3-3	30 Dec 1-3	2 Jan 3-3	7 Apr 0-1
Albion Rovers	1 Jan 3-2	X	19 Aug 0-1	14 Oct 1-3	28 Oct 2-4	9 Dec 3-1	13 Jan 2-2	11 Nov 3-10	30 Sep 0-5	18 Nov 4-3	16 Sep 2-0	2 Sep 0-3	10 Feb 2-3	27 Jan 0-4	25 Nov 0-0	23 Dec 1-0
Celtic	28 Oct 4-2	2 Dec 5-0	X	23 Sep 2-4	30 Dec 2-1	17 Feb 2-1	16 Dec 5-3	12 Aug 4-1	14 Oct 1-1	6 Jan 6-1	10 Feb 1-1	7 Apr 3-0	2 Apr 3-0	9 Sep 0-4	27 Jan 2-1	26 Aug 1-0
Clyde	2 Sep 4-0	20 Jan 2-3	23 Dec 0-3	X	2 Jan 7-1	16 Sep 5-1	21 Oct 7-1	4 Nov 5-1	25 Nov 2-3	3 Feb 1-0	19 Aug 5-3	7 Oct 4-1	11 Nov 3-1	13 Jan 0-2	30 Sep 3-2	9 Dec 1-2
Dumbarton	23 Dec 2-0	3 Feb 3-2	16 Sep 0-3	18 Nov 3-0	X	1 Jan 1-4	28 Apr 0-2	21 Apr 3-2	2 Sep 0-3	21 Oct 0-4	25 Nov 2-6	19 Aug 4-1	7 Oct 2-2	17 Feb 3-6	9 Dec 3-1	30 Sep 2-5
Falkirk	21 Apr 2-1	26 Aug 7-1	11 Nov 2-1	30 Dec 3-0	9 Sep 5-1	X	23 Sep 9-1	6 Jan 2-2	7 Oct 1-3	16 Dec 1-0	14 Oct 1-3	2 Jan 2-1	2 Dec 5-1	12 Aug 2-3	5 May 2-0	4 Nov 3-1
Hamilton Academical	25 Nov 5-0	7 Oct 8-4	2 Sep 6-2	21 Apr 5-3	10 Feb 3-3	23 Dec 1-1	X	18 Nov 2-2	9 Dec 1-1	11 Nov 4-2	1 Jan 1-0	30 Sep 3-4	28 Oct 5-3	14 Oct 2-4	16 Sep 5-2	19 Aug 5-2
Heart Of Midlothian	19 Aug 3-2	17 Feb 2-1	25 Nov 2-0	10 Feb 6-2	14 Oct 4-0	30 Sep 1-2	2 Jan 4-2	X	1 Jan 3-0	7 Oct 2-1	9 Dec 3-3	23 Dec 3-3	7 Apr 2-1	28 Oct 1-1	2 Sep 7-0	16 Sep 4-1
Hibernian	11 Nov 3-2	6 Jan 4-1	20 Jan 2-4	12 Aug 0-4	16 Dec 0-0	13 Jan 3-0	26 Aug 3-1	9 Sep 3-1	X	2 Dec 0-1	18 Nov 0-1	21 Oct 8-0	30 Dec 2-0	23 Sep 4-1	4 Nov 6-2	3 Feb 2-4
Morton	9 Dec 4-2	2 Jan 3-0	30 Sep 4-3	28 Oct 2-3	7 Apr 2-1	2 Sep 4-2	17 Feb 1-2	13 Jan 5-1	19 Aug 3-2	X	23 Dec 1-3	16 Sep 2-0	14 Oct 4-1	10 Feb 1-4	1 Jan 3-0	25 Nov 3-1
Motherwell	13 Jan 5-1	30 Dec 7-2	4 Nov 2-1	2 Dec 2-3	12 Aug 4-3	7 Apr 5-2	9 Sep 4-2	26 Aug 4-1	2 Jan 3-0	23 Sep 4-2	X	3 Feb 2-1	16 Dec 4-2	6 Jan 0-4	17 Feb 2-0	21 Oct 4-6
Partick Thistle	10 Feb 1-2	16 Dec 4-1	13 Jan 0-3	9 Sep 4-2	2 Dec 1-2	18 Nov 1-2	6 Jan 3-1	23 Sep 2-1	28 Apr 5-1	30 Dec 3-2	28 Oct 1-3	X	12 Aug 2-1	2 Apr 1-4	14 Oct 3-0	17 Feb 2-6
Queen's Park	30 Sep 2-1	4 Nov 8-1	9 Dec 0-2	17 Feb 2-0	13 Jan 2-0	19 Aug 2-1	3 Feb 4-0	21 Oct 1-1	16 Sep 0-2	20 Jan 2-1	2 Sep 2-4	25 Nov 5-2	X	18 Nov 1-4	23 Dec 4-2	1 Jan 4-0
Rangers	16 Sep 2-0	21 Oct 3-0	1 Jan 0-1	7 Apr 3-0	11 Nov 5-2	25 Nov 4-0	20 Jan 2-0	3 Feb 4-0	23 Dec 5-0	4 Nov 2-4	30 Dec 1-1	9 Sep 2-0	2 Jan 0-1	X	19 Aug 6-1	2 Sep 0-0
St Mirren	18 Nov 2-1	12 Aug 1-2	21 Oct 2-1	6 Jan 2-3	26 Aug 4-2	28 Oct 2-0	30 Dec 7-1	16 Dec 1-2	10 Feb 1-1	9 Sep 2-2	11 Nov 2-1	21 Apr 1-2	23 Sep 2-2	2 Dec 0-1	X	13 Jan 0-0
Third Lanark	14 Oct 3-5	23 Sep 2-1	18 Nov 1-2	2 Apr 1-2	6 Jan 0-2	10 Feb 2-1	2 Dec 2-1	30 Dec 1-2	28 Oct 3-6	12 Aug 2-3	5 May 1-1	11 Nov 4-1	9 Sep 2-0	16 Dec 1-4	7 Oct 1-2	X

		P	W	D	L	F	A	Pts
1	Rangers	30	23	3	4	88	27	49
2	Celtic	30	20	2	8	70	42	42
3	Motherwell	30	18	5	7	83	54	41
4	Clyde	30	18	0	12	80	61	36
5	Heart of Midlothian	30	14	7	9	75	60	35
6	Hibernian	30	15	5	10	69	51	35
7	Morton	30	16	1	13	71	60	33
8	Falkirk	30	14	3	13	67	57	31
9	Hamilton Academical	30	12	5	13	77	86	29
10	Queen's Park	30	12	4	14	60	62	28
11	Partick Thistle	30	12	1	17	55	74	25
12	Third Lanark	30	11	3	16	55	65	25
13	Dumbarton	30	9	3	18	51	84	21
14	St Mirren	30	7	6	17	45	71	20
15	Albion Rovers	30	7	2	21	42	104	16
16	Airdrieonians	30	4	6	20	43	73	14

The Scottish Southern Football League Cup 1944-45

Section A	Albion R	Hibernian	Rangers	Third Lanark
Albion Rovers	X	31 Mar 1-8	17 Mar 1-3	3 Mar 2-3
Hibernian	10 Mar 1-1	X	3 Mar 1-1	17 Mar 3-1
Rangers	24 Feb 2-1	24 Mar 2-0	X	10 Mar 2-0
Third Lanark	24 Mar 3-3	24 Feb 2-1	31 Mar 2-4	X

		P	W	D	L	F	A	Pts
1	Rangers	6	5	1	0	14	5	9
2	Hibernian	6	2	2	2	14	8	6
3	Third Lanark	6	2	1	3	11	15	5
4	Albion Rovers	6	0	2	4	9	20	2

Section B	Celtic	Clyde	Falkirk	Partick Th
Celtic	X	17 Mar 1-1	3 Mar 3-2	31 Mar 1-2
Clyde	24 Feb 0-0	X	10 Mar 1-2	24 Mar 6-1
Falkirk	24 Mar 1-0	31 Mar 5-1	X	24 Feb 2-1
Partick Thistle	10 Mar 0-1	3 Mar 2-0	17 Mar 1-2	X

		P	W	D	L	F	A	Pts
1	Falkirk	6	5	0	1	14	7	10
2	Celtic	6	2	2	2	6	6	6
3	Clyde	6	1	2	3	9	11	4
4	Partick Thistle	6	2	0	4	7	12	4

Section C	Airdrieonians	Hamilton Ac	Morton	Queen's Park
Airdrieonians	X	24 Feb 1-3	10 Mar 0-3	24 Mar 1-1
Hamilton Academical	17 Mar 3-2	X	3 Mar 2-6	31 Mar 2-4
Morton	31 Mar 1-0	24 Mar 1-0	X	24 Feb 0-2
Queen's Park	3 Mar 4-1	10 Mar 4-2	17 Mar 2-1	X

		P	W	D	L	F	A	Pts
1	Queen's Park	6	5	1	0	17	7	11
2	Morton	6	4	0	2	12	6	8
3	Hamilton Academical	6	2	0	4	12	18	4
4	Airdrieonians	6	0	1	5	5	15	1

Section D	Dumbarton	Hearts	Motherwell	St Mirren
Dumbarton	X	3 Mar 0-0	17 Mar 2-2	10 Mar 5-1
Heart of Midlothian	24 Mar 6-2	X	31 Mar 2-4	24 Feb 2-0
Motherwell	24 Feb 2-1	10 Mar 1-1	X	24 Mar 4-1
St Mirren	31 Mar 3-1	17 Mar 0-1	3 Mar 1-3	X

		P	W	D	L	F	A	Pts
1	Motherwell	6	4	2	0	16	8	10
2	Hearts	6	3	2	1	12	7	8
3	Dumbarton	6	1	2	3	11	15	4
4	St Mirren	6	1	0	5	7	16	2

Semi-final
Played on 21 Apr at Hampden Park, Glasgow
Rangers v Queen's Park 3-0
Played on 28 Apr at Hampden Park, Glasgow
Motherwell v Falkirk 1-0

Final
Played on 12 May 1945 at Hampden Park, Glasgow
Att 70,000
Rangers 2 *(Gillick, Venters)*
Motherwell 1 *(Watson)*

Rangers: Jenkins, Young, Shaw, Little, Woodburn, Symon, Waddell, Gillick, Smith, Venters, Johnstone
Motherwell: Johnstone, Kilmarnock, Shaw, Ross, Paton, Miller, Gibson, Watson, Mathie, Gillan, McCulloch

The Scottish North Eastern Football League 1944-45

First Series	Aberdeen	Arbroath	Dundee	Dundee U	Dunfermline A	East Fife	Falkirk 'A'	Hearts 'A'	Raith R	Rangers
Aberdeen	X	12 Aug 2-0	28 Oct 2-3	30 Sep 5-1	26 Aug 3-2	9 Sep 7-1	2 Dec 7-0	7 Oct 2-0	9 Dec 2-0	4 Nov 4-1
Arbroath	25 Nov 0-3	X	16 Sep 1-4	19 Aug 2-1	28 Oct 2-1	21 Oct 2-1	7 Oct 1-1	2 Sep 5-2	23 Sep 3-5	11 Nov 3-3
Dundee	19 Aug 2-1	14 Oct 6-2	X	4 Nov 2-2	9 Dec 3-1	25 Nov 1-1	23 Sep 1-2	30 Sep 6-0	21 Oct 4-6	2 Sep 5-3
Dundee United	11 Nov 0-5	18 Nov 2-5	26 Aug 1-2	X	2 Dec 2-7	12 Aug 2-1	9 Sep 1-2	28 Oct 4-3	7 Oct 5-1	16 Sep 3-0
Dunfermline Athletic	21 Oct 3-3	30 Sep 0-0	11 Nov 3-4	2 Sep 2-2	X	23 Sep 5-2	14 Oct 3-3	25 Nov 3-2	19 Aug 3-2	7 Oct 2-0
East Fife	16 Sep 5-4	4 Nov 4-0	7 Oct 1-0	14 Oct 2-5	18 Nov 1-5	X	11 Nov 1-0	9 Dec 1-1	2 Sep 2-2	19 Aug 1-5
Falkirk 'A'	2 Sep 0-5	9 Dec 0-0	18 Nov 1-2	21 Oct 4-2	16 Sep 0-3	30 Sep 0-3	X	19 Aug 1-5	28 Oct 0-1	25 Nov 0-1
Heart of Midlothian 'A'	18 Nov 0-7	2 Dec 1-4	9 Sep 1-3	23 Sep 3-0	12 Aug 3-4	26 Aug 2-2	4 Nov 3-1	X	11 Nov 0-2	21 Oct 3-0
Raith Rovers	14 Oct 2-1	9 Sep 2-0	12 Aug 2-4	25 Nov 1-1	4 Nov 3-1	2 Dec 1-2	26 Aug 4-1	16 Sep 3-0	X	30 Sep 4-1
Rangers 'A'	23 Sep 1-2	26 Aug 5-0	2 Dec 0-1	16 Dec 2-0	9 Sep 1-1	28 Oct 2-0	12 Aug 4-0	14 Oct 1-2	18 Nov 2-1	X

		P	W	D	L	F	A	Pts
1	Dundee	18	13	2	3	53	30	28
2	Aberdeen	18	13	1	4	65	21	27
3	Raith Rovers	18	10	2	6	42	32	22
4	Dunfermline Athletic	18	8	5	5	49	36	21
5	Rangers 'A'	18	7	2	9	32	32	16
6	East Fife	18	6	4	8	31	44	16
7	Arbroath	18	6	4	8	30	43	16
8	Dundee United	18	5	3	10	34	49	13
9	Heart of Midlothian 'A'	18	5	2	11	31	49	12
10	Falkirk 'A'	18	3	3	12	16	47	9

1944-45 Second Series	Aberdeen	Arbroath	Dundee	Dundee U	Dunfermline A	East Fife	Falkirk 'A'	Hearts 'A'	Raith R	Rangers
Aberdeen	X	3 Mar 2-2	1 Jan 5-0	5 May 6-0	21 Apr 0-1	31 Mar 2-2	7 May 7-0	24 Mar 3-1	17 Feb 8-0	14 Apr 1-0
Arbroath	2 Jan 2-2	X	28 Apr 2-1	7 Apr 0-2	24 Mar 0-3	6 Jan 0-1	24 Feb 5-0	17 Feb 3-2	21 Apr 1-4	12 May 2-1
Dundee	7 Apr 1-4	31 Mar 4-2	X	2 Jan 4-1	12 May 1-2	21 Apr 3-2	6 Jan 5-1	24 Feb 5-1	5 May 4-0	10 Mar 2-3
Dundee United	10 Feb 1-9	1 Jan 1-0	3 Mar 0-4	X	17 Feb 6-3	17 Mar 3-1	14 Apr 2-5	28 Apr 0-0	13 Jan 5-2	24 Mar 1-1
Dunfermline Athletic	24 Feb 1-4	5 May 2-2	14 Apr 2-0	31 Mar 3-1	X	2 Jun 4-2	2 Jan 3-1	1 Jan 1-1	10 Mar 2-2	28 Apr 1-1
East Fife	28 Apr 1-0	10 Mar 1-1	10 Feb 1-4	12 May 6-1	7 Apr 3-2	X	24 Mar 6-2	2 Jan 0-0	1 Jan 3-1	24 Feb 2-1
Falkirk 'A'	10 Mar 2-1	13 Jan 8-2	17 Mar 1-2	2 Jun 0-1	3 Mar 1-3	17 Feb 1-3	X	10 Feb 2-1	7 Apr 2-4	1 Jan 1-2
Heart of Midlothian 'A'	17 Jul 3-1	14 Apr 5-2	13 Jan 5-3	10 Mar 0-3	17 Mar 1-0	3 Mar 1-2	5 May 2-2	X	12 May 2-0	2 Jun 2-2
Raith Rovers	17 Mar 1-4	10 Feb 1-2	24 Mar 2-1	24 Feb 5-2	6 Jan 5-2	14 Apr 0-3	28 Apr 5-1	31 Mar 6-0	X	2 Jan 1-2
Rangers 'A'	27 Jan 1-2	17 Mar 3-0	17 Feb 2-5	6 Jan 5-1	10 Feb 4-2	13 Jan 3-0	31 Mar 3-2	21 Apr 4-0	3 Mar 3-0	X

		P	HW	AW	HD	AD	L	F	A	Pts
1	Aberdeen	18	6	5	2	1	3	61	19	31
2	Rangers 'A'	18	6	4	2	1	5	41	25	29
3	East Fife	18	7	3	0	3	5	39	29	28
4	Dundee	18	6	4	0	0	8	49	36	24
5	Dunfermline Athletic	18	5	4	3	0	6	37	35	24
6	Dundee United	18	4	3	2	0	9	31	54	19
7	Raith Rovers	18	5	2	0	1	10	39	47	18
8	Heart of Midlothian 'A'	18	5	0	2	2	9	27	39	18
9	Arbroath	18	4	1	1	3	9	28	43	18
10	Falkirk 'A'	18	3	1	0	1	13	32	57	11

3 points were awarded for an away win, 2 points for an away draw

The Scottish North Eastern League Cup 1944-45

Supplementary Cup
First Round - 2 legs
First leg played on 16 Dec, second on 23 Dec
Dundee v Raith Rovers 2-1, 2-0
Dunfermline Athletic v Aberdeen 2-1, 0-2

Final
Played on 30 Dec at Dens Park, Dundee
Att 19,098
Aberdeen 5 *(Waldron 4, Williams)*
Dundee 0

Aberdeen: Johnstone, Cooper, Dyer, Russell, Dunlop, Taylor, Miller, Pattillo, Waldron, Green*, Williams
Dundee: Bennett (Anderson), Thomson, Westwater, McKenzie, Gray, Cox, Moir, Ewen, Turnbull, Smith, Hill

NOTE this competition was played between the top four clubs in the Autumn Series of the League

Mitchell Cup
First Round - 2 legs
First leg played on 19 May, second on 26 May
Arbroath v Raith Rovers 1-4, 2-4
Dundee United v Falkirk 'A' 3-2, 1-3
East Fife v Aberdeen 2-1, 2-3
Heart of Midlothian 'A' v Dundee 3-0, 2-3
Rangers 'A' v Dunfermline Athletic 1-0, 1-1

Second Round
Played on 2 Jun
Aberdeen v Raith Rovers 3-1
Falkirk 'A' bye
Heart of Midlothian 'A' bye
Rangers 'A' bye

Semi-final - 2 legs
First leg played on 9 Jun, second on 16 Jun
Falkirk 'A' v Aberdeen 2-1, 0-7
Heart of Midlothian 'A' v Rangers 'A' 1-2, 2-0

Final - 2 legs
First leg, 23 Jun 1945 at Pittodrie Park, Aberdeen
Att 8,000
Aberdeen 3 *(Pattillo 2 , McMahon)*
Heart of Midlothian 3 *(Aikman 2, McFarlane)*

Aberdeen: G Johnstone, D Johnstone, McKenna, Taylor, Dunlop, Cruikshank, Pattillo, Bremner, Williams, McMahon, Munro
Hearts: Watters, McSpadyen, Black, Cox, Gilmour, Neilson, McFarlane, Conn, Aikman, McCrae, Walker

Second leg, 30 Jun 1945 at Tynecastle Park, Edinburgh
Att 12,000
Heart of Midlothian 0
Aberdeen 1 *(Baird)*

Hearts: Watters, McSpadyen, Black, Cox, Gilmour, Neilson, McFarlane, Conn, Aikman, McCrae, Walker
Aberdeen: Johnstone, McKenna, Dyer, Bremner, Dunlop, Taylor, Munro, Pattillo, Armstrong, Baird, Williams

Other Scottish Competitions 1944-45

SUMMER CUP

First round - 2 legs
First leg played on 26 May, second on 2 Jun
Albion Rovers v Celtic 1-1, 2-4
Clyde v Queen's Park 2-1, 2-5
Heart of Midlothian v Airdrieonians 3-0, 2-0
Morton v Hamilton Academical 6-1, 4-2
Partick Thistle v Dumbarton 4-4, 2-1
St Mirren v Hibernian 4-2, 0-7
Third Lanark v Falkirk 2-1, 0-5

Second round - 2 legs
First leg played on 9 Jun, second on 16 Jun
Hibernian v Falkirk 3-1, 0-1
Morton v Queen's Park 1-0, 0-0
Partick Thistle v Heart of Midlothian 3-0,1-2

Semi-final
Played on 23 Jun
Hibernian v Celtic 2-0 *(at Tynecastle Park, Edinburgh)*
Partick Thistle v Morton 1-0 *(at Hampden Park, Glasgow)*

Final
30 Jun 1945 at Hampden Park, Glasgow
Att 30,000
Partick Thistle 2 *(Johnson 2)*
Hibernian 0

Partick Thistle: Steadward, McGowan, Curran, Shankly, Parker, Husband, Johnson, Brown, Sharp, Candlin, McGeachie
Hibernian: Brown, Govan, Hall, Howie, Baxter, Finnigan, Weir, Combe, Smith, Peat, Caskie

Semi-final - 2 legs
First leg played on 2 Oct, second on 9 Oct
Dundee v Dundee United 2-1, 2-1
Arbroath bye

FORFARSHIRE CUP

Final
Played at Dens Park, Dundee
Dundee v Arbroath 6-0

GLASGOW CUP

First round
Played on 26 Aug
Queen's Park v Clyde 3-2
Partick Thistle v Rangers 1-2

Semi-final
Played on 25 Sep
Third Lanark v Celtic 1-2
Queen's Park v Rangers 0-3

Final
Played on 7 Oct at Hampden Park, Glasgow
Rangers v Celtic 3-2

GLASGOW CHARITY CUP

First round
Played on 2 Apr
Celtic v Third Lanark 5-0
Played on 28 Apr
Rangers v Queen's Park 1-0

Semi-final
Played on 5 May
Rangers v Clyde 4-0
Partick Thistle v Celtic 1-1 *(Celtic won 9-2 on corners at Hampden Park, Glasgow)*

Final
Played on 21 May at Hampden Park, Glasgow
Rangers v Celtic 2-1

EAST OF SCOTLAND SHIELD

Semi-final
Played on 10 Feb
Hibernian v Edinburgh City 5-3

Final
Played on 16 Apr at Easter Road, Edinburgh
Hibernian v Heart of Midlothian 3-1

RENFREWSHIRE CUP

Final
Played on 12 May at Cappielow Park, Greenock
Morton beat St Mirren

WILSON CUP

Played on 18 Sep at Tynecastle Park, Edinburgh
Heart of Midlothian v Hibernian 2-6

PAISLEY CHARITY CUP

Played on 19 May at St Mirren Park, Paisley
St Mirren v Clyde 2-0

Northern Ireland 1944-45

NORTHERN REGIONAL FOOTBALL LEAGUE

	Belfast Celtic	Cliftonville	Derry City	Distillery	Glentoran	Linfield
Belfast Celtic	X	16 Dec 2-0 / 6 Jan 1-0	18 Nov 2-2 / 13 Jan 3-1	3 Apr 3-1 / 25 Dec 2-2	9 Dec 7-3 / 3 Mar 4-1	2 Dec 2-0 / 24 Feb 1-1
Cliftonville	11 Nov 0-2 / 10 Mar 1-2	X	9 Dec 2-3 / 3 Mar 1-4	18 Nov 0-1 / 13 Jan 1-3	2 Dec 2-1 / 24 Feb 2-3	3 Apr 0-6 / 25 Dec 0-4
Derry City	23 Dec 3-3 / 31 Mar 1-0	4 Nov 3-1 / 30 Dec 2-3	X	7 Apr 3-1 / 26 Dec 0-5	25 Nov 4-0 / 3 Feb 2-1	16 Dec 0-5 / 10 Mar 0-2
Distillery	25 Nov 1-5 / 3 Feb 2-2	23 Dec 3-1 / 31 Mar 4-2	2 Dec 0-1 / 24 Feb 4-2	X	11 Nov 5-0 / 6 Jan 3-5	9 Dec 1-3 / 3 Mar 0-3
Glentoran	4 Nov 1-2 / 30 Dec 1-2	7 Apr 9-3 / 26 Dec 6-2	3 Apr 6-2 / 25 Dec 6-3	16 Dec 3-4 / 10 Mar 2-1	X	18 Nov 1-5 / 13 Jan 1-2
Linfield	7 Apr 3-1 / 26 Dec 2-2	25 Nov 4-2 / 3 Feb 6-0	11 Nov 3-3 / 6 Jan 5-2	4 Nov 7-1 / 30 Dec 7-1	23 Dec 9-2 / 31 Mar 3-3	X

		P	W	D	L	F	A	Pts
1	Linfield	20	15	4	1	81	24	34
2	Belfast Celtic	20	13	5	2	54	27	31
3	Derry City	20	8	3	9	41	53	19
4	Distillery	20	8	1	11	44	58	17
5	Glentoran	20	7	1	12	55	67	15
6	Cliftonville	20	2	0	18	23	69	4

SUBSTITUTE GOLD CUP

	Belfast Celtic	Cliftonville	Derry City	Distillery	Glentoran	Linfield
Belfast Celtic	X	14 Oct 2-0	28 Oct 4-6	19 Aug 1-2	16 Sep 2-2	7 Oct 3-2
Cliftonville	2 Sep 1-5	X	19 Aug 7-4	7 Oct 2-5	28 Oct 4-0	16 Sep 0-3
Derry City	23 Sep 5-3	30 Sep 4-3	X	21 Oct 3-5	26 Aug 2-5	2 Sep 3-3
Distillery	30 Sep 1-2	26 Aug 4-0	16 Sep 3-0	X	14 Oct 3-2	28 Oct 0-3
Glentoran	21 Oct 0-1	23 Sep 6-1	7 Oct 4-3	2 Sep 2-0	X	19 Aug 0-4
Linfield	26 Aug 2-1	21 Oct 4-1	14 Oct 5-2	23 Sep 3-0	30 Sep 7-0	X

		P	W	D	L	F	A	Pts
1	Linfield	10	8	1	1	36	10	17
2	Distillery	10	6	0	4	23	18	12
3	Belfast Celtic	10	5	1	4	24	21	11
4	Glentoran	10	4	1	5	21	27	9
5	Derry City	10	3	1	6	32	42	7
6	Cliftonville	10	2	0	8	19	37	4

Northern Ireland 1944-45

IRISH FA CUP

First round – 2 legs
First leg played on 30 Dec, second on 6 Jan
Bangor reserves v Ards 2-3, 3-2
Glentoran II v Bangor
NOTE Glentoran II were successful in a claim that Bangor failed to supply a list of players

Larne bye

Second round – 2 legs
First leg played on 13 Jan, second on 3 Feb
Ards v Infantry Training Centre 5-3, 5-2
Larne v Glentoran II 6-0, 4-4

Third round – 2 legs
First leg played on 10 Feb, second on 17 Feb
Ards v Linfield 0-8, 0-2
Derry City v Cliftonville 5-0, 3-2
Distillery v Belfast Celtic 4-1, 3-4
Larne v Glentoran 3-4, 3-5

Semi-final
Played on 24 Mar
Glentoran v Distillery 3-0
Linfield v Derry City 4-0

Final
Played on 14 Apr at Celtic Park, Belfast
Linfield v Glentoran 4-2

INTER CITY CUP

Derry City played all their home matches in Belfast
All League of Ireland clubs' home games were played at Dalymount Park, Dublin

First round – 2 legs
First leg played on 21 Apr, second on 27 Apr
Derry City v Shelbourne 1-3, 3-3
First leg played on 21 Apr, second on 25 Apr
Distillery v Dundalk 5-2, 1-2
First leg played on 28 Apr, second on 5 May
Shamrock Rovers v Belfast Celtic 0-3, 0-5
Cliftonville v Bohemians 2-3, 1-1
First leg played on 28 Apr, second on 30 Apr
Glentoran v Limerick 2-1, 1-2 *(Limerick won on corners)*
First leg played on 5 May, second on 7 May
Linfield v Cork United 8-2, 1-5

Second round - 2 legs
The first round winners were joined by the best Northern losers (Glentoran) and Southern losers (Cork United)

First leg played on 12 May, second on 19 May
Shelbourne v Belfast Celtic 0-0, 2-4
Glentoran v Bohemians 1-0, 2-3 *(Bohemians won on corners)*
First leg played on 12 May, second on 14 May
Linfield v Cork United 3-0, 2-1
First leg played on 19 May, second on 21 May
Distillery v Limerick 5-0, 1-1

Semi-final - 2 legs
First leg played on 23 May, second on 26 May
Bohemians v Distillery 5-1, 3-2
Linfield v Belfast Celtic 2-2, 3-5

Final - 2 legs
First leg played on 30 May, second on 2 Jun
Belfast Celtic v Bohemians 2-2, 0-1

NOTE First leg played at Windsor Park, Belfast

1945-46

The Victory season saw a re-organization of the Football League competitions in England. The First and Second Division clubs (of 1939 status) were placed into North and South sections of 22 clubs each. However the Third Divisions were split into further regional sections. The FA Cup effectively replaced the League Cup while the local cups were no longer included within the overall standings as before. The Third Divisions also ran cup competitions, with the North section also running a Second Championship which included the cup results as well as scheduled matches.

The Scottish Football League restarted and took over the running of the combined Southern and North Eastern Leagues which was now divided into 'A' and 'B' Divisions. Unlike the Football League in England, pre-war status was not used to determine which division which club was placed. Several clubs had pushed for the formation of a 'super league' of sixteen clubs however this didn't come to fruition. An Eastern League composed of clubs excluded from this set-up was also played.

The Northern Irish Northern Regional League also operated. There was also an international competition involving clubs from the Republic of Ireland.

WINNERS OF THE PRINCIPAL COMPETITIONS

FA Cup	Derby County
Football League –	
North	Sheffield United
South	Birmingham City
Third Division (Northern Section) –	
West	Accrington Stanley
East	Rotherham United
Second Championship	Rotherham United
Third Division (Northern Section) Cup	Rotherham United
Third Division (Southern Section) –	
North	Queen's Park Rangers
South	Crystal Palace
Third Division (Southern Section) Cup	Bournemouth & Boscombe Athletic
Scottish Victory Cup	Rangers
Scottish League –	
A Division	Rangers
B Division	Dundee
Scottish League Cup	Aberdeen
Irish FA Cup	Linfield
Northern Regional League	Linfield
Substitute Gold Cup	Belfast Celtic
Inter City Cup	Shamrock Rovers

The Football League 1945-46

NORTH

	Barnsley	Blackburn R	Blackpool	Bolton W	Bradford	Burnley	Bury	Chesterfield	Everton	Grimsby T	Huddersfield T	Leeds U	Liverpool	Manchester City	Manchester United	Middlesbrough	Newcastle U	Preston NE	Sheffield United	Sheffield Wed	Stoke C	Sunderland
Barnsley	X	4 May 4-0	15 Dec 1-1	27 Apr 0-3	12 Jan 3-0	6 Apr 3-0	29 Dec 1-3	30 Mar 2-2	19 Apr 2-0	8 Dec 1-0	16 Mar 3-2	15 Sep 1-0	26 Dec 2-0	2 Feb 2-2	22 Sep 2-2	10 Nov 1-3	16 Feb 1-5	25 Aug 3-5	20 Oct 4-0	2 Mar 3-3	17 Nov 4-2	13 Oct 4-2
Blackburn Rovers	1 Jan 3-1	X	15 Sep 1-1	20 Feb 0-1	10 Nov 1-2	20 Oct 4-2	6 Oct 2-3	17 Sep 0-7	12 Jan 2-1	25 Aug 3-2	25 Dec 1-6	23 Feb 0-0	22 Sep 0-5	24 Nov 0-0	16 Mar 1-3	19 Apr 3-3	1 Dec 1-2	16 Feb 0-2	13 Apr 0-0	22 Dec 1-2	20 Apr 5-1	23 Mar 2-1
Blackpool	22 Dec 1-1	8 Sep 5-2	X	12 Sep 1-1	29 Sep 0-1	22 Apr 2-1	1 Sep 3-1	1 Dec 0-1	25 Dec 5-2	13 Apr 5-0	24 Nov 4-2	19 Jan 1-1	20 Apr 1-1	6 Oct 5-4	27 Mar 1-5	26 Mar 3-1	27 Oct 1-1	27 Aug 6-3	23 Feb 1-2	3 Nov 5-1	30 Mar 4-0	16 Feb 4-0
Bolton Wanderers	20 Apr 2-0	2 Feb 1-2	29 Dec 1-1	X	13 Mar 0-0	8 Sep 2-0	12 Jan 1-0	22 Apr 1-0	1 Sep 3-1	1 Jan 0-0	6 Apr 2-1	13 Oct 6-0	29 Apr 1-0	27 Mar 3-1	20 Apr 1-1	8 Dec 2-1	10 Apr 0-0	22 Sep 0-0	17 Nov 1-4	30 Mar 2-2	15 Dec 2-2	10 Nov 1-2
Bradford	19 Jan 2-1	3 Nov 2-1	22 Sep 3-0	16 Feb 0-5	X	17 Nov 7-0	20 Oct 6-0	27 Aug 1-0	3 Apr 1-2	15 Sep 3-2	12 Sep 2-2	16 Mar 9-4	13 Oct 0-2	1 Dec 2-3	23 Mar 2-1	27 Apr 1-1	27 Mar 5-3	23 Feb 3-1	19 Apr 0-2	25 Dec 3-2	25 Aug 1-0	13 Apr 1-0
Burnley	13 Apr 3-2	27 Oct 1-4	19 Apr 1-1	15 Sep 2-2	14 Nov 2-1	X	22 Sep 2-3	16 Mar 3-1	27 Apr 1-0	30 Mar 1-2	26 Jan 4-3	10 Nov 2-3	25 Aug 1-3	15 Dec 1-0	8 Dec 2-2	2 Feb 8-1	29 Dec 3-2	13 Oct 0-0	4 May 0-1	12 Jan 2-2	1 Apr 1-0	26 Dec 2-3
Bury	12 Sep 1-1	13 Oct 3-2	25 Aug 1-4	19 Jan 0-2	27 Oct 2-3	29 Sep 1-0	X	25 Dec 2-3	4 May 3-1	27 Apr 1-1	22 Dec 3-1	16 Feb 2-1	25 Sep 1-3	3 Nov 1-1	23 Feb 1-1	13 Apr 2-1	24 Nov 1-1	2 Feb 1-1	23 Mar 2-2	1 Dec 1-2	19 Jan 2-3	16 Mar 3-0
Chesterfield	23 Mar 1-1	29 Dec 4-0	8 Dec 0-3	19 Apr 1-2	4 May 2-0	19 Mar 3-0	26 Dec 3-1	X	13 Apr 1-1	17 Nov 0-2	2 Mar 0-0	25 Aug 3-1	15 Dec 1-1	12 Jan 0-1	15 Sep 1-1	20 Oct 1-0	2 Feb 2-0	27 Apr 1-0	13 Oct 0-0	20 Feb 1-1	10 Nov 1-1	22 Sep 3-0
Everton	22 Apr 0-4	19 Jan 4-1	26 Dec 7-1	25 Aug 3-2	2 Feb 0-0	20 Apr 2-0	1 Jan 3-1	6 Apr 4-0	X	15 Dec 2-1	30 Mar 5-2	22 Sep 0-2	29 Dec 2-2	9 Feb 4-1	13 Oct 3-0	17 Nov 1-1	2 Mar 4-1	15 Sep 1-1	10 Nov 1-0	9 Mar 2-2	8 Dec 6-1	20 Oct 4-0
Grimsby Town	1 Dec 0-0	1 Sep 2-0	6 Apr 4-2	25 Dec 0-2	8 Sep 2-1	23 Mar 1-1	20 Apr 1-1	24 Nov 3-3	22 Dec 1-2	X	3 Nov 5-3	26 Jan 3-2	22 Apr 1-1	29 Sep 0-2	19 Jan 1-0	23 Feb 1-1	6 Oct 0-2	4 May 1-0	16 Feb 1-6	27 Oct 1-2	16 Mar 0-2	3 Mar 4-1
Huddersfield Town	9 Mar 2-1	26 Dec 0-2	17 Nov 2-4	13 Apr 2-4	29 Dec 1-1	16 Feb 4-2	15 Dec 3-0	23 Feb 1-2	16 Mar 0-1	10 Nov 3-2	X	27 Apr 3-2	8 Dec 3-1	4 May 3-0	25 Aug 3-2	13 Oct 7-0	12 Jan 1-4	23 Apr 2-0	22 Sep 1-4	2 Feb 3-2	20 Oct 3-1	15 Sep 4-1
Leeds United	8 Sep 1-2	2 Mar 1-4	12 Jan 1-2	6 Oct 2-1	1 May 3-1	3 Nov 1-2	9 Feb 3-3	1 Sep 1-3	29 Sep 2-3	9 Mar 2-2	3 Apr 3-2	X	2 Feb 3-0	30 Mar 1-3	17 Nov 3-3	25 Dec 1-0	6 Apr 0-3	20 Oct 2-1	15 Dec 2-4	22 Apr 0-1	29 Sep 0-0	1 Dec 4-2
Liverpool	25 Dec 5-2	29 Sep 4-0	27 Apr 4-0	29 Aug 2-2	6 Oct 4-1	1 Sep 2-3	8 Sep 1-1	22 Dec 2-2	12 Sep 2-1	19 Apr 2-0	1 Dec 4-1	10 Apr 1-1	X	27 Oct 0-5	16 Feb 0-5	23 Mar 1-2	3 Nov 3-0	12 Jan 4-2	16 Mar 0-3	24 Nov 0-2	13 Apr 4-1	23 Feb 2-2
Manchester City	13 Mar 2-3	17 Nov 4-2	13 Oct 1-4	23 Feb 1-0	8 Dec 6-0	22 Dec 1-2	10 Nov 4-1	19 Jan 1-0	16 Feb 1-3	28 Sep 0-2	22 Sep 3-2	1 Jan 5-1	23 Mar 1-0	X	13 Apr 1-3	25 Aug 2-1	25 Dec 4-3	16 Mar 3-0	27 Apr 2-1	12 Jan 1-5	15 Sep 0-2	19 Apr 0-2
Manchester United	29 Sep 1-1	9 Mar 6-2	2 Feb 4-2	27 Oct 2-1	30 Mar 4-0	1 Dec 3-3	2 Mar 1-1	8 Sep 0-2	6 Oct 0-0	12 Jan 5-0	2 Sep 2-3	24 Nov 6-1	9 Feb 2-1	6 Apr 1-4	X	29 Dec 4-1	22 Apr 4-1	3 Nov 6-1	26 Dec 2-3	20 Apr 4-0	4 May 2-1	15 Dec 2-1
Middlesbrough	3 Nov 2-5	22 Apr 5-1	9 Mar 4-2	1 Dec 1-0	20 Apr 3-0	10 Apr 2-1	6 Apr 3-0	27 Oct 0-4	24 Nov 0-0	2 Mar 3-1	6 Oct 2-8	26 Dec 4-1	30 Mar 2-5	1 Sep 2-2	1 Sep 2-1	X	8 Sep 0-6	15 Dec 0-1	19 Jan 3-0	29 Sep 2-0	1 May 3-1	1 Jan 1-0
Newcastle United	1 May 1-1	8 Dec 8-1	20 Oct 2-2	16 Mar 3-4	15 Dec 4-0	12 Sep 0-1	17 Nov 4-2	26 Jan 3-2	23 Feb 1-3	13 Oct 6-2	13 Jan 4-1	10 Nov 6-2	26 Dec 1-1	19 Apr 0-1	15 Sep 1-1		X	23 Mar 2-1	25 Jan 6-0	1 Jan 2-0	22 Sep 9-1	27 Apr 4-1
Preston North End	1 Sep 2-3	31 Mar 3-1	3 Sep 5-0	29 Sep 1-2	11 Apr 4-6	6 Oct 4-0	17 Sep 1-2	20 Apr 1-0	8 Sep 0-2	29 Dec 1-2	22 Apr 2-0	27 Oct 8-2	12 Jan 2-1	9 Mar 5-1	10 Nov 2-2	22 Dec 0-1	30 Mar 3-1	X	8 Dec 5-2	6 Apr 0-1	26 Dec 2-4	17 Nov 1-1
Sheffield United	27 Oct 1-1	6 Apr 2-1	2 Mar 4-2	24 Nov 2-3	22 Apr 1-1	1 Jan 5-1	30 Mar 2-1	6 Mar 1-1	3 Nov 4-0	9 Feb 7-1	29 Dec 4-1	22 Mar 6-2	9 Apr 3-1	20 Apr 2-3	25 Dec 1-0	12 Jan 2-7	1 Sep 3-0	1 Dec 2-0	X	8 Sep 1-3	2 Feb 4-2	13 Sep 4-0
Sheffield Wednesday	27 Feb 0-3	5 Dec 1-1	10 Nov 3-2	1 Apr 0-0	26 Dec 3-0	12 Jan 1-1	8 Dec 2-0	16 Feb 1-0	16 Mar 0-0	20 Oct 4-1	4 Feb 3-0	23 Apr 2-0	17 Nov 2-3	29 Dec 1-1	27 Apr 1-0	15 Sep 2-1	4 May 2-3	13 Apr 2-0	15 Sep 2-1	X	13 Oct 1-0	25 Aug 6-3
Stoke City	24 Nov 4-0	27 Apr 5-0	23 Mar 6-3	22 Dec 4-1	1 Sep 3-0	23 Feb 0-0	22 Apr 2-0	3 Apr 6-1	1 Dec 2-3	15 Oct 4-2	27 Oct 6-2	13 Sep 2-1	6 Apr 0-1	8 Sep 2-0	20 Sep 1-2	16 Feb 1-4	29 Dec 3-1	25 Sep 6-0	8 Apr 0-3	6 Oct 3-0	X	12 Jan 0-0
Sunderland	6 Oct 1-0	30 Mar 2-2	13 Mar 3-1	3 Nov 1-0	6 Apr 1-0	25 Dec 1-1	9 Mar 2-1	29 Sep 0-5	27 Oct 0-4	2 Feb 2-0	8 Dec 0-2	8 Dec 5-1	2 Mar 0-2	22 Apr 4-0	22 Dec 4-2	4 May 0-1	20 Apr 1-0	24 Nov 0-1	29 Dec 1-2	1 Sep 1-0	17 Oct 4-2	X

Bury v Everton on 29 Aug was abandoned because of poor light after 75 mins with the score at 2-3 and replayed at a later date

The Football League 1945-46

SOUTH

	Arsenal	Aston Villa	Birmingham	Brentford	Charlton Athletic	Chelsea	Coventry City	Derby County	Fulham	Leicester City	Luton Town	Millwall	Newport County	Nottingham Forest	Plymouth Argyle	Portsmouth	Southampton	Swansea Town	Tottenham Hotspur	WBA	West Ham United	Wolverhampton W
Arsenal	X	22 Jan 2-4	26 Jan 0-3	29 Apr 1-1	20 Oct 1-2	9 Mar 1-2	1 Sep 0-0	22 Apr 0-1	10 Nov 2-0	20 Apr 1-2	8 Sep 0-2	30 Mar 4-0	26 Dec 7-0	15 Dec 2-2	17 Nov 3-0	8 Dec 4-3	6 Apr 1-1	2 Oct 4-1	9 Feb 1-1	12 Jan 2-0	4 May 2-1	29 Dec 3-2
Aston Villa	29 Sep 5-1	X	12 Jan 2-2	17 Apr 1-1	13 Oct 0-2	27 Mar 0-3	20 Apr 0-0	6 Apr 4-1	20 Oct' 3-0	22 Apr 3-0	1 Sep 7-1	1 May 2-0	19 Dec 5-2	1 Dec 3-1	10 Nov 4-2	17 Nov 3-2	30 Mar 2-0	8 Feb 6-3	2 Feb 5-1	5 Sep 3-3	29 Dec 2-2	26 Dec 1-1
Birmingham City	13 Mar 0-1	19 Jan 3-1	X	27 Oct 1-0	16 Feb 1-0	3 Nov 5-2	29 Dec 2-0	22 Dec 1-0	23 Feb 2-0	25 Dec 6-2	3 Sep 3-2	24 Nov 4-0	19 Apr 3-2	13 Apr 3-1	16 Mar 0-1	10 Apr 1-0	8 Dec 4-0	29 Sep 5-0	2 Oct 8-0	9 Sep 4-0	2 Aug 0-1	27 Apr 0-1
Brentford	23 Feb 6-3	16 Feb 0-1	20 Oct 2-1	X	16 Mar 1-1	1 Dec 4-4	19 Jan 1-2	13 Sep 0-0	23 Mar 1-2	6 Sep 1-2	24 Apr 6-1	15 Dec 7-0	25 Aug 2-1	27 Apr 5-1	13 Apr 3-2	19 Apr 0-2	25 Dec 1-4	24 Nov 2-2	10 Nov 1-3	13 Oct 2-0	9 Sep 1-1	15 Sep 0-0
Charlton Athletic	27 Oct 6-2	6 Oct 0-0	29 Apr 0-0	10 Apr 4-3	X	30 Mar 0-0	8 Sep 3-1	20 Apr 2-1	17 Nov 4-2	1 Sep 2-1	29 Sep 5-1	6 Apr 2-3	29 Dec 2-0	26 Dec 2-0	1 Dec 4-0	15 Dec 2-0	22 Apr 1-1	3 Nov 5-0	17 Apr 1-0	2 Feb 1-1	19 Jan 3-0	4 May 1-1
Chelsea	16 Mar 1-2	23 Feb 2-2	16 Nov 2-3	8 Dec 4-2	3 Apr 0-1	X	10 Apr 2-1	19 Sep 3-0	13 Apr 0-0	19 Jan 4-0	26 Feb 2-1	25 Dec 3-0	13 Sep 2-0	25 Aug 0-4	19 Apr 2-0	27 Apr 3-0	12 Sep 1-0	22 Dec 3-4	17 Nov 3-4	20 Oct 7-4	13 Oct 1-2	22 Sep 1-1
Coventry City	25 Aug 2-0	27 Apr 2-2	12 Sep 2-3	17 Jan 1-0	15 Sep 1-1	2 Feb 2-0	X	14 Mar 3-1	22 Sep 3-1	30 Mar 0-1	4 Apr 0-3	9 Feb 7-2	15 Nov 7-1	10 Nov 1-4	2 Oct 3-1	20 Apr 3-1	2 Mar 0-1	6 Apr 2-2	4 May 0-1	26 Dec 3-2	15 Dec 2-5	8 Dec 1-0
Derby County	19 Apr 1-1	13 Apr 0-1	15 Dec 0-2	29 Dec 3-2	1 May 3-1	4 May 1-1	16 Mar 3-0	X	25 Apr 5-2	10 Apr 4-1	3 Apr 4-3	12 Jan 8-1	20 Oct 4-1	13 Oct 3-2	15 Sep 3-1	22 Sep 3-1	2 Feb 8-1	16 Feb 2-1	26 Dec 2-0	8 Dec 3-3	17 Nov 5-1	10 Nov 2-0
Fulham	3 Nov 5-2	27 Oct 1-4	15 Apr 3-2	30 Mar 2-2	24 Nov 2-4	6 Apr 3-2	29 Sep 2-0	1 Sep 2-1	X	8 Sep 1-1	2 Oct 4-1	22 Apr 7-0	4 May 3-1	29 Dec 3-3	15 Dec 4-0	26 Dec 5-2	20 Apr 3-1	1 Dec 5-2	9 Mar 1-1	9 Feb 1-4	2 Feb 0-1	12 Jan 3-1
Leicester City	26 Jan 4-5	23 Apr 0-1	26 Dec 0-1	4 May 1-3	25 Aug 2-3	12 Jan 1-7	23 Mar 1-3	23 Feb 1-1	15 Sep 0-1	X	13 Apr 0-2	2 Feb 2-6	16 Nov 2-0	10 Oct 0-0	29 Sep 2-2	13 Oct 3-2	9 Feb 1-2	16 Mar 0-2	29 Dec 4-0	15 Dec 1-3	8 Dec 4-1	17 Nov 1-2
Luton Town	15 Sep 1-2	25 Aug 1-1	4 May 0-3	2 Feb 1-4	22 Sep 1-4	23 Mar 3-1	19 Apr 1-2	30 Mar 1-1	13 Oct 2-2	6 Apr 2-1	X	2 Mar 0-1	1 May 1-0	17 Nov 1-4	27 Oct 0-0	10 Nov 1-1	9 Mar 4-2	20 Apr 3-1	12 Dec 3-1	29 Dec 1-2	26 Dec 1-4	15 Dec 1-0
Millwall	23 Mar 1-1	16 Mar 2-2	17 Nov 5-1	22 Dec 3-1	13 Apr 2-2	26 Dec 0-8	16 Feb 1-1	19 Jan 1-2	19 Apr 0-1	15 Sep 2-2	23 Feb 2-0	X	22 Sep 4-0	15 Sep 2-1	20 Apr 6-1	25 Aug 4-0	8 Apr 5-3	10 Dec 5-1	8 Dec 3-2	10 Nov 1-4	20 Oct 0-0	13 Oct 2-0
Newport County	25 Dec 1-2	22 Dec 0-4	22 Apr 0-1	1 Sep 0-5	13 Sep 2-1	8 Sep 1-3	22 Nov 1-3	27 Oct 1-4	30 Aug 1-5	3 Nov 2-0	1 Dec 4-0	29 Sep 3-1	X	16 Feb 2-4	19 Jan 2-1	26 Jan 4-2	2 Oct 2-6	23 Mar 3-1	20 Apr 1-4	6 Apr 0-3	30 Apr 2-2	9 Mar 1-3
Nottingham Forest	22 Dec 3-2	8 Dec 1-3	6 Apr 1-0	20 Apr 2-0	25 Dec 0-2	1 Sep 0-1	3 Nov 0-0	2 Oct 1-1	12 Sep 1-1	27 Sep 1-1	24 Dec 0-2	8 Sep 2-2	23 Apr 7-2	X	17 Sep 2-0	19 Jan 3-0	29 Sep 4-0	26 Jan 2-2	22 Apr 0-2	30 Mar 0-2	9 Mar 1-1	2 Feb 0-0
Plymouth Argyle	24 Nov 0-4	3 Nov 0-3	1 Sep 2-3	6 Apr 1-1	8 Dec 1-5	22 Apr 1-4	13 Oct 1-1	8 Sep 0-4	22 Dec 0-2	22 Sep 2-3	20 Oct 1-1	27 Apr 1-2	12 Jan 0-3	4 May 3-2	X		29 Dec 1-3	1 Sep 0-3	25 Mar 1-3	30 Mar 0-1	2 Feb 1-2	2 Feb 3-2
Portsmouth	1 Dec 1-1	24 Nov 2-3	30 Mar 3-4	22 Apr 2-0	22 Dec 0-3	20 Apr 3-0	27 Oct 1-1	29 Sep 3-0	25 Dec 2-2	2 Oct 0-2	3 Oct 2-1	1 Sep 1-1	2 Feb 2-3	12 Jan 2-2	12 Sep 6-1	X	8 Sep 3-2	29 Aug 5-0	6 Apr 0-1	9 Feb 3-0	2 Mar 2-3	9 Dec 0-2
Southampton	13 Apr 1-1	23 Mar 3-5	1 Dec 1-1	26 Dec 3-4	19 Apr 3-1	29 Dec 7-0	23 Feb 4-3	29 Apr 4-2	27 Apr 1-1	16 Mar 3-1	16 Apr 2-2	4 May 2-4	13 Oct 0-0	22 Sep 5-2	25 Aug 5-5	15 Sep 3-1	X	19 Jan 5-2	15 Dec 3-2	17 Nov 1-2	10 Nov 3-3	20 Oct 2-4
Swansea Town	13 Oct 3-2	15 Sep 5-4	22 Sep 2-4	17 Nov 4-1	10 Nov 1-1	15 Dec 5-3	13 Apr 3-2	21 Feb 2-3	8 Dec 2-2	9 Mar 4-3	27 Apr 2-0	29 Dec 5-0	2 Mar 3-0	2 Feb 3-3	26 Dec 0-0	4 May 3-0	12 Jan 4-1	X	20 Oct 4-1	1 Sep 2-4	19 Apr 2-3	23 Mar 2-5
Tottenham Hotspur	16 Feb 2-0	20 Apr 3-0	13 Oct 0-1	3 Nov 1-1	23 Feb 2-1	24 Nov 3-2	26 Jan 2-0	25 Dec 2-5	16 Mar 1-3	12 Jan 6-2	19 Dec 2-3	1 Dec 5-1	27 Apr 1-0	19 Apr 3-2	23 Mar 2-0	13 Apr 2-0	22 Dec 4-3	27 Oct 3-1	X	29 Sep 4-2	15 Dec 2-3	25 Aug 1-4
West Bromwich Albion	19 Jan 0-1	29 Aug 1-0	15 Sep 0-0	2 Oct 3-4	15 Apr 2-5	27 Oct 8-1	24 Dec 2-2	1 Dec 2-3	16 Feb 3-1	22 Dec 3-2	12 Sep 3-1	3 Nov 3-1	13 Dec 6-0	23 Apr 1-0	23 Mar 5-2	16 Feb 2-0	24 Nov 5-2	25 Aug 4-1	22 Sep 5-0	X	27 Apr 1-2	23 Apr 1-1
West Ham United	27 Aug 1-1	10 Sep 1-2	1 Sep 3-2	29 Sep 0-2	19 Jan 2-0	2 Oct 2-4	22 Dec 6-3	24 Nov 2-3	29 Apr 3-5	1 Sep 2-2	25 Dec 3-4	27 Oct 3-1	23 Mar 4-1	16 Mar 1-3	16 Feb 7-0	23 Feb 3-1	3 Nov 3-1	22 Apr 3-0	8 Sep 1-1	20 Apr 1-1	X	13 Apr 2-1
Wolverhampton Wanderers	3 Sep 1-1	25 Dec 1-2	20 Apr 3-3	8 Sep 1-0	27 Aug 1-2	29 Sep 1-0	1 Dec 1-0	3 Nov 1-0	19 Jan 1-0	24 Nov 2-0	22 Dec 3-0	2 Oct 1-2	16 Mar 5-2	23 Feb 4-0	29 Apr 1-1	16 Feb 4-0	27 Oct 3-2	30 Mar 1-0	1 Sep 4-2	22 Apr 0-0	6 Apr 3-3	X

The Football League 1945-46

NORTH

Final Table

		P	W	D	L	F	A	Pts
1	Sheffield United	42	27	6	9	112	62	60
2	Everton	42	23	9	10	88	54	55
3	Bolton Wanderers	42	20	11	11	67	45	51
4	Manchester United	42	19	11	12	98	62	49
5	Sheffield Wednesday	42	20	8	14	67	60	48
6	Newcastle United	42	21	5	16	106	70	47
7	Chesterfield	42	17	12	13	68	49	46
8	Barnsley	42	17	11	14	76	68	45
9	Blackpool	42	18	9	15	94	92	45
10	Manchester City	42	20	4	18	78	75	44
11	Liverpool	42	17	9	16	80	70	43
12	Middlesbrough	42	17	9	16	75	87	43
13	Stoke City	42	18	6	18	88	79	42
14	Bradford	42	17	6	19	71	84	40
15	Huddersfield Town	42	17	4	21	90	89	38
16	Burnley	42	13	10	19	63	84	36
17	Grimsby Town	42	13	9	20	61	89	35
18	Sunderland	42	15	5	22	55	83	35
19	Preston North End	42	14	6	22	70	77	34
20	Bury	42	12	10	20	60	85	34
21	Blackburn Rovers	42	11	7	24	60	111	29
22	Leeds United	42	9	7	26	66	118	25

SOUTH

Final Table

		P	W	D	L	F	A	Pts
1	Birmingham City	42	28	5	9	96	45	61
2	Aston Villa	42	25	11	6	106	58	61
3	Charlton Athletic	42	25	10	7	92	45	60
4	Derby County	42	24	7	11	101	62	55
5	West Bromwich Albion	42	22	8	12	104	69	52
6	Wolverhampton W	42	20	11	11	75	48	51
7	West Ham United	42	20	11	11	94	76	51
8	Fulham	42	20	10	12	93	73	50
9	Tottenham Hotspur	42	22	3	17	78	81	47
10	Chelsea	42	19	6	17	92	80	44
11	Arsenal	42	16	11	15	76	73	43
12	Millwall	42	17	8	17	79	105	42
13	Coventry City	42	15	10	17	70	69	40
14	Brentford	42	14	10	18	82	72	38
15	Nottingham Forest	42	12	13	17	72	73	37
16	Southampton	42	14	9	19	97	105	37
17	Swansea Town	42	15	7	20	90	112	37
18	Luton Town	42	13	7	22	60	92	33
19	Portsmouth	42	11	6	25	66	87	28
20	Leicester City	42	8	7	27	57	101	23
21	Newport County	42	9	2	31	52	125	20
22	Plymouth Argyle	42	3	8	31	39	120	14

The Football League 1945-46

THIRD DIVISION (NORTHERN SECTION) WEST

	Accrington S	Barrow	Chester	Crewe Alex	Oldham Ath	Rochdale	Southport	Stockport Co	Tranmere R	Wrexham
Accrington Stanley	X	1 Dec 4-1	3 Nov 5-2	1 Jan 0-1	29 Sep 1-1	26 Dec 4-2	27 Oct 1-0	6 Oct 3-0	1 Sep 2-3	8 Sep 2-1
Barrow	29 Dec 0-4	X	29 Sep 1-3	20 Oct 0-0	25 Dec 3-2	10 Nov 2-1	15 Sep 3-3	1 Sep 2-3	13 Oct 0-2	1 Jan 1-0
Chester	10 Nov 3-3	22 Sep 3-1	X	13 Oct 0-0	22 Dec 2-2	27 Oct 3-3	1 Sep 5-3	25 Dec 4-2	8 Sep 5-1	1 Dec 4-1
Crewe Alexandra	22 Dec 1-2	27 Oct 7-0	6 Oct 2-0	X	1 Sep 0-0	1 Dec 1-4	29 Sep 3-0	8 Sep 1-2	3 Nov 5-3	25 Dec 2-1
Oldham Athletic	22 Sep 0-3	26 Dec 3-1	29 Dec 2-3	25 Aug 4-2	X	15 Sep 2-1	1 Jan 3-0	3 Nov 4-1	27 Oct 1-2	13 Oct 0-0
Rochdale	25 Dec 2-0	3 Nov 3-0	20 Oct 3-1	29 Dec 3-2	8 Sep 4-2	X	13 Oct 5-0	29 Sep 4-2	19 Aug 0-0	1 Sep 3-1
Southport	20 Oct 0-0	8 Sep 2-1	25 Aug 3-5	22 Sep 2-7	1 Dec 3-0	6 Oct 1-2	X	22 Dec 0-4	25 Dec 0-1	10 Nov 2-2
Stockport County	13 Oct 0-0	25 Aug 2-3	26 Dec 1-1	15 Sep 4-5	10 Nov 3-1	22 Sep 7-0	15 Dec 1-1	X	29 Dec 2-1	20 Oct 1-2
Tranmere Rovers	25 Aug 1-3	6 Oct 1-1	15 Sep 3-0	10 Nov 4-1	20 Oct 2-1	22 Dec 3-2	26 Dec 1-2	1 Dec 3-1	X	22 Sep 2-3
Wrexham	15 Sep 1-0	22 Dec 1-1	24 Dec 2-0	26 Dec 2-3	6 Oct 1-1	25 Aug 4-1	3 Nov 3-0	27 Oct 3-2	29 Sep 2-0	X

THIRD DIVISION (NORTHERN SECTION) EAST

	Bradford City	Carlisle U	Darlington	Doncaster R	Gateshead	Halifax T	Hartlepools U	Lincoln C	Rotherham U	York C
Bradford City	X	29 Dec 2-3	10 Nov 2-5	6 Oct 3-3	20 Apr 5-1	1 Sep 5-1	29 Sep 2-0	8 Sep 5-1	27 Oct 0-4	26 Dec 6-0
Carlisle United	1 Dec 2-2	X	1 Jan 3-3	27 Oct 2-4	26 Dec 3-2	15 Sep 4-1	6 Oct 1-3	29 Oct 4-3	3 Nov 3-2	1 Sep 0-2
Darlington	3 Nov 3-2	22 Dec 7-1	X	15 Sep 2-1	25 Aug 2-4	20 Oct 1-2	26 Dec 5-2	1 Dec 6-1	13 Oct 6-1	29 Sep 3-1
Doncaster Rovers	13 Oct 3-1	20 Oct 3-0	8 Sep 1-2	X	10 Nov 2-2	15 Dec 3-0	1 Sep 2-0	25 Dec 3-1	22 Sep 0-3	1 Dec 1-1
Gateshead	22 Dec 3-2	25 Dec 3-1	1 Sep 4-2	3 Nov 3-1	X	29 Sep 3-3	27 Oct 3-1	6 Oct 6-1	1 Dec 4-1	8 Sep 1-3
Halifax Town	25 Aug 0-0	8 Sep 5-2	22 Dec 2-3	27 Oct 6-5	22 Sep 1-6	X	1 Dec 3-2	3 Nov 6-2	25 Dec 1-4	13 Oct 3-1
Hartlepools United	22 Sep 3-2	13 Oct 3-2	25 Dec 0-0	25 Aug 1-1	20 Oct 0-2	8 Dec 0-0	X	1 Jan 1-4	15 Sep 2-4	3 Nov 0-2
Lincoln City	15 Sep 2-3	22 Sep 5-0	29 Dec 1-3	26 Dec 4-0	13 Oct 1-4	10 Nov 1-2	22 Dec 4-2	X	25 Aug 1-1	27 Oct 2-2
Rotherham United	20 Oct 4-1	10 Nov 5-0	6 Oct 1-2	29 Sep 7-1	1 Jan 3-1	26 Dec 6-3	8 Sep 3-0	1 Sep 1-0	X	22 Dec 3-2
York City	25 Dec 2-2	25 Aug 3-3	22 Sep 3-4	29 Dec 1-2	15 Sep 2-1	6 Oct 0-0	10 Nov 5-0	20 Oct 3-0	20 Feb 1-1	X

	WEST	P	W	D	L	F	A	Pts			EAST	P	W	D	L	F	A	Pts
1	Accrington Stanley	18	10	4	4	37	19	24		1	Rotherham United	18	12	2	4	56	28	26
2	Rochdale	18	10	2	6	43	35	22		2	Darlington	18	12	2	4	61	36	26
3	Crewe Alexandra	18	9	3	6	43	31	21		3	Gateshead	18	11	2	5	51	34	24
4	Chester	18	8	5	5	44	38	21		4	Doncaster Rovers	18	8	4	6	34	35	20
5	Wrexham	18	8	4	6	30	25	20		5	York City	18	6	6	6	34	34	18
6	Tranmere Rovers	18	9	2	7	33	31	20		6	Halifax Town	18	7	4	7	39	46	18
7	Stockport County	18	6	3	9	38	38	15		7	Bradford City	18	6	4	8	45	40	16
8	Oldham Athletic	18	5	5	8	29	32	15		8	Carlisle United	18	5	3	10	34	58	13
9	Barrow	18	4	4	10	21	44	12		9	Lincoln City	18	4	2	12	34	54	10
10	Southport	18	3	4	11	22	47	10		10	Hartlepools United	18	3	3	12	22	45	9

The Football League 1945-46

THIRD DIVISION (SOUTHERN SECTION) NORTH

	Clapton Orient	Ipswich T	Mansfield T	Northampton T	Norwich C	Notts Co	Port Vale	QPR	Southend U	Walsall	Watford
Clapton Orient	X	27 Oct 2-1	1 Sep 0-0	3 Nov 1-0	29 Dec 3-0	20 Dec 3-3	6 Oct 1-1	5 Sep 0-2	8 Sep 2-2	29 Sep 2-0	10 Jan 4-0
Ipswich Town	20 Oct 3-1	X	20 Feb 1-1	22 Sep 2-1	19 Dec 0-0	8 Sep 1-0	1 Sep 0-1	13 Oct 2-1	26 Dec 3-1	29 Dec 5-3	10 Nov 4-2
Mansfield Town	25 Aug 2-2	22 Dec 1-2	X	25 Dec 2-0	13 Oct 4-1	27 Oct 2-3	1 Dec 1-2	12 Sep 2-6	3 Nov 2-2	19 Sep 6-1	15 Sep 1-2
Northampton Town	10 Nov 6-1	29 Sep 3-3	26 Dec 4-0	X	1 Jan 4-1	6 Oct 1-2	8 Sep 1-0	20 Oct 0-2	29 Dec 6-2	1 Sep 1-0	17 Sep 3-0
Norwich City	13 Sep 4-0	1 Dec 4-0	6 Oct 5-1	22 Dec 2-1	X	29 Sep 5-1	30 Aug 3-4	25 Dec 1-1	27 Oct 6-1	3 Nov 2-1	25 Aug 8-1
Notts County	1 Dec 1-0	15 Sep 1-1	20 Oct 1-0	13 Oct 2-1	22 Sep 2-2	X	19 Sep 3-1	10 Nov 0-1	4 Oct 4-1	24 Dec 2-0	26 Dec 1-2
Port Vale	13 Oct 4-0	25 Aug 3-2	24 Dec 2-0	15 Sep 0-0	3 Sep 2-2	29 Dec 3-0	X	22 Sep 0-0	1 Jan 1-1	26 Dec 0-1	20 Oct 2-1
Queen's Park Rangers	19 Sep 2-0	6 Oct 2-0	29 Dec 3-2	27 Oct 4-1	26 Dec 1-2	3 Nov 6-0	29 Oct 4-1	X	1 Sep 4-1	8 Sep 4-0	1 Jan 1-1
Southend United	15 Sep 1-1	25 Dec 2-0	10 Nov 1-1	5 Sep 0-1	20 Oct 1-4	12 Sep 2-3	22 Sep 2-0	25 Aug 1-2	X	1 Dec 0-1	22 Sep 6-2
Walsall	22 Sep 5-3	12 Sep 3-0	27 Sep 2-0	25 Aug 1-1	10 Nov 1-2	22 Dec 3-3	25 Dec 1-5	15 Sep 1-1	8 Dec 6-0	X	13 Oct 0-3
Watford	22 Dec 5-2	3 Nov 4-3	8 Sep 2-1	29 Aug 4-2	1 Sep 2-1	25 Dec 7-2	27 Oct 2-2	1 Dec 0-2	29 Sep 0-1	6 Oct 2-1	X

THIRD DIVISION (SOUTHERN SECTION) SOUTH

	Aldershot	Bournemouth	Brighton & HA	Bristol City	Bristol Rovers	Cardiff C	Crystal Palace	Exeter C	Reading	Swindon T	Torquay U
Aldershot	X	15 Sep 2-2	10 Nov 4-2	20 Oct 2-1	29 Dec 3-2	29 Sep 1-5	1 Sep 2-5	`5 Sep 3-5	26 Dec 1-3	10 Apr 1-1	6 Oct 1-1
Bournemouth & Boscombe Ath	8 Sep 7-0	X	13 Oct 3-0	22 Sep 8-1	5 Jan 3-5	1 Sep 1-5	26 Dec 2-1	20 Oct 3-1	8 Dec 4-1	24 Oct 2-4	29 Dec 0-2
Brighton & Hove Albion	3 Nov 4-2	6 Oct 4-2	X	19 Sep 4-3	8 Sep 3-4	27 Oct 2-3	22 Sep 7-3	19 Dec 3-2	1 Sep 1-0	29 Dec 4-3	1 Dec 3-0
Bristol City	27 Oct 3-0	29 Sep 1-1	5 Sep 3-1	X	1 Sep 3-0	6 Oct 3-2	8 Sep 1-2	27 Dec 5-1	29 Dec 3-3	26 Dec 4-1	3 Nov 6-2
Bristol Rovers	10 Sep 4-5	22 Dec 2-2	15 Sep 2-4	25 Aug 0-3	X	25 Dec 2-2	1 Dec 1-1	22 Sep 2-1	10 Nov 3-3	20 Oct 2-0	17 Sep 3-0
Cardiff City	22 Sep 4-1	25 Aug 9-3	20 Oct 4-0	13 Oct 2-4	26 Dec 4-2	X	29 Dec 6-1	10 Nov 0-0	15 Dec 2-1	8 Dec 3-0	8 Sep 6-0
Crystal Palace	25 Aug 0-0	25 Dec 4-1	29 Sep 5-1	15 Sep 0-1	19 Dec 1-0	12 Sep 3-0	X	13 Oct 2-1	5 Sep 2-2	10 Nov 10-1	22 Dec 5-0
Exeter City	19 Sep 1-4	27 Oct 0-3	22 Dec 3-2	1 Dec 1-0	29 Oct 2-2	3 Nov 3-2	6 Oct 0-1	X	8 Sep 5-1	1 Sep 1-1	26 Dec 0-2
Reading	25 Dec 2-4	1 Dec 3-2	25 Aug 1-2	12 Sep 6-2	3 Nov 2-2	22 Dec 3-1	19 Sep 3-4	15 Sep 1-1	X	13 Oct 1-2	27 Oct 4-1
Swindon Town	22 Dec 2-0	7 Nov 2-1	12 Sep 3-2	25 Dec 4-3	27 Oct 2-3	1 Dec 1-2	3 Nov 1-3	25 Aug 1-4	6 Oct 3-0	X	29 Sep 1-1
Torquay United	13 Oct 2-2	12 Sep 3-2	27 Oct 0-0	10 Nov 0-1	29 Aug 0-3	15 Sep 0-7	15 Dec 1-2	25 Dec 3-1	20 Oct 4-1	22 Sep 0-2	X

NORTH

		P	W	D	L	F	A	Pts
1	Queen's Park Rangers	20	14	4	2	50	15	32
2	Norwich City	20	11	4	5	54	31	26
3	Port Vale	20	9	6	5	34	25	24
4	Watford	20	10	2	8	42	47	22
5	Ipswich Town	20	8	4	8	33	36	20
6	Notts County	20	8	4	8	39	47	20
7	Northampton Town	20	8	3	9	37	34	19
8	Clapton Orient	20	5	6	9	28	42	16
9	Walsall	20	6	3	11	31	42	15
10	Southend United	20	5	5	10	33	49	15
11	Mansfield Town	20	3	5	12	29	42	11

SOUTH

		P	W	D	L	F	A	Pts
1	Crystal Palace	20	13	3	4	55	31	29
2	Cardiff City	20	13	2	5	69	31	28
3	Bristol City	20	11	2	7	51	40	24
4	Brighton & Hove Albion	20	10	1	9	49	50	21
5	Bristol Rovers	20	7	6	7	44	44	20
6	Swindon Town	20	8	3	9	35	47	19
7	Bournemouth & Boscombe A	20	7	3	10	52	50	17
8	Aldershot	20	6	5	9	38	56	17
9	Exeter City	20	6	4	10	33	41	16
10	Reading	20	5	5	10	43	49	15
11	Torquay United	20	5	4	11	22	52	14

The Football League Third Division (Northern Section) Cup 1945-46

WEST

	Accrington S	Barrow	Chester	Crewe Alex	Oldham Ath	Rochdale	Southport	Stockport Co	Tranmere R	Wrexham
Accrington Stanley	X	16 Mar 5-3	9 Mar 2-1		2 Feb 3-3		23 Feb 4-0		26 Jan 1-0	
Barrow	12 Jan 0-5	X			16 Feb 0-3		9 Mar 0-3	26 Jan 1-2	2 Feb 4-0	
Chester	2 Mar 4-1		X	2 Feb 8-3		19 Jan 2-0		12 Jan 1-2		16 Feb 4-2
Crewe Alexandra			9 Feb 5-5	X	12 Jan 3-1	23 Feb 3-1	19 Jan 1-1	2 Mar 3-2		
Oldham Athletic	9 Feb 2-1	23 Feb 0-0		5 Jan 1-1	X				9 Mar 1-2	19 Jan 2-1
Rochdale		26 Jan 6-1	16 Feb 2-2			X	12 Jan 1-3	2 Feb 2-3		2 Mar 1-2
Southport	16 Feb 3-0	2 Mar 4-2		26 Jan 2-1		16 Mar 0-2	X			9 Feb 3-1
Stockport County		19 Jan 5-2	8 Dec 2-0	9 Mar 4-1		9 Feb 2-2		X	23 Feb 4-0	
Tranmere Rovers	6 Mar 1-2	9 Feb 2-1			2 Mar 3-3		16 Feb 3-0		X	16 Mar 3-2
Wrexham			23 Feb 2-0		26 Jan 1-2	9 Mar 2-1	2 Feb 1-1		12 Jan 7-3	X

EAST

	Bradford City	Carlisle U	Darlington	Doncaster R	Gateshead	Halifax T	Hartlepools U	Lincoln C	Rotherham U	York C
Bradford City	X	2 Feb 3-2	12 Jan 4-5				2 Mar 6-2		9 Mar 5-1	9 Feb 0-0
Carlisle United	26 Jan 6-2	X	9 Mar 5-1		23 Feb 3-0		16 Feb 1-3			19 Jan 3-1
Darlington	19 Jan 2-1	5 Jan 1-3	X		9 Feb 3-1		26 Jan 3-1	23 Feb 7-2		
Doncaster Rovers				X	26 Jan 4-2	16 Feb 1-1		19 Jan 3-0	23 Feb 0-0	16 Mar 3-1
Gateshead		2 Mar 0-2	16 Feb 3-1	9 Mar 3-3	X	12 Jan 2-2			2 Feb 6-4	
Halifax Town				9 Feb 4-1	19 Jan 0-1	X	5 Jan 2-5	26 Jan 1-3		23 Feb 0-1
Hartlepools United	23 Feb 0-0	9 Feb 5-3	2 Feb 5-1			9 Mar 1-1	X		19 Jan 2-3	
Lincoln City			2 Mar 6-2	12 Jan 2-3		2 Feb 2-3		X	9 Feb 1-5	13 Mar 2-2
Rotherham United	7 Mar 2-4			2 Mar 1-3	16 Mar 1-3		12 Jan 1-1	16 Feb 6-1	X	
York City	16 Feb 2-2	12 Jan 1-2		2 Feb 1-3		2 Mar 1-1		9 Mar 6-2		X

WEST

		P	W	D	L	F	A	Pts
1	Stockport County	10	7	1	2	26	15	15
2	Southport	10	6	2	2	20	13	14
3	Accrington Stanley	10	6	1	3	24	17	13
4	Oldham Athletic	10	4	4	2	18	15	12
5	Crewe Alexandra	10	3	4	3	23	27	10
6	Wrexham	10	4	1	5	21	20	9
7	Chester	10	4	1	5	26	25	9
8	Tranmere Rovers	10	4	1	5	17	25	9
9	Rochdale	10	2	2	6	18	20	6
10	Barrow	10	1	1	8	13	29	3

EAST

		P	W	D	L	F	A	Pts
1	Doncaster Rovers	10	6	3	1	24	15	15
2	Carlisle United	10	7	0	3	30	17	14
3	Bradford City	10	4	3	3	27	22	11
4	Hartlepools United	10	4	3	3	25	21	11
5	Gateshead	10	4	2	4	21	23	10
6	Darlington	10	5	0	5	26	31	10
7	Rotherham United	10	3	2	5	24	26	8
8	York City	10	2	4	4	16	18	8
9	Halifax Town	10	2	4	4	15	18	8
10	Lincoln City	10	2	1	7	21	38	5

The Football League Third Division (Northern Section) Cup 1945-46

First round – 2 legs
First leg played on 23 Mar, second on 30 Mar
  Accrington Stanley v York City 1-0, 1-3
  Carlisle United v Tranmere Rovers 5-1, 1-2
  Chester v Bradford City 3-0, 2-2
  Crewe Alexandra v Hartlepools United 1-2, 3-3
(aet, 90 mins 2-1)
  Darlington v Southport 2-1, 1-3 *(aet, 90 mins 1-2)*
  Oldham Athletic v Gateshead 2-2, 0-3
  Rotherham United v Wrexham 4-0, 2-0
  Doncaster Rovers v Stockport County 2-2, 2-2
(aet, 90 mins 2-2)
REPLAY on 3 Apr
  Doncaster Rovers v Stockport County 4-0

Second round – 2 legs
First leg played on 6 Apr, second on 13 Apr
  Carlisle United v Gateshead 1-2, 1-2 *(aet, 90 mins 1-0)*
  Chester v York City 4-0, 0-1
  Doncaster Rovers v Rotherham United 0-0, 0-2
  Hartlepools United v Southport 1-2, 1-1

Semi-final – 2 legs
First leg played on 19 Apr, second on 22 Apr
  Chester v Southport 3-0, 4-2
  Gateshead v Rotherham United 2-2, 1-3

Final – 2 legs
Third Division (Northern Section) Cup 1945-46
First leg, 27 Apr 1946 at Millmoor, Rotherham
Att 12,000
Rotherham United 2 *(J Shaw 2)*
Chester 2 *(Bett, Hamilton)*

Rotherham United: Warnes, Selkirk, Hanson, Edwards, H Williams, Mills, Guest, J Shaw, Adron, Burke*, Dawson
Chester: Scales, James*, McNeil, Marsh, Walters, Lee, Bett*, Leahy, Burden*, Astbury, Hamilton

Second leg, 4 May 1946 at Sealand Road, Chester
Att 12,650
Chester 2 *(Leahy, Bett)*
Rotherham United 3 *(Dawson, Burke, J Shaw)*

Chester: as first leg
Rotherham United: as first leg except D Williams for Edwards, Wilson* for Guest

The Football League Third Division (Northern Section) 1945-46
Second Championship

Played on 23 Mar and 30 Mar
  Lincoln City v Halifax Town 1-1, 3-2
  Rochdale v Barrow 2-1, 2-1
Played on 6 Apr and 13 Apr
  Bradford City v Barrow 2-3, 0-2
  Crewe Alexandra v Wrexham 2-1, 0-0
  Halifax Town v Oldham Athletic 1-0, 1-1
  Rochdale v Lincoln City 2-3, 2-1
  Accrington Stanley v Darlington 2-2, 3-4
  Tranmere Rovers v Stockport County 3-0, 2-6
Played on 19 Apr and 22 Apr
  Accrington Stanley v Bradford City 3-1, 0-2
  Hartlepools United v Barrow 3-1, 1-2
  York City v Doncaster Rovers 5-1, 1-1
  Carlisle United v Darlington 4-0, 2-2
  Crewe Alexandra v Stockport County 4-2, 1-0
Played on 20 Apr and 22 Apr
  Lincoln City v Tranmere Rovers 3-0, 0-3
  Rochdale v Oldham Athletic 3-1, 4-0

Played on 20 Apr
  Darlington v Hartlepools United 4-1
Played on 22 Apr
  Wrexham v Halifax Town 1-1
Played on 20 Apr and 27 Apr
  Halifax Town v Stockport County 0-1, 2-3
  Crewe Alexandra v Carlisle United 2-1, 1-3
Played on 27 Apr and 4 May
  Accrington Stanley v Lincoln City 2-1, 1-5
  Barrow v Gateshead 2-3, 2-4
  Oldham Athletic v Doncaster Rovers 2-1, 1-5
  Southport v Rochdale 2-0, 1-2
  Tranmere Rovers v Darlington 3-0, 3-2
  Wrexham v Bradford City 3-1, 2-4
  York City v Hartlepools United 2-3, 2-6
Played on 4 May
  Stockport County v Carlisle United 1-2

		P	W	D	L	F	A	Pts
1	Rotherham United	8	5	3	0	18	7	13
2	Rochdale	8	6	0	2	17	10	12
3	Carlisle United	9	5	1	3	20	11	11
4	Crewe Alexandra	8	5	1	2	14	11	11
5	Chester	8	4	2	2	20	10	10
6	Gateshead	8	4	2	2	17	13	10
7	Tranmere Rovers	8	5	0	3	16	17	10
8	Lincoln City	8	4	1	3	17	13	9
9	Hartlepools United	9	4	1	4	20	18	9
10	Stockport County	9	3	2	4	17	17	8
11	Darlington	9	3	2	4	17	21	8
12	York City	8	3	1	4	14	17	7
13	Southport	8	3	1	4	11	14	7
14	Accrington Stanley	8	3	1	4	13	18	7
15	Barrow	8	3	0	5	14	17	6
16	Doncaster Rovers	8	1	4	3	12	15	6
17	Halifax Town	7	1	3	3	8	10	5
18	Bradford City	8	2	1	5	12	18	5
19	Wrexham	7	1	2	4	7	14	4
20	Oldham Athletic	8	1	2	5	7	20	4

This table also includes the normal-time results of matches from the knock-out stages of the Third Division (Northern Section) Cup

The Football League Third Division (Southern Section) Cup 1945-46

NORTH

	Clapton Orient	Ipswich T	Mansfield T	Northampton T	Norwich C	Notts Co	Port Vale	QPR	Southend U	Walsall	Watford
Clapton Orient	X		9 Feb 0-2	13 Apr 2-1	12 Jan 2-1		9 Mar 0-0	20 Apr 0-0	30 Mar 0-3	23 Feb 0-1	2 Feb 4-3
Ipswich Town		X	9 Mar 2-1		16 Feb 4-0	30 Mar 1-2	23 Feb 1-0	19 Jan 1-0	2 Feb 2-1		13 Apr 2-2
Mansfield Town	16 Feb 1-2	16 Mar 3-0	X	30 Mar 3-1		19 Jan 2-0	6 Apr 2-1	23 Feb 0-0		2 Feb 1-2	22 Apr 1-0
Northampton Town	6 Apr 0-2		23 Mar 1-1	X	2 Feb 1-1	9 Mar 2-1			19 Jan 0-1	20apr 1-4	16 Feb 4-1
Norwich City	19 Jan 3-4	9 Feb 1-0		26 Jan 2-1	X	22 Apr 2-1			2 Mar 0-1	13 Apr 1-1	30 Mar 3-0
Notts County		23 Mar 1-0	12 Jan 1-2	16 Mar 1-2	19 Apr 0-1	X	2 Feb 3-2	13 Apr 0-3		16 Feb 1-0	23 Feb 2-1
Port Vale	16 Mar 2-2	2 Mar 4-1	13 Apr 0-0		26 Jan 2-1		X	30 Mar 0-2	20 Apr 2-1	19 Jan 1-0	
Queen's Park Rangers	22 Apr 6-0	12 Jan 4-1	2 Mar 3-0			6 Apr 3-1	23 Mar 4-2	X	16 Feb 4-0		16 Mar 2-1
Southend United	23 Mar 2-1	26 Jan 2-1		12 Jan 4-3	23 Feb 1-0		22 Apr 1-1	17 Apr 00	X	9 Mar 2-2	
Walsall	5 Jan 4-3		26 Jan 2-2	22 Apr 3-1	6 Apr 4-2	9 Feb 2-0	12 Jan 3-1		16 Mar 2-0	X	
Watford	19 Apr 2-0	6 Apr 0-1	20 Apr 0-3	9 Feb 1-0	23 Mar 2-1	2 Mar 6-2		9 Mar 1-3			X

SOUTH

	Aldershot	Bournemouth & BA	Brighton & HA	Bristol City	Bristol Rovers	Cardiff C	Crystal Palace	Exeter C	Reading	Swindon T	Torquay U
Aldershot	X	19 Jan 2-1	4 May 2-2				3 Apr 0-3	20 Apr 5-3	23 Feb 2-7	9 Mar 1-3	6 Apr 1-1
Bournemouth & Boscombe Ath	12 Jan 3-0	X	19 Apr 4-3	20 Apr 3-2	9 Mar 3-3		2 Mar 4-0	6 Apr 1-1	30 Mar 3-2	16 Feb 6-1	
Brighton & Hove Albion	16 Feb 4-6	2 Feb 1-4	X		22 Apr 1-3		12 Jan 2-2	2 Mar 2-2	16 Mar 1-2		23 Mar 4-0
Bristol City		22 Apr 1-0		X	30 Mar 1-2	9 Mar 3-2	13 Apr 2-2	16 Feb 3-0		19 Jan 2-1	2 Mar 5-1
Bristol Rovers		16 Mar 1-2	20 Apr 6-1	23 Mar 0-0	X	23 Feb 1-0		12 Jan 2-1		6 Apr 0-0	19 Apr 3-1
Cardiff City			16 Mar 3-2	2 Mar 3-0		X	22 Apr 3-0	2 Feb 5-1	13 Apr 5-2	30 Mar 2-0	16 Feb 3-0
Crystal Palace	2 Feb 6-0	23 Feb 2-1	19 Jan 6-1	6 Apr 1-2		20 Apr 1-1	X	23 Mar 3-0	9 Feb 3-3		
Exeter City	22 Apr 1-0	13 Apr 3-1	23 Feb 0-0	9 Feb 3-0	19 Jan 0-1	26 Jan 2-1	30 Mar 2-3	X			9 Mar 1-1
Reading	2 Mar 5-1	23 Mar 1-1	9 Mar 4-1			6 Apr 3-2	16 Feb 0-2		X	2 Feb 5-0	19 Jan 6-0
Swindon Town	16 Mar 4-0	9 Feb 0-0		12 Jan 1-1	13 Apr 2-1	23 Mar 3-2			26 Jan 3-2	X	22 Apr 0-0
Torquay United	13 Apr 1-1		30 Mar 1-0	23 Feb 4-2	26 Jan 1-0	9 Feb 1-0		16 Mar 0-2	12 Jan 3-1	20 Apr 4-1	X

On 2 Feb, Bristol Rovers v Torquay United was abandoned at 2-1 and replayed at a later date.

THIRD DIVISION (SOUTHERN SECTION) CUP (NORTH AND SOUTH)

Played on 12 Jan and 19 Jan
Watford v Cardiff City 1-7, 2-0
Played on 2 Feb and 19 Apr
Bristol City v Queen's Park Rangers 2-0, 2-4
Played on 9 Feb and 16 Feb
Bristol Rovers v Port Vale 4-2, 0-1
Played on 23 Feb and 2 Mar
Swindon Town v Northampton Town 1-4, 1-5

Played on 9 Mar and 16 Mar
Crystal Palace v Norwich City 2-3, 1-6
Played on 23 Mar and 30 Mar
Aldershot v Walsall 1-1, 1-3
Played on 6 Apr and 13 Apr
Brighton & HA v Southend United 2-2, 1-1
Played on 20 Apr and 22 Apr
Reading v Ipswich Town 2-0, 1-2

The Football League Third Division (Southern Section) Cup 1945-46

Final Tables

	NORTH	P	W	D	L	F	A	Pts		SOUTH	P	W	D	L	F	A	Pts
1	Queen's Park Rangers	16	11	3	2	38	11	25	1	Bournemouth & Boscombe A	16	8	4	4	37	20	20
2	Walsall	16	10	4	2	34	18	24	2	Bristol Rovers	16	8	3	5	27	19	19
3	Mansfield Town	16	8	4	4	24	15	20	3	Reading	16	8	2	6	46	29	18
4	Southend United	16	7	5	4	22	21	19	4	Crystal Palace	16	7	4	5	37	30	18
5	Norwich City	16	7	2	7	27	25	16	5	Cardiff City	16	8	1	7	39	22	17
6	Ipswich Town	16	7	1	8	19	24	15	6	Bristol City	16	7	3	6	30	27	17
7	Clapton Orient	16	6	3	7	22	31	15	7	Torquay United	16	6	4	6	19	30	16
8	Port Vale	16	5	4	7	21	25	14	8	Exeter City	16	5	4	7	22	28	14
9	Northampton Town	16	5	2	9	27	29	12	9	Swindon Town	16	5	4	7	21	35	14
10	Watford	16	5	1	10	23	35	11	10	Aldershot	16	3	4	9	23	48	10
11	Notts County	16	5	0	11	17	31	10	11	Brighton & HA	16	1	6	9	23	45	8

Semi-final
Played on 27 Apr
  Bristol Rovers v Walsall 1-3
Played on 27 Apr, REPLAY on 1 May
  Bournemouth & Boscombe Athletic v Queen's Park Rangers 1-1, 1-0 *(aet, 90 mins 0-0)*

Final
4 May 1946 at Stamford Bridge, London
Att 19,715
Bournemouth & BA 1 *(McDonald)*
Walsall 0

Bournemouth & BA: Bird, Marsden, Sanaghan, Woodward, Wilson, Gallacher, Currie, Paton, Kirkham, Tagg, McDonald
Walsall: Lewis, Methley, Shelton, Crutchley, Foulkes, Newman, Hancocks, Talbot, Mullard, Wilshaw*, Alsop

The FA Challenge Cup 1945-46

First round – 2 legs
First leg played on 17 Nov, second on 24 Nov
  Barnet v Queens Park Rangers 2–6, 1-2
  Barrow v Netherfield 1–0, 2-2
  Bath City v Cheltenham Town 3–2, 2-0
  Brighton & Hove Albion v Romford 3–1, 1-1
  Carlisle United v North Shields 5–1, 3-2
  Chorley v Accrington Stanley 2–1, 0-2
  Crewe Alexandra v Wrexham 4–2, 0-3
  Darlington v Stockton 2–0, 6-1
  Doncaster Rovers v Rotherham United 0–1, 1-2
  Gateshead v Hartlepools United 6–2, 1-2
  Halifax Town v York City 1–0, 2-4
  Kettering Town v Grantham 1–5, 2-2
  Leyton Orient v Newport (IOW) 2–1, 0-2
  Lovell's Athletic v Bournemouth & Boscombe Athletic 4–1, 2-3
  Mansfield Town v Gainsborough Trinity 3–0, 2-4 *(aet)*
  Marine v Stalybridge Celtic 4–0, 3-3
  Northampton Town v Chelmsford City 5–1, 5-0
  Notts County v Bradford City 2–2, 2-1
  Port Vale v Wellington Town 4–0, 2-0
  Reading v Aldershot 3–0, 3-7
  Shrewsbury Town v Walsall 5–0, 1-4
  South Liverpool v Tranmere Rovers 1–1, 1-6
  Southport v Oldham Athletic 1–2, 1-3
  Stockport County v Rochdale 1–2, 1-1
  Sutton United v Walthamstow Avenue 1–4, 2-7
  Swindon Town v Bristol Rovers 1–0, 1-4
  Torquay United v Newport County 0–1, 1-1
  Trowbridge Town v Exeter City 1–3, 2-7
  Watford v Southend United 1–1, 3-0
  Willington v Bishop Auckland 0–5, 2-0
  Wisbech Town v Ipswich Town 0–3, 0-5
  Yeovil & Petters United v Bristol City 2–2, 0-3
  Yorkshire Amateur v Lincoln City 1–0, 1-5
First leg played on 17 Nov
  Bromley v Slough United 2–1 *(abandoned after 80 mins)*
REPLAYED first leg played on 19 Nov, second on 24 Nov
  Bromley v Slough United 6–1, 0-1

Second round – 2 legs
First leg played on 8 Dec, second on 15 Dec
  Aldershot v Newport (IOW) 7–0, 5-0
  Barrow v Carlisle United 4–2, 4-3
  Bishop Auckland v York City 1–2, 0-3
  Bristol City v Bristol Rovers 4–2, 2-0
  Bromley v Watford 1–3, 1-1
  Gateshead v Darlington 1–2, 4-2
  Grantham Town v Mansfield Town 1–2, 1-2
  Lovell's Athletic v Bath City 2–1, 5-2
  Newport County v Exeter City 5–1, 3-1
  Northampton Town v Notts County 3–1, 2-3
  Oldham Athletic v Accrington Stanley 2–1, 1-3
  Port Vale v Marine 3–1, 1-1
  Queens Park Rangers v Ipswich Town 4–0, 2-0
  Rotherham United v Lincoln City 2–1, 1-1
  Shrewsbury Town v Wrexham 0–1, 1-1
  Tranmere Rovers v Rochdale 3–1, 0-3
  Walthamstow Avenue v Brighton & Hove Albion 1–1, 2-4

The FA Challenge Cup 1945-46

Third round – 2 legs
First leg played on 5 Jan, second on 7 Jan
Bradford v Port Vale 2–1, 1-1
Charlton Athletic v Fulham 3–1, 1-2
Huddersfield Town v Sheffield United 1–1, 0-2
Northampton Town v Millwall 2–2, 0-3
Stoke City v Burnley 3–1, 1-2
First leg played on 5 Jan, second on 8 Jan
Bury v Rochdale 3–3, 4-2
Coventry City v Aston Villa 2–1, 0-2
First leg played on 5 Jan, second on 9 Jan
Accrington Stanley v Manchester United 2–2, 1-5
Aldershot v Plymouth Argyle 2–0, 1-0
Birmingham City v Portsmouth 1–0, 0-0
Bolton Wanderers v Blackburn Rovers 1–0, 3-1
Cardiff City v West Bromwich Albion 1–1, 0-4
Chester v Liverpool 0–2, 1-2
Chesterfield v York City 1–1, 2-3 *(aet, 90 mins 2-2)*
Grimsby Town v Sunderland 1–3, 1-2
Leeds United v Middlesbrough 4–4, 2-7
Lovell's Athletic v Wolverhampton Wanderers 2–4, 1-8
Luton Town v Derby County 0–6, 0-3
Newcastle United v Barnsley 4–2, 0-3
Norwich City v Brighton & Hove Albion 1–2, 1-4
Preston North End v Everton 2–1, 2-2 *(aet, 90 mins 1-2)*
Rotherham United v Gateshead 2–2, 2-0
First leg played on 5 Jan, second on 9 Jan
Southampton v Newport County 4–3, 2-1
West Ham United v Arsenal 6–0, 0-1
Wrexham v Blackpool 1–4, 1-4
First leg played on 5 Jan, second on 10 Jan
Mansfield Town v Sheffield Wednesday 0–0, 0-5
Bristol City v Swansea Town 5–1, 2-2
Chelsea v Leicester City 1–1, 2-0
Tottenham Hotspur v Brentford 2–2, 0-2
Manchester City v Barrow 6–2, 2-2
First leg played on 5 Jan, second on 9 Jan
Nottingham Forest v Watford 1–1, 1-1 *(aet, abandoned)*
REPLAYED second leg on 16 Jan
Nottingham Forest v Watford 0-1
First leg played on 5 Jan, second on 9 Jan
Queens Park Rangers v Crystal Palace 0-0, 0-0 *(aet, abandoned)*
REPLAYED second leg on 16 Jan
Queens Park Rangers v Crystal Palace 1-0

Fourth round - 2 legs
First leg played on 26 Jan, second on 28 Jan
Millwall v Aston Villa 2–4, 1-9
Stoke City v Sheffield United 2–0, 2-3
First leg played on 26 Jan, second on 29 Jan
Sunderland v Bury 3–1, 4-5 *(aet, 90 mins 3-5)*
First leg played on 26 Jan, second on 30 Jan
Southampton v Queen's Park Rangers 0–1, 3-4
Sheffield Wednesday v York City 5–1 ,6-1
Bolton Wanderers v Liverpool 5–0 ,0-2
Derby County v West Bromwich Albion 1–0, 3-1
Brighton & Hove Albion v Aldershot 3–0, 4-1
Manchester United v Preston North End 1–0, 1-3 *(aet)*
Chelsea v West Ham United 2–0, 0-1
Bradford v Manchester City 1–3, 8-2
Charlton Athletic v Wolverhampton Wanderers 5–2, 1-1
Birmingham City v Watford 5–0, 1-1
First leg played on 26 Jan, second on 31 Jan
Bristol City v Brentford 2–1, 0-5
Barnsley v Rotherham United 3–0, 1-2
First leg played on 26 Jan, second on 30 Jan
Blackpool v Middlesbrough 3–2, 2-3 *(aet, abandoned)*
REPLAY on 4 Feb
Blackpool v Middlesbrough 0–1 *(at Elland Road, Leeds)*

Fifth round - 2 legs
First leg played on 9 Feb, second on 11 Feb
Stoke City v Sheffield Wednesday 2–0, 0-0
First leg played on 9 Feb, second on 12 Feb
Chelsea v Aston Villa 0–1, 0-1
First leg played on 9 Feb, second on 13 Feb
Bolton Wanderers v Middlesbrough 1–0, 1-1
Sunderland v Birmingham City 1–0, 1-3
Barnsley v Bradford 0–1, 1-1
First leg played on 9 Feb, second on 14 Feb
Preston North End v Charlton Athletic 1–1, 0-6
Queen's Park Rangers v Brentford 1–3, 0-0
Brighton & Hove Albion v Derby County 1–4, 0-6

Sixth round - 2 legs
First leg played on 2 Mar, second on 6 Mar
Aston Villa v Derby County 3–4, 1-1
Charlton Athletic v Brentford 6–3, 3-1
Stoke City v Bolton Wanderers 0–2, 0-0
First leg played on 2 Mar, second on 9 Mar
Bradford v Birmingham City 2–2, 0-6

Semi-final
Played on 23 Mar
Charlton Athletic v Bolton Wanderers 2-0
(at Villa Park, Birmingham)
Played on 23 Mar, REPLAY on 27 Mar
Derby County v Birmingham City 1-1
(at Hillsborough, Sheffield)
Derby County v Birmingham City 4-0
(at Maine Road, Manchester)

Final
27 Apr 1946 at Wembley Stadium, London
Att 98,215
Derby County 4 *(H Turner og, Doherty, Stamps 2)*
Charlton Athletic 1 *(H Turner)*
aet, 90 mins 1-1
Derby County: Woodley, Nicholas, Howe, Bullions, Leuty,
Musson, Harrison, Carter, Stamps, Doherty, Duncan
Charlton A: Bartram, Phipps, Shreeve, H Turner, oakes,
Johnson, Fell, Brown, A Turner, Welsh, Duffy

Other English Competitions 1945-46

LANCASHIRE CUP

Preliminary round – 2 legs
First leg played on 29 Aug, second on 5 Sep
  Chester v Wrexham 2-2, 3-2

First round – 2 legs
First leg played on 3 Sep, second on 24 Sep
  Blackburn Rovers v Bury 0-3, 1-6
First leg played on 3 Sep, second on 25 Sep
  Bolton Wanderers v Accrington Stanley 2-0, 0-1
First leg played on 12 Sep, second on 19 Sep
  Chester v Crewe Alexandra 5-1, 1-3
First leg played on 5 Sep, second on 19 Sep
  Southport v Manchester City 3-2, 0-5
First leg played on 19 Sep, second on 26 Sep, REPLAY on 20 Feb
  Everton v Liverpool 3-3, 1-1, 0-4 *(at Anfield Road, Liverpool)*
First leg played on 16 Aug, second on 17 Sep
  Burnley v Blackpool, 1-0, 1-0
First leg played on 3 Sep, second on 10 Sep
  Oldham Athletic v Barrow 1-2, 3-1
First leg played on 5Sep, second on 1 Jan
  Manchester United v Rochdale 5-1. 0-2

Second round – 2 legs
First leg played on 2 Apr, second on 10 Apr
  Oldham Athletic v Manchester City 3-1, 1-4
First leg played on 6 Mar, second on 12 Mar
  Manchester United v Bury 4-1, 1-0
First leg played on 16 Feb, second on 11 Mar
  Chester v Burnley 0-1, 1-2
One leg only, played on 11 Mar
  Liverpool v Bolton Wanderers 3-1

Semi-final
Played on 27 Mar
  Burnley v Liverpool 3-2 aet
Played on 1 May
  Manchester United v Manchester City 3-0

Final
Played on 11 May at Maine Road, Manchester
  Manchester United v Burnley 1-0

LIVERPOOL SENIOR CUP

Semi-final – 2 legs
Played on 3 Apr
  Liverpool v Southport 2-0
First leg played on 13 Mar, second on 8 Apr
  Everton v Tranmere Rovers 2-2, 3-3 *(both games played at Goodison Park)*
REPLAY on 15 Apr
  Tranmere Rovers v Everton 3-3
SECOND REPLAY on 25 Apr
  Tranmere Rovers v Everton 1-2

Final
Played on 1 May at Goodison Park, Liverpool
  Everton v Liverpool 1-3

CHESHIRE BOWL

Semi-final – 2 legs
First leg played on 19 Apr, second on 22 Apr
  Crewe Alexandra v Stockport County 4-2, 1-0
First leg played on 6 May, second on 8 May
  Tranmere Rovers v Chester 2-1, 2-6

Final
Played on 11 May at Sealand Road, Chester
  Chester v Crewe Alexandra 3-1

DURHAM SENIOR CUP

Semi-final
Played on 17 Apr
  Sunderland v Gateshead 3-0

Final
Played on 8 May at Roker Park, Sunderland
  Sunderland v Darlington 0-2

DEVON PROFESSIONAL CHAMPIONSHIP

Semi-final – 2 legs
Played on 10 Apr
  Exeter City v Plymouth Argyle 2-1

Final
Played on 4 May at Exeter
  Torquay United v Exeter City 4-0

The Scottish Football League 1945-46

A DIVISION

	Aberdeen	Celtic	Clyde	Falkirk	Hamilton A	Hearts	Hibernian	Kilmarnock	Morton	Motherwell	Partick Th	QOS	Queen's Park	Rangers	St Mirren	Third Lanark
Aberdeen	X	15 Dec 1-1	20 Oct 1-2	8 Sep 2-0	17 Nov 4-0	9 Feb 2-1	22 Dec 2-1	1 Dec 2-0	3 Nov 3-1	22 Sep 4-1	2 Jan 3-0	26 Jan 7-1	5 Jan 5-0	12 Jan 4-1	25 Aug 6-1	11 Aug 3-0
Celtic	1 Sep 1-1	X	18 Aug 2-2	27 Oct 2-1	15 Sep 2-0	29 Dec 3-5	2 Feb 0-1	16 Feb 1-1	24 Nov 2-1	10 Nov 3-0	6 Oct 4-1	29 Sep 2-0	8 Dec 3-3	1 Jan 0-1	20 Oct 2-2	12 Jan 3-2
Clyde	19 Jan 0-0	1 Dec 3-3	X	13 Feb 6-2	26 Jan 3-2	3 Nov 3-1	22 Sep 2-2	22 Dec 3-0	9 Feb 4-3	2 Jan 3-0	8 Sep 0-2	17 Nov 2-2	25 Aug 4-4	5 Jan 0-1	11 Aug 2-3	5 Jan 1-2
Falkirk	1 Jan 3-1	26 Jan 4-2	1 Sep 4-1	X	18 Aug 7-0	24 Nov 3-5	6 Oct 2-1	20 Oct 3-4	15 Sep 3-2	12 Jan 3-3	17 Nov 2-1	8 Dec 3-2	29 Sep 1-1	29 Dec 0-3	9 Feb 1-3	3 Nov 3-1
Hamilton Academical	16 Feb 3-3	22 Dec 0-1	27 Oct 2-4	1 Dec 3-1	X	12 Jan 2-0	25 Aug 1-1	22 Sep 4-4	20 Oct 2-2	8 Sep 3-6	11 Aug 0-1	6 Oct 2-2	10 Nov 3-4	2 Feb 1-4	15 Dec 0-3	2 Jan 0-1
Heart of Midlothian	10 Nov 1-2	22 Sep 2-2	2 Feb 1-1	11 Aug 4-1	13 Oct 4-1	X	8 Sep 0-2	2 Jan 1-4	6 Oct 6-0	25 Aug 0-0	1 Dec 4-1	15 Apr 0-3	27 Oct 3-3	16 Feb 2-0	22 Dec 2-2	15 Dec 2-1
Hibernian	15 Sep 1-1	3 Nov 1-1	29 Dec 3-2	5 Jan 4-1	8 Dec 1-2	1 Jan 1-0	X	12 Jan 4-1	29 Sep 5-0	20 Oct 0-0	9 Feb 3-1	24 Nov 6-1	1 Sep 4-0	18 Aug 2-1	17 Nov 3-2	26 Jan 4-0
Kilmarnock	18 Aug 1-4	17 Nov 2-1	15 Sep 0-0	6 Apr 6-2	29 Dec 0-2	29 Sep 2-2	13 Oct 3-4	X	8 Dec 1-1	6 Oct 2-5	26 Jan 2-1	1 Jan 1-1	24 Nov 2-2	1 Sep 0-7	3 Nov 6-4	9 Feb 1-3
Morton	2 Feb 3-2	11 Aug 1-1	10 Nov 1-1	22 Dec 3-3	19 Jan 3-1	5 Jan 4-2	2 Jan 4-1	25 Aug 6-1	X	1 Dec 3-3	15 Dec 1-1	13 Oct 7-1	16 Feb 1-2	27 Oct 2-2	8 Sep 0-1	22 Sep 4-4
Motherwell	29 Dec 1-3	9 Feb 1-3	29 Sep 3-2	13 Oct 1-1	1 Jan 0-0	8 Dec 5-4	19 Jan 0-0	5 Jan 2-2	18 Aug 2-1	X	3 Nov 2-1	1 Sep 2-1	15 Sep 1-2	24 Nov 1-2	26 Jan 5-1	17 Nov 1-3
Partick Thistle	29 Sep 1-1	5 Jan 0-3	1 Jan 2-1	16 Feb 4-3	24 Nov 5-1	18 Aug 1-3	10 Nov 0-2	27 Oct 5-3	1 Sep 2-2	2 Feb 3-0	X	15 Sep 2-1	29 Dec 1-3	8 Dec 1-5	12 Jan 1-0	20 Oct 6-2
Queen of the South	27 Oct 3-2	2 Jan 0-0	16 Feb 1-2	25 Aug 0-2	5 Jan 5-1	20 Oct 3-3	11 Aug 3-0	8 Sep 2-1	12 Jan 2-3	15 Dec 1-4	22 Dec 5-3	X	2 Feb 3-3	10 Nov 2-4	22 Sep 5-1	1 Dec 5-3
Queen's Park	25 Dec 3-1	16 Aug 2-0	12 Jan 1-2	2 Jan 2-0	9 Feb 3-2	26 Jan 0-1	23 Apr 2-4	11 Aug 2-3	17 Nov 3-4	22 Dec 4-0	22 Sep 1-1	3 Nov 2-3	X	20 Oct 0-2	1 Dec 3-0	1 Jan 1-1
Rangers	13 Oct 3-1	8 Sep 5-3	25 Dec 3-1	22 Sep 1-0	3 Nov 5-1	17 Nov 1-1	1 Dec 3-2	15 Dec 5-1	26 Jan 4-4	11 Aug 0-3	16 Aug 4-2	9 Feb 5-2	19 Jan 2-1	X	2 Jan 3-1	22 Dec 1-0
St Mirren	8 Dec 4-1	19 Jan 1-2	24 Nov 2-1	10 Nov 0-0	1 Sep 2-3	15 Sep 3-1	16 Feb 0-3	2 Feb 4-1	1 Jan 2-4	27 Oct 0-0	13 Oct 0-2	29 Dec 4-1	18 Aug 2-3	29 Sep 2-2	X	6 Oct 3-4
Third Lanark	24 Nov 3-1	13 Oct 0-2	8 Dec 1-6	2 Feb 2-3	29 Sep 7-2	1 Sep 1-2	27 Oct 2-1	10 Nov 4-1	29 Dec 2-1	16 Feb 0-2	19 Jan 4-2	18 Aug 5-1	8 Sep 1-0	15 Sep 1-5	5 Jan 3-1	X

		P	W	D	L	F	A	Pts
1	Rangers	30	22	4	4	85	41	48
2	Hibernian	30	17	6	7	67	37	40
3	Aberdeen	30	16	6	8	73	41	38
4	Celtic	30	12	11	7	55	44	35
5	Clyde	30	11	9	10	64	54	31
6	Motherwell	30	11	9	10	54	55	31
7	Heart of Midlothian	30	11	8	11	63	57	30
8	Queen's Park	30	11	8	11	60	60	30
9	Third Lanark	30	14	2	14	63	68	30
10	Morton	30	9	11	10	72	69	29
11	Falkirk	30	11	5	14	62	70	27
12	Partick Thistle	30	11	4	15	54	65	26
13	Queen of the South	30	9	6	15	62	82	24
14	St Mirren	30	9	5	16	54	70	23
15	Kilmarnock	30	7	8	15	56	87	22
16	Hamilton Academical	30	5	6	19	44	88	16

The Scottish Football League 1945-46

B DIVISION

	Airdrieonians	Albion Rovers	Alloa	Arbroath	Ayr U	Cowdenbeath	Dumbarton	Dundee	Dundee United	Dunfermline A	East Fife	Raith Rovers	St Johnstone	Stenhousemuir
Airdrieonians	X	1 Jan 2-5	12 Jan 3-0	3 Nov 5-0	17 Nov 3-2	13 Oct 5-2	19 Jan 3-2	1 Sep 3-3	22 Dec 1-1	15 Sep 1-1	29 Dec 2-0	24 Nov 4-2	22 Sep 5-5	18 Aug 6-0
Albion Rovers	8 Sep 3-2	X	11 Aug 6-2	15 Dec 1-1	8 Dec 3-2	1 Dec 4-0	10 Nov 3-0	20 Oct 0-2	25 Aug 1-0	5 Jan 2-0	29 Sep 3-2	2 Jan 3-0	27 Oct 1-6	6 Oct 0-0
Alloa	20 Oct 2-1	17 Nov 0-2	X	6 Oct 4-4	18 Aug 1-3	27 Oct 2-0	29 Sep 2-1	15 Sep 0-1	8 Dec 3-1	1 Sep 1-5	3 Nov 1-1	5 Jan 6-0	24 Nov 3-1	1 Jan 4-0
Arbroath	2 Jan 0-5	15 Sep 1-0	29 Dec 1-2	X	19 Jan 2-4	29 Sep 4-1	8 Dec 0-3	18 Aug 1-4	13 Oct 4-1	24 Nov 3-1	12 Jan 2-6	17 Nov 2-1	1 Jan 0-1	1 Sep 0-3
Ayr United	11 Aug 0-3	22 Sep 3-1	10 Nov 2-6	27 Oct 4-1	X	25 Aug 1-1	8 Sep 4-1	29 Dec 2-1	1 Dec 1-1	22 Dec 2-1	15 Dec 1-1	20 Oct 1-0	2 Jan 1-0	5 Jan 10-1
Cowdenbeath	5 Jan 2-3	1 Sep 1-0	19 Jan 1-1	22 Dec 4-2	24 Nov 1-1	X	20 Oct 1-5	2 Jan 2-2	6 Oct 4-2	1 Jan 1-0	22 Sep 1-3	18 Aug 2-1	15 Sep 3-3	17 Nov 5-1
Dumbarton	27 Oct 1-2	18 Aug 4-0	22 Dec 2-0	22 Sep 1-3	1 Jan 3-1	12 Jan 3-1	X	24 Nov 0-1	3 Nov 2-1	6 Oct 2-1	13 Oct 3-0	1 Sep 6-3	17 Nov 3-5	15 Sep 1-1
Dundee	1 Dec 4-1	12 Jan 2-0	15 Dec 5-1	10 Nov 8-0	6 Oct 1-4	3 Nov 5-0	25 Aug 5-2	X	8 Sep 1-0	19 Jan 3-1	11 Aug 2-1	22 Dec 7-0	13 Oct 5-1	8 Dec 6-1
Dundee United	29 Sep 4-2	24 Nov 2-3	22 Sep 2-5	5 Jan 4-1	1 Sep 3-2	29 Dec 0-2	2 Jan 4-1	1 Jan 2-3	X	17 Nov 1-2	27 Oct 5-2	15 Sep 0-7	18 Aug 3-4	20 Oct 7-0
Dunfermline Athletic	15 Dec 5-2	13 Oct 5-2	1 Dec 2-3	25 Aug 6-1	29 Sep 2-3	8 Sep 4-1	29 Dec 1-1	27 Oct 0-6	11 Aug 7-0	X	10 Nov 0-4	8 Dec 8-1	12 Jan 0-1	3 Nov 5-1
East Fife	6 Oct 2-1	22 Dec 1-0	2 Jan 1-1	20 Oct 8-0	15 Sep 2-0	8 Dec 0-1	5 Jan 6-2	17 Nov 1-4	19 Jan 2-0	18 Aug 0-0	X	1 Jan 4-0	1 Sep 2-1	24 Nov 7-2
Raith Rovers	25 Aug 4-0	3 Nov 0-1	13 Oct 1-2	11 Aug 3-2	12 Jan 2-3	10 Nov 3-2	1 Dec 1-4	29 Sep 0-5	15 Dec 5-0	22 Sep 3-2	8 Sep 0-2	X	29 Dec 4-5	27 Oct 1-2
St Johnstone	8 Dec 0-0	19 Jan 3-0	25 Aug 0-4	8 Sep 4-6	3 Nov 3-2	15 Dec 1-1	11 Aug 3-3	5 Jan 4-1	10 Nov 3-0	20 Oct 1-1	1 Dec 1-4	6 Oct 5-3	X	29 Sep 4-1
Stenhousemuir	10 Nov 0-2	29 Dec 0-1	8 Sep 3-2	1 Dec 3-2	13 Oct 0-6	11 Aug 4-3	15 Dec 2-2	22 Sep 1-5	12 Jan 2-2	2 Jan 1-3	25 Aug 1-2	19 Jan 2-2	22 Dec 4-1	X

		P	W	D	L	F	A	Pts
1	Dundee	26	21	2	3	92	28	44
2	Ayr United	26	15	4	7	69	43	34
3	East Fife	26	15	4	7	64	34	34
4	Airdrieonians	26	14	5	7	69	50	33
5	Albion Rovers	26	14	2	10	45	41	30
6	St Johnstone	26	12	6	8	66	60	30
7	Alloa Athletic	26	12	4	10	59	53	28
8	Dumbarton	26	11	4	11	59	54	26
9	Dunfermline Athletic	26	10	4	12	63	47	24
10	Cowdenbeath	26	8	5	13	43	62	21
11	Stenhousemuir	26	6	5	15	36	89	17
12	Dundee United	26	6	3	17	46	70	15
13	Arbroath	26	6	2	18	40	88	14
14	Raith Rovers	26	6	2	18	48	80	14

The Scottish Football League Cup 1945-46

DIVISION A

Section A

Section A	Falkirk	Hamilton AC	Hearts	St Mirren
Falkirk	X	30 Mar 2-1	23 Mar 2-2	23 Feb 3-1
Hamilton Academical	9 Mar 2-1	X	23 Feb 3-2	23 Mar 0-1
Heart of Midlothian	2 Mar 3-1	16 Mar 1-0	X	9 Mar 3-1
St Mirren	16 Mar 2-1	2 Mar 0-0	30 Mar 1-1	X

		P	W	D	L	F	A	Pts
1	Heart of Midlothian	6	3	2	1	12	8	8
2	St Mirren	6	2	2	2	6	8	6
3	Hamilton Academical	6	2	1	3	6	7	5
4	Falkirk	6	2	1	3	10	11	5

Section B

Section B	Morton	Motherwell	QOS	Rangers
Morton		23 Feb 3-0	23 Mar 7-1	30 Mar 1-1
Motherwell	16 Mar 3-1		30 Mar 3-1	2 Mar 0-3
Queen of the South	2 Mar 1-3	27 Mar 1-1		16 Mar 0-2
Rangers	9 Mar 1-0	23 Mar 4-2	23 Feb 4-0	

		P	W	D	L	F	A	Pts
1	Rangers	6	5	1	0	15	3	11
2	Morton	6	3	1	2	15	7	7
3	Motherwell	6	2	1	3	9	13	5
4	Queen of the South	6	0	1	5	4	20	1

Section C

Section C	Aberdeen	Hibernian	Kilmarnock	Partick Th
Aberdeen	X	2 Mar 4-1	16 Mar 1-0	9 Mar 2-1
Hibernian	23 Mar 3-2	X	30 Mar 4-0	23 Feb 1-0
Kilmarnock	23 Feb 1-1	9 Mar 1-0	X	23 Mar 2-2
Partick Thistle	30 Mar 0-0	16 Mar 0-1	2 Mar 3-0	X

		P	W	D	L	F	A	Pts
1	Aberdeen	6	3	2	1	10	6	8
2	Hibernian	6	4	0	2	10	7	8
3	Partick Thistle	6	1	2	3	6	6	4
4	Kilmarnock	6	1	2	3	4	11	4

Section D

Section D	Celtic	Clyde	Queen's Park	Third Lanark
Celtic	X	2 Mar 4-0	16 Mar 2-0	30 Mar 1-1
Clyde	23 Mar 6-2	X	9 Mar 5-1	23 Feb 7-3
Queen's Park	23 Feb 3-1	30 Mar 2-3	X	23 Mar 1-4
Third Lanark	9 Mar 0-4	16 Mar 1-0	2 Mar 2-2	X

		P	W	D	L	F	A	Pts
1	Clyde	6	4	0	2	21	13	8
2	Celtic	6	3	1	2	14	10	7
3	Third Lanark	6	2	2	2	11	15	6
4	Queen's Park	6	1	1	4	9	17	3

The Scottish Football League Cup 1945-46

DIVISION B

Section A	Alloa	Cowdenbeath	East Fife	Raith R
Alloa	X	23 Mar 3-2	23 Feb 1-2	30 Mar 3-2
Cowdenbeath	2 Mar 0-1	X	9 Mar 3-7	16 Mar 2-4
East Fife	16 Mar 2-0	30 Mar 7-1	X	2 Mar 4-2
Raith Rovers	9 Mar 0-3	23 Feb 4-2	23 Mar 3-2	X

		P	W	D	L	F	A	Pts
1	East Fife	6	5	0	1	22	10	10
2	Alloa	6	4	0	2	11	8	8
3	Raith Rovers	6	3	0	3	15	16	6
4	Cowdenbeath	6	0	0	6	10	24	0

Section B	Ayr U	Dumbarton	Dundee United	Stenhousemuir
Ayr United	X	16 Mar 3-1	2 Mar 2-0	30 Mar 2-2
Dumbarton	23 Feb 0-1	X	30 Mar 1-2	23 Mar 1-3
Dundee United	23 Mar 2-1	9 Mar 3-2	X	23 Feb 4-0
Stenhousemuir	9 Mar 2-3	2 Mar 0-2	16 Mar 1-1	X

		P	W	D	L	F	A	Pts
1	Ayr United	6	4	1	1	16	5	9
2	Dundee United	6	4	1	1	12	7	9
3	Stenhousemuir	6	1	2	3	8	13	4
4	Dumbarton	6	1	0	5	7	12	2

Section C	Airdrieonians	Albion R	Dunfermline Ath	St Johnstone
Airdrieonians	X	23 Mar 5-1	9 Mar 5-1	23 Feb 4-0
Albion Rovers	2 Mar 1-0	X	16 Mar 3-0	30 Mar 0-0
Dunfermline Athletic	30 Mar 0-0	23 Feb 3-1	X	23 Mar 2-0
St Johnstone	16 Mar 2-2	9 Mar 9-0	2 Mar 1-0	X

		P	W	D	L	F	A	Pts
1	Airdrieonians	6	3	2	1	16	5	8
2	St Johnstone	6	2	2	2	13	8	6
3	Albion Rovers	6	2	1	3	6	17	5
4	Dunfermline Ath	6	2	1	3	6	10	5

Section D	Arbroath	Dundee	Stirling Alb
Arbroath	X	23 Mar 1-3	9 Mar 1-0
Dundee	2 Mar 0-0	X	16 Mar 8-1
Stirling Albion	30 Mar 3-1	23 Feb 2-0	X

		P	W	D	L	F	A	Pts
1	Dundee	4	2	1	1	11	4	5
2	Stirling Albion	4	2	0	2	6	10	4
3	Arbroath	4	1	1	2	3	7	3

Quarter final
Played on 6 Apr
 Heart of Midlothian v East Fife 3-0
 Aberdeen v Ayr United 2-0
 Clyde v Airdrieonians 0-1
 Rangers v Dundee 3-1

Semi-final
Played on 27 Apr
 Rangers v Heart of Midlothian 2-1
 (aet, 90 mins 1-1, at Hampden Park, Glasgow)
 Aberdeen v Airdrieonians 2-2
 (aet, 90 mins,2-2, at Ibrox Park, Glasgow)
 REPLAY on 30 Apr
 Aberdeen v Airdrieonians 5-3
 (aet, 90 mins 2-2, at Ibrox Park, Glasgow)

Final
Played on 11 May 1946 at Hampden Park, Glasgow
Att 121,000
Aberdeen 3 *(Baird, Williams, Taylor)*
Rangers 2 *(Duncanson, Thornton)*

Aberdeen: Johnstone, Cooper, McKenna, Cowie, Dunlop,
Taylor, Kiddie, Hamilton, Williams, Baird, McCall
Rangers: John Shaw, Gray, Jock Shaw, Watkins, Young,
Symon, Waddell, Thornton, Arnison, Duncanson, Caskie

Victory Cup 1945-46

Preliminary Competition
(Scottish Football League clubs' results only)
First round
Played on 22 Sep
  Brechin City v Montrose 1-7
  Duns v Edinburgh City 1-6
  Stirling Albion v Glasgow University 10-2
  Leith Athletic v Peebles Rovers scr-wo

Second round
Played on 6 Oct
  East Stirlingshire v Stirling Albion 5-4
  Montrose v Forfar Athletic 3-4

Third round
Played on 20 Oct
  East Stirlingshire v Edinburgh City 3-2
Played on 27 Oct
  Clachnacuddin v Forfar Athletic 3-2

Semi-final
  Tarff Rovers v East Stirlingshire 1-9

Final - 2 legs
First leg played on 24 Nov, second on 1 Dec. REPLAY on 2 Jan
  Clachnacuddin v East Stirlingshire 3-3, 2-2, 2-5

Competition Proper
First round – 2 legs
First leg Played on 20 Apr, second on 22 Apr
  Cowdenbeath v Queen's Park 0-0, 5-3
  Stenhousemuir v Rangers 1-4, 1-4
First leg Played on 20 Apr, second on 24 Apr
  Aberdeen v Hamilton Academical 2-0, 2-0
  Airdrieonians v Dumbarton 4-0, 1-1
  Alloa Athletic v Heart of Midlothian 3-1, 0-5
  Ayr United v Morton 1-3, 2-4
  Clachnacuddin v Partick Thistle 2-2, 1-7
  Clyde v Albion Rovers 4-2, 2-1
  St Johnstone v Celtic 2-8, 0-5
First leg Played on 20 Apr, second on 27 Apr
  Arbroath v Raith Rovers 3-4, 1-3
  Dundee United v Queen of the South 2-1, 1-3
  East Fife v Kilmarnock 2-0, 0-3
  Falkirk v Motherwell 2-1, 4-2
  Hibernian v Dundee 3-0, 0-2
  St Mirren v East Stirlingshire 3-1, 2-2
  Third Lanark v Dunfermline Athletic 1-2, 2-0

Second round
Played on 4 May
  Airdrieonians v Rangers 0-4
  Celtic v Queen of the South 3-0
  Falkirk v Third Lanark 3-2
  Hibernian v Heart of Midlothian 3-1
  Raith Rovers v St Mirren 2-1
Played on 4 May REPLAY on 8 May
  Cowdenbeath v Partick Thistle 1-1, 1-2
Played on 4 May REPLAY on 11 May
  Clyde v Morton 0-0, 2-0
Played on 4 May REPLAY on 13 May
  Aberdeen v Kilmarnock 1-1, 3-0

Third round
Played on 18 May, REPLAY on 25 May
  Clyde v Aberdeen 4-2
  Falkirk v Rangers 1-1, 0-2
  Partick Thistle v Hibernian 1-1, 0-2
  Raith Rovers v Celtic 0-2

Semi-final
Played on 1 Jun, REPLAY on 5 Jun
  Hibernian v Clyde 2-1 *(at Tynecastle Park, Edinburgh)*
  Rangers v Celtic 0-0, 2-0 *(at Hampden Park, Glasgow)*

Final
15 Jun 1946 at Hampden Park, Glasgow
Att 90,000
Rangers 3 *(Duncanson 2, Gillick)*
Hibernian 1 *(Aitkenhead)*

Rangers: Brown, Cox, Shaw, Watkins, Young, Symon, Waddell. Gillick, Thornton, Duncanson, Caskie
Hibernian: Kerr, Govan, Shaw, Howie, Aird, Finnigan, Smith, Peat, Milne, Aitkenhead, Nutley

The Eastern Football League 1945-46

First Series	Brechin City	Dundee 'A'	East Stirlingshire	Edinburgh City	Forfar Ath	Montrose	Stirling Albion
Brechin City	X	8 Sep 1-5	17 Nov 1-4	10 Nov 2-3	1 Dec 5-1	25 Aug 3-5	29 Sep 4-3
Dundee 'A'	27 Oct 3-0	X	15 Sep 5-1	1 Sep 5-1	29 Dec 2-1	24 Nov 6-2	20 Oct 4-2
East Stirlingshire	15 Dec 5-0	10 Nov 3-1	X	22 Dec 2-0	NOT PLAYED	8 Sep 1-4	13 Oct 4-2
Edinburgh City	13 Oct 5-3	3 Nov 2-3	29 Sep 7-1	X	25 Aug 5-6	27 Oct 6-3	24 Nov 1-2
Forfar Athletic	15 Sep 3-1	13 Oct 2-2	1 Sep 3-3	17 Nov 3-5	X	29 Sep 7-3	10 Nov 4-8
Montrose	20 Oct 1-1	17 Nov 3-5	8 Dec 2-1	15 Sep 5-2	3 Nov 4-3	X	1 Sep 2-3
Stirling Albion	3 Nov 0-1	25 Aug 1-2	27 Oct 5-1	18 Aug 8-3	8 Sep 7-1	1 Dec 5-1	X

First Series		P	W	D	L	F	A	Pts
1	Dundee 'A'	12	10	1	1	43	19	21
2	Stirling Albion	12	7	0	5	46	28	14
3	East Stirlingshire	11	5	1	5	26	30	11
4	Montrose	12	5	1	6	35	43	11
5	Edinburgh City	12	5	0	7	40	43	10
6	Forfar Athletic	11	3	2	6	34	45	8
7	Brechin City	12	3	1	8	22	38	7

Second Series		P	W	D	L	F	A	Pts
1	East Stirlingshire	12	7	3	2	47	26	17
2	Dundee 'A'	12	6	1	5	40	31	13
3	Brechin City	11	5	4	2	18	18	14
4	Forfar Athletic	11	5	3	3	32	26	13
5	St Johnstone 'A'	12	4	3	5	27	34	11
6	Montrose	11	3	2	6	22	32	8
7	Edinburgh City	11	1	2	8	19	38	4

Second Series	Brechin City	Dundee 'A'	East Stirlingshire	Edinburgh City	Forfar Ath	Montrose	St Johnstone	Stirling Albion
Brechin City	X	12 Jan 1-0	16 Mar 1-1	16 Feb 1-1		9 Mar 4-3	26 Jan 2-1	
Dundee 'A'	30 Mar 5-1	X	23 Mar 5-2	14 May 2-2	8 May 3-2	23 Feb 6-1	9 Mar 7-0	5 Jan 5-4
East Stirlingshire	19 Jan 2-2	2 Mar 6-1	X	2 Feb 6-2	9 Mar 4-3	30 Mar 7-2	5 Jan 5-1	
Edinburgh City	5 Jan 1-4	9 Feb 1-4	23 Feb 0-3	X	26 Jan 2-5	16 Mar 2-4	30 Mar 4-2	
Forfar Athletic	23 Mar 1-1	2 Feb 7-3	9 Feb 3-2	2 Mar 4-2	X	5 Jan 3-1	16 Mar 4-4	
Montrose	9 Feb 0-1	19 Jan 3-2	12 Jan 3-6		16 Feb 0-0	X	2 Mar 4-0	
St Johnstone	23 Feb 3-0	1 Jan 5-2	16 Feb 3-3	23 Mar 3-2	12 Jan 4-0	2 Feb 1-1	X	
Stirling Albion			1 Jan 6-2					X

Stirling Albion resigned from the League in Jan 1946 in order to compete in the Scottish Southern League Cup and there record was expunged

EASTERN LEAGUE CUP

First Series
First round
Played on 8 Dec
Forfar Athletic v Edinburgh City 5-1
Stirling Albion v Brechin City 7-2

Semi-final
Played on 15 Dec
Montrose v Dundee 'A' 3-5
Forfar Athletic v Stirling Albion 3-2

Final – 2 legs
First leg played on 22 Dec, second on 29 Dec
Forfar Athletic v Dundee 'A' 3-5, 1-2

Second Series
First round – 2 legs
First leg played on 6 Apr, second on 15 Apr
Edinburgh City v Dundee 'A' 4-3, 0-5
First leg played on 6 Apr, second on 17 Apr
Brechin City v East Stirlingshire 0-1, 3-0
Montrose v Forfar Athletic 5-5, 0-6

Semi-final – 2 legs
First leg played on 20 Apr, second on 27 Apr
Forfar Athletic v St Johnstone 'A' 3-4, 0-3
First leg played on 24 Apr, second on 1 May
Dundee 'A' v Brechin City 3-1, 1-1

Final – 2 legs
First leg played on 4 May, second on 11 May
St Johnstone 'A' v Dundee 'A' 5-0, 2-0

Other Scottish Competitions 1945-46

SCOTTISH FOOTBALL LEAGUE B DIVISION SUPPLEMENTARY CUP

First round - 2 legs
First leg played on 26 Jan, second on 2 Feb, REPLAYS on 6 Feb
Stenhousemuir v Dumbarton 1-6, 2-2
Cowdenbeath v Dundee 1-4, 2-2
St Johnstone v Ayr United 2-2, 1-2
East Fife v Dunfermline Athletic 3-0, 0-3
Dundee United v Raith Rovers 1-4, 3-0, 3-3 *(4-4 on corners, Raith won on toss of a coin)*
Albion Rovers v Airdrieonians 2-1, 3-4, 1-1 (Airdrie won 8-5 on corners)
Arbroath v Alloa Athletic 1-3, 3-3, 4-2

Second Round
Played on 9 Feb
Dundee v Alloa Athletic 6-2
Raith Rovers v Airdrieonians 0-4
Ayr United v East Fife 0-1
Dumbarton bye

Semi-Final
First leg played on 16 Feb, REPLAY on 20 Feb
East Fife v Dumbarton 0-1
Dundee v Airdrieonians 1-1, 1-2

Final
17 Apr 1946 at Ibrox Park Glasgow
Att 25,000
Airdrieonians 2 *(Peters, Aitken)*
Dumbarton 1 *(Bootland)*

Airdrieonians: Moodie, Peters, Hadden, Peden, Brennan, Clapperton, McCulloch, Dalgleish, Aitken, Picken, Watson
Dumbarton: Henderson, Wallace, Ray OR Douglas, Ross, Donaldson, Campbell, Getty, McDonald, Neil, McGowan, Bootland

FORFARSHIRE CUP

First round – 2 legs
First leg played on 2 Jan, Second on 7 May
Montrose v Dundee 0-3, 2-2
First leg played on 16 Feb, second on 4 May
Arbroath v Dundee United 2-2, 6-0

NOTE This season's competition was completed the end of season 1946-47.

Semi-final – 2 legs i
First leg played on 11 May, second on 15 May
Brechin City v Forfar Athletic 3-2, 0-5
First leg played on 4 Sep 1946, second on 11 Sep 1946
Arbroath v Dundee 3-4, 2-3

Final
Played on 16 Apr 1947 at Dens Park, Dundee
Dundee v Forfar Athletic 6-1

GLASGOW CUP

First round
Played on 25 Aug
Third Lanark v Partick Thistle 1-2
Rangers v Celtic 3-1

Semi-final
Played on 24 Sep, REPLAY on 1 Oct
Partick Thistle v Queen's Park 0-0, 1-2
Clyde v Rangers 4-3

Final
Played on 6 Oct at Hampden Park, Glasgow
Queen's Park v Clyde 2-0

GLASGOW CHARITY CUP

First round
Played on 1 May
Partick Thistle v Third Lanark 0-1
Played on 6 May
Rangers v Queen's Park 4-1

Semi-final
Played on 8 May
Third Lanark v Clyde 3-1
Played on 13 May
Celtic v Rangers 1-3

Final
Played on 8 Jun at Hampden Park, Glasgow
Rangers v Third Lanark 2-0

DEWAR SHIELD

Semi-final – 2 legs
First leg played on 15 Aug, second on 16 Aug
Dundee v Falkirk 5-2, 0-4
St Johnstone v Aberdeen 2-1, 0-4

Final – 2 legs
First leg played on 13 Apr, second on 23 Sep 1947, both games at Pittodrie Park, Aberdeen
Aberdeen v Falkirk 2-0, 1-1

NOTE this competition was completed at the start of season 1946-47.

FIFE CUP

Semi-final – 2 legs
First leg played on 16 Feb, second on 6 Apr
Cowdenbeath v Dunfermline Athletic 2-0, 5-0
First leg played on 11 May, second on 5 Apr 1947
Raith Rovers v East Fife 0-0, 2-7

Final
Played on 30 Apr 1947 at Central Park, Cowdenbeath
East Fife v Cowdenbeath 3-0

NOTE this competition was completed at the start of season 1946-47.

Other Scottish Competitions 1945-46

EAST OF SCOTLAND SHIELD
Final
Played on 11 May at Tynecastle Park, Edinburgh
Heart of Midlothian v Hibernian 3-2

STIRLING CHARITY CUP
Played on 14 May at Annfield Park, Stirling
Stirling Albion v Airdrieonians 1-0

PENMAN CUP
First round – 2 legs
First leg played on 6 Apr, second on 15 Apr, REPLAY on 26 Apr at Annfield Park, Stirling
Alloa Athletic v Stirling Albion 1-0, 1-2, 1-4

Semifinal
Played on 6 Apr
Raith Rovers v Stenhousemuir 0-1
Played on 4 May
Stirling Albion v East Fife 6-1

Final
Played on 10 May at Annfileld Park, Stirling
Stirling Albion v Stenhousemuir 1-1

NOTE as there was no replay due to fixture congestion, the trophy was shared

STIRLINGSHIRE CUP
First round – 2 legs
First leg played on 5 Sep, second on 12 Sep
Stirling Albion v Dumbarton 3-2, 0-4
Single leg only played on 11 Sep
Stenhousemuir v East Stirlingshire 8-1

Semi-final
Alloa Athletic v Stenhousemuir
Played on 11 May
Falkirk v Dumbarton 2-1

COMPETITION ABANDONED

RENFREWSHIRE CUP
Final
Played on 16 Aug at St Mirren Park, Paisley
St Mirren v Morton 4-0

WILSON CUP
Played on 15 Aug at Easter Raod, Edinburgh
Hibernian v Heart of Midlothian 4-1

PAISLEY CHARITY CUP
Played on 8 Jun at St Mirren Park, paisley
Airdrieonians v St Mirren 4-2

Northern Ireland 1945-46

NORTHERN REGIONAL FOOTBALL LEAGUE

	Belfast Celtic	Cliftonville	Derry City	Distillery	Glentoran	Linfield
Belfast Celtic	X	4-1 / 15 Dec 5-0	2-1 / 22 Dec 5-0	24 Nov 4-3 / 9 Feb 5-0	29 Dec 3-1 / 2-2	3-0 / 0-2
Cliftonville	10 Nov 0-4 / 5 Jan 0-3	X	4-1 / 3-2	1-1 / 0-6	1 Dec 2-3 / 2 Mar 1-1	22 Dec 1-3 / 2-3
Derry City	17 Nov 1-4 / 12 Jan 2-2	24 Nov 5-2 / 9 Feb 5-2	X	1-0 / 4-1	15 Dec 4-3 / 1-2	19 Jan 1-4 / 3-5
Distillery	1-3 / 0-0	29 Dec 1-1 / 4-2	8-4 / 1 Dec 2-1	X	17 Nov 4-1 / 12 Jan 3-3	15 Dec 1-6 / 3-2
Glentoran	2-5 / 2-2	5-0 / 1-1	10 Nov 9-5 / 5 Jan 5-4	22 Dec 2-2 / 1-3	X	24 Nov 1-7 / 9 Feb 0-3
Linfield	1 Dec 2-1 / 2 Mar 0-1	17 Nov 5-0 / 12 Jan 8-1	4-3 / 5-0	10 Nov 3-2 / 5 Jan 8-2	5-0 / 4-2	X

		P	W	D	L	F	A	Pts
1	Linfield	20	17	0	3	79	27	34
2	Belfast Celtic	20	14	4	2	58	20	32
3	Distillery	20	7	5	8	47	52	19
4	Glentoran	20	5	6	9	46	58	16
5	Derry City	20	5	1	14	48	72	11
6	Cliftonville	20	2	4	14	24	73	8

SUBSTITUTE GOLD CUP

	Belfast Celtic	Cliftonville	Derry City	Distillery	Glentoran	Linfield
Belfast Celtic	X			8 Sep 3-0	18 Aug 2-1	27 Oct 3-1
Cliftonville	25 Aug 1-3	X	20 Oct 1-2	29 Sep 2-4		
Derry City		8 Sep 6-2	X	27 Oct 2-4		18 Aug 1-3
Distillery	20 Oct 1-2	18 Aug 8-0		X		
Glentoran	29 Sep 3-5	27 Oct 3-4	25 Aug 4-2		X	8 Sep 1-3
Linfield			29 Sep 2-0	25 Aug 4-1	20 Oct 0-3	X

Belfast Celtic were declared winners

Northern Ireland 1945-46

IRISH FA CUP

First round- 2 legs
First leg played on 19 Jan, second on 26 Jan
Cliftonville v RAF Aldergrove 3-2, 3-1
Glentoran v Belfast Celtic II 3-2, 1-5
Derry City v Distillery ?-?, 4-8

Semi-final
Played on 23 Mar, REPLAY on 30 Mar
Linfield v Belfast Celtic 2-0
Distillery v Belfast Celtic II 0-0, 1-0

Final
Played on 13 Apr at Celtic Park, Belfast
Linfield v Distillery 3-0

INTER CITY CUP

Derry City played all their home matches in Belfast
All League of Ireland clubs' home games were played
at Dalymount Park, Dublin

First round – 2 legs
First leg played on 27 Apr, second on 4 May
Shamrock Rovers v Derry City 5-1, 1-1
First leg played on 1 May, second on 10 May
Linfield v Drumcondra 2-1, 1-0
First leg played on 1 May, second on 11 May
Dundalk v Belfast Celtic 0-5, 5-2
First leg played on 4 May, second on 11 May
Distillery v Cork United 5-0, 2-1
First leg played on 6 May, second on 11 May
Cliftonville v Shelbourne 1-4, 0-3
First leg played on 8 May, second on 11 May
Bohemians v Glentoran 1-0, 1-3

Second round - 2 legs
The first round winners were joined by the best losers
(Bohemians and Drumcondra)

First leg played on 15 May, second on 18 May
Bohemians v Linfield 1-7, 1-4
First leg played on 17 May, second on 20 May
Distillery v Drumcondra 4-3, 1-1
First leg played on 18 May, second on 21 May
Shelbourne v Belfast Celtic 0-2, 0-8
First leg played on 18 May, second on 22 May
Shamrock Rovers v Glentoran 3-1, 4-3

Semi-final - 2 legs
First leg played on 25 May, second on 28 May
Belfast Celtic v Linfield 5-1, 1-0
NOTE First leg played at Dalymount Park, Dublin, second
leg at Celtic Park, Belfast
First leg played on 25 May, second on 27 May
Distillery v Shamrock Rovers 2-1, 1-5

Final - 2 legs
First leg played on 1 Jun, second on 3 Jun
Belfast Celtic v Shamrock Rovers 1-3, 1-0

NOTE First leg played at Windsor Park, Belfast, second
leg at Dalymount Park, Dublin

Appendices

Appendix 1

Non-Participating Football League Clubs

During both wars, a number of Football League clubs were either excluded from the mainstream competitions for geographical reasons or else chose to close down for the duration of the war.

The Great War

Aston Villa 1915-1918
Birmingham 1915-1918
Blackburn Rovers 1915-16
Bristol City 1916-1919
Middlesbrough 1915-1918

Newcastle United 1915-1918
Sunderland 1915-1918
West Bromwich Albion 1915-1918
Wolverhampton Wanderers 1915-1919

The Second World War

1939-40
Aston Villa
Derby County
Exeter City
Gateshead
Ipswich Town
Sunderland

1940-41
Accrington Stanley
Aston Villa
Barrow
Bristol Rovers
Carlisle United
Darlington
Derby County
Exeter City
Gateshead
Hartlepools United
Ipswich Town
Newport County
Plymouth Argyle
Port Vale
Sunderland
Swindon Town
Torquay United
Wolverhampton Wanderers

Blackpool and Bolton Wanderers took part in the second half of the season only

1941-42
Accrington Stanley
Aston Villa
Barrow
Birmingham
Bristol Rovers
Carlisle United
Coventry City
Crewe Alexandra
Darlington
Derby County
Exeter City
Hartlepools United
Hull City
Ipswich Town
Newport County
Notts County
Plymouth Argyle
Port Vale
Southend United
Swindon Town
Torquay United

Coventry City didn't take part in the second half of the season

1942-43
Accrington Stanley
Barrow
Bournemouth & Boscombe Athletic
Bristol Rovers
Carlisle United
Darlington
Exeter City
Hartlepools United
Hull City
Ipswich Town
New Brighton
Newport County
Norwich City
Plymouth Argyle
Port Vale
Preston North End
Southend United
Swindon Town
Torquay United

1943-44
Accrington Stanley
Barrow
Bournemouth & Boscombe Athletic
Bristol Rovers
Carlisle United
Exeter City
Hull City
Ipswich Town
New Brighton
Newport County
Norwich City
Plymouth Argyle
Port Vale
Preston North End
Southend United
Swindon Town
Torquay United

1944-45
Barrow
Bournemouth & Boscombe Athletic
Bristol Rovers
Carlisle United
Exeter City
Ipswich Town
New Brighton
Newport County
Norwich City
Plymouth Argyle
Southend United
Swindon Town
Torquay United

1945-46
Hull City
New Brighton

Appendix 1

Non-Participating Football League Clubs - Aston Villa

Rather than competing in the Football League's competition, Aston Villa chose to spend two seasons, 1940-41 and 1941-42 in the local Birmingham & District Football League before returning to the Football League North in 1942.

1940-41 Birmingham & District Football League

14 Sep	Hednesford T	A	1-6		22 Feb	Revo Electric	A	4-1
21 Sep	Revo Electric	A	4-8		1 Mar	RAF Hednesford	H	5-1
12 Oct	RAF Cosford	H	0-1		15 Mar	Worcester C	A	3-5
9 Nov	Wellington T	H	1-4		5 Apr	RAF Bridgnorth	H	8-1
16 Nov	RAF Cosford	A	1-3		12 Apr	Wellington T	A	2-4
14 Dec	RAF Hednesford	H	3-4		14 Apr	WBA reserves	A	3-4
21 Dec	Worcester C	A	2-3		26 Apr	WBA reserves	H	6-1
15 Feb	RAF Bridgnorth	H	3-1		3 May	Hednesford T	A	0-2

		P	W	D	L	F	A	Pts
1	Hednesford Town	16	12	1	3	52	16	25
2	Wellington Town	16	11	1	4	54	32	23
3	RAF Cosford	16	9	3	4	52	30	21
4	Worcester City	16	10	1	5	53	36	21
5	Revo Electric	16	6	3	7	56	60	15
6	West Bromwich Albion reserves	16	7	1	8	45	54	15
7	**Aston Villa**	16	5	0	11	46	49	10
8	RAF Bridgnorth	16	4	2	10	30	52	10
9	RAF Hednesford	16	1	2	13	16	75	4

Birmingham reserves withdrew during the season and their record deleted

BIRMINGHAM LEAGUE CUP

26 Oct	Worcester C	A	0-2
2 Nov	Worcester C	H	2-2

WORCESTER CUP

7 Dec	Revo Electric	A	1-2

WORCESTER INFIRMARY CUP

10 May	Worcester C	A	1-2

1941-42 Birmingham & District Football League

6 Sep	Hednesford T	A	3-0		3 Jan	Wolverhampton reserves	A	3-1
13 Sep	RAF Hednesford	H	2-1		10 Jan	Hednesford T	H	8-0
20 Sep	Revo Electric	A	5-1		14 Feb	RAF Hednesford	H	7-0
27 Sep	Wellington T	H	5-1		21 Feb	Revo Electric	H	3-0
4 Oct	Wellington T	A	0-5		24 Mar	RAF Lichfield	H	19-2
11 Oct	WBA reserves	H	2-3		11 Apr	Worcester C	H	2-0
18 Oct	RAF Cosford	H	3-0		18 Apr	RAF Lichfield	H	9-0
1 Nov	Worcester C	A	8-1		25 Apr	RAF Cosford	H	0-0
25 Dec	WBA reserves	A	2-0		16 May	Wolverhampton reserves	H	6-1

		P	W	D	L	F	A	Pts
1	**Aston Villa**	18	15	1	2	87	16	31
2	Revo Electrics	18	13	1	4	72	37	27
3	Worcester City	18	11	2	5	63	41	24
4	Hednesford	17	10	1	6	56	37	21
5	RAF Cosford	17	7	2	8	31	35	16
6	West Bromwich Albion reserves	18	6	2	10	35	44	14
7	Wolverhampton Wanderers reserves	17	4	0	13	39	65	8
8	RAF Hednesford	17	3	0	14	30	75	6
9	RAF Lichfield	18	3	0	15	29	120	6

BIRMINGHAM LEAGUE CUP

8 Nov	Wellington T	H	5-0
22 Nov	Wellington T	A	1-2
17 Jan	RAF Hednesford	H	14-1
31 Jan	Hednesford T	H	3-2
9 May	Worcester C	H	4-2

WORCESTER CUP

13 Dec	Revo Electric	H	1-2

WORCESTER INFIRMARY CUP

2 May	Worcester C	A	3-0

KEYS CUP

6 Dec	Worcester C	H	6-0
24 Dec	Worcester C	A	4-1
28 Feb	Revo Electric	A	2-
23 May	Hednesford T	H	5-0

Appendix 1

Non-Participating Football League Clubs - Norwich City

Norwich City were excluded from the Football League competitions from 1942-43 to 1944-45 seasons due to their geographical location on the east coast. However they did manage to arrange enough friendly matches, mainly against services XIs for a sufficient fixture list.

1942-43			1943-44			1944-45		
12 Sep	Navy (Suffolk) XI	8-1	4 Sep	Army XI	6-3	16 Sep	RAF XI	9-1
19 Sep	Navy (Suffolk) XI	3-0	11 Sep	Navy (Suffolk) XI	3-3	23 Sep	REME XI	5-0
3 Oct	Chelmsford	4-3	18 Sep	Army XI	10-1	30 Sep	RAF XI	10-1
24 Oct	RAF XI	6-1	25 Sep	Navy (Suffolk) XI	1-0	14 Oct	RAF XI	8-1
31 Oct	RAF XI	1-2	9 Oct	RA XI	3-0	21 Oct	Cambridge University	6-2
7 Nov	RAF XI	0-0	23 Oct	RAF XI	3-4	28 Oct	RAC XI	3-5
14 Nov	Army XI	5-3	30 Oct	Cambridge University	7-3	4 Nov	RAC XI	5-1
21 Nov	Army XI	6-1	6 Nov	Royal Navy XI	5-2	11 Nov	Norwich League XI	8-1
28 Nov	Army XI	4-1	13 Nov	King's Royal Rifles XI	2-2	18 Nov	RAF XI	8-2
5 Dec	RAF XI	8-2	20 Nov	RA XI	9-1	9 Dec	Lowestoft Services League XI	3-4
12 Dec	Services XI	3-4	27 Nov	United Services XI	3-4	16 Dec	RAF XI	2-2
19 Dec	Army XI	3-1	4 Dec	RA XI	2-3	23 Dec	RAF XI	1-5
26 Dec	Norwich League XI	5-6	18 Dec	East Lancashire Regiment	6-3	26 Dec	RAF XI	3-3
2 Jan	Army XI	?-?	27 Dec	Eastern Command XI	3-2	30 Dec	REME XI	7-0
9 Jan	Norwich League XI	7-1	8 Jan	RAF XI	9-3	6 Jan	REME XI	8-1
16 Jan	Cambridge University	3-2	15 Jan	RAF XI	5-1	20 Jan	Royal Corps of Signals XI	3-3
23 Jan	Army XI	3-2	22 Jan	RA XI	2-0	3 Feb	Ely & District XI	4-1
30 Jan	Army XI	8-1	5 Feb	King's Royal Rifles XI	3-0	10 Feb	United Services XI	2-2
6 Feb	Eastern Command XI	8-3	12 Feb	RA XI	3-4	17 Feb	Mine Sweepers XI	5-0
6 Mar	Army XI	5-4	19 Feb	Reconnaissance Corps XI	9-4	24 Feb	Royal Navy XI	4-1
13 Mar	Army XI	2-4	26 Feb	East Lancashire Regiment	5-2	3 Mar	Metropolitan Police	0-1
20 Mar	Army XI	4-2	11 Mar	Norwich League XI	6-2	10 Mar	Army XI	0-4
3 Apr	Army XI	2-0	18 Mar	Anti-Tank Regiment XI	2-1	17 Mar	RA XI	7-2
17 Apr	Army XI	3-2	8 Apr	RAF XI	7-3	24 Mar	REME XI	11-1
24 Apr	Eastern Command XI	3-1	15 Apr	Lothian Regiment XI	4-4	2 Apr	Royal Corps of Signals XI	1-2
1 May	Army XI	4-3	22 Apr	RA XI	4-0	7 Apr	Royal Navy XI	3-4
8 May	Army XI	5-2	29 Apr	Army XI	9-0	21 Apr	Army XI	4-2
			6 May	RASC XI	4-0	5 May	Norwich League XI	3-5

Non-Participating Scottish Football League Clubs

In Scotland the following clubs did not participate during the seasons shown.

Aberdeen 1917-1919, 1940-41
Alloa Athletic 1940-1945
Arbroath 1940-1944
Ayr United 1939-1945
Brechin City 1939-1945
Cowdenbeath 1918-19, 1940-1945
Dundee 1917-1919, 1940-1944
Dundee Hibernian / United 1918-19, 1940-41

Dunfermline Athletic 1918-19
East Fife 1940-41
East Stirlingshire 1917-1919, 1940-1945
Edinburgh City 1939-1945
Forfar Athletic 1939-1945
Kilmarnock 1939-1944
King's Park 1940-1945
Leith / Leith Athletic 1916-1919, 1939-41, 1942-1945

Lochgelly United 1917-1919
Montrose 1939-1945
Queen of the South 1939-1945
Raith Rovers 1917-1919, 1940-41
St Bernard's 1917-1919, 1940-41 (Disbanded in 1942)
St Johnstone 1940-1945
Stenhousemuir 1940-1945

Kilmarnock

After being forced to sit out the war as their ground had been taken over for military purposes, Kilmarnock didn't competeagain until 1944-45 when theiy entered their first XI in the Glasgow & District Reserve League. They returned to mainstream Scottish Football League for season1945-46.

1944-45 Glasgow & District Reserve Football League

2 Sep	St Mirren 'A'	A	4-4	4 Nov	Celtic 'A'	A	2-3	3 Feb	Partick Th 'A'	A	1-3
9 Sep	Airdrieonians 'A'	H	2-2	18 Nov	Queen's Park Str	H	5-1	10 Feb	Partick Th 'A'	H	0-2
23 Sep	Celtic 'A'	H	2-3	9 Dec	Third Lanark 'A'	A	3-3	17 Feb	Morton 'A'	H	4-2
30 Sep	Hibernian 'A'	A	0-2	16 Dec	St Mirren 'A'	H	7-0	24 Feb	Queen's Park Strollers	A	2-2
7 Oct	Dumbarton 'A'	H	6-0	23 Dec	Airdrieonians 'A'	A	1-1	3 Mar	Hibernian 'A'	H	2-4
14 Oct	Motherwell 'A'	A	2-5	30 Dec	Dumbarton 'A'	A	3-4	10 Mar	Motherwell 'A'	H	2-0
21 Oct	Motherwell 'A'	H	1-1	6 Jan	Morton 'A'	A	2-2	24 Mar	Celtic 'A'	A	0-2
				13 Jan	Hibernian 'A'	H	1-4	31 Mar	Partick Th 'A'	A	2-6

		P	W	D	L	F	A	Pts
1	Motherwell 'A'	24	18	4	2	86	26	40
2	Hibernian 'A'	23	18	3	2	82	28	39
3	Partick Thistle 'A	24	15	0	9	72	46	30
4	Celtic 'A'	22	12	2	8	57	53	26
5	Morton 'A'	24	9	6	9	57	44	24
6	St Mirren 'A'	24	7	5	12	47	76	19
7	Third Lanark 'A'	22	8	3	11	51	79	19
8	**Kilmarnock**	23	5	7	11	54	56	17
9	Dumbarton 'A'	23	6	3	14	50	84	15
10	Queen's Park Strollers	24	5	4	15	43	87	14
11	Airdrieonians 'A'	23	4	5	14	48	68	13

Appendix 2

Representative and Friendly Matches 1914-1919

1914-15

Played on 8 Aug
St Bernard's v Leith Amateurs 4-1

Played on 22 Aug
Tottenham Hotspur v The Arsenal 1-5

Played on 9 Sep
Broxburn Shamrock v Hibernian 1-1

Played on 2 Nov
The Arsenal v West Ham United 1-0

Played on 19 Dec
The Arsenal v Swindon Town 1-2

Played on 4 Apr
Abercorn v Renton 0-3

Played on 17 Apr
Rangers v Notts County 1-1

Played on 19 Apr
Hibernian v Bradford City 5-3

Played on 24 Apr
East Fife v Raith Rovers 1-3
St Johnstone v Arthurlie 2-2
Third Lanark v Clydebank 3-2
Airdrieonians v Albion Rovers 1-1

Played on 15 May
Scottish Football League XI v Celtic 0-1
(at Hampden Park, Glasgow)
Dumbarton v Dunbartonshire Select 2-2

1915-16

Played on 11 Sep
Luton Town v EMBFA (RAMC) XI 5-0

Played on 18 Sep
Luton Town v Tottenham Hotspur 3-1

Played on 25 Sep
Luton Town v Leicester Fosse 3-2

Played on 2 Oct
Northampton Town v Luton Town 2-1

Played on 9 Oct
Luton Town v Footballers Battery XI 3-2

Played on 16 Oct
Luton Town v Bedfordshire Regiment XI 10-1

Played on 23 Oct
Luton Town v Northampton Town 4-0

Played on 30 Oct
Luton Town Clapton Orient 6-1

Played on 6 Nov
Luton Town v Portsmouth 3-1

Played on 13 Nov
Luton Town v Kettering 4-0

Played on 20 Nov
Clapton Orient v Luton Town 2-2

Played on 4 Dec
Luton Town v 59th Northamptonshires XI 8-0

Played on 11 Dec
Portsmouth v Luton Town 2-1

Played on 18 Dec
Luton Town v Ashbourne Yeomanry XI 9-2

Played on 25 Dec
Luton Town v Northampton Town 9-2

Played on 26 Dec
Northampton Town v Luton Town 8-2

Played on 4 Jan
Rangers v Rest of Glasgow XI 3-2

Played on 8 Jan
Luton Town v 3/2 London RFC XI 8-0
St Bernard's v Clydebank 1-0

Played on 15 Jan
Luton Town v 1st Wash RA XI 3-2
Vale of Leven v HLI (Dumfries) 4-1

Played on 22 Jan
Luton Town v Midland Railway XI 11-0

Played on 29 Jan
Luton Town v Watford 3-1
Chelsea v Brentford 1-2
The Arsenal v Fulham 2-0
Crystal Palace v Croydon Common 2-0
West Ham United v Queen's Park Rangers 0-0
Tottenham Hotspur v Clapton Orient 0-1
Millwall v Reading 3-1

Played on 19 Feb
Eastern League XI v West of Scottish League XI 4-1
(at Cowdenbeath)
Albion Rovers v Wishaw Thistle 2-1

Played on 26 Feb
East Stirlingshire v Albion Rovers 2-1

Played on 4 Mar
Stevenston United v Queen's Park Strollers 3-0

Played on 18 Mar
West of Scotland League XI v Eastern League XI 2-2
(at Coatbridge)
East Fife v Highland Cyclist (Fifeshire) Battalion XI 3-3
Dunfermline Athletic v 7th Argyll & Sutherland Highlanders XI 0-2
Clydebank v St Bernard's 1-1

Played on 1 Apr
East Stirlingshire v Queen's Park Rangers 2-2

Played on 8 Apr
Leith v Civil Service Strollers 1-0
East Fife v Denbeath Star 6-0
Johnstone v Abercorn 4-3
Dykehead v Stevenston United 2-0

Played on 22 Apr
Armadale v Clydebank 2-2
Dumbarton v Vale of Leven 1-0
Dunfermline Athletic v Dunfermline Junior XI 3-2

Played on 29 Apr
Hibernian v Parkhead 3-1

Played on 6 May
The Arsenal v Rest of London Combination XI 2-2
Millwall v Scots Guards XI 5-1
Chelsea v Fulham 2-0
Clapton Orient v Tottenham Hotspur 3-2
Liverpool v Everton 1-3
Newcastle United v Sunderland 1-1
Birmingham v Leicester Fosse 6-3
Sheffield United v The Wednesday 3-0
English XI v Scottish XI 4-4 (at Bradford)
Blackburn Rovers v Burnley 9-3
Bristol Rovers v Army Service Corps Remounts 3-0
Nottingham Forest v Notts County 1-2
Manchester City v Manchester United 2-2
Southampton v Royal Flying Corps 5-2
Grimsby Town v Armay & Navy XI 4-1
Rotherham County v Chesterfield Town 1-3
Bristol City v 3rd Bristol Officers' TC 6-3
Luton Town v RA XI 5-1
Dundee v Aberdeen 3-4

Played on 13 May
Dundee v Aberdeen 1-0

Played on 20 May
Rest of the Scottish League XI v Celtic 0-1 (at Hampden Park, Glasgow)
Ayr United v Queen's Park 3-1
Broxburn United v Armadale 3-4

Played on 27 May
Scottish Football League East XI v SFL West XI 3-4
(at Tynecastle Park, Glasgow)
Lanarkshire XI v Glasgow XI 0-1 *(at Fir Park, Motherwell)*
St Mirren v Renfrewshire Select 1-5
Eastern League XI v West of Scotland League XI 0-2
(at Volunteer Park, Armadale)
Vale of Leven v Rangers 1-2
Dumbarton v Clydebank 6-0
Raith Rovers v Junior Internationalists XI 1-1

Appendix 2

Representative and Friendly Matches 1914-1919

1916-17

Played on 3 Jan
Home Scots XI v Anglo Scots XI 2-1 (at Hampden Park, Glasgow)
Heart of Midlothian v Bathgate 3-4

Played on 27 Jan
St Bernard's v Royal Fusiliers 3-1

Played on 10 Feb
Dunfermline Athletic v Rosyth League Select 3-2

Played on 3 Mar
Broxburn United v Royal Fusiliers 1-1

Played on 10 Mar
East Fife v Cowdenbeath 4-0
Albion Rovers v Royal Albert 2-0

Played on 17 Mar
Queen's Park Strollers v Stevenston United 1-1

Played on 24 Mar
St Bernard's v Royal Fusiliers 4-1

Played on 31 Mar
Dunfermline Athletic v Rosyth 1-1

Played on 7 Apr
Albion Rovers v Airdrieonians 2-0

Played on 14 Apr
Rangers v Army XI 3-1

Played on 16 Apr
St Bernard's v Military XI 2-1

Played on 21 Apr
Heart of Midlothian v Military XI 2-2
Falkirk v East Stirlingshire 4-0
Clydebank v Stevenston United 2-0

Played on 28 Apr
Hibernian v St Bernard's 2-0
Ayr United v Kilmarnock 0-2
Motherwell v Wishaw Thistle 3-1
Arthurlie v Cadet XI 4-1

Played on 5 May
Everton v Leeds United 2-3
Chelsea v Fulham 3-1
Millwall v Crystal Palace 1-4
West Ham United v Tottenham Hotspur 3-3
West Bromwich Albion v Birmingham 0-1
Sheffield United v The Wednesday 1-2
Motherwell v Celtic 0-5
Aberdeen v Dundee 1-2
Morton v Rangers 1-0
St Mirren v Aberorn 4-1

Played on 12 May
Dundee v Aberdeen 3-0

Played on 19 May
Military XI v Scottish Football League XI 4-3 (at Tynecastle Park, Edinburgh)
Arthurlie v St Mirren 3-1
Morton v Clyde 0-0

Played on 26 May
Celtic v Rest of Scottish League XI 1-2
Ayr United v Stevenston United 4-2

1917-18

Played on 11 Aug
Dumbarton v Dumbarton Harp 5-4
Motherwell v Partick Thistle 2-1
St Mirren v Third Lanark 3-0
Kilmarnock v Ayrshire Junior XI 3-2

Played on 18 Aug
Armadale v Bathgate Juniors 3-1

Played on 8 Sep
Cowdenbeath v Argyll & Sutherland Highlanders 6-1

Played on 15 Nov
British Army XI v Belgian Army XI 4-1 (at Stamford Bridge, London)

Played on 17 Nov
British Army XI v Belgian Army XI 1-2 (at Celtic Park, Glasgow)

Played on 24 Nov
British Army XI v Belgian Army XI 1-6 (at Birmingham)

Played on 22 Dec
Aberdeen v Military XI 4-3

Played on 16 Mar
Falkirk v Ayr United 4-2

Played on 30 Mar
East Fife v Scottish Rifles XI 2-1

Played on 13 Apr
Albion Rovers v Queen's Park Strollers 1-1
Cowdenbeath v Falkirk 1-0
Brentford v Clapton Orient 0-1
Chelsea v Tottenham Hotspur 1-1
West Ham United v Fulham 2-0
The Arsenal v Millwall 4-3
Crystal Palace v Queen's Park Rangers 2-1

Played on 20 Apr
Clapton Orient v Brentford 5-3
Tottenham Hotspur v Chelsea 0-1
Fulham v West Ham United 1-1
Millwall v The Arsenal 0-1
Crystal Palace v Queen's Park Rangers 3-1

Played on 27 Apr
Cowdenbeath v Heart of Midlothian 2-2
Motherwell v Hamilton Academical 6-0
Kilmarnock v Ayr United 3-3
Third Lanark v St Mirren 3-3
Manchester City & United XI v Leeds United 3-0
Everton v Sheffield United 1-1
The Arsenal v Brentford 3-1
West Ham United v Chelsea 3-3
Crystal Palace v Clapton Orient 2-0
Fulham v Tottenham Hotspur 3-0
Queens's Park Rangers v Millwall 4-3

Played on 4 May
Kilmarnock v Clydebank 4-2
Dumbarton v Dumbarton Harp 2-0
Liverpool v The Wednesday 1-1
Manchester City v Stockport County 1-0
Sheffield United v Everton 2-0
Chelsea v West Ham United 4-1
Brentford v The Arsenal 1-1
Clapton Orient v Crystal Palace 0-2
Millwall v Queen's Park Rangers 3-1
Tottenham Hotspur v Fulham 2-3
Leicester Fosse v Coventry City 0-3
Albion Rovers v Lanarkshire Select XI 3-1

Played on 11 May
Scottish Football League East XI v SFL West XI 1-2 (at Tynecastle Park, Edinburgh)
Cowdenbeath v Dunfermline Athletic 3-0
Clydebank v St Mirren 2-1
Stevenston United v Celtic 2-3
The Wednesday v Liverpool 3-1
Lincoln City v Grimsby Town 1-0
Manchester City v Stockport County 4-3
Newcastle United v Middlesbrough 3-3
West Ham United v RA XI 3-2
Leicester Fosse v Notts County 3-2
Fulham v Chelsea 4-0
Millwall v Crystal Palace 0-0

Played on 18 May
Cowdenbeath v Raith Rovers 2-2

Appendix 2

Representative and Friendly Matches 1914-1919

1918-19

Played on 10 Aug
Motherwell v Partick Thistle 2-1

Played on 25 Dec
Portsmouth v Southampton 5-1

Played on 2 Jan
Heart of Midlothian v Canadian XI 3-3

Played on 3 Jan
Glasgow XI v T Morley's English XI 4-0 *(at Hampden Park, Glasgow)*

Played on 22 Feb
Football League XI v Scottish League XI 3-1 *(at Birmingham)*

Played on 1 Mar
Hibernian v Dundee Hibernian 6-2
East of Scotland Junior XI v Cowdenbeath 4-2

Played on 8 Mar
Scottish Command XI v RAF XI 7-2 *(at Celtic Park, Glasgow)*
Cowdenbeath v HMS Conqueror 0-0
Heart of Midlothian 'A' v East Fife 4-3

Played on 9 Mar
Lutetians v RAF XI 1-3 *(at Paris)*

Played on 22 Mar
Raith Rovers v East of Scotland Junior XI 3-1
Arbroath v Dundee Hibernian 2-1

Played on 29 Mar
Falkirk v Third Lanark 3-1
Dundee v Aberdeen 3-2
Raith Rovers v East Fife 6-0

Played on 30 Mar
French Army XI v British Army XI 1-2 *(at Paris)*

Played on 5 Apr
Dundee v Clyde 3-2
Raith Rovers v Cowdenbeath 2-1
Dundee Hibernian v Arbroath 0-0
Aberdeen v 3rd Canadian Command Depot XI 1-0

Played on 6 Apr
Belgian Military XI v English Military XI 2-4 *(at Brussels)*

Played on 7 Apr
Dundee v Raith Rovers 4-4

Played on 12 Apr
Heart of Midlothian v Dundee 4-3
The Wednesday v Sheffield United 0-1

Played on 14 Apr
Dundee v Rangers 2-1
Dundee Hibernian v Hibernian 0-3

Played on 19 Apr
Cowdenbeath v Hibenian 0-0
Dundee v Third Lanark 2-1
Clydebank v Motherwell 1-2
East Fife v Raith Rovers 1-2
Aberdeen v Queen's Park Strollers 1-0

Played on 26 Apr
Brentford v The Arsenal 3-3
Cowdenbeath v Falkirk 2-3
Dundee v Raith Rovers 6-0

Played on 28 Apr
Hibernian v Hull City 3-3

Played on 29 Apr
Rangers v Everton 4-0

Played on 1 May
Musselburgh District XI v Heart of Midlothian 3-3 *(at Musselburgh)*

Played on 3 May
Dundee v Motherwell 1-1
Cowdenbeath v Third Lanark 3-1
St Johnstone v Clyde 2-2
Bathgate v Falkirk 2-0
Aberdeen v Albion Rovers 2-1
Fulham v Chelsea 0-4
West Ham United v The Arsenal 1-0
Millwall v Crystal Palace 0-2
Manchester City v Sheffield United 1-0
Everton v Rangers 4-3
Aston Villa v Birmingham 1-3
Oldham Athletic v Bolton Wanderers 3-3

Played on 10 May
Fulham v Tottenham Hotspur 2-2
The Arsenal v West Ham United 3-2
Crystal Palace v Millwall 0-4
Stoke v Chelsea 4-1
Liverpool v Manchester Uniyed 4-0
South Shields District XI v Players Union XI 4-2 *(at South Shields)*

Played on 12 May
Musselburgh District XI v Hibernian 1-0

Played on 17 May
The Arsenal v Chelsea 1-2
Millwall v West Ham United 4-0
Manchester United v Liverpool 3-1

Played on 24 May
The Arsenal v Tottenham Hotspur 0-0

Appendix 3

Representative and Friendly Matches 1939-1946

1939-40

Played on 16 Aug
Southerd United v Colchester United 2-2

Played on 19 Aug
For the Football League Jubilee Fund
Aston Villa v West Bromwich Albion 1-1
Blackpool v Preston North End 0-1
Bolton Wanderers v Bury 2-1
Brentford v Chelsea 1-5
Charlton Athletic v Millwall 1-1
Coventry City v Birmingham 3-2
Derby County v Leicester City 4-6
Grimsby Town v Lincoln City 3-2
Liverpool v Everton 2-1
Manchester United v Manchester City 1-1
Middlesbrough v Sunderland 3-3
Southampton v Portsmouth 0-3
Stoke City v Wolverhampton Wanderers 2-4
Tottenham Hotspur v Arsenal 0-1
Cardiff City v Swansea Town 1-1
Chesterfield v Barnsley 1-1
Ipswich Town v Norwich City 2-1
Newcastle United v Gateshead 3-0
Notts County v Nottingham Forest 1-1
Sheffield Wednesday v Sheffield United 2-4
Stockport County v Oldham Athletic 4-6
Watford v Luton Town 2-1
West Ham United v Fulham 3-3
Aldershot v Reading 3-3
Brighton & Hove Albion v Crystal Palace 3-3
Bristol Rovers v Bristol City 4-0
Queen's Park Rangers v Northampton Town 3-2
Southend United v Clapton Orient 1-1
Torquay United v Bournemouth & BA 3-1
Walsall v Mansfield Town 5-1
Accrington Stanley v Southport 6-1
Crewe Alexandra v Port Vale 6-1
Hartlepools United v Darlington 6-1
New Brighton v Tranmere Rovers 2-1
Rochdale v Halifax Town 3-1
Rotherham United v Doncaster Rovers 3-1
Wrexham v Chester 2-3
York City v Hull City 2-2
Huddersfield Town v Leeds United 5-0
Bradford v Bradford City 3-2
Burnley v Blackburn Rovers 3-1
Exeter City v Plymouth Argyle 1-2

Played on 9 Sep
Queen's Park Rangers v Army XI 10-2

Played on 16 Sep
Aldershot v Queen's Park Rangers 0-1
Barnsley v Huddersfield Town 2-1
Barrow v Preston North End reserves 1-0
Blackpool v Everton 2-1
Bolton Wanderers v Manchester United 2-2
Bournemouth & BA v Southampton 2-2
Bristol Rovers v Bristol City 3-2
Brighton & HA v Fulham 3-3
Burnley v Accrington Stanley 2-1
Bury v Manchester City 2-4
Cardiff City v Newport County 2-0
Chelmsford City v Arsenal 0-4
Chester v Liverpool 0-5
Chesterfield v Sheffield United 2-0
Doncaster Rovers v Bradford 0-0
Guildford City v Millwall 2-2
Halifax Town v Leeds United 3-2
Leicester City v Aston Villa 3-0
Luton Town v Brentford 3-2
Peterborough United v Nottingham Forest 4-3
Plymouth Argyle v Torquay United 3-2
Preston North End v Blackburn Rovers 3-1

Played on 16 Sep (continued)
Reading v Chelsea 0-4
Rochdale v Oldham Athletic 1-2
Shrewsbury Town v Port Vale 3-0
Southend United v Norwich City 6-2
Stoke City v Coventry 3-1
Swindon Town v Cheltenham 2-0
Stockport County v Southport 4-1
Clyde v Partick Thistle 3-1
St Mirren v Morton 3-4
St Johnstone v An Army XI 0-2

Played on 18 Sep
Blackburn Rovers v Preston North End 1-1

Played on 23 Sep
Accrington Stanley v Rochdale 6-4
Aldershot v Chelsea 2-3
Barnsley v Sheffield Wednesday 1-2
Barrow v Workington 6-3
Blackpool v Blackburn Rovers 1-1
Bournemouth & BA v West Ham United 1-2
Bradford City v Burnley 1-4
Brentford v Arsenal 3-0
Brighton & HA v Millwall 6-1
Bristol Rovers v Torquay United 1-1
Bury v Everton 3-2
Cardiff City v Swansea Town 1-1
Carlisle United v Preston North End 1-1
Chelmsford City v Tottenham Hotspur 4-2
Crewe Alexandra v New Brighton 5-2
Doncaster Rovers v Notts County 4-2
Guildford City v Crystal Palace 5-0
Halifax Town v Bradford 3-3
Huddersfield Town v Sheffield United 1-2
Leicester City v Birmingham 6-4
Liverpool v Bolton Wanderers 3-0
Luton Town v Charlton Athletic 3-2
Manchester United v Oldham Athletic 3-1
Millwall v Charlton Athletic 1-1
Newcastle United v Leeds United 2-2
Nottingham Forest v Grimsby Town 1-2
Plymouth Argyle v Bristol City 7-1
Portsmouth v Southampton 2-3
Preston North End v Manchester City 3-0
Reading v Newport County 5-0
Rotherham United v Chesterfield 1-3
Shrewsbury v Coventry City 0-6
Southend United v Fulham 4-3
Southport v Stockport County 0-0
Stoke City v Port Vale 3-2
Swindon Town v Queen's Park Rangers 1-0
West Bromwich Albion v Wolverhampton W 3-5
Wrexham v Chester 0-2
Aberdeen v Arbroath 4-0
Edinburgh City v Tank Corps XI 7-1
Heart of Midlothian v Hibernian 2-4
Celtic v Partick Thistle 4-2
Queen's Park v Third Lanark 3-4
Rangers v Falkirk 1-4
St Johnstone v Scottish Junior XI 3-3

Played on 25 Sep
Accrington Stanley v Blackburn Rovers 2-1

Played on 30 Sep
Accrington Stanley v Southport 1-3
Aldershot v Army PT Staff XI 2-2
Barrow v Carlisle United 4-3
Blackburn Rovers v Liverpool 0-5
Blackpool v Bolton Wanderers 2-0
Bradford v Grimsby Town 4-2
Brentford v Crystal Palace 3-0
Brighton & HA v Southampton 1-4
Bristol City v Plymouth Argyle 1-5

Played on 30 Sep (continued)
Burnley v Bury 1-3
Charlton Athletic v Fulham 1-1
Chelsea v Tottenham Hotspur 4-2
Chelmsford City v Charlton Athletic 1-1
Chester v Wrexham 3-2
Chesterfield v Huddersfield Town 1-0
Coventry City v Leicester City 3-3
Darlington v Hartlepools United 3-2
Derby County v Leeds United 1-3
Doncaster Rovers v Bradford City 1-2
Everton v Preston North End 3-3
Halifax Town v Sheffield United 1-1
Lincoln City v Nottingham Forest 0-6
Luton Town v Millwall 1-2
Manchester United v Manchester City 2-3
Newcastle United v Barnsley 1-2
Newport County v Birmingham 2-2
Notts County v Wolverhampton W 1-4
Oldham Athletic v Rochdale 5-3
Port Vale v Crewe Alexandra 5-0
Portsmouth v Chelsea 5-2
Reading v Arsenal 1-3
Rotherham United v Sheffield Wednesday 4-2
Southend United v Queen's Park Rangers 3-2
Swansea Town v Cardiff City 4-1
Swindon Town v Bristol Rovers 1-0
Tranmere Rovers v New Brighton 4-1
Torquay United v Bournemouth & BA 6-2
Watford v Northampton Town 4-0
West Bromwich Albion v Stoke City 6-0
West Ham United v Millwall 2-1
Hamilton Academical v Motherwell 2-3
Queen of the South v Preston North End 3-3
Morton v Rangers 4-2
Dundee v St Johnstone 4-2
Hibernian v St Mirren 5-1
Aldershot v Army Physical Training Corps 2-2

Played on 7 Oct
Aldershot v Millwall 1-2
Barnsley v Grimsby Town 2-2
Blackpool v Queen of the South 2-1
Bournemouth & BA v Torquay United 4-1
Bradford City v Leeds United 3-1
Bristol City v Bristol Rovers 5-5
Bury v Burnley 4-2
Cardiff City v Plymouth Argyle 1-1
Chelmsford City v Southend United 5-3
Chelsea v Arsenal 0-3
Chester v West Bromwich Albion 0-2
Chesterfield v Birmingham 3-2
Clapton Orient v Walthamstow Avenue 0-2
Coventry City v Wolverhampton W 0-4
Crewe Alexandra v Port Vale 2-0
Crystal Palace v Brighton & HA 2-2
Guildford City v Charlton Athletic 4-3
Halifax Town v Oldham Athletic 1-1
Hartlepools United v Darlington 1-1
Huddersfield Town v Blackburn Rovers 5-0
Hull City v Bradford 2-2
Leicester City v Sheffield United 2-2
Liverpool v Everton 1-4
Luton Town v Fulham 5-2
Millwall v Brentford 8-4
Newcastle United v Middlesbrough 3-2
New Brighton v Preston North End reserves 3-1
Newport County v Swansea Town 5-3
Northampton Town v Notts County 6-0
Nottingham Forest v Sheffield Wednesday 1-2
Preston North End v Bolton Wanderers 6-1
Queen's Park Rangers v Birmingham 2-3
Reading v Portsmouth 6-3
Rochdale v Accrington Stanley 1-1
Rotherham United v Doncaster Rovers 3-5

Appendix 3

Representative and Friendly Matches 1939-40 continued

Played on 7 Oct (continued)
Southend United v Watford 1-2
Stockport County v Manchester City 0-5
Stoke City v Manchester United 2-2
Swindon Town v Southampton 3-0
Tottenham Hotspur v West Ham United 0-2
Tunbridge Wells Rangers v Charlton Athletic 1-0
Wrexham v Tranmere Rovers 5-3
Heart of Midlothian v Partick Thistle 4-2
St Mirren v Hibernian 3-3
Kilmarnock v Clyde 5-5
Dunfermline Athletic v Rangers 'A' 2-1
Edinburgh City v Murrayfield Amateurs 2-4

Played on 11 Oct
Aldershot v Army Physical Training Corps 0-2

Played on 14 Oct
Accrington Stanley v Bradford City 3-2
Barrow v Preston North End reserves 2-0
Blackburn Rovers v Bury 2-2
Blackpool v Manchester United 6-4
Bolton Wanderers v Manchester City 2-2
Bournemouth & BA v Southampton 3-2
Bradford v Chesterfield 0-1
Brighton & HA v Southend United 0-4
Bristol Rovers v Cardiff City 1-2
Cardiff City v Swindon Town 3-1
Chelsea v Millwall 1-1
Carlisle United v Clyde 4-4
Chester v New Brighton 1-2
Clapton Orient v Finchley 6-1
Crewe Alexandra v Liverpool 0-1
Crystal Palace v Brentford 1-1
Doncaster Rovers v Rotherham United 3-2
Everton v Burnley 4-0
Guildford City v Aldershot 3-1
Halifax Town v Barnsley 2-1
Leeds United v Grimsby Town 2-2
Leicester City v Port Vale 2-2
Luton Town v Queen's Park Rangers 1-2
Middlesbrough v Hartlepools United 3-2
Newcastle United reserves v An Army XI 0-1
Norwich City v Northampton Town 6-1
Nottingham Forest v Notts County 2-1
Portsmouth v Bristol City 5-1
Preston North End v Newcastle United 4-0
Reading v Fulham 2-2
Scunthorpe United v Lincoln City 5-2
Sheffield Wednesday v Huddersfield Town 5-4
Southport v Oldham Athletic 4-0
South Shields v Darlington 3-2
Southend United v Shorts Sports 1-4
Stockport County v Rochdale 3-2
Stoke City v Birmingham 3-2
Swansea Town v Newport County 2-0
Torquay United v Plymouth Argyle 2-2
Tranmere Rovers v Wrexham 4-2
Watford v Charlton Athletic 2-0
West Ham United v Charlton Athletic 9-2
West Bromwich Albion v Coventry City 4-2
Wolverhampton W v Birmingham 1-0
York City v Sheffield United 2-4
Heart of Midlothian v Celtic 5-2
Falkirk v Alloa Athletic 4-4
Dumbarton v Rangers 'A' 4-3
Raith Rovers v Dunfermline Athletic 2-0
Hibernian 'A' v Leith Athletic 3-3

Played on 18 Oct
FA XI v Combined Services XI 1-0 *(at Aldershot)*

Played on 21 Oct
Barnsley v Leeds United 5-4

Played on 28 Oct
Bradford v Army XI 2-0

Played on 2 Nov
Chelsea v Metropolitan Police 4-1

Played on 4 Nov
Football League XI v All-British XI 3-3 *(at Goodison Park, Liverpool)*
Bury v York City 4-1
Doncaster Rovers v Huddersfield Town 5-1
Halifax Town v Chesterfield 0-2
Hartlepools United v Middlesbrough 4-5
Lincoln City v Rotherham United 6-3
Manchester City v Preston North End 2-2
New Brighton v Rhyl 4-2
Notts County v Birmingham 1-0
Sheffield United v Manchester United 3-0
Tranmere Rovers v Crewe Alexandra 5-4
Chelmsford City v Nottingham Forest 1-4
Chester v Stockport County 3-2

Played on 11 Nov
Sheffield United v Bradford City 4-1

Played on 18 Nov
Middlesbrough v vStockton 6-3
Bristol City v Nottingham Forest 3-9

Played on 25 Nov
Bishop Auckland v Darlington 3-3
FA XI v Army XI 4-1

Played on 2 Dec
Doncaster Rovers v FA XI 2-2
Scunthorpe United v Bradford 2-1

Played on 16 Dec
Barnsley v Bradford 2-3
Bolton Wanderers v Army XI 3-3
Bradford City v Rotherham United 3-2
Burnley v Manchester City 0-2
Chester v Bury 3-4
Chesterfield v Halifax Town 1-1
Crewe Alexandra v Shrewsbury Town 3-1
Doncaster Rovers v Huddersfield Town 2-2
Grimsby Town v Leeds United 5-5
Hull City v Notts County 4-5
Liverpool v Preston North End 0-1
Manchester United v Sheffield United 1-2
Nottingham Forest v Stockport County 6-0
Port Vale v West Bromwich Albion 1-4
Rochdale v Tranmere Rovers 2-0
Sheffield Wednesday v Stoke City 1-2
South Shields v Hartlepools United
York City v Lincoln City 3-3
Carlisle United v Newcastle United 2-5
Played on 23 Dec
Rotherham United v Bradford 1-2

Played on 25 Dec
Accrington Stanley v Preston North End 2-3
Bath City v Cardiff City 1-3
Blackburn Rovers v Doncaster Rovers 5-0
Blackpool v Preston North End 3-2
Bolton Wanderers v Stoke City 3-0
Bradford City v Huddersfield Town 1-4
Burnley v Barnsley 2-3
Bury v Leeds United 4-1
Carlisle United v Queen of the South 1-3
Chester v Birmingham 1-1
Chesterfield v Rotherham United 1-1
Crewe Alexandra v Rochdale 3-2
Darlington v Middlesbrough 1-5
Liverpool v Everton 2-3
Grimsby Town v Hull City 1-5

Played on 25 Dec (continued)
Luton Town v Chelsea 4-2
Manchester City v Manchester United 1-1
Mansfield Town v Lincoln City 2-2
Newcastle United v Gateshead 1-1
Notts County v Coventry City 1-1
Plymouth Argyle v Torpedo Depot XI 5-1
Port Vale v Northampton Town 1-1
Sheffield United v Sheffield Wednesday 2-1
Shrewsbury Town v Wrexham 0-3
Southport v New Brighton 2-0
Stockport County v Oldham Athletic 5-1
Tranmere Rovers v South Liverpool 4-1
Walsall v Darlington 2-1

Played on 26 Dec
Football League XI v All-British XI 3-2
Barnsley v Burnley 5-1
Cardiff City v Wolverhampton Wanderers 2-5
Coventry City v Notts County 8-2
Darlington v Bishop Auckland 6-2
Doncaster Rovers v Blackburn Rovers 2-1
Huddersfield Town v Sheffield United 5-0
Hull City v Grimsby Town 0-0
Leeds United v Bury 4-4
Everton v Liverpool 2-1
Manchester United v Manchester City 3-1
Newcastle United v Middlesbrough 1-1
Northampton Town v Port Vale 5-1
Nottingham Foreest v Leicester City 3-1
Oldham Athletic v Stockport County 0-0
Preston North End v Blackpool 1-1
Rhyl v New Brighton 1-4
Rochdale v Crewe Alexandra 2-2
Rotherham United v Bradford City 1-3
Southport v South Liverpool 2-1
Stoke City v Bolton Wanderers 1-5
Tranmere Rovers v Chester 6-3
Wrexham v Shrewsbury Town 3-1
York City v Carlisle United 3-3
Lincoln City v Mansfield Town 4-1

Played on 30 Dec
Accrington Stanley v New Brighton 4-2
Bradford City v Doncaster Rovers 5-2
Bury v Stoke City 7-6
Carlisle United v York City 4-2
Chesterfield v Rochdale 2-2
Darlington v Newcastle United 1-2
Everton v Blackpool 2-3
Halifax Town v Sheffield Wednesday 0-0
Middlesbrough v Barnsley 4-2
Notts County v West Bromwich Albion 4-0
Peterborough United v Lincoln City 4-1
Port Vale v Nottingham Forest 1-3
Preston North End v Liverpool 1-3
Rotherham United v Hull City 1-0
Sheffield United v leeds United 3-0
Stockport County v Bradford 7-4

Played on 1 Jan
Blackburn Rovers v Huddersfield Town 4-2
Barnsley v Sheffield Wednesday 5-0
Bolton Wanderers v Preston North End 3-1
Bury v Bradford 3-3
Chesterfield v Leicester City 7-2
Darlington v Leeds United 3-1
Carlisle United v Bradford City 2-2
Manchester United v Blackpool 1-4
Middlesbrough v Newcastle United 5-2
New Brighton v Accrington Stanley 6-0
Southport v Everton 2-2
Manchester City v Stockport County 7-2

Appendix 3

Representative and Friendly Matches 1939-40 continued

Played on 6 Jan
Cardiff City v Birmingham 4-5
Chelmsford City v FA XI 0-5
Newport County v Wolverhampton Wanderers 1-3
West Bromwich Albion v Sheffied Wednesday 0-3 *(abandoned)*

Played on 13 Jan
Chester v Shrewsbury Town 4-2
Everton v Tranmere Rovers 4-4
New Brighton v Liverpool 1-4
Accrington Stanley v Barnsley 2-1
Blackburn Rovers v Manchester City 1-2
Blackpool v Leeds United 0-1
Chesterfield v Bradford 5-0
Huddersfield Town v Grimsby Town 1-0 *(abandoned in the second half)*
Lincoln City v York City 4-3
Nottingham Forest v Birmingham International XI 0-1
Preston North End v Stoke City 2-1
Rochadale v Sheffield United 2-0
Newcastle United v Gateshead 3-1

Played on 20 Jan
England XI v Army XI 4-3

Played on 8 Feb
London Amateur XI v London Professional XI 2-4

Played on 17 Feb
Blackpool v Bolton Wanderers 2-1
Manchester United v Blackburn Rovers 6-2
Newcastle United v Preston North End 4-1
Manchester City v Sheffield Wednesday 3-1

Played on 18 Feb
French Army XI v British Army XI 1-2 *(at Lille, France)*

Played on 24 Feb
Accrington Stanley v Bradford 3-3
Oldham Athletic v Blackburn Roves 6-0

Played on 2 Mar
Football League XI v All-British XI 4-4 *(at Bradford)*

Played on 9 Mar
Football League XI v British Army XI 2-5 *(at Liverpool)*
Chelmsford City v West Bromwich Albion 3-1
Sheffield Wednesday v Bolton Wanderers 3-3
Swindon Town v Army XI 1-2

Played on 16 Mar
Scottish FA XI v Army XI 2-2 *(at Netherdale, Galashiels)*
Nottingham Forest v Army XI 3-0
Plymouth Argyle v United Services XI 9-1

Played on 18 Mar
League of Ireland v Irish League 2-0 *(at Dalymount Park, Dublin)*

Played on 22 Mar
All-British XI v Football League XI 1-1 *(at Bloomfield Road, Blackpool)*
Accrington Stanley v Halifax Town 5-2
Burnley v Huddersfield Town 2-3
Bury v Manchester United 3-1
Chelmsford City v Luton Town 5-4
Chester v Blackburn Rovers 0-0
Chesterfield v Stoke City 3-1
Doncaster Rovers v Leeds United 2-0
Everton v Wolverhampton Wanderers 4-2
Manchester City v Blackpool 5-3
Oldham Athletic v Rochdale 5-2
Plymouth Argyle v Royal Navy XI 3-0
Preston North End v Queen of the South 5-1
Stockport County v Bradford City 3-0
Swindon Town v Northampton Town 3-1

Played on 25 Mar
Blackpool v Manchester City 0-3
Cardiff City v West Bromwich Albion 1-1
Halifax Town v Bradford 2-1
Kettering v Mansfield Town 3-1
Leeds United v Doncaster Rovers 6-2
Leicester City v Sheffield Wednesday 5-2
Liverpool v Bolton Wanderers 0-1
Manchester United v Preston North End 5-1
Newcastle United v Sheffield United 2-1
Northampton Town v Swindon Town 5-2
Plymouth Argyle v Army XI 3-1
Rochdale v Oldham Athletic 3-1
Shrewsbury Town v Crewe Alexandra 1-1
Wolverhampton Wanderers v Everton 2-2

Played on 26 Mar
Huddersfield Town v Burnley 2-1
Barnsley v Grimsby Town 3-0

Played on 20 Apr
Scottish FA XI v Army XI 5-1 *(at Shielfield Park, Berwick)*
French Air Force XI v RAF XI 3-0 (at Paris)
Guildford City vAldershot 3-3

Played on 24 Apr
Scotland XI v Army XI 4-1 *(at Tynecastle Park, Edinburgh)*

Played on 27 Apr
Aberdeen v Rangers 'A' 5-1

Played on 4 May
Chelmsford City v Southampton 5-1
Oldham Athletic v Liverpool 2-4

Played on 6 May
East of Scotland FA XI v Army XI 6-2 *(at Tynecastle Park, Edinburgh)*

Played on 10 May
Kilmarnock v Ayrshire Juniors XI 5-5

Played on 11 May
Bedford Town v Mansfield Town 4-5
Chelmsford City v Charlton Athletic 1-1
Guildford City v Southampton 4-1
Millwall v Luton Town 4-4
New Brighton v Southport 2-2
Oldham Athletic v Preston North End 4-1
Falkirk v Stenhousemuir-Alloa XI 4-1
Fifeshire XI v Army XI *(at Stark's Park, Kirkcaldy)*

Played on 18 May
Millwall v Chelsea 2-3

Played on 25 May
Aldershot v Guildford City 6-1
Brentford v Brighton & Hove Albion 4-1
Northampton Town v Sheffield Wednesday 2-7

Played on 1 Jun
Birmingham v West Bromwich Albion 2-2
Clapton Orient v Millwall 2-3

Played on 30 Mar
FA XI v RAF XI 2-3
Bradford v Doncaster Rovers 1-1
Halifax Town v Accrington Stanley 3-1
Newcastle United v Sunderland 2-0

Played on 6 Apr
Hartlepools United v Sunderland 4-2

Appendix 3

Representative and Friendly Matches 1940-41

Played on 17 Aug
Watford v RAMC XI 9-1

Played on 24 Aug
Watford v RASC XI 0-0 (abandoned)

Played on 31 Aug
Birmingham v RAF XI 1-1
Chesterfield v Army XI 3-2

Played on 7 Sep
Southernd United v Highland regiment XI 1-0
(abandoned after 60 mins)

Played on 10 Sep
Lord Rosebery's XI v Polish Army XI 6-0 (at
Tynecastle Park, Edinburgh)

Played on 21 Sep
Notts County v Army XI 1-1

Played on 12 Oct
Lovell's Athletic v Swansea Town 5-1

Played on 19 Oct
Lincoln City v Nottingham Forest 2-3

Played on 26 Oct
Leeds United v Army XI 5-0
Bournemouth & BA v Army XI 10-0
British Army XI v Norwegian Army XI 8-4

Played on 2 Nov
Cardiff City v Army XI 18-1

Played on 9 Nov
Northampton Town v RAF XI 3-5
Nottingham Forest v RAF XI 1-4

Played on 23 Nov
Stoke City v RAF XI 2-2
Norwich City v Army XI 2-3
Army XI v RAF XI 6-1 (at Anlaby Road, Hull)

Played on 30 Nov
Army in Scotland v Army in England 1-4 (at Ibrox
Park, Glasgow)
Watford v Army XI 3-2
Brentford v RAF XI 1-2
Tranmere Rovers v Stoke City 2-2
RAF XI v Nottingham Forest 1-4

Played on 7 Dec
Army XI v RAF XI 2-1 (at Nottingham)
Army XI v Army XI 2-4 (at Manchester)
Halifax Town v RAF XI 1-3
Lincoln City v Army XI 6-5
Cambridge Town v Southend United 5-1

Played on 14 Dec
Scottish FA XI v Army XI 4-2 (at Stark's Park,
Kirkcaldy)
Notts County v FA XI 2-1
Southport v RAF XI 2-2
Swansea Town v RAF XI 5-2
Walsall v Army XI 5-1
Played on 21 Dec
Aldershot v Army XI 3-5
Chester v RAF XI 2-3
Bristol City v RAF XI 2-3
Newcastle United v Sunderland 3-1

Played on 28 Dec
Halifax Town v Bolton Wanderers 4-1
Metropolitan Police v Army XI 5-1

Played 11 Jan
Royal Navy XI v Army XI 1-5 (at Portman Road,
Ipswich)

Played on 18 Jan
All-British XI v Football League XI 3-5

Played on 25 Jan
Scottish FA XI v Army XI 1-0
Cambridge University v Luton Town 4-3

Played on 8 Feb
Stoke City v RAF XI 9-1
Swansea Town v RAF XI 4-2
RAF XI v Army XI 4-2
Shorts Sports v Norwich City 6-1

Played on 15 Feb
Army XI v FA XI 4-3

Played on 1 Mar
Rochdale v RAF XI 3-1

Played on 8 Mar
Notts County v Army XI 3-1
Army XI v RAF XI 2-2

Played on 15 Mar
Army XI v Huddersfield Town 1-6
Lincoln City RAF XI 3-4
Swansea Town v RAF XI 4-4
British Army XI v Allied Armies XI 8-2 (at
Stamford Bridge, London)

Played on 17 Mar
League of Ireland v NI Regional League 3-8 (at
Dalymount Park, Dublin)

Played on 22 Mar
RAF XI v Royal Navy XI 2-4
Norwich City v Czechoslovak Army XI 6-0

Played on 29 Mar
Northampton Town v Lincoln City (RAF) 2-4
D Compton's XI v Cullis' XI 4-4

Played on 5 Apr
Army XI v RAF XI 3-1
Royal Navy XI v Army XI 2-1
Norwich City v Dutch Army XI 7-0

Played on 12 Apr
Catterick Garrison v Middlesbrough 1-8
Stoke City v Army XI 7-2
Walsall v RAF XI 6-0

Played on 14 Apr
Newcastle United v Sunderland 3-4
Tranmere Rovers v RAF XI 4-4
Wrexham v Stoke City 5-2
NI Regional League v League of Ireland 2-1 (at
Windsor Park, Belfast)

Played on 19 Apr
Aldershot v Army XI 5-6
Football League XI v All-British XI 9-7

Played on 26 Apr
West Bromwich Albion v Aston Villa 1-6
Crystal Palace v RAF XI 3-2
United Services XI v RAF XI 2-3

Played on 3 May
Army XI v York City 1-0
Grimsby Town v RAF XI 4-2
Rochdale v RAF XI 6-1
Shorts Sports v Crystal Palace 2-3

Played on 10 May
Brighton & HA v Army XI 3-2
Services XI v Norwich City 4-1
Middlesbrough v Sunderland 3-4

Played on 17 May
Walsall v Aston Villa 4-3
Rotherham United v RAF XI 2-1
FA XI v Army XI 4-2
Scottish FA XI v Army XI 5-0

Played on 24 May
Brighton & HA v Army XI 4-1
Newcastle United v Services XI 0-4
West Bromwich Albion v RAF XI 6-1
Norwich City v RAF XI 0-4

Played on 31 May
Cardiff City v Wolverhampton W 5-1

Played on 2 Jun
Shorts Sports v Watford 6-3

Played on 4 Jun
RAF XI v Metropolitan Police XI ?-? (at Wembley
Stadium, London)

Played on 7 Jun
Brighton & HA v Allied Services XI 7-1

Appendix 3

Representative and Friendly Matches 1941-42

Played on 2 Aug
Heart of Midlothian v Arsenal 0-1

Played on 6 Sep
Birmingham v Czechoslovak Army 3-2
Bournemouth & BA v Army XI 2-3

Played on 13 Sep
Birmingham v Wolverhampton W 4-0
Troops in N Ireland v Army XI 1-4 *(at Windsor Park, Belfast)*
Cardiff City v Czechoslovak Army XI 0-0
Army XI v Southampton 5-2

Played on 15 Sep
Troops in N Ireland lost to Army XI

Played on 18 Sep
Troops in N Ireland lost to Army XI

Played on 20 Sep
Scottish FA XI v Army XI *(at Palmerston Park, Dumfries)*
Wolverhampton W v Birmingham 2-4

Played on 23 Sep
Irish FA XI v Army XI

Played on 27 Sep
Birmingham v RAF XI 2-0
Nottingham Forest v RAF XI 1-2

Played on 4 Oct
Birmingham v Army XI 2-4

Played on 11 Oct
Football League XI v Scottish Southern League XI 3-2 *(at Bloomfield Road, Blackpool)*

Played on 18 Oct
Army in Scotland XI v RAF XI 3-2 *(at Palmerston Park, Dumfries)*
Army XI v Bristol City 1-2
Northampton Town v Czechoslovak Army 5-2

Played on 25 Oct
Bristol City v Army XI 6-1

Played on 1 Nov
Bristol City v RAF XI 9-2
Nottingham Forest v RAF XI 3-1
West Bromwich Albion v Czechoslovak Army 3-1
Swansea Town v Belgian Army 10-1
Birmingham v Birmingham Works FA XI 3-0

Played on 8 Nov
Army in Scotland XI v Army in England XI 1-3 *(at Ibrox Park, Glasgow)*
Birmingham v All-Welsh XI 2-3
Southampton v Southampton Police 5-2
Bournemouth &BA v Army XI 5-1

Played on 15 Nov
Aston Villa v Birmingham 7-0
Army XI v Southampton 3-3
Swansea Town v Army XI 7-5
RAF XI v Army-Navy XI 5-1

Played on 22 Nov
Birmingham v Czechoslovak Army 4-0
FA XI v RAF XI 2-7
Norwich City v RAF XI 9-2

Played on 29 Nov
Birmingham v Aston Villa 0-1
Royal Navy XI v Norwich City -3

Played on 6 Dec
Birmingham v Army XI 3-6
Southampton v Royal Navy XI 4-5
Metropolitan Police XI v Army XI 4-1
Fenerbachce v British Army XI 2-2 *(at Istanbul, Turkey)*

Played on 13 Dec
FA XI v RAF XI 2-2 *(at Elland Road, Leeds)*
Leicester City v Czechoslovak Army 8-1
Southampton v Army XI 3-2
Norwich City v Army XI 4-3
Notts County v Polish Army 1-3

Played on 20 Dec
Army XI v Norwich City 1-6
West Bromwich Albion v Birmingham 4-1
Bournemouth & BA v Army XI 7-3
Scottish Command XI v AA Command XI 3-1

Played on 25 Dec
Bournemouth & BA v RAF XI 4-0
Norwich City v The Gunners XI 4-2
Nottingham Forest v Mansfield Town 3-0

Played on 26 Dec
Aston Villa v Birmingham 4-1
Netherlands XI v W Swann's XI 0-5

Played on 10 Jan
Norwich City v Army XI 6-3
Rotherham United v Army XI 1-4
Southampton v Army XI 1-3
Derby County v Czechoslovak Army 11-4
RAF XI v Free French Air Force 9-1
Army XI v RAF XI 0-0

Played on 17 Jan
RAF XI v Lincoln City 2-5
England XI v Scotland XI 3-0 *(at Wembley Stadium, London)*

Played on 24 Jan
Swansea Town v RAF XI 1-4
Royal Navy XI v Dutch Army 5-3

Played on 7 Feb
Derby County v AA Command XI 1-4

Played on 14 Feb
Northampton Town v AA Command XI 7-1
Army XI v RAF XI 1-1

Played on 21 Feb
Northern Command XI v Scottish Command XI 1-1 *(at Elland Road, Leeds)*
RAF XI v Bristol City 6-1
Coventry City v Czechoslovak Army 4-1
Shorts Sports v Metropolitan Police XI 2-4
Derby County v Belgian Army 3-3
Army XI v RAF XI 4-1 *(at Bristol)*

Played on 28 Feb
RAF XI v Bristol City 2-2

Played on 7 Mar
Cardiff City v RAF XI 3-3
Norwich City v Army XI 0-2

Played on 14 Mar
Army XI v FA XI 3-1
Aston Villa v Birmingham 4-0
Army XI v Norwich City 0-13
Lincoln City v RAF XI 1-2
Southampton v Royal Navy XI 6-1
Wolverhampton W v RAF XI 3-4

Played on 17 Mar
League of Ireland v NI Regional League 2-2 *(at Dalymount Park, Dublin)*

Played on 21 Mar
Derby County v Birmingham 2-2
Rotax Cyfarthfa v Wolverhampton W 1-9

Played on 28 Mar
Norwich City v Army XI 7-4
West Bromwich Albion v Aston Villa 1-2
Wolverhampton W v Army XI 1-0

Played on 4 Apr
Army in England XI v Army in Scotland XI 4-1 *(at Sheffield)*
Birmingham v RAF XI 1-1
Bournemouth & BA v Army XI 2-2

Played on 6 Apr
Bournemouth & BA v Army XI 5-3
Birmingham v Aston Villa 2-1
Royal Navy XI v Free French Forces 8-3
Derby County v RAF XI 0-0
Luton Town v Metropolitan Police XI 6-2
NI Regional League v League of Ireland 5-2 *(at Windsor Park, Belfast)*

Played on 18 Apr
Netherlands v France 2-0 *(at London)*
Chester v Birmingham 3-3
Army XI v Southampton 2-6
E Command XI v London Command XI 1-2

Played on 25 Apr
Millwall v Arsenal 2-2

Played on 2 May
Football League XI v W Command XI 5-3 *(at Molineux Grounds, Wolverhampton)*
Birmingham v Leicester City 0-3
Aldershot v Southampton 3-1
Crystal Palace v Chrlton Athletic 1-3
N Command XI v Barnsley 1-5 *(at Doncaster)*
Portsmouth v West Ham United 2-1
Derby County v N Command XI 3-2

Played on 9 May
Brentford v Chelsea 2-0
Leicester City v Birmingham 4-2
Reading v Aldershot 0-0
Southampton v Army XI 3-2
West Ham United v Fulham 4-2
Tranmere Rovers v Army XI 5-0
Clapton Orient v Leyton 0-1

Played on 16 May
Bolton Wanderers v RAF XI 1-4
Charlton Athletic v Millwall 4-1
E Command XI v Norwich City 8-1
Portsmouth v Aldershot 4-4
Reading v Crystal Palace 1-2
West Ham United v Chelsea 5-2

Played on 23 May
Aldershot v Reading 1-0
Bolton Wanderers v RAF XI 2-3
West Ham United v Millwall 6-2
Everton v W Command XI 3-7
Portsmouth v Army XI 3-3
Welsh Services XI v Police XI 3-6 *(at Cardiff)*
RAF Arsenal XI v RAF Select XI 1-1 *(at White Hart Lane, London)*

Appendix 3

Representative and Friendly Matches 1941-42 continued

Played on 25 May
Bristol City v E Davis' XI 1-2
Coventry City v Birmingham 4-2
Crystal Palace v Tottenham Hotspur 3-5
Derby County v Stoke City 2-1
Everton v Bolton Wanderers 7-3
Fulham v Chelsea 4-1
Millwall v Charlton Athletic 4-2
Preston North End v Blackburn Rovers 2-1
West Bromwich Albion v Aston Villa 3-4

Played on 30 May
Aston Villa v RAF XI 1-2
Grimsby Town v RAF XI 2-2
Welsh XI v W Command XI 4-1
West Bromwich Albion v Birmingham 4-1
Newcastle United v Aberdeen 1-1

Played on 6 Jun
FA XI v RAF XI 6-6 *(at Luton)*
Liverpool v Royal Artillery XI 2-3
Bristol City v Football League XI 3-8
W Command XI v Welsh XI 0-2 *(at Wrexham)*

Representative and Friendly Matches 1942-43

Played on 1 Aug
Hibernian v RAF XI 1-3
St Mirren v Services XI 3-4

Played on 5 Sep
FA XI v Civil Defence XI 4-1 *(at Griffin Park, Brentford)*

Played on 12 Sep
Irish FA XI v ArmyXI 3-2 *(at Windsor Park, Belfast)*

Played on 19 Sep
Scottish XI v Army XI 1-3 *(at Palmerston Park, Dumfries)*

Played on 26 Sep
Wales v RAF XI 1-3 *(at Vetch Field, Swansea)*

Played on 17 Oct
N Command XI v Football League XI 2-9 *(at Bootham Crescent, York)*

Played on 7 Nov
Scottish Army XI v Dutch Army XI 8-0 *(at Cappielow Park, Greenock)*
Metropolitan Police XI v Royal Artillery XI 7-0

Played on 14 Nov
Army XI v Civil Defence XI 8-2 *(at The Den, London)*
Metropolitan Police XI v Dutch United Services XI 5-0

Played on 21 Nov
FA XI v RAF XI 4-3 *(at Victoria Ground, Stoke)*
National Police XI v N Command XI 3-2 *(at Oakwell, Barnsley)*
Navy (Suffolk) XI v Dutch Army XI 2-0 *(at Portman Road, Ipswich)*

Played on 28 Nov
N Command XI v Polish Army XI 6-1 *(at Anlaby Road, Hull)*
Belgian Army XI v Czechoslovak Army XI 5-0 *(at Somerton Park, Newport)*
W Command XI v Football League XI 2-0 *(at Ninian Park, Cardiff)*
Metropolitan Police XI v RN & RM Portsmouth 2-1

Played on 5 Dec
RAF XI v Scotland XI 4-0 *(at St James' Park, Newcastle)*
SE Command XI v AA Command XI 4-7 *(at Elm Park, Reading)*
Royal Artillery XI v Royal Marines XI 1-4

Played on 12 Dec
Netherlands v Belgium 0-0 *(at Griffin Park, Brentford)*
RAF XI v W Command XI 6-1 *(at Bloomfield Road, Blackpool)*
Infantry Training Centre XI v Dundee United 3-5 *(at Muirton Park, Perth)*

Played on 19 Dec
Belgians v Norwegians 2-1 *(at Newport)*
Dundee United v Midland Junior Select 4-2

Played on 26 Dec
Army XI v RAF XI 3-1 *(at Elland Road, Leeds)*

Played on 1 Jan
Army XI v RAF XI 1-1 *(at Gayfield Park, Arbroath)*

Played on 23 Jan
E Command XI v London District XI 2-1 *(at Watford))*

Played on 30 Jan
RAF XI v National Police XI 2-0 *(at Upton Park, London)*

Played on 6 Feb
Army XI v Belgian Army XI 5-0 *(at Recreation Ground, Aldershot)*

Played on 13 Feb
E Command XI v Football League XI 2-2 *(at Portman Road, Ipswich)*

Played on 20 Feb
France v Netherlands 5-4 *(at Dulwich Hamlet)*

Played on 27 Feb
SE Command XI v London District XI 6-3 *(at Recreation Ground, Aldershot)*

Played on 13 Mar
Mansfield Town v Army XI 1-2
Northampton Town v E Command XI 5-6
Metropolitan Police Amateur XI v United States Army XI 3-0 *(at Imber Court, London)*

Played on 17 Mar
League of Ireland v NI Regional League 0-1 *(at Dalymount Park, Dublin)*

Played 27 Mar
Bolton Wanderers v RAF XI 7-3
Cardiff City v RAF XI 1-3
Rotax v Wolverhampton Wanderers 3-5
E Command XI v Navy (Suffolk) XI 5-5 *(at Portman Road, Ipswich)*

Played 3 Apr
Cardiff City v W Command 5-4
Royal Artillery XI v RNAS XI 0-7

Played on 10 Apr
Bury v Bury Amateurs 3-2
National Police XI v Army XI 2-1
Shorts Sports v Wolverhampton Wanderers 2-5
Southport v RAF XI 4-3

Played on 17 Apr
Aldershot v Watford 4-2
Brentford v Crystal Palace 3-0
Brighton & HA v Fulham 0-9
Luton Town v Arsenal 1-4
Preston North End v Burnley 3-0
Queen's Park Rangers v Tottenham Hotspur 1-1
Southampton v Millwall 9-3
West Ham United v Portsmouth 1-1
Aberdeen v Morton 3-1

Played on 24 Apr
Aldershot v Fulham 3-3
Crystal Palace v Brentford 2-2
Everton v Preston North End 4-0
Millwall v Clapton Orient 2-2
Portsmouth v Southampton 0-0
Reading v West Ham United 3-0
Tottenham Hotspur v Charlton Athletic 2-1
E Command XI v SE Command XI 4-7 *(at Layer Road, Colchester)*

Played on 26 Apr
Norwegian Forces XI v Belgian Army XI 1-0 *(at Stamford Bridge, London)*
Bolton Wanderers v RAF XI 5-2
Crystal Palace v Millwall 4-2
Doncaster Rovers v Nottingham Forest 3-3
Portsmouth v Aldershot 3-2
Queen's Park Rangers v Watford 3-2
Preston North End v Blackburn Rovers 3-3
Tottenham Hotspur v Fulham 3-0
West Ham United v Southampton 4-0
NI Regional League v League of Ireland 2-2 *(at Windsor Park, Belfast)*

Played on 1 May
Brentford v Millwall 5-3
Grimsby Town v RAF XI 5-1
Portsmouth v Reading 4-2
Preston North End v Bury 2-4
Southampton v West Ham United 5-1
Tottenham Hotspur v Clapton Orient 4-3
Shorts Sports v Crystal Palace 0-6
Bath City v Army XI 1-2
Rochdale v RAF XI 2-2
N Command v W Command 4-3 *(at St James' Park, Newcastle)*

Played on 8 May
France v Belgium 0-7 *(at Shepherd's Bush, London)*
Army XI v Chester 4-11 *(at Buckley)*
Aston Villa v Portsmouth 1-1
Coventry City v RAF XI 2-1
RAF XI v Derby County 0-3 *(at Fauld)*
Tottenham Hotspur v Arsenal 1-2
Tranmere Rovers v Preston North End 6-1
Clapton Orient v Shorts Sports 2-5

Played on 15 May
Bath City v Bristol City 5-1
Chester v W Command 1-3
Derby County v National Police XI 2-0
Wrexham v Stoke City 1-2
Army XI v Military Police XI 5-4

Played on 22 May
Aberdeen Select v Army XI 4-5

Appendix 3

Representative and Friendly Matches 1943-44

Played on 7 Aug
Heart of Midlothian v RAF XI 3-2

Played on 11 Sep
Northern Ireland XI v Army XI 4-2 *(at Windsor Park, Belfast)*
RAF XI v Civil Defence XI 6-0 *(at Selhurst Park, London)*

Played on 2 Oct
AA Command XI v RAF North West XI 3-3 *(at Blackpool)*

Played on 9 Oct
England XI v Scottish-Welsh XI 3-6 *(at Chesterfield)*

Played on 23 Oct
Scottish Command XI v N Command XI 3-4 *(at Dens Park, Dundee)*

Played on 30 Oct
Cardiff City All Guest Team v W Command XI 1-0
E Command XI v AA Command XI 1-4 *(at Ipswich)*
AA XI v West Riding XI 3-2

Played on 6 Nov
Scottish XI v RAF XI 1-2 *(at Hampden Park, Glasgow)*

Played on 13 Nov
N Command XI v W Command XI 3-4
Aberdeen v Scottish Command XI 0-5

Played on 27 Nov
FA XI v Civil Defence Force XI 5-4 *(at Luton)*

Played on 11 Dec
E Command XI v Belgian Army XI 6-2 *(at Norwich)*
RAF XI v Military XI 3-1 *(at Grimsby)*
W Command XI v AA Command XI 3-5 *(at Victoria Ground, Stoke)*

Played on 18 Dec
Infantry Training Centre XI v RA XI 6-3

Played on 25 Dec
East Fife v Raith Rovers 1-3

Played on 1 Jan
Scottish Command v W Command 0-0 *(at Somerset Park, Ayr)*

Played on 8 Jan
AA Command v S Command XI 1-1 *(at Bristol)*

Played on 22 Jan
FA XI v RAF XI 2-4 *(at Bristol)*
W Command XI v RAF XI 6-1 *(at Chester)*

Played on 29 Jan
E Command XI v SE Command XI 4-6 *(at Wrexham)*
N Command XI v Polish Forces XI 3-2 *(at Catterick)*

Played on 5 Feb
Army XI v Civil Defence Force XI 4-3 *(at Derby)*

Played on 12 Feb
N Command XI v National Police & NFS XI 01 *(at Grimsby)*
SE Command XI v AA Command XI 1-0 *(at Chatham)*
W Command XI v RAF North West XI 3-5 *(at Wolverhampton)*

Played on 26 Feb
Scottish Command XI v AA Command XI 2-2 *(at Dumfries)*
Gillingham v London Fire Force XI 3-1

Played on 4 Mar
Scottish Command XI v AA Command XI 2-2 *(at Greenock)*
Gillingham v RA Depot (Woolwich) XI 1-6

Played on 11 Mar
FA XI v Army XI 2-5 *(at Stoke)*
London District XI v E Command XI 5-0 *(at Brentford)*
Gillingham v Belgian Army XI 4-1

Played on 17 Mar
League of Ireland v NI Regional League 3-4 *(at Dalymount Park, Dublin)*

Played on 1 Apr
Army XI v RAF XI 4-0 *(at Tynecastle Park, Edinburgh)*
Blackburn Rovers v Blackpool Services 3-0
Crystal Palace v Millwall 7-0
Gillingham v Royal Navy XI 5-2
Preston North End v Chester 2-3
Brighton & HA v Clapton Orient 4-2

Played on 8 Apr
British United Services XI v Allied United Services XI 3-3 *(at Reading)*
Blackpool Services v Blackburn Rovers 1-2
Brentford v Queen's Park Rangers 2-1
Gillingham v Ford Sports 4-1
Luton Town v Fulham 2-2
Portsmouth v Southampton 2-1
West Ham United v Watford 4-2
Wolverhampton W v Wath Wanderers 7-2

Played on 10 Apr
E Command XI v London District XI 1-4 *(at Ipswich)*
Mansfield Town v AA XI 3-2
Newcastle United v Preston North End 2-2
Millwall v Tottenham Hotspur 0-0
Blackpool Services v Burnley 4-1
Gillingham v Northampton Town 1-2
NI Regional League v League of Ireland 2-2 *(at Windsor Park, Belfast)*

Played on 15 Apr
Scotland ATC XI v England ATC XI 0-2
Aldershot v Fulham 3-3
Crystal Palace v West Ham United 4-1
Preston North End v Blackburn Rovers 1-6
Southampton v Portsmouth 3-0
Gillingham v AA XI 8-2

Played on 22 Apr
Gillingham v AA XI 2-5
Shropshire XI v Crewe Alexandra 1-1 *(at Shrewsbury)*

Played on 29 Apr
Gillingham v AA XI 5-2
England XI v Combined Services XI 3-1 *(at Stamford Bridge, London)*
Scottish Command XI v Netherlands XI 7-0 *(at Dumfries)*

Played on 6 May
Gillingham v AA XI 9-4
Grimsby Town v RAF XI 0-4
Tranmere Rovers v RAF XI 1-3

Played on 13 May
RN & RM XI v Civil Defence XI 4-4
Aston Villa v Portsmouth 3-3
Derby County v Huddersfield Town 3-4
Newcastle United v North east XI 3-3
Wolverhampton W v RAF XI 2-1

Played on 20 May
W Command XI v RAF XI 2-3 *(at Liverpool)*
Scottish Command XI v Celtic 3-3 *(at Ayr)*

Appendix 3

Representative and Friendly Matches 1944-45

Played on 5 Aug
Dundee v Army XI 0-7
Edinburgh Select XI v Aston Villa 3-4

Played on 19 Aug
Army XI v Selected XI 3-6
Burnley v National Police 3-2
Coventry City v Tottenham Hotspur 3-1
Everton v Liverpool 2-5
Lincoln City v RAF XI 6-2
Manchester City v Manchester United 2-2
Sheffield Wednesday v Huddersfield Town 3-2
RAF XI v W Command XI 2-2

Played 2 Sep
Wales v RAF XI 1-1

Played on 9 Sep
Ireland XI v Combined Services XI 4-8 *(at Belfast)*

Played on 30 Sep
Cumberland Services XI v W Command XI 1-1 *(at Whitehaven)*

Played on 7 Oct
E Command XI v AA Command XI 2-8 *(at Ipswich)*
London District XI v SE Command XI 5-1 *(at Brentford)*

Played on 21 Oct
N Command XI v W Command XI 6-1
National Police v NFS & CD XI 3-1

Played on 28 Oct
Canadian Forces XI v Norwegian Forces XI 6-1
Metropolitan Police v London Fire Service XI 1-3

Played on 11 Nov
W Command XI v AA Command XI 3-3 *(at Bolton)*

Played on 18 Nov
S Command XI v RN & RM XI 9-0 *(at Portsmouth)*

Played on 25 Nov
E Command XI v SE Command XI 2-10 *(at Luton)*
RAF XI v Scotland XI 1-7 *(at Sheffield)*

Played on 9 Dec
FA XI v Army XI 1-1 *(at Bradford)*

Played on 16 Dec
E Command XI v National Police XI 3-1 *(at Ipswich)*
N Command XI v Scottish Command XI 5-2 *(at Darlington)*
Belgium XI v Army-RAF XI 2-1 *(at Brussels)*

Played on 23 Dec
Dundee United v Celtic 'A' 2-1
Arbroath v Arbroath Junior XI 2-2

Played on 26 Dec
Bath City v League West XI 1-5
Bristol Rovers v Bristol City 0-5
Swansea Town v RAF XI 4-4

Played on 1 Jan
Scottish Command XI v W Command XI 0-2 *(at Ayr)*

Played on 6 Jan
Belgium v Scottish Services XI 2-3 *(at Brussels)*
Played 13 Jan
AA Command XI v SE Command XI 3-6 *(at Selhurst Park, London)*
London District XI v E Command XI 6-7 *(at Brentford)*

Played on 20 Jan
FA XI v RAF XI 4-6 *(at Coventry)*

Played on 10 Feb
N Command XI v AA Command XI 2-2 *(at Mansfield)*

Played on 17 Feb
Royal Navy XI v Army XI 0-2 *(at Ipswich)*
Metropolitan Police v Royal Netherlands Navy XI 3-1

Played on 24 Feb
W Command XI v N Command XI 2-0 *(at Wolverhampton)*

Played on 3 Mar
Sheffield United v Polish AF XI 2-1

Played 10 Mar
Army XI v RAF XI 0-0 *(at Newcastle)*
Rotherham United v Polish AF XI 4-1

Played on 17 Mar
W Command XI v London District XI 5-0 *(at Stoke)*
N Command XI v Combined Universities XI 2-3 *(at Bishop Auckland)*
Luton Town v Fulham 1-0
Notts County v Aston Villa reserves 4-1
League of Ireland v NI Regional League 2-1 *(at Dalymount Park, Dublin)*

Played on 24 Mar
Diables Rouge v FA Services XI 1-8 *(at Bruges)*

Played on 25 Mar
Belgium v FA Services XI 2-3 *(at Brussels)*

Played on 2 Apr
Barnsley v Charlton Athletic 4-0
Coventry City v Polish AF XI 2-2
E Command XI v London District XI 2-3
Gillingham v Clapton Orient 4-3
Northampton Town v Watford 3-3
Southampton v Brighton & HA 3-2
NI Regional League v League of Ireland 3-5 *(at Windsor Park, Belfast)*

Played on 7 Apr
Crystal Palace v Tottenham Hotspur 3-1
Fulham v Arsenal 0-3
Portsmouth v Southampton

Played on 21 Apr
Diables Rouge v FA Touring XI 0-0 *(at Liege)*
Tranmere Rovers v South Liverpool 0-0
S Command XI v London District XI 4-2

Played on 5 May
Millwall v Queen's Park Ranges 3-2
Portsmouth v Crystal Palace 4-5
Nottingham Forest v Chelmsford City 3-0
East Fife v Queen's Park 1-1
Hibernian v Scottish Services XI 2-2

Played on 9 May
Victory in Europe Cup
Celtic v Queen's Park 1-1 *(Celtic won on corners)*

Played on 12 May
England ATC XI v Scotland ATC XI 8-0 *(at Tottenham)*
RAF XI v Services XI 8-2 (at Montrose)
Maidstone United v Arsenal 1-1

Played on 19 May
RAF XI v Queen's Park 5-1 *(at Inverness)*
Fulham v Queen's Park Rangers 0-3
Leicester City v Crystal Palace 0-1
Plymouth Argyle v Cardiff City 1-2
Tottenham Hotspur v Arsenal 4-0

Played on 21 May
Charlton Athletic v Millwall 2-2
Cardiff City v League West XI 5-4
Southampton v Chelsea 4-6

Played on 26 May
Cardiff City v Plymouth Argyle 2-2
Crystal palace v Leicester City 1-4
Gillingham v Charlton Athletic 7-3
Luton Town v E Command XI 2-7
West Ham United v Brentford 0-5
Tottenham Hotspur v Fulham 2-2

Played on 9 Jun
France v British Army 4-2

Played on 7 Jul
Scotland ATC v Wales ATC 2-2 *(at Tynecastle Park, Edinburgh)*

Played on 14 Jul
RAF v Royal Navy 7-1

Appendix 3

Representative and Friendly Matches 1945-46

Played on 2 Aug
Combined Services XI v Arsenal 1-6

Played on 4 Aug
Edinburgh Select v Huddersfield Town 4-0
(at Tynecastle Park, Edinburgh)

Played on 11 Aug
Stirling Albion v Airdrieonians 'A' 3-1

Played on 25 Aug
Stirling Albion v Dundee 'A' 1-2
Brechin City v Montrose 3-5
Edinburgh City v Forfar Athletic 5-6

Played on 15 Sep
Stirling Albion v Celtic XI 3-4

Played on 16 Sep
Oslo XI v Scottish Command 1-2 *(at Oslo)*

Played on 25 Sep
Rangers v Newcastle United 3-2

Played on 1 Oct
Dundee v Army XI

Played on 13 Oct
Belgian Army XI v British Army XI 2-3 *(at Anderlecht)*

Played on 13 Nov
Chelsea v Moscow Dynamo 3-3

Played on 17 Nov
Cardiff City v Moscow Dynamo 1-10
Coventry City v Chester 1-5
Norwich City v Crystal Palace 2-5
Army XI v Royal Navy XI 2-3 *(at Ipswich)*

Played on 21 Nov
Arsenal XI v Moscow Dynamo 3-4

Played on 24 Nov
Crystal Palace v Norwich City 4-0
Chester v Coventry City 3-2

Played on 28 Nov
Rangers v Moscow Dynamo 2-2

Played on 8 Dec
Bradford City v Doncaster Rovers 5-4
Crystal Palace v Clapton Orient 5-1
Torquay United v Polish Navy XI 3-1

Played on 15 Dec
Bradford City v Chester 2-2
Crewe Alexandra v Walsall 2-3
Norwich City v Southend United 4-3
Chelmsford City v Clapton Orient 2-1

Played on 22 Dec
Queen's Park Rangers v Bristol City 1-2

Played on 25 Dec
Gillingham v Brighton & HA

Played on 29 Dec
Watford v Polish Sir Force XI 6-2

Played on 1 Jan
Scottish Command XI v W Command XI 3-4

Played on 5 Jan
Sunderland v Reading 5-4
Tranmere Rovers v Southport 3-0

Played on 26 Jan
Bournemouth & BA v Argyll & Sutherland Highlanders 4-0
Everton v Fulham 10-1
Plymouth Argyle v Crystal Palace 4-7

Played on 9 Feb
Luton Town v Chesterfield 0-2
Newcastle United v Huddersfield Town 2-3

Played on 20 Feb
W Command XI v Royal Engineers XI 4-2

Played on 2 Mar
Stirling Albion v ITC XI 4-2
Fulham v Arsenal 2-1
Preston North End v Leicester City 2-3
Tottenham Hotspur v Chelsea 4-2
Burnley v Polish Air F\orce XI 6-1

Played on 7 Mar
E Command v AA Command *(at Colchester)*

Played on 9 Mar
Millwall v Newcastle United 1-7

Played on 13 Mar
S Command XI v London District XI 1-3
Army XI v RAF XI 3-0 *(at Stamford Bridge, London)*

Played on 16 Mar
Crewe Alexandra v Bradford City 4-0
Oldham Athletic v Stockport County 0-3

Played on 18 Mar
League of Ireland v NI Regional League 1-2 *(at Dalymount Park, Dublin)*

Played on 23 Mar
Stirling Albion v St Roch's 6-2
Montrose v RAF XI 4-3

Played on 30 Mar
Clachnacuddin v Dundee 0-4
Edinburgh City v St Johnstone 'A' 4-2

Played on 6 Apr
English XI v APTC XI 3-5
St Johnstone v Queen's Park 2-0

Played on 22 Apr
NI Regional League v League of Ireland 3-0 *(at Windsor Park, Belfast)*

Played on 1 May
Torquay United v Fulham 2-3

Appendix 4

International Matches

THE GREAT WAR
MILITARY INTERNATIONAL
Played on 13 May 1916 at Goodison Park, Liverpool att 22,000
England v Scotland 4-3

NOTE this was a match played between two military XIs

VICTORY INTERNATIONALS
Played on 26 Apr 1919 at Goodison Park, Liverpool att 45,000
England v Scotland 2-2

Played on 3 May 1919 at Hampden Park, Glasgow att 80,000
Scotland v England 3-4

Played on 11 Oct 1919 at Ninian Park, Cardiff att 20,000
Wales v England 2-1

Played on 19 Oct 1919 at The Victoria Ground, Stoke att 16,000
England v Wales 2-0

THE SECOND WORLD WAR
Played on 11 Nov 1939 at Ninian Park, Cardiff att 28,000
Wales v England 1-1

Played on 18 Nov 1939 at The Racecourse Ground, Wrexham att 17,000
Wales v England 2-3

Played on 2 Dec 1939 at St James' Park, Newcastle att 15,000
England v Scotland 2-1

Played on 13 Apr 1940 at Wembley Stadium, London att 40,000
England v Wales

Played on 11 May 1940 at Hampden Park, Glasgow att 75,000
Scotland v England 1-1

Played on 08 Feb 1941 at St James' Park, Newcastle att 25,000
England v Scotland 2-3

Played on 16 Apr 1941 at City Ground, Nottingham att 13,016
England v Wales 4-1

Played on 03 May 1941 at Hampden Park, Glasgow att 78,000
Scotland v England 1-3

Played on 07 Jun 1941 at Ninian Park, Cardiff att 20,000
Wales v England 2-3

Played on 04 Oct 1941 at Wembley Stadium, London att 65,000
England v Scotland 2-0

Played on 25 Oct 1941 at St Andrews, Birmingham att 25,000
England v Wales 2-1

Played on 17 Jan 1942 at Wembley Stadium, London att 64,000
England v Scotland 3-0

Played on 18 Apr 1942 at Hampden Park, Glasgow att 91,000
Scotland v England 5-4

Played on 09 May 1942 at Ninian Park, Cardiff att 30,000
Wales v England 1-0

Played on 10 Oct 1942 at Wembley Stadium, London att 75,000
England v Scotland 0-0

Played on 24 Oct 1942 at Molyneux Grounds, Wolverhampton att 25,097
England v Wales 1-2

Played on 27 Feb 1943 at Wembley Stadium, London att 75,000
England v Wales 5-3

Played on 17 Apr 1943 at Hampden Park, Glasgow att 105,000
Scotland v England 0-4

Played on 08 May 1943 at Ninian Park, Cardiff att 25,000
Wales v England 1-1

Played on 25 Sep 1943 at Wembley Stadium, London att 80,000
England v Wales 8-3

Played on 16 Oct 1943 at Maine Road, Manchester att 60,000
England v Scotland 8-0

Played on 19 Feb 1944 at Wembley Stadium, London att 80,000
England v Scotland 6-2

Played on 22 Apr 1944 at Hampden Park, Glasgow att 133,000
Scotland v England 2-3

Played on 06 May 1944 at Ninian Park, Cardiff att 50,000
Wales v England 0-2

Played on 16 Sep 1944 at Anfield Road, Liverpool att 38,483
England v Wales 2-2

Played on 14 Oct 1944 at Wembley Stadium, London att 90,000
England v Scotland 6-2

Played on 03 Feb 1945 at Villa Park, Birmingham att 65,780
England v Scotland 3-2

Played on 14 Apr 1945 at Hampden Park, Glasgow att 133,000
Scotland v England 1-6

Played on 05 May 1945 at Ninian Park, Cardiff att 25,000
Wales v England 2-3

Appendix 4

International Matches continued

VICTORY INTERNATIONAL
Played on 26 May 1945 at Wembley Stadium, London att 65,000
England v France 2-2

UNOFFICIAL INTERNATIONAL FOR THE SWISS FA 50th ANNIVERSARY
Played on 21 Jul 1945 at Berne, Neufeld Stadion, Berne att 35,000
Switzerland v England 3-1

UNOFFICIAL INTERNATIONAL
Played on 24 Jul 1945 at Grasshoppers Stadium, Zurich
Switzerland 'B' v England 0-3

NOTE The two games listed against Switzerland were later re-classed as Services XI, but at the time were viewed as being official matches.

VICTORY INTERNATIONAL
Played on 15 Sep 1945 at Windsor Park, Belfast att 45,061
Northern Ireland v England 0-1 ENGLAND

VICTORY INTERNATIONAL
Played on 20 Oct 1945 at The Hawthorns, West Bromwich at 54,611
England v Wales 0-1

VICTORY INTERNATIONAL
Played on 10 Nov 1945 at Hampden Park, Glasgow att 97.000
Scotland v Wales 2-0

VICTORY INTERNATIONAL
Played on 19 Jan 1946 at Wembley Stadium, London att 85,000
England v Belgium 2-0

VICTORY INTERNATIONAL
Played on 23 Jan 1946 at Hampden Park, Glasgow att 49,000
Scotland v Belgium 2-2

VICTORY INTERNATIONAL
Played on 2 Feb 1946 at Windsor Park, Belfast att 53,000
Scotland v Wales 2-0

VICTORY INTERNATIONAL
Played on 13 Apr 1946 at Hampden Park, Glasgow att 139,468
Scotland v England 1-0

BOLTON DISASTER MATCH
Played on 24 Apr 1946 at Maine Road, Manchester att 70,000
England v Scotland 2-2
NOTE Not a War-Time or Victory International

VICTORY INTERNATIONAL
Played on 4 May 1946 at Ninian Park, Cardiff att 45,000
Wales v Northern Ireland 0-1

VICTORY INTERNATIONAL
Played on 11 May 1946 at Stamford Bridge, London att 75,000
England v Switzerland 4-1

VICTORY INTERNATIONAL
Played on 15 May 1946 at Hampden Park, Glasgow att 113.000
Scotland v Switzerland 3-1

VICTORY INTERNATIONAL
Played on 19 May 1946 at Stade Olympique, Paris att 58,481
France v England 2-1

INTERNATIONAL CHAMPIONSHIP

	P	W	D	L	F	A	Pts
Scotland	3	3	0	0	6	2	6
Northern Ireland	3	1	0	2	3	4	2
England	3	1	0	2	1	2	2
Wales	3	1	0	2	1	3	2

Appendix 5

Military Competitions 1919

Army Cup
Organized by Sir Herbert Plummer
Final
Played on 28 Mar at Blucher Park, Cologne, Germany
1st Battalion, Cameron Highlanders 2
8th Battalion, Black Watch 1

International Army Tournament
Round robin tournament played at Stamford Bridge, London
Played on 3 May
British Army v Belgian Army 1-2
Played on 6 May
French Army v Belgian Army 0-0
Played on 8 May
British Army v French Army 3-2

Belgian Army were declared winners

Inter Theatre of War Cup
Played on 17 Apr
BEF v BEF, India 2-0
Played on 17 Apr
BEF, France v BEF, Salonica 4-2
Played on 22 Apr
BEF v BEF, Italy 3-1
Played on 17 Apr
BEF v BEF, Egypt 1-0

Final
Played on 1 May at Stamford Bridge, London
BEF, France v BEF, Egypt 1-0

Bull Dog Cup
Final
Played on 17 May
RAF (Roehampton) v Scots Guards 2-5

Appendix 5

Inter-Allied Services Cup

1940-41

First round
Played on 19 Apr
 Royal Netherlands XI v Polish Air Force 3-4
Polish Air Force possibly withdrew

Semi-final
Played on 24 May
 British Army v Belgian Army 4-1
 RAF v Civil Defence 4-2

Final
Played on 2 Jun at Stamford Bridge, London
Att 8,000
British Army 8 *(Edelston 3, D Compton 2, Birket, Welsh, Hagan)*
RAF 2 *(Fenton, Kitchen)*

1941-42

First round
Played on 28 Feb
 Belgian Army v RAF 3-6 *(at Wolverhampton)*
Played on 7 Mar
 British Army v Czechoslovak Army 3-1 *(at Dulwich)*

Second round
Played on 14 Mar
 Police v Fire Service 3-0
Played on 28 Mar
 AA Command v British Army 0-4 *(at Derby)*
Played on 4 Apr
 Canadian Army v Norwegian Army 2-5 *(at Hove)*
Played on 6 Apr
 RAF v Polish Land Forces 2-1 *(West Ham, London)*

Semi-final
Played on 25 Apr
 British Army v Norwegian Army 7-1
(at Palmerston Park, Dumfries)
 Police v RAF 2-0 *(at Derby)*

Final
Played on 16 May at Stamford Bridge, London
Police 6 *(L Compton5, ____)*
British Army v Police 2

Police: Fairbrother *(Preston NE)*, Hiles *(Fulham)*, F Dawes *(C Palace)*, Nicholas *(Derby Co)*, Smith *(Preston NE)*, Weaver *(Chelsea)*, Fisher *(Millwall)*, A Dawes *(C Palace)*, L Compton *(Arsenal)*, Harris *(Birmingham)*, Spence *(Chelsea)*
British Army: Whitehead, Burchill, Firth, Gerrais, Fuller, Kirkham, Glasby *(Aldershot)*, Eccleston *(Reading)*, Osborne *(Millwall)*, Matthews, Hopper *(Reading)*

1942-43

First round
Played on 27 Feb
 Fighting French v Norwegian Forces 0-1
(at Elm Park, Reading)
 Police v Civil Defence v RAF 2-4
(at Leeds Road, Huddersfield)

Second round
Played on 20 Mar
 Czechoslovakians v Belgians 0-1 *(at Dovercourt)*
Played on 27 Mar
 British Army v United States Army 11-0
(at The Dell, Southampton)
 Norwegian Forces v Canadians 10-2
(at Upton Park, London)
 Royal Netherlands Brigade v RAF 1-15
(at Griffin Park, Brentford)

Semi-final
Played on 3 Apr
 British Army v Norwegian Forces 11-0
(at Selhurst Park, London)
Played on 10 Apr
 RAF v Belgians 3-1 *(at Carrow Rd, Norwich)*

Final
Played on 26 Apr at Stamford Bridge, London
Att 30,812
British Army 2 *(Hagan, Mercer)*
RAF 2 *(Carter 2)*
There was no replay and the trophy was shared

1943-44

First round
Played on 19 Feb
 National Fire Service v Canadian Army 6-3
Played on 26 Feb
 British Army v Norwegian Forces 10-0 *(at Dulwich)*
 RAF v Netherlands Forces 6-1 *(at Upton Park, London)*
 Belgian Army v Police 2-1 *(at Ramsgate)*

Semi-final
Played on 18 Mar
 RAF v Belgian Army 3-0 *(at Selhurst Park, London)*
Played on 25 Mar
 National Fire Service v British Army 3-4 *(at Brentford)*

Final
Played on 10 Apr at Dulwich
RAF 3 *(Horseman 2, Finch)*
British Army 0

RAF: Streten *(Notts Co)*, Mennie *(Queen's Park)*, Manderson *(Queen's Park)*, Thorpe, Joy *(Arsenal)*, Whittaker, Gearing, Turner *(Chelsea)*, Horsman *(Bradford)*, Bacon *(Chelsea)*, Finch
British Army: Smith, Waymouth, Robbins, White *(Tottenham)*, Fuller, Kirkham, Ashcroft *(Tranmere)*, Glasby *(Aldershot)*, Bryant, Hardisty *(Middlesbrough)*, Hopper *(Reading)*

Index of Competitions

Aberdeenshire Cup 15
Army Cup 285
Ayr Charity Cup 32, 65, 81
Ayrshire Cup 15
B Division Supplementary Cup 262
Bass Charity Cup 77
Belfast & District League 35, 53, 67, 82
Belfast City Cup 35, 53, 67, 82, 105
Birmingham Charity Cup 11
Blenheim Cup 17, 33
Bull Dog Cup 285
Cheshire Bowl 97, 126, 174, 204, 235, 255
Coatbridge Express Cup 34
Combined Counties Cup 126, 148, 173, 204
Cup Winners' Match 149, 175, 205, 233
Devon Professional Championship 255
Dewar Shield 103, 130, 262
Dunbartonshire Charity Cup 32, 50, 62, 81
Dunbartonshire Cup 14, 32, 102, 240, 262
Dunedin Cup 11, 65
Durham Senior Cup 77, 255
East of Scotland City Cup 15, 154
East of Scotland Shield 15, 51, 65, 80, 103, 154, 180, 209, 240, 263
Eastern League 31, 49, 64, 261
Eastern League Cup 31, 49, 64, 261
FA Cup 10, 253
Falkirk Infirmary Shield 17, 33, 51, 103
Fife Cup 16, 33, 51, 103, 262
Fife League 52
Football League
  East Midland 91
  First Division 5, 87
  Lancashire Principal 21, 39, 57, 71
  Lancashire Subsidiary 22, 42, 59, 73
  League Championship 138
  League Championship Cup 60, 74
  Midland Principal 23, 40, 58, 72
  Midland Subsidiary 24, 43, 60, 74
  North (Second Championship) 163, 190, 219
  North 135, 159, 185, 215, 245
  North Eastern 94
  North Regional 109
  North Western 93
  Second Division 6, 87
  South 123, 145, 170, 200, 230, 246
  South 'A' 89
  South 'B' 89
  South 'C' 90
  South 'D' 90
  South Regional 116
  South Western 95
  Third Division (Northern Section) 88, 248
  Third Division (Northern Section) 2nd Championship 251
  Third Division (Southern Section) 88, 249
  West 171, 201, 231
  Western 92
Football League Cup 97, 125, 147
Football League North Cup 172, 202, 233
Football League South Cup 174, 205, 230, 234, 246
Football League West Cup 173, 203, 233
Forfarshire Cup 14, 32, 102, 240, 262
Fraser Charity Cup 65, 80
Gardeners Cup 51
Glasgow Charity Cup 14, 32, 50, 66, 80, 102, 130, 154, 180, 209, 240
Glasgow Cup 14, 32, 50, 66, 80, 102, 130, 154, 180, 209, 240
Gold Cup 18, 36, 54, 68, 82, 105
Hampshire Cup 126

Inter Allied Services Cup 286
Inter City Cup 156, 182, 212, 242, 265
Inter County League 52
Inter Theatre of War Cup 285
International Army Tournament 285
Irish FA Cup 35, 53, 67, 82, 104, 131, 156, 182, 211, 142, 265
Irish League 18, 104
Lanarkshire Charity Cup 50, 66, 81
Lanarkshire Cup 15, 33, 50, 66, 81, 102
Lancashire Cup 11, 73, 97, 127, 148, 175, 204, 235, 255
Lincolnshire Cup 11
Linlithgowshire Cup 34, 52
Liverpool Senior Cup 11, 77, 97, 126, 148, 174, 204, 235, 255
Loftus Cup 17
London Combination 25, 44, 61, 75
London Cup 11, 127, 149
London League 146
London Victory Cup 76
Menzies Trophy 34
Midland Cup 126, 204, 235
Midland Victory League 76
Northern Regional League 131, 155, 181, 211, 241, 264
Northern Victory League 76
Paisley Charity Cup 16, 34, 51, 66, 103, 240, 263
Penman Cup 16, 34, 51, 66, 103, 263
Renfrewshire Cup 15, 50, 65, 81, 103, 130, 154, 180, 209, 240, 263
Renfrewshire Victoria Cup 33, 50, 65, 81
Robertson Cup 13, 33
Rosebery Charity Cup 15, 34, 51, 66, 80, 103, 154, 180, 209
Scottish FA Qualifying Cup 17
Scottish League
  First / 'A' Division 12, 28, 46, 62, 78, 99, 256
  North & East Division 101
  Second / 'B' Division 13, 99, 257
  West Division 100
Scottish League Cup 258
Scottish North Eastern League 152, 178, 208, 238
Scottish North Eastern League Cup 153, 179, 209, 239
Scottish Southern League 128, 150, 176, 206, 236
Scottish Southern league Cup 129, 151, 177, 207, 237
Sheffield Cup 126, 175, 204, 235
Southern League
  First Division 8
  Second Division 9
South Wales & Monmouthshire Cup 126
South Western Combination 27
Staffordshire Cup 97
Stirlingshire Consolation Cup 17
Stirlingshire Cup 17, 103, 263
Substitute Gold Cup 155, 181, 211, 242, 264
Summer Cup 130, 154, 179, 210, 240
Sunderland Hospital Cup 11
Third Division (Northern Section) Cup 250
Third Division (Southern Section) Cup 252
Tyne, Wear & Tees Cup 204, 235
Victory Cup 80, 260
War Emergency Cup 102
War Fund Shield 14, 65
Welsh FA Cup 11, 97
Wemyss Cup 16, 34, 52, 66
West Fife Charity Cup 33, 51, 66
West of Scotland League 30, 48, 63, 79
West Riding Cup 77
Western Cup 48, 63, 79
Western Regional League 124
Western Regional League Cup 124
Wilson Cup 15, 32, 51, 65, 80, 103, 130, 209, 240, 263
Wishaw Charity Cup 17